TRAIL OF HOPE

1334
DAYS

120,000
PEOPLE

12,500
KILOMETRES

NORMAN
DAVIES

TRAIL OF HOPE

THE ANDERS ARMY
AN ODYSSEY ACROSS THREE CONTINENTS

OSPREY
PUBLISHING

AUTHOR NORMAN DAVIES AND PHOTOGRAPHER JANUSZ ROSIKOŃ in Jerusalem (January 2014). Together they visited many (though not all) of the sites along the 'Trail of Hope'.

INTRODUCTION

I HAVE LONG WANTED TO PRODUCE A BOOK ON GENERAL ANDERS AND HIS ARMY, BUT FOR MANY YEARS WAS UNABLE EITHER TO FIT IT INTO MY SCHEDULE OR TO DECIDE ON ITS FORM AND CONTENT.

A **book proposal for an academic** study of the subject, which would have been similar to my work on the Warsaw Rising – *Rising '44* – failed quite recently to find favour with my British publishers, and I was forced to think again. But I did not lose my conviction that a comprehensive survey of the Anders story was long overdue.

The decision to give preference to a popular, richly illustrated album was inspired by three factors. First, I was greatly pleased by my earlier cooperation with Rosikon Press over *To and From*, an album, which presented modern Polish history through the medium of philately and postal history. Secondly, I became aware that the number of eyewitness memoirs was multiplying fast, providing valuable insights into every stage of the saga. And thirdly, having noticed the abundance of unpublished photographic materials, I realised that a visual approach could be more effective than the traditional academic route. I found the title – *Trail of Hope* or *Szlak nadziei* – long before any detailed plans had been laid.

I also felt strongly that my work should strike a different tone from that of its predecessors. Most of the existing literature concentrates on two episodes – either on the martyrology of Poles deported to the USSR in 1940–1941, or on the culminating Battle of Monte Cassino in May 1944. These remain vital elements within the whole. Yet I was determined to show more. I wished to convey something of the geographical grandeur of the 'Trail', which led from Russia and Central Asia through half a dozen Middle Eastern countries to Italy, England, and eventually to more distant continents. I wished to explain the wartime context of the adventures of the *Andersowcy* (the Anders Army), whose destiny was shaped by successive shifts in the strategic framework: by Operation Barbarossa in 1941; by German defeats at Stalingrad, Kursk, and El Alamein in 1942; by the Allied offensive in Italy in 1943–1944; and by the Yalta Agreement of 1945. Above all, I wished to demonstrate not only the rich diversity of people, who answered to Anders' command, but also the extraordinary variety of their experiences and emotions, from death and despair, to fear and longing, ordeals and self-sacrifice, and, at the end, to a mixture of relief, resignation, bitterness, and hope.

The main text was written at pace, without any laborious research, drawing on knowledge that had accummulated in my head over the decades. My task was assisted by the fact that in the previous year I had presented a course of twenty lectures on the subject at the Oriental Institute of the Jagiellonian University in Kraków. In the second stage, flesh was added to the bones by inserting scores of substantial extracts from memoirs and eyewitness reports, thereby counterbalancing the historian's views with the voices of people who had completed the Trail in person. Each of the 20 chapters was then embellished by hundreds of pictures, many collected by an Internet appeal. The sheer weight of the pictorial material ensures that the historian's contribution does not dominate.

AS PART OF MY PREPARATION, I thought it essential, if not to tramp the trail from start to finish, at least to visit a selection of the key sites in person. With this purpose in mind, I succeeded in travelling in the company of Mr Janusz Rosikoń and his camera to Russia, to Iran, to Israel, to Italy, and to several evocative places in England. Our expeditions enabled us to add an extra dimension to the pictorial stock, where the old black-and-white images of yesteryear can be compared and contrasted to the vivid colour of today's digital wonders. They equally helped to sensitise us to the times and places that figure in the album. It is one thing to write factual sentences such as 'General Anders was held prisoner in Moscow by Stalin's NKVD'; it is something else to stand in front of the newly painted Lubyanka, to see that Felix Dzierzhynski is still honoured there, and to realise that today's Russia is far from changing 'all its spots'. In Iran, we not only travelled the road from the port of Pahlevi (now Bandar-e Anzali) to Tehran and Isfahan; we saw with our own eyes the glorious snow-capped mountains and fabulous Islamic art that sweetened the exiles' pain. In Israel, while seeking out some of the survivors, the journey gave us ample food for thought to grasp that the Jewish state, about which some of Anders' soldiers could only dream, is now a reality. And in Italy, we not only attended the annual commemoration of Monte Cassino; we walked round the flower-filled cloisters of St Benedict's rebuilt foundation, and recalled the spine-chilling moment when a Polish trumpeter had scaled the heights and with a marvellous sense of appropriateness had sounded the *hejnał mariacki* (St. Mary's Trumpet Call).

We have agreed on the popular term, 'the Anders Army', for the simple reason that all the alternatives would be infernally complicated. The force, over which Anders was given command in August 1941, was officially called 'The Polish Armed Forces in the USSR'. When the Army was evacuated to Persia it became *Polskie Siły Zbrojne na Bliskim Wschodzie*. One also meets the simple PSZ na Wschodzie, 'in the East'. In March 1943, however, the Army was divided into two: the Polish II Corps, which was to be attached to the British VIII Army, and the Polish III Corps, which was to remain in the Middle East.

General Anders and his army now belong to history. The pain and strivings of his followers have come to an end. For which reason, it is all the more important that the new generation should learn what happened, and pay tribute to a triumph of the human spirit. If the Poles of today knew their history better, perhaps they would be less inclined to decry their nation's achievements in the last 25 years.

NORMAN DAVIES
OXFORD, JUNE 2015

PHOTOGRAPHER JANUSZ ROSIKOŃ AND AUTHOR NORMAN DAVIES confer over the layout towards the end of three years' preparation. (As usual, the whole of the text of *Trail of Hope* was written by hand with pen and ink).

TABLE OF CONTENTS

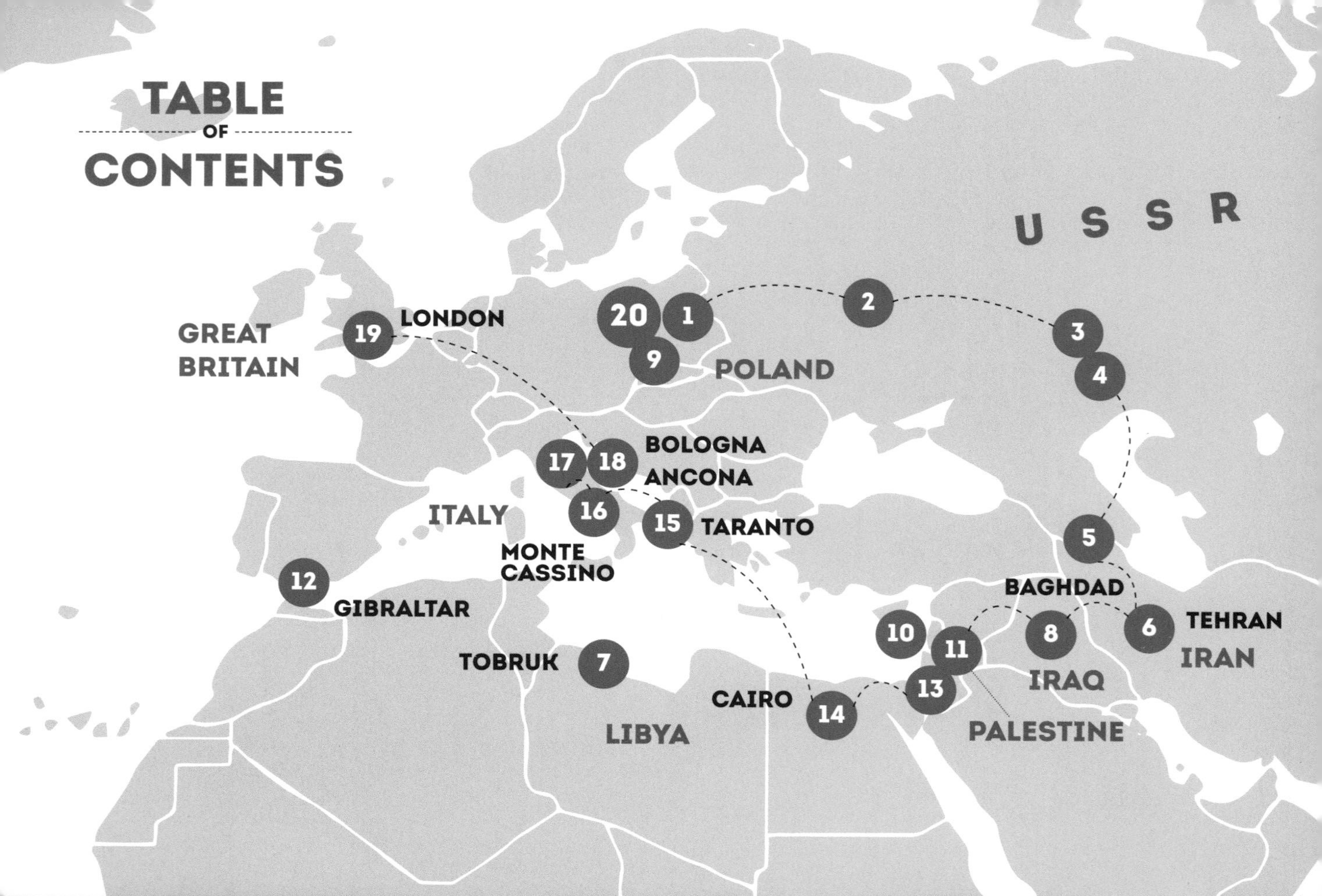

10 INDIA

10 NEW ZEALAND

TRAIL OF HOPE

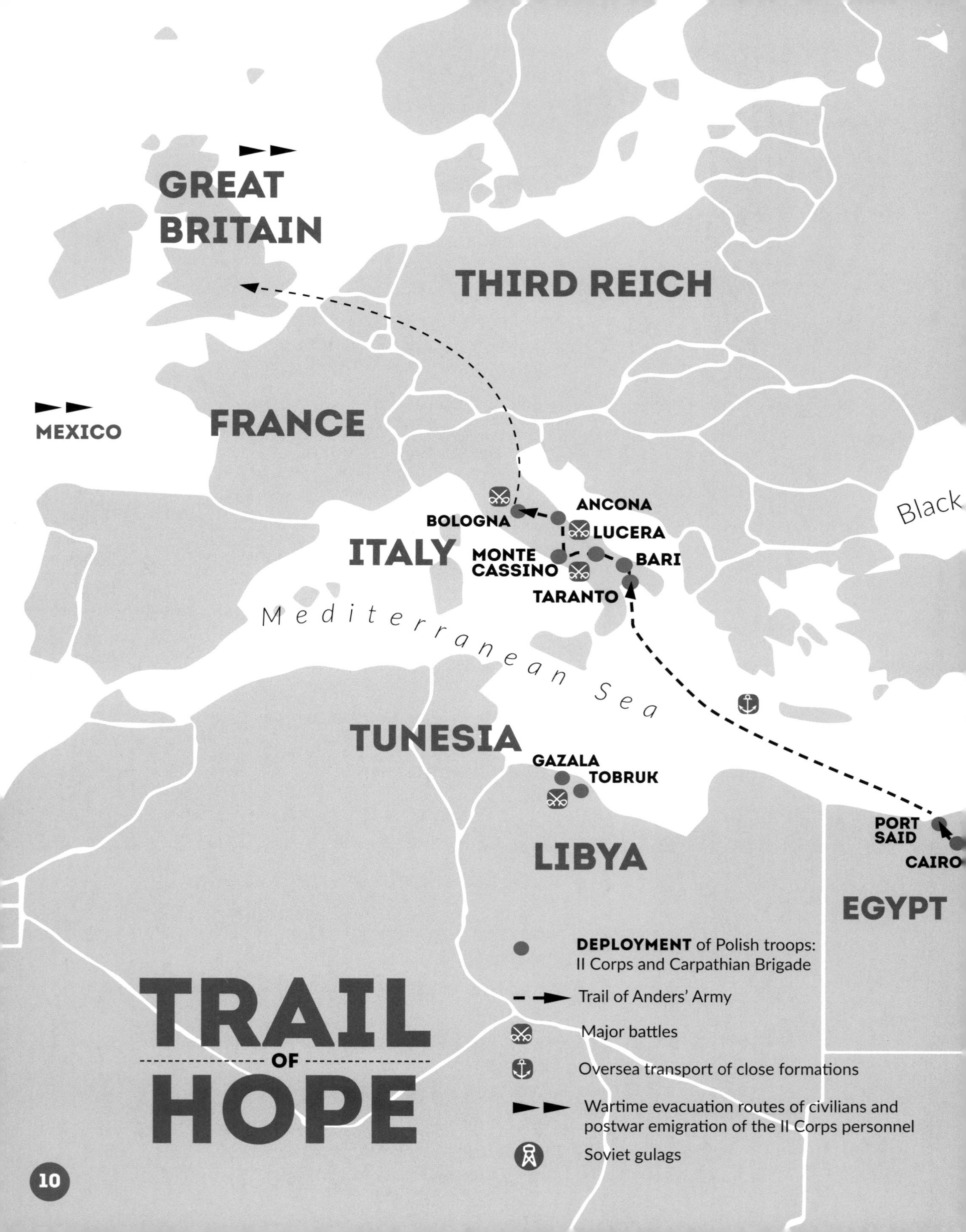
GREAT BRITAIN
THIRD REICH
MEXICO
FRANCE
ITALY
BOLOGNA
ANCONA
LUCERA
MONTE CASSINO
BARI
TARANTO
Black
Mediterranean Sea
TUNESIA
GAZALA
TOBRUK
LIBYA
PORT SAID
CAIRO
EGYPT
DEPLOYMENT of Polish troops: II Corps and Carpathian Brigade
Trail of Anders' Army
Major battles
Oversea transport of close formations
Wartime evacuation routes of civilians and postwar emigration of the II Corps personnel
Soviet gulags

USSR
MOSCOV
FIRST HQ OF THE POLISH ARMY IN THE USSR
KUYBYSHEV
KOLTUBANKA
BUZULUK
TOTSKOYE
TATISHCHEVO
SHALKAR
Aral Sea
LUGOVOYE
KARABALTY
CHOK-PAK
TASHKENT
JALAL-ABAD
MARGELAN
VREVSKOYE
KERMINE
KOROSU
SHAHRIZYABS
GUZAR
Sea
Caspian Sea
KRASNOVODSK
TURKEY
PAHLAVI
ASHABAD
MOSUL
KAZWIN
TEHRAN
KIRKUK
HAMADAN
KANAGIN
ARAK
ISFAHAN
MESHED
ALESTINE
KIZIL RIBOT
BAGHDAD
AHWAZ
GAZA
KOMAMSZAHR
ERUSALEM
IRAQ
IRAN
INDIA
RHODESIA
SOUTH AFRICA
KENYA
NEW ZEALAND

PROLOGUE

IN DECEMBER 1943, the port of Taranto, on the toe of Italy, was in British hands. It had been captured earlier that year as a result of the military operation, that had driven the Germans and Italians from Sicily, and had brought British and American forces onto the Italian mainland.

Y**et the Allied cause was not prospering** to the extent that its leaders had hoped. The burden of fighting against the Axis powers was being carried almost exclusively by Stalin's Red Army, and Stalin was exasperated by the failure of his Western allies to open a new Western Front. The Italian campaign, which was tying down fewer than 20 German divisions, bore no comparison in scale to the titanic struggles in the East, where over 150 German divisions were deployed against a still larger Soviet opponent. But it was politically and psychologically important. It was aimed at detaching Italy from the Axis camp, and it provided the only practical evidence that the Western Allies were serious in their promises of accepting a share of the war against Germany.

The Italian campaign, however, was not going well. The British and Americans were making slow progress in mountainous terrain, where the Germans could build effective defence lines and inflict heavy casualties. Two costly attempts to outflank the German lines by amphibious landings, first at Salerno near Naples and later further north at Anzio, had not brought the expected benefits. The direct road to Rome in the middle of the peninsula was blocked by the massive natural fortress of Monte Cassino. To put the problem simply: the Allies did not possess either the troops or the firepower to dislodge the Germans from their positions, still less to sweep them from the field. Reinforcements were needed urgently.

And reinforcements were finally coming. British officers, nervously pacing the harbourside at Taranto, had been informed that large convoys of troopships had started to leave Alexandria at the eastern end of the Mediterranean, carrying about 50,000 trained men to boost Allied fortunes in Italy. The arrival of the first convoy was awaited with bated breath. The shipping lanes of the Mediterranean had been cleared of enemy attacks only recently; and it was just a matter of weeks since German and Italian ships and planes based in Taranto had made life on the nearby island of Malta a misery.

The British VIII Army of General Oliver Leese, which held Taranto and its surroundings, was a composite force of soldiers from many nationalities. Among others, it included a large formation from India, a Maori battalion from New Zealand, and the Free French *Bataillon du Pacifique* from Tahiti. So, exotic allies were not unusual. But a special sense of mystery surrounded the identity and origins of the force that was now drawing close. The newcomers had been officially designated as the Polish II Corps, and had already been placed under British command. Their leader was General Władysław Anders, who had led his men into the British orbit two years earlier in Persia. But how, when, and why they had found their way to Persia was near-impossible to understand. There were liaison officers present who could explain the outlines of the history of the II Corps. But for most of the harbourside watchers the explanations would have been incomprehensible. The word was that these were 'reinforcements from Siberia', and the question had been posed, as on similar previous occasions whether or not they would arrive with snow on their boots.

Westerners' knowledge of the war in the East was, to put it mildly, limited.

FIRST FRUIT OF THE NAZI–SOVIET PACT

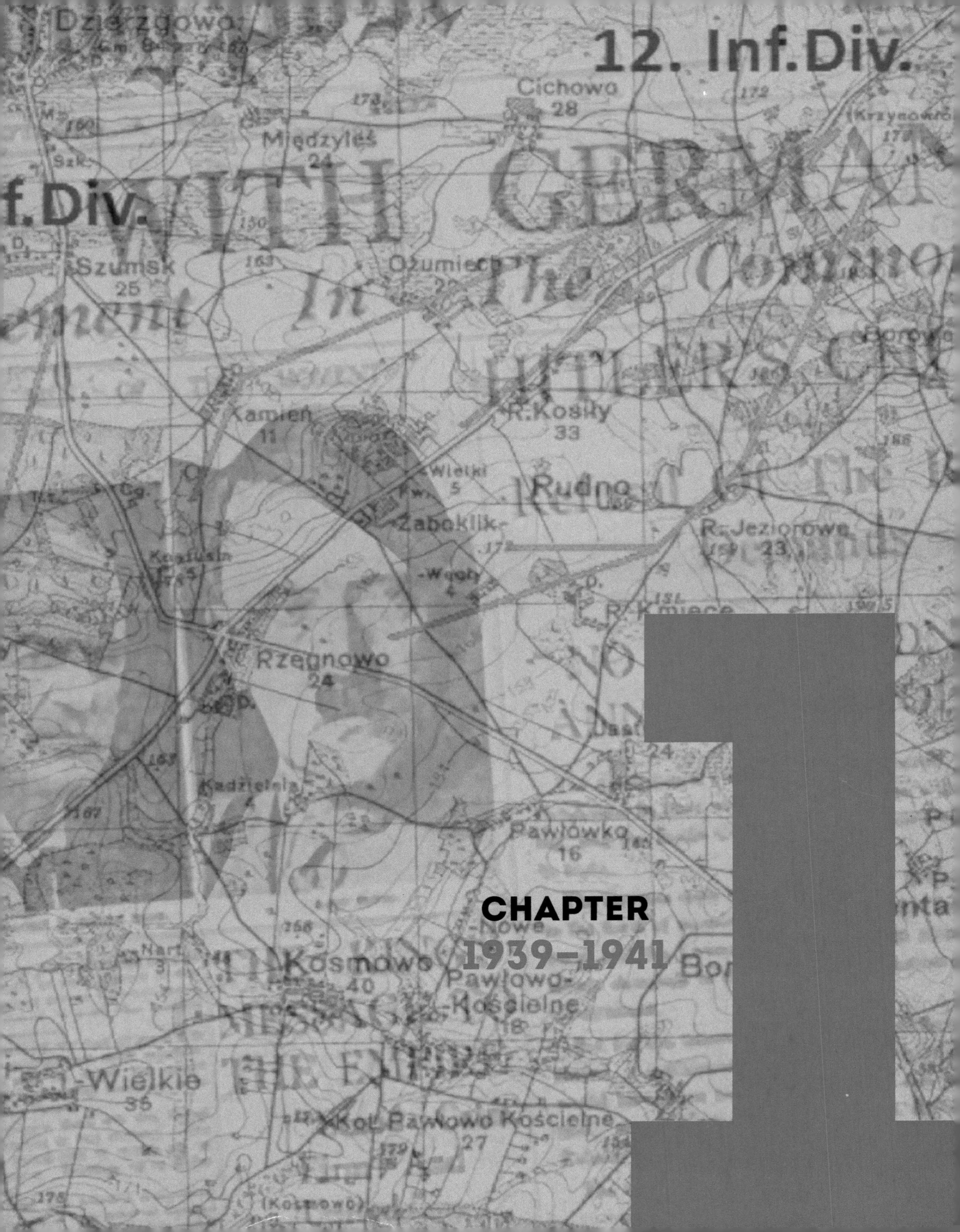

CHAPTER 1

1939–1941

PARTITION OF POLAND, 28 September 1939: German zone of occupation (left), Soviet occupation zone (right).

SOVIET POSTAGE STAMP issued in 1940: "The Liberation of Fraternal Nations in Western Ukraine and Western Byelarus, 17.IX.1939", otherwise known as the Soviet Occupation of Eastern Poland.

CHAPTER 1

1939–1941

FIRST FRUIT OF THE NAZI–SOVIET PACT

WARS SET PEOPLE IN MOTION. ARMIES MARCH. OFFENSIVES INVITE COUNTER-OFFENSIVES. FEAR AND VIOLENCE SPREAD. CIVILIANS FLEE. WITHIN DAYS, TENS OF THOUSANDS OF MEN, WOMEN AND CHILDREN, BOTH MILITARY AND NON-MILITARY, ARE ON THE MOVE.

This is what happened in the first week of September 1939, when the German Army invaded Poland, thereby starting the Second World War.

Then, of course, more armies march. More fear and worse violence ensue. And the stream of refugees turns into a tide of humanity heading for destinations and experiences that they could never have imagined. This is what happened after the third week of September 1939, when Stalin's Red Army unexpectedly joined the *Wehrmacht*'s invasion of Poland, thereby bringing an end to Polish resistance and ensuring the destruction of the Polish state.

The outbreak of the Second World War, in fact, set several such tides of humanity in motion. One stream ran to the north to the Baltic States, which offered a further escape route into Scandinavia. Another flowed over Poland's southern frontiers into neighbouring Hungary and Romania, whence the refugees hoped to reach Allied territory. Among them were thousands of Polish soldiers together with the Polish government, which left Warsaw on 18 September, crossed the Romanian frontier, and eventually found an exiled home first in Paris and then in London. A third tide, over 300,000 strong, flowed eastwards, fleeing before the German advance and seeking refuge in the Soviet Union. It contained a large contingent of Polish Jews, fearful of the Nazis' discriminatory policies that had already surfaced in Germany.

Yet by far the largest tide started to flow with some delay out of Soviet-occupied eastern Poland, whence, under the auspices of Stalin's security services, between one and two million people were forcibly deported to distant parts of the USSR, the largest country on Earth. Unlike their compatriots who had left their homes under duress of war, these deportees were not refugees in any normal sense of the term; they were victims of official Soviet policies, which actively sought to rid the newly occupied territories of wholesale human categories judged socially or politically undesirable. They were a clear example of the fact that, whereas Nazi ideology condemned various categories of people according to pseudo-racial criteria, Soviet ideology condemned other human categories according to pseudo-sociological criteria. And their ordeal was often destined not to cease

THE NAZI-SOVIET PACT, 23 August 1939, Moscow. Molotov signs, Ribbentrop (left) inscrutable, Stalin smiles. The interpreter stays neutral. Lenin presides over the whole thing.

when they reached their initial place of exile. It would continue far beyond Soviet Russia – to Central Asia, Persia, Iraq, Palestine, and Egypt, and eventually to every continent in the world – to India, Africa, America, Western Europe, and even to Australasia. It was an essential element of the drama that none of its participants could have known whether they would live or die, or where and when their involuntary wanderings would cease. This volume tells their story.

Western Europeans have grown accustomed to the false notion that nothing much happened in the first months of the Second World War. They talk of *la drôle de guerre* or 'the Phoney War', and they rarely lift their eyes beyond the confines of their own region. The two Western Powers, Britain and France, declared war on Germany on 3 September 1939, demanding that the *Wehrmacht* be withdrawn from Poland, but they did not react in like manner to the Soviet invasion and did not demand that the Red Army also be withdrawn. When the Polish Ambassador, Count Raczyński, visited Britain's Foreign Office on 17 September attempting to invoke the British Guarantee of his coun-

GERMAN TROOPS destroy a Polish factory.

try's independence, he provoked astonishment among British officials. "Britain has guaranteed Poland's independence", he was told, "not her frontiers." Which was a nice piece of sophistry. The Ambassador was left in no doubt that the Guarantee was intended to apply exclusively to actions by Germany, and that neither London nor Paris was prepared to judge 'Russia' by the same harsh standards that they judged Germany. Prominent voices, including that of the former Prime Minister, David Lloyd George, expressed the view in the press that while the German attack was despicable, the Soviet attack was somehow understandable. Not for the last time, the Polish government was faced by the painful realisation that many Western politicians saw Russia through 'rose-coloured spectacles' and were incapable of seeing Stalin for the tyrant that he was. Their attitude derived partly from strong sentiments established by the strategic set-up of the First World War, in which Russia had been a friendly ally, partly from the lack of accurate reporting on the Great Terror and other horrors of the 1930s, and partly from the fact that the secret terms of the Nazi–Soviet Pact of 23 August 1939 remained secret.

Nowadays, no serious historian can doubt the reality of the Nazi–Soviet Pact. Yet its importance continues to be minimised. It is often presented merely as a cynical political device, which facilitated Hitler's plan to invade Poland, which set the Second World War rolling, and which bought Stalin time to strengthen Soviet defences. It was much more than that. Among other things, it included an agreement to divide Eastern Europe into German and Soviet spheres of influence, and in the process to partition the Polish state. In effect, it was Poland's death sentence.

DURING THE BRIEF September Campaign which followed the signing of the Pact, Hitler's *Wehrmacht* invaded Poland from the west and north on the 1st, and Stalin's Red Army followed suit on the 17th. (The Germans were furious at the delay, which was probably caused by Stalin's insistence on terminating the conflict with Japan in Mongolia before he joined the war on Poland.)

The Western Powers declared war on Germany, but not on the USSR, and did virtually nothing to assist their beleaguered Polish ally. British assistance was limited to dropping leaflets over Berlin urging the Führer to desist. Caught between the pincers of Europe's two largest armies, the Polish armed forces could

AFTER THE BATTLE IN MUŻYŁOWICE. On the night of 15 September 1939 Polish troops crushed a crack German armoured regiment, the SS Germania.

not prolong resistance, and a joint German-Soviet victory parade was staged at Brest-Litovsk even before Warsaw had capitulated. The aggressors thereon declared that Poland had ceased to exist, and proceeded to carve up the country between them.

According to the German–Soviet Treaty of Friendship signed 28 September 1939, the eastern half of the defunct Polish Republic was arbitrarily annexed to the USSR and renamed as 'Western Byelorussia' and 'Western Ukraine'. It comprised a broad swathe of territory some 77,612 square miles (201,015 km^2) bordered in the north by Lithuania, in the west by the Nazi-run General Government, and in the south by Hungary and Romania. It was roughly equivalent in size to modern-day Belarus or Senegal, and was inhabited by some 15 million people — Poles, Belarusians, Ukrainians, and Jews. The principal cities were Wilno (now Vilnius) and Lwów (now L'viv). In a deft political manoeuvre Stalin initially handed Wilno to Lithuania, but in June 1940, having destroyed the Republic of Lithuania as he had helped to destroy the Republic of Poland, he added it to the Soviet Union.

THE TERRITORIES ANNEXED by the USSR were known to the Poles as the Kresy or eastern 'Marches'. Historically, they had formed part of the ancient Polish–Lithuanian Commonwealth, which had been dismembered during the Partitions of the late 18th century, and they were deeply bound up with the romantic traditions of Poland's historic role as the *antemurale christianitatis*, the 'Bulwark of Christianity'. Before they succumbed to the Partitions, they had withstood the hostile onslaughts of Turks, Tartars, and Muscovites for centuries. In the 19th century, though submerged by the wave of Russian expansion, they never attracted a significant number of Russian settlers, and most of the population remained staunchly opposed to the Tsar and all his works. Similarly, after the Bolsheviks had overrun Russia, the traditional society of the Kresy provided few enthusiasts for Communism. The Bolsheviks' advocacy both of atheism and of land collectivisation ensured that the landown-

SOVIET POSTER: "Our army is one that liberates working people." J. Stalin.

ers, peasants, and orthodox Jews of the region were all unimpressed. In the Polish-Soviet War of 1919–1920, when Lenin's Red Army marched through the Kresy and reached the outskirts of Warsaw, the Kresowiacy had its first taste of Communist medicine, and reacted strongly against it. The failure of Leninist propaganda was one of the reasons for the Bolsheviks' defeat in that war and memory of the defeat was one of the reasons why the Kresy were treated so brutally when the Soviets returned in 1939.

In the 1920s and 1930s, the Polish element among the population of the Kresy was strengthened by the plantation of numerous colonies of military veterans, who were rewarded with land for their service, and Poles became the largest single ethnic group. At the same time, thanks to the rise of nationalism among all communities, tensions rose between the state-backed Poles and the others. The Jewish community, for example, became increasingly influenced by Zionism. In the case of the Ukrainians, open conflict broke out in 1931–1932, when the Polish Army conducted so-called pacification campaigns in some disaffected rural areas. Yet nothing occurred that might be compared to the horrors that were being perpetrated both in Nazi Germany to the west or in the USSR to the east. The big development in eastern Poland in those years was the advent of universal schooling and the near-elimination of illiteracy.

IN THE SEPTEMBER CAMPAIGN of 1939, almost all the fighting took place in western Poland against the *Wehrmacht*; the Kresy remained largely free of military operations. After the intervention of Soviet forces on 17 September, confusion was more common than combat. The terms of the Nazi–Soviet Pact were not known. Red Army commanders sowed misinformation on all sides, often giving the impression that they had come to assist Poland against the Germans. The Soviet press was filled with weasel words of friendship and brotherhood. Stalin's real intentions did not become clear until it was too late to react against them.

Many history books, especially from the USA and from Russia, skip over the years 1939–1941 as if nothing really worth mentioning occurred in that period. Both Americans and Russians have been taught to think that the Second World War only started when their own countries became openly involved. Europeans know better. In reality, Hitler attacked and subjugated eight countries during the currency of the Nazi–Soviet Pact, and Stalin did the same to five. As soon as Poland was subdued, the Red Army invaded Finland in the so-called Winter War. The moment a truce with Finland was arranged in the spring of 1940, the German *Wehrmacht* crashed first into Denmark and Norway and then into the Netherlands, Belgium, and France. That summer, when Hitler's forces were entering Paris, Soviet forces were taking over the three Baltic States and parts of Romania. If not for the Battle of Britain, in which the *Luftwaffe* was repulsed, the United Kingdom would have joined the long list of subjugated states. In the early months of 1941, Hitler's ally, Mussolini ran into trouble in Albania, which he had earlier invaded, launching a Balkan crisis that led

JOINT GERMAN–SOVIET victory parade, 22 September 1939, Brest. Generals Guderian and Krivoshein.

POLISH POWS shot by the *Wehrmacht*, Ciepielów. Neither the Germans nor the Soviets respected the Geneva Conventions.

to the German occupation both of Yugoslavia and Greece. Far from being quiet and peaceful, therefore, the 21 months between September 1939 and June 1941 were filled with military actions, brutal occupations, death, fear, misery, and the maltreatment of civilians on a grand scale. Neither the Nazis nor the Soviets respected the Geneva Conventions.

By the same token, many historians who accept the significance of the Nazi–Soviet Pact nonetheless repeat the mealy-mouthed arguments later produced by Soviet propagandists when their guilty secret leaked out. The USSR, they say, was never an aggressor; it was a 'peace-loving state', and prior to the German attack of June 1941 had practiced neutrality. The Red Army did not 'invade Poland' in 1939; it entered Western Byelorussia and Western Ukraine to liberate the population from the oppression of feudal Polish lords, and only after the Fascist Polish state had collapsed. The Ribbentrop–Molotov Pact was signed for

TRIUMPHAL ARCH in Volhynia, erected to welcome Soviet troops by a pro-Soviet element in the local population.

one reason and one reason only: to win time for preparing the USSR against the inevitable Nazi onslaught that everyone knew was coming. These sorts of argument were to be welcomed by Western opinion in the days when the Red Army's courageous stand against Nazi Germany was widely admired, when Stalin the Bloody Dictator became 'Dear Old Uncle Joe', and when bad-mouthing the Soviet regime was unacceptable. But they do not hold up to rational examination; they are built on sheer delusion. One can only quote the Duke of Wellington, who was once mistaken in the street and addressed as 'Mr. Jones'. "If you believe that," said the Duke, "you can believe anything."

When the Nazi-Soviet Pact was signed, it is highly unlikely that either Hitler or Stalin imagined that the arrangements would be permanent. Each of Europe's two great totalitarians harboured ambitions which were incompatible with the indefinite toleration of a major rival. Yet equally, neither thought that the Pact would be short-lived. German re-armament was on course to reach a peak in 1942–1943 or in three–four years' time, and the Red Army, which was suffering the effects of a deadly officers' purge, was still less prepared for early action. In any case, both Berlin and Moscow expected that Hitler's known intention of following his attack on Poland with a major offensive against the Western Powers would necessarily embroil Germany in a prolonged conflict of uncertain outcome. Everyone in 1939 was conscious of the miscalculation of their predecessors in 1914, who imagined that the Great War would be over by Christmas. So the general feeling was that an extended breathing space would open up in the East. Hence, while the Nazis began organising the General Government for the short term and preparing their strategic 'Generalplan Ost' for the long term, the Soviets set about transforming eastern Poland beyond all recognition.

THE POLICIES ADOPTED BY STALIN in the new Soviet territories were as radical in vision as they were ruthless in execution. They aimed at the total overthrow not simply of the previous political system but also of the existing social, economic, and cultural structures. A phoney referendum was staged to approve the incorporation of the region into the USSR. All Polish laws were declared null and void. All

KAMIEŃ POMORSKI: Polish signs torn down by the passing *Wehrmacht.*

Polish institutions were disbanded or replaced, and their directors dismissed. All Polish banks were closed, and the currency abolished. All landowners were stripped of their property in preparation for the compulsory collectivisation of agriculture, and all economic enterprises, large and small, were subject to state control. All schools and universities were sovietised, and all churches and synagogues were closed. Russian was introduced as the principal language and all the inhabitants, irrespective of their wishes, were registered as Soviet citizens. Anyone who dared to object was promptly arrested, and sent to the camps. All men of military age were ordered to report for conscription into the Red Army. Confusion was attended by penury and despair. All decisions were placed in the hands of the all-powerful Communist Party. The tentacles of the NKVD (the People's Commissariat for Internal Affairs) spread into every town and village. Local militias were recruited to do the NKVD's bidding. And, in a state where children were encouraged to inform on their parents, networks of snitchers and blackmailers were set up to keep people in line. For the duration of the process of 'social cleansing', a special police cordon was established to isolate Western Byelorussia and Western Ukraine from the rest of the USSR.

One needs to remember that measures of such a drastic nature could only have been contemplated in a country where the instruments of mass repression were already firmly in place. In this regard, the Soviet Union was years ahead of the Third Reich. The unlimited powers of the Soviet security services could be traced to the Red Terror of 1918–1919. The vast network of state concentration camps, the notorious Gulag,

WARSAW, 2015. Monument to the Fallen and Murdered in the East. Each sleeper bears the name of a Siberian destination.

had been established during the Civil War under Lenin, before being expanded by Stalin. The practice of uprooting millions from their homes by administrative decree had become routine during the collectivisation campaigns of the early 1930s. The pseudo-judicial system of false accusations and fake trials had been refined during the Great Terror of 1937–1939, and the capacity of the Soviet railways to cope with vast quantities of human freight was well proven. Therefore the horrific measures which rained down on the people of eastern Poland, were not exceptional; they were but a continuation of the many oppressions which had overtaken numerous groups and regions in the USSR ever since the Bolshevik Revolution.

FOR THE PURPOSES OF THE PRESENT STORY, however, the most pernicious of the NKVD's policies was embodied in the decree which ordered that the whole population of the annexed territories be filtered for 'undesirables' and that all unwanted persons be physically removed. Five main categories of victim were involved. The first were so-called illegal migrants. These in large part were the refugees who had flooded across the Soviet western frontier in September and October 1939, fleeing the German advance. Many were Jewish, and most had gained entry to the USSR without the requisite permission or documents. Some who were willing to work for the new Communist agencies were permitted to stay. But most were unceremoniously despatched to far off destinations in the Urals or Central Asia, often without means of support.

The shockingly arbitrary nature of the treatment of these migrants is beautifully described in a memoir written after the war called *Mink Coats and Barbed Wire*. The author, Ruth Turkow-Kamińska, was the daughter of a famous actress, Ida Kamińska, star of the Yiddish Theatre in Warsaw, and wife of Adolf 'Eddie' Rosner, a popular jazz trumpeter. To begin with, unlike most of their fellow fugitives, the family were warmly welcomed. Though jazz was officially banned, Rosner was in great demand in private party clubs. He played in Leningrad during the siege, and even performed for Stalin himself. As darlings of the Soviet elite, they were showered with caviar and champagne and

SOVIET LOCOMOTIVE named "To Work or to Die", at work during the deportations.

lavish presents. Yet when he revealed that he hoped to return to Poland at the end of the war, he was promptly arrested, accused of treachery and cosmopolitanism, and thrown into the Gulag where he spent eight years.[1]

The second category of deportees consisted of prisoners-of-war. At the end of the September Campaign in 1939, about 250,000 Polish soldiers were held in Soviet captivity. Many of them had been captured on the southern frontier, whence they were trying to escape to Romania or Hungary. They were interned in various parts of the western USSR. Yet the officers were invariably separated from the ranks, and some 22,000 of them were sent to three special camps at Kozielsk and Ostaszków in Russia and at Starobielsk in Ukraine. There, in the winter of 1939–1940, they were permitted – since the postal service worked normally between the Soviet and German zones of occupation – to conduct limited correspondence with their families. They were also interrogated systematically by the NKVD and found lacking in pro-Soviet sentiments. Then suddenly, in the

WARSAW, 2015. Norman Davies beside the Monument to the Fallen and Murdered in the East, "17 IX 39".

spring of 1940, they disappeared; their correspondence came to an abrupt end and their fate was unknown. The Polish government was unable to discover their whereabouts.

THOSE IN THE THIRD CATEGORY were, in the eyes of the Soviet regime, 'social criminals'. Some 400,000 strong, they consisted of Polish citizens who by any normal standards were entirely innocent. They were arrested for no other reason than for belonging to groups that the NKVD rated inimical to the 'socialist' system. They included: all state employees such as civil servants, policemen, teachers, and railwaymen; all politicians irrespective of their party, not excepting Communists; all professionals such as doctors, lawyers, bankers, engineers, architects, company managers, and academics; all major aristocrats and owners of private firms; all gamekeepers (who might have protected runaways in the woods); and all members of occupations such as philatelists, esperantists, and linguists, who maintained foreign contacts. Most of them were hauled before a peremptory court, accused of imaginary offences such as spying, sabotage, or defaming the Soviet state, and in the course of two or three minutes awarded draconian sentences of 10, 15, or even 25 years of hard labour.

After that, with no chance to defend themselves, they were transported to the arctic camps of the Gulag. Soviet civil law at the time did not recognise death sentences. But, since the average life expectancy in the Gulag was one winter, everyone knew that a large proportion of the people who were sent 'to see the Great White Bear' would not return.

SEVERAL SPINE-CHILLING accounts of life and death in the Gulag were written by Poles, who were taken away in that period. Józef Czapski's *The Inhuman Land* (1951) and Gustaw Herling-Grudziński's *A World Apart* (1951) would later become classics. Joseph Scholmer's *Vorkuta*, was published in English in 1955 and was an eyeopener for many who still denied the realities of Stalinism. Menachem Begin (1913–1992), the future Prime Minister of Israel, who was a Polish citizen and a native of Brest, was arrested in 1940 and sent to the Gulag for his activities as a Zionist youth leader. His memoir entitled *White Nights* (1957; English translation 1977) provides perhaps the best description of the NKVD's methods of interrogation, to which he was subjected during his confinement in a Soviet camp.[2] Needless to say, none of these titles could be published officially in Poland before 1989.

FIRST SIGHT of a Soviet camp.

Among countless absurdities of the Soviet system stands the fact that the death penalty had been abolished and that, notwithstanding, millions died at the hands of the state. Very few inmates of the Gulag were shot, killed, or executed as had been routine during the prewar 'Great Terror'. Yet conditions were so indescribably harsh, that dying was a daily, not to say hourly experience:

"Throughout the Gulag's existence, the prisoners always reserved a place at the very bottom of the camp hierarchy for the dying — or rather for the living dead. A whole sub-dialect of camp slang was invented to describe them. Sometimes, the dying were called *fitili* or 'wicks', as in the wick of a candle, soon to be blown out... [But] most often they were called *dokhodyagi* from the Russian verb *dokhodit*, 'to reach' or 'attain' [the end], a word usually translated as 'goners'...

Put simply, the *dokhodyagi* were starving to death, and they suffered from all the diseases of starvation and vitamin deficiency: scurvy, pellagra, diarrhoea. In the early stages, these diseases manifested themselves in the form of loosened teeth and skin sores... In later stages, prisoners would lose their ability to see in the dark. Gustav Herling remembered 'the sight of the night-blind, walking slowly through the zone in the early morning, their hands fluttering in front of them'...

In the final stages, the *dokhodyagi* took on a bizarre and inhuman appearance, becoming the physical fulfilment of the de-humanizing rhetoric used by the state: in their dying days, the enemies of the people ceased to be people at all. Their skin was loose and dry. Their eyes had a strange gleam. They became demented, ranting and raving... They ate anything — birds, dogs, garbage... and could not control their bowels or their bladders, [thereby] emitting a terrible odour. They stopped washing, stopped having normal reactions to insults...

Despite prisoners' efforts, many many deaths went unmarked, unremembered and unrecorded... The names, the lives, the individual stories, the family connections, the history — all were lost."[3]

IN THE 1940S, the outside world was largely oblivious to the Gulag's realities. People who survived the Gulag, and reached the West, were to find that telling the truth led to blank stares of incomprehension.

My own introduction to these matters was provided by a Polish man, whom I met in Oxford in the late 1950s. I was a history student, and he was the manager of the foreign department of Blackwell's Bookshop; though 30 years my senior, he later became a friend, a neighbour, and a bottomless well of information on Polish history. Mr Kazimierz Michalski was born and raised in Jarosław in the Podkarpacie Region, had studied law at the university in Lwów, and in 1939 had just been appointed to his first position as a junior circuit judge in south-east Poland. When the Soviets arrived, he was an obvious target for the NKVD teams who were rounding up 'enemies of the people'. He was arrested without warning, imprisoned, tried in a perfunctory court-hearing, in which he was not allowed to speak, sentenced to 15 years hard labour, and frog-marched to the waiting cattle trucks. His destination was a camp near Pechora in the north-west of Arctic Siberia.

The fourth category of deportees consisted of the associates and families of persons already convicted in the courts. They had committed no known offence even according to Soviet law, but, being judged guilty by association; it was

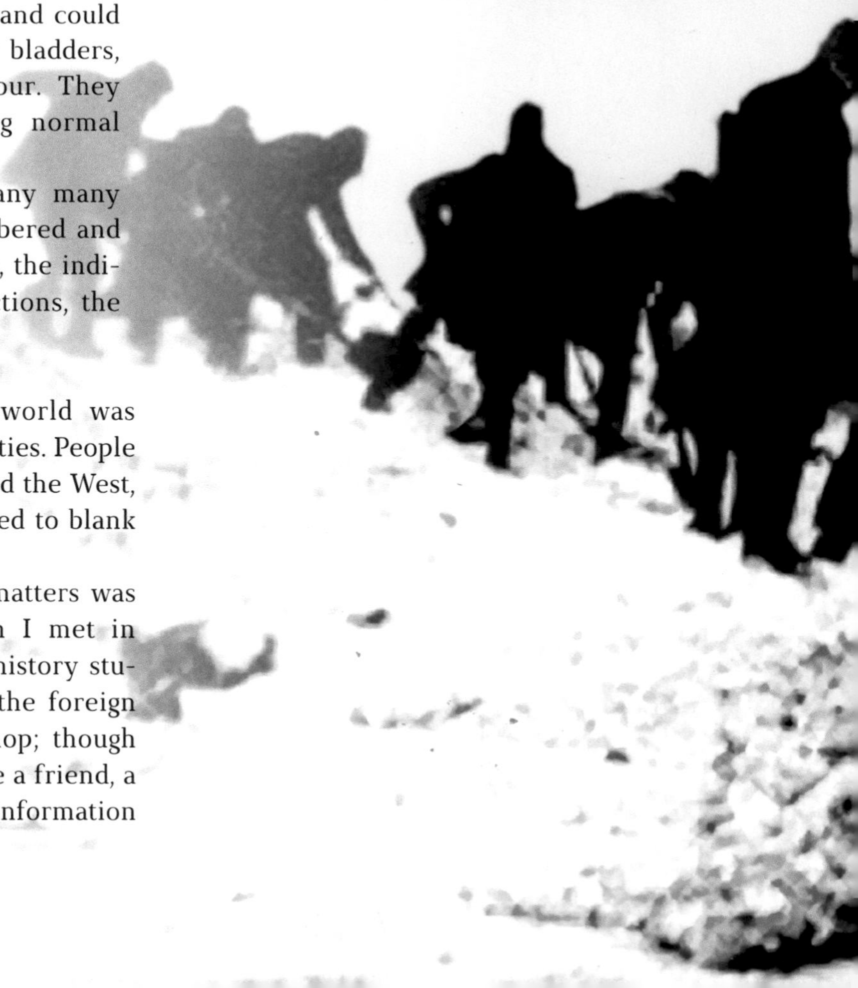

the practice of the NKVD to round them up and to deport them by administrative order to the republics of Central Asia. Their numbers were not counted, but were clearly several times greater than those of the convicts (Category 3). In the nature of things, they were the most vulnerable elements of society: women, children, and the elderly. Nonetheless, they were taken from their homes, usually in the early hours of the morning; were given 10 or 15 minutes to pack; and were marched under guard to the waiting trains, onto which they were loaded – 50, 60 or 70 to a wagon. Their chances of survival were not high.

The family of a military officer was high on the list of people to be targeted:

"When then war broke out, all hell broke loose. My father, an officer of the reserve, returned home [after the September Campaign], but immediately discovered that the NKVD, were looking for officers and other 'intelligentsia', so he went into hiding... My mother went back to work as a teacher to keep the family going.

During February and March 1940, my mother underwent several interrogations

"HE WHO does not work, does not eat".

by the local NKVD, both about her work as a teacher and the whereabouts of her husband. In March, the NKVD declared her politically unfit to teach, and she lost her job at school.

On 13 April 1940, the second mass deportation began. The NKVD arrived early in the morning, [reading] out the sentence of deportation and internal exile in Russia and allowing 30 minutes to pack essentials and enough food for a journey of up to four weeks. Everyone living in the family home was arrested; my mother with my sister Krysia, my mother's eldest sister and their parents... They were marched to the local railway station and loaded into cattle trucks.

back of the head by the NKVD [in the Katyń massacres]...

After a journey of two to three weeks... they were taken off the train with five other families, at Martuk in the district of Aktubinsk in Kazakhstan. From Martuk, they walked 7 km to a small village or *posiołek* called Nagorny. This was an agricultural *kolchoz* — a state-owned farm — where they were immediately set to work in the fields. Initially, they were given a shepherd's hut because in the summer, the shepherd was out on the steppe with his flock. Later, they were moved into a cottage... that belonged to a peasant who had been deported into internal exile. Everyone on the *kolkhoz* had to work."[4]

POLISH EXILES in Kazakhstan.

When my father heard of the arrests, he gave himself up to the NKVD in the hope that he would be allowed to join his family in exile. But that was the last reliable report we had of him, until [many years later] we found his name on the list of officers shot in the

Another of my friends and neighbours in Oxford, Mr Michał Giedroyć, belonged to this same category. He was the son and heir of a prominent landed family, whose residence lay at Łobzów near Nowogródek (now in Belarus). In 1939, he was 10 years old. As an aristocrat and a Polish officer, his father was doubly sus-

MOSCOW (2015). Norman Davies in front of the newly restored Lubyanka: HQ of Russia's FSB, formerly of the Soviet NKVD and KGB.

pect in the eyes of the NKVD, and was soon arrested. The family estate was thereon sequestrated. Michał and his mother took refuge in the local town, fearing the worst. And in due course, in April 1940, they were picked up and taken away. As their train pulled past the Castle of Minsk, which was being used as a prison, Michał's mother pointed out the tower where his father was being held and, unbeknown to them, would shortly be shot. Their destination was Nikolaevka in Kazakhstan.[5]

MR MICHALSKI'S WIFE, meanwhile, was suffering a similar fate from a starting-point in Lwów, 300 miles to the south. Mrs Joanna Michalska was 30 years old at the time. She was deported with her mother and two-year-old son, Andrzej. Packed like sardines into a wagon lacking water or sanitation, she and her family had no information either about her husband's whereabouts or about the length or direction of their journey. Many of her fellow passengers perished on the way. But after six weeks the train came to a halt somewhere on the open steppe. Forty years later, she would recount to her incredulous British neighbours how the doors of the wagon were dragged open to reveal a landscape of deep, pristine snow. The guards forced the passengers to descend into the snow, before they themselves climbed aboard as the train pulled slowly away into the distance. A couple of thousand half-starving, half-frozen wretches were left behind huddled in the drifts beside the track. Mrs Michalska and her charges were among those who refused to succumb. On the second day, the sun came up, warming them with its reflected rays, and miraculously they saw a posse of Kazakh horsemen riding their hardy ponies over the snowfields. Soon the horsemen were searching for the living among the dead. Mrs Michalska, clutching her infant son, was hauled to her feet, wrapped in furs and led on horseback to an encampment of yurts, where she was revived with mare's milk and hot sweet tea.

She did not know where she was; she could not speak with her rescuers; and she had no possible inkling of what the future might hold.

The fifth, much smaller category was made up of what might be called 'accidentals'. When the NKVD arrived in eastern Poland, they came armed with lists of thousands of names and addresses of people who were slated for arrest. When they knocked on doors in the middle of the night, they would usually read the names aloud from their list before telling the people to pack. Yet the lists, which had clearly been in preparation for years, were often inaccurate or out of date, and an NKVD team, which had been ordered to arrest a given number of bodies, was reluctant to report back with anything less than its quota. So it would pick up victims on the street or at random. Stories abound of people being taken simply because they happened to be visiting when the NKVD appeared, or because they took the place of some sick or infirm relative. One also hears that if someone managed to jump from the train when it started moving, the NKVD found it easier, rather than chase the getaway, to kidnap a passing peasant or an unsuspecting cyclist just to make up the numbers.

Stories also abound about people who slipped through the NKVD's net. My future parents-in-law, Mr and Mrs Stefan and Janina Korzeniewicz, were among them. Both, by NKVD standards, were suspicious, bourgeois characters. He was a graduate of the John II Casimir University in Lwów and a qualified engineer; she was the daughter of a Polish Army colonel. Fortunately for them, when the NKVD first called in October 1939 in the little town of Brody, the soldiers went to an old address. Stefan and Janina were tipped off, and left town immediately. Next year, when the NKVD tracked them down to a relative's house in Lwów, they were lucky to have a senior Soviet military officer lodging with them. The NKVD hammered on the door in the early hours of the morning. The angry officer, disturbed in his sleep, opened the door, told them to 'go to hell' (or the Russian equivalent thereof) and assured them that no-one of the given description was living there. The dog, amazingly, did not bark. (The scene is identical to one that Andrzej Wajda included in his film, *Katyń*.)

THE EFFECT OF THE DEPORTATION on the folks left behind can only be imagined. Ryszard Kapuściński gave us a glimpse of it. In 1939–1940, aged 7, he was a schoolboy in Pińsk, the main town of the Pripet Marshes, where the Red Army marched in at the beginning of the school year. Every week thereafter he noticed that one or two children disappeared from the

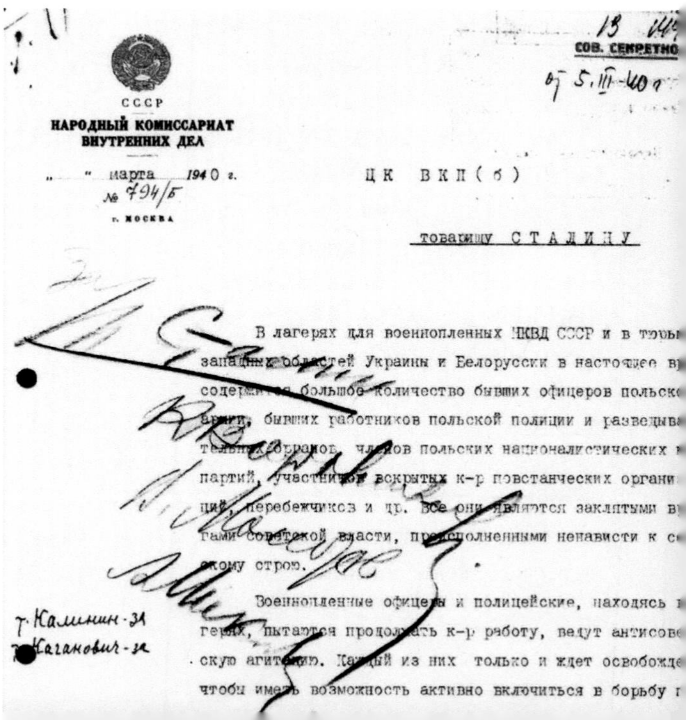

13 14
СОВ. СЕКРЕТНО
от 5.III-40 г.

СССР
НАРОДНЫЙ КОМИССАРИАТ
ВНУТРЕННИХ ДЕЛ

" " марта 1940 г.
№ 794/Б
г. Москва

ЦК ВКП(б)

товарищу СТАЛИНУ

В лагерях для военнопленных НКВД СССР и в тюрь
западных областей Украины и Белоруссии в настоящее в
содержится большое количество бывших офицеров польско
армии, бывших работников польской полиции и разведыва
тельных органов, членов польских националистических
партий, участников вскрытых к-р повстанческих органи
ций, перебежчиков и др. Все они являются заклятыми в
гами советской власти, преисполненными ненависти к с
скому строю.

Военнопленные офицеры и полицейские, находясь
герях, пытаются продолжать к-р работу, ведут антисове
скую агитацию. Каждый из них только и ждет освобожде
чтобы иметь возможность активно включиться в борьбу

г. Калинин - за
г. Каганович - за

5 MARCH 1940. Stalin's signature on the NKVD order to liquidate 20,000 Polish prisoners.

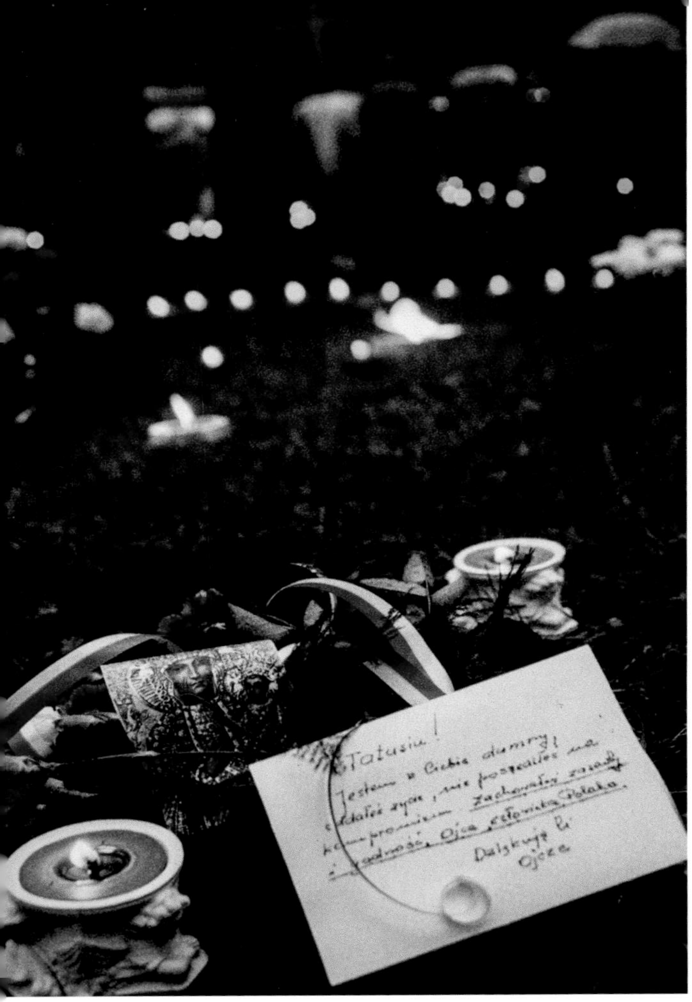

KATYŃ THEN AND NOW.
In Soviet times, the memorial was dedicated to Polish soldiers murdered by the Germans.

classroom. By the New Year, the class was half empty, and his lady teacher told those remaining not to be afraid. Then came the day when the teacher herself disappeared. Running as fast as his little legs could carry him, Ryszard found her standing by the open door of a cattle wagon in the station siding, and he tried to jump in and join her. She kindly helped him to scramble back down, and persuaded him not to go. The teacher was lost, but her pupil lived to become a world-famous writer. Had he stayed aboard, he too would have been one of the 'accidentals'.[6]

Many deportees spent time in prison either en route to the Gulag or as the result of a court sentence. Life in a Soviet prison consisted of a strange mixture of deprivation, brutality and ideological indoctrination. Most inmates were supervised by a 'senior' who received privileged treatment in return for evangelising his fellow convicts. A Polish officer, who had successfully disguised his rank and identity, listened for several months to the daily rants of a particularly persistent indoctrinator:

> "At first I was shut in Cell no. 23. Moshe Moseyevitch (son of Moshe) Nizgorodskij, a Russian Jew about fifty years old, was the senior of this cell. He had been a bookkeeper in some Soviet corporation, and now he was kept in prison, still under interrogation, for 'carelessness', because he had committed some error in the accounts. Originally he had been accused of the far greater crime of 'sabotage'... We asked him what kind of a sentence he expected.

POLISH EXILES at Kostousovo in the Urals, 1940 or 1941.

'A small one, I don't think more than three years.'

A nice prospect! He called it 'a small one' — three years in prison! Just for making an error in book-keeping...

He stayed in our cell for about three months. During this time he explained to us, for several hours daily, the principles of Leninism and Stalinism, often quoting Marx and Engels. He talked of the life of the Soviet people, their happiness, and the freedom every citizen enjoyed. His speeches were intelligent and beautifully phrased. He always had a ready answer or explanation to questions; with the patience and indulgence of an experienced teacher, he treated us as unlettered children. It appeared that we were complete ignoramuses from the capitalist world, who could not, and would not, appreciate the achievements of the Revolution. Moshe Moseyevitch immediately started to enlighten us on this subject.

One thing struck us, however: he would never listen to any accounts of conditions of life prevailing in our country. When some of our crowd, exasperated by his boasting, wanted to tell our story, he immediately interrupted him, saying:

'Comrade, stop it! Now you live here; you must change your outlook. Your previous life will never return.'

We were told by him that before the days of Marx and Engels the world had been ignorant, reactionary, and lacking in culture; the people were cruelly exploited by the aris-

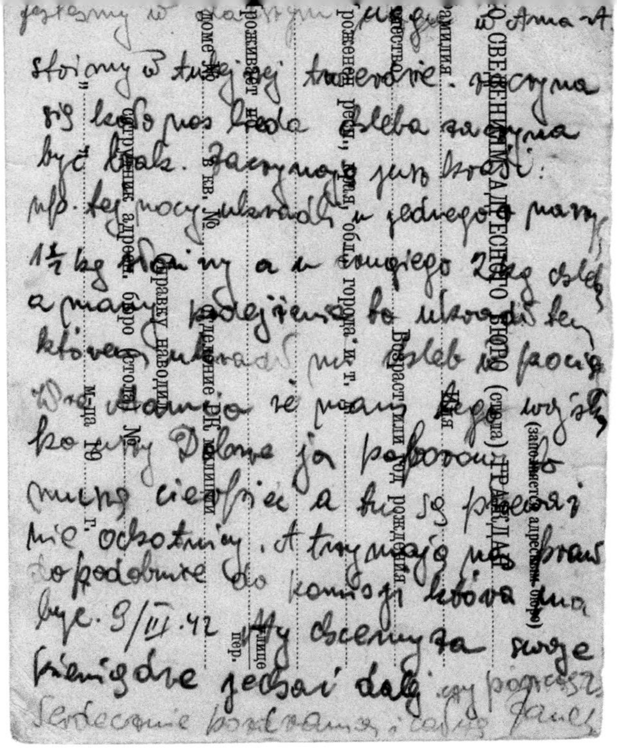

LETTER DATED 8 March 1942, sent by a Pole stranded in Siberia: "Bread is running out and stealing has started."

tocracy, and imperialistic wars raged. Only Lenin and Stalin had succeeded in liberating a part of the world and introducing real happiness. Obviously, this was not perfect yet, because we were still living in a period of Socialism, which is only the first step to complete Communism — which, when universal, will bring paradise on earth.

He expounded such marvellous visions to us that once one of our simpletons, fascinated by them, asked: 'How many years will it take to achieve?'

Such a question was probably not foreseen in the training of a 'pro-agit' (Communist agitator) which was probably the education Moshe has received. 'It will come when it will,' he replied. And added: 'When Stalin orders it.'"[7]

For obvious reasons, few of the deportees were in a fit state to keep a diary or to give a

SOVIET CAMP utensils.

coherent account of their journey. For much of the time, they could only look through the slats of the wagon and, from the angle of the sun, guess if they were travelling east, south, or north (but never west). Whenever the train stopped and the doors were thrown open for water to be distributed or for a bowl of gruel to be served, the guards would never say where they were or how far they had travelled. But there were exceptions. Mrs Czesława Panek (née Wierzbińska), who now lives in Oamaru on the South Island of New Zealand, was deported with nine other members of her family from a village called Chmielów near Jezupol in the Stanisławów district. She and her sisters kept a log, which 60 years later she would translate into English for the benefit of her grandchildren.

The Wierzbińskis were deported because their father fitted the NKVD's profile of an enterprising, self-reliant and religious bourgeois family; he was exactly the sort of man whom they aimed to eliminate. He had spent some years working in the USA, and was using his

NKVD LIST of deportees (in part).

savings to build a large, 16-room house. He had a wife and eight children, five boys and three girls, of whom Mrs Panek was the youngest. Still worse, he was a professional politician, working as a local official of the Polish Peasant Party (PSL), which had a strong following among independent small farmers. “He wanted to improve the life of the poorest people,” Mrs Panek told us; “he was strongly opposed to the Communists all his life.” And that was his undoing. In the eyes of the NKVD, he was a dupe of the so-called kulak class, whom Stalin had sworn to abolish. At least such was the family’s presumption. They were never tried in a court, or told why they were being so brutally uprooted.

The fateful day dawned on 10 February 1940, bright and very cold. The only member of the family to escape was the eldest son, Mieczysław, who left home at dawn. He would not see the sister who kept the diary until long after the war. He did not even know that they had been taken. He passed a group of NKVD soldiers at the local railway station, but thought nothing of it. When he returned home from school in the afternoon, the house was empty. By that time, his parents and siblings were already trundling towards the East in a monster convoy of over 100 trains carrying over 200,000 people:

> “**10-2-1940 Chmielów**
> Mietek left for Dubowce station
> to catch the train to
> high school in Stanisławów
> before the soldiers arrived
> banging on the door.
> [They] gave us
> very short time
> to pack, before taking us to Jezupol.

POLISH CHILDREN on a Soviet deportation train.

Jezupol
They packed us into cattle wagons
& bolted the door.
Train left that afternoon.

Feb 1940 Szepetówka
Travelled through
Szepetówka (Poland).

Zlatoust (Ural)
Went through Zlatoust (in Ural).

Mid-March 1940, Bredy
Arrived in Bredy in middle of March.
Were locked in the station building
[which] burnt down that night.

Next day,
Dzytagara on River Tobol.
Kazakhstan, Kustanaiska Oblast.
Travelled by tractor drawn sleighs.
Were allotted a room in barracks.
Gold mining place.

Stayed there
until autumn 1941.

[March 1941. Mama died]"[8]

SUCH WAS THE EXPERIENCE of one family among tens of thousands. Their journey of nearly 2,000 miles had been shorter than most. It took them almost due east, probably passing through Kiev, Saratov, and Magnitogorsk. (Zlatoust is a small station on the mainline near Chelyabinsk.) They spent five weeks in the cattle wagons, travelling at an average of 50 miles per day or 2 miles per hour; before depositing them at Bredy, the train had taken them beyond Europe, but did not go far into Siberia or Central Asia. The final stage on sleighs took them over the border between Russia and the north-western corner of Kazakhstan. Dzetygara (now Zhetikara) is a small mining settlement in the upper reaches of the basin of the Irtysh, a tributary of the Ob, the principal river of western Siberia. (Nearby Tobolsk was the first fort to be captured at the start of Russia's conquest of Siberia under Ivan the Terrible.)

Yet this was no comfortable resting place. The climate was extreme, sinking to -50°C in the winter and rising to +35°C in the summer. Living conditions were primitive. The exhausted mother died within the first year. The father, who was not accustomed to physical labour, was wilting under the back-breaking work which he was forced to do in a slave gang. He was only saved by the generosity of a fitter compatriot who volunteered to take his place in the mine. The children did not go to school and were not properly fed. Their future was unknown, but extremely bleak.

Soon after her arrival in northern Kazakhstan, one exiled woman dreamed that her husband, a serving Polish officer, was already dead. She would learn many years later that he had indeed been killed in the Katyń Forest. In the meantime, she had to contend with fearsome climactic conditions, for which she and her daughter were completely unprepared:

> "Winter in North Kazakhstan came early in 1940. Snow fell at the end of September and the ground became ice-bound. It was hard to imagine how we could survive in our hut with limited reserves of fuel, *kiziak*, and food sufficient for two months at the most. We knew that winter in these parts was not only very long and severe, the temperature falling to minus 50°C, but in addition that very strong winds and snow storms were a regular occurrence. These snow storms, called *bourans*, paralysed daily life, and if we had to go out of the hut during one, the whole world disappeared from view, and we found it advisable to tie a rope to ourselves, like dogs on chains, to find our way back to the hut. It was only too easy to become disorientated and wander into the steppe, which could be fatal. As storms came without warning, trips to Troitsk and other places were cut to an absolute minimum. In summer, people moved along beaten tracks but in winter these disappeared under the snow. Gradually the snow on the tracks would compact and the only means of recognising the way was by feeling the hard path under one's feet. Winds that blew dust in summer now carried snow from the endless steppe and often buried the entire village."[9]

Living through such a winter, she came to understand the fatalism of the local Russians:

> "We had to admit that the saying frequently repeated by the natives in Novo-Troitski, '*Nichevo privikniesh*' (It is nothing, you will get used to it), had a lot of truth in it. The other saying when life seemed unbearable was, 'You can't go into the grave alive.' Could there be a stronger way of expressing one's utter resignation?"[10]

EVERY SEASON BROUGHT ITS OWN MISERY. The snow had melted by May, and it was a great achievement for the exiles to rid themselves of the lice that had plagued them for months:

> "But I then had to face another enemy, fleas. For some reason the area round my bed was singled out as a breeding ground. It looked as if they were dormant during the winter, and, with the arrival of warmer days they came back to life with a vengeance. I became an obvious target, and dreaded the thought of bedtime, for as soon as I approached my bed, I was assailed by hundreds of them. I had to invent some

EXILES: "ENSLAVEMENT in Russia" (above).

VIRGIN MARY AND CHILD fashioned from old tin cans and ex-Red Army uniform buttons.

method of defence. The best I could think of was to brush the fleas off with a very quick movement of both hands, and lift the leg promptly on to the bed, and repeat the same manoeuvre with the other leg. In that way I was able to rid myself of most of these parasites. Inexplicably they never jumped on to the bed... As if this was not enough, very soon the mosquitoes and other flying insects made their appearance. Somehow, nothing in this country seemed to have any sense of moderation, and now they came in millions and tormented us day and night, not only stinging, but getting into eyes and ears as well. They eased off only for a couple of hours at dawn and this was the only time I could get some rest. Once, after several sleepless nights, my body burning from their bites, I jumped out of bed, ignoring the fleas, to see how the others were faring. I was amazed to find they were all asleep with mosquitoes sitting on their faces and any other exposed parts of their bodies."[11]

Summer was the opposite of what winter had been, but no more comfortable:

"July arrived, and with it the sweltering heat from which there was no escape. The steppe which only a short time ago had been green, now turned into a desert under the scorching sun. Tormented by heat and horse flies, the cows, with tails erect, stampeded home, raising clouds of dust as they abandoned the pastures at midday. Sudden and very hot gusts of wind blew dust and made breathing very difficult. At night we were drenched in perspiration, and often now I was joined outside the hut by other members of the family who, like me, were not able to sleep. We could not sit for a moment

SURVIVORS

FOLLOWING THE DEPORTATIONS of 1940–1941, tens of thousands of destitute Polish children, including countless orphans, were scattered in the remote areas of the Soviet Union. General Anders was to issue an order to rescue as many of them as possible.

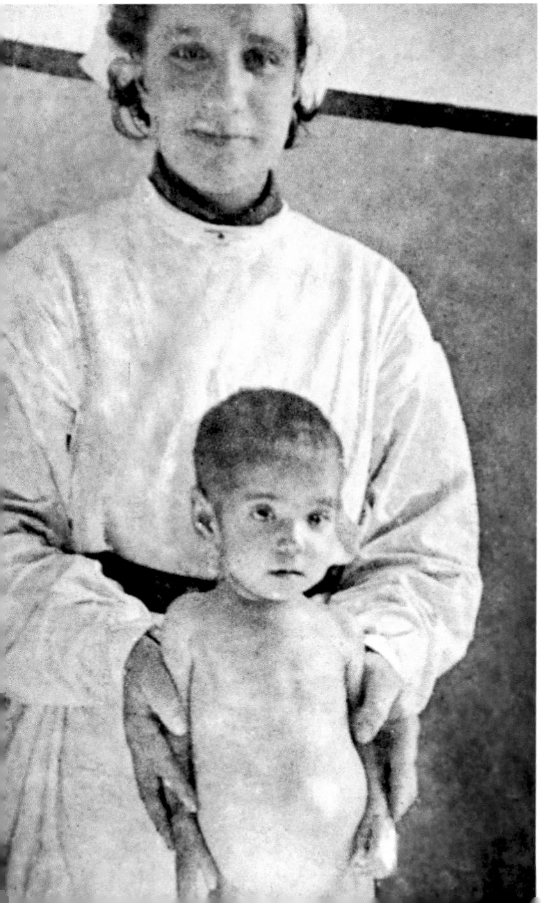

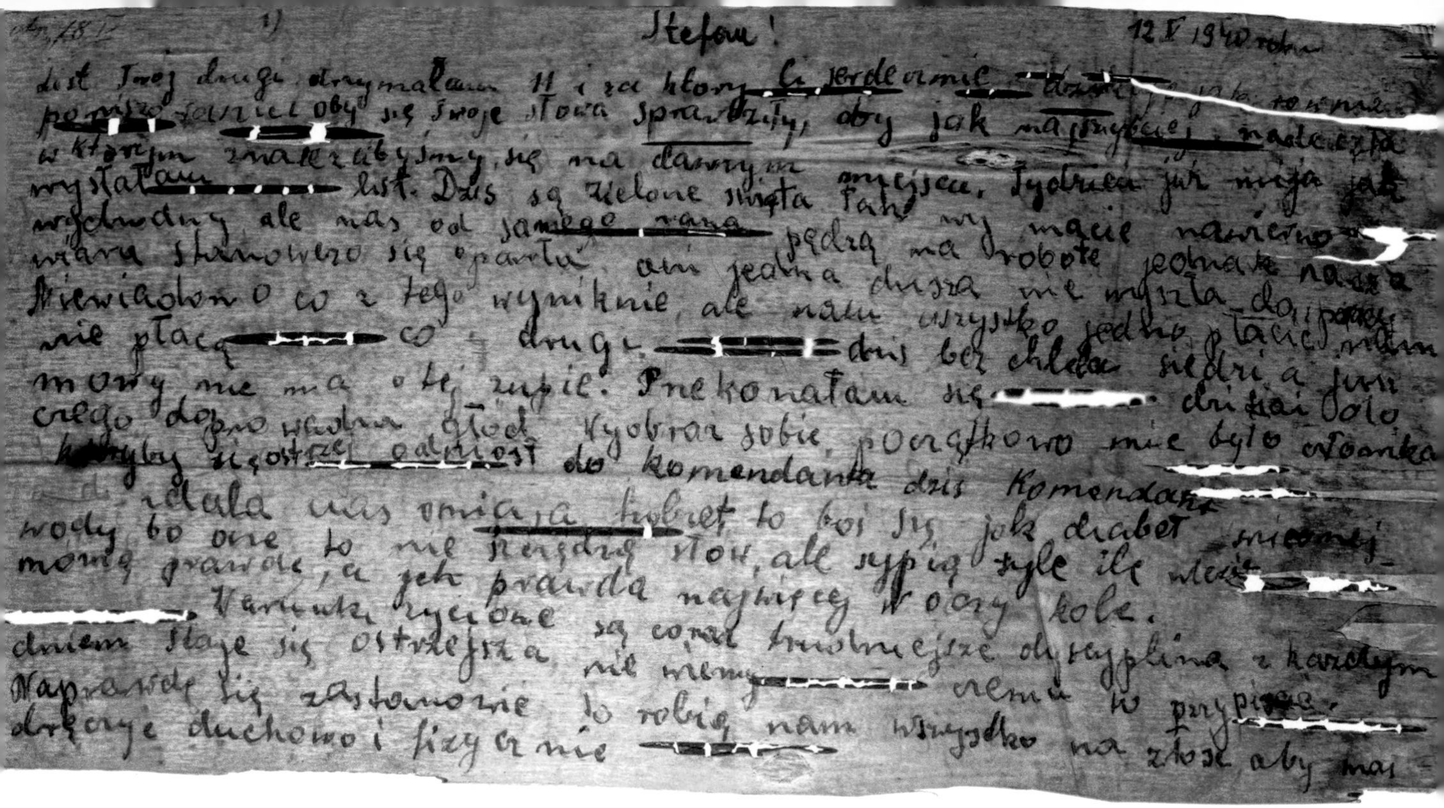

A LETTER from Siberia written on birch bark.

because of the mosquitoes, but as nights were as light as days, we wandered along the edge of the steppe until, completely worn out, we returned to our beds of torture hoping to snatch a few hours of badly needed sleep."[12]

In such surroundings, every simple task played on people's nerves and drained their energy. To walk from the farmhouse to the well to collect water, for example, required an elaborate routine:

"During the day everybody suffered equally from mosquitoes and midges which made going to the well particularly unpleasant. To make the trip worthwhile the normal procedure was for two people to take three buckets, one on either side and one in the middle carried between them. An escort of two additional people was necessary to defend the water-carriers, whose hands were occupied, by waving pieces of cloth, bunches of wormwood or other grass as available. Both the water carriers and escort came back utterly exhausted from this mission and with half the water spilled. Similar protection had to be given to anyone doing the cooking on our small stove in the open. Even smoke did not deter the pests. Kazakhstan was a cruel and uncharitable country."[13]

Living in the remote outback of Kazakhstan, far from the urban centres, the Polish exiles often mixed with the native population, gradually won their confidence, and learned something of their complicated history:

"The Kazakhs (whose name has the same origin as that of the Cossacks) are a people (formerly called Kirgiz by the Russians) living in Kazakhstan and numbering (1959) 3.6 million. They are Sunni Muslims, but Islam has not taken such deep roots among them as among, for example, the Uzbeks. Until the collectivization of agriculture... in the early 1930s they were a nomadic pastoral people, and they are still predominantly engaged in animal husbandry – sheep, horses, camels – though since the 19th century there had been some agriculture, and many Kazakhs now work in industry. Ethnically and linguistically the Kazakhs are a very homogenous people, although remnants still exist of their complicated clan system. The Kazakhs broke off from the 'Mongol' Golden Horde in 1456 and part of them moved east and south-east to occupy the whole of present-day Kazakhstan. During the following century three primitive states gradually developed among them: the Junior Hundred, the most numerous, in the original Kazakh territory of present north-west Kazakhstan; the Middle Hundred, in the present northern and central Kazakhstan; and the Senior Hundred in south-east Kazakhstan. In 1723 the strong Dzungarian (Kalmyk) state attacked the Kazakhs, and conquered large parts of their territory, but rather than submit the Senior Hundred withdrew to the west, returning later after the rout of the Kalmyks by the Chinese... the Junior and Middle Hundreds asked for Russian protection in the 1730s, but Russian rule did not become a reality until the 19th century, while the Senior Hundred, situated between the advancing Russians and the expansionist Kokand Khanate, chose to submit to the Russians in 1846. Russian rule was indirect and had little impact until the beginning of Russian colonization of the fertile northern Kazakhstan and Semirech'ye in the late 19th and early 20th centuries. Russian–Kazakh relations deteriorated, and in 1916 the anti-Russian uprising in Turkestan spread to the Kazakhs, where it was led by Imanov. During the civil war an autonomous anti-Bolshevik Kazakh government was set up by the local intelligentsia, which cooperated with the Whites. Outstanding national figures of the past have been the leaders of anti-Russian uprisings, K. Kasimov and S. Datov, the orientalist and explorer Ch. Valikhanov (1837–65), and Abay Kunanbayev (1845–1904), the founder of modern Kazakh literature; the venerable folk-singer Dzhambul Dzhabayev (1846–1945) was used by the Communist authorities in the 1930s as a leading propagandist of the Stalin cult. Nationalist tendencies are strong among the Kazakhs, and especially manifested themselves during the collectivization of agriculture and the Virgin Land Campaign."[14]

THE LAST GREAT TRAIN CONVOY pulled out of Soviet-occupied eastern Poland on 21 June 1941. The human cargo it carried would not have been aware of the extent to which German-Soviet relations had deteriorated, although some might have heard the widespread rumours about German divisions massing on the frontier. German planes had been overflying for weeks. As would soon be revealed, the Ribbentrop-Molotov Pact was on the point of collapse. Having defeated the Western Powers in record time and at very little cost, Hitler had decided to accelerate his plans and to turn the full weight of his war machine on the Soviet Union. And the Soviet zone of Poland would be in the first line of the onslaught. Stalin, however, refused to believe it. He ordered his forces to hold their current positions, ignored all warnings, and took no basic precautionary measures. The very next day the Wehrmacht launched Operation Barbarossa, the mightiest offensive in European history. When Stalin learned that his Nazi partner had deceived him, he was said to have suffered a nervous breakdown. And the alliances of the war were transformed.

THE CONSEQUENCES OF BARBAROSSA

CHAPTER 2

1941

CHAPTER 2

1941

THE CONSEQUENCES OF BARBAROSSA

HITLER'S ATTACK ON THE SOVIET UNION BROUGHT ALL THE ASSUMPTIONS OF THE PREVIOUS TWO YEARS GRINDING TO A HALT. IT TURNED THE TITANIC CONTEST ON THE EASTERN FRONT BETWEEN THE *WEHRMACHT* AND THE RED ARMY INTO THE BIGGEST OF ALL MILITARY THEATRES. IT DROVE ALL OF THE NAZIS' ENEMIES TO UNITE.

It increased the chances of the USA being drawn into the war in Europe, and it encouraged the Japanese to think that the time had come for them to launch a similar, strategic offensive in the Pacific. At the same time, it planted the first seeds of hope in the hearts of all those people who had been suffering from the effects of the close cooperation of the Nazis and Soviets. Among those sufferers, none were more alert to the new possibilities than the vast cohorts of Polish citizens who had been deported into the depths of the USSR since 1939.

At the time of Barbarossa, London was the sole Allied capital still free from Axis occupation. It was home to a dozen allied governments, including that of Poland. Thanks to the Royal Navy and the RAF, the United Kingdom had avoided invasion. But the British Expeditionary Force had been lost in France, and the Army was greatly weakened; very few troops remained to man the defences, the Royal Navy was fully occupied by the campaign against German U-boats in the Atlantic, and Bomber Command did not yet have the capacity to carry the war to the German heartland. The Prime Minister, Winston Churchill, bristled defiance, but knew in his heart that the cause would be lost without the support of further allies. He valued the Poles, whose gallant airmen had performed particularly well in the Battle of Britain; and he respected the Polish Prime Minister and Commander-in-Chief, General Sikorski. Even so, neither the British nor the Polish governments possessed the 'big battalions' that were needed to compete in the top league of continental warfare. In the second half of 1941, therefore, Churchill strained every sinew to achieve two goals: to make common cause with the USSR, and to persuade a reluctant USA to enter the war on the Allied side. He was destined to succeed on both fronts.

Churchill was no lover of Communism. On the contrary, he was a seasoned anti-Com-

GERMAN POSTAGE (preceding page) stamps overprinted in late 1941 for 'Ostland' (i.e., the occupied Baltic States and Belarus) and for Ukraine. (German forces never exercised effective control over Russia, and never issued stamps overprinted 'Russland'.) From 1941 to 1944, Polish eastern territories which had been annexed by the USSR in 1939, were governed either by the Reichskommisariat Ostland or by the Reichskommisariat Ukraine.

SOVIET POWS (above) captured by the Wehrmacht during Barbarossa. Their numbers were staggering, topping a million in the first few months, leading experts to conclude that the Red Army could not survive.

GERMAN ROAD SIGNS (left) in Soviet territory.

munist. During the Russian Revolution, he had called the Bolsheviks "a bloody, barbaric baboonery". On the other hand, he would have been aware that Western public opinion was generally more sympathetic to the Soviet Union than he, and as a former First Lord of the Admiralty, he was well versed in geopolitical realities. He had long understood that Germany's formidable military might could only be contained by the combined resources of West and East. In 1914, the Allies had fielded a combination of the British, French, and Russian Empires, with the USA and Italy joining during the final stages. In 1941, with France already eliminated, Britain's only hope was to bring in America and the Soviet Union, together with supporting players such as the Poles and the Free French. There was no other practical alternative.

THE MAKING of this Grand Coalition, as Churchill called it, was packed with acute political dilemmas. The rhetoric of the Western Powers, as embodied in the Atlantic Charter of August 1941, spoke of 'freedom and democracy' and the altruism of 'the united nations'. Yet it was self-evident that Stalin's totalitar-

JOSEPH STALIN, Dictator, General Secretary of the Soviet Communist Party, and briefly, holder of the subordinate position of Prime Minister of the USSR.

A SOVIET camp photographed illegally from a train by a Polish officer sent from Britain via Murmansk.

ian regime, which had committed any number of mass crimes, was totally incompatible with such ideals. Similarly, from Stalin's point of view, it was obvious that the Western Powers constituted the 'capitalist enemy' against which all Marxist-Leninists were supposed to direct their struggle. Yet the logic of necessity was stronger than any ideals or ideology. As the German spearheads drove east with frightening speed, both Churchill and Stalin saw that West and East were condemned to cooperate. Stalin's Red Army alone possessed the reserves of manpower that might check Hitler's advance, and 'the hyenas of capitalism' alone controlled the sources of money and material that could assist the Red Army's fight for survival. So the deal had to be done. In the House of Commons, Churchill announced that he was "ready to sup with the Devil". And on 12 July 1941, less than two years after the Molotov–Ribbentrop Pact, the same Vyacheslav Molotov signed an agreement in Moscow with the British Ambassador, Sir Stafford Cripps. The agreement stated that the British Empire and the Soviet Union were to take common action against the Third Reich, and that no separate peace was to be contemplated. In due course, it led to the Anglo–Soviet Treaty of Mutual Assistance (1942).

Negotiations for Britain's rapprochement with the Soviet Union, however, took place in parallel to similar talks for a rapprochement between the Soviet Union and Britain's first ally, Poland. Talks began in London early in July between General Sikorski and the Soviet Ambassador to London, Ivan Maisky. Here, the political dilemmas were more than acute; they were excruciating. The Polish side would have to drop its principled stand of regarding the USSR as an aggressor, with whom it was in a state of war, and the Soviet side would have to eat its words about the Polish Republic having ceased to exist. Indeed, the Nazi–Soviet Pact itself would have to be renounced. Any form of Polish–Soviet agreement would imply a measure of mutual recognition. But now, in the interests of Allied solidarity, the quarrel had to be patched up somehow. General Sikorski faced a decision that was every bit as uncomfortable as Churchill's. If he said 'No' to an arrangement, he would anger the British, who regarded cooperation with the Soviets as a matter of life and death, and who as hosts, controlled every aspect of the Polish government's presence in Great Britain. If he said 'Yes', he would anger a large section of his ministers and supporters, who regarded

NKVD MUGSHOT: 5953, Anders, Vladyslav Albertovich, [born] 1892.

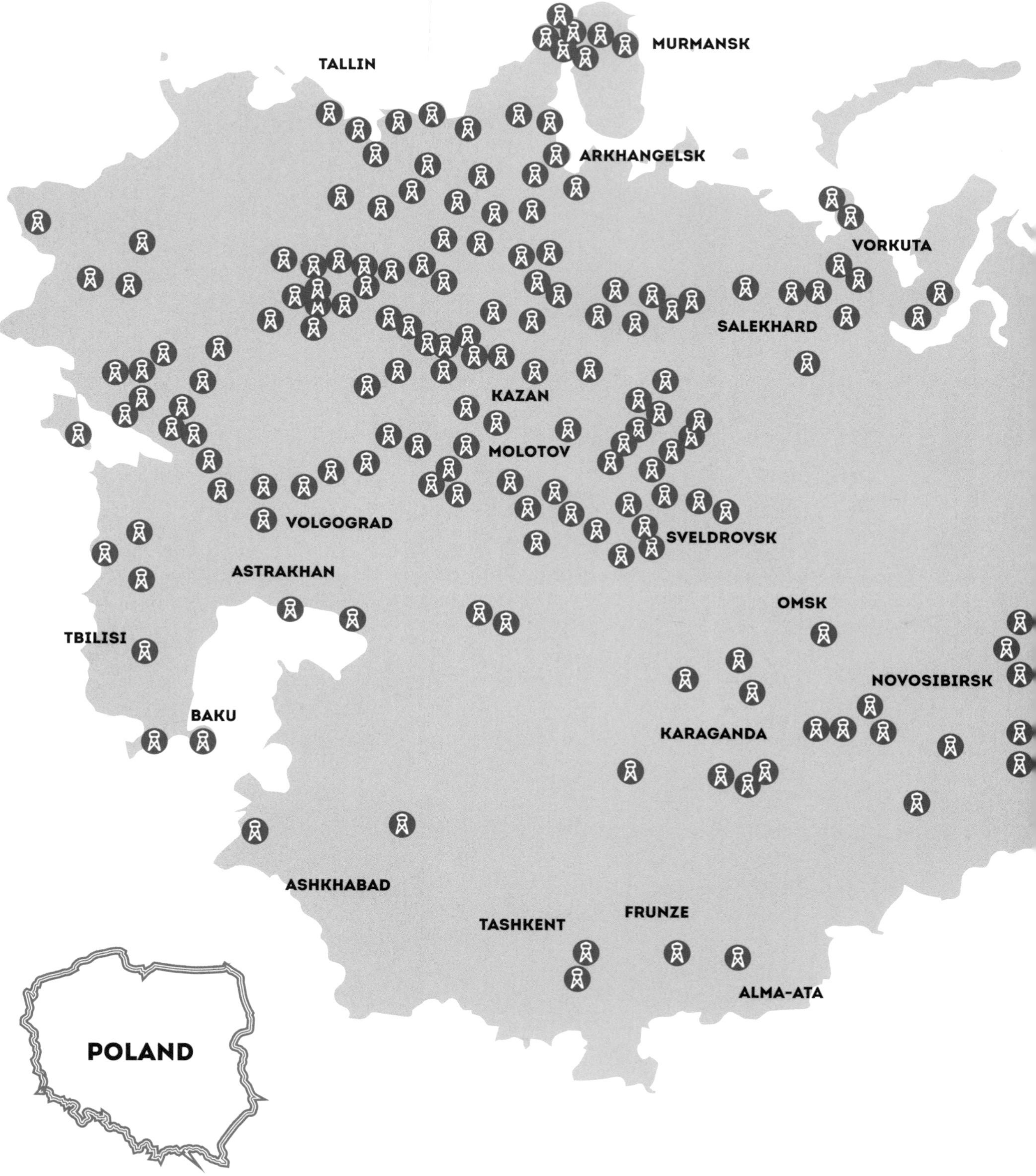
MURMANSK
TALLIN
ARKHANGELSK
VORKUTA
SALEKHARD
KAZAN
MOLOTOV
VOLGOGRAD
SVELDROVSK
ASTRAKHAN
OMSK
TBILISI
NOVOSIBIRSK
BAKU
KARAGANDA
ASHKHABAD
FRUNZE
TASHKENT
ALMA-ATA
POLAND

THE GULAG ARCHIPELAGO

EACH OF THE MAIN CAMPS was supplied from dozens or scores of other camps.

Numer 324, Londyn, Czwartek, 31 lipca, 1941 r

DZIENNIK POLSKI

CENA PRICE 1 PENNY

5, PORTUGAL ST., W.C.2

63, LINCOLN'S INN FIELDS, LONDON, W.C.2

THE POLISH DAILY—No. 324 Thursday, 31 July, 1941

Umowa między Polską a Z.S.R.R.

Układy między Z.S.R.R. a Niemcami o zmianach terytorialnych w Polsce nieważne — Stosunki dyplomatyczne nawiązane — Współdziałanie w wojnie przeciw Niemcom — Armia Polska na terytorium Z.S.R.R. — Uwolnienie wszystkich obywateli polskich, jeńców, uwięzionych i zesłanych — Oświadczenie Rządu Brytyjskiego, że nie uznaje zmian terytorialnych w Polsce od sierpnia 1939 r.

Polska Agencja Telegraficzna donosi:

Doniesienie urzędowe Foreign Office

Treść układu między Rządem Polski a Rządem Z.S.R.R.

Jak się odbyło podpisanie

Izba Gmin wita porozumienie

Mowa Gen. Sikorskiego

Życzenia Amb. Biddle

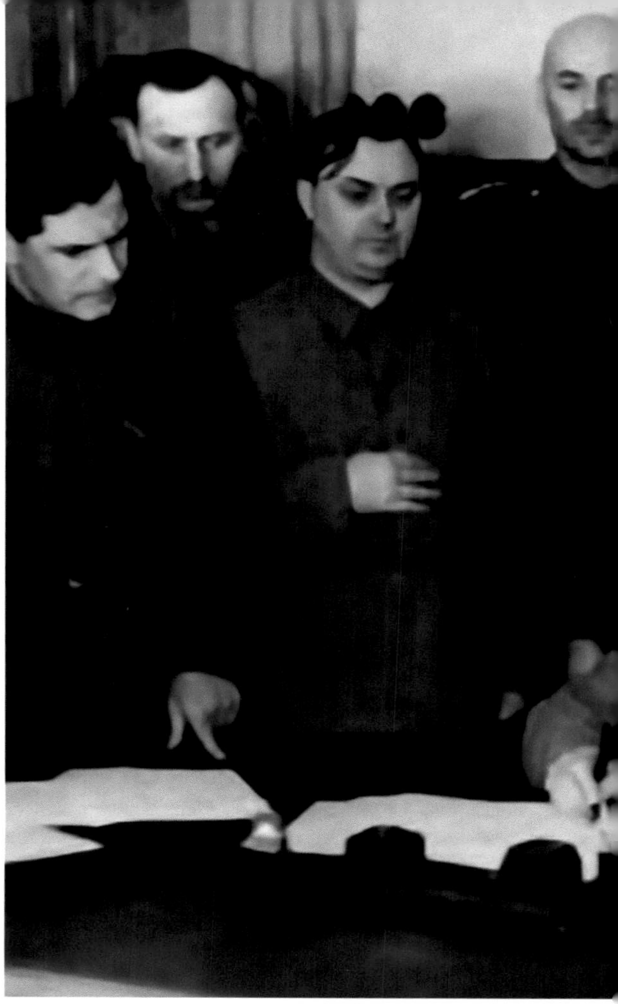

Stalin and all his works as anathema. The debates in the Polish cabinet, as among exiled Poles in general, were fierce. But in the end, Sikorski resolved to swallow the bitterest of pills and to gain what benefits were available. Agreement with the Soviets would strengthen Poland's position in the Allied camp. But also, by reopening diplomatic relations in Moscow, it would provide an opportunity to pursue the mystery of the missing officers and to bring relief to hundreds of thousands of prisoners. The essential bargain was that the Soviets should release the prisoners, and that in return, the Polish authorities would raise a 'Polish Army' from their ranks. The Army was to be led and organised by Polish military staff, but was intended to fight on the Eastern Front under Soviet operational command. Sikorski and Maisky signed the papers on 30 July.

Without delay, a Polish Embassy to the USSR was opened, initially in Kuibyshev, and Professor Stanisław Kot (1885–1975), a prominent member of the PSL, was appointed ambassador. In conjunction with the embassy, the Polish Consular Service was reestablished after 22 months' closure. The role of the consular officials was crucial. They were charged with protecting and assisting all Polish citizens on Soviet territory. In order to do so, they had first to determine how many such citizens there were, and where, in the vastest of lands, they were located. Between one and two million Poles had been removed from eastern Poland since 1939. It was an open question how many were still alive and how they could be helped.

Within a fortnight, the Soviet authorities

POLISH DAILY, London, 31 July 1941, "Agreement between Poland and the USSR" (far left).

STALIN SIGNS the Polish–Soviet Convention, 14 August 1941, Moscow. Watching with interest, Georgij Malenkov and Ivan Maisky, Anders (at the back) and Sikorski (right).

appeared to keep their side of the bargain by issuing an 'Amnesty' whereby all Polish detainees were to be released. Very soon, it emerged that the decree, dated 12 August 1941, was open to a variety of different interpretations. What is more, great offence was caused among Poles by the word 'Amnesty', which implied that real crimes had been committed.

THE SOVIET GOVERNMENT may have been changing its policy toward the Poles, but had no intention of admitting the impropriety of its earlier actions. According to the testimony of Sikorski's secretary, Józef Retinger, the term 'Amnesty' had crept into the text of the Agreement not through Soviet insistence, but through the negligence of a Polish official. One way or the other, large numbers of people, held either in the Gulag or in remote places of exile, were now going to be freed.

The man chosen to head the Polish Army in the USSR was General Władysław Anders (1892–1970), an officer of great fortitude and determination, who was lucky to have escaped the fate of his comrades murdered at Katyń. Appointed on 4 August before the Amnesty had taken place, he was chosen because he was a man of undoubted courage, having been wounded in action eight times, because he had no close political ties with the prewar Sanacja regime, and above all because he had an expert knowledge of Russia. Twenty-five years earlier Anders had been serving as a cavalry officer in one of the elite guards regiments of the Tsar's Army. More recently, ever since his capture in October 1939, he had been the inmate of Soviet prisons, first

POLISH PRIME MINISTER and Commander-in-Chief Władysław Sikorski (right) greets the Polish Ambassador to the USSR, Prof. Stanisław Kot. Moscow, December 1941.

L

of the Brigidki in Lwów and later of the Lubyanka, the NKVD's headquarters, in Moscow. Anders was lucky. In June 1941, he was lingering in the Lubyanka's dungeon expecting to be taken out any day and shot. Barbarossa saved him. As soon as the Soviet regime realised that a deal with the Polish government could not be avoided, he became a valuable asset. He was taken from his cell, brushed down, given a good meal, and told that he was going to command an army.

Anders recalled the moment of his release:

"It was 8 pm when the car left the NKVD building. It was already dark, and the street lights were dim. There were very few passers-by, but quite a number of vehicles, all army ones, and all making much use of their klaxon horns. For nearly two years I had lived in prison cells. Now the fresh air, the noise of the streets and the traffic almost intoxicated me. How strange it was to be free again."[15]

SUCH A BREATHTAKING CHANGE of fortune was not especially exceptional in Stalin's USSR. Exactly the same thing happened to Anders' contemporary, Konstanty Rokossowski (1896–1968), another ex-Tsarist cavalryman who had been brought up in Warsaw. In 1940, Rokossowski had been lingering in the Gulag, a victim of Stalin's officer purge, and heading for oblivion. In 1941, when the Red Army des-

THE POLISH EMBASSY, Kuibyshev (now Samara), 1941–1943.

perately needed every officer it could find, he was let out, rehabilitated, given a vacation in the Crimea to recover, and handed the first of several high commands which made him a Marshal of the Soviet Union.

Anders, like Rokossowski, did not match any of the standard Polish stereotypes. He was the son of a polonised German family, originally from Livonia, and was brought up as a Protestant. He was born in Wielkopolska, then in Germany, where his father was employed as an estate manager, but as a boy he moved with the family to Lithuania, in the Russian Empire. There, as a teenager, he caught the eye of a visiting Russian general, who was impressed by the skill and strength with which he took control of some bolting horses. He saw front-line combat against the Kaiser's *Wehrmacht*, received high decorations for valour, including a golden sabre, and in 1917 was sent as a cadet to Russia's staff college. If not for the Revolution, he would probably have found his way to a commission in the highest ranks of the Tsar's Army. Instead, and unlike Rokossowski, who chose to serve the Bolsheviks, he resigned and made for newly independent Poland.

Anders' service in the Polish Army saw several ups and down. In 1920, during the Bolshevik War, he was seriously wounded. During the May Coup of 1926, when commanding the presidential guard at the Belvedere Palace, he stayed loyal to the government, and rejected overtures to join Piłsudski's force. In September 1939, he commanded several operational cavalry groups with great dash and daring, and according to critics, with repeated disregard for his orders. He evaded capture by the Germans, but fell into the hands of the Red Army while attempting to re-group in the south.

In August 1941, when he received his unexpected command, he was subject to orders sent from his Commander-in-Chief, General Sikorski, and to dispositions made from the Polish Ministry of War in London. But for practical purposes he was entirely dependent on assistance from the Soviet military and on the NKVD minders, who were appointed to watch him. At the outset, he had no staff, no soldiers, no arms or equipment, no bases and no independent sources of supply. He started, as the English say, 'from scratch'.

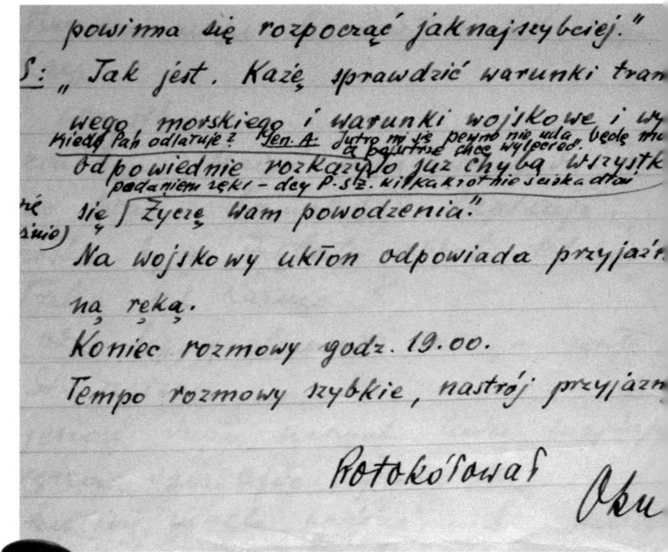
powinna się rozpocząć jaknajszybciej."
S: „Jak jest. Każę sprawdzić warunki tran
wego morskiego i warunki wojskowe i wy
odpowiednie rozkazy. To już chyba wszystk
się / Życzę Wam powodzenia."
Na wojskowy ukłon odpowiada przyjaź
na ręką.
Koniec rozmowy godz. 19.00.
Tempo rozmowy szybkie, nastrój przyjazn
Protokółował

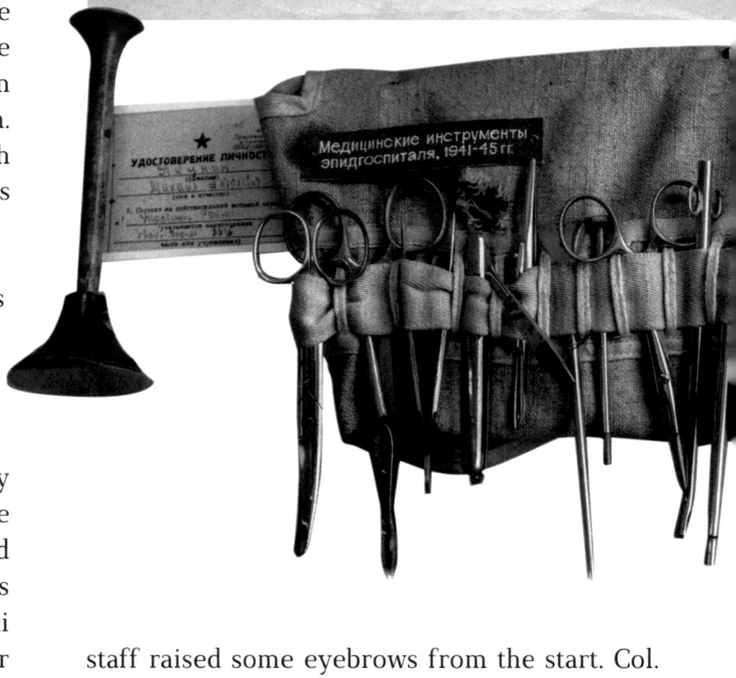

The task of forming the Army began before Anders was free to take charge. Early in August, General Michał Karaszewicz-Tokarzewski (1893–1964), another Polish general who had recently been freed by the NKVD, made his way to a POW camp at Totskoye in the Orenburg Oblast, where Polish soldiers were being held. Gaining their release, he organised them into the initial core from which the Army would subsequently grow. Tokarzewski was a man of great enterprise. Like Anders he had fought in the September Campaign, but after going into hiding, was instrumental in forming the clandestine ZWZ or Union of Armed Struggle, which in due course developed into the Home Army, Poland's underground resistance movement. Tokarzewski was picked up by the NKVD in March 1940, when trying to cross from the Soviet into the German zone of occupation. Now, he created the Army HQ at Totskoye, which was already at work by the time that Anders arrived to take over two weeks later.

BY THE END OF AUGUST, the barebones of an Army Staff had been formed. Right from the outset, it was clear that large numbers of officers known to have been taken into Soviet captivity in 1939 were missing. But enough senior men reported for duty at the Moscow Embassy for Anders to make his appointments. Many of them had survived by concealing their officer's status. The Army's Chief-of-Staff was to be Col. Leopold Okulicki (1898–1946), a man with a rich and tragic war service in front of him. Some 20 officers were to head each of the main military departments: quartermaster, transport, artillery, armour, and medical services, etc; and two were commissioned to command the Army's first two infantry units: General Mieczysław Boruta-Spiechowicz (1894–1985) the 5th Wilno Infantry Division and General Tokarzewski the 6th Lwów Infantry Division. Tokarzewski's divisional chief-of-staff raised some eyebrows from the start. Col. Zygmunt Berling had received especially favourable treatment during his internment by NKVD. And those who suspected that the Army had a Communist cuckoo in its nest were to be proved absolutely correct.

In the next step, the Red Army put three further military bases at Anders' disposal. In addition to Totskoye, he was offered a main base at Buzuluk in the Orenburg Oblast, and two more at Tatishchevo and Chkalov. He and

AIDE-MEMOIRE (top left) of General Okulicki of Anders's meeting with Stalin [18 III 1942]: "Fast tempo, friendly atmosphere".

MEDICAL INSTRUMENTS from the Epidemiological Hospital in Buzuluk, 1941–1945 (bottom left).

KOLTUBANOVKA NEAR Samara (2015). Former Polish Hospital, 1941 (above).

his staff thereon moved to the new quarters at Kultubanka, in the immediate vicinity of Buzuluk.

The recruitment of soldiers could then begin. The early stages were relatively straightforward because the first wave of recruits was made up almost exclusively of POWs who had seen active military service. Commissions toured a number of POW camps and by mid-September 24,828 men had signed up. This number was approaching the initial quota of 30,000, as agreed with the Soviet authorities.

But, given the fact that the pool of POWs was estimated at quarter of a million, it was extremely small as 90 per cent of potential recruits had not been located. As soon became clear, the death rate among prisoners during the winters of 1939–1940 and 1940–1941 had been high.

Pictures of the men who reported for duty show gaunt, exhausted, lice-ridden, and malnourished individuals dressed in rags. They did

RUSSIA

GENERAL ANDERS' flat in Buzuluk with its current Russian occupants (top left).

MOSCOW BY night (February 2015). Norman Davies in a Mongol fur cap. In the 13th century the Mongols destroyed Moscow, going on to sack the Polish capital of Kraków (top center).

ORTHODOX CATHEDRAL of Christ the Saviour, rebuilt in 2000. During my first visit in 1965 I swam in a heated winter pool. After the October Revolution the bolsheviks destroyed nearly all of the 1000 churches in Moscow (bottom left).

SCHOOL AND ARMY HOSPITAL in Buzuluk (from 24 July 1941 to 26 November 1946).

GENERAL OKULICKI'S tomb in a cemetery in Moscow.

KOLTUBANOVKA: CONSUL Rafał Kosiba removes snow from the tomb of Polish soldiers.

TOTSKOYE, 1941. General Anders with walking stick, inspects army quarters.

not look like good material from which an efficient fighting force could be formed.

These first steps of the 'Anders Army' were taken at the height of German successes on the Eastern Front. In the first months of Operation Barbarossa, the *Wehrmacht* carried all before it. Whole Soviet armies were encircled and annihilated. Hundreds of thousands of Soviet soldiers were taken prisoner or deserted. Leningrad was besieged and the spearheads were moving on Moscow. Stalin considered abandoning the capital, as Tsar Alexander had once done. In this period of the Soviets' greatest distress, it is understandable that minimal attention and few resources could be spared for the nascent Polish Army.

Yet the exceptional circumstances also gave Anders greater freedom than might otherwise have applied. The vigilance of the NKVD in rear areas was weakened; many of its operatives were sent to the front to man the notorious 'blocking divisions', which prevented Red Army men from deserting. In any case, the times were abnormal. That a collective Amnesty should have been granted to a large group of prisoners, many of them in the Gulag, was unprecedented in Soviet history. So, too, was the fact that a foreign army could be raised on Soviet soil without the imposition of the usual Soviet practices of embedded political commissars, of supervision by the Military-Political Committee, and of dual command posts. Soviet commanders were obliged to sleep in the same bunker as the 'political member', whose signature was required to validate all orders. General Anders and his men were free of all such impositions.

MEANWHILE, hundreds of thousands of deportees remained oblivious to the existence of an 'Amnesty' or were unable to benefit from it. For the time being their aim was simply to survive. To begin with, many did not even know where they were:

> "I accosted a man in my broken Russian, and asked him where I was... And he patiently explained that the place used to be called Nikolaevka, but now was renamed *Kolkhoz Krasnoye Znamya* – The Collective Farm of the Red Banner... In the spring of 1940 it was just a large village in the middle of nowhere, clinging to an insignificant lake called Kubysh — its water supply, but not, alas, a source of fish... Nikolaevka's link with the outside world was the Trans-Siberian railway, connecting the southern Urals with Novosibirsk and beyond... Administratively, Nikolaevka (no one ever took the name Krasnoe Znamya seriously) was included in the District of Presnovka of the North Kazakhstan Region. Geographically, it lay on the southern edge of the West Siberian Plain.
>
> The village consisted of three long 'streets' running more or less along the east–west axis, in harmony with the elongated shape of Lake Kubysh on its southern perimeter. Each street was cut into two sections by the *maidan* in the middle. They were known by their traditional names of *Verkhnaya* (Upper), *Srednyaya* (Middle), and *Nizhnyaya* (Lower), thus designating their respective elevations above the lake. I recall that *Nizhnyaya* was renamed by the Soviets *Proletarskaya* (Proletarian, I suppose), but this ideological allusion was generally ignored... The three streets were mirror images of the *maidan* — no more than wide stretches of rough ground, uneven and, in bad weather, impassable.
>
> The dwellings were clustered irregularly along the edges of the streets. Some of them could be described as cottages (*izba* in Russian) but most were primitive hovels thrown together with no attempt at making them look tidy, let alone pleasing to the eye. The better *izbas* were made of wood, but the majority relied on the staple bonding material in those parts: an unfired brick of clay and straw. The roofs were covered with *plasty* — pieces of turf harvested in the surrounding steppe during the summer, and applied so that the earth was exposed to the elements...
>
> Two or three dwellings were proper houses remembering better times. One of them — the residence of a pre-revolution grain trader perhaps — was converted into the main office of the Commune. It had large windows, high ceilings, and some old birches at the entrance. The other became the main building of the local *desyatiletka*, the Soviet-style secondary school taking children from the age of seven to eighteen.
>
> Nikolaevka's newest architectural embellishment was a wooden pedestal with a red star on the top, marking half a dozen or so unnamed graves of revolutionary heroes who had died for the cause of the Proletariat. This memorial was placed at the head of the *maidan* close to the desecrated church, presumably to supersede the latter as a new spiritual and social focus for the 'gatherings of the masses'...
>
> The seat of Soviet power, concentrated near the memorial across Verkhnaya street, comprised two forbidding wooden dwellings: the office of *Sel'sovet* (pronounced 'Sielsoviet'

– the governing body of the *kolkhoz*) with the private quarters of its chairman under the same roof, and the *Radiotochka*, a separate building housing the single central radio transmitter/receiver and its shadowy operator.

NIKOLAEVKA'S CHAIRMAN WAS A WOMAN. She was lame, domineering, and skilled at deploying her Wagnerian baritone. It was common knowledge that the radio operator was the local KNVD agent in mufti, whose principal job was to keep a malevolent eye on the village and on the chairman of its *Sel'sovet*. This sinister duo was served by a dedicated bureaucrat, the *sekretar'* (secretary) of the *Sel'sovet*; he, too, was lame. The ruling triumvirate was surrounded by an exclusive circle of courtiers: the *kolkhoz brigadiers*. These were robust frontiersmen of the Siberian plain, placed in charge of the agricultural teams (brigades) allocated to different geographic or functional sectors of the enterprise. Officialdom was served by a fleet of horsedrawn light vehicles exclusive to each member. In these handsome conveyances our oligarchs criss-crossed the village and their fiefdoms at breakneck speed. The rural proletariat observed their betters with a mixture of fear and oriental respect.

The *kolkhoz* establishment ruled with two levers of power. One was the allocation of grain surplus — after heavy dues to the state — among the households of the *kolkhozniks*, members of the collective. The other was the control of information. Newspapers came late and irregularly, and the only contact with the outside world was in the gift of the radio controller. Loudspeakers were encouraged in private dwellings, through which selective propaganda was fed to the households at the discretion of the controller. This sophisticated system was imposed on a village which at the time had no electricity.

Lavka, the village shop, could have been another economic weapon, but it was not — due to chronic shortages of consumer goods. The only two commodities readily available were colouring crayons and books on Leninism-Stalinism. What Nikolaevka really craved was vodka, and that precious nectar occasionally appeared on the shelves without warning.

Work would then cease, and an enormous queue would instantly form, panting with anticipation and occasionally erupting into conflict... To our great surprise the occasional availability of *odekolon* (eau-de-cologne) was greeted by the male population of Nikolaevka with almost equal enthusiasm.

ON THE way to the Anders Army. A Polish couple, the Szeligas, mourn the death of their son, 1941 or 1942.

YANGI-YUL (UZBEKISTAN). Winter, 1942. A soldier heads for the communal baths from the tented camp.

We soon discovered that it was consumed in lieu of vodka... Close to the central offices was the tiny post office hidden behind the *Radiotochka*. For us this soon became the most important lifeline. Nearby was the *bol'nitsa,* a tidy cottage hospital run by a good paramedic. It dispensed warm and dedicated terminal care and little else, because there were no medicines, let alone any up-to-date equipment. For me the *bol'nitsa* will always remain associated with my earliest introduction to the Russian language. My new local friends insisted that I should memorise their latest pop song which began thus: '*Na gore stoit bol'nitsa / pod bol'nitsoi burdachok...*', of which the English translation would be: 'There on a hill stands a hospital / and behind it – a little bordello.' The song went on to list the services available in this establishment, together with their prices. Nearby stood the veterinary centre. There was also a dairy, equipped to separate cream from milk (our *kolkhoz* had a small herd of cows, inaccessible even to the members of the collective; no one quite knew the destination of the cream.)

On the northern perimeter of the village the 'motor park' held large quantities of rusty farm equipment, and the occasional tractor — usually under repair. Beyond, at the high edge of the open steppe, stood four windmills watching over the village at their feet. Three windmills were old and magnificent in their decrepitude. The fourth was a recent investment by the *kolkhoz*. It was equipped with an advanced multi-blade propeller, and Nikolaevka was justly proud of it. Close to the oldest windmill lay the village cemetery, which in due course took in those deportees that were not strong enough to bear the cold and the hunger.

Nikolaevka had its own Soviet-style class system. Members of the *kolkhoz* were the privileged class. Indeed, the *kolkhozniks* and their families had access to the one overriding privilege: the means for survival. They qualified for the collective's grain and potato surplus, and for an allocation of *kizyaki* –dried cowdung-and-straw brickettes used as fuel. They were allowed modest private gardens, in which they grew cabbages, carrots, onions, and more potatoes. Some kept chickens, and occasionally a goose or two. The ownership of a cow — a sign of wealth beyond the dreams of ordinary mortals — was rare.

In comparison with the living standards of our smallholders in eastern Poland, the life of a *kolkhoznik* of Nikolaevka was no more than harsh subsistence; a subsistence subjected to the vagaries of the Siberian climate and to the ruthless and erratic exploitation by the economic dictatorship imposed from Moscow. But to the underclass of our village the status of a *kolkhoznik* seemed one of extravagant luxury.

The underclass consisted of two groups, the deportees, and the *odinolichniks*, who were the

MOTORCYCLE EXCURSION in the footsteps of Anders' Army, organised by Father Canon Wiesław Lenartowicz. Buzuluk (2010).

W TYM BUDYNKU
W OKRESIE IX 1941 - I 1942
MIEŚCIŁO SIĘ DOWÓDZTWO I SZTAB
ARMII POLSKIEJ W ZSRR
FORMOWANEJ PRZEZ GENERAŁA
WŁADYSŁAWA ANDERSA
В ЭТОМ ЗДАНИИ
В ПЕРИОД С IX 1941 ПО I 1942
НАХОДИЛОСЬ КОМАНДОВАНИЕ И ШТАБ
ПОЛЬСКОЙ АРМИИ В СССР
ФОРМИРОВАННОЙ ГЕНЕРАЛОМ
ВЛАДИСЛАВОМ АНДЕРСОМ

SYMBOLIC GATE to former Polish Army camp. Buzuluk, 2015 (top left).

GENERAL ANDERS' headquarters in Buzuluk, 1941–1942 (top right).

original 'refuseniks'. Not prepared to trade political subservience for permission to subsist, they would not — could not — join the collective farm. The enraged establishment declared them social pariahs, to be left to fend for themselves and to be discriminated against at every turn. In Nikolaevka there were only one or two of them and no wonder. They survived mainly because of the surreptitious help extended to them by their relations and friends in the collective.

Such help was not available to the lowest caste of Nikolaevka's social pyramid: the deportees. We were the untouchables; the undesirable flotsam resistant to reeducation. The NKVD kept us under constant surveillance, but at arm's length. We were not allowed to leave the *kolkhoz*. There was no need to force us to work. The powers knew very well that the deportees would be desperate to do anything for bread. But these 'rewards' were insufficient for survival. This was a well-tried Soviet formula, through which the 'enemies of the people' were deliberately drained of their ever-decreasing strength.

On the first morning of our exile my mother ventured out to look for accommodation. Someone told her that *Odinolichnik* Samoilov would probably take her family in. The sly message that the underclasses belonged together went above her head because she did not know as yet what an *odinolichnik* was. But she duly went in search of the Samoilov cottage, and found it on Lower Street, which refused to be renamed Proletarskaya, on the very edge of Lake Kubysh. On the doorstep of that cottage my mother met her prospective landlord, they looked each other up and down, and each recognised in the other more than a match. I remember that meeting very clearly. Rodion Samoilov was a tall bearded man in his sixties. I do not know his patronymic – my mother addressed him as *Khozyain* (Landlord), which for all of us became his appellation. He called her *Barynya*, the Russian for Lady of the Manor. It was a signal of recognition. Later he upgraded it to *Panya*, a light-hearted derivative of the Polish *Pani*, which approximates to 'Madame'."[16]

One might imagine that exiles who were directed to work on collective farms, were in a favourable position and would be properly fed. This was not always the case. In Uzbekistan, for example, the Soviet planners had turned many collective farms over from food production to cotton production, assuming that they could obtain their food supplies from the local market. In practice, food production had fallen so low that no surplus was available for sale, and the cotton-farmers starved. Elsewhere, *kolkhozniks* received such paltry rations that they, too, hovered at starvation level:

"As daily wages for their labour, they received, according to the prevailing custom on the *Kolchoz* farms, anything from 2 oz. of *jugary* (a kind of millet) to 14 oz. meal made from various kinds of corn. In theory, they were also entitled to one pint of milk daily and some meat, but in fact they hardly ever received these. No cash wages were paid at all. When workers lived on such rations, they lost their strength: they were then simply driven away to small towns and left to the care of Providence. 'No work, no food.' And so they died."[17]

EVEN IN PLACES where workers received regular food or pay, working conditions were often inhumanely harsh:

"The same day we had a big Workers' Meeting. The manager was the speaker. He spoke about the heroic efforts of the Red Army, which had fought so successfully against the Fascist-Nazi invaders, and about the necessity for the united efforts of all of us to support the achievements of the Red Army. He therefore begged us to vote for the abolition of our one free day in the week, which would mean working on Sundays, and to give the earnings of this day to a special "fund" for the State.

'Victory will be with us,' he concluded. 'Now, who is against the motion?'

Nobody opposed it, so the motion was carried.

From this time on, we had no Sundays."[18]

The Soviet Union prided itself on being 'the workers' state', and in theory was run in the workers' interests. The reality was very different. As many exiles found to their cost, even if they found paid employment in a mine or a factory or in some other sort of state enterprise, they had no certainty of being paid. One Pole, who had been released from prison and had been sent to the industrial town of Kirov (formerly Vyatka) in the Urals, described how payday looked:

AN NKVD food coupon from the Gulag.

AN ORPHANED Polish deportee eating lunch provided by the Army.

"At last, on Saturday, we went to the office to collect our pay. There was a long queue outside the cashier's office. We waited patiently for the window to be opened.

At last the cashier's head appeared. 'There is no money today, we haven't received it from the *Gosbank* (State Bank).' And the window was closed again.

I thought there was probably not sufficient money sent. The workers, however, started to shout: 'It's not true! We want the manager! How shall we buy bread, or pay for our food? What shall we give to our children?!' Eventually the manager arrived, and after much argument everybody was paid 'on account' five to ten roubles of his earnings.

Later I heard that at almost every payday such scenes occurred. The workers lived by payments 'on account' and the Works always owed them money. It was wrong for anyone to possess too much money: he might think himself free, and stop working, or run away from the Works, which might thus run the risk of being involved in difficulties. And so the money was kept, as in a Savings Bank; and thus the management ran no risk of losing their workers."[19]

The shocking deficiencies of Soviet economic life could only be properly described by people who had experienced them. They were far worse

WOULD-BE RECRUITS to the Polish Army in the USSR.

than anything the deportees had encountered in prewar Poland, even though Poland lagged well behind the more developed west European countries. And they were worlds apart from the fantasies that inspired leading Western intellectuals, like Sidney and Beatrice Webb, who had published their starry-eyed book, *Soviet Communism: A New Civilisation,* in 1935:

"Lenin's noble-sounding motto, that had seduced so many English intellectuals, 'To everyone according to their needs, from everyone according to their abilities', had been translated on the ground into a much more practical '*nie rabotayet, nie kushayet*' – if you don't work, you don't eat. So those who reported for work received half a loaf of bread a day, and the foreman would turn a blind eye to small amounts of food taken home at the end of the day. This food had to be shared with any member of the family who for some reason was unable to work.

Each 'Work Day' was recorded, and in the autumn everyone received farm produce for the winter, according to the number of Work Days they had put in. During the summer of 1940 our family had earned a sack of rye and a sack of potatoes. In October, after I was born, my mother was allocated 250 gm (10 oz.) of bread, half a litre of full cream milk and two litres of skimmed milk a day for the baby. Her own ration was, of course, still subject to the 'don't work, don't eat' rule.

We survived that first winter thanks to a sack of flour that my grandfather had the foresight to take when they were arrested, and to parcels sent by my mother's two sisters, who were still in Poland... Money came from selling anything that was not strictly necessary for survival like my grandfather's suit, the sugar and other little luxuries from the parcels.

PROFESSOR STANISŁAW GRABSKI (left), brother of a Polish Premier, released from internment in Russia.

The Kazakh villagers were indifferent to us, but there were two or three Russian families without whose help we could not have survived... It is likely that they had been sentenced to internal exile, just like us, but it was better not to ask. They helped in many small ways. We were not allowed to buy things in the village shop, so they bought things for us. On one occasion, my aunt went to Martuk to sell grandfather's suit... and found herself in serious trouble because we weren't allowed to leave the village without permission... [The

Russians'] greatest contribution was to introduce us to *kiziak*. *Kiziak* is made... by collecting dried animal dung on the steppe, soaking it in water, then mixing it with straw and forming it into briquettes which were then dried in the sun. This was to be our fuel for the winter... Without it, the whole family would have frozen to death in the -30°C temperatures...

Hope came with Germany's invasion of Russia in June 1941. Suddenly and unexpectedly we became Russia's allies... We were now free to buy in the village shop, and to travel to Martuk. My uncle was released from prisoner-of-war camp to join the Polish Army, and he managed to come and see us in Nagorny just before the snows fell. He helped making kiziak, brought money, and most importantly papers to join the Army as his family. Wisely, it was decided not to travel that winter... The Russian authorities were providing rations for soldiers, so many [civilians] who travelled that winter perished from cold, hunger and exhaustion."[20]

ALL THE INHABITANTS of these remote Soviet settlements, both locals and exiles, became hardened to the fact that Death stalked the land with monotonous regularity:

"We were housed in a wooden hut which only had a few beds, a table and a little coal stove [in a village near a forest not far from the town of Sverdlovsk]. Early each morning my Mother and Father had to work deep in the forest collecting pitch resin from fir trees in heavy buckets. They had to visit all

POLISH ARMY railway transport, Russia, 1941 or 1942 (above).

PERSONAL IDENTITY DOCUMENT permitting the bearer, Bolesław Jakunowicz, to leave the Gulag and to buy a railway ticket. 15 October 1941 (opposite).

the trees in their patch and collect full buckets to be credited with food allowances. They worked from dawn till dusk in freezing conditions for very little food and practically no pay. The overriding feeling was that of perpetual hunger and fear. At times, I was forced to chew on grass to kill the hunger pains. Malnutrition… became so bad that owing to the lack of essential vitamins my Mother partly lost her sight… Every morning I had to look after my younger brother and dress him and take him to the kindergarten where we

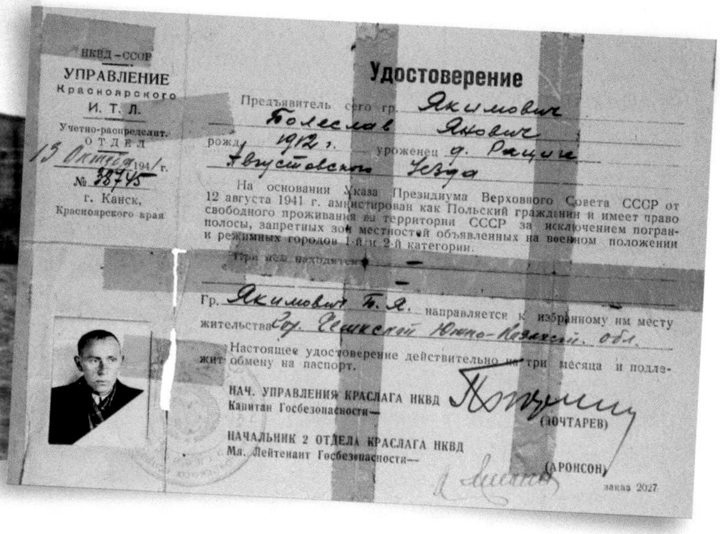
НКВД – СССР
УПРАВЛЕНИЕ
Красноярского
И. Т. Л.
Учетно-распределит.
ОТДЕЛ
13 Октября 1941 г.
№ 38745
г. Канск,
Красноярского края

Удостоверение

Предъявитель сего гр. Якимович Болеслав Янович
рожд. 1912 г. уроженец

На основании Указа Президиума Верховного Совета СССР от 12 августа 1941 г. амнистирован как Польский гражданин и имеет право свободного проживания на территории СССР за исключением погранполосы, запретных зон местностей объявленных на военном положении и режимных городов 1-й и 2-й категории.

Гр. Якимович Б. Я. направляется к избранному им месту жительства

Настоящее удостоверение действительно на три месяца и подлежит обмену на паспорт.

НАЧ. УПРАВЛЕНИЯ КРАСЛАГА НКВД
Капитан Госбезопасности— (ПОЧТАРЕВ)

НАЧАЛЬНИК 2 ОТДЕЛА КРАСЛАГА НКВД
Мл. Лейтенант Госбезопасности— (АРОНСОН)

заказ 2027

were taught to speak Russian and were taught Russian history.

My older brother Stasio went to the infant school [where] he became ill with scarlet fever and died as there were very little medicines. He was just seven years old.

After a few months of coping with severe frost, hunger, fear, lack of medical attention, hard work and inhuman conditions… my Father's health deteriorated; he developed pneumonia and, after a few weeks in hospital without medication, he passed away in 1941."[21]

One of the few benefits of the Soviet system, however, lay in the provision of universal, free education. It did not involve education as understood in the free world, and included heavy doses of indoctrination and coercion. But it did provide children with the basic skills of reading and writing, and it presented parents with an acute dilemma:

"My mother's decision to send me to the Soviet school was a radical step. Most deportee children were kept at home through a mixture of defiance and fear of indoctrination. My mother was prepared to take the risk. She explained to me that she expected selective learning, without submission to brainwashing. I was proud of her confidence in me, and was determined not to let her down.

The opportunity arose soon enough. I was instructed to join the Pioneers, the first step on the ladder towards party membership. I refused. The teacher, under pressure no doubt to 'deliver' the children, ordered me to stay behind after lessons. She sat at her table, I at mine. She told me that I would not be released until I signed up. So we sat there, eyeing one another. Time went by and my teacher became tired and hungry. Eventually I was released – and on return home commended by my mother. I had won my first confrontation with the System.

BUT THIS WAS ONLY A PRELUDE. During my second year of Soviet education I was elected by my peers (no doubt with some encouragement from the authorities) to the office of *klasnyi organizator* (head of class). I did not seek the job and I declined to accept. This was unheard of, and my classmates became concerned for my future. Sure enough, I was hauled before *zav-uch*, short for *zaveduyushchii uchennikami* – the all-powerful political boss of the school. He told me to sit down, moved over close to me, his legs wide apart, and began shouting: '*Tebya massy izbirayut!*' (You are being elected by the masses!) I stood my ground, only just, and was eventually released. My mother was very pleased, but also worried about possible repercussions. There were none, and I was left alone to get on with my studies, which by then I was starting to enjoy.

In September 1940, I was still unable to read or write in Russian. I was extremely unsure of myself. My first dictation was a disaster, and my chances were pronounced bleak. But I was fascinated by this new language, and I began applying myself. In the spring of 1941 my grade in the Russian language rose to 'good' (second in the scale of five). Other subjects were at least 'good'. There were no *otuchniks* – those with only 'very goods' among us.

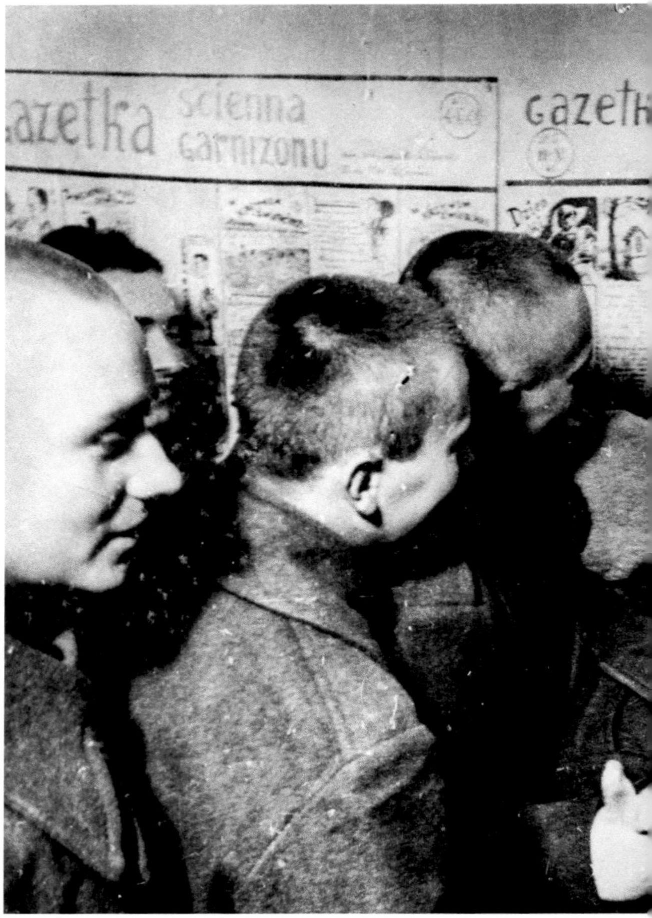

The other *udarnik* was a Kazakh boy called Akhmetov, a village aristo in shiny high boots with beautifully soft leggings. Our relationship was one of mutual respect, which eventually, and slowly, blossomed into friendship. In the meantime I was befriended, swiftly this time, by Kol'ya Glotov. He had only one eye, but in spite of this disability – indeed perhaps because of it – he was a boy of some standing. We two coopted Grishka Palej, the math wizard. The three of us set the tone, so to speak: the two deportees delivering results, presided over by the street-wise and respected Kol'ya.

GARRISON WALL NEWSPAPER AT a Polish camp in the USSR.

A RUSSIAN heating stove used on the railways.

The fourth member of the class deserving a mention was our Hercules, Karpachev. He was good-natured but not too quick-witted, and for that reason disqualified from our inner circle. On one occasion he challenged me to a friendly wrestling match, presumably to win some respect. Everyone assumed that I had no chance. But then I remembered one particular 'throw', shown me by my riding instructor at Łobzów.

It was more of a Ju-Jitsu throw than a legitimate wrestling hold, and it amounted to locking one's right arm around the opponent's neck and then twisting the victim anticlockwise onto the ground over one's right knee. I deployed this against Karpachev and soon had him on his back. My success became a sensation...

WINTER ARRIVED EARLY. There was nothing tentative about snow east of the Urals. It came down suddenly and copiously, and soon muffled the *izbas* to the rooftops. It was like an instant 'makeover', to use a modern term. Ugly blemishes and wrinkles were buried. Temporarily. Relentless frost followed soon after, settling at below 20 degrees Centigrade, often plunging to minus 40. Old men spoke of minus 60... The snow became hard, and on calm days the sky was blueish – occasionally bright blue. But there was an ugly side to the Siberian winter: the *buryan*, a snow storm without snowfall. At ground level icy wind pumps a dust of tiny particles of hardened snow at anyone who dares to confront it. Visibility is low, frostbite virtually inevitable. Death is seldom far away. During *buryan* any self-respecting *Sibiryak* stays inside; and when he has to go out, he makes sure that he wears appropriate clothing: warm underwear, *pimy* (long stiff felt boots), a *fufyaka* (padded jacket), a fur hat with earflaps, and an assortment of woollen scarves.

To us deportees all these necessities were inaccessible. Indeed, in Nikolaevka *pimy* were like gold-dust, a valued inheritance subject to a brisk repair business, and only very occasionally for resale. So our commune settled down to hibernation, now faced with the double threat of hunger and cold. Anuśka and Tereska huddled in their corner, writing interminable letters, awaiting replies, and taking their turn at the 'Polish flying library'. This involved the few books that had accompanied the exiles all this way (although none had come with us). They were carefully split into many slender instalments, which were then discreetly circulated among the Polish-speaking community, weather permitting. It was the Nikolaevka flying library that introduced me to Sienkiewicz's *Quo Vadis,* the novel that won him the Nobel Prize. Parcels from my mother's family in Wilno were the joyful milestones. We went to bed early: there was no light apart from my *puzyrek,* which in any case was for my homework. Early bed was also a way of keeping warm; and of killing time.

All this time my mother stitched her duvets, and tried to defuse the occasional conflict. There were not many of these. Everyone understood that calm was one of the weapons for survival. Hala produced the occasional poem, and we sent copies to Wilno and elsewhere. I wonder if any of them reached their destinations. My mother was sometimes persuaded to stop sewing, and instead to sketch a little with crayons. She drew her three children, which attracted the attention of our *Khozyain.* Eventually he too was persuaded to sit for her. His little portrait was the best of them all.

We dreaded the approach of Christmas. Back home it was the happiest event of the liturgical cycle: the exuberant coming together of the material and the spiritual. Tentative, and very modest, preparations were put in hand. Some bits from the parcels were put aside for *Wigilia,* the Vigil celebrated on 24th December at the sighting of the first star of the evening. There was no problem with that: the cold Siberian sky was crystal-clear. Khozyayushka invited our women to make (under her supervision) some real Russian *bliny,* delicious pancakes. Władek's bench was commandeered and transformed into a banqueting table under a white sheet. There was plenty of hay under the 'table cloth', a

REV. STANISŁAW BOGUCKI, prewar photo (below) and photo on arrival at the Polish Army Camp where he died (1941).

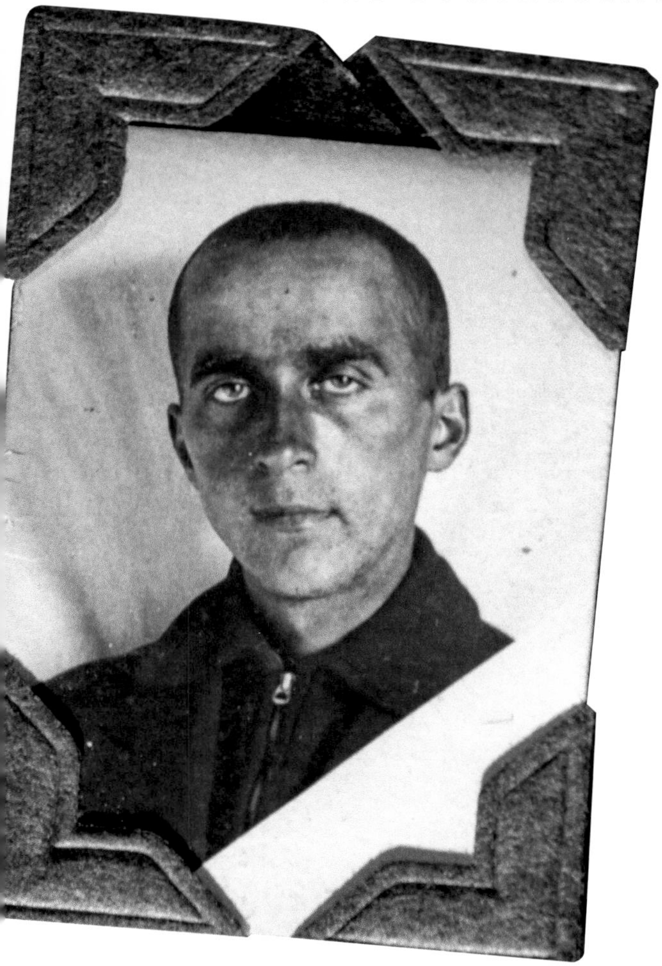

reminder of the stable at Bethlehem. The Samoilovs, after ritual refusals out of politeness, were persuaded to join in. Prayers were said, and *opłatek* (a wafer symbolising Communion, safely received from Wilno) was shared. Wishes were exchanged (along the lines of 'next year in Jerusalem'), carols were sung pianissimo and tears were shed. Our first Siberian *Wigilia* remains a happy, bittersweet memory to this day.

Two years later, at the age of fourteen, I wrote a description of our daily life in Siberia: 'During the winter, in a small room covered in mould where the ten of us lived together and where hands were stiff with cold, I studied by the *puzyrek* from the occasional textbook which I was able to borrow from some fellow-deportees. Most of the time we were hungry. The fight for survival was interspersed with illnesses. Deported from Poland without warm clothes, we suffered during Siberian winters regular frost-bites on the face, the hands and the feet.'

I faced frostbite every day on my trek to school, which I persisted in attending because I had discovered the pleasures of learning. My clothes were inadequate; other children had *pimy*, I had to make do with my father's old riding boots... The Russian language was the main challenge, and its conquest a source of exhilaration. This in turn led me to the school library, stocked mainly with Marxist-Leninist texts, but containing some classics of Russian literature, and even a few foreign books. In my spare time I began my systematic forays into Russian *belles-lettres*: Pushkin, Lermontov, Gogol, Tolstoy... In Nikolaevka I also discovered Shakespeare, Dickens, and Robbie Burns – in Russian translation."[22]

THE IMPLEMENTATION of the Amnesty was chaotic, prolonged and never completed. Following the announcement of 12 August 1941, the Soviet government issued directives to district commissars and to camp commanders stating that all Poles were to be released. Yet the directives were either obeyed or ignored or postponed according to the whim of officials, and the process dragged on throughout 1941 and 1942. The Soviet press publicised the Amnesty. But the word spread slowly, especially in the most distant provinces, and the releases, if they happened, were not coordinated with Army recruitment. Most people who benefited from the Amnesty left their places of exile with little information about where or when the Polish Army was going to be formed. All they knew was that a chance to escape had fallen from heaven, and that they must somehow leave the

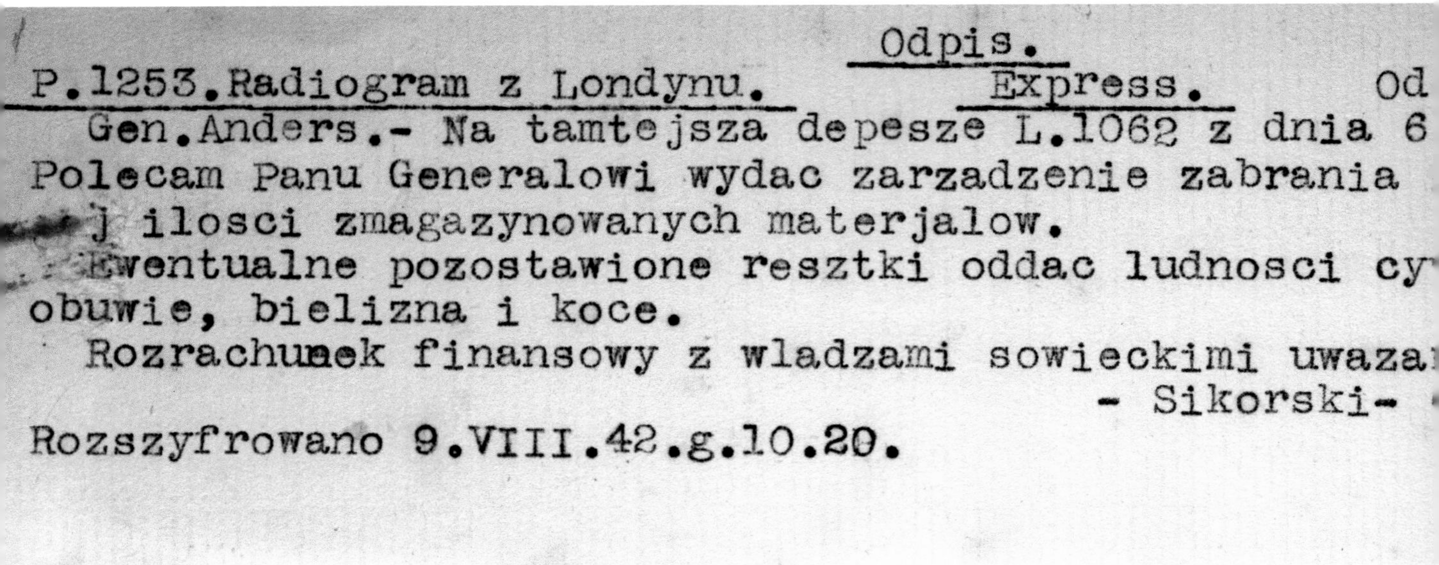

Odpis.

P.1253.Radiogram z Londynu. Express. Od

Gen.Anders.- Na tamtejsza depesze L.1062 z dnia 6

Polecam Panu Generalowi wydac zarzadzenie zabrania

j ilosci zmagazynowanych materjalow.

Ewentualne pozostawione resztki oddac ludnosci cy

obuwie, bielizna i koce.

Rozrachunek finansowy z wladzami sowieckimi uwaza

\- Sikorski-

Rozszyfrowano 9.VIII.42.g.10.20.

RADIOGRAM FROM LONDON, received 9 August 1942. "I consider the financial accounts [agreed] with the Soviet authorities as fiction. (Signed) Sikorski, [Prime Minister and Commander-in-Chief].

Arctic before the onset of the next murderous winter. In some cases, the camp commandants refused to release them or to give them the necessary documents. In others, rumours spread that Jews were being given preferential treatment. As often as not, however, freed prisoners were given no food rations or money for transportation. They were pushed through the gates of their camps into the wilderness and left to fend for themselves. Some began to walk across the taiga. Some built rafts, on which they could float down the great rivers of the north. Most tried to hitch a lift, or to climb onto the back of a passing lorry and to make for the nearest railhead.

Great assistance was provided at this stage by Polish consular officials and so-called *Mężowie Zaufania* (Persons of Trust), who had fanned out to all the main railway junctions and cities of northern Russia and Siberia to receive them.

Wherever the weary, half-starved travellers could reach these meeting points, they were greeted with a smile and handed life-saving food, tickets, money, and instructions to continue their journey. Yet the officials found once more that the numbers were far less than expected.

The late Ryszard Kaczorowski (1919–2010), for instance, who would later rise to be President of the Republic of Poland, had been deported at the age of 21 from Białystok. After a journey of many months, which took him to the Pacific port of Magadan and thence by boat to the terrible camps of Kolyma in the goldfields of Yakutia, he had arrived in north-eastern Siberia in mid-1940 in a group of over 300 deportees. Shortly before his tragic death in the air crash at Smoleńsk in 2010, he told me how a year after his deportation he had returned from Siberia in a group of only 18 survivors.[23]

Among the many long-distance walkers, none had a more remarkable tale to tell than the late Sławomir Rawicz (1915–2004). Indeed, Rawicz's tale was so remarkable that it was regularly dis-

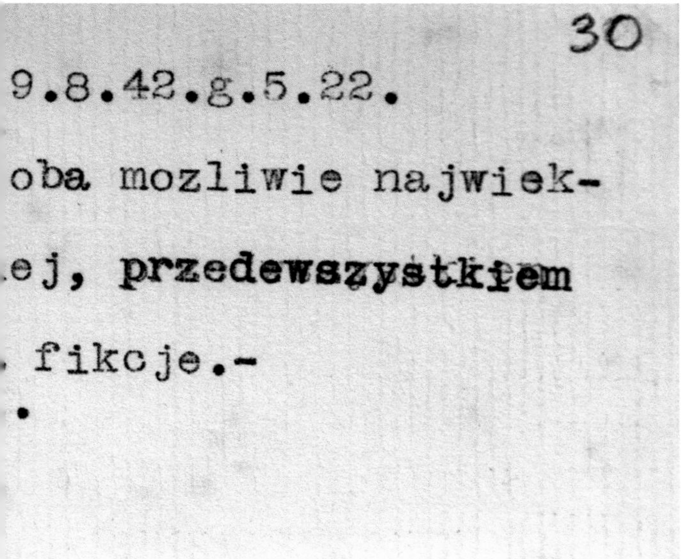

30
9.8.42.g.5.22.
oba mozliwie najwiek-
ej, przedewszystkiem
fikcje.-

missed as a fake. Setting off from northern Siberia with a group of companions, he claimed to have crossed the Gobi Desert, the Tibetan plateau, and the high Himalayas, and after two years on the road to have walked into British India. When his book, *The Long Walk*, was published in London in 1956, many reviewers judged it incredible. It certainly contained numerous inconsistencies and embellishments, that raised the possibility that Rawicz did not make the journey himself. Nonetheless, as the archives from 1943 confirm, incredulous British officials in places as far apart as Delhi and Kabul reported the arrival of footsore Polish refugees, who said that they had escaped from the USSR. In 2010 the story formed the basis of a popular film called *The Way Back*.[24]

ANOTHER SURVIVOR once explained to me how assistance could sometimes be provided by sympathetic Soviet officials. The Gulag complex at Pechora on the Arctic Sea, for instance, was exceptional in that it was linked by rail to the main Siberian thoroughfares far to the south. Freight trains ran along the 890-mile line to Omsk carrying canned fish and timber. According to the informant, the camp commandant offered to requisition a number of cattle wagons and to attach them to the departing freight trains. But in order to do so, he needed to fill in the paperwork and to name a destination. "Where do you want to go to?" he asked the would-be passengers. "As far as possible", was the reply. "In that case, I shall send you to Alma-Ata!" And in due course they reached Alma-Ata. Now called Almaty, it was then the capital of Kazakhstan, and it lies on the frontier of China, some 2,300 miles from Pechora. Only there did they learn that the nearest collection point for the Polish Army lay not in Kazakhstan but in neighbouring Uzbekistan. So they moved on to Uzbekistan.[25] Such unverified accounts invite questions. But the fact remains that by the middle of 1942, thousands of such hardy trav-

POLISH SOLDIERS in the USSR with their Soviet trucks.

ellers were streaming into the collection centres from all over the Union.

MRS ZOFIA LITEWSKA benefited from local help in a different way. Born in Barwałd near Kęty in Western Galicia, she had trained as a teacher before being posted to the Kresy. In 1939, she was living happily with her husband and four children in a village on the banks of Niemen south of Wilno, and was working as the village schoolmistress. On 1 September, her husband, who was a forester and a reserve officer, mounted his horse and rode off to join his regiment. Before she could learn whether he was dead or alive, the NKVD arrived, and

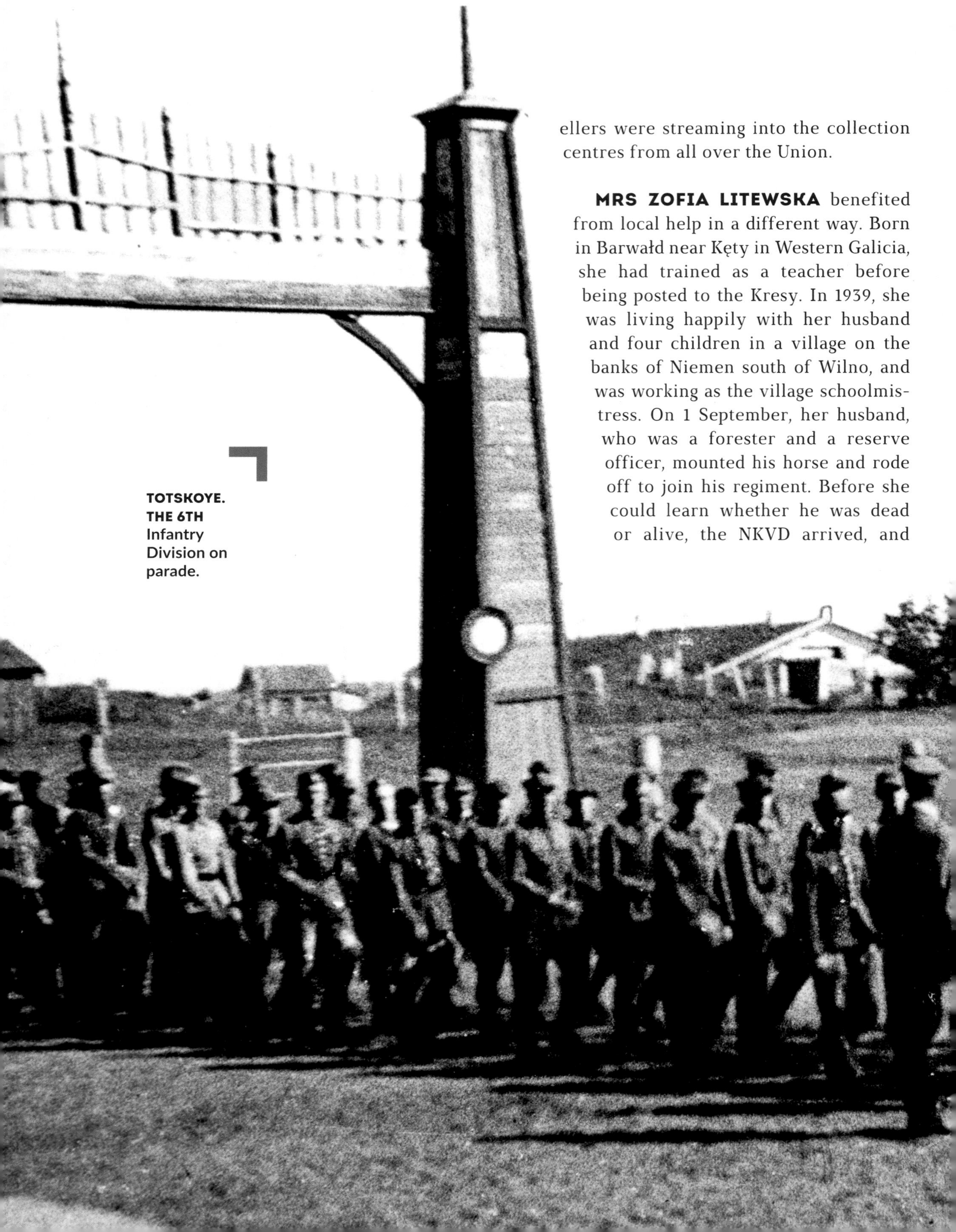

TOTSKOYE. THE 6TH Infantry Division on parade.

sent her and her children to a labour camp in Arctic Russia, somewhere beyond Archangel. After her release from the camp in the autumn of 1941, she tried to make her way south, but being penniless made little progress. She and her brood were saved by the generosity of a young Russian man, whom they encountered in the middle of a forest on his way to be conscripted. "*Zhenshchyna*," he cried, emptying his pockets; "Woman, I shall not need any money when I'm killed." With the money he gave her, she was able to buy the rail tickets whereby they escaped the Arctic. The ordeal, however, was not over. In the winter of 1941–1942, she kept her family alive by working on Russian collective farms and gradually moving south in stages. At some point she met up with her husband, who had been released from the Gulag, and together, after nearly two years on the road, they made it to the Polish Army. Her husband was to die soon afterwards from exhaustion.[26] (Thirty years later she was my son's Polish language teacher in Oxford.)

JUDGE KAZIMIERZ MICHALSKI was one of the men who travelled from Pechora to Uzbekistan, where in the spring of 1942 he joined the Army. After signing up, however, he learned from an incoming recruit that his wife and family were stranded in a remote settlement in north-eastern Kazakhstan. So he took leave and set out on a second long trek in the direction from which he had come. His journey there and back covered another 3,000 miles. But he located his family, and in the spring of 1943 arrived back at his army camp in time to join the

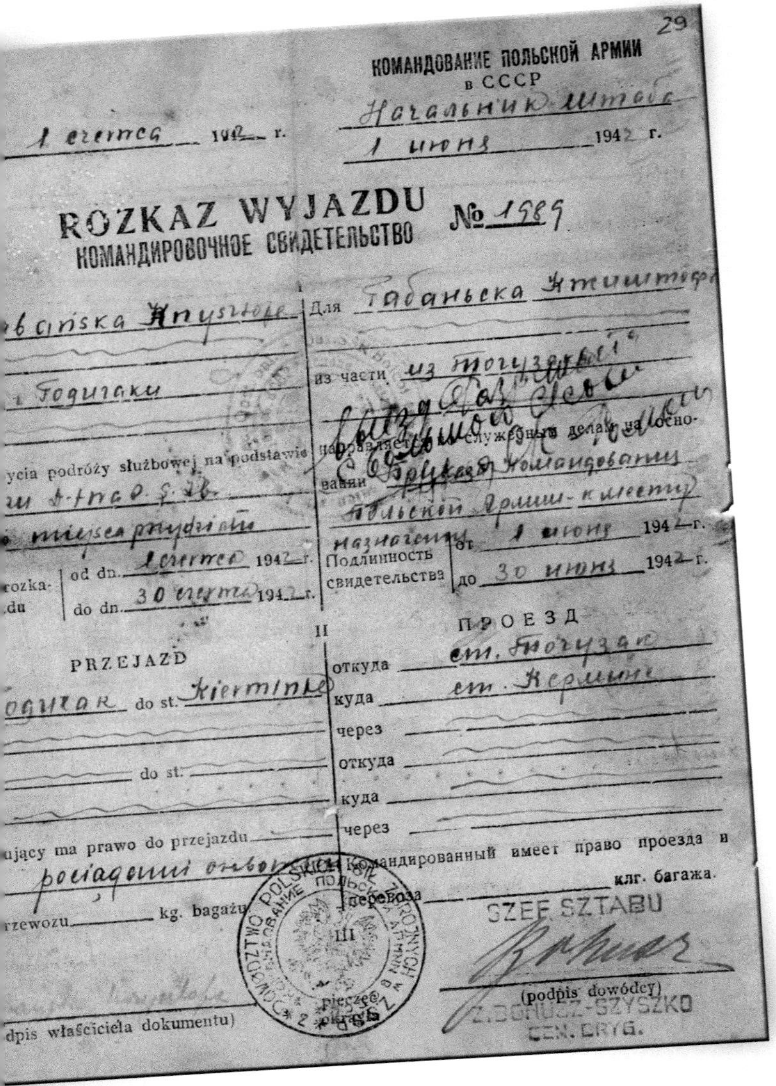
29
КОМАНДОВАНИЕ ПОЛЬСКОЙ АРМИИ
в СССР
Начальник штаба
1 czerwca 1942 r.
1 июня 1942 г.
ROZKAZ WYJAZDU
КОМАНДИРОВОЧНОЕ СВИДЕТЕЛЬСТВО № 1989
...bańska Krzysztofa — Для Габаньска Кшиштофа
из части
...ycia podróży służbowej na podstawie — направляется в служебную командировку на основании
Подлинность свидетельства от 1 июня 1942 г. до 30 июня 1942 г.
...rozka... od dn. 1 czerwca 1942 r. do dn. 30 czerwca 1942 r.
II
PRZEJAZD — ПРОЕЗД
откуда ст. Тогузак
...oguzak do st. Kiermine — куда ст. Кермине
через
do st.
откуда
куда
через
...ujący ma prawo do przejazdu pociągiem osobowym
Командированный имеет право проезда в ... перевоза ... клг. багажа.
...rzewozu ... kg. bagażu
SZEF SZTABU
(podpis dowódcy)
Z. BOHUSZ-SZYSZKO
GEN. BRYG.
pieczęć
...dpis właściciela dokumentu)

EXIT PASS No. 1989, issued on 1 June 1942 to Krzysztofa Gabańska, valid one month, for the trip from Toguzak to Kermine in Uzbekistan.

last evacuation. He had performed a superhuman feat, but as he always stressed in later life, all members of his family survived and they were among the fortunate few.

FOR MANY OTHERS, the Amnesty presented a terrible dilemma. It was often the case that younger members of an exiled family were fit to travel, while the older ones were not. Heartbreaking decisions were called for. The Bogdanowicz family, for example, were living in the district of Semipalatinsk, halfway between Alma-Ata and Novosibirsk. The father and son received a conscription order and decided that their duty was to head for the Army. But the grandparents felt too frail to be moved. Their daughter volunteered to stay behind and care for them. At every stage of their journey, however, the men sent a postcard to the loved ones from whom they were separated, and this correspondence has survived. The cards were posted in Barabinsk, Semipalatinsk, Barnaul, Almata, Lugovaya Camp (Uzbekistan), and eventually in Tehran.[27]

Such experiences were not unique. Sixty years after these events, I received a telephone call from Bradford in England, from a British man of Polish descent, who had been looking through the papers of his late grandfather. As often happened, the grandfather had said little in his lifetime of his years in the USSR, preferring to forget them. But his papers revealed not only that a younger sister had accompanied him during their deportation to Central Asia, but also that the sister had been left behind. The grandson's question was: "Is it possible that my granddad's sister is still alive?" And the answer was obviously 'Yes'. A girl who had been 10 years old in 1940 would have reached the age of 70 in the year 2000.

Rafters' tales feature prominently in the repertoire, and they undoubtedly contain more than a grain of truth. As recounted by a friend who now lives in Wrocław, one party built their rafts with a view to reaching the White Sea coast and thence a railway head, but found that the camp authorities regarded the intended voyage as illegal. When they left, the guards opened fire. The adults were all paddling at the sides for dear life, the children were lying flat on the deck to duck the bullets, and everyone was singing *Jeszcze Polska nie zginęła* (the Polish national anthem *Poland is not yet lost*).[28]

In the autumn of 1941, as reported, another group of amnestied Poles was sailing down the River Volga on rafts, heading for the Caspian Sea. One day, as they floated past, they spotted a tractor standing in a riverside field; its engine was running, but with no sign of a driver. Upon investigation, they discovered an abandoned village, whose inhabitants had just been deported only hours, or even minutes, earlier. Unfinished meals stood on the tables; the doors of the houses were open or unlocked; and all around were indications of a sudden evacuation. This was the Volga German Autonomous Soviet Socialist Republic (between Voronezh and Kuybyshev), which Stalin had recently ordered to be liquidated. The entire population of some 400,000 people, mainly harmless farmers, had been removed by the NKVD to the Altai Region of southern Kazakhstan in conditions reminiscent of the deportations from eastern Poland. Poles were not the only object of Stalin's oppressions. In the very same week, Stalin had signed one decree condemning the Volga Germans, and another that brought the Amnesty to the Poles.

FOR SOME POLES, however, the Amnesty ushered in a period of acute distress. It encouraged the Wierzbiński family, for instance, to make an abortive dash for freedom that had disastrous consequences. Already a widower, and weak from overwork, the father decided to take his seven remaining children on a journey of some 1,200 miles in the hope of crossing the Soviet-Iranian frontier. The girls' log gives no details, but from the Kustanaiska Oblast they travelled south along the Aral Railway to Tashkent, and from there westwards into Turkmenistan, which shares a border with Iran. At the border post, heartbreak awaited them. They were told that the Amnesty permitted them to travel inside the USSR, but not to leave it. They were ordered to return

WOMEN EXILES fed by the Army in Buzuluk.

POLISH WOMEN volunteers attached to the 7th Infantry Regiment (Russia).

and to reside on a series of collective farms in Uzbekistan, which was hit that winter by an outbreak of typhoid fever:

> **"September 1941**
> Travelled south but turned back from Iranian border.
>
> **Autumn 1941,**
> Jacubat Station, Uzbekistan
> Frania, 4 years of age died on the station.
> Buried on a hill by
> the station, just wrapped up in a sheet.
>
> **Czenkient district**
> Sent to kolhoz (collective farm)
> about 100 km from
> Tashkent. Worked picking cotton.
>
> **Czarapchana Kolchoz**
> Bolek died, 2.1.1942. Aged 6.
> Zdziszek died, end of January 1942,
> aged 15.
>
> **Dad died,** 7 Feb 1942.
> Stasia died, end of February 1942, Aged 11.
> Three of us left on our own.
>
> **Spring 1942,** Ajtanas commune
> Uncle Antek came for us.
>
> (Kamienne Lustro) [Stone Mirror]
> Stayed with them until autumn.
>
> (Molotow Kolchoz, Kazakhstan)
> **Autumn 1942,** Dzegergen
>
> Picked up three girls
> of our own age.
> Walked with our aunt and their
> older sister 40 km
> to appointed settlement.

KOLTUNBANOVKA ARMY CAMP, Russia: **7TH INFANTRY** Regiment in Russian uniforms (bottom left) and the same in British battledress (bottom right).

LIFE IMPROVES, Polish Army in the USSR.

Tashkent
Travelled there by train
(cattle wagons only
not locked this time) and walked quite
a long way to an orphanage.

Aszchabad
Arrived in a big Polish orphanage
with over
100 children.

[1942–1943]
4 July, when General Sikorski was killed,
adults from the orphanage were imprisoned. Our future was uncertain."[29]

After being orphaned in early 1942, the troubles of the three surviving sisters continued. They were rescued by a relative, Uncle Antek, who must have heard of their fate and who took them back to Kazakhstan. After six months there, they moved south again to orphanages, first in Tashkent in Uzbekistan and then in Ashkabad in Turkmenistan. By this time, they were clearly in Polish as opposed to Soviet care, and the death of General Władysław Sikorski in July 1943 provided them with a lasting memory point.

Individual experiences, however, can only hint at the ocean of human misery endured by the flood of ex-prisoners and ex-deportees. Many of them fell by the wayside, stricken by exhaustion, disease, and utter despair. But many kept going, drawn to 'our Army' as to a

magnet that gave them hope and a sense of purpose. None of them could have imagined all the further journeys that still awaited them.

Once the first wave of recruitment, in the POW camps, was accomplished the 'Polish Army in the USSR' had to steel itself to cope with increasing hordes of desperate people who were besieging its bases.

IN THESE EARLY DAYS, Jewish refugees, who had fled Poland in 1939, formed the largest group that was pleading with the Army for assistance, and it seems, for a time, that Jewish recruits formed a noticeably prominent element among successful applicants. Yet the army staff soon realised that more would have to be rejected than accepted, and that tensions would rise accordingly. The principles, however, remained clear; the Army opened its ranks to all men and to some women who were both Polish citizens and medically fit for service; and priority was given to persons with previous military experience. Among the civilians, it undertook to care for the dependants of enlisted personnel, but not for unlimited numbers of unattached refugees, for whose welfare other Polish agencies were in theory responsible.

In November 1941, General Anders supposedly issued a secret Order of the Day on the Jewish Question. In it, he allegedly said that he "understood" his officers' feelings, while urging

GENERAL ANDERS reads a report. USSR, 1941 or 1942.

them to recognise the sensitivities of Poland's allies, and promising that after the war "we shall deal with the Jewish problem in accordance with the size and independence of our homeland." Whatever that meant. When a text of the purported Order was published two years later, Anders dismissed it as a forgery.

Early in December 1941, General Sikorski visited the USSR for talks with Stalin at Kuybyshev, and Anders was invited to attend. Great events were in progress. The Battle for Moscow was in full swing. The Japanese had bombed Pearl Harbor, thereby ending isolationism in the USA. And the Anglo-Soviet Occupation of Iran was completed. The British had informed Stalin that they wanted Polish troops to contribute to the Iranian theatre. Notwithstanding, the talks went well. Sikorski was given four full hours. Stalin was in a genial mood. "You conquered Moscow twice," he mused, "and we have been in Warsaw several times. We always used to fight each other. We ought to be done with the past."[30] Permission was granted for a limited number of Polish units to transfer to Iran. A Soviet government loan was made available to expedite the supply of food and equipment. And the two leaders agreed to meet again.

After talks, the time was ripe for parades. General Anders conducted the first review of his troops at Buzuluk, and the Commander-in-Chief was present to take the salute. The ground was deep in snow. Genuine weapons were scarce; many men carried wooden dummy-guns, as per Soviet training practice, though the front ranks shouldered rifles with fixed bayonets. But they wore newly arrived British Army overcoats, fur *ushankas*, crowned eagle hat badges, and stout British boots. They stepped out with pride to the strains of the march songs *Warszawianka* [Varsovienne] and of *Pierwsza Brygada* [The First Brigade].

Recruitment, meanwhile, gathered pace and numbers steadily increased. Yet it was bedevilled – as the historiography of the subject still is – by persistent charges of anti-Semitism. General Anders and his officers, it was said, did not want to accept Jewish recruits, and blatantly discriminated against them. Historians, who should know better, often repeat the accusations at face value.[31] In his otherwise brilliant memoir, *White Nights*, Menachem Begin has the *chutzpah* to state that "in essence Jews were not accepted"; and he says it, knowing full well that he himself was taken on together with thousands of other Jews.[32] At the other end of the scale, one can quote the testimony of Ambassador Mordechai Palzur, the son of Captain Alexander Plutzer: "We never experienced any form of maltreatment."[33]

THE ROOTS OF THE BICKERING lay partly in pre-war Polish politics, and partly in the presence among the Jews of militant Zionists, like Begin, and among the Poles of militant nationalists of the 'Endek' and 'Nara' tendencies. The former were given to mouthing their mantra of 'Polish anti-Semitism' at every possible opportunity, and the latter to harbouring conspiracy theories. Neither of them saw that their mutual animosities were skilfully encouraged by the NKVD. In Soviet practice, citizenship was clearly distinguished from nationality. The former referred to the state, to which a citizen belonged, and the latter was a matter of personal identity. In 1939, therefore, when Soviet citizenship was imposed on the whole population of eastern Poland, people were issued documents that recorded both their citizenship, which could only be 'Soviet', and their 'nationality', which had to be one of a long list of approved categories including 'Polish', 'Jewish', 'Ukrainian', or 'Byelorussian'. Two years later it turned out that the NKVD was sticking to the same guidelines, insisting that the Polish Army should only accept recruits of Polish nationality. In NKVD eyes, men of Jewish, Ukrainian, or Byelorussian nationality should be serving in the USSR's Red Army. In this way, Polish Jews found themselves in the same predicament as Polish Ukrainians or Polish Byelorussians. They faced rejection, not as many assumed from naked anti-Semitism, but rather from the workings of Soviet bureaucracy.[34]

What is more, most of the medical doctors who served on the recruitment commissions were NKVD appointees, and they were inclined to adhere to Soviet guidelines. Applicants of Polish nationality were more likely to be given 'Grade A' or 'Grade B', i.e., fit for military service, while anyone whose papers indicated a different nationality, had a good chance of receiving a 'Grade D'.

GENERAL ANDERS himself never wavered. He was adamant that a Polish Army should be subject to Polish, not Soviet law, and he steadfastly upheld the rule that all Polish citizens should be eligible irrespective of race, religion, or politics. Far from blocking the recruitment of non-Poles, he sought to override Soviet obstructions wherever possible.

Anders was equally aware of numerous political complexities. He must have known that Poland's prewar Sanacja regime had close links with extreme Zionist Revisionists (to whom Begin belonged), and that in 1936–1939 the Polish Army had been training Zionist guerrillas for action against the British in Palestine. He did not need to ask his British allies for their views on that. Equally, he would have known that the prewar Polish Communist Party (KPP) had been liquidated on Stalin's orders in 1938, and that several thousand Polish Communist leaders, including many Jews, trapped in the USSR, had subsequently disappeared, exactly as his officer POWs had disappeared. He did not shrink from 'reminding' his subordinates, therefore, that a substantial element among Polish Jews had welcomed the Soviet invasion of 1939 and that such attitudes were incompatible with a soldier's oath of loyalty. Yet, when a Zionist proposal was put to him to create separate Jewish units, he did not oppose it outright. One such experimental unit was formed at Koltubanka, only to be disbanded later at British request.

On one point, however, Anders did not disagree with his Soviet partners, namely that applicants of German nationality should not be admitted. Around 2 per cent of Poland's prewar population was German, mainly from Silesia, and a few individuals from that community were pres-

ent in Soviet POW camps. Under the pressure of Operation Barbarossa, however, Stalin was taking action against his own citizens of German nationality, and, though Anders himself possessed German ancestry, it was not surprising that he concurred in the exclusion of some 300 Polish Germans.

FORTUNATELY OR UNFORTUNATELY, circumstances at the recruitment centres were often chaotic. Applicants did not always reveal the facts. Application forms could be doctored. Officials could turn a blind eye. Arguments and confusion were rife. Prejudice of one sort or another surfaced, and some individuals undoubtedly had good reason to complain.[35] Yet the NKVD did not always get its way. And in the end, with the exception of Germans, the composition of the Polish Army in the USSR was broadly representative of the country's population as a whole. The successful recruits included a majority of ethnic Poles, a substantial contingent of Byelorussians and Ukrainians, some 5,000 Jews and 22 Tatars.

The multi-ethnicity of the rank and file was reflected in the make-up of the Army's Chaplaincy Department. The Dean of the Department, ks. Włodzimierz Cieński, who had been interned in the USSR, took up his post at Buzuluk early in September 1941. By the end of the year, he was supported by a score of Catholic chaplains, two Greek Catholics (Uniates), two Orthodox, one Protestant, and five rabbis.[36]

Father Michał Wilniewczyc (1912–1997) came from the district of Nowogródek, the third son of

FIRST AID bag of a Polish soldier (opposite).

POLISH CEMETERY. Kuibyshev, 1942.

a peasant family from the village of Dąbrowica. Trained in seminaries at Nowogródek, Drohoczyn and Pińsk, he was ordained in 1937 and served as the parish priest in Hajnówka near Białystok. During the September Campaign, he rode a bicycle through the German lines and reached Dąbrowica, only to be told by his mother to return to his parishioners. He was arrested in Hajnówka on 11 November on an invented charge of spreading anti-Soviet propaganda. He was then thrown into the prison at Wolkowysk, interrogated, and on 29 June 1940 deported by train to the East. One of the 'crimes' to which he confessed was that of 'eating eggs in Poland' (*Kuszał jaiczka w Polszy*). In his interrogator's way of thinking, a man who accepted a basket of eggs every morning from his parishioners was self-evidently an 'exploiter of the proletariat'. For this offence, he was condemned to a labour camp in a forest near Kotlas in the Urals. Released by the 'Amnesty' on 8 September 1941, he travelled with a group of fellow Poles in a train laid on by the NKVD, arriving in Totskoye on the 24th. As he later recalled, the first snow of winter fell two days later.[37]

IN ITS TIME AT TOTSKOYE, the 6th Division employed six Catholic chaplains. They served their flock in the most primitive conditions. Father Wilniewczyc celebrated Christmas mass in a corridor of the camp hospital. In his homily, he said: "This Christian night has such power that the guns will fall silent... and the opposing nations will bow their heads before the Great Mystery." The communion stole which he fashioned for himself from a scrap of cloth was to travel with him for the rest of his life – to Tashkent, to Isfahan, to New Zealand, to Beirut, to Rome, and eventually full circle to the seminary at Drohiczyn on the Bug river.

Tensions between Anders' staff and their Soviet counterparts, nonetheless, continued to mount. Practical problems aggravated basic differences of attitude. In Polish eyes, Soviet officialdom was needlessly obstructive and negligent of its obligations. In Soviet eyes, the Polish Army was an upstart outfit that refused to respect Soviet norms. It was particularly

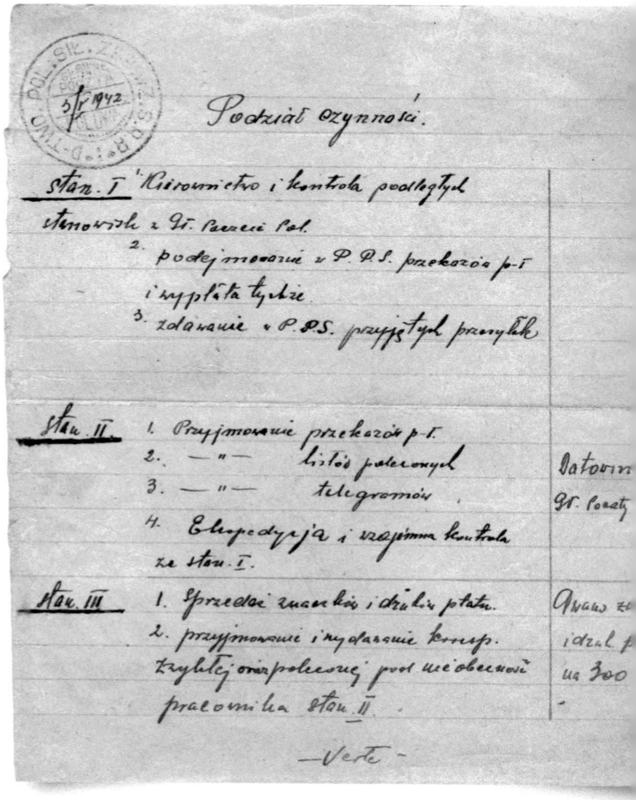
Podział czynności.

stan. I 1. Kierownictwo i kontrola podległych ... z Gł. Pocztą Pol.
2. podejmowanie w P.P.S. przekazów p-t i wypłata tychże
3. zdawanie w P.P.S. przyjętych przesyłek

stan. II. 1. Przyjmowanie przekazów p-t.
2. — " — listów poleconych
3. — " — telegramów
4. Ekspedycja i wzajemna kontrola ze stan. I.

stan. III 1. Sprzedaż znaczków i druków płatn.
2. przyjmowanie i wydawanie koresp. zwykłej oraz poleconej pod nieobecność pracownika stan. II.

— Verte —

POLISH ARMY POST in the USSR: postmaster's plan.

disliked, one supposes, by the NKVD, which until recently had been charged with rounding up its soldiers, and, as many must have suspected, shooting them in cold blood. Only a few months previously these Poles had been convicts and outlaws, and now they were strutting around in their funny hats, behaving once again like *Pany*, 'lords': making demands, talk-

A HOMEMADE SLEIGH.

ing of international agreements, and expecting to be treated as equals. What was worse, they were singing dubiously patriotic songs, saluting a foreign flag, and holding religious services, for which ordinary Soviet people could be punished. Where on earth, the NKVD men must have thought, had all those priests come from?

With regard to practical matters, the Soviet logistical organisations proved incapable of supplying sufficient rations, even for the 30,000 soldiers originally agreed. It was completely beyond their means to keep pace with the rising number of recruits and civilians. Anders' underfed soldiers found themselves sharing their meagre diet with their dependants. The Soviets were equally slow in supplying weapons and training facilities. At every step, the NKVD appeared to have its own priorities. None of Anders' men were transferred to combat duties in 1941. But fears arose that the Soviet staff were planning to disperse Polish units, instead of sending them to the front as one coherent entity.

Above all, suspicions were rife about the fate of the 20,000 missing officers. Over the two previous years, every Pole in the Soviet Union had picked up scraps of information and misinformation about the various categories of humanity that had been destroyed in the Collectivisation Campaign, the Moscow Trials and the Great Terror. They were more inclined to ask: 'Why should the Polish officers have been reprieved?' rather than 'Is it possible that they had been murdered?' Everyone knew that murder was a possibility. When Anders and Sikorski met, they resolved next time to ask Stalin about it face to face.

CENTRAL ASIA

CHAPTER 3

1942–1943

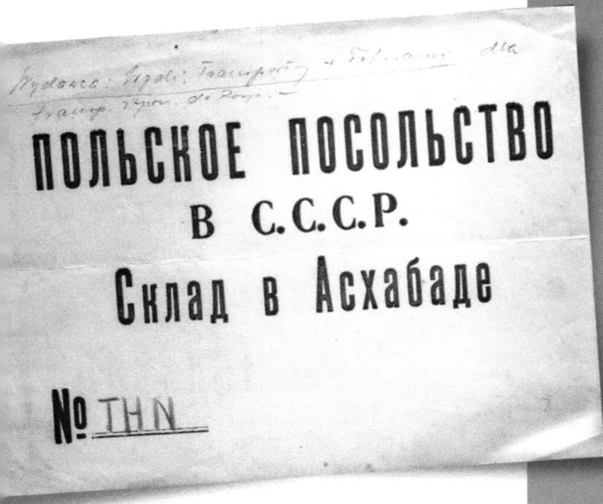
ПОЛЬСКОЕ ПОСОЛЬСТВО
В С.С.С.Р.
Склад в Асхабаде
№ THN

POLISH EMBASSY in the USSR – Askabad Store: the collection point for aid sent from Iran.

THE KALON Minaret, Bokhara, AD 1127: one of the few great monuments spared by Genghis Khan. In Soviet times, the adjoining mosque was used as a warehouse.

CHAPTER 3

1942–1943

CENTRAL ASIA

IN THE WINTER OF 1941–1942, THE GEOPOLITICS OF THE EASTERN FRONT CHANGED, AND THE CENTRAL ASIAN REPUBLICS OF THE USSR — KAZAKHSTAN, UZBEKISTAN, TURKMENISTAN, KIRGHIZSTAN, AND TAJIKISTAN — BECAME AN IMPORTANT REAR AREA TO THE FIGHTING.

After its failure to conquer Moscow, the Wehrmacht turned its attention to the south and south-east, giving top priority to the capture of the oilfields of Baku, Iran, and northern Iraq. Berlin's plan was to close on the Middle East through a giant pincer movement: one arm of which was aimed at the Caucasus via Ukraine and southern Russia, and the other, in the hands of the Afrikakorps, which was ordered to advance from North Africa to the Suez Canal. This strategic shift dominated discussions between London and Moscow on how best to deploy the growing army of General Anders.

Another critical change had recently taken place in Iran. In August 1941, fearing that the reigning Shah was sympathetic to Germany's plans, the British and the Soviets decided on joint military action to prevent Iran and Iranian oil from falling into the German sphere of influence. In Operation *Countenance*, a British force landed on the northern shore of the Persian Gulf, and made its way to Tehran, while a Soviet force invaded from the north, from Azerbaijan. As a result, Iran became an Anglo-Soviet protectorate. Shah Reza Khan was deposed, and replaced by his son, Mohammad Reza Pahlavi whose government was dependent on the orders of British and Soviet controllers. This was the time of Barbarossa, however, and, for the British, a time of maximum stress due to the Japanese attack on Malaya and Singapore and to Axis successes in North Africa. Neither the British nor the Soviets had sufficient troops to spare to keep Iran secure. Both were amenable to the idea of sending Anders south.

THE CHANGING STRATEGIC SITUATION was already evident when General Sikorski returned to Russia at the start of December 1941. His meeting with Stalin in the Kremlin on 3 December, in the company of Molotov, Ambassador Kot, and General Anders, is best remembered for the exchange concerning the 20,000 missing Polish officers. "They may have escaped to Manchuria," Stalin said wryly (knowing full well that he had signed the order for their mass murder in March of the previous year). But on other subjects the conversation was workmanlike. Without making a final decision about the Army's fate, the two leaders agreed that Anders' men should move to the south. And they established that the Army's standing should be raised to six divisions. Stalin showed a definite liking for Anders:

ON THE road to Central Asia: a railway bridge linking Europe and Asia.

ROADSIGN (2015): Koltubanovski 8, Samara 156 (opposite).

"I regret that I have not met you before," the dictator said.

"It is not my fault," Anders replied, "that I was not instructed to meet you earlier."

Stalin knew of the Pole's youthful career in the Tsarist cavalry, of course, and made him a present of two thoroughbred riding horses and an old Packard limousine.[38]

IN THAT SAME WEEK, the Japanese bombed the US Navy base at Pearl Harbor in Hawaii, thereby bringing a new dimension to the war. Hitler gleefully declared war on the United States in an act of supreme stupidity, and convinced President Roosevelt that military aid should immediately be sent to the Red Army to slow the

German advance. The USA and the USSR were never formal allies. But they were facing the same enemy, and American aid played a substantial role in underpinning the Red Army's recovery. What is more, when the Americans were seeking the best route for sending in supplies to the Eastern Front, they decided on the so-called Persian Corridor which ran through Iran to Soviet Central Asia. Some months passed before the convoys of ammunition, fuel, and transport vehicles began to roll in earnest. But the operation brought Central Asia to the attention of Allied leaders at the very time that General Anders was preparing to move there.

General Anders left Totskoye with his HQ staff on 15 January 1942, travelling on a train journey that took 5–6 days. His destination was Yangi-Yul, a vacant military camp some 12.5 miles from Tashkent in Uzbekistan. He was leaving Russia with its snows and sorrows for a warmer land, whose climate, people, and culture were entirely exotic for Europeans. In Soviet military parlance, he was moving into the territory of the Central Asian War District (SAVO).

On the journey, an army signals unit set up a radio station next to the General's carriage. Antennae were fixed to the roof of the moving train and contact was established with the Polish Legation in Tehran, and then with the Radio Centre of the Polish government in London. This was not just an outstanding technical achievement; it was an act of defiance which must have caused the NKVD serious concern. No one in the Soviet Union was supposed to have independent communication with the outside world.

On arrival in Central Asia, branch camps were allocated over a wide area to all the divisions and military departments. Polish units were stationed not just in Uzbekistan, but in all the neighbouring republics:

- **5th Infantry Division**
Dzhalyal Abad (Kirghizia)
- **6th Infantry Division**
Shachrizyabs (South Uzbekistan)
- **7th Infantry Division**
Kermine (Central Uzbekistan, near Samarkand)
- **8th Infantry Division**
Pachta, then Chok-Pak (Kirghizia)
- **9th Infantry Division**
Ferghana (Uzbekistan)
- **10th Infantry Division**
Lugovoy (South Kazakhstan)
- **Artillery Centre**
Karasu (Tadzhikistan)
- **Army Training & Engineers**
Vrevskoye (East Uzbekistan)
- **Armoured Forces**
Otar (West Kirghizstan, near Alma-Ata)
- **Army Depot**
- **Women's Auxilliary Service**
Guzar (South Uzbekistan).

ARMY RECRUITMENT and Evacuation Collecting centres, 1941–1942, and evacuation routes 1942–1943.

THE DISTANCES BETWEEN THESE PLACES were enormous. The nearest army base to Yangi-Yul at Szachrizyabs was 400 miles away. The journey between Dzhalyal Abad and Kermine stretched for 1,600 miles.

It was there, in the spring and summer of 1942, that the Polish Army in the USSR began to take shape. New recruiting posts were opened to deal with the constant stream of newcomers. New disputes arose with the NKVD over who

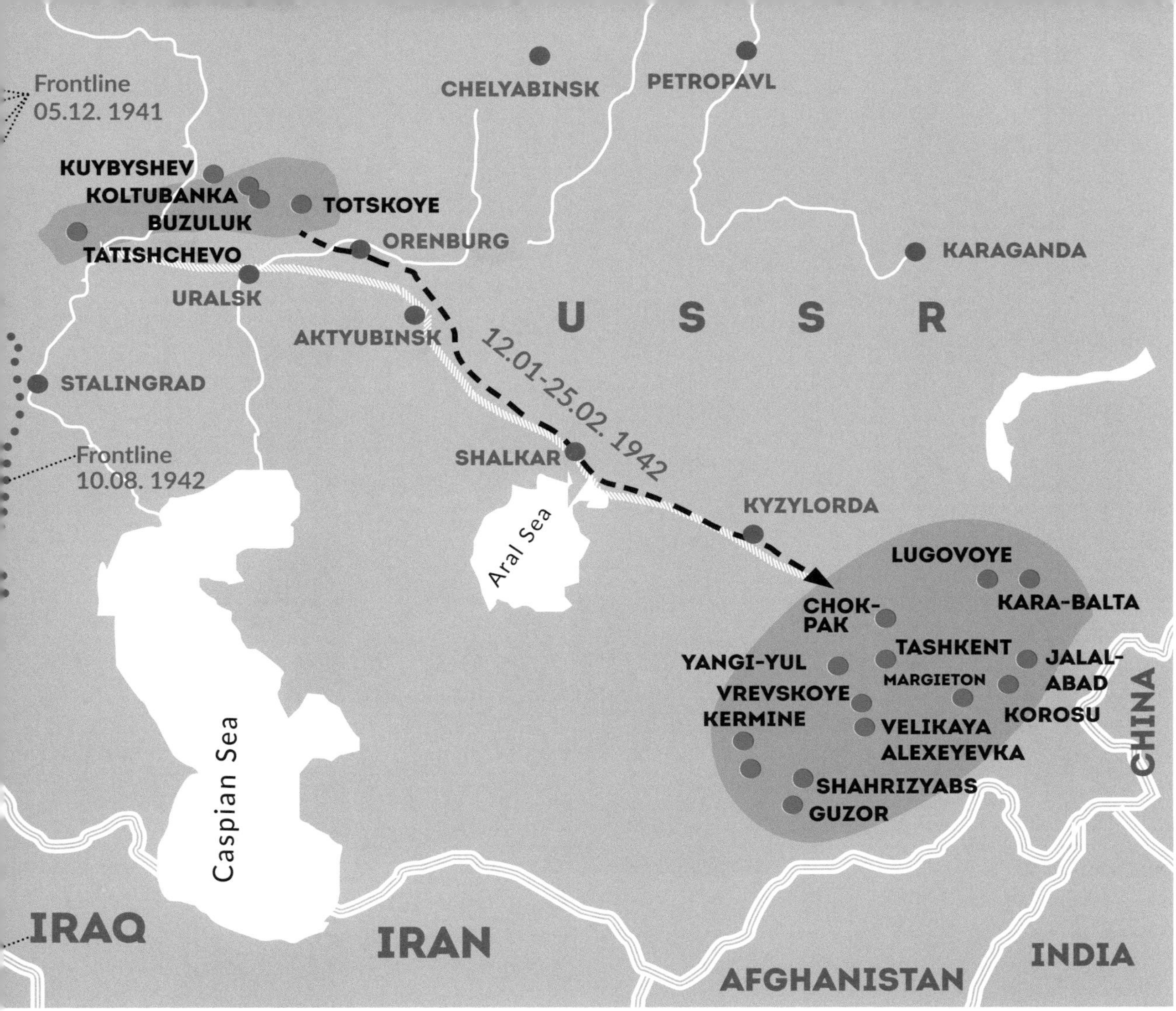

could or could not be admitted. And new provisions were made for the formation of a Women's Auxiliary Service and for the care of dependants. Above all, the men could eat regularly, rest, recover their strength, and train. Uniforms, weapons, and other supplies were delivered by the British Army via Iran.

News of the Polish Army's formation gradually filtered through to all parts of the USSR, inspiring many of the stranded exiles to undertake a hazardous journey to try and reach it. Many travelled as would-be recruits. But most were moved by the expectation of finding shelter and security by simply being in the vicinity of their compatriots. The journey demanded careful preparations, much courage, and a strong dose of good fortune:

"For my mother the decision in the summer of 1942 to travel to Central Asia must have been painful. She always considered it her first duty to be as near to her husband as possible; now she was about to abandon that duty. But circumstances had changed. She knew that my father was neither in the Polish Army nor in the Embassy. If he were still alive, he could be anywhere between Archangel and Kamchatka... In these circumstances, she decided that her next priority was to get her children out of the

Soviet Union; in other words, to attempt a journey from Nikolaevka via Novosibirsk towards Tashkent and beyond...

For us the last few days of June were extremely busy. My mother called on the chairwoman of the *kolkhoz* and, having secured her counter-signature on our precious papers, proceeded to convert her 'iron reserve' — the few gold coins put aside for a crisis such as this — into wheat flour to be transformed into dry biscuits, and into a Soviet currency more stable and even more valuable than gold — pure alcohol. There was no money left for transport to the rail station at Petukhovo. So, in anticipation of a 100-plus km trek on foot, we reduced our bundles to a minimum. My balalaika had to go. By then my mother was not too strong on her legs, and the prospect of a long walk was extremely daunting. Help came unexpectedly from our fellow exile, the Jewish merchant of Oszmiana. He offered to hire a *podvoda,* a one-horse cart, on the understanding that we would repay him sometime, somewhere... It was an act of great generosity. I do not remember the name of our benefactor, but 65 years later I still offer a prayer for him every Sunday.

The *podvoda* appeared at midday on July 2, complete with two silent and sullen Kazakhs. The bundles were placed on the cart, my mother was deposited on top of the bundles, and we set off across the village, past the *Radiotochka* and on towards the three rickety windmills, saying our goodbyes on the hoof as we passed the dwellings of various friends. The windmills waved their last farewell as we confronted the steppe and set off into the

A RAILWAY transport of Polish families arriving in Central Asia, 1942 (left).

RAILWAY TICKET (below).

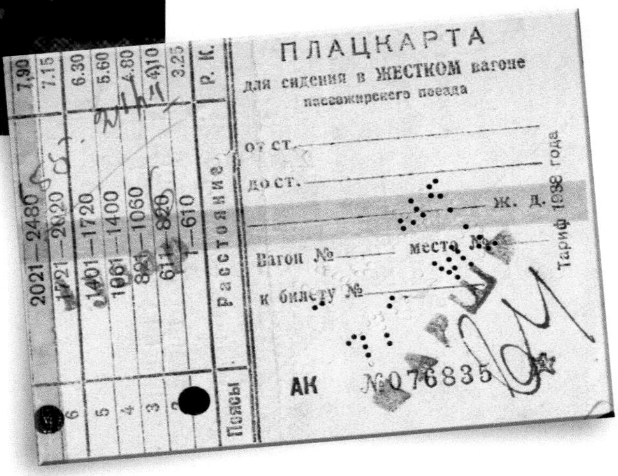

unknown. As the sky darkened, we began our second great journey.

We stopped for the night on the edge of a Siberian forest, sharing the shack of some hospitable woodcutters. If I remember rightly, they were deportees from Lithuania. Early next morning we set off again under a heavy sky. Soon the rain came down, and our march became a muddy slog into the wind. Late in the afternoon we were overtaken by some fellow-travellers in a cart pulled by two strong horses. They took pity on us foot soldiers, and offered a lift... My mother followed behind with the two silent Kazakhs.

After her children were lost from sight, my mother's two minders stopped the cart, unharnessed the horse, and told her that the three of them would spend the night where they stood. My mother sensed danger and — after a short and particularly fervent prayer — said to the duo: 'Look up there. That person on the top of the hill is my son who is coming to be with his mother.' And so it was. Feeling uneasy about leaving her behind on her own, I began retracing my steps. As I marched down towards them, the two Kazakhs quickly reharnessed the horse and resumed the journey. Thereafter my mother insisted that on that wet afternoon I saved her life.

TOWARDS THE END of the next day, which was July 4, we reached the railway station of Petukhovo, where two and a half years earlier we had been tossed out of the cattle truck. The two Kazakhs were paid off, and we spent the night in an outbuilding of a house belonging to a railwayman. The next morning we joined a large and impatient crowd of would-be passengers besieging the ticket office. A few dispirited Poles assured my mother that our chances of getting tickets were virtually nil. But she persisted, joining the crowd at the ticket booth whenever the news went round that the next eastward train was due. We took turns to accompany her during these depressing vigils.

The routine was becoming monotonous, but then a burly NKVD man appeared on the scene. Wishing to restore order, he shouted: '*Kto zdes' voennyi?*' (Any military personnel

(L.L.)

Ankudowicz Wacł. s. Leopol. 1878 (5)
Bratkozor Stanisł. s. Jana 1906 (2)
+ Butrym Bohdan s. Anton. 1887 (3)
+ Dawidowicz Jul. s. Aleks. 1912 (2)
Dobkiewicz Donat s. Jana 1883 (2)
Bieliński Franc. s. Stan. 1900
+ Grynhoff Stanisł. s. Stanisł. 1915
+ Hoppen Antoni s. Kazim. 1897 (5)
Iwankiewicz Kazim. s. Kazim. 1909 (3)
Iwankiewicz Stanisł. s. Józef 1891 (2)
+ Jakubowski Wacław s. Jana 1899 (2)
Jankowski Saturnin s. Miecz. 1890 (4)
Jaworski Kazim. s. Kazim. 1904 (3)
Janowicz Maciej s. Kazim. 1895 (4)
Jarudas Zygm. s. Gust. 1898 (2)
Jasiński Zygm. s. Wojc. 1883 (1)
Jasieński Stanisł. s. Stan. 1896 (2)
Jankowski Herkul. s. Adama 1890 (3)
Koźmian Wacł. s. Jana 1891 (4)
+ Kossakowski Michał s. Zygm. 1915 (2)
Lutyk Ign. s. Stan. 1887 (3)
+ Narkiewicz Kazim. s. Kaz. 1893 (2)
+ Parczewski Dr.
+ Plater-Zyberk Stan. s. Ludw. 1889 (3)
Paszkiewicz Kazim. s. Józefa 1880 (4)
Romanowski Edward s. Witolda 1888 (2)
+ Kraczkowski Witold s. Wacł. 1896 (3)
+ Rusnecz Gustaw s. Ign. 1885
Stankiewicz Kaz. s. Stanisł. 1884 (2)
Sobolewski Stan. s. Zygm. 1907 (1)
+ Szwoynicki Jerzy s. Romana 1909 (1)
Sienkiewicz Alfons s. Witolda 1885
Wojtkowicz Stan. s. Jul.
Żebrzycki Czesław s. Józefa 1874 (4)
Wahrman Dr. 1904 (2)
Szemiota (Tad.)
Stefanowicz Witold 1879

EXHAUSTED EXILES outside an Army camp (above centre).

9 SEPTEMBER 1941. "That's what I looked like after being released from the Gulag – Tosiek" (above right).

HANDWRITTEN LIST of would-be recruits at one of the Polish Army collecting centres (left). † denotes a recruit who died.

here?) In the hush that followed I heard my mother's tremulous voice: *'Ya voennaya'* (I am military personnel). The representative of internal order looked her up and down and said, 'Come with me.' The crowd parted and my mother was ushered to the window where her papers were scrutinised and four tickets issued to Guzar at the end of the world. The price was minimal. With the tickets came *kompostirovka* – the NKVD endorsement – but only for the first leg of the journey to

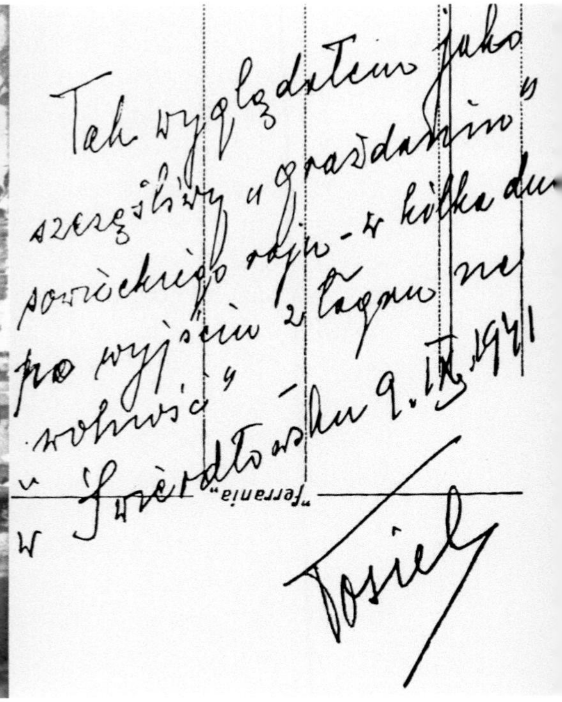

nearby Omsk. The full significance of this limitation was to become apparent at our next stop. In the meantime, we happily clambered up to a real passenger carriage designated *zhostkii,* a Soviet euphemism for third class. My mother said: 'Tadzio's sign of the cross from the Słonim prison has launched us on our way.'

I WAS ECSTATIC. The sun was shining, the wheels were tappety-tapping along. From my vantage point on the steps of our carriage – strictly forbidden, of course – I was taking in the Siberian summer countryside rolling by at a leisurely speed. We stopped almost casually at Petro-Pavlovsk (now for some reason renamed Petropavl) and eventually arrived at Omsk very late on July 6. Here we became specks in a large crowd heaving and pushing for access to trains... What was now required was a double endorsement from the NKVD: the next *kompostirovka* and a *sanobrabotka* (sanitary inspection), i.e., a delousing-cum-shower.

After several attempts it became obvious that the NKVD were routinely refusing *kompostirovkas* to Polish civilians attempting to travel to Tashkent and beyond. My mother decided that the time had come for her pure alcohol. By diluting a measure of this nectar, she converted it into a *chakushka* (quarter litre) of respectably strong vodka. With this prize she proceeded to corrupt the station personnel – in the event a surprisingly easy task. *San-obrabotka* and *kompostirovka* were brushed aside and in the depth of the night we were smuggled by our relaxed new friends onto the train destined for Novosibirsk, some 700 km due east. My mother did not know that *en route* we now faced the risk of being picked up by the NKVD as illegal passengers. The train pulled out of Omsk in the early hours of July 8...

The race was on. We had been extremely lucky so far: there were no ticket checks along this sector of the journey. But in comparison

with Omsk, the station of Novosibirsk was a nightmare. And for us, a critical point of the whole undertaking. Novosibirsk was an important rail junction, besieged by a mass of humanity demanding transport. Because of its strategic significance, it was strictly controlled by the NKVD. My mother soon discovered that her *chakushkas*, though welcome, were not enough. For a day or two she fought for official permits, while we three, and our bundles, were continuously moved by the police around the pavements near the station. We seemed to have reached the end of the road.

THEN A POLISH SERGEANT in a British uniform came up to us and asked if he could be of any help. I do not remember his name but I feel bound to put on record his talents as a sculptor. Learning of our predicament, and showing little surprise, he produced a potato, on which he proceeded to carve a replica of the *kompostirovka* stamp. The result was impeccable. He then applied this stamp to our tickets, added signatures with a flourish, and said to my mother: 'The secret door to Tashkent is open.'

My mother understood how dangerous this was. But in Novosibirsk she had come to the conclusion that our journey was no longer a battle of wits with hostile authorities, but a hazardous game with life itself as the stake. Our cicerone escorted us with full pomp onto the train bound for Tashkent 1,200 miles away. Over the next few days he travelled with us. Inspections were frequent and the tickets were scrutinised with great care. We missed several heartbeats at every check, but the potato stamp created by our guardian angel in battledress passed the test every time...

In Novosibirsk we... turned sharply south onto the 'Turk-Sib' Railway. It was then a tedious single-line route, interspersed with occasional

PARADE AT Kermine, 3 May 1942, with American, Soviet and Polish flags (above).

IDENTITY DOCUMENT of Corporal Bogdan Doliński, b. 1924, bachelor, 'in active service with the Polish Army in the USSR'. (below)

CORPUS CHRISTI procession, 1942, led by the band of the 6th Battalion of 'the Children of Lwów' (right).

Удостоверение личности
Фамилия, имя, отчество
Состоит на военной действительной службе Польской Армии в С. С. С. Р.
Чин
Назначение
Должность
Родился: год, месяц, число
Место рождения
Холост или женат
1942 г.

'waiting sidings' and windswept towns. Of these I vaguely remember the depressing Semipalatinsk. Progress was slow and stops at the sidings long — we always seemed to be early for the rendezvous with oncoming traffic. During such interruptions I developed the habit of getting off to stretch my legs. I was the only one to do so, or so it seemed. It was enjoyable

but could be risky. On one occasion – our driver having moved off with no warning – I had to run along the moving train in order to remount it several carriages downstream of ours...

The other distraction was the pursuit of food at the stations. Some of these offered a soup kitchen, but the demand was such that a thirteen-year-old [like me] had little chance in the mêlée. So I developed a cunning plan. I would wait for the final whistle when the crowd would rush back to the train, get my bowl filled, and then run very fast to clamber back onto the moving wagons – more often than not pulled up by friendly passengers...

One afternoon a limitless expanse of water appeared to starboard. Someone explained that it was Lake Balkhash. More of a sea than a lake, really; and for me a new experience of water on such a scale. On that day the lake was restless, and its waves lapped quite close to the wheels of our carriage.

I was mesmerised. Later, past Alma-Ata, the snow-clad approaches to the mighty Tyan-Shan range came into view. Our journey now acquired a dramatic backcloth. The train turned westwards and travelled along the foothills of these majestic mountains all the way to Tashkent.

Fifty miles short of our destination, at Chimkent, we were confronted for the first time with an abundance of watermelons, and also jugfuls of rough local wine; all very cheap. Alas there was no bread... The sight was seductive and we – inexperienced newcomers – overdid the melons. The price was diarrhoea, to which many succumbed, including myself. My mother, not quite knowing how to deal with the situation, told me to try some red wine. I put away a large mug, fell sound asleep, and woke up several hours later totally cured...

ARMY TENTS at Yangi-Yul.

We rolled into Tashkent station exhausted by the long journey and disoriented by the heat. The huge square in front of the station was full of squatters waiting for their chance of onward travel. There we established our private space. Around us we noticed many Poles in uniform. Indeed, Tashkent station seemed almost Polonised, which was not surprising because General Anders' HQ was in nearby Jangi-Jul', no more than 30 km away. It was cheering to see the NKVD take a back seat.

Tashkent seemed full of clanging trams... The new Soviet-style squares I found overbearing, and the old Tashkent, with its low houses and high walls of sun-dried mud, uninviting. But the bazaars were magnificently colourful. I could not keep my eyes off the men's *tibeteikas* (skull-caps), the sultanas and dried apricots arranged in pyramids, and the teahouse sub-culture around the edges...

In the meantime our sergeant presented my mother, by way of a farewell gift, with fresh fake endorsements for the next leg of the journey. The following morning, after warm good-byes and embraces, we boarded the train for Samarkand.

About 70 km out of Tashkent we crossed the mighty River Syr-Darya. It was an awe-inspiring encounter. At the time I did not quite realise that we were about to enter one of the great playing fields of history: 'Transoxiana' to the men of the Mediterranean. It is a vast stretch of Asian steppe between the ancient rivers Oxus and Jaxartes, today called the Amu-Darya and the Syr-Darya. Most of the region is a desert, the Kyzyl-Kum, stretching northwards to the sea of Aral. Its southern belt is blessed with important oases, Samarkand and Bukhara, and the fertile valley of Fergana...

POLISH SOLDIERS with a captured lizard, Kenimech.

We caught only a glimpes of Samarkand from the train windows; I remember it as a city nestling among trees. No wonder: it stands in the middle of a great oasis. Here... our last bag of dried biscuits from Nikolaevka was stolen. By then it did not matter all that much.

We moved on, and eventually got off at a small station in the middle of nowhere called Karshi... On 15 July 1942, we had no difficulty in catching the local train to Guzar, where we arrived late in the afternoon, 13 days after leaving Nikolaevka. On that day, 15 July, General Anders issued his orders for the Second Evacuation. We heard the news at the station."[39].

IF THE TRUTH WERE TOLD, the travellers who managed to board a train had a relatively comfortable journey. Others, who were trying to reach the Army overland, had a much harder time. Stanisława Jasionowicz, for example, then aged 10, belonged to a family which had been deported to Central Asia, and which, moving gradually, stage by stage, had a much shorter distance to cover:

"As far as I can remember, the town that we were in was called Farab... They put us on these cattle barks and we were supposed to sail on the Amu-Darya in an unknown direction. The conditions were inhuman: hunger, stuffy air, fleas, illnesses, no toilets, terrible. People died on the way. They would stop the boat and put the cadavers in the fields, covering them with grass, accompanied by the family's tears and utter despair.

The journey on the Amu-Darya took two weeks. When the boat stopped from time to time, people would get off to find something to eat. Sometimes they did not make it back in time and despite their pleas, they were left behind. Desperate scenes. I remember this man who wanted to go back for his son. He fell off the boat and drowned.

The Amu-Darya is a terrible memory... days of utter despair, which we, children, felt also. Hopelessness, fear, hunger, no information

SOLDIERS RECEIVE a delivery of rifles, Kermine.

where we were going did not make us want to go on living. People normally courageous enough suffered from a terrible indifference.

Finally we reached some small town and port. There we were packed onto arbas and taken in different directions. Our family was assigned to some Uzbeks who spoke no Russian at all. We communicated with them by sign language. We got one 'room' in their mud hut. Some responsible Uzbek came along and told us that starting at dawn the next day we were supposed to go to work, pick cotton, that is. We had an assigned quota. For us, children, it was a hard deal because we had to break open the hard shell protecting the small swab of cotton wool. Our fingers kept being bloody and we were not supposed to stain the cotton! Mother wrapped them in rags and so we went to do our 'Stakhanov' quota. We were to get money to buy groats for our work. I think it was called *uruk*...

We were sick with dysentery and ulceration. Constantly hungry and tired.

Once our host asked us to a meal. With his dirty hands he reached into the bowl first, then gave each one of us a piece of greasy mutton meat; we were sitting all around it on mats. We ate greedily, although we were disgusted by the way it was all done. We all

A CRACOVIAN dance ensemble in Central Asia.

were terribly sick afterwards, because our hungry stomachs could not take this luxury...

Soon the 'predsedatel' [representative] came and told us, we had to go. Mother had just washed our raggedy clothes in water with ashes and had put them out on the grass to dry. Frost that night made everything stiff and we had to sit on these stiff things on the cart. Once again a journey into the unknown. A nightmare. The mule pulling the arba walked slowly through the mud, driven on by the Uzbek. The roads were terrible. The arba sank in the mud more and more. We had to get off and push. My brother had a fever and could barely walk. We had nothing to eat. The night was drawing near. We were left with the stubborn mule and the Uzbek in some forest. I was petrified with fear. The Uzbek was cursing, shouting at us and getting angry at the mule. God only knows how we managed to get through that night. I remember praying all the time...

WE REACHED THE PORT FINALLY. We made the same horrible journey, by the same river Amu-Darya. The same nightmare all over again. We were flea-ridden, stinking, but most of all hungry. We kept dreaming of bread and all we talked about once we woke up was bread. You could eat your fill in your sleep. Bread was the only dream in our lives...

They took us somewhere near Tashkent. I watched these strangely dressed women with fear. They had these long black dresses, faces covered completely, stiff thick nets falling to the ground from their foreheads! They looked terrible. I was afraid to go near them, because I thought they were witches of some kind. In this part of the USSR, we first lived in a yurt, that is, a shelter made of bamboo, a few families in each one – it was very crowded!

I remember our second Christmas in Russia in such a yurt (1941). Someone did not forget

CHRONICLE

RYŚ, the handwritten and hand-illustrated "Field Gazette of the 13th Battalion of the Polish Army in the East", Year 1, No. 8, November 1942.
The chronicle was started in Buzuluk in 1941.

SAMOCHODEM PRZEZ PERSJĘ
Moja Persia nie była krainą
stolic i wielkich miast. Była pasmem
gór dzikich i groźnych, rozsianem po-
nowanych w przełęczach obczyzy - gór-
skich wiosek do stromych stoków jak
jaskółcze gniazda przyklejonych. Krajem
osłów i baranich dzwonków, winogron
i bananów. Kalejdoskopem przelotnym
śnieżnym. Wyjeżdżamy z Pahlewi 16-go
września wczesnym rankiem.
Samochody wojskowe podjeżdżają
pod. Potężne długodystansowe trans-
portowce, zielone, czerwone o karoseriach
kurniki pozbijanych z łat. Lecą
pokład <mańele> i skaczą żołnierze.
bowi zachrypniętym głosem wykrzy-
czy. Kolumny kolejno ruszają.
bogata w wodę. Ciemno-zielony
bujnych drzew i krzewów rzuca
na szosę. Zrzadka z prętów splecione
ki. Śniady żołnierz hinduski
uśmiechem. Jasno-szmaragdowa
ryżowych pól. Garbate yaki.
Melodyjne dzwonki baraniego sta-
da. Na puszystym ośle kobieta kar-
miąca dziecko. Mężczyzna prowadzi
osiołka za wodę. Motyw biblijny.
Małe chłopaki niosą do miasteczka
olbrzymie kosze jarzyn i owoców.
Piramidy winogron zielonych i si-
nych, wieńce cebul błyszczących,
jak mosiądz, brunatne rogalki ba-
kłażanów i ogórkowe łyków długości
dziecka. Pachnie lato.
Resztę mijamy pobieżnie, po ślicznej
Szosa biegnie w górę. Początkowo góry
jeszcze swojskie, okrągłe zielone.
Drzewa trochę jak akacje, trochę jak pa-
procie. Nad drogą kiście jasno-różowych
kwiatów. Stoki w dół opadają łagodnie
ku rzece. U wylotu szosy horyzont szero-
ki, otwarty. W gospodzie gorąca herbata
i wino. Szosa pnie się odważnymi spi-
ralami w górę. Zachwyt zapiera dech.
Jedziemy jak we śnie. Góry nagie, skaliste,
spiętrzone, jak by wczoraj wysadzone
z ziemi straszliwym wybuchem. Pok-
pane w płyty, postrzępione w zęby.
Potworne, powywracane głazy - pobojo-
wisko zbuntowanych olbrzymów. Szosa
biegnie wąską łaźnią nad urwiskiem,
nad głową strome ściany sięgające
nieba. Ostre igły sterczą i tafle jak noże.
Szczerzy zęby głowa leżącego sfinksa.
Szosa biegnie w górę. Zachwyt trwa i
ochłonąć trudno, ale w tym zachwycie
i postrach i groza. Groza przytłacza.
Coś się rodzi jakby chęć ucieczki. A dwo-
ma budzi się zrogłpienie, czy tę szosę
budowali ludzie. Kierowca żadnych
wątpliwości nie ma bierze ostro wiraże
z fantazją. Wspina się i w dół opuszcza
jak na piskliwym saneczkowym torze
i obliczą trafnie na zakrętach siłę
odśrodkową. Mądry szach kazał wy-

Rosja
Polska

…łowiek z szalonym apetytem
…się do niewoli. Pojecha-
…na wschód, na zachód,
…południe. Lecz gdzie
…głodny wszędzie
…nienajedzony
…a się już do licha ni-
…m.
…się do Polskiego Woj-
…le pomogło! Siedzę
…tu jeść. Tu nie, tu
…na dostać się do
…ry pomysł. Tam
bym podjadł chociaż raz, chociaż
dwa - grunt by pojeść.
Byłem i tam i znów głodny
pomyślałem - nie pomoże, chyba
ja w tym kraju nigdy się nie na-
jem.
Pewnego razu na wykładzie
pogadanka o wyjeździe. Słucha-
pilnie - gdzie? Czy już do Polski?
Jeszcze nie - to do doliny raju.
Hm - nazwa piękna. Pytam z
zaciekawieniem, gdzie to jest?
Mówią że w środkowo-azjatyc-
kiej S.S.R.
Wszystko stracone - znów będę
głodny.
…prawdziwa
o dwóch alarmach
Było to tak:
Jak nocny ptak
Nasz „Pe-De-k" pocichu
Nie mówiąc nic…ni chu-chu
Przez zaspy się śnieżne przekrada
Do kompanii pogotowia wpada
I…„alarm!" krzyczy „alarm!! powia-
da
Kompania cała
Spała
I o tem że ma pogotowie
Ani jej w głowie
Aż tu raptem krzyk na dworze
-„Co tam się dzieje"?.. o Boże!?
Allaarm!!!
Alarm - trza wstać nic nie pomoże
I zaczęli się na alarm wybierać
Zimno….
Ciemno…
Nieprzyjemno!
Ani butów swych pozbierać
Ni kamizelki znaleźć - trzeba broń
pobierać
Trzebaby dowódcę kompanii poszu-
kać
Namiot z pod śniegu odgrzebać
- postukać popukać
Może wstanie
(Pomyśli, że śniadanie)
….Tymczasem „Pe-De-k"
wściekły i zły
Na mrozie stoi
Od mrozu kapią mu łzy
A może łzy rozpaczy
Bo się boi
Że tego pogotowia prędko nie
zobaczy
Dość, że się nie może doczekać
A tu mu pilno i nie może zwlekać
Więc wybiegł, delikatnie mówiąc do
„dwóchz…"
A rano „O.p.-er"
„Drogą służbową" wszystkim się do-
stało
- Taki alarm?! półtora chłopa?!
to trochę za
mało
I znowu wtedy
Kiedy
Przyszły angielskie mundury
(Oczko w głowie od dołu do góry
„Pe-De-K" spać nie może
No, bo to…. broń Boże
Magazyn zapalić się może
Więc „Pe-De-K" znowu w nocy
(Ciemno….wykol oczy)
Przychodzi do magazynu mundu-
rowego
Odszukał inspekcyjnego
Paallii się!!!
(na niby)
MAGAZYN MUNDUROWY
I na niego jak burza wali
-„Alarm!!" krzyczy, - magazyn
się pali
Inspekcyjny osłupiał
……zgłupiał
-„Co nasze mundury? na..asze
swetery
Alaaarm!! pali się do jasnej cholery
Co pan robi dalej
„W myśl instrukcji!" No to już, bo
przecież się pali
Telefon poszedł
w ruch
Gońce pędzą jak
wariaty
Od namiotu do
„ziemianki" od chaty do chaty
I kiedy wieść w kształt gromu
Lotem błyskawicy do wszystkich
dociera
Nikt nie zostaje w domu
Każdy się na alarm wybiera
By ratować mundury

SOLDIERS DRAWN up to swear the Army's oath, Kermine.

about the date. It was a very sad day. No chance of Christmas Eve. We did not have anything to eat. My brother and I were running all over the place, hoping to catch a dog to kill, but we failed.

Finally they took us somewhere in the *arbas*. We travelled a long time through complete wilderness. We stopped in the field, where there was a stable in very bad condition. That is where we were supposed to live. The ground was covered with very dirty straw, the door broken, the window openings closed with sheaves of straw. When it rained, water poured onto our heads. We would put out all the vessels we had to catch the water so that the rest of our bedclothes would not get wet. A few other families joined us. No toilets whatsoever. Water came from a very deep well and to get a bucket of very muddy water you had to get the men, because it was a great effort.

The native people lived at a distance... these were the Kirgiz, the people of Kirghizstan. They lived in bamboo shelters and dressed strangely. They were very amused to see us and they would often come to the stables in groups, sit on their haunches and laugh, which irritated us a great deal. They pointed at us with their fingers and talked in their own language. One of the men once asked our supervisor, who spoke Russian, what should we do with them. He said to get a pig's foot and show it to them. It was the only medicine...

ONE EVENING... Janina was baking some pancakes from barley flour she got somewhere miraculously... The kids unable to wait any longer surrounded her by the fire and sang joyfully 'The old bear is sleeping deeply'. Just then someone on horseback stopped by us and started to listen to our singing and to look at us with interest. After a minute he got off his horse and came up to us to ask what we were doing here, where our parents were and who took care of us. We pointed out Janina to him. This man took her aside and told her he would send a mule the next day and she was supposed

OBELISK MARKING the Europe–Asia boundary (2015).

CAMEL RIDE in Kermine.

to pack the younger kids onto the mule and the rest should walk to Shahrizyabs, because they were organizing a soldiers' camp there and took care of civilians. And so it happened. The mule and arba came at four in the morning. The tiny tots and the luggage, that is, what was left of our rags, were packed on the mule and arba and we, the older kids, went on foot. It was about 40 km... travelling on the *arba* was very difficult. Our cousin Hela was very sick and lay curled up in great pain. The Uzbek who was driving the small children often told Hela to get up and walk behind the arba, because the mule was finding it very difficult. Hela had no strength left and was collapsing from exhaustion.

Monika was carrying *kumis*, mare's milk, in a can; we got it on the previous evening in return for a mirror. The people there wanted to buy it because it was glossy. They had no idea what it was, because they had never seen a mirror in their lives...

Far from the civilized world, all alone, without adult care, we knew nothing about the amnesty, about General Anders and his efforts to get civilians out of the forced labour camps and about the chances to leave the USSR. It followed from the Sikorski–Mayski agreement of 30 July 1941.

The man who found us in this 'inhumane land' was one of the mustered soldiers. If not for him... I don't know how long we could have gone on living like that, stealing oil cake from the cows, drinking awful muddy water, eaten by lice and all kinds of vermin. I don't know...

Organized groups of civilians, children in particular, were supposed to save these human skeletons from inevitable death.

Our journey to a camp like that was very hard. The heat was terrible, we had nothing to eat, our legs were bloodied and cut by the merciless stones in the road, they could not carry us any longer. At first we walked behind the mule, but when we lost it from sight, we panicked from fear. We asked occasional passers-by for directions. Once we even went off the road intentionally, seeing some huts in the distance. We wanted to get a drink of water, if nothing else. They seemed to be Gypsies. They set a dog on us, which did not bite us, but made us very scared and tore the rest of the ragged clothes we had. Crying we went back on our pilgrimage, totally exhausted. It was truly the Way of the Cross!

The river crossing was an epilogue to this journey. There was a guy there with a raft, but we had no money to pay him. So he showed us where the water was shallow and we started to get across. Water reached up to our necks, but we got across safely. On the other side we sat down on the rocks to rest and recover from the emotional stress. That's when I started to feel very weak and I told my sister I would not move from the spot. It didn't matter one way or another. I did not want to live anymore. My guardian was desperate, frightened by my decision, begging me any which way to get up. She told me she would carry me on her back, that she would take me there, if I could not do it myself. Nothing helped. She kept saying: 'See the light there? That is where the camp is and Monika is there for sure and crying for us. Let us pray, put ourselves in the care of the Lord and let's go.'

I woke up in some tent. Janina and Monika were with me, worried but smiling. I didn't know where I was or what had happened. I could not remember anything. Later I found out that I had lost consciousness after running to the camp in the night and I slept for two whole days."[40]

TAMERLANE'S TOMB, Samarkand, (2015).

IT IS A MATTER of speculation how far the Poles in Central Asia had the time or inclination to take an interest in their new surroundings. Many of them, who had come out of Russia, remained in a state of exhaustion; disease was rife; and everyone was kept very busy with training, exercising, and organising. Nonetheless, for those who wished to take stock of their predicament, there were interesting political, cultural, and historical things to be seen:

"Szachrizyabs was a little town about fifty miles south-east from Samarkand, previously governed by the Emir of Bukhara; it was about three miles from the railway terminus in Kitab, and was mostly inhabited by Uzbeks. An English translation of the town's name would be 'Carrot Town'.

In olden times, Szachrizyabs was, after Samarkand, the largest metropolis of Tamerlaine. Now it is only a small Asiatic town, modelled on Russian–Soviet lines. It is partially destroyed, some parts of it being almost abandoned. The houses were built, as is usual in the East, of clay; the streets were narrow and winding. The whole town was surrounded by a defensive clay wall, reminiscent of bygone centuries. Vines climbed up it, mingling with the green of the mulberry and *uruk* trees.

Wandering along the streets, one came across charming spots, among them the ruins of a minute mosque, with open-work pillars and, high up, slender minarets. In the centre of the town were the ruins of the colossal castle of Tamerlaine, whose turret of imposing magnitude and beauty was covered with small tiles, glazed in blue enamel and scrolled with beautiful arabesques.

This charming sight was enhanced by the colourful, trailing clothes of men and women, walking about or riding on *ishaks* (small donkeys). These people belonged to a completely different world from ours – to Asia – and it was difficult for a European to see through the dividing screen. It took a long time to realise how much they knew about their glorious past and how proud they were of it. Later on they told us that the Emirate of Bukhara lost its independence only in 1922. Even as recently as 1932, the whole territory between Karashi and the Pass of Samarkand had been under the rule of the Bassmatshi, who, having their headquarters in inaccessible mountains, had come down to the valleys and killed all the alien population – mostly Russians – and occupied a territory equal in size to one-third of Poland. Budionnyj's army, however, bloodily suppressed this rising, destroyed all the monuments to Uzbek greatness, and strengthened Soviet rule.

In the beginning the Uzbeks were suspicious of us and watched us cautiously. When everything became clear to them, friendship was born... Our soldiers became friendly with the *bayans* (men) in colourful gowns and the *marzias* (girls) in *carsafs*...; they became openhearted and Uzbek hamlets were open to us...

Later, probably some of them paid the price for it and for the hopes which had been aroused, by

A POLISH chaplain, Fr. Czesław Kulikowski, poses with Uzbek children.

being deported to the banks of the Kolyma River."[41]

The Central Asian Republics, like Russia itself, were ruled by the centralised dictatorship of the Soviet Communist Party (Bolsheviks) and by the coercive organs of state including the Red Army and the ubiquitous NKVD. In each of the republican capitals, like Tashkent or Dushanbe, the Party House was the most important seat of power. At the same time Party-controlled local governments, legislative assemblies, and administrations were allowed to function. Whilst Russian was the language of the Party elite, native languages such as Uzbek, Kazakh, or Tadzik operated on lower levels. As one wag put it, 'In the Soviet Union, you can speak seventy languages, so long as you say nothing in any of them.'

A popular postwar encyclopaedia published in Britain after the sojourn of the Polish Army emphasised that the Central Asian Republics were very different from Russia:

"**UZBEKISTAN,** Union Republic of the USSR, lying in the central part of Central Asia with deserts in the north-west (adjacent to the Aral Sea), a chain of fertile and densely populated oases roughly along latitudes 40°–42° (Khorezm, Zeravshan, Tashkent, Fergana Valley), and a mountainous area between Zeravshan and the middle course of the River Amu-Dar'ya; there are large deposits of natural gas near Bukhara, brown coal near Tashkent and oil in the Fergana Valley, also rich deposits of copper, lead and rare metals near Tashkent. Area 158,100 sq. m.; population (1959) 8,106,000 (fourth among the Union Republics of the USSR; 1939, 6,336,000; 34 per cent urban). In 1959, the ethnic composition was as follows: Uzbeks, 62 per cent; Russians, 14 per cent; Tatars, 5.5 per cent; Tadzhiks, 4 per cent; Kazakhs, 4 per cent; Kara-Kalpaks, 2 per cent; there are also Koreans (2 per cent), etc.

The principal feature of the republic's economy is cotton production, both cultivation and industries associated with it. Cultivated land takes up about one-ninth of the area, and over a half of it is irrigated. The irrigated land is chiefly used for cotton and other industrial and fodder crops, while the non-irrigated land is almost entirely taken up by grain crops. The cotton-growing area was more than doubled between 1913 and 1941, and the cotton crop was nearly trebled... the republic is also the biggest silk-producing area of the USSR (about one-half of the total). Fruit and grapes (for raisins) are also produced on a large scale. The main branch of animal husbandry is the breeding of Astrakhan sheep... Engineering and metal-working industries (mostly agricultural machinery and cotton-processing equipment) employ

one-third of all industrial workers... Coal and oil extraction have been developed since the 1930s... The chemical industry of the republic is largely concentrated upon fertilizers. Uzbekistan is chiefly served by the Trans-Caspian Railway, with its branches to the Fergana Valley, Stalinabad and the Khorezm oasis; navigation on the Amu-Dar'ya also plays a role. The capital of the republic is Tashkent... and it is divided into the Tashkent, Samarkand, Bukhara, Fergana, Andizhan, Khorezm, and Surkhan-Dar'ya oblasts and the Kara-Kalpak Autonomous Republic... The Uzbek Republic was formed in 1924 during the National Delimitation of Central Asia... and included Tadzhikistan as an Autonomous Republic; the latter became a Union Republic in 1929. The Kara-Kalpak Autonomous Republic was transferred from the R.S.F.S.R. to Uzbekistan

POLISH SOLDIERS and local elders (above).

THE ARK FORTRESS of the Emir of Bokhara, 5th century AD (left).

in 1936. Throughout the 1920's and early thirties Uzbekistan was the main centre of the anti-Bolshevik Basmachi... guerrilla warfare. The Great Purge (q.v.) of the late 1930's was very severely felt in Uzbekistan, which until then had been ruled by National Bolsheviks."[42]

As the Poles were to discover, each of the republics was different from its neighbours, possessing its own specific history and characteristics:

"**KIRGIZ,** Turkic-speaking people living in the Kirgiz Republic and numbering

UZBEKISTAN
KIRGHIZSTAN
KAZAKHSTAN
TURKMENISTAN

THE WALLS of Samarkand, the oldest inhabited city on the Silk Road, Uzbekistan (top).

YOUNG SHEPHERDS, Uzbekistan (top right).

THE POLISH CEMETERY in Kitab, Uzbekistan (top centre).

THE CEMETERY in Shokpak, Kazakhstan (bottom).

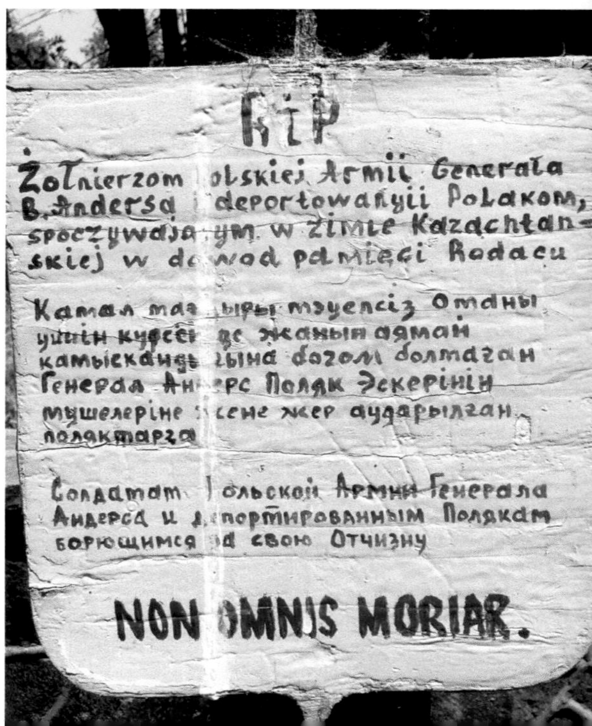

THE NARIN RIVER gorge, Kirghizstan (top left).

THE HORSE is still the most reliable mode of transport in Kirghizstan (top).

ASHCHABAD BY night, Turkmenistan (bottom left).

SHEPHERDS IN THE KARAKUM desert, Turkmenistan (bottom right).

THE CENTRAL ASIAN REPUBLICS, which were coerced into joining the Soviet Union in the 1920s, were subject to Soviet rule when the Anders Army passed through. As of 1991 they are free again. Kirghizstan borders China in the south, and is elsewhere surrounded by Uzbekistan, Kazakhstan and Turkmenistan. Kazakhstan, the largest Soviet republic after Russia, was the destination of most Polish deportees in 1940–1941.

(1959) 974,000 (884,000 in 1939). They are Muslims and are still mostly pastoral people. The Kirgiz are of a clearly Mongoloid racial type, and are probably the product of a mixture between Mongol tribes which invaded Semirech'ye... in the 12th and 13th centuries and the Turkic-speaking Kirgiz who in the 7th–17th centuries lived in the upper Yenisey area and some of whom came with the Mongol invaders.

Kirgizia, Union Republic of the USSR. lying in Central Asia and bordering upon China, predominantly in the Tien-Shan mountain system but including a part of the Fergana Valley in the south-west and the upper parts of the Chu and Talas river valleys in the north. It is traversed by the River Naryn, a headstream of the Syr-Dar'ya, and the lake Issyk-Kul' lies in the north-east. Kirgizia has the richest pastures in Central Asia, and varied mineral deposits (coal, oil, ozokerite, antimony, mercury, lead, sulphur, arsenic and building materials). Area 76,600 sq. m.; population (1959) 2,066,000 (34 per cent urban; 1939, 1,458,000), Kirgiz (about 40.5 per cent in 1959), Russians (30 per cent) and Ukrainians (7 per cent) in the north, Uzbeks (11 per cent) and Tadzhiks in the Fergana Valley, also some Uygurs and Dungans. Animal husbandry is the main agricultural pursuit (sheep, goats, cattle, horses, bees); over a half of the cultivated area is irrigated, and cotton, sugar-beet, tobacco, fruit and grapes are grown and sericulture carried on, while grain crops (wheat, oats, barley, maize) are cultivated in the unirrigated regions. There are metal-working and engineering (agricultural machinery, food industry equipment) industries, largely confined to the capital of the republic, and also varied food, textile and mining industries. While the north of the republic and the Fergana Valley are served by railways, the mountainous areas are traversed by the Frunze-Naryn-Kashgar (in China), the Pamir (Osh-Khorog) and the new Frunze-Osh highways. The capital of the republic is Frunze, and there are two oblasts, Osh, comprising the Kirgiz part of the Fergana Valley, and Tien-Shan. In the 1940s and 1950s there were also Frunze, Talas, Issyk-Kul' and Dzhalal-Abad oblasts.

The area was gradually annexed by Russia in 1855–76. Russian and Ukrainian agricultural colonization was resented by the indigenous population, and in 1916 the Kirgiz took part in the uprising prompted by the mobilization of native peoples (hitherto exempt from military service) for labour battalions. As a result of the 'National Delimitation of Central Asia'... in 1924, the Kirgiz (then called Kara-Kirgiz) Autonomous Oblast was established within the R.S.F.S.R., which in 1926 was raised to the status of Autonomous Republic and in 1936 to Union Republic."[43]

CULTURALLY, DESPITE THE INROADS of the Russian language and of state-sponsored atheism, the mass of Central Asian society clung to traditional Islam, to local customs and to their native languages. In the 1920s, when the Bolsheviks reconquered Central Asia, they did not subject Islam to the same murderous repressions that they inflicted on the Christian churches in Russia. The political power of the imams was clipped, of course; but the mosques and the religious schools were not closed, and a *modus vivendi* achieved. Women were not subjected to the restrictions prevalent in more traditional societies. Ever since, Central Asian Islam has enjoyed a reputation for religious moderation. Nonetheless, as Poles often commented, the local population knew all about deportations and oppressions and welcomed the Polish arrivals with sympathy and warm hospitality.

Historically, Central Asia was a wonderland filled with the remains of ancient civilisations. Russian expansion into the region dated only from mid-19th century, and Russian culture was no more than skindeep. For those with a moment

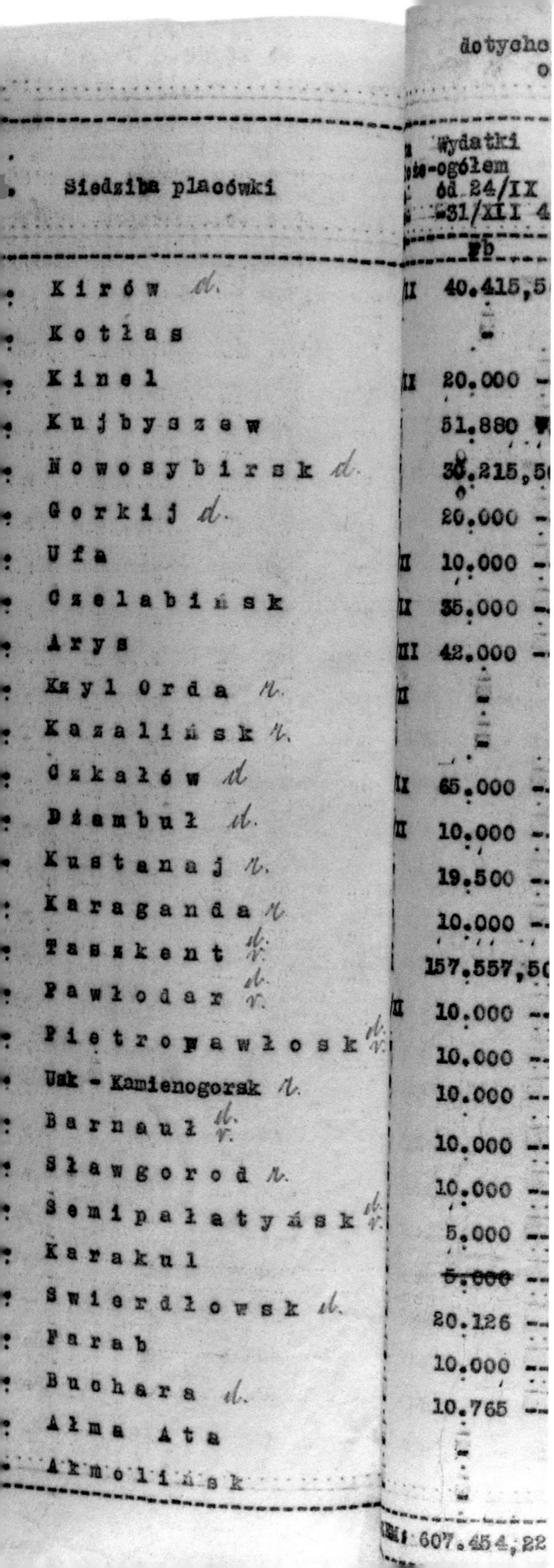

Siedziba placówki	Wydatki ogółem od 24/IX – 31/XI 4.. Rb
Kirów	40.415,5
Kotłas	-
Kinel	20.000
Kujbyszew	51.880
Nowosybirsk	30.215,5
Gorkij	20.000
Ufa	10.000
Czelabińsk	35.000
Arys	42.000
Kzyl Orda	-
Kazalińsk	-
Czkałów	65.000
Dżambuł	10.000
Kustanaj	19.500
Karaganda	10.000
Taszkent	157.557,5
Pawłodar	10.000
Pietropawłosk	10.000
Ust-Kamienogorsk	10.000
Barnauł	10.000
Sławgorod	10.000
Semipałatyńsk	5.000
Karakul	~~5.000~~
Swierdłowsk	20.126
Farab	10.000
Buchara	10.765
Ałma Ata	-
Akmolińsk	-
	607.454,22

for reflection, the sights spoke eloquently about human vanity and the impermanence of political powers. For people who had been suffering in the gulags only weeks or months earlier, or who had lingered in the remoteness of steppe and tundra, it was no small excitement to wander for a couple of hours through the bazaars of Tashkent, or to stand for a snapshot before the magnificent Tomb of Tamerlane in Samarkand.

Tashkent, the city with which the Poles had the closest connections, was not an inspiring sight in the early 1940s:

> "After leaving the Polish Delegate's office, I visited the town. It covered a wide area but was rather dreary. Mostly there were low wooden bungalows, with some ordinary town houses. There were only a few shops, all of them typical Soviet-nationalised cooperative ones. Everywhere one could discern misery and destitution.
>
> In one part of the town there were several modern blocks, probably offices, but they did not improve the general view. This part of the town looked as if it had been modernised by force, lacking as it did any of the beauty of Asiatic folklore or architecture, and presenting a colourless suburban appearance.
>
> The Uzbek part of the town had probably once been beautiful, but now it was in ruins. Dilapidated houses, with Eastern arches and canopies, courtyards with mulberry, almond or bread-fruit trees, and half-demolished mosques decorated with a few blue enamelled tiles, bore witness to the old culture.
>
> Many street vendors sold *shashlyk* (mutton cooked on iron grills and dripping with fat), *uruk* (small fruit similar to olives) and *kyshmysh* (raisins and walnuts). There was Eastern mobility

EXPENSES FOR Army Collecting Centres, February–March 1942.

and noise. Little donkeys passed, succumbing under the heavy weight of their freight or their riders; and sometimes a small caravan of camels, attached one to another by strings and heavily loaded with cotton. The streets were narrow, one could hardly move in them; along them were many cafés serving green tea or coffee, where one could sit on worn mats.

It was the East, but not the ancient East, where, alongside misery, one could have seen splendour and riches."[44]

Nonetheless, visitors with their ears to the ground could learn much about the region's recent history. They found that Poles were not alone in their feelings of oppression:

"During my wanderings in the ancient part of the town, I met an old Uzbek dentist. When he realised that I was a Pole and not a Soviet Russian, he invited me to his room and told me about his country and its slavery. He spoke about the last Uzbek rising, in 1924, and about the bloody 'pacification' performed by Budionnyj, in which all the old mosques, dating from Tamerlane's times, and other national monuments were destroyed. In its place, the new Soviet way of life was inculcated, utterly alien to local traditions.

He believed that the Uzbeks would one day recover their freedom, and hoped that this war would bring it about. He was surprised that we Poles were going to help the Bolsheviks to fight against the Germans, instead of the reverse: he ascribed it to our peculiarly different political situation. Surprised that he was so outspoken,

KIRGHIZ YURT (above).

MAUSOLEUM AND STATUE to the Kirghiz hero, Manas Ordo, Talas (opposite top).

KIRGHIZ MOUNTAINS, one of the western ranges of the Tian Shan.

I asked whether he was not afraid to talk so freely; but he said he knew to whom he was talking, as he knew Polish history and could trust us. Polish traditions were vivid to him because they were connected with the golden age of Uzbek history under the reign of the Gengis Khan dynasty. He certainly knew far more about Poland than I did about Uzbekistan.

His national pride was enthusiastically expressed, and he fervently believed that soon freedom would come to his country.

This was the first time in the Soviet Union that I had met views expressed in such a way. Perhaps it was due to the fact that for the first time we were outside the national limits of Russia. It was a new and interesting discovery within the 'voluntary and spontaneous Union of Republics'."[45]

Anders, who loved riding, saw things that he was not supposed to see:

"During my stay at Yangi-Yul, Stalin made me a present of two horses, and I tried to ride every day... to free myself from my NKVD escort. Sometimes I rode by concentration camps where I saw thousands of people in rags, just as my soldiers had looked on arrival not long before... Once I came across a camp which attracted my attention because the inmates were in uniform... they were all Soviet officers.

INFANTRY PARADE, Yangi-Yul: soldiers in British uniforms (above).

PRIEST ACTING as an Agent of the Polish Embassy, Karshy (Uzbekistan), 4 July 1942 (right).

Their insignia of rank had... been removed on arrest, but from traces of the badges on their collars, I could see many were colonels and generals... When I got back, I asked... Colonel Volkovysky who they were. He answered that they were Hitlerites and cowards..."[46] The next day, Anders was told not to ride in that direction.

For the exiles, however, the search for food and for money on which to live was unending. Enterprising individuals set up little businesses, unaware of the risks they were running:

"The woman whom we had taken into the room with us conceived a plan for making food to sell in the market. We bought horse meat, onions and garlic, and chopped this up very finely. Using the last of the dried bread we had been given and which we soaked in water, we mixed these ingredients together. We had no eggs, but even so the meatballs were wonderful – big and tasty. It was the first time I had ever eaten horse meat, but it was good.

We cooked them and I put them in a bowl covered with a scarf and took them to market to sell. I came home with lots of roubles...

Next day there were still some meatballs left, so I went again to the market. A very tall Russian man accompanied by a woman came to me. 'Please come with us', he whispered to me.

I could sense that they were friendly, and I went with them.

A short distance away they stopped... 'Please, we beg of you, don't risk this again', the man told me. 'We saw you yesterday in the market and we noticed that the NKVD men were watching you. If you continue in this way you will be arrested and sent back to the place where you came from.'

The thought of being sent back to Siberia terrified me, but I was loathe to abandon my enterprise. 'I have a lot of meatballs left', I said. But the woman told me not to worry. 'I have friends in town, and I will tell them about the food, and they will come to you and buy', she reassured me. 'They will follow us. We cannot go all together because it will make the NKVD suspicious'.[47]

Others came much closer to the brink of disaster. By this time, Danuta (Skiba) and her Mother were the only two left from a family of six.

"We would not have survived if not... for the formation of a Polish Army... The army was being formed in Kermine, and the families of enrolled soldiers were issued with train tickets... We did not have anybody in the army, so we had to find another way to get to Kermine. We [boarded] the train without tickets, and hid when the conductor came to check.

[In Kermine], we were not allowed onto the Polish Army camp, so we found a shady tree near the camp and stayed there for days. I used to wonder if some kind [person] would give me some soup. My Mother talked to one of the Polish soldiers to see if there was any way that we could leave with the registered families [otherwise] we would have to stay and probably die. The soldier registered us as his sister and niece."[48] And so they were saved.

WHEN GENERAL ANDERS reached Yangi-Yul, there is no reason to suppose that he intended anything other than to honour the Polish–Soviet convention agreed the previous summer. He had transferred to Central Asia to feed and train his men more efficiently, and still assumed that most of them, when ready for battle, would be sent into action on the Eastern Front.

In the following months, however, severe disillusionment set in and he became convinced that the Soviets were neither able nor willing to keep their side of the bargain. In January he had already refused a Soviet demand for the immediate transfer of one division to the front. He did so partly because, in his judgement, his men were not yet ready for combat and he abhorred the possibility that, like third-rate Soviet divisions, they would be driven under German fire. He was also afraid that the Soviets intended to separate the men into smaller units and distribute them among larger Soviet formations. In the latter case, they would not have been fighting as an integrated Polish force under Polish officers, and would have been subjected to the Soviet military–political system. Anders was not in the least prepared to see patriotic Poles put at the mercy of Beria's dreaded *politruks*.

Yet other factors weighed as well. For one thing, the British, who were doing much to keep Anders supplied, let it be known that his soldiers would be more than welcome in the Middle East. In the spring of 1942, the Polish Carpathian

Brigade was impressing the British command of its mettle. For another, despite the move to Central Asia, the physical condition of the men was actually deteriorating through poor diet and persistent epidemics. Still under extreme pressure to keep their own armies in the field, the Soviet logistical organisations were incapable of giving priority to the Poles, and failed to deliver food and equipment in the necessary quantities. Worst of all, Polish men and women under Anders' command were dying at the rate of 300 or 400 a month. A dozen Polish cemeteries in Central Asia received over 3,000 burials before a single shot was fired in battle. The death rate was intolerable.

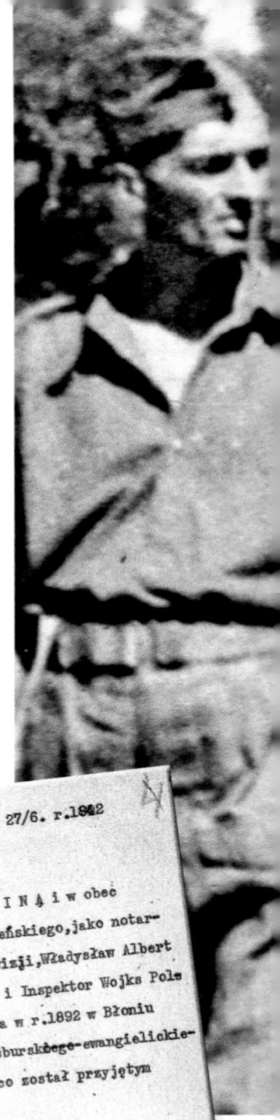

FIELD BISHOP Józef Gawlina, Yangi-Yul, June 1942.

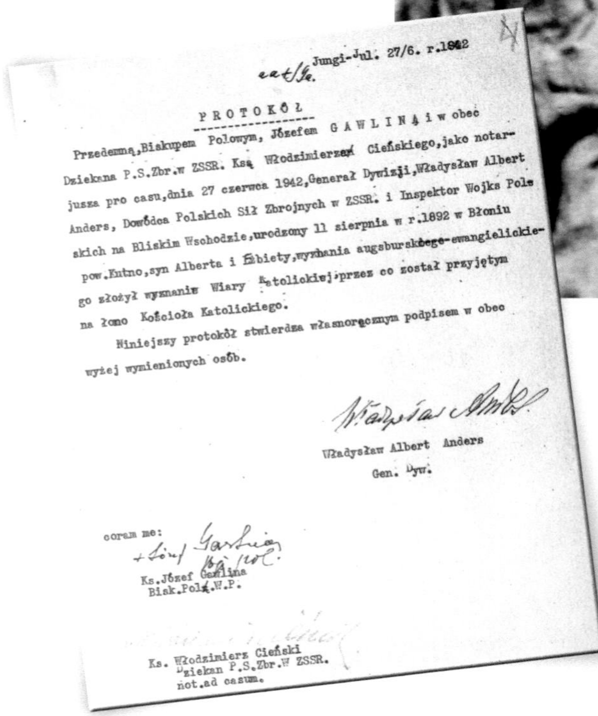

Jungi-Jul. 27/6. r.1942

PROTOKÓŁ

Przedemną, Biskupem Polowym, Józefem GAWLINĄ i w obec Dziekana P.S.Zbr.w ZSSR. Ks. Włodzimierza Cieńskiego, jako notarjusza pro casu, dnia 27 czerwca 1942, Generał Dywizji, Władysław Albert Anders, Dowódca Polskich Sił Zbrojnych w ZSSR. i Inspektor Wojks Polskich na Bliskim Wschodzie, urodzony 11 sierpnia w r.1892 w Błoniu pow. Kutno, syn Alberta i Elżbiety, wyznania augsburskiego-ewangielickiego złożył wyznanie Wiary Katolickiej, przez co został przyjętym na łono Kościoła Katolickiego.

Niniejszy protokół stwierdza własnoręcznym podpisem w obec wyżej wymienionych osób.

Władysław Albert Anders
Gen. Dyw.

coram me:
Ks. Józef Gawlina
Bisk.Pol.W.P.

Ks. Włodzimierz Cieński
Dziekan P.S.Zbr.W ZSSR.
not.ad casum.

PROTOCOL DATED 27 June 1942, recording the induction of Władysław Anders into the Roman Catholic faith.

THE PROBLEM WAS RESOLVED by a further meeting between Anders and Stalin on 18 March 1942. To begin with, Stalin tried to bargain, first by threatening to reduce the number of Polish rations to 26,000 and then by offering to raise them to 44,000. Anders found no difficulty in showing that 80,000 rations were needed, and asked what might happen to the 30–40,000 Poles who would go unfed. Stalin suggested that they be sent to collective farms, but on hearing staunch opposition to the idea, relented and accepted that roughly 40,000 soldiers and their dependants be evacuated to the British zone of Iran. Anders must have breathed a huge sigh of relief.

In this way, the 'Polish Army in the USSR' was divided in two: one half being despatched to Iran, and the other half remaining in Central Asia, dispirited and unfit for action. This situation could not last indefinitely.

As 1943 wore on, the plight of the Polish units who had remained in the USSR grew from bad to worse. Colonel Rudnicki, who was in command of them, despaired from the fearful combination of Soviet obstructionism and of epidemics:

"By now we had realised that our continued existence in Russia was futile. Eleven months of attempted cooperation with the Soviets had stripped us of all illusions. No longer could it be concealed: the experiment had been a failure. There was no possibility of real cooperation with Soviet Russia. One could only fight against her, or surrender unconditionally – there was no alternative.

During these terrible eleven months both sides had mutually disclosed their doubts: we

averred we would never surrender to them, and they declared they did not want us as we are. Both parties revealed their attitude.

Under these circumstances, there was no hope of our carrying out our own decisions. Fatalistically, we expected some drastic, final settlement.

When our Embassy's delegates were arrested on the pretext of spying, we prepared for the worst. We decided to offer stiff resistance, if the Soviets attempted to take us by force, and to hack our way through to Afghanistan or Iran. We even began to prepare plans for such an emergency. Under the pretext of excursions, we reconnoitred the passes and roads to the Afghan frontier, and studied the possibility of taking over by force the trains running to Ashhabad *en route* to the Persian frontier. We reconnoitred the disposition of the nearest Soviet garrisons, and their stores where we could secure necessary equipment.

This secretly designed plan was quite fantastic, and could hardly have been carried out in practice , especially as many soldiers were at the time laid low by malaria."[49]

The onset of disease only served to increase anxiety:

"In the spring, diseases again began to decimate our Division; first typhus, then typhoid fever, brought to us by new recruits and civilians. Later on, when swarms of mosquitoes had bred; various kinds of malaria, jaundice, deadly coma, dysentery, etc., spread rapidly. The doctors were almost helpless; there were no medicines, the nurses were ill themselves and over-fatigued; there was no room for new patients in the Divisional hospital or in the units. For a long time, 10–20 people died each day. About 95 per cent of the Division's strength, including Tokarzewski and myself, were attacked by these diseases, and there were days when there were not enough healthy men to perform the most necessary administrative jobs to keep going the daily existence of the Division and the civilians.

Kitab, Tshirakshi and Shachrizyabs were the worst affected by disease, as they were next to the water, which provided good breeding grounds for mosquitoes.

Well do I remember how I inspected the 16th Infantry Regiment in Kitab when the epidemics were raging at their worst. What a macabre sight! I walked round the regimental encampment, which was unguarded, without duty officer or N.C.O. The offices and kitchens were deserted, and the quarters were strewn with half-conscious people lying one beside the other, feverishly delirious or in coma. It was one vast, silent death camp!"[50]

The impression is sometimes given that death and starvation was faced exclusively by civilian exiles. Yet the Army was vulnerable, too. Conditions deteriorated on the eve of the Second Evacuation:

"The situation of the dangerously ill was also very tragic. People with a high temperature, typhus, dysentery or some undiagnosed tropical disease, were obviously excluded from the evacuation. When they heard that the Army was leaving the USSR, they left their huts in a hurry, pretending to be healthy in order not to be left behind: all they wanted was to be evacuated and thus saved. Many of them were detained in Soviet hospitals in Kitab and Tshirakshi, and they, most of all, were tormented by the uncertainty of their fate, as it was most difficult to simulate good health there. We had less trouble with the patients kept in our hospitals: they grinned, their colleagues propped them inconspicuously under their arms, holding them up during the last parade before the entrainment; then they were pushed into the trucks, where they collapsed on the floors, but happy that they

OVERTAKING
in Central Asia.

were going, and not being left behind. We knew what was happening, but we had not the heart to prevent it, and so they went.

We ourselves visited Soviet hospitals with our doctors, selecting people fit to travel. We walked round the wards, from one patient to another, meeting mute imploring from burning eyes, or had to listen to their barely audible petitions: 'Take me with you! Death is better than being left behind... Take me, *please...*'"[51]

In these circumstances, it was obvious that the original concept of sending the Anders Army to the Eastern Front, and of placing it under Soviet command, had ceased to be a viable option. As soon as the transfer could be arranged, all the Polish units that had stayed on in Central Asia, together with their civilian dependants, would be ordered to rejoin their comrades in Iran.

General Anders himself did not leave Central Asia until 19 August 1942, when he flew to

MOUNTAIN TERRAIN between Central Asia and Iran, over which General Anders flew in August 1942.

Tehran. His ironic comments on that flight were inimitable:

"As we flew over the high mountains dividing Russia from Persia, the sound kept ringing in my ears of a song familiar to all who had been in Russian concentration camps. It was broadcast every day from every Soviet wireless station and heard every morning by the 20 million slaves who were daily driven like cattle to work for the greatness of the Soviet Union:

Dear native land, thy plains are wide;
Thy forests, fields and streams abound.
I know no other land beside
Where such free room to breathe is found."[52]

CONSOLIDATION OF THE ARMY

CHAPTER 4
1941–1943

CHAPTER 4

1941–1943

CONSOLIDATION OF THE ARMY

DURING THE 5–6 MONTHS THAT IT WAS BASED IN RUSSIA, IN THE VOLGA REGION, THE POLISH ARMY IN THE USSR HAD REMAINED A SKELETON FORCE.

It was woefully undersupplied, and the General Staff spent most of its time either with political problems or with the basic tasks of registering, sheltering, feeding, and clothing the men. Above all, it had to conduct a running battle with the NKVD whose liaison officers could not understand that the Army was disinclined to accept their unquestioned control.

The problems of isolation in the wilderness that is Russia had to be seen to be believed. One senior officer, who was issued with a car together with petrol vouchers and special passes, found that the 925-mile drive from Moscow to Buzuluk was all but impossible in winter and that the car was more of a burden than a privilege. He left Moscow on 14 October 1941:

> "There was a good road only as far as Gorkij (about 300 miles from Moscow); from there to Kazan, it could hardly be called a road. Only with difficulty could the car move over the frozen mud. On the ferry over the Volga at Kazan, we were detained, with our car, suspected of espionage. After [the guard] checked up on us... [they] let us proceed. Driving for 20 miles on the road to Ulyanovsk, we had to return to Kazan as the road was completely impassable. Only by using force, efficiently assisted by the NKVD, did we manage to embark with our car on the SS *Lomonosov*, sailing down the Volga to Kuibyshev..."[53]

The Soviet government and president Kalinin, together with all foreign embassies, had been evacuated to Kuibyshev, and the city was crammed to overflowing. There was 'a terrific snowstorm', and the General slept on the floor of the Polish Embassy, waiting for better weather. In the end, he abandoned his car, and travelled to Buzuluk by rail, arriving on November 1, on the 18th day of the journey.

In the course of those months, several new categories of potential recruits made their appearance. One was a group of some 400 officers, who, like Zygmunt Berling, had been preserved and set aside by the NKVD in the belief that they had Communist or at least pro-Soviet sympathies. Apart from Berling, they included one general, Jerzy Wołkowicki, five colonels and fourteen lieutenant colonels. A second, larger group was made up of officers who had been interned in 1939–1940 in Lithuania and Latvia and who only fell into Soviet hands after the NKVD's murder campaign. They included one

AN ARMY review at Totskoye, Spring 1942.

POLISH POST in the USSR, 50 kopeck stamp inscribed: 1941–1942 *Dojdziemy*! (We will get there!).

THE VOLGA frozen over. Samara (2015).

general, Wacław Przeździecki, and a substantial number of older men above military age.

In these circumstances, General Anders was severely constrained in his choice of senior officers. He was fortunate in having a close circle of trusted colleagues on whom he could rely implicitly. These included General Leopold Okulicki (1898–1946), his Chief-of-Staff, General Michał Karaszewicz-Tokarzewski (1893–1964), who commanded the 6th Division, and Col. Klemens Rudnicki (1897–1992), commander of the 5th Division. All three had been involved in 1939–1940 in the underground, Anti-Soviet resistance movement, and, like Anders himself, had proved their patriotism and loyalty under Soviet captivity. In addition, he had General Zygmunt Bohusz-Szyszko (1893–1982), who had been sent to Russia from London by the Commander-in-Chief. But beyond that inner circle, many officers had question marks hanging over them. Anders took a pragmatic line. He did not exclude men who had graduated from courses at the NKVD's 'Villa of Bliss'. He gave them the benefit of the doubt, and ordered everyone else to stop spreading rumours. Lt Col. Zygmunt Berling was made Chief-of-Staff of the 5th Division, Col. Eustachy Gorczyński, Head of the Engineers, and Lt Col. Leon Tyszyński, Head of the IVth Section. Of these, only a handful proved disloyal. Col. Berling was to be sentenced in absentia. Lt Col. Leon Bukojemski was jailed while the Army was still in the USSR. Major Rosen-Zawadzki was jailed when it reached Palestine.

A third group, of non-commissioned soldiers, possibly 200,000 strong, was made up of young Polish men who had been conscripted

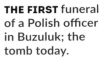

THE FIRST funeral of a Polish officer in Buzuluk; the tomb today.

SUPPLY TRUCK from 1941 in the Museum in Orenburg (right).

into the Red Army after the Soviet takeover of the Kresy. Anders could not hope to gain access to men who were fighting in Soviet units at the height of the German onslaught. But news arrived that a substantial proportion of those Polish conscripts had been withdrawn from the front because of the NKVD's suspicions about their loyalty, and that they were now serving as virtual slave-labourers in penal *stroybataliony*. It was hoped that some of these unfortunates could now be released.

Anders and his staff were assailed by two quite different political problems. The first derived from acute political conflicts within the Army's own ranks. The second was the natural product of the brutal and callous treatment of Poles by Stalin's regime in the preceding period.

General Sikorski, now Prime Minister and Commander-in-Chief, had belonged to Poland's prewar opposition, and had distanced himself from military service under Piłsudski and Piłsudski's successors. Together with Ambassador Stanisław Kot, whom he had appointed in Moscow, he was extremely suspicious of officers who had connections either with Piłsudski's Legions or with the Sanacja government. He insisted, therefore, that he personally vet all appointments to the higher positions. Anders took a different line. Beset by the drastic (and as yet unexplained) shortage of officers, he was prepared to give a chance to all trained officers, including those with radical right-wing or left-wing leanings, and to withhold all action against them, unless and until they gave proof of manifest disloyalty or incompetence.

ALMOST EVERY MAN AND WOMAN who served in the Anders Army, had the strongest grounds for despising the Soviet regime, which had brought such untold misery upon them. Once they were free, they were naturally inclined to vent their disgust on every possible occasion. General Anders, however, who undoubtedly shared their feelings, was equally conscious of the dangers. The Army was stationed in a country where an unguarded word about Stalin could land people in a concentration camp, and where any mention of Soviet crimes was severely punished. Moreover, it was supervised by NKVD liaison officers who were clearly outraged by what they frequently overheard. Anders ordered his subordinates, therefore, to hold their tongues. In his Officers Order No. 1 of 29 December 1941, he stated that criticism of the Soviet Union showed disrespect for the Commander-in-Chief and was contrary to the spirit of the Sikorski–Maisky Pact. "I have issued orders to all commanders", he stated, "to report to me immediately and to list the names of all officers who do not conform to my wishes."[54]

Similar arrangements were made with the Army chaplains, to ensure that 'anti-Soviet outbursts' were not delivered from the pulpit. But particular difficulties were encountered in the lyrics of songs that enjoyed great popularity among troops attending recreational concerts. Already in Buzuluk, a satirical puppet show was attracting attention, not least for its risqué doggerel. One day, a puppet dressed in the rags of a Gulag inmate (*lagiernik*) sang a 'Song of Gratitude':

I thank you for everything
For all that's good or ill.
I thank you for the prison,
And time there night and day.
I thank you for the Gulag camps,
For the convoys and the dogs,
And thank you for the fleas and lice.
And now that there's an amnesty,
Thanks for your gracious gesture![55]

The song caused a storm. A senior NKVD officer mounted the stage, and demanded a copy of the text. Anders took the author of the song into his own car for safety, and the company worked all night, changing all references to the NKVD into comments about the Gestapo.

Some forms of indiscipline had more drastic consequences. Men who had survived the Gulag were used to stealing food and to sharing the loot with their friends. But when certain individuals mounted large-scale night-time raids on the Army's food stores, presumably to facilitate illicit trade with the local population, the General Staff decided to make an example of them. Court-martials were held; death sentences were passed; and execution squads carried out their duty. The numbers involved were small, but the view has been expressed that Anders exceeded his due powers.

Observers noted, however, that the soldiers were no longer prepared to accept the sort of discipline that had prevailed in the prewar army. "They were of the opinion", wrote the young journalist, Zdzisław Bau, "that 'blind obedience' had ended once and for all in September 1939, and that in the 'March to Poland', which was constantly proclaimed, they were the nation that had to be consulted."[56]

TOTSKOYE (NOVEMBER 2011). A group of visitors from the Polonia in Russia with veteran, Wojciech Narębski, 'Little Wojtek'.

SUMMER AT LAST. The 6th Infantry Division still in Russia prior to its transfer to Uzbekistan.

THE PORT of Murmansk as seen from a British navy porthole.

2ND LT. MIECZYSŁAW ZAKRZEWSKI, a graduate of the AGH University of Science and Technology in Kraków, who had travelled from Britain with a camera, on the rail journey from Murmansk to Uzbekistan, February 1942.

The decision to move south was taken (in December 1941) three months before the later decision to evacuate part of the Army from the USSR. Anders always denied that he had intended to escape from the outset. He took the Army to Uzbekistan for simple logistical reasons, and had no other plans than to prepare his troops for service under Soviet command on the Eastern Front. He estimated that they would need six months of preparation and training.

In Uzbekistan, the Army passed under the supervision of SAVO, the Red Army's Central Asian Military District, whose officers and agents sought to oversee all operations. Recruitment and registration, for instance, was now organised through the joint Polish–Soviet *Voyenkom* or Military Commission, where all the old arguments revived about who was or was not entitled to serve.

ONCE THE GENERAL STAFF reached Central Asia, recruitment to the Army resumed, and all the quarrels surrounding it revived. Colonel Rudnicki, who had the unenviable task of negotiating with Soviet officers in SAVO, left a record of the problems:

"Two basic decisions were intimated to me. According to SAVO's representative, these decisions had been reached in Moscow and must be strictly adhered to. The first one stated that new recruits must be enlisted only through Soviet Army offices – the *Voyenkomaty* – and not directly by the Polish Divisions.

The second one defined who might be recruited, *viz.* only Poles who before 1939 had lived to the west of the Ribbentrop-Molotov demarcation line. All Poles living to the east of this line could join the Polish Army only if they were undoubtedly of Polish origin. All Jews, from any part of Poland, were deprived of this right.

We had no doubts about the meaning of this decision. The sovereignty of our Army, which, according to the Agreement reached, had the right to incorporate into her ranks all Polish citizens able to bear arms, was thus put into jeopardy. Entrusting the enlistment of new recruits to Soviet military authorities meant that we should receive only as many new recruits as the Soviet authorities were willing to let us have, and they need only enlist those men they wished to. This would enable the Soviets to prevent the increase of our Army to 100,000, which was the figure agreed during the Kremlin talks.

The differentiation of Poles in accordance with the German–Soviet demarcation line before 1939, and the denial to Polish national minorities of the right to serve in the Polish Army and thus fulfil their duty towards the country, was a political act, disclosing the will of the USSR to annex the Eastern Polish territories. A denial of the rights of Jews to join the Polish Army was also calculated to exacerbate

Polish–Jewish relations and cast a slur on our nation in the West, especially in the USA.

I immediately lodged a protest against both these decisions. SAVO's representative then announced that he could not discuss these questions, they being outside the scope of his competence. That being the case, I adjourned the conference and sent a report to General Anders by wireless, asking him for further instructions. The General replied promptly, informing me that a protest had been lodged at the highest level. Nevertheless, I must aim at a speedy settlement of the recruiting organisation, even under the conditions thrust upon us, because the growth of our Army was the most important matter; all other questions were comparatively minor.

I considered this decision to be the right one. We should leave the Governments to exchange diplomatic notes, meanwhile doing everything in our power to increase our Army to 100,000 men without delay. I thought this possible of achievement, in spite of the regulations about the *Voyenkomaty*, because it was obvious that, once volunteers heard that recruitment for the Polish Army had begun, they would join that Army by hook or by crook, disregarding orders...

I therefore resumed discussion with SAVO along these lines, and we very soon reached agreement. We settled the mixed recruitment commissions in each *Voyenkomat*. To each of those commissions we had to send a Polish doctor to work with a Soviet one, and an officer to verify the nationality of the volunteers.

There were some amusing incidents during the drafting of instructions for these commissions. For instance, the Soviets wanted to insert a clause giving the commissions the right to reject not only national minorities, but also Poles who might cause suspicion by professing 'pro-Fascist tendencies'. I asked them what they meant by 'pro-Fascist tendencies'. Did they mean that, if a volunteer were asked which he preferred, a *Kolchoz* or an individually-owned farm, and declared himself in favour of private enterprise, he would be regarded as a Fascist and for this reason not enlisted in the sovereign Polish Army? I

THE TOP BRASS: General Bohusz-Szyszko (right), Colonel Okulicki (centre), and Col. Nikodem Sulik (left), greeted by schoolchildren.

GENERALS SIKORSKI and Anders in Buzuluk, early 1942. British, Polish, Soviet and American flags flying overhead (far left).

TOTSKOYE TODAY, Polish officer lays a wreath at the memorial, 15 August 2010 (left).

also asked what they meant by 'Fascist': was it everybody who was not a Communist?"[57]

THE MOST COMMON WAY of slipping through the NKVD's net was to declare one's previous identity papers to be lost or stolen – which was frequently true – then to modify inconvenient details on the registration forms. Belarusians and Ukrainians typically adopted Polish Christian names like 'Stanisław' or 'Jerzy' and spelled their surnames in standard Polish orthography. Jews would state that they were Catholics or of 'no religion'; and Poles would often change their place of birth. Before 1918, for example, there had been large Polish communities in St Petersburg, Kiev, Odessa, and Baku, and 25 years later the NKVD were still likely to treat people born in such places as Soviet citizens (even if they had never resided in the Soviet Union). The safest policy was to declare one's birthplace as Poznań (in Germany) or Kraków (in Austria), and thereby to avoid any chance of an argument. Polish officers were instructed to close their eyes to the practice. As a result, the Polish Army had more than its share of recruits of dubious identity, and so long as the NKVD was hovering in the vicinity, no one asked any questions.

Despite the well-established facts of the case, charges of anti-Semitic discrimination were, and are, endlessly directed at General Anders and his Army's recruitment policy. Sixty years after the event, the eminent Cracovian, professor of literature, Henryk Markiewicz, was still saying that his ethnic origin was the cause of his rejection:

"The draft into the Polish Army began in the spring of 1942. Only Zygmunt was drafted, because he had a higher education and a driver's licence. Father and I were rejected, most probably because of our origins. I had no idea at the time that it was at the request of the Soviet side, but the Polish military authorities appeared quite willing, understandably as a matter of fact: if all men of Jewish origin had been accepted, they would have overwhelmed in number the others in the army ranks. I was discouraged by this decision, to be honest, more by the discriminatory form than the refusal as such. I wanted to join the army out of a sense of duty and to avoid death

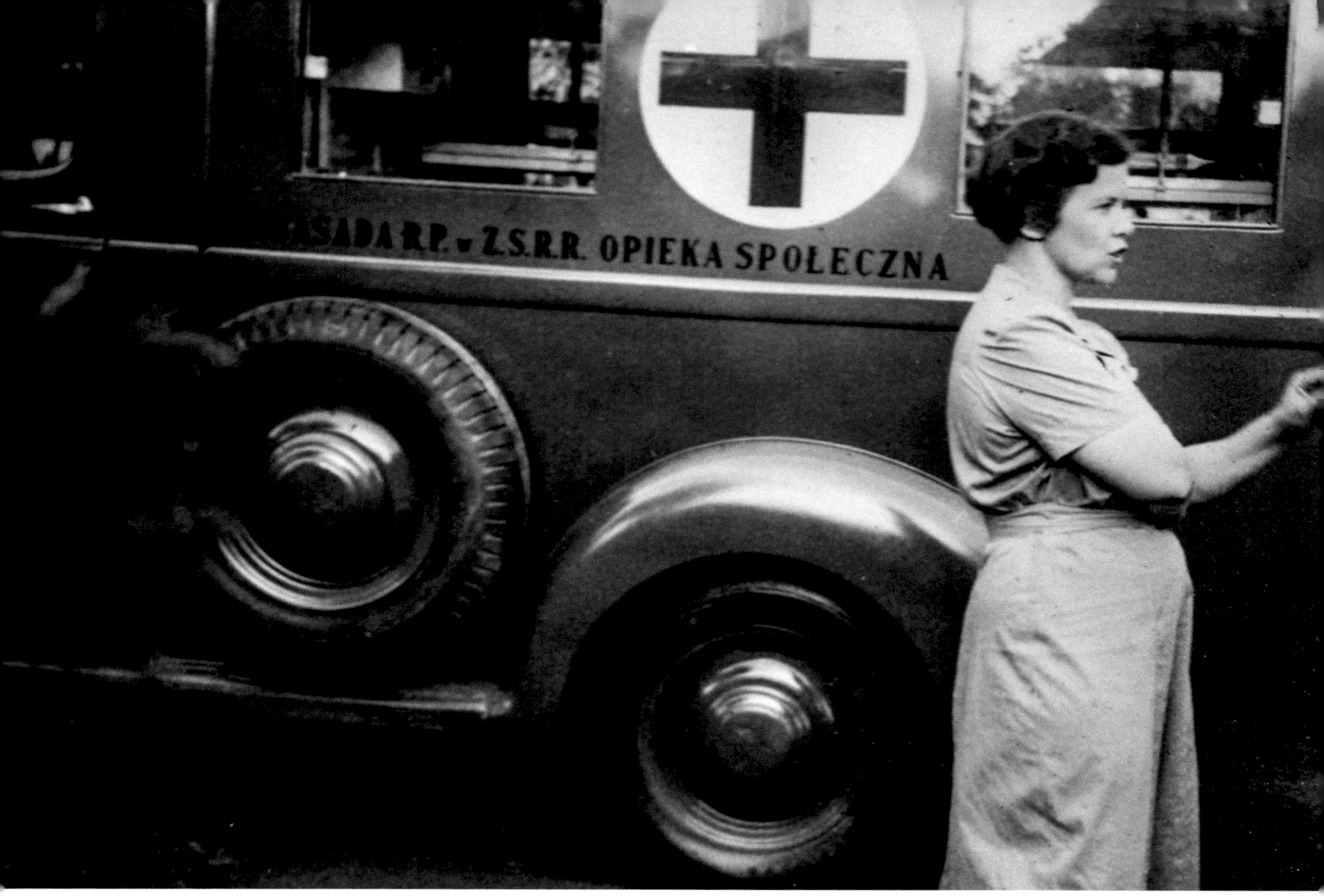

by starvation, and to escape from the Soviet Union. But I was worried that my helplessness and oafishness, magnified by a pitiful weakness and shortsightedness, would make it extremely difficult for me to fulfill my soldierly duties. I was not afraid to die at war, but I was afraid that I would become a klutz. That is what would have happened, you know.

Shorty after that Father died of a heart condition in the hospital at Andijan, and I was also in the forecourts of death, because of starvation."[58]

WHAT CAN ONE SAY? People like Professor Markiewicz are manifestly honest and sincere, but they are reporting their subjective feelings, not objective reality. Tens of thousands of others, Jews and non-Jews, were stranded like him in Uzbekistan and dying of starvation. Everyone who was rejected felt that they, too, were victims of injustice.

Another group, meanwhile, was more fortunate. It consisted of the wives and families of Rudnicki's own regiment, whom he had last seen in 1939 at the regimental base at Trembowla, and who qualified for Army support being dependants of serving officers:

"This news came in a letter written by the wives of several officers and NCOs in Aya-Guz, near Semipalatinsk, in the Kazak S.S. Republic. They had all been dragged there in the spring of 1940 from Trembowla, when the Bolsheviks began to clear the town from 'rotting elements'. The letter told of their misery, and expressed tremendous joy that they had discovered me: 'Now we know we shall not get lost.'

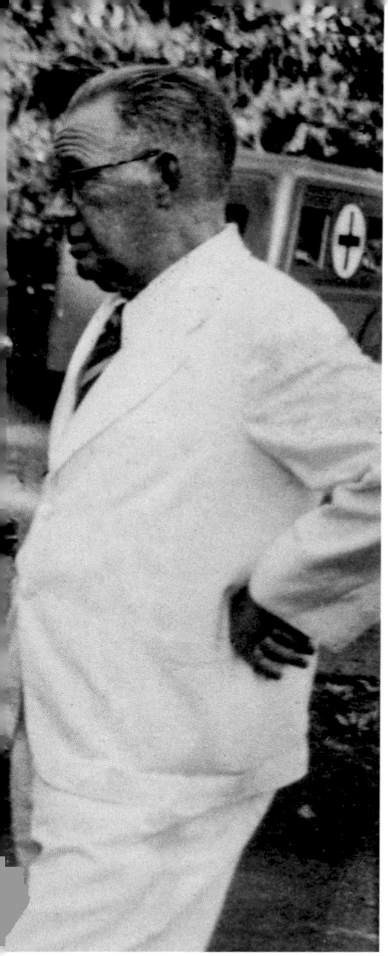

MS KIRA BANASIŃSKA and Mr Boyd Walker, who accompanied a convoy of vehicles and supplies from Britain. August 1942.

AMERICAN DODGE WC-series half-ton trucks from the Lend-Lease programme.

Among them were the wives of Capt. Ksyk with their six-year-old boy; of Capt. Zahorski with their boy; and of the late Capt. Poborowski with a little daughter. The wife of Capt. A. Bielecki had been with them but had died of starvation, leaving behind two little sons under Our Lord's protection. There was also the wife of my pre-war second-in-command, Lt Col. Golaszewski, with their son and her sister; the wife of Capt. A. Rogawski, another old 9th Lancers officer; and many more. And there were the wives of many NCOs: Tyblewski, Sobol, Ostafin, Maznas, and many others."[59]

Their good fortune was not the result of favouritism, but of sensible rules laid down in near-impossible circumstances.

Notwithstanding the obstacles, numbers began to increase rapidly, reaching 1,000–1,500 recruits daily in March 1942. A substantial proportion of the newcomers had been conscripted by the Soviet authorities in Kazakhstan, where many deportees were concentrated.

The expansion of the Army proceeded through the creation of four new infantry divisions – the 7th, 8th, 9th, and 10th – and of numerous other technical and logistical formations. All of them had to be allocated bases, which had been vacated by Soviet units and which were scattered over a very wide area.

Very soon, however, the drawbacks of the move to Central Asia were made painfully obvious. The army had jumped from the Russian freezer into an oriental frying-pan. Conditions were hardly conducive to a healthy and trouble-free life:

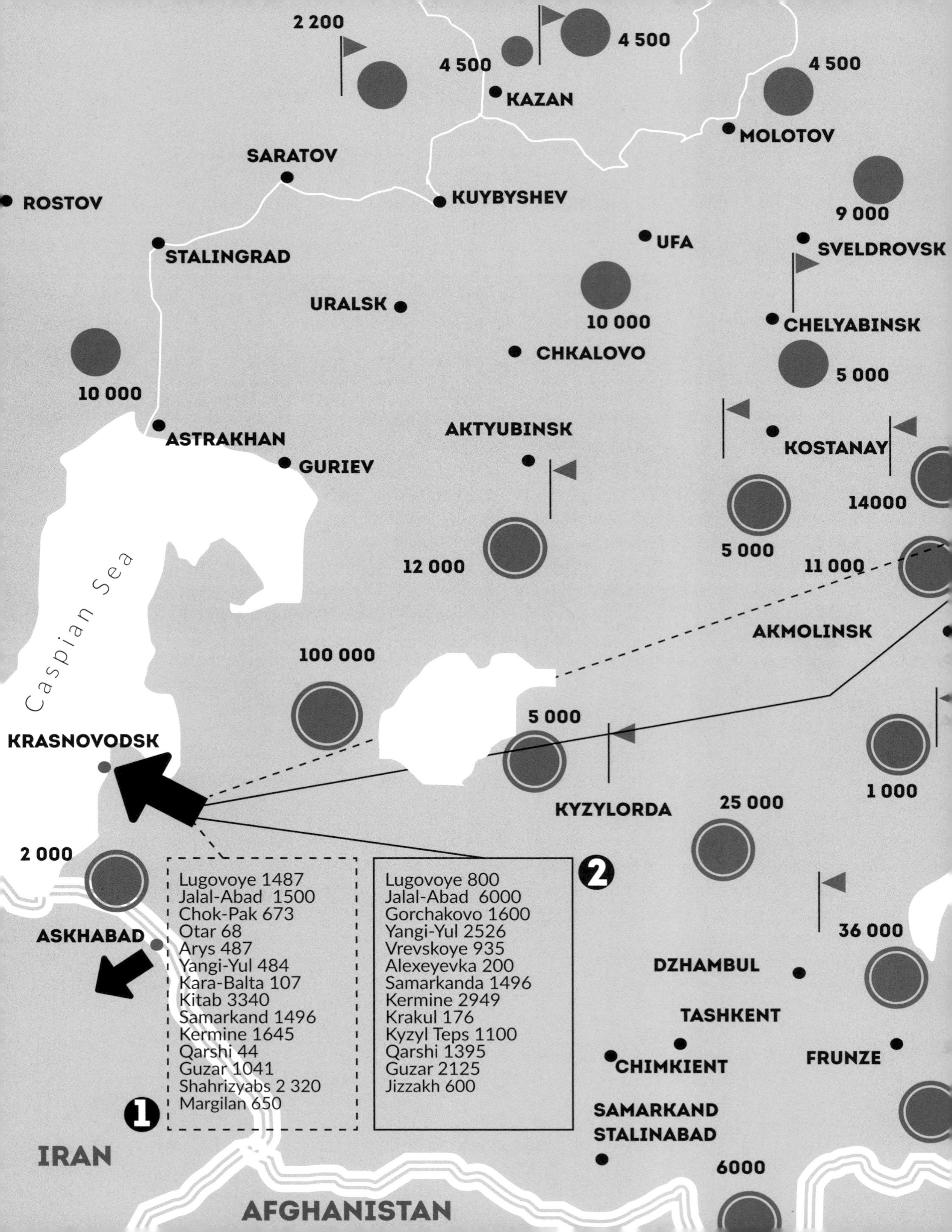

2 200
4 500
4 500
4 500
KAZAN
MOLOTOV
SARATOV
ROSTOV
KUYBYSHEV
9 000
UFA
SVELDROVSK
STALINGRAD
URALSK
10 000
CHELYABINSK
CHKALOVO
5 000
10 000
ASTRAKHAN
AKTYUBINSK
KOSTANAY
GURIEV
14000
5 000
12 000
11 000
Caspian Sea
AKMOLINSK
100 000
5 000
KRASNOVODSK
KYZYLORDA
25 000
1 000
2 000
2
Lugovoye 1487
Jalal-Abad 1500
Chok-Pak 673
Otar 68
Arys 487
Yangi-Yul 484
Kara-Balta 107
Kitab 3340
Samarkand 1496
Kermine 1645
Qarshi 44
Guzar 1041
Shahrizyabs 2 320
Margilan 650
Lugovoye 800
Jalal-Abad 6000
Gorchakovo 1600
Yangi-Yul 2526
Vrevskoye 935
Alexeyevka 200
Samarkanda 1496
Kermine 2949
Krakul 176
Kyzyl Teps 1100
Qarshi 1395
Guzar 2125
Jizzakh 600
ASKHABAD
36 000
DZHAMBUL
TASHKENT
CHIMKIENT
FRUNZE
1
SAMARKAND
STALINABAD
IRAN
6000
AFGHANISTAN

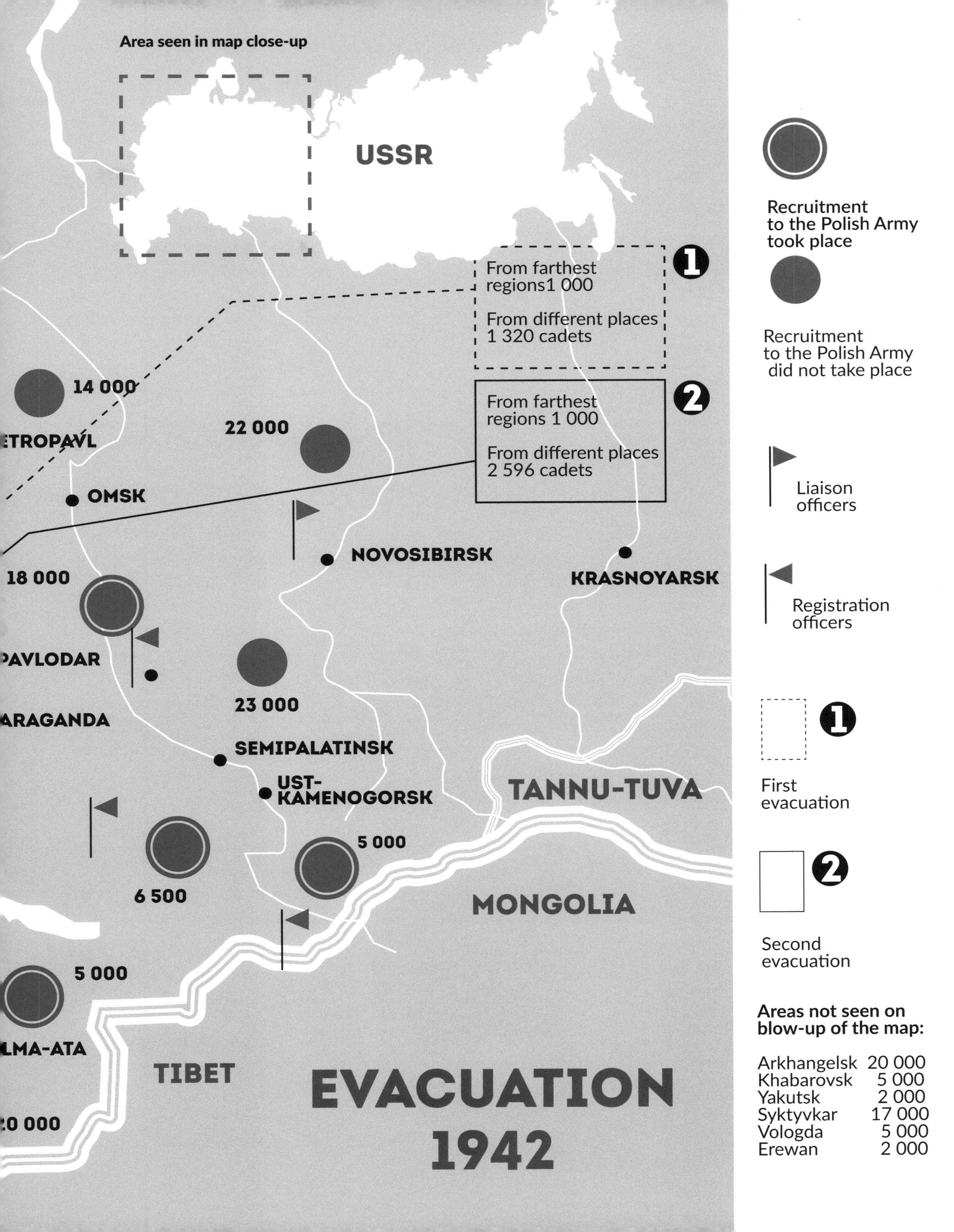

Area seen in map close-up
USSR
From farthest regions1 000
From different places 1 320 cadets
From farthest regions 1 000
From different places 2 596 cadets
14 000
ETROPAVL
22 000
OMSK
NOVOSIBIRSK
KRASNOYARSK
18 000
PAVLODAR
23 000
ARAGANDA
SEMIPALATINSK
UST-KAMENOGORSK
TANNU-TUVA
5 000
6 500
MONGOLIA
5 000
LMA-ATA
TIBET
20 000
EVACUATION 1942
Recruitment to the Polish Army took place
Recruitment to the Polish Army did not take place
Liaison officers
Registration officers
First evacuation
Second evacuation
Areas not seen on blow-up of the map:
Arkhangelsk 20 000
Khabarovsk 5 000
Yakutsk 2 000
Syktyvkar 17 000
Vologda 5 000
Erewan 2 000

"Kitab was the terminus of a local railway-line siding from the main Tashkent–Ashkhabad–Krasnovodsk line. It was our nearest garrison: only about three miles away [from the General Staff].

The 16th Infantry Regiment was under canvas on the borders of the river Kashka-Darya, about six miles from Kitab. Only the Regimental HQ and the Medical Inspection Room were billeted in the wooden building of a wine factory. There were very few trees and practically no shade and the heat made life in the tents unbearable. The nearby river and the channels for irrigating the fields soon proved to be plague spots — breeding-grounds for malarial mosquitoes.

Yakobak was a station on the same railway-line, about 12 miles from Shachrizyabs, but completely in the desert, without water, trees, or green shrubs. Water for drinking, cooking and washing, had to be carried in big barrels on wheels, drawn by mules, from an oasis a couple of miles distant. This was where the tents of the 17th Infantry Regiment and the 6th Field Artillery Regiment were erected — dirty, second-hand Soviet tents. Men made dugouts for themselves to secure a little coolness.

Tshirakshi, about 10 miles beyond Yakobak, was the name of a small Uzbek town near which the 18th Infantry Regiment was encamped. As at Kitab, the River Kashka-Darya flowed by the tents, and again there were many irrigation channels. But here there was plenty of green and shade. Also, Tshirakshi was full of folklore, and provided entertainment for our soldiers, which was completely missing in Yakobak. Here, on market days, one could watch the poor Asiatic people riding on their little donkeys to the town's bazaar, carrying baskets full of melons, grapes, or nuts. Sometimes they brought homespun silken handkerchiefs in beautiful pastel colours, *carsafs*, bracelets, earrings, and other wonders. In the evenings one could listen to Uzbek tunes, played on pipes, which to European ears sounded monotonous, like a kind of lamentation or prayer."[60]

Each division consisted of two or more constituent infantry regiments, and was supported

SNOWBOUND YANGI-YUL. General Anders, sitting on the snow talks to soldiers wearing British Army helmets, with Soviet officers in attendance. Spring 1942.

by its own sections of artillery, cavalry and engineers. The 5th Division, for example, was composed of three infantry regiments (16th, 17th, and 18th), of the 6th Artillery Regiment, one battalion of Signals, one battalion of Engineers, the Provost Company, transport and stores units and a Field Hospital. When it arrived in Central Asia, it had only 8,000 men, though the strength would rise to 14,000.

The constituent units of the Division were distributed between four centres. The Divisional HQ and Services were in Shakhrisabz. The infantry regiments were distributed to Kitab, Yakobak, and Tshirakshi.

POLISH SOLDIERS in the USSR: 'The alarm is sounded.' Passed by the Polish Ministry of Information censorship office.

THE LIST OF 'SERVICES' on which an army depends is a long one; no fighting force would be able to operate for long without the support of administrative and logistical departments, engineers, transport companies, intelligence and signals sections, the Medical Corps, Military Police, and women's auxiliaries.

Poland had a long tradition of female military service, and in 1938 the law on conscription applied to women as well as men.. The *Pomocnicza Służba Kobiet* (PSK, Women Auxiliary Service), the equivalent of the British Army's Auxiliary Territorial Service (ATS), therefore, came into being from the very beginning at Buzuluk. Its commandant was Major, later Lieutenant Colonel, Władysława Piechowska neé Buttowt-Andrzeykowicz (1900–1987), a woman with a long history of patriotic service going back to the clandestine Polish Military Organisation (POW) in 1917–1918. Born in Volhynia, she was serving in 1939 with a Women's Battalion in Lwów, where she was arrested by the NKVD and sent to a penal camp at Vyatka. Members of the PSK were affectionately known as *pestki* or 'apple pips'. Their traditional duties centred on the medical sphere as nurses and orderlies, but rapidly expanded into clerical work, the messenger service, vehicle maintenance, and driving. Their initial numbers reached about 2000.

The Army's Justice Department was the ultimate arbiter of military discipline. Its officers were charged with the enforcement of regulations, the supervision of the *żandarmeria* (Military Police) and provost marshalls, the administration of military courts, and the management of jails. The director was Col. Stanisław Rohm (1891–1969).

Owing to the extreme difficulty in Russia of securing basic supplies, heavy responsibility fell onto the Army's Quartermaster General, Lt Col. Stanisław Pstrokoński (1897–1952).

The General Staff's III Department (Operations) was headed by Lt Col. Kazimierz Wiśniowski (1896–1964); the I Department (Training) by Lt Col. Władysław Krogulski

(1894–1962). They had the reputation of holding extreme nationalist views.

The Army's Medical Corps was charged with caring for the health of the troops both at the frontline and at the rear. Since the prospect of frontline fighting in Russia was not immediate, the attention of the staff – doctors, nurses, ambulance drivers and stretcher bearers – was fully stretched, dealing with malnutrition, exhaustion, frostbite, and outbreaks of malaria and typhus. The Chief Surgeon of the Corps was Lt Col. Prof. Bolesław Szarecki (1874–1960).

INTELLIGENCE, AS ALWAYS, had prime importance, and the 2nd Section of the General Staff (the *Dwójka*) played a vital role in the Army's activities. Anders' intelligence officers were charged with collecting information both on all aspects of the soldiers' conduct, and on all external matters relating to the Army's existence. They needed to keep their superiors up to date on developments in the German–Soviet War, and in Poland, which by 1942 was entirely subject to German occupation. In normal circumstances, as part of the interallied intelligence network, the *Dwójka*, would have

VOLGA INDUSTRIAL region (2015) (top).

MOTORCYCLING ON the trail of General Anders (2009) (above).

THE URAL RIVER near Orenburg (right).

worked closely with the NKVD. But circumstances in Stalin's realm were not normal, and the NKVD did not treat their Polish counterparts as trusted partners. On the contrary, the NKVD did everything in its power to restrict and filter information.

The *Dwójka* also acted as the principal link between the Polish Army in the USSR and the Polish government in London. For this reason, it was often seen as General Sikorski's Trojan Horse, and was suspected, especially in the early phase of the Army's formation, of influencing appointments to the detriment of officers with pro-Sanacja sympathies. These suspicions subsided with the elevation to Chief of Intelligence of Lt Col. Wincenty Bąkiewicz (1897–1974), an officer of great tact and competence who was to keep his position until the war's end. Like Anders, Bąkiewicz had served in the Tsarist Army, was fluent in the Russian language, and very familiar with Soviet affairs. Before the war, he had worked in the Polish Army's historical section and was markedly more neutral in political matters than his predecessor, Lt Col. Jan Axentowicz, known as 'Majonez', whose prewar career lay in the Intelligence Service of the Sanacja.

The *Dwójka's* work was dependent to a high degree on good communications. Fortunately, the Army's Communication Section possessed a number of talented operators, who managed to overcome the primitive conditions in which they worked. Headed by Lt Col. Mieczysław Zaleski, who was specially sent out from England in March 1942, it was based in Yangi-Yul, and was divided into two sections. The external section, which had started life in Buzuluk,ran *Radio Buz* and established communication with the Commander-in-Chief's central station at Stanmore near London, the Polish Embassy in Kuibyshev, the Polish Embassy in Tehran, and the Evacuation Base at Krasnovodsk. It possessed two transmitters, one an old British SA apparatus, and the other, an AI

Polish-produced 'Pipstick', which General Anders smuggled into the USSR in his personal baggage after his trip to Britain in May 1942. Its transmissions in encoded Morse were not authorised by the NKVD, who constantly tried to interrupt it by cutting off the electricity supply. It survived by sharing the output of the Army Press Office's generator. Its recognised stars were the two Łapiński brothers from Wilno, who had been short-wave radio enthusiasts before the war. For two months, from April to May 1942, they also succeeded in talking daily to a clandestine Home Army station, *Radio Ada,* in German-occupied Warsaw. The information from *Radio Ada* was regularly passed on to Marshal Zhukov.

The internal section of *Radio Buz* used standard Soviet equipment to each of the Army's bases scattered round Central Asia. It transmitted in 'open mode', and was not harassed by the NKVD.

The Army Press Office operated a complementary monitoring service, which gathered information about the progress of the war by listening to a wide variety of Allied and enemy radio stations. Zdzisław Bau, who specialised in English-language broadcasts, recalled how his heart beat with excitement when he first tuned into the BBC in London, and heard the BBC's famous 'Three Knock' call signal. Apart from the BBC, the Poles huddled over their receivers in Yangi-Yul under the starlit Central Asian sky and listened with ease to Wehrmacht stations on the Eastern Front, to the *Afrikakorps,* to Soviet broadcasts, to the British Army in Cairo, and even to the Americans in Iceland.

Supervision by the NKVD caused a non-stop headache, not least because they habitually 'bugged' all the premises used by the Polish Army. An NKVD Colonel called Volkovyski lived per-

AN ARMY football team in full kit.

MARCHING SOLDIERS urged on by trumpets and watched by children. Chirakchi, Uzbekistan (opposite).

manently in a room inside General Anders's HQ; he was head of the Soviet Military Mission. He was a Jew and, as his adopted name suggests, came from a small Polish town (now called Vavkavysk, in Belarus), not far from Białystok. He understood Polish, though seldom spoke it, and was excessively polite. He was particularly deferential to Anders. In General Rudnicki's opinion, "his behaviour was that of a sly fox, sometimes insolent, sometimes servile". He "pretended to be friendly", gossipped a great deal, and peppered his conversation with political propaganda. He was constantly urging his Polish hosts to express their solidarity with the USSR.

Yet experience was to show that the NKVD was by no means as friendly as its officers purported to be:

"In several places in our HQ our experts found microphones installed for the interception of private talks. For instance, one ingeniously fitted microphone was found in General Anders' room in the ventilator above his desk. The wires led to a room in the basement which was not occupied by us because, allegedly, the town's records were kept there, as no other place could be found for them.

Instead of records, the telephone exchange had amplifiers for the interception of our talks. We disconnected the microphones, and General Anders hid them in the drawer of his desk. Then he asked Col. Volkovyski for an interview, in the presence of Okulicki and me.

After we had discussed various questions, the General took the incriminating microphones from his drawer and smilingly handed them over to Wolkowyski. He said, jokingly, that his Staff had found these innocent toys – one even in his own room. He apologised for having

WOMEN VOLUNTEERS

WOMEN VOLUNTEERS (Ochotniczki). The Polish Auxiliary Women's Service (PSK) was the equivalent of the British ATS or the American WIMSA, and it formed part of the 'Anders Army' from the beginning. It was an essential element of its logistical and psychological make-up.

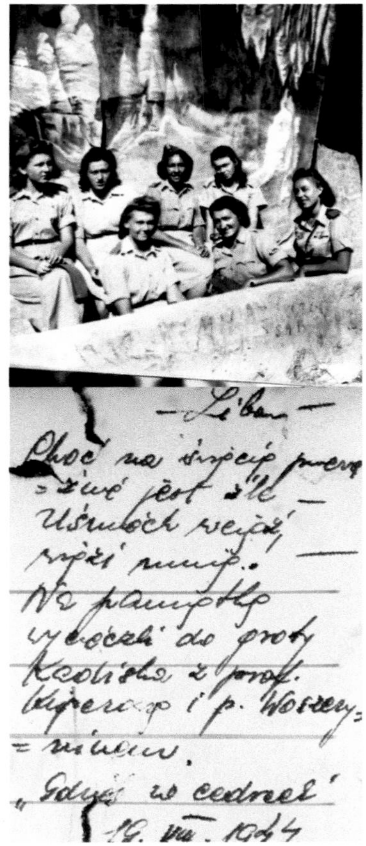
– Liban –
Na pamiątkę
wycieczki do groty

taken them down, and wished to return them to their rightful owners. He averred that he was not annoyed; he could well understand the need for caution. But he could assure Volkovyski that we had nothing to conceal; our approach to the cooperation and organisation of our Army was quite sincere, and Volkovyski could obtain any information he required by asking us directly without having recourse to any such subterfuges.

Volkovyski reacted instantly. He said there must be a tragic misunderstanding somewhere, which had nothing to do with him, and our assumption was a direct offence to the Soviet authorities. He thanked us for having discovered the microphones; he would immediately report to Moscow about the incident and ask for an enquiry to be made, to establish how the instruments had found their way into the HQ building.

Indeed, the Court of Enquiry came from Moscow three days afterwards. After making a 'thorough investigation', it communicated its findings to General Anders.

It was 'irrefutably' established that the net of microphones dated from old – probably Revolutionary – times; they had never been used since, and had only through carelessness been left in the building handed over to us. The Court of Enquiry was most apologetic, and assured the General that the culprits would be severely punished."[61]

Another disturbing incident arose when the NKVD informed General Anders that three Polish officers had been intercepted after crossing the Eastern Front from the German side, and were claiming to be couriers sent by the Home Army in Poland. They were carrying a

KENIMECH : Field training (Below) and a soldiers' meal (right).

COMING TO grips with a Soviet mortar (opposite top)

microfilm, which the NKVD had obviously read, and which carried a message to Anders urging him to attack the Red Army at the rear. They claimed that the message was just a ruse which had persuaded the Gestapo to assist their mission. What exactly they were up to was hard to determine, though they were clearly connected in some way with an underground intelligence unit in Poland known as 'The Musketeers', and with the unit's leader, Dr Stefan Witkowski (1903–1942), pseudonym "Tęczyński". Having checked with London that their mission had not been approved by the Home Army, Anders decided to put them on trial. Two of the three were acquitted on the grounds that they were innocent dupes, but their commander, a Captain Zaremba, was found guilty of collaboration with the enemy and sentenced to 25 years' detention. He was lucky not to have been shot.

Shortly afterwards, another dubious visitor presented himself at Buzuluk and asked to join the Army. Professor Leon Kozłowski (1892–1944), a distinguished archaeologist, had been a fervent supporter of the Sanacja regime, and had briefly served, in 1934, as Poland's Prime Minister. Arrested by the NKVD in Lwów, he had been tortured and threatened with the death sentence, and had only been released from the Lubyanka through the personal intervention of General Anders. He was restored to his prewar rank of lieutenant, and given a desk job in Staff HQ.

But then, to everyone's embarassment, Kozłowski vanished. Soviet intelligence reported that he had been seen crossing the frontline near Tula and surrendering to the Germans. Berlin Radio duly confirmed his defection. So what was his game? It is assumed that he was one of the few known Polish collaborators. If so, his treachery led nowhere. He died in Germany in murky circumstances in 1944, allegedly from Allied bombing.

There was even a prolonged dispute over the name of the 6th Infantry Division. The dispute was all the more bizarre because in 1941–1944 the city of Lwów was living under German occupation. Nonetheless, Col. Volkovyski let it be known that it was unacceptable to call the unit the '6th (Lwów) Division'. The city in question, he argued, had been formally incorporated into Soviet Ukraine in November 1939. On the contrary, his interlocutors replied, the Polish government had never issued a document that might have recognised the cession of Lwów to the USSR. Volkovyski tried to insist that 'the People's Will' trumped all such trifles. So stalemate ensued. The men of the division were livid. They had first been brought together in a battalion called 'the Children of Lwów'; and their encampment was festooned with the city's motto, '*Semper Fidelis*' and with reproductions of the city's coat-of-arms. In defiance, on 2 May 1942, General Tokarzewski published a communication to the Army's CO: "The soldiers of the 6th Division", it read, "kindly request that our division be called the 'Dywizja lwów'." By altering the capital letter to a small one, they

Jeśli zapomnę o Nich, ty, Boże w niebie, zapomnij o mnie.
Adam Mickiewicz
Szlakiem Generała Andersa

kept the sound of the name while changing its meaning to the 'Division of Lions'.

These episodes underline the extreme vulnerability of the Army's leaders to the political intrigues that were swirling around them. Fortunately, Anders and his inner circle stood firm against all the internal threats and external dangers, and the Army did not disintegrate. As early as November 1941, when Anders flew to Tehran to talk with Sikorski before their meeting with Stalin, he took a memorandum with him summarising the fears of his closest advisers. The memorandum listed three points:

1. The USSR was unwilling to implement the Polish–Soviet Military Agreement, or else intended to carry it out in a different way, to serve its own, unknown aims.
2. The Polish military authorities were completely cognisant of the situation, and would never allow themselves to be used as unwilling tools for an alien policy.
3. Only a decisive move at the highest level could safeguard the continued existence of a strong and sovereign Polish Army in the USSR.

Despite the dangers, it is a matter of fact that a series of moves at the highest level, involving Polish, Soviet, and British leaders, did succeed in ensuring the Army's survival.

In the meantime, the Poles were forced to observe the impassable gulf which separated them from the political culture of their hosts. While the General Staff was still in Central Asia, a delegation of senior Polish officers was invited to attend a four-hour session in the Tashkent Opera House, where festivities were taking place for the 25th Anniversary of the formation of the Red Army. The President of the Uzbek S.S. Republic presided. Speaker after speaker rose to praise the glorious victories of the Red Army, the incomparable achievements of the Soviet Union, and the untrammeled happiness of all Soviet citizens. Each one finished with the same rhetorical question: "To whom are we indebted for all of this?" and followed it with the same formulaic answer: "To our dearest comrade Stalin, the Sun and Leader of the Nations!" At every stage of the proceedings, the Chairman put the same question to the assembly, "Anyone against?" and received a deathly

FORMER POLISH hospital at Buzuluk.

LOCAL TEENAGERS greet an expedition from Poland. Koltubanka (2013) (opposite).

silence in response. Every speaker proposed the same resolution, to send a telegram of gratitude to Stalin. Colonel Rudnicki, who was present, described the event as "unbearably nauseating". "People in the Soviet Union", he wrote, "were perfectly trained, hopelessly patient, tragically enduring, and pathetically obsequious."[62]

The most serious problem centred on food rations, and could only be settled at the highest level. But a multitude of other obstacles raised their heads.

The Army, for one, did not receive even the first instalment of the promised loan from the Soviet State Bank for months. It had no money with which to pay its men or to order supplies. Still worse, it found its officers sent from Britain were entitled to British rates of pay converted to roubles. There was no way that equivalent pay scales could be offered to other officers.

Most annoyingly, it soon became clear, though British supplies arrived regularly via Archangel, that the level of supplies proposed by the Soviet Army proved woefully inadequate. The Polish staff worked out that the allocations of food and equipment made to each division fell far below the norms which had prevailed in the Polish Army before 1939. What is more, the NKVD practised all sorts of chicanery to curtail the delivery of supplies. For example, it would routinely purloin a large part of the British shipments and keep them 'in reserve'. At the same time, it consistently failed to honour its own promises in full. Polish forage parties would be told to collect supplies from this or that *kolkhoz*, only to find on arrival that absolutely nothing was waiting for them.

Driven to desperation by the impossible task of feeding the hungry mouths of both soldiers and civilians, the Polish leadership moved inexorably to the conclusion that a general exodus from the USSR offered the only practical solution.

THE CRISIS OF THE 'POLISH ARMY IN THE USSR' developed in the context of very shaky relations between the Western Allies and the Soviet Union. In 1941–1942, those relations were dominated by two issues: first, the Arctic convoys, which brought substantial aid from Britain to the ports of Murmansk and Archangel, and second, the prospect of a so-called 'Second Front' in the West, which Stalin repeatedly demanded to relieve hard-pressed Soviet forces on the Eastern Front. In this early period of the German–Soviet War, prior to Stalingrad, few observers reckoned that the Red Army's chances of survival would be high, if this Western support failed. Yet the convoys delivered less than was expected, and the Second Front – explicitly promised by President Roosevelt in May 1942 – was constantly postponed. In July 1942, the disaster of convoy PQ17, in which 24 out of 35 vessels were sunk, caused the suspension of the convoys, and in August 1942, the calamity of the Dieppe Raid, in which the Canadian expeditionary force suffered 68 per cent casualties, showed that German defences on the Atlantic coast were very strong.

Allied diplomacy in this period operated on the unwritten principle that only the Anglo-Saxon powers could discuss major issues with Stalin. Yet London and Washington put their trust in a series of pretty inexperienced and eccentric negotiators.

THE FIRST IMPORTANT MEETING TOOK PLACE IN MOSCOW IN OCTOBER 1941, when London was represented by the Canadian press baron, Lord Beaverbrook, and Washington by the ex-Governor of New York and racehorse owner, Averell Harriman. Beaverbrook was Churchill's Minister of Supply, but Harriman was no more than President Roosevelt's personal 'ambassador at large'. Beaverbrook and Harriman were treated to a lavish Kremlin banquet at a time when the *Wehrmacht* was launching its main attack on the Soviet capital, and when food riots had broken out in Moscow's streets. Both came away expressing strong sympathy for 'Russia'. Harriman promised increased aid from the Arctic convoys; he reacted with irritation after learning that a small part of the convoys' shipments were destined for the Polish Army. The tone of the visit was marked by North American-style 'joshing' and forced bonhomie. At the banquet, Beaverbrook asked Stalin, if President Kalinin had a mistress. "No", the jovial Georgian replied, "he's too old. But how about you?"

The second big meeting was delayed until 12–17 August 1942, when Prime Minister Churchill arrived in Moscow with Harriman in tow. The visitors were obliged to make some tricky explanations. Churchill had to explain why the Arctic convoys had been suspended, and Harriman to explain why the Western Powers were fighting in North Africa but not in continental Europe. Churchill's wife, Clementine, had labelled the trip 'a visit to the Ogre's Den', but it surmounted the prevailing tensions. Churchill offloaded the bad news at the very beginning, announcing that the Chiefs of Staff had ruled out a cross-Channel offensive that year. He immediately fired off a telegram to London saying "I expect to establish a solid and sincere relationship with this man."

MAX AITKEN, Lord Beaverbrook, a London press baron and Churchill's Minister of Supply, visited Moscow with Averill Harriman in October 1941.

Stalin launched a verbal broadside on the second day, accusing the British forces of cowardice and the Western Allies of bad faith. Churchill countered by pardoning Stalin's words "on account of the bravery of the Russian Army".

As a sign of protest, he attended the state banquet in the Kremlin not in evening dress, but in his one-piece, working boiler-suit. The British Ambassador calmed the Prime Minister down by saying (privately) that Stalin was just a 'peasant' in a palace. Surprisingly, perhaps,

STALIN WITH Averill Harriman (left), Wendell Wilkie (right), who had a riotous evening with Stalin in the Kremlin.

a further appointment was made, and it lasted eight hours, from 7 p.m. to 3 a.m. During those long hours of carousal, in Stalin's private apartment, the Dictator admitted to the mass killing of kulaks, apologised for the Nazi–Soviet Pact, and made fun of Molotov as 'a gangster'. Churchill came away with a 'slight headache', with a sense of achievement, and a conviction that the war could be fought in the spirit of 'comradeship'. Nothing was said about Poland or about Stalin's demand for recognition of territorial gains in 1939.

A third high-level meeting in September 1942 saw Stalin receiving Roosevelt's latest emissary, Wendell Wilkie, in the Kremlin. Wilkie had been the defeated Republican candidate in the presidential election of 1940, and Roosevelt was using him, as he used Harriman, as a 'roving ambassador'. Wilkie had once said, "It is from weakness that people reach for dictators... Only the strong can be free, and only the productive can be strong." When he had the good fortune of meeting a Dictator face to face, however, his judgement wobbled. "I am rather glad your lot was not cast in America," he told him; "you would have been a tough competitor." But the encounter then turned to farce. Wilkie himself boasted of drinking 53 toasts, and of still being able to walk to his car. At one point, he asked if he could see the famous Kalashnikov submachine gun. Stalin ordered a gun to be brought in. The British Ambassador checked to ensure that the magazine was empty, before Wilkie put an apple on his assistant's head, sat down, took aim and pulled the trigger. "You ought to be more careful carrying a machine-gun in the Kremlin." "What do I care", Wilkie replied, "the apple isn't mine!" At which, according to an official British report, "Stalin laughed so much he almost rolled on the floor."

When pressed by the Soviets to send troops to the Eastern Front, General Anders had countered by saying that none of the Polish divisions would be ready for action before June 1942. But June 1942 was long past and there were still no Polish units in a fit condition for frontline service.

CHAPTER 5

1942–1943

EVACUATION FROM THE USSR

CHAPTER 5

1942–1943

EVACUATION FROM THE USSR

MUCH HAS BEEN SAID AND WRITTEN ABOUT THE ARBITRARY HABITS OF THE NKVD, AND OF THE SOVIET UNION'S CHAOTIC WARTIME BUREAUCRACY. BUT IN ONE SPHERE THEY SHOWED GREAT EFFICIENCY; THANKS TO MUCH PRACTICE THEY HAD MASTERED THE ART OF TRANSPORTING HUGE NUMBERS OF PEOPLE OVER GREAT DISTANCES.

Theirs was a branch of tourism with no frills. But it worked. Within six days of Stalin issuing orders for the 'First Evacuation', groups of deportees were on the move. Between 24 March and 5 April 1942, a total of 44,000 Polish soldiers and civilians were taken by train and by ship from Central Asia to Iran.

Priority during the First Evacuation was given to certain categories of trained personnel – pilots, engineers, mechanics, and wireless operators – whom the British wished to send on directly to Great Britain. In second place, military administrators were sent to Iran to set up bases and prepare the ground for the influx of larger formations. And thirdly, among the civilians, preference was given to children and to the sick, whose lives were in danger from staying longer in the Soviet Union.

The itinerary required a three-stage journey. The first stage, by truck, took the deportees to a variety of Central Asian railway stations. The second, by cattle wagon, familiar from the mass deportations of 1940–1941, took them in two, three, or four days to the port of Krasnovodsk on the eastern shore of the Caspian Sea. And the third, by steamer, took them from Krasnovodsk to the Iranian port of Pahlevi.

Despite the beautiful climate, Krasnovodsk was no holiday resort. It served as an entrepôt for state-run commerce on the Caspian, and a base for a fleet of ageing vessels that carried heavy industrial goods, oil, and coal between Baku in Azerbaijan and Astrakhan at the mouth of the Volga. It had no luxury hotels or guest houses where travellers could rest their weary heads.

THE VOYAGE FROM KRASNOVODSK to Pahlavi, over a distance of 250 miles, lasted some three days, provoking extreme feelings both of hope and discomfort. The vessels were packed to overflowing with men, women, and children who were forced to stand on the deck or in the hold, and, if lucky, to find a patch of iron grating on which to sleep. But the destination was 'Freedom', an escape from 'the Inhuman Land'; and the exhausted travellers, peering towards the southern horizon were prepared to bear every deprivation in order to reach their goal.

The beach and waterfront at Pahlavi, however, did not present a picture of paradise. Reception centres set up by British officers struggled to

PREPARING TO leave. Anxious faces.

POLISH POSTAGE stamp, 2000: commemorating the 60th Anniversary of the Evacuation of the Polish Army from the USSR.

cope with crowds of hungry, thirsty, and bewildered people. Some individuals simply lay down on the sand and died. Others rushed to buy or barter for things, like fresh fruit, that they had not seen since leaving Poland; then fell violently ill. Makeshift hospitals began to fill up. And the largest of Polish cemeteries in the Middle East received its first victims. The long years of maltreatment in Russia were taking their toll.

THE JOURNEY, which took soldiers and civilians out of the Soviet Union, was full both of excitement and of discomfort. Many were to recall it as if it had been a dream:

> "About five thirty the following morning, the soldiers came with horses and carts and took us and our few bundles to the station.
>
> 'Are you sure we are going to Pahlevi?' I asked the driver.
>
> 'Yes, I am sure', he reassured me. 'Look, you can see the soldiers guarding the train... Your brothers are on their boat, probably already at sea.'
>
> But the thought of boarding a train that was to take us away from Tony, [the brother, who was lost, and] to leave him alone in Russia was almost more than I could bear. I was torn in both directions, to follow after the little boys or to stay and try and find Tony. But I had my mother to think of, and I knew she could not cope without me.
>
> Even so as we boarded the train, both of us turned simultaneously and said aloud, 'Tony, please forgive us.'
>
> The soldier who was escorting us, heard us.
>
> 'Please don't be too unhappy', he told us. 'Whatever Sergeant Paluch says is true. He has promised you he will find [Tony] and he will.'
>
> We reached the sea at Krasnovodsk on the eastern shore of the Caspian Sea, just in time to see the boat with the boys on board moving away from the dock. It was one of two boats containing children who had survived the camps and had been orphaned or taken into care in Russia. One ship held boys, the other girls.
>
> We crossed the Caspian on a Russian boat. Pahlevi was about 800 km away on the opposite shore, a journey that took four days. As well as the officers' families, the boat was packed to capacity with Polish and Jewish civilian refugees.
>
> We watched the shore of Persia grow closer, and we saw the beautiful white beaches and palm trees at Pahlevi.
>
> We disembarked in little boats since the big boat could not dock, and my mother and I were amongst the first off, following perhaps twenty others, who like us were so thin and weak that they staggered as they lifted the little bundles that contained all they had left in the world.

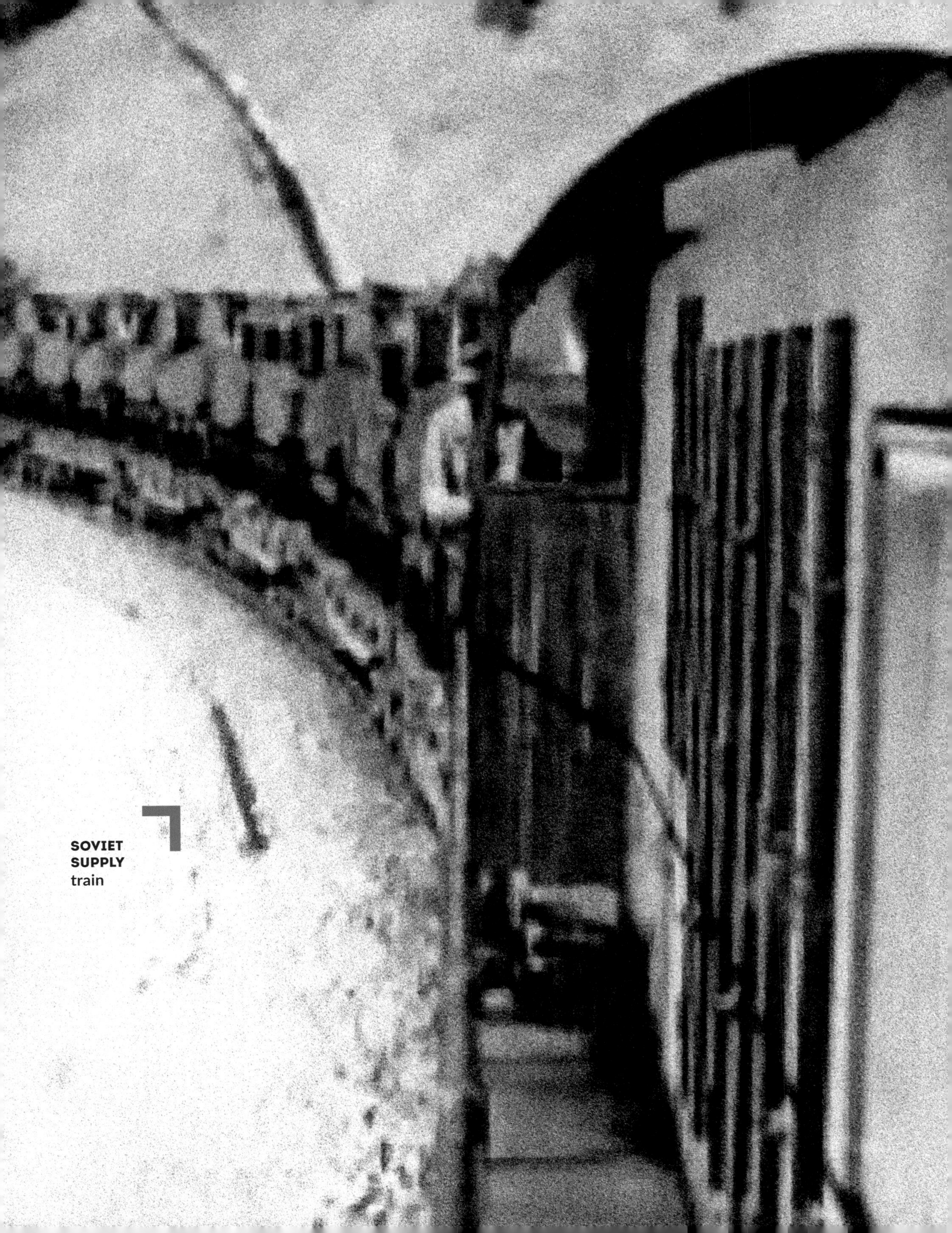
SOVIET
SUPPLY
train

There were about a thousand of us in all. Standing watching as we were unloaded were three British Army officers, a Colonel, a Major and a Captain. The Colonel had a swagger stick under his arm. He looked very official as he watched us, but as I passed him I saw that he had tears rolling unashamedly down his face.

We stepped onto the jetty and down onto the hot, fine sand. We had left Russia and all its horrors behind. We were free. Yet even the moment's intense rush of joy and elation was tempered by remembrance of our loved ones who had died in that terrible country".[63]

MOST OF THE SOLDIERS AND REFUGEES knew very little about their prospective evacuation until the very last minute. They were pre-occupied with the daily struggle to survive, and, after a series of earth tremors in Uzbekistan, they were worried by the possibility of a major quake. In the end, the joyful day often arrived as a surprise.

"Staff Sergeant Paluch tried to reassure us, telling us that he was doing all he could... [But] one evening he came to see us, almost running in his anxiety to get to us.

My mother and I looked at his face, unable to read his expression, and together we said, 'What is it? What has happened?'

'The boys are going to the station on Saturday morning', he blurted out. 'They are going to catch a ship... and you will follow them the next morning.'...

We bombarded him with questions.

'I can tell you that you are going to Persia', he told us, 'to Pahlevi, travelling with the officers' families in my name.'

We thanked him with all our hearts, saying goodbye to him, and hugging him. After that we went to see the boys, but they were unaware of what was going to happen.

'We're not going anywhere', Marian exclaimed. I told him to be quiet. 'You will be told soon', I promised him".[64]

And for tens of thousands of anxious people, the days of deliverance did arrive. They were packed into steamships like sardines into a can. Few remembered much of the voyage except the crush, the stench, and the discomfort:

"We went from Krasnovodsk (now Turkenbashi), a port on the Caspian Sea... There were only four toilets on board, so with people and children suffering from dysentery and other disorders, it was simply impossible for everybody to avail themselves of the toilet facilities. We docked at Pahlavi, Port Pahlavi, in Persia (now Iran)...".[65]

Hardly anyone knew where they might be going after they landed.

Nonetheless, some of those who benefited from it realised that they had witnessed not only a remarkable operation, but one that had stirred up a major political dispute:

"There followed the so-called First Evacuation. It was a Soviet *tour de force*. Within a week 34 trains were laid on by the NKVD, and between 24th March and 5th April half the Polish Army on Soviet soil was transported to Krasnovodsk, then to Pahlavi, an Iranian port on the Caspian Sea, in 17 or 18 shiploads. The extraordinary aspect of this exodus was that Anders managed to include in it some 11,000 civilians. Stalin certainly knew about this, but chose to ignore it. Not so the Polish government in London. Orders were issued that no civilians were to be evacuated. Apparently the London Poles did not wish to upset the British government, which had expressed doubts about its capacity to cope with a sudden influx of humanity in great distress. Anders ignored the orders of his political masters, and more than 11,000 older men, women and children were saved. To those thus rescued, Anders became a latter-day Moses. The rest of the world came to call this event 'the Polish Dunkirk'. The British – presented with a *fait accompli* – coped with their side of the task in their usual way: humanely and without fuss."[66]

The scenes on the beach at Pahlevi presented an extraordinary mixture of joy and distress. Some of the new arrivals were already celebrating with a picnic, or happily paddling in the sand. Others were wandering around aimlessly, while still more were visibly sick or too weak to stand. Everyone was looking for friends or loved ones. Helena Czuprin remembers having an urgent commercial transaction to conduct. She had no money, but had saved one valuable item from her family's belongings.

"I was carrying my dead father's enormous fur coat, and I was so hot. All of us longed for a drink...

There was a Persian standing close by with lemonade and ice cream. We had been instructed on the ship not to buy ice cream because of the health risk, and so I bought two bottles of lemonade and returned to where my mother was sitting...

'We have father's fur coat...' I said to her after a while. 'Shall we sell it?'

'We have too', she said. 'If we don't the authorities will burn it', she told me, nodding towards the bonfire of filthy and lice ridden refugee clothing that had been lit on the beach.

THE OLD road between Pahlevi and Tehran (2015).

I put the coat on and walked five hundred yards in it, sweltering in the heat. A Persian bought it and gave me thirty tooman which was a lot of money. We were thrilled. We thought we could buy half the country with that.

I bought a suitcase from another refugee, and we turned our bundles into it. We had sold almost everything we possessed now, but it was amazing how you held on to tiny little things that were reminders of another life.

The British soldiers had built showers for us in a building that they had erected on the beach. We lined up to go through them. Our clothes were taken away from us, and we were inspected by doctors who also examined our hair. If there were lice present, the hair was shaved off. The water in the shower had some disinfectant in it. It smelt like Lysol.

Everything we had brought with us was burnt. The doctors were terrified of typhus breaking out amongst us, knowing that in our weakened state it would spread rapidly.

We were issued with clothes from a huge pile on the sand that had been donated from America. There were some lovely clothes amongst them. We had underclothes, dresses and shoes, whatever you wanted you were given. I remember that my dress had a raspberry background with little yellow and blue flowers on it. I had a scarf, and a thin, silky cardigan...

Afterwards we sat down on the beach in the sun. It felt wonderful – the warmth seemed to penetrate right into your bones. My hair was still wet from the shower, and I spread it with my fingers. It was dry almost immediately.

We slept the night on the beach. The next morning lorries arrived. Another boat was due in and the beaches had to be cleared. We were to go on to the next stage. I did not meet anyone I knew, except for one woman who had been working in the hospital in Russia.

The lorries set off in convoy, some open, others covered, and we learned that we were bound for Tehran".[67]

Evacuation prompted the repeat of an old problem that had caused great friction during Army recruitment. It is not easy to learn where the exact truth lies, but the version of events as presented by a Polish divisional commander shows no doubts as to where he thought the blame lay:

"Another difficulty that we encountered which enraged us, was the Jewish problem. The Soviet authorities forbade us most rigorously to include any Jewish families in our transports. If we attempted to bypass this order, the convoy would be stopped. After much bargaining, they agreed that the wives and children of Jewish soldiers on active service in our Division might be admitted in transports with their husbands or fathers. This was subject to a severe inspection of nominal rolls at the entrainment. Parents, or more remote relatives, were denied this opportunity, to which the families of non-Jewish soldiers were entitled. It was a new tragedy.

There were quite a few families of Polish Jews who had no relatives in the Division; they lived in Samarkand, or Bukhara, or other places in the vicinity. Many of them, having heard that the Division was evacuating civilians, came to Shachrizyabs and begged us to take them with us, adjuring us in the name of humanity to save them. When we refused to admit them to our transports, citing the orders received and the threat that were we to take them our transports might be stopped, they went to the N.K.V.D. There they met with a civil reception, and were told that the Soviet authorities had nothing against their evacuation, but that it was the Polish military authorities who refused them passage as they hated the Jews so intensely. The Jews came

CHILDREN UNDER the Army's care.

back, cursing us and ascribing their tragedy to us. Our denials had no effect: they believed the Soviets. This was one of the most cunning and treacherous of the Soviet tricks, intended to smear the Poles throughout the world with the indictment that Polish soldiers were 'Fascist anti-Semites'."[68]

THE SPRING OF 1942 was not a happy season for Allied armies. The German 9th Army was heading for the middle Volga at Stalingrad, from which it could then advance rapidly to the Caspian Sea. The 11th Army had recently conquered Crimea, and was clearing the Black Sea coast in a movement that would take it to Georgia. And the spearheads of the 17th Army had been ordered to drive hell-for-leather for Baku. The Americans were struggling to get a foothold in the eastern Pacific against the Japanese, and had still not sent a single soldier to Europe. The Battle of the Atlantic against German U-Boats was raging at its height in face of an uncertain outcome. The British, having lost Singapore, were fearful for the safety of India, and were stretched to the limit to keep the sea-lanes open in the Mediterranean between Gibraltar and Suez. They had no hope of creating a Second Front without American support, and decided for the time being that the only way to mount telling attacks against Germany was to switch all resources to the strategic bombing offensive. Three years into the war, no one could dream of final victory.

Poland in 1942 was completely crushed by a Nazi-German occupation which was employing genocidal campaigns of unparalleled ferocity. Thanks to information brought out by couriers like Jan Karski and Jan Nowak-Jeziorański, the Polish government was able to tell the world not only of the Jewish Holocaust, but also of Nazi plans to transform the ethnic make-up across Eastern Europe. The Polish Resistance Movement, though growing in strength, was not yet capable of organising a major operation. And the Polish Forces Abroad, though re-forming and training in Britain, were still recovering from the catastrophe caused by the Fall of France.

Both the Axis powers and the Allies could see that the modern warfare of tanks, aeroplanes, and oil-fired battleships was ultimately dependent on the control of oil. Hitler's Command had made the conquest of the oilfields its prime objective. The British knew that their presence in Iran and Iraq would come under enormous pressure. And the Americans had decided that the supply of fuel via the Persian Corridor was the best way of keeping the Red Army in the field.

Once the First Evacuation was complete, therefore, General Anders travelled to London to discuss further developments with both the British and Polish governments. During his stay, he discovered serious differences of opinion. Generally speaking, the senior British figures whom he met, like General Sir Alan Brooke, the Chief of the Imperial General Staff and the Prime Minister, Winston Churchill, agreed with him that his army had no fruitful prospects in the Soviet Union, and should be transferred to the Middle East in its entirety. Senior Polish figures, in contrast, held to the opposite. They were concerned that total withdrawal would damage Polish-Soviet relations to the detriment of the hundreds of thousands of Polish citizens still stranded there. General Sikorski advised Anders to stay in London to strengthen the activities of the General Staff. Anders insisted on returning to the USSR, to finish the task.

General Anders, back in his tent at Yangi-Yul brooding and awaiting Stalin's decision, did not need to be told that he was sitting in a strategic hot-spot. He was not, as many of his men may have thought, in the 'middle of nowhere', in a place of no consequence. He knew that he would not be left alone for long.

During the stand-off, the initiative was taken by the British. Churchill penned a personal letter to Stalin, suggesting that it would be in the best interests of all if the bulk of the Anders Army were moved to the Middle East. Spring 1942 was a moment when Axis forces were engaged in major offensives both on the 'road to Baku' and in North Africa. But Stalin refused; he still had hopes that a major cohort of Poles could be sent to reinforce the Eastern Front. Churchill, however, persisted. If the Poles now in Central Asia could not be used to strengthen the defences of the oilfields in Iran and Iraq, he argued, British divisions would to be diverted, thereby weakening preparations to open a Second Front in Western Europe. This was high-risk political blackmail. Churchill was well aware of Stalin's annoyance at the absence of a Second Front, but calculated rightly that the Soviet dictator had little room for manoeuvre so long as the *Wehrmacht* was still making progress. After much delay, therefore, Stalin was forced to concede; and on 7 July 1942, Anders was officially informed that all his remaining forces, and their dependants, could now be withdrawn to Iran.

An observer, whose fate depended on the outcome of these political manoeuvres, describes in greater detail how events developed:

> "On 8th June a telegram from the Polish Prime Minister in exile in London arrived at Jangi-Jul' ordering the Polish Army to remain in the Soviet Union. This was a political decision, taken 4,000 miles away by men unaware of local realities and unable to read the Soviet mind. Anders knew better, and decided to ignore the order. He suspected that the British authorities had already arrived at the same conclusion. So, on his own initiative, he requested

an interview with Sir Archibald Clark-Kerr, British ambassador to the Soviet Union, to take the matter further. This act of insubordination took place on 7 July – and had an instant and dramatic effect. That same night, the night of 7–8 July 1942, Stalin gave his agreement to the transfer of Anders's entire army to Iran. Orders for the Second Evacuation were issued to the Polish units on the 15th.

Stalin's motives for these decisions are unlikely ever to be fathomed. The instant response to the Anders – Clark-Kerr conversation suggests that in this case British and Soviet objectives were identical and urgent. The Polish historian Zbigniew Siemaszko recently suggested that Stalin's intelligence service anticipated the discovery by the Germans of the Katyń graves. Stalin would have been seriously concerned about the effect of this news on the Polish Army within the Soviet Union. So he chose the 'lesser evil' – the removal of Anders' 80,000 or so men from Soviet territory."[69]

In that same period, the USA's entry into the war began to make itself felt. In February 1942, Count Raczyński visited Washington, and was pleased to report the warm words with which

WOMEN AND children waiting by the wayside.

THE STORY OF A BAG

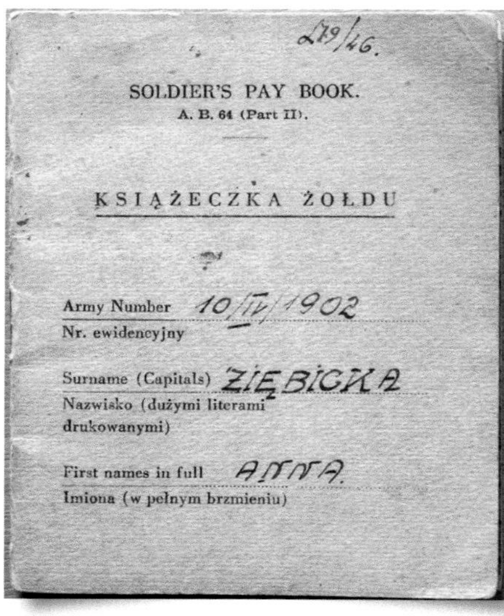

279/46.

SOLDIER'S PAY BOOK.
A. B. 64 (Part II).

KSIĄŻECZKA ŻOŁDU

Army Number 10/IV/1902
Nr. ewidencyjny

Surname (Capitals) ZIĘBICKA
Nazwisko (dużymi literami drukowanymi)

First names in full ANNA.
Imiona (w pełnym brzmieniu)

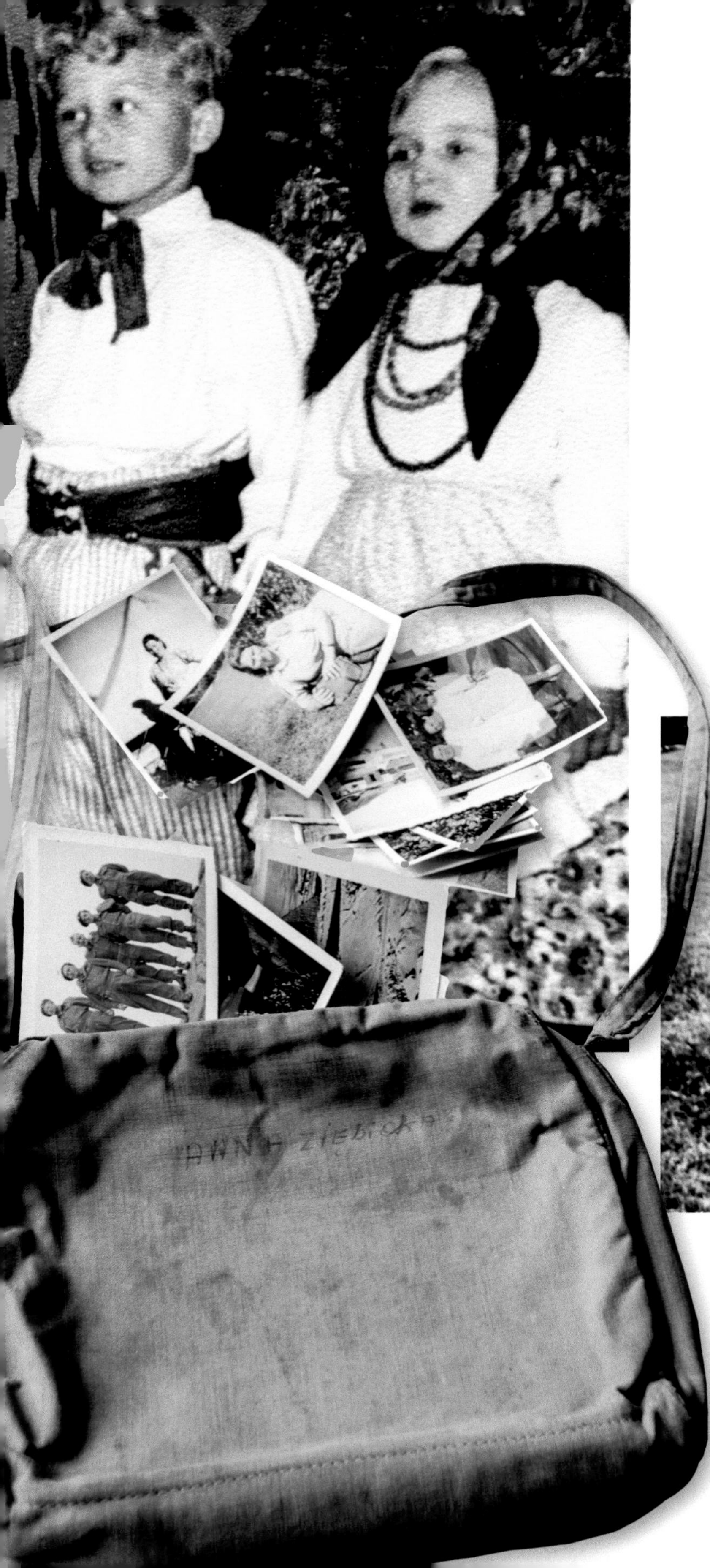

THE STORY of the Bag. Discovered by chance in 1981, in the English town of Exeter, an old unassuming shoulder bag looked like any other piece of nondescript lost property. Yet it contained a lifetime's collection of photos and souvenirs that had once belonged to the late Anna Ziębicka, a Polish woman, from a military settlement in Volhynia, who had been deported with her husband to the USSR, had served in the PSK under General Anders, had been evacuated to Iran, and had eventually reached England. It even contained a photo of Anna Ziębicka holding her precious bag, .'Lost Memories Found in a Small Bag", <www.polishresettlementcampsintheuk.co.uk/stories/ziebicka.htm>.

President Roosevelt praised the Polish war effort. He was given encouragement to think that the USA, though not a formal ally, was certainly a reliable friend. He might have thought differently had he known what Roosevelt was saying in private. Roosevelt, even more than Churchill, was extremely dismissive of what he called the small states'. Despite having launched the 'Declaration by the United Nations' at the beginning of the year, and giving its 26 signatories the impression that they were joining a club of equals, he really did not intend to let policy-making slip from the hands of the chosen few. On hearing of the dispute over the Polish–Soviet frontier, he casually admitted what he would never have said in public: "It is up to the great powers to decide what Poland should be", and "I have no intention of going to a peace conference and bargaining with Poland or the other small states... Poland is to be set up in a way that will maintain the peace of the world." As Piotr Wandycz concludes in his magisterial study, *The United States and Poland* (1980): "The President was committed to a vague and ill-defined policy that led with inexorable logic to Tehran and Yalta, and contained within in it the seeds of the Cold War." For good or ill, Anders and his men knew nothing of this.

In the interval between the First and Second Evacuation, thousands of Poles were still trekking across Russia in the hope of reaching the Army in time. Thousands more were milling around in Uzbekistan hoping against hope that the Army would take pity on them. Danuta Skiba, whose father had already perished, belonged to a dwindling family, which was one of these thousands:

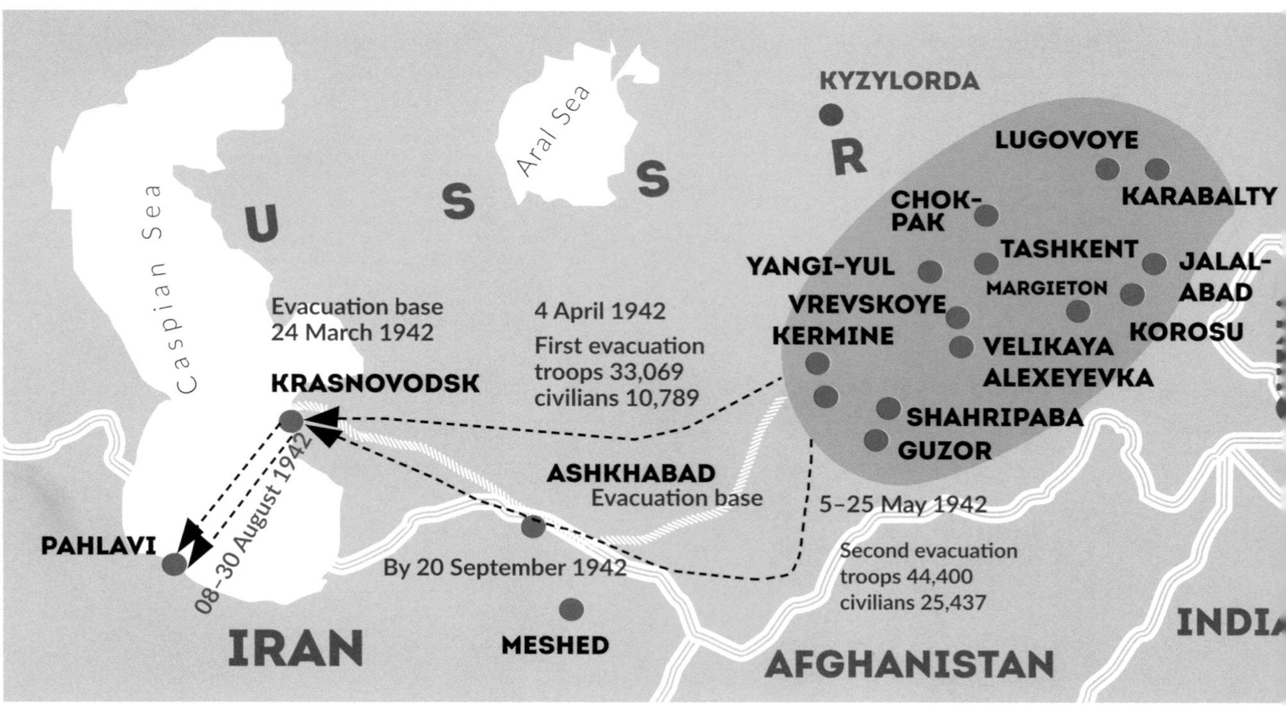

EVACUATION TO IRAN

"The journey was dreadful: people were squashed into wagons, the train was speeding and very uncomfortable. When it stopped for a while, the people could only get some hot water and occasionally a small piece of bread... My Mother had a little money, but I would not let her leave the train, being terrified that she would not be able to get back on... My Grandfather got off at one of the stations, and did not [return] before the train left. We never learnt what happened to him.

ON THAT JOURNEY, my little brother Adaś developed a bad cold and was very poorly... When we arrived at the destination, which was in Uzbekistan, they left us under the open sky; the train [stopped] and we had nowhere to go. My little brother was much worse, but a kindly Uzbek woman [said] that there was a hospital a few miles away, and... she carried him all the way there, leaving him in the care of nurses... When we [reached] the hospital, little Adaś was dead.

We were then taken, with another elderly man, by an Uzbek with a horse and cart, to his village, and put into an Uzbek hut. There was straw on the floor for sleeping, and a depression in the middle for a fire.

My Mother had to get up early in the morning to go to work at a building site. I was left sleeping on the floor... When I woke up, always feeling hungry, I dressed myself and walked to the building site, sitting on the steps, crying... and waiting for my Mother. Many times I was chased by hungry dogs... When the whistle blew, the workers went to the canteen for a bowl of watery soup, [where] I was allowed to share the soup with my Mother...

Some days, I and [another girl] would go into the Uzbek teahouses, where they used to sit on the floor, crossed legged, drinking and eating dried sultanas. Some of them were very kind, and would give us a few sultanas, and others... chased us out. Many a time, all my Mother and I had before going to bed, was water."[70]

Danuta and her mother were lucky. At the very last moment, a Polish soldier saw them squatting forlornly under a tree, and came over to talk to them. Since he had no dependants of his own, he agreed to register them as his relatives. And thus they were able to leave.

In June 1942, in the last month before news of the Second Evacuation, the 'Polish Army in the USSR' received an important guest. Field Bishop Józef Gawlina (1892–1964), a Silesian, was the highest ranking priest in the Polish Armed Forces, and commander of all military chaplains. Appointed in 1933, he had followed the government into exile in France and England in 1939 but not before making a solemn declaration of Holy War against Germany. "God is our witness", he said defiantly, "that we Poles wanted peace. Our hands are clean. The war did not break out through our misdoing... Our war is a Holy War!"[71]

THREE COLONELS: from left, Stanisław Lechner (Polish Army), Kirieyev (Red Army), Alexander Ross (British Army), 6 October 1942.

TURKMENBASHI, FORMERLY Krasnovodsk (2011).

Arriving in Yangi-Yul Bishop Gawlina was paying a pastoral visit to soldiers and civilians who had been deprived of regular contact with their Church. In three weeks, he visited scores of camps and settlements in Central Asia, confirmed 11,000 soldiers, and gave First Communion to 5,000 children. He presided at field masses, parades, and festivities. On 27 June, he attended aName Day party for General Anders. The next day, he formally admitted the General into the Catholic faith, and celebrated his First Communion. Just over one week later, he was present when the announcement was made that all army units that had remained in the USSR would soon be leaving for Iran.

THE 'SECOND EVACUATION', which began in mid-July 1942 and continued for a couple of months, involved a similar number of military personnel as the preceding wave but a much reduced number of civilians. The figures for estimated totals, as calculated by Siemaszko, are shown in the table opposite.

This time the main route lay along the direct railway line from Tashkent to the border city of Mashhad in the north-east corner of Iran. The distance between the two cities was only 600 miles, and could be covered in one or two days. Only a minority of evacuees were directed to Krasnovodsk and thence by sea to Pahlavi.

The departure of General Anders himself was delayed by yet another round of the Jewish question. On 3 August a delegation of rabbis appeared demanding that the number of Jewish evacuees be increased. Anders offered to talk again to the Soviet authorities, whilst pointing out that great damage has been done by unguarded Jewish criticism abroad. On the 19th, at a meeting between the NKVD's chief liaison officer, Zhukov and General Bohusz-Szyszko, the rabbis' representative heard himself that it was the Soviet side which was obstructing the exit of national minorities. As a special favour, Zhukov told him that he would permit the departure of Jews who had been living prior to November 1939 to the west of the Molotov-Ribbentrop Line. In the view of the late Harvey Sarner, who was well versed in these matters, the root cause of the problem was political, not discriminating:

> "In the political sphere, therefore, it [the Polish–Jewish dispute] was not really an issue connected to antisemitism but rather to the

EVACUATIONS:	I	II	TOTAL
Officers and men	40,500	30,000	70,500
Women's Auxiliary Service	2,000	1,000	3,000
Male + female cadets	2,500	2,000	4,500
Total military	45,000	33,000	78,000
Families	16,000	8,000	24,000
Children under 14	9,500	3,000	12,500
Total civilians	25,500	11,000	36,500
Overall	70,500	44,000	114,500[72]

"FULL STEAM ahead".

territorial dispute between the USSR and Poland. For persons who had been refused permission to leave, of course, this made little difference. All they knew was that they had been pulled off a train by an officer in Polish uniform."[73]

When General Anders finally left in early September, he went by sea, and he took the Army's military band with him. One of the band's members, a trumpeter called Feliks Bilos, who had bought his instrument in Buzuluk for 50 roubles and a bar of soap, left a description of the event:

"It [had been] a cruel time in Yangi-Yul, what with sickness, exhaustion and starvation. We had our hands full playing funeral marches and paying our last respects to dozens of friends. Finally, after months of painful waiting we were ready to leave for Krasnovodsk. General Anders had received special permission from [NKVD] General Zhukov... to take with him the band and a set of musical instruments.

As we were about to board the ship, we learned that we were not allowed to take Soviet money abroad. At the same time, our conductor found out that Russian rubles were good money in Persia. So many of us decided to hide our rubles, and stuffed our instruments full of banknotes... Then, with the ship ready to sail, we were ordered to play the Soviet and Polish national anthems. The [bandsmen] turned pale with fright, but did not lose their cool. The clarinets, saxophones and other thin instruments led the way, supported by drums and percussion, while we, with trumpets and trombones silent... tried to imitate them with our voices... We certainly fooled them... After landfall, we [played] with full force, marching at the head of a long column of soldiers."[74]

ON THAT SAME OCCASION, as related by Irena Ehrlich, a company of women auxiliaries (PSK) was about to board the boat, when an NKVD officer shouted out *Zhenshchiny niet* (no women) for no reason at all. Intense negotiations followed. But an open clash was avoided by a large contingent of soldiers standing in parallel lines and forming a corridor through which women and children could pass.

After Anders' departure, the exit road to Iran remained open for a further 7 months. Though the Soviet authorities were no longer organising large-scale convoys, they did not prevent smaller groups from crossing the frontier. Among the last-minute travellers were stragglers who had trekked from distant parts of the Soviet Union: officials and camp staff, who had stayed behind at a diminishing number of reception centres and assembly points; engineers employed in dismantling premises or packing up equipment; and doctors, nurses, and patients fit to travel from field hospitals.

Colonel Klemens Rudnicki, Commander of the 6th Division, was the last man to join the last organised group of evacuees on the last ship from Krasnovodsk. He had been suffering both from malaria and dysentery, and was lucky to have been declared fit to travel. And one last surprise awaited him:

"At last, we embarked. Some of the soldiers were able to walk up the gangway; others had to be carried. Soon the boat was really overloaded, like the barges on the Petsera or the Amur-Darya. I was the last to be embarked. Col. Berling, C.O. of the Polish Evacuation Centre, accompanied by NKVD officers, bade me farewell.

'When and how will you link up with us?' I asked Berling.

'By train *via* Ashkhabad. Now I have to go to Yanghi Yul to return to the Commission winding up the Polish Army in the USSR, to give them all the documents relating to this recent evacuation', he said. And so we parted.

OVERLOADED STEAM SHIP *Zdanov* docks at Pahlevi.

NORMAN DAVIES at the same port, now Bandar-e Azali (2014).

The boat left the landing-stage slowly and streamed out of the port. Only then did we realise how much of our equipment was left behind: thousands of bales of English uniforms, blankets and underwear, tinned food, and all the Service and Ordnance Corps supplies which had come from Great Britain to Archangel for the 100,000 men of the Polish Army in the USSR. All the stores had come, with our convoys, to Krasnovodsk; there we were told it was impossible for us to take them with us; and everything was confiscated by the Red Army.

Our soldiers, watching the horizon and the disappearing nightmare of the Soviet coast, which had stolen from every one of them three years of life in the most inhuman conditions, said: 'May they choke themselves with our goods!'

If anyone asked me what were my strongest impressions of this country, I would probably say the treacherous deceit which has grown into a system, deprived men of dignity, and ill-treated and degraded them. Everybody and everything had lied, from the very moment I passed the threshold of this *régime*... till the moment when Berling told me his own lie when taking leave of me, knowing quite well that he would be taking over the stores left behind in the port of Krasnovodsk, and would try to build up a new Soviet-Polish Army...

Delightedly we watched the disappearing shores of this country of lies and deceit, knowing that we were now sailing towards the free world, to which we wholeheartedly belonged."[75]

Whether or not Iran was a member of the 'Free World' is open to question.

The struggle to reach the evacuation points often demanded titanic efforts. In the case of two brothers, Paweł and Adam Chlipalski, it was touch-and-go to the very last moment whether or not they would make it:

"We arrived in Tashkent, Uzbekistan. We were planning with our mother to escape to China/Mongolia. My brother Adam as he was older joined the Polish army in Narpay Uzbekistan and I was staying with my mother in Kermine. The terrible onslaught of contagious diseases killed many Polish soldiers. The Majority of us were deprived of clean water and ample nourishment... Adam and I

soon contracted a number of these sicknesses of which typhus and dysentery were more prevalent and very destructive. I got very ill... with bloody Dysentry. I was on the toilet 80-100 times a day to the point I was not passing food, only blood.

We met again as patients in the hospital that was preparing for evacuation to Iran... We were taken to Krasnovodsk, Turkmenistan on the Caspian Sea and were dumped on the sand dunes on the outskirts of town without water or food in the scorching heat of the sun. At that point I started to show signs of total exhaustion and dehydration. I was emaciated and barely coherent. In the afternoon came the order to march to the port area several kilometers away from where we were but... neither Adam or I had the strength to [do it]. If it was not for some compassionate person carrying us inside the car we would never have reached our destination. The sight from train's window which was considerably higher than the sea shore revealed the path of marching soldiers [strewn with] dead or exhausted. When finally we boarded the ship (called Kaganovic) I had to be dragged along to the top deck and Adam laid me down under the ventilator, completely limp, apparently lifeless. In due course the sanitary commission came and examined me and... they demanded that I be carried to the ship's mortuary. Adam protested and refused to allow them to take me..."[76] So the brothers sailed away and thousands didn't.

IN THE MEANTIME, a critical situation had been mounting at the other end of the exit route. The Hospital at Pahlevi was one of the saddest stops on the whole 'Trail of Hope'. It had been set up to care for the hordes of sick and starving that were pouring out of the USSR, and to set them on the road to recovery. Instead, through an epidemic of typhus, it became the haunt of perpetual death. Helena Czupryn worked there as a military nurse; 'working as a sister in the tents that were being used as temporary wards':

"And all the time the ships of the refugees kept coming. Thousands, tens of thousands, hundreds of thousands, emaciated, broken, desperately sick, but still living people, victims of mass deportations and labour camps whom Russia had chewed up and now spat out, Polish citizens whom she claimed had been invited as 'guest workers' of the Soviet Union. I knew the truth: that for every one survivor at least ten had died.

I was put on a rota, two weeks on the Children's Ward, two weeks on Men's, two weeks on Officers'. There were fifty-two

ON BOARD ship: relieved looks between Krasnovodsk and Pahlevi (right).

WAITING TO leave the boat at Pahlevi (opposite).

patients in each tent ward, often two to a bed because we were still chronically short of space to accommodate such overwhelming numbers.

Despite all our efforts, most of our patients were just too weak to live. Many of them seemed to have hung on just long enough to reach freedom, and I found myself remembering the men from the salt mines and their desperate efforts to get home to their families, and often I wept for all these poor people.

The matron was a kindly as well as a wise woman. Knowing that so many of the men especially had been beaten and treated like animals, she tried to ensure that they retained their dignity. I will always remember her saying one day with passionate intensity, 'We have all been through the same ordeal. We in this camp have seen the worst of human nature, and at times have been privileged to glimpse the best... Because of that it is vitally important that we treat each other with respect.'

You nursed almost automatically, as professionally as you could, so concerned with the terrible fight against death that was in so many cases inevitable, that your feelings were submerged. That was the only way you could survive with your mind intact. But there was always one case that twisted your heart strings...

The boy in the last bed on the Children's Ward was one such patient. I never knew his name but day after day I saw him fighting desperately hard to stay alive.

Each day when I came on duty I expected him to have gone, just another corpse in a body bag, but each day he hung on, little more than skin and bone, but with eyes that burned with the intensity of his struggle.

Then one day he made signs to me that he would like a biscuit. I took one and crumbled it into tiny pieces for him. I know that if he had asked me then I would have baked a mountain of biscuits for him. I put the crumbs gently onto his tongue.

The sun was in his eyes and I got up for a moment to lower the blind. When I looked back he was dead.

Typhus broke out. We worked frantically but our chronically malnourished patients had no defence against it, and it ran through the wards like fire in a tinder dry forest. We were asleep on our feet, but all hands were needed. I snatched an hour's sleep when I could and went back onto the wards. I was on the Men's Ward, and I found myself trying to care for desperately sick men who were so worried about their missing families that it was impossible to reassure them...

Still the constant stream of refugees continued with no sign of abating. Each refugee who came off the ship had to be bathed, and showered. His hair had to be cut, and all bodily hair shaved off before he went on the wards.

Two English officers came to help me.

'You do the ladies, we'll do the men', they told me. They worked side by side with me, and I had immense respect for them. They

kept an eye on me. When they saw that my back was soaking wet with perspiration, they would insist that I should go and change. They were so kind. They and the good Polish soldiers who so patiently carried the sick to the hospital, kept me sane.

It was miraculous, but I didn't become sick. People who came to work in the hospital usually only lasted a week before catching typhus. One of the doctors I worked with gave me a daily injection to help build me up, and perhaps that was what kept me healthy, but then I thought back to Russia and remembered that even in the labour camp I had not had so much as a headache!

Then abruptly the flood of refugees stopped. Russia had quite simply refused to let out any more Polish people, civilians or army."[77]

HOLY MASS celebrated on the Pahlevi beach. Easter, 5 April 1942.

The escape route had been closed. Due to the dispute over the Katyń Affair, Stalin severed relations with the Polish government on 25 April 1943. The Amnesty of 1941 was revoked, and the possession of Polish citizenship offered no-one protection against hostile Soviet officials. The gates of the frontier posts slammed shut, and the Anders Army was cut off completely from the compatriots which it left behind.

IT IS IMPORTANT TO RECOGNISE that the Poles who remained in the USSR far exceeded those who had managed to leave. A few of them, like Col. Zygmunt Berling, chose to stay, having thrown in their lot with the Soviet regime, or with Soviet-run Polish Communist organisations. Berling, who had been working with the NKVD from the time of Katyń, was branded a traitor by Anders, who had once welcomed him into his service.

He stood on the waterfront at Krasnovodsk, watching the last steamer sail off to Pahlavi. He would soon be put in command of a new Polish formation, the so-called Kościuszko Division, which was raised in Russia under Communist auspices.

A larger group of individuals had been slowly making their way across the vastness of Eurasia in the hope of joining Anders. Before reaching their goal, they heard that diplomatic relations had been severed, and that the frontier was closed.

Among them was 20-year-old Wojciech Jaruzelski, who had been deported to arctic Siberia with his parents in 1940. He claimed to have berated Anders for the rest of his life "for not waiting". At all events, barred from leaving the USSR, Jaruzelski reported to Soviet recruiting, was trained as an infantry officer of the Kościuszko Division, and returned to Poland in 1945 as a promising figure of the Communist establishment.

By far the largest number of stranded Poles, however, was made up of people who had been unable to benefit from the Amnesty, and who were eking out a living on collective farms or in remote districts. The Polish Consular Service, before being expelled from Moscow, took steps to help these scattered citizens. It appointed a new set of *Mężowie Zaufania*, 'Persons of Trust', who fanned out across the USSR to seek information and to render assistance. Not surprisingly, these brave men became an easy target for the NKVD. For the most part, they were rounded up, cast into the Gulag, and disappeared.

The poet, Aleksander Wat (1900–1967), was one of the employees of the Polish Consular Service who was stranded in Central Asia. A pre-war Communist who described himself as 'a Jew-Jew and Pole-Pole', he had spent lengthy spells in prison both in pre-war Poland (as a Communist) and in the Soviet Union (as a Pole). He had made his way to Alma-Ata, the capital of Kazakhstan in search of his deported family, and, after finding them, was taken on by the Delegate's Office.

Afflicted by a heart condition that had been diagnosed as incurable, he could not think of joining the Polish Army, like his colleague Broniewski. Instead he stayed on, and awaited an uncertain fate.

In 1943, Wat was undergoing an intense spiritual transformation that would lead him far from his earlier convictions. According to his biographer, he was greatly influenced by *De Imitatione Christi* of Thomas à-Kempis – a book which had been shipped to the USSR by the Polish Government-in-Exile, "together with old shoes and cans of corned beef", and which was almost the only book in his possession in Kazakhstan. The influence of the mediaeval ascetic is clearly visible in his poems of that period:

For long I protected myself from Thee
For long I did not desire to know Thee
For long I escaped Thee
into blind alleys
into the absinthe of poetry
and into the fury of struggle
and into the uproar of a fair
where an entrepreneur
and a somnambulist lady
call forth by their magic
A lost paradise.[78]

Wat and his family did not wait long to learn of the Soviets' changed attitude towards them. For a time, after the arrest of his colleagues at the Delegate's Office, he was 'one of only two representatives of the Polish Government-in-Exile for the entire territory of Kazakhstan'. Then it was the Wats's turn. Aleksander was cast into the notorious Third Section of the jail in Alma-Ata for refusing to accept a Soviet passport. The experiences of his wife Ola "did not differ too much from those of people in Nazi death camps". But they were lucky. They were released after three months, probably through Aleksander's long talks with the NKVD Colonel, who had been sent from Moscow to examine the 'unanimous refusal' of Polish exiles to accept Soviet citizenship. They were permitted to return to the small town of Ili, not far from the Chinese frontier, where they had briefly lived before their arrest, and where they would now reside for the next three years:

"Ili was inhabited almost exclusively by observant Jews deported from eastern Poland, many of them Hasidim. Wat wore a cross, which would have been considered a punishable insult in most Jewish neighborhoods in independent Poland, where strict Talmudic rules still prevailed. But, an ecumenical spirit had developed in Ili, which had the flavor of antiquity before the division of faiths. Wat even became a leader of the community,

ALEKSANDER WAT, poet — one of the hundreds of thousands left behind in the USSR.

almost a patriarch. With good reason, he later defined the year 1943 as 'the most important, heroic year' without equal in his life."[79]

MANY OF THE POLES stranded in the USSR simply died, or disappeared without trace, like Grandfather Skiba, who was left on the platform when his train shot off without warning. What could have happened to him? Did he just lie down on the platform and close his eyes? Was he picked up by the NKVD, and sent to a death-ridden jail? Was he beaten up by robbers and left for dead? Or did he find a niche in that God-forsaken Russian backwater – whose name his grieving relatives had not even noticed – and calmly live out the rest of his natural life? God only knows.

A significant proportion of the exiles, however, returned to post-war Poland, where they rarely talked of their experiences. Theirs was the guilt of survivors who couldn't bear to think of those who had perished. It is often the lot of children and grandchildren to count the losses of their families and to set the record straight:

"I am the grand-daughter of Bronisław Kordoński. The whole Kordoński family was deported on 10 February 1940 from their property at Piłatowicze near Nowa Mysz in the district of Baranowicze (now Baranovichi in Belarus), [and sent] to the *spetsposiolek* or special settlement of Poludniavitsa (postal address Lubtiuk) in the Gorkovsky District [of the Oblast' of Omsk in south-western Siberia]. There, my mother's sisters, Franciszka and Zofia, died of hunger.

They all worked in the taiga. [But] at the end of 1941 they got permission to travel to the South and found themselves in Uzbekistan. They worked in the Askar kolkhoz, whence Bronisław Kordoński and his son Piotr were sent to the Anders Army, [more exactly] to the army camp at Guzar. There, both of them died. (Unfortunately, on the memorial tablets at the Military Cemetery [in Guzar] only the name Junak Piotr Kordoński can be found.) Tadeusz, Edward and Filip departed with an Anders Army orphanage to South Africa. My mother only learned of the death of her father and brother, and of the fate of the orphans, in 1949 after long searches through the International Red Cross in Cairo.

My mother, together with her mother, Paulina, worked in Bukhara, whence they returned in 1947 to Poland. Grandma died in 1956. Mama is 85 years old."[80]

IRAN

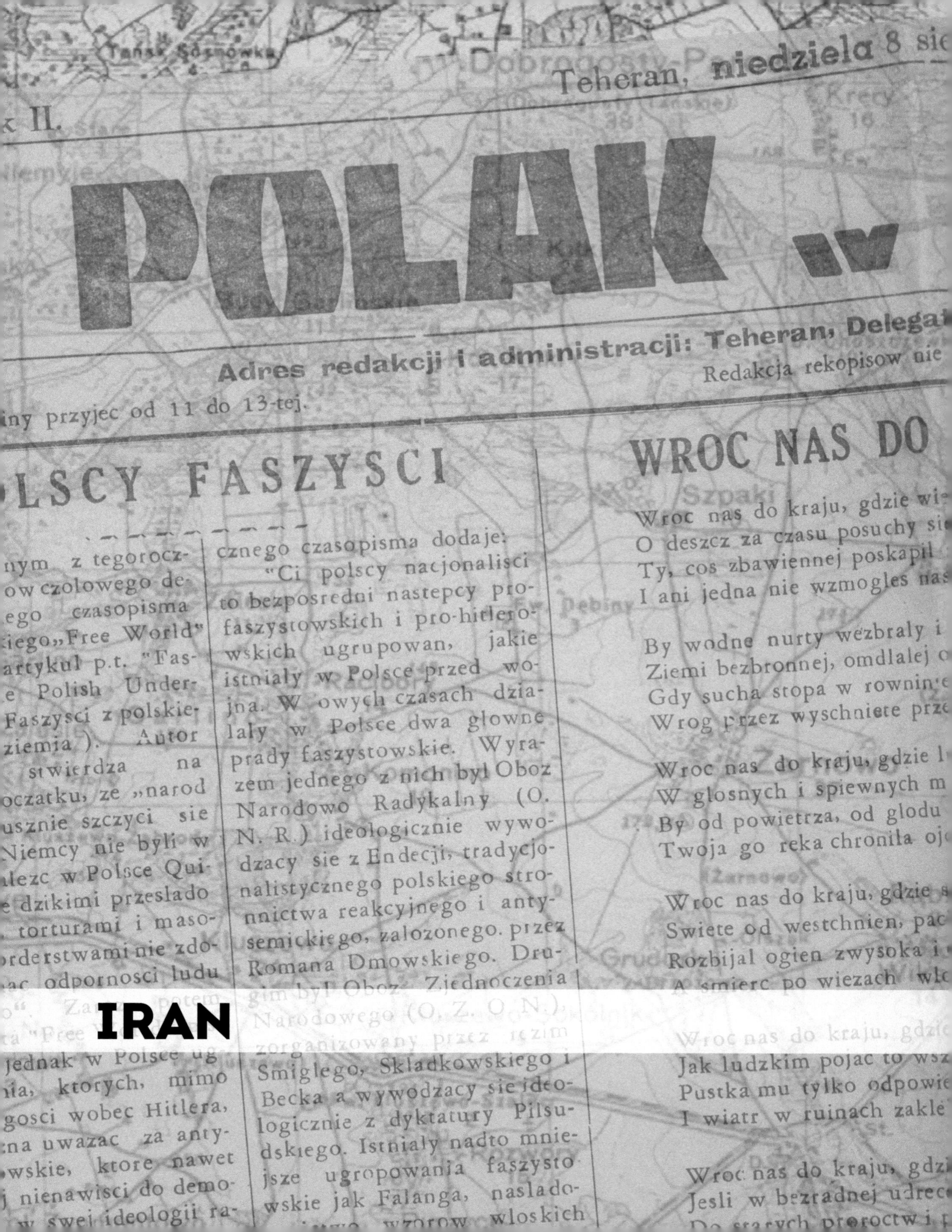
Teheran, niedziela 8 sie
POLAK
Adres redakcji i administracji: Teheran, Delegat
Redakcja rekopisow nie
POLSCY FASZYSCI
WROC NAS DO

CHAPTER 6

1942–1943

SOLDIERS OF Cyrus the Great (6th century BC) – mosaic from Susa (Iran) (left).

POLISH–IRANIAN FRIENDSHIP: commemorative plaque dedicated to the Persian bard Firdusi (AD 940–1020) by "Polish soldiers from distant Sarmatia, 1943".

CHAPTER 6

1942–1943

IRAN

IRAN, IN 1942–1943, WAS NOT A HAPPY LAND. OCCUPIED SINCE THE PREVIOUS YEAR BY BRITISH AND SOVIET FORCES, IT WAS NOT THE MASTER OF ITS FATE. THE YOUNG SHAH, MOHAMMAD REZA PAHLAVI, IF NOT A PUPPET, WAS A DEPENDANT FIGURE, AND HIS GOVERNMENT HAD TO BALANCE THE COMPETING INTERESTS OF THE COUNTRY AND ITS FOREIGN CONTROLLERS.

A **sophisticated elite** (rightly) suspected the British, through the Anglo-Iranian Petroleum Company, of aiming to keep the lion's share of the oil-wealth for themselves; and they (rightly) suspected the Soviets, in the best traditions of Russian imperialism, of aiming to swallow the north-western province of Azerbaijan. (Historic Azerbaijan had once belonged to the Persian Empire in its entirety. But in the Russo–Persian Wars of the 18th century, the smaller northern section centred on Baku had been taken by Russia, while the larger, southern section centred on Tabriz had remained in Persia.) Stalin, who had spent several pre-revolutionary years in Baku, was known to be an advocate of expanding Soviet Azerbaijan, and of merging it with Iranian Azerbaijan.

Despite their long and proud history, the Iranians were isolated in the region. Devotees of the Shia branch of Islam, they were historic rivals both of Turkey and of the neighbouring Sunni-ruled Arab states. Their only close friends were the fellow Shias of southern Iraq, where the holiest Shiite shrines of Karbala and Najaf were located. Above all, they were deeply hostile to Russia, which throughout modern times had launched unceasing schemes to penetrate and subordinate their country.

On entering Iran, therefore, the Polish Army found itself in a somewhat anomalous position. It had not arrived at the invitation of the Shah's government, but as a guest of the British occupiers, and came inevitably under suspicion of being there to strengthen the British garrison. At the same time, it was made up of people who were known to have suffered greatly in Russia, and in that capacity attracted considerable local sympathy. The Iranian government asked in vain for a formal treaty with the Poles to confirm their presence in the country. But personal relations between Poles and Iranians were friendly.

POLISH SOLDIERS on Pahlevi Beach: undressed and awaiting de-lousing (above); the same (opposite) fully dressed in new uniforms.

The Polish newcomers saw little of Iran's high politics, but it was not difficult to learn the outlines. One boy had his first political lesson on the day of his arrival:

"Early in the morning we were woken by a familiar song [that we had often heard in Russia]:

Hey, vy pola,
Zheleniye pola
Krasna kavaleria
Saditsya na konia...
(Oh you, steppes!
You green, green steppes.
The Red Cavalry
Are mounting their steeds...)

I wiped my eyes in wonder. The measured tread of soldiers' boots was mingled with their singing. I looked outside. A company of soldiers in fur caps and Russian uniforms was marching past. Where had they come from? After all, we'd only just crossed the frontier.

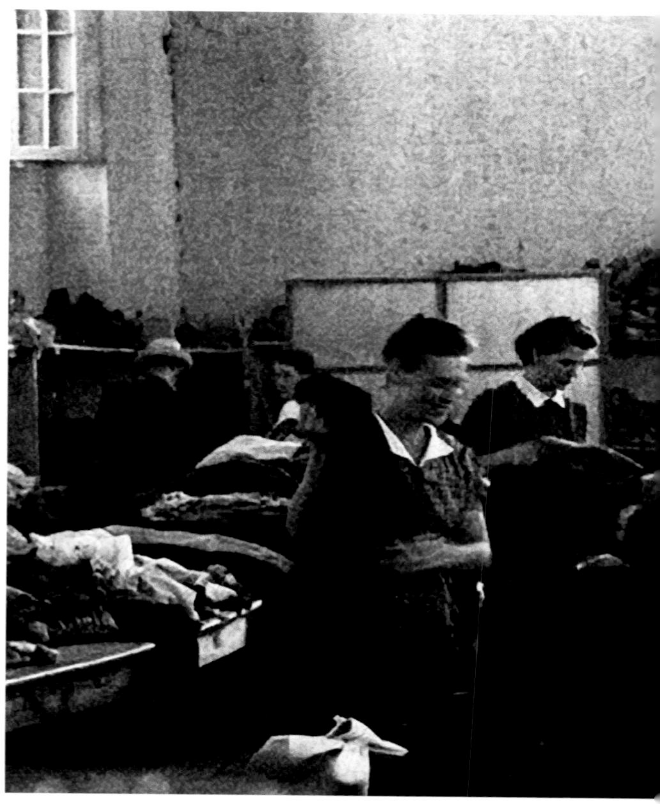

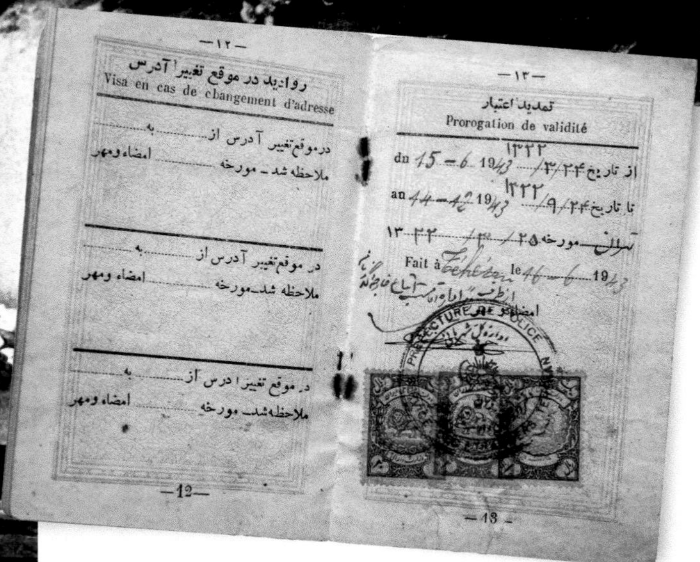

POLISH OFFICER'S Iranian identity card, validated for six additional months, 1942–1943, by the Prefecture of Police, Tehran (left).

WOMEN CHOOSING clothes sent by an American charity (Pahlevi).

The words of the song had not yet faded away, when another column appeared from the other direction. At its head, marched a noisy collection of local troops. Behind them, urged on by a tooting horn, a line of military trucks was pushing its way through the crowd. From one of these trucks, I heard a different song:

It's a long way to Tipperary,
It's a long way to go
(without your mother!)
It's a long way to Tipperary
To the sweetest girl I know...

The English soldiers were trying to outshout the hubbub of the street and the vehicles. A real Tower of Babel. Someone later explained to us that the Eastern Front had been growing closer from the north-west, and that Persia had been divided into Russian and English spheres, where units from each of the two powers were stationed."[81]

Those Poles who were informed about politics, saw a country which was undergoing the pains not only of foreign occupation, but also of social and cultural conflict. The Anglo–Soviet overlords, who had forced the old Shah into exile on Mauritius, imprisoned several hundred politicians whom they judged pro-German; but they left governmental structures intact. In the words of the British ambassador, Reader Bullard: "The Iranians expect, in compensation for the invasion of their country, that we rescue them from the tyranny of the Shah." The Allies only partially succeeded. Under the new dispositions the 20-year-old Moham Reza Shah was left in full control of the Iranian Army, and of his father's much-feared police force. The fortress and prison of Ghasr-e Kadziar, which

GENERALS SIKORSKI (in tropical helmet) and Anders — 3 km to central Tehran, 4,371 km to Warsaw. 1943.

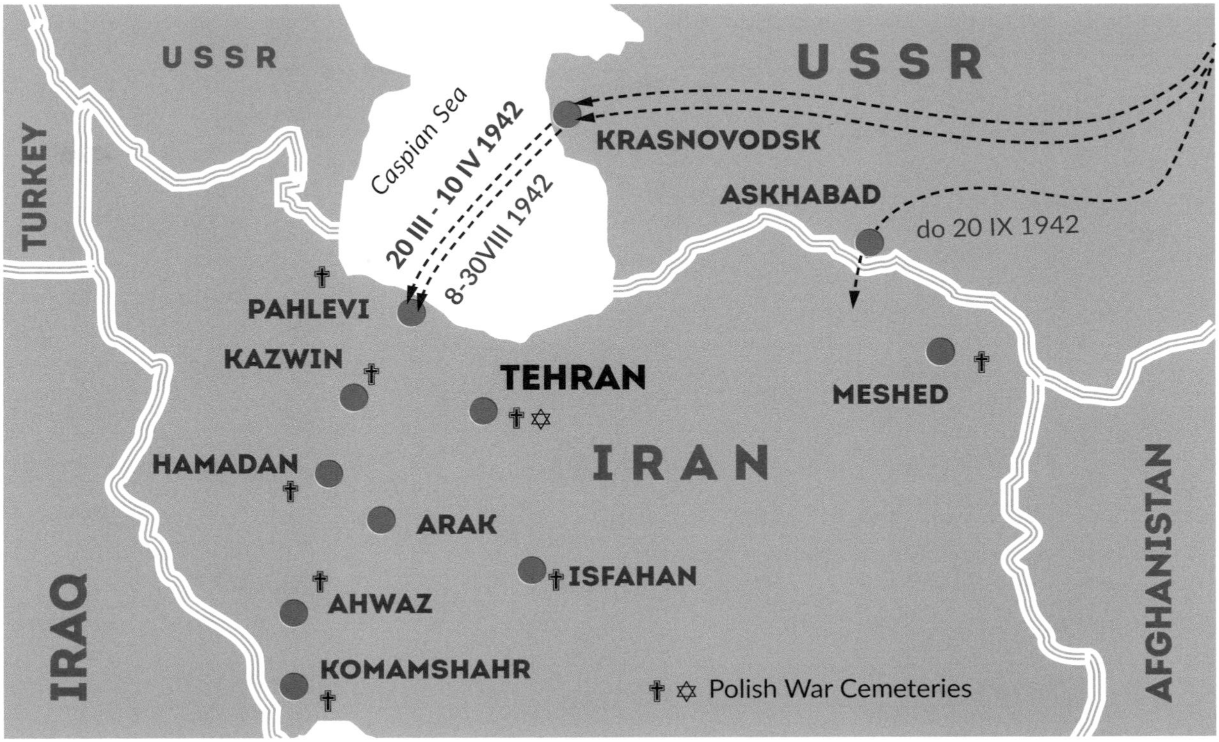

overlooked central Tehran from the neighbouring mountainside, continued to cow the inhabitants, who called it the *faramush chane*, 'The House of Oblivion'. At the same time, the new Shah was stripped of his control of the Government, Ministries and Parliament, which fell back into the hands of the old aristocratic families. In 1943, when the Shah's glamorous queen, Fauzia, left for her native Egypt to sue for divorce, he was left an isolated and forlorn figure. Like the Poles, he was no more than a pawn on the world stage.

The Polish visitors would equally have noticed that Iran was in the throes of a social revolution driven from above. As from 1934, the Shah's father had launched far-reaching reforms and grandiose building projects that aimed to modernise the country by decree, somewhat in the spirit of Kemal Ataturk in neighbouring Turkey. Roads, railways, and bridges were everywhere under construction. Children were going to school in unprecedented numbers. And women were discouraged from wearing the veil. They still covered their heads, but they risked being caned on the street by the Shah's police, if they reverted to the most traditional Islamic habits. A programme of 'Persification' led to wholesale changes in place-names and personal names. The province of Arabestan became Chuzestan; the town of Sultanabad became Arak; and the port of Pahlevi, where the Poles had landed, had been called Enzeli until five or six years earlier. The Prime Minister in 1942–1943, whom the Poles knew as 'Ghawam Ahmad', a cousin of the future premier, Mossadeq Mohammad, had called himself Ghawam al-Sultane until recently. The spirit of these reforms was strongly nationalist, and they aimed to undermine the so-called forces of reaction: namely the Shiite clergy, the tribal system of the countryside, the backward infrastructure, and the inertia of a largely illiterate population.

L

ISLAMIC ART, 16th-century mosaics in the hah (or Jameh) Mosque, Isfahan.

One wonders if any of the Poles saw parallels with the problems of their own country. One thing, however, would have struck them most forcefully: many districts of Tehran were still not supplied with running water.[82]

Iran, like Central Asia, possessed a number of astonishing cultural and historical sights. Persepolis, the capital of Darius the Great from 518 BC, contained extraordinary ruins. Isfahan, holy city of the Shias, was a treasure house of Islamic art. The Poles had little time for sightseeing. But those who were stationed near the sites, or could take a couple of days' leave, did not miss the opportunity.

Isfahan, in particular, was the city which the Poles most wished to visit and which welcomed thousands of them for educational purposes. Its main square dominated by the Masq-e-Shah Mosque, the Imperial Bazaar, and the Ali Qapu Palace is universally regarded as masterpiece of Islamic Art.

In 1942–1946, the city was home to four Polish boarding schools that were established for the education of the sons and daughters of serving soldiers. No fewer than 2,600 pupils passed through their classrooms; the Armenian community opened its churches to Catholic worshippers; and the children who were educated there never forgot it.[83]

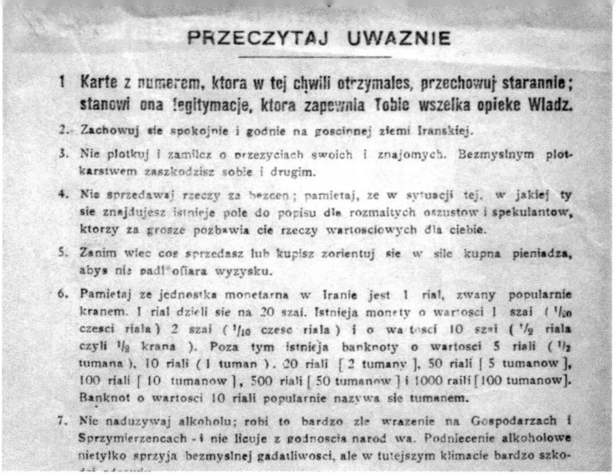

PRZECZYTAJ UWAZNIE

1 Karte z numerem, ktora w tej chwili otrzymales, przechowuj starannie; stanowi ona legitymacje, ktora zapewnia Tobie wszelka opieke Wladz.

2. Zachowuj sie spokojnie i godnie na goscinnej ziemi Iranskiej.

3. Nie plotkuj i zamilcz o przezyciach swoich i znajomych. Bezmyslnym plotkarstwem zaszkodzisz sobie i drugim.

4. Nie sprzedawaj rzeczy za bezcen; pamietaj, ze w sytuacji tej, w jakiej ty sie znajdujesz istnieje pole do popisu dla rozmaitych oszustow i spekulantow, ktorzy za grosze pozbawia cie rzeczy wartosciowych dla ciebie.

5. Zanim wiec cos sprzedasz lub kupisz zorientuj sie w sile kupna pieniadza, abys nie padl ofiara wyzysku.

6. Pamietaj ze jednostka monetarna w Iranie jest 1 rial, zwany popularnie kranem. 1 rial dzieli sie na 20 szai. Istnieja monety o wartosci 1 szai (1/20 czesci riala) 2 szai (1/10 czesc riala) i o wartosci 10 szai (1/2 riala czyli 1/2 krana). Poza tym istnieja banknoty o wartosci 5 riali (1/2 tumana), 10 riali (1 tuman). 20 riali [2 tumany], 50 riali [5 tumanow], 100 riali [10 tumanow], 500 riali [50 tumanow] i 1000 raili [100 tumanow]. Banknot o wartosci 10 riali popularnie nazywa sie tumanem.

7. Nie naduzywaj alkoholu; robi to bardzo zle wrazenie na Gospodarzach i Sprzymierzencach - i nie licuje z godnoscia narodowa. Podniecenie alkoholowe nietylko sprzyja bezmyslnej gadatliwosci, ale w tutejszym klimacie bardzo szko-

READ CAREFULLY! Soldiers' instructions (top).

MEMORIAL TABLET to the sojourn of Poles in hospitable Iran, 1942–1945.

SOLDIERS IN transit (above right). For many, Iran was just a stopping-place on the way to Iraq.

SOLDIERS STILL in British trench coats (below right).

Iran, above all, was the place where the paths of Polish soldiers and civilians diverged: for many, a painful parting of the ways. The soldiers made ready for service in various countries of the Middle East. The civilians, who could not be easily accommodated in Iran, prepared to be sent to various parts of the British Empire. Families were regularly split up. As often as not, they could not be reunited until the war had ended, three and four years later.

As the port of Pahlevi continued to receive daily shiploads of desperate exiles, a further overland route had been opened up between Ashkabad in Turkmenistan and the Iranian city of Meshed. Wiesław Stypuła (born in 1931 in Równe, Volhynia) was an 11-year-old boy when he was taken out of the USSR on the back of a British Army truck:

"Those of us preparing to leave were reminded by our teachers that, for sanitary reasons, it was not permitted to take any 'old things' with us. With the greatest grief, therefore, I was separated from a couple of faithful and invaluable companions – a pair of battered felt hats, which had been cleverly sewn up and which had long served me as shoes. Then someone tore open the side of my footwear, and pulled out a real treasure: a tiny, damaged photograph of my family. That was happiness!

We drove out onto the main road leading towards the frontier. 'What frontier's that?' we ask. 'It's the frontier with Persia', our guardian replies. 'Yes, yes, the frontier of legendary Persia...'

Outside the town, a halt is made. Everyone jumps out and stands in rows. The commandant of the column steps forward, and introduces himself as Captain Konarski... He's a well-built man in middle age. A large revolver hangs by his hip in its holster. The older lads are fascinated by it.

The commander outlines the route and the regulations. We are heading for the Persian city of Meshed, about 500 km (310 miles) along the road between Ashkabad and Tehran. The track is very mountainous and dangerous. Rigorous discipline will be observed. The lorries must stick to their numbered position in the column. No stopping! No overtaking!...

After one-and-a-half hours, we pull up in front of the low buildings of the frontier post. We hear raised voices. Then Capt. Konarski orders us to stand beside our vehicles and not to move. The formalities drag on. First the commander presents the permit for crossing the frontier. Then the adults' passports are checked, and finally, the lists of children's names. Something doesn't add up [and we have to wait].

As we later learn, Capt. Konarski had decided at the last minute to add 10-year-old Jasio to the column, so as to keep him with his elder brother. Jasio had been ill, and wasn't supposed to travel.

SHAH-IN-SHAH MOHAMMAD PAHLAVI,
Portrait by Bolesław Kersen.

Portrait de S. M. I.
ChahinChah Mohammed
Reza Pahlavi
Kersen Boleslа

IRANIAN '*PERMIS DE SÉJOUR*' for Mr I. Kościałkowski.

But he was hidden under a pile of blankets... [And the guards had to be diverted when they were trying to count heads.]

Several kilometers down the road we reach the final checkpoint. Jasio, wrapped in a blanket, is lying behind other boys' legs. Two elderly soldiers collect the passes, count heads once again, and eventually raise the barrier, allowing us to cross. Everyone is banging the backdrops of the lorries from sheer joy. Then someone screams, and another responds. And for ten minutes, a tumult of hysterical shouting broke out, before our teachers calmed us down, and called us to repeat 'Our Father'...

[One of the drivers is a dark-skinned Indian,] 'black as night', wearing an English uniform and chewing gum. We observe him closely, since we have never seen such a person before... Before he leaves us, he gives us some chocolates. The temptation is too great to refuse...

At last, on flatter ground, the first lights begin to appear in the night. Untidy buildings. People's voices. This is Sabzevar".[84]

Both at Meshed and at Pahlevi an important task was udertaken under the supervision of British officials. Every child who entered Iran with the Anders Army was required to register their arrival by filling out simple forms with details of their name, sex, date of birth, place of birth, and schooling. Questions were also asked about their parents and siblings. If they had lost their parents or become separated from them, they were asked 'where' and 'when'. Lines of trestle tables and benches were lined up on the beach at Pahlevi, and the boys and girls were sat down by the hundred. Any illiterate children, who had never been to school – of whom there were droves – had to find an older, literate person to help them fill in the forms. In all, some 40,000 documents of one sort or another were collected, and are now deposited in the archive of the Hoover Institution at Stanford, California. They provided Jan and Irena Gross with the documentary material that is included in their classic book, *War Through Children's Eyes* (Stanford, 1981). Michał Giedroyć, then 14 years old, was one of the better schooled children, who could help others. More than sixty years later, when he was preparing his own memoir, *Crater's Edge*[85], he was able to contact the Hoover archive, to retrieve the form that he had filled in in 1943, and to subject it to textual criticism.

ON ENTERING IRAN, the 'Polish Army in the USSR' passed under British command, and in particular under that of Lt Gen. Sir Henry Pownall, commander of the Persia and Iraq

Force (PAI) whose HQ was at Baghdad. The army, whose name was changed to 'Polish Army in the Middle East', had about 80,000 men under arms.

General Pownall, who had been Chief-of-Staff of the defeated British Expeditionary Force in France, had taken a keen interest in the progress of the Anders Army, and had once suggested to London that it be deployed in the Caucasus. He now wrote to Anders, somewhat patronisingly, pointing out that the Poles lacked experience in battle and that a rigorous training programme was essential.

The Chargé d'Affaires of the British Embassy in Tehran, (Lord) Robin Hankey, was better informed. He had served in Warsaw before 1939, knew the Poles well, and unlike most Britishers, fully understood the appalling events which surrounded the creation of the Anders Army in the USSR. He wrote to London expressing admiration for the Army's morale and its eagerness to see action against Germany.

To facilitate cooperation, the 26 British Liaison Unit (26 BLU) was assigned to the Polish Army. It was headed by Brigadier Eric Frith and his staff of 14 officers. It had no executive authority. Its function was to explain orders, to

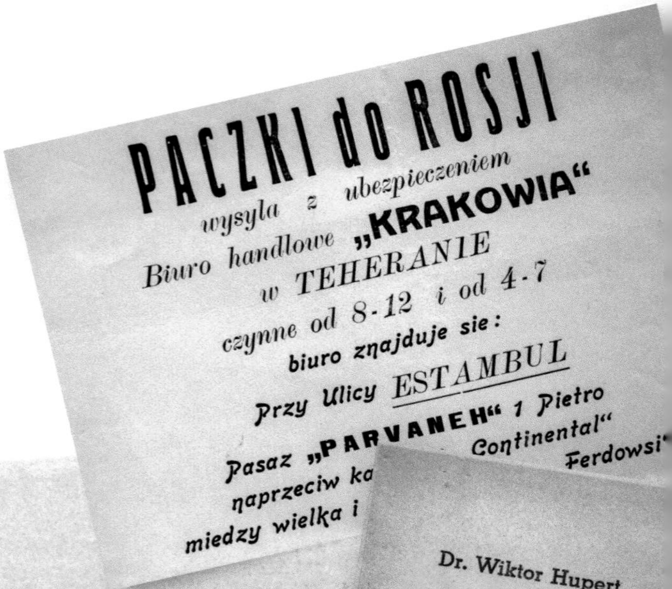
PACZKI do ROSJI
wysyla z ubezpieczeniem
Biuro handlowe „KRAKOWIA"
w TEHERANIE
czynne od 8-12 i od 4-7
biuro znajduje sie:
Przy Ulicy ESTAMBUL
Pasaz „PARVANEH" 1 Pietro
naprzeciw ka... Continental"
miedzy wielka i ... Ferdowsi"

Dr. Wiktor Hupert
O Higienie
w Krajach
Tropikalnych
Cena 5 sls.
Teheran 1943
Société Anonyme Tchap

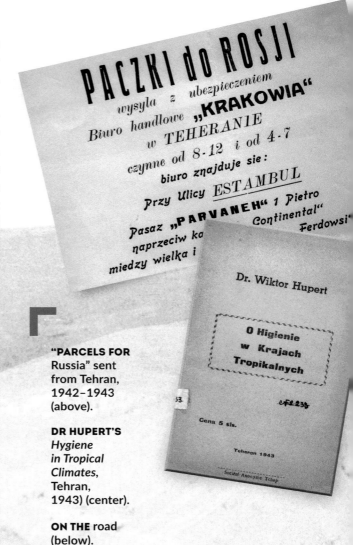

"PARCELS FOR Russia" sent from Tehran, 1942–1943 (above).

DR HUPERT'S *Hygiene in Tropical Climates*, Tehran, 1943) (center).

ON THE road (below).

assess capabilities, and to facilitate liaison with other Allied formations. All its work, however, was conducted in English; and since Anders was no longer permitted to communicate with his government using Polish radio and codes, it came to control most links with the outside world. (It remained at Anders' side until the end of the Italian campaign.)

THE POLISH ARMY, however, was not assigned to any special duties in Iran. It was not deployed in the south-west region to guard the Abadan oilfields, and the leadership knew fairly soon that its next destination would likely be Iraq. This meant that it only set up temporary transit camps in northern and central Iran, while the main body of troops were preparing to be transferred further west to Iraqi Kurdistan. Some units travelled direct from Port Pahlevi to Iraq without ever setting foot on Iranian soil.

For most Polish soldiers, therefore, Tehran was little more than a temporary transit station. But for most civilians, it was the first lively, civilised, and peaceful place of residence that they had seen in three or four years. They loved it, and more than one was to call it their 'Persian Paradise':

"We arrived in Tehran in May 1942... The streets were lined with people who had gathered to welcome us. We looked into their faces, as they waved and cheered us, and we saw that they were beautiful, free and happy.

We were taken to the Persian University, nestling in the foothills of the mountains, which had been converted to receive us. As our convoy drove through gates which closed behind us, we saw magnificent buildings, lawns, and trees with ripe apricots...

As we disembarked, to be met by Polish soldiers, we were warned, 'Do not eat the fresh fruit. We will give you fruit in the dining room – eat only that. Do not buy anything from the hands of local traders.' We learned later that this later precaution was because of the venereal disease that was endemic in this country. We were even warned not to sit on seats that were still warm...

Within hours of our arrival dozens of cars had besieged the gates of the University offering gifts of clothes and food and other

IRAN 2015

IRAN, 2015. Norman Davies gazing in wonder, in the Mausoleum of Sahi Ibn Ali. Scenes from Yazd (opposite top), the Bazaar at Isfahan and a view of modern Tehran (opposite bottom).

ترمه وسرمه
ترمه

DOWN WITH
THE U.S.A
مرگ بر آمریکا

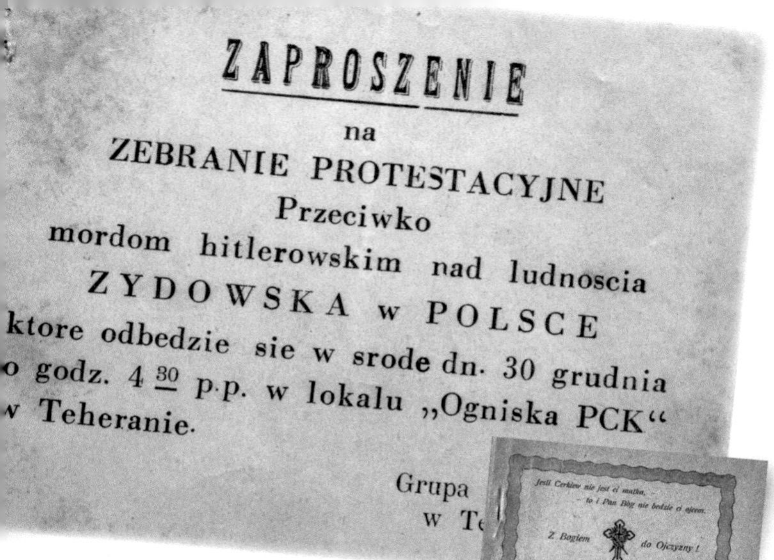
ZAPROSZENIE

na

ZEBRANIE PROTESTACYJNE

Przeciwko

mordom hitlerowskim nad ludnoscia

ZYDOWSKA w POLSCE

ktore odbedzie sie w srode dn. 30 grudnia

o godz. 4 30 p.p. w lokalu „Ogniska PCK“

w Teheranie.

Grupa

w T

INVITATION TO a protest meeting against the Hitlerite murders of the Jewish population in Poland, issued by the Bund Group. Tehran, 30 December 1942.

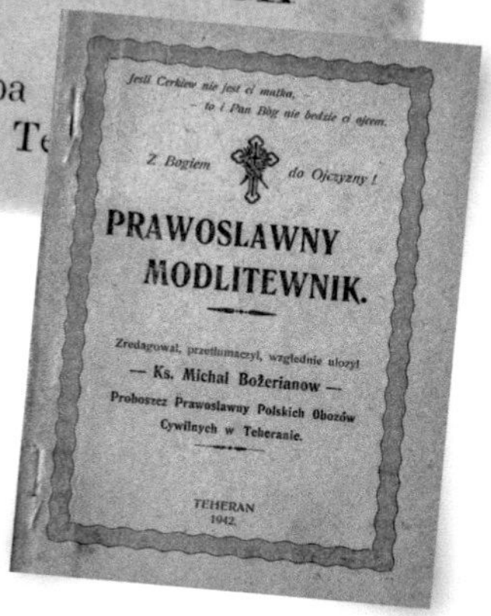
Z Bogiem do Ojczyzny!

PRAWOSLAWNY MODLITEWNIK.

— Ks. Michal Bożerianow —

Proboszcz Prawosławny Polskich Obozów Cywilnych w Teheranie.

TEHERAN 1942

ORTHODOX PRAYER book: edited by Rev. Michał Bozerianov, Orthodox Vicar of Polish civilian and military camps, Tehran, 1942.

necessities. The people's kindness was overwhelming.

We were told that the boys had arrived the day before and that they were in No. 1 Camp, across the road from Tehran Airport, where we were bound, and knowing that they were safe gave us a tremendous boost.

We soon had our own community, with priests. We built an altar to Our Lady, and we sang hymns and held a service of thanksgiving.

We had food, rice, salad and other things that had been donated to us. We had everything we needed. But so many of us had broken hearts and could hardly touch the food."[86]

Tehran would also be remembered as a place of frantic searching, where refugees hoped to be reunited with their nearest and dearest and where everyone wanted information about those with whom they had lost contact:

"As more refugees arrived from Russia, we went to them immediately, besieging them with questions… 'Where did you come from?'… 'Have you news of this person, or that person?'… 'Did you hear this name…?'

At the end of May the Polish Army came to our church service, and it was then that I met someone who came from our own village, a [Belarussian] in the Polish Army whose father had also been a Legionnaire, and who had been taken to Siberia at the same time as us.

'Oh, Aloshya, it's wonderful to meet you', I told him. 'What are you doing here?'

I questioned him about Stanislaw [my husband], but he could not help me. But he did tell me that although his battalion was actually moving on, other Polish Army soldiers would soon be arriving.

Waiting for the soldiers to arrive, I continued to question the new refugees in the hope of getting some information about [my brother] Tony from them.

A Jewish rabbi came and assembled his flock. Several girls whom I had not ever expected to be Jewish declared their faith. 'Come, Helenka', one of them said to me, 'soon we will be going home to Israel.'

But the rabbi lost one disciple fairly quickly... Anne was a Jewish woman with a little girl who

'ALLIES' – a Sikh from Britain's Indian Army with a Polish soldier in Iran (above).

IRANIAN HARVEST (left).

was very sick. As the child was dying she told her, 'Mummy, Jesus is here and He says He loves me.' The rest of the Jews soon flew to Palestine, but Anne stayed behind to convert to Catholicism".[87]

Nonetheless, for those families who had not been struck down by bereavement or by serious illness, Tehran was a veritable 'God's Playground':

"The so-called Civilian Camp No. 3, to which we were assigned, was the result of our General's endeavours, the latest addition to two earlier camps situated in the city's industrial suburbs. No. 3 was by far the most congenial. It was set up in the grounds of a magnificent country residence, the property of an Iranian notable whose family had fallen on hard times. A high wall surrounded an extensive park, in which tall cypresses guarded the ruins of the big house. The estate was several kilometers to the north of the city, on the newly asphalted road to Darband, the Shah's summer residence. Amongst the avenues and *aryks* – fast streams of ice-cold water running down from the snow-clad peaks of Elburz – an instant city of army tents mushroomed under sympathetic British supervision. In the centre stood the communal canteen, alongside the administration block, hot shower, and an open-air stage for theatricals and film-shows with a natural amphitheatre of hills around it.

WE ENTERED THIS IDYLLIC SETTING in a blaze of publicity. The appearance in Iran of former Soviet prisoners and deportees was an event attracting world attention. Film crews, mainly American, were poised at the gates to record our arrival. Only the other day I saw on British TV an old clip showing one such event at the gate of glorious No. 3. This particular piece of visual evidence remains today a confirmation of what General Anders said about the state of his civilians: 'My most urgent task was to organise proper medical care and accommodation for the civilian dependants. The condition of the newly-arrived was appalling and often beyond rehabilitation. People were dying of exhaustion and the after-effects of hunger... In a matter of weeks over one thou-

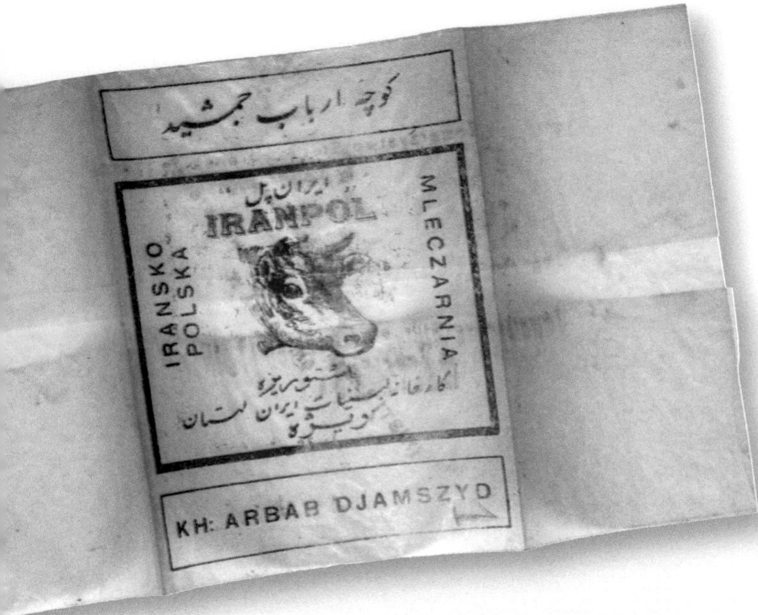

IRANPOL: POLISH-IRANIAN dairy label (left).

TEMPORARY MILITARY camp in Iran (below).

ISFAHAN: ARMENIAN Cathedral (top).

THE CATHEDRAL'S founder, Archbishop Khachatour Kesaratsi (1590–1646).

sand crosses rose at the new Polish cemetery of Tehran.'

The young orderly with an armband who took our contingent in hand at the gate was none other than my friend Muś Łętowski, one of our fellow refugees at Słonim and a member of Father Adam Sztark's contingent of altar boys. Later we discovered in Tehran a number of 'fellow-travellers' who had shared the Soviet experience: from Słonim the Łętowskis, the Bitner-Glindziczes and the Rudlickis; from Dereczyn the Zięciaks; from Nikolaevka Mrs Tubielewicz with her two daughters; and, last but not least, Mrs Bazylewska and guitar! A feeling of camaraderie prevailed.

Muś led us to our new quarters. These amounted to a space on the ground covered with matting, in a long communal tent. There was no furniture in the tent, the nearest 'sitting room' being a bench in the central canteen. Stacks of

NAKLAD PO KONFISKACIE!

Cena 2 Rls

SŁOWO POLSKIE

POLAKIEM JESTEM
I NIC CO POLSKIE
NIE JEST MI OBCEM
R. DMOWSKI

PISMO POSWIECONE SPRAWOM NARODOWYM

ROK II. TEHERAN 1-GO LUTEGO 1943 R. Nr 2 (3)

„WIELKIEJ POLSKI MOC TO MY"

Oni to duchem twardzi
i sercem jak klos prosci
bagnetami sie upomna
o prawo do wolnosci.
Eugeniusz Malaczewski.

Wyrosl On z najzdrowszej czesci spoleczenstwa polskiego, tj. warstwy sredniej, rzemieslniczej i mieszczanskiej. Ojciec Jego był brukarzem. Czesto opowiadal nam Dmowski o tym jak ojciec Jego pracujac przy brukowaniu starych drog i goscincow Wielko-

SŁOWO POLSKIE (*The Polish Word*), *a Journal of National Affairs*, **Year II, No. 2(3), Tehran, 1 February 1943. Published after Confiscation. "I am a Pole, and nothing Polish is foreign to me." (R. Dmowski). A press organ of the Nationalists.**

used clothes of high quality awaited the women – American generosity again. Soon my mother and sisters began to look thoroughly presentable, although the total image took some while to achieve. The other day I found in my mother's papers one of her early Tehran photographs, in which she is topped with an elegant summer hat and tailed with a pair of tired plimsolls.

The plimsolls did not inhibit contacts with Iranian high society. Local young blades sought out the exotic Polish girl: Anuśka caught the eye of a colonel in shiny riding boots, who offered outings in his equally shiny American car. Anuśka was allowed to accept the invitation, but 'her mother came too' – as did Tereska, the collective view being that there was safety in numbers. My mother's chaperoning tended to inhibit these budding opportunities.

I in the meantime made new friends and we began thumbing lifts to the city below. I soon discovered that lifts came more easily to individual travellers, so I began exploring the capital alone. This suited me well until one day a chauffeur-driven car pulled up. I remember its number: 1888. A corpulent man in a striped three-piece suit invited me in with fulsome cordiality, and began making sexual advances. I turned to the driver and demanded that he should stop at once. Which he did. On return I told my mother what had happened, and she reported the incident to the authorities. 'Ah, yes', they said with amusement, 'the old 1888 again'.

OTHERWISE LIFE WAS BLISSFUL. Camp food was plentiful, the weather perfect, and there were good friends galore. As an occasional treat at the camp shop we had a drink called 'Sinalco', a delicious fizzy concoction brewed locally under German licence, to which I became addicted.

After a month's hard work I obtained promotion to the second year, which my mother celebrated by giving me a slap-up luncheon at the camp shop, by then extended to include a 'café-restaurant'. The main dish was a Wiener Schnitzel with a slice of lemon on it. This blow-out was followed by a foray *en famille* to Cafe Ferdosi in the heart of Tehran, where the Giedroyćes astounded both the waiters and

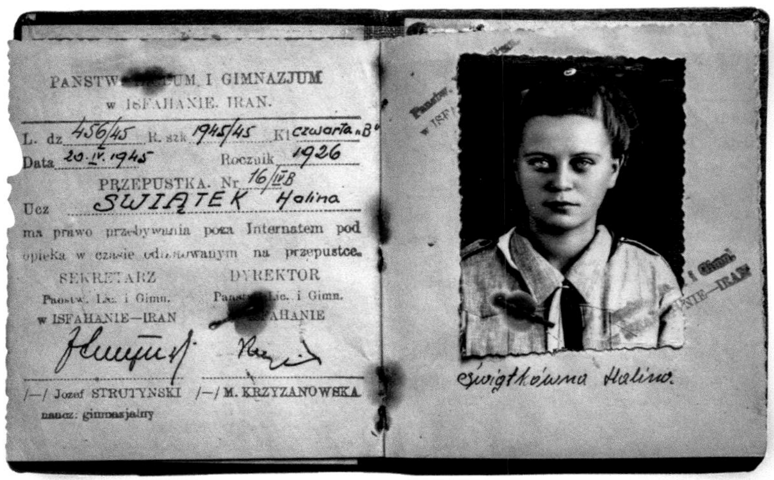

PANSTW... UM. I GIMNAZJUM
w ISFAHANIE. IRAN.

L. dz. 456/45 R. szk. 1945/45 Kl. czwarta „B"
Data 20.IV.1945 Rocznik 1926
PRZEPUSTKA. Nr. 16/IVB
Ucz. SWIĄTEK Halina
ma prawo przebywania poza Internatem pod opieka w czasie odznaczonym na przepustce.

SEKRETARZ
Panstw. Lic. i Gimn.
w ISFAHANIE—IRAN
/—/ Jozef STRUTYNSKI
naucz: gimnasjalny

DYREKTOR
Panst... Lic. i Gimn.
...AHANIE
/—/ M. KRZYZANOWSKA

Świątkówna Halina.

POLISH CROWNED eagle: stamp printed for parcels sent to Polish POWs in German camps, 3 May 1943.

HALINA ŚWIĄTEK, aged 19. Identity card from the State *Gimnazjum* in Isfahan, 1945.

There was a serious side to camp existence: the alfresco secondary school organised by the Polish Authorities and manned by devoted teachers who had survived the Soviet exile. Classrooms were pitched under the shadiest trees. In view of my academic successes at Nikolaevka, I was assigned to the first year of the Polish secondary system, younger by at least two years than my classmates. This time the Polish language was my main challenge, but somehow I managed to please the demanding Mrs Korczewska...

the patrons by their unrestrained demands for fresh mountains of cakes.

Extramural activities laid on by a school anxious to improve our minds were, on the other hand, less exciting. The well-meant random lecturers we found boring, although we welcomed with enthusiasm the pomp of Bishop Gawlina, chaplain to the Polish Armed Forces, who came to administer confirmations — in most cases long overdue...

یا اباعبدالله الحسین

IRAN 2015

ISFAHAN (top left) **ANCIENT PERSEPOLIS** (centre); scenes from the Shia Festival of the Martyr Hussein (bottom and opposite).

Then there was the memorable performance by the Review Theatre which had sprung up on the fringes of the Polish Army. It featured a number of prewar artists of high calibre (many of Jewish origin) who came out of the Soviet Union with the Army. The star of the show was a platinum blonde (of Polish-Ukrainian origin) called Renata Bogdańska, the darling of the Polish Forces and the future Mrs Anders.

Enjoying life as never before, I was unaware that to my sisters, and to my mother, things looked very different. Communal living, and the prospect of a sterile existence as refugees, was not what they – one aged 22 and the other 20 – expected after two and a half years of suspended animation. They became restless and my mother began to look for a means of returning to some kind of normality...."[88]

IRENA VALDI was another entertainer who made good in Tehran. A professional singer, who had performed before the war with the Warsaw Opera, she possessed an inimitably deep contralto voice; she reached Iran in the company of her sister, Maria Żórawska, an accomplished pianist, and together they put on an act that greatly appealed to Iranian audiences. Billed as the *chanteuse polonaise*, she lived well from her music-making, appearing both on Radio Tehran and at the Shah's palace, and staying in Iran until 1945, when she moved to Beirut. Before leaving, Irena Valdi-Gołębiowska née Żórawska (1891–1977) applied for a passport at the Polish Consulate in Tehran where she declared her birth date to be 1905, thereby subtracting 14 years from her official age.

Valdi was not alone by staying on when the Army left. Numerous young Polish women

EN ROUTE to Iraq.

married Iranian men, and spent the rest of their lives in Iran. We met some of them during our visit in October 2014. Their life has been recreated in a stunning film, *Mit Iranske Paradis* (2008), 'My Iranian Paradise' by Danish director Katia Forbert Petersen. Ms Petersen, born 1949, is the daughter of a Polish mother who came to Iran with the Anders Army, and of a Danish father, an engineer, who was employed on the grand project to build a North–South railway from one end of the country to the other. She remembers her childhood in Tehran as uninterrupted bliss. "To me Iran is the happiest place under the sun." She lived there until the Revolution of 1979, when the family fled to Denmark. She returned more than quarter of a century later to record what had happened to her 'Paradise' under the Islamic régime, and, in particular to discover the disturbing experiences of the Iranian,

THE WHITE Rose Choir, Camp No. 2, Tehran (top).

PLAYING VOLLEYBALL (above).

whom she had known in a totally different pre-revolutionary world.

The biggest group of Poles who stayed on in Iran after the bulk of the Army had left, consisted of three to four thousand schoolchildren and their teachers, whose primary and secondary education had been organised by the Polish School Commission in 1942. Many of them were placed in four large boarding schools, the most prominent of which, the Polish School for Girls in Isfahan, has inspired a fascinating volume of history and memoirs. I heard about it from our good friend, Zofia Litewska, who taught there after the death of her husband.

"LONG LIVE our saviours" — a tribute to visiting Polish soldiers from primary schoolchildren, Tehran.

ISFAHAN, the 'pearl of Iranian cities', occupies a verdant oasis at the foot of the Zagros Mountains some 340 km to the south-west of Tehran. It is a city of turquoise-domed mosques and flower-filled gardens. Its incomparable Islamic art and architecture dates from the 16th century, when Shah Abbas the Great made it the capital of his empire.

Despite the idyllic eulogies of Katia Petersen, life in the 'City of Polish Children'

CHAPEL OF THE SISTERS OF CHARITY in Isfahan, next to the Polish Girls' School. From left: Norman Davies, Polish Ambassador in Tehran Juliusz Gojło and Sister Giuseppina.

could be uncomfortable. Polish girls who went out in the town wearing their scout uniforms were showered with stones, and berets were torn from their heads. The Poles found support from local Christian Armenians; and a chapel in the Armenian cathedral was set aside for Polish Catholic services. The Convent of the Sisters of Charity was another place of safety; Our Lady of Częstochowa hangs in their chapel to this day. The hillside Armenian Cemetery, which looks down on Isfahan, bears witness to the Polish presence. It also shelters the tomb of Teodor Miranowicz, Ambassador of the Commonwealth of Poland–Lithuania, who died there in 1686.

The Poles of wartime Isfahan, however, could not be described as an embattled community. It is said that Iranians called them 'the sad people'. But they created a vibrant hive of activity; there were Polish bakeries, Polish baths, Polish sewing rooms (*szwalnie*), a Polish carpet factory, and, unusually for Iran, a Polish pig farm. They were honoured in 1943 by visits both of the Duke of Gloucester and the Shah with his new bride, Queen Soraya. A memorial volume, *Isfahan, City of Polish Children*, was published in England in 1987.[90]

Monika and Stanisława Jasionowicz were pupils in the girls' school in Isfahan, where 'my Mrs Litewska' was a teacher. They had lost contact with their mother in Uzbekistan; they had last seen her in a 'terminal ward' in a Soviet hospital. They both assumed, since leaving the USSR with an Anders Army orphanage, that, apart from their sister, they were completely

THE BIG THREE

THE BIG THREE. The Soviet Embassy in Tehran, November 1943.

AT THE RUSSIAN EMBASSY in Tehran, 5 October 2014. Ambassador Levan Dzhagaryan as Stalin, Mrs Patrycja Ozcan as Roosevelt, Norman Davies as Churchill (below).

AMBASSADOR LEVAN DZHAGARYAN (right) shows Norman Davies mementoes of the Tehran Conference.

STALIN TOAST the Allie Nations at Churchill's birthday party, the British Legation (centre left).

THE EMBASSY'S main building about 1940 (centre right).

THE EMBASSY'S main hall where the Tehran Conference was held (below).

STILL HEADING for Iraq.

DIRECTIVE OF the Government-in-Exile for the evacuation of Polish refugees from Iran, 6 March 1943.

alone in the world. Then one day, long after the closing of the Iranian–Soviet frontier, they received a shock:

“Monika and I were living at number nine when we were told one day that there was a woman waiting for us downstairs. We didn’t know anyone, so we went to the gate feeling quite surprised. We saw a tall, thin figure with shaved head.

She was dressed in a bathrobe and some kind of slippers. She was holding a bundle in her hands. We stood there looking, we at her and she at us. Then she said: ‘You don’t know me, you don’t recognize me?’ Suddenly I was afraid and I wanted to run. It felt like she was a ghost from another world. ‘You don’t know who I am... don’t you?’ Then I knew. ‘Mother!’ I called out to Monika. We hugged her and apologized. We laughed and we cried for joy. Sitting in the garden, we told her about what had happened in the past year. Mother had left Russia with the last transport, must have been the fall of 1943.

They closed the border after that. It was Divine Providence that guided us, led us through the tragedies of the ‘inhuman land’ and let us meet again. Our family gradually came back to life.

We didn’t know anything about our father. Edward was already on this side, that was

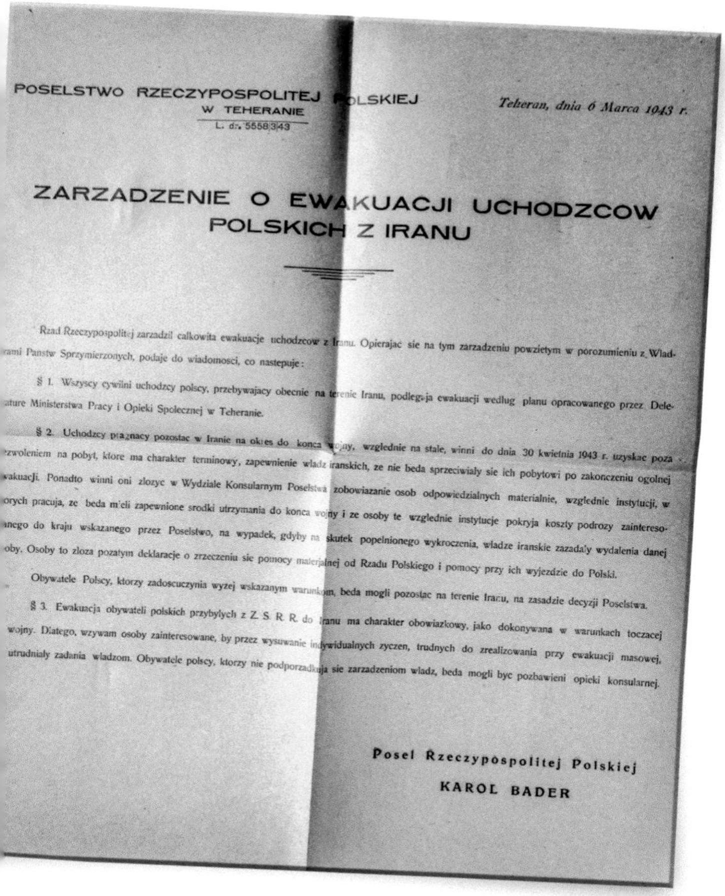

POSELSTWO RZECZYPOSPOLITEJ POLSKIEJ
W TEHERANIE
L. dz. 5558/3/43

Teheran, dnia 6 Marca 1943 r.

ZARZADZENIE O EWAKUACJI UCHODZCOW POLSKICH Z IRANU

Rzad Rzeczypospolitej zarzadził całkowita ewakuacje uchodzcow z Iranu. Opierajac sie na tym zarzadzeniu powzietym w porozumieniu z Wład- rami Panstw Sprzymierzonych, podaje do wiadomosci, co nastepuje:

§ 1. Wszyscy cywilni uchodzcy polscy, przebywajacy obecnie na terenie Iranu, podlegaja ewakuacji wedlug planu opracowanego przez Dele- ature Ministerstwa Pracy i Opieki Spolecznej w Teheranie.

§ 2. Uchodzcy pragnacy pozostac w Iranie na okres do konca wojny, wzglednie na stale, winni do dnia 30 kwietnia 1943 r. uzyskac poza zwoleniem na pobyt, ktore ma charakter terminowy, zapewnienie wladz iranskich, ze nie beda sprzeciwiały sie ich pobytowi po zakonczeniu ogolnej wakuacji. Ponadto winni oni zlozyc w Wydziale Konsularnym Poselstwa zobowiazanie osob odpowiedzialnych materialnie, wzglednie instytucji, w orych pracuja, ze beda mieli zapewnione srodki utrzymania do konca wojny i ze osoby te wzglednie instytucje pokryja koszty podrozy zainteresoanego do kraju wskazanego przez Poselstwo, na wypadek, gdyby na skutek popelnionego wykroczenia, wladze iranskie zazadaly wydalenia danej oby. Osoby to zloza pozatym deklaracje o zrzeczeniu sie pomocy materjalnej od Rzadu Polskiego i pomocy przy ich wyjezdzie do Polski.

Obywatele Polscy, ktorzy zadoscuczynia wyzej wskazanym warunkom, beda mogli pozostac na terenie Iranu, na zasadzie decyzji Poselstwa.

§ 3. Ewakuacja obywateli polskich przybyłych z Z. S. R. R. do Iranu ma charakter obowiazkowy, jako dokonywana w warunkach toczacej wojny. Dlatego, wzywam osoby zainteresowane, by przez wysuwanie indywidualnych zyczen, trudnych do zrealizowania przy ewakuacji masowej, utrudniały zadania wladzom. Obywatele polscy, ktorzy nie podporzadkuja sie zarzadzeniom wladz, beda mogli byc pozbawieni opieki konsularnej.

Posel Rzeczypospolitej Polskiej
KAROL BADER

certain, but we didn't have any news from him from Egypt. Mother was hired to work in one of the shelters for children and she came to visit us from time to time.

I remember the joyful frenzy on May 18, 1944, when the II Corps took Monte Cassino! It seemed we would be going home to Poland pretty soon!"[91]

The sisters referred to General Anders as '*Nasz Zbawiciel*' (Our Saviour). They attended his funeral. Fifty years after arriving in Iran, Stanisława, long since re-baptised as 'Sister Maria Teresa', was elevated to the position of Mother Superior (*Przełożona Generalna*) of the Order of the Most Holy Family of Nazareth.

It was during the Army's time in Iran, that news arrived of what Churchill was to call 'The Turning of the Tide'. Ever since the Army's creation in 1941, the Allied cause had been battling against the odds, with few signs of success. The Axis Powers had seemed invincible. But in October 1942, Anders heard of Montgomery's victory at El Alamein and of Rommel's retreat in North Africa. One of the imminent threats to the Middle East was lifted. In February 1943, he heard of the Red Army's stunning victory at Stalingrad, and of the surrender of a whole German army group. Another menace to the oilfields disappeared, and Stalin's standing in Allied counsels rose sharply. And two months later, he was informed of the landings of US forces in Morocco, and of the subsequent surge of Operation Torch. The Allies' tentative hold on the Mediterranean was improving. The Anglo-Americans were at last talking of mounting an attack on Hitler's 'Fortress Europe'. Anders must surely have wondered what part he and his soldiers might play in the new, more optimistic phase.

DURING THE MIDDLE YEARS of the war, Tehran acted as one of the principal hubs of interallied transport and communication in the Middle East. Despite the expanding traffic between the Western Powers and the Soviet Union, no Allied plane could fly directly from London to Moscow. The usual route involved a laborious five-day series of flights from London via Gibraltar, Cairo, and Tehran, and from Tehran to Russia.

In 1943, the flow of American Lend-Lease Aid to the Soviet Union via the Persian Corridor was gathering pace. The sheer scale of the shipments is hard to comprehend. It is a matter of dispute whether American aid was a decisive element in the Red Army's remarkable recovery that year. But it is beyond dispute, despite Washington's intentions, that the continuing flow of military supplies helped to give Stalin's armies overwhelming superiority by 1944–1945.

It is not surprising, therefore, that Tehran was chosen in November 1943 as the venue of the first wartime conference of the Allied 'Big Three'. By that time, General Anders had left Iran, but many of his subordinates were still there, and can only have followed proceedings with bated breath.

The main issue at the Tehran Conference had nothing to do with Poland. Roosevelt, Churchill, and Stalin were preoccupied by arrangements for launching the so-called 'Second Front' in Western Europe (France). But, from the strictly Polish point of view, three things are notable.

FIRST, THE BIG THREE operated a closed monopoly on all discussions. Allied diplomacy was stuck in the mode of the Congress of Vienna where a handful of so-called Powers felt free to determine the fate of a whole continent. No other delegations were admitted; no Polish representative was present to offer an opinion. In this, the Poles were treated in the same dismissive manner as the French, the Canadians, the Czechs and, indeed, the Iranians.

Secondly, in the wake of Stalingrad and Kursk, Stalin enjoyed a position of unprecedented prestige. He was the only leader of the Three whose armies were fighting against the main German force, and as such, he was treated with unusual deference.

He had ten times the number of troops in the field as did the British and Americans combined, and assumed an unchallenged air of superiority. What is more, Stalin was the only leader to have a serious stake in Eastern Europe. All three assumed, if the Western Powers were to have a free hand in the West, that Stalin must have a free hand in the East.

Thirdly, despite the difficulties, Churchill raised the thorny question of Poland's future. Unlike Roosevelt, he was a formal ally of the Poles, and felt a sense of duty towards them. It is NOT true, as one often hears, that Churchill and Stalin reached agreement on the Polish–Soviet frontier and hence on the fate of Poland's eastern territories.

What Churchill proposed was: the 'Curzon Line' can be the basis for discussion; in other words, when detailed negotiations began, the negotiators could start by discussing Soviet demands for the Curzon Line, i.e. the line of the Bug , but prior to a final agreement, the whole issue would remain open. (It would be interesting to know how Stalin's interpreter translated the key phrase, 'basis for discussion'.) At the time, the British leaders took it for granted that all such territorial matters would be the subject of a grand, postwar Peace Conference (like the Peace Conference at Paris held in 1919 at the end of the First World War).

In the meantime, Churchill ordered his Foreign Office to prepare a series of draft proposals on the Polish–Soviet frontier. All four such drafts, prepared in London in 1943–1944, left Lwów but not Wilno on the Polish side of the frontier.

What is true is that President Roosevelt approached the same issue in an unforgivably nonchalant fashion. On the day after Churchill's talk with Stalin, Roosevelt met the Generalissimo on his own, and assured him that 'frontier matters will cause no trouble'. With these casual words, he certainly gave Stalin the impression that Churchill's proposed 'discussions' could be safely ignored. And so it proved.

Anders was not privy to everything said at Tehran, and he can only have resented Poland's subordinate ranking within the Coalition. His considered reaction, as contained in his memoirs, expresses both stoicism and regret.

Apart from anything else, he was opposed to the very concept of a 'Second Front', which was a typical product of Soviet 'agitprop' speak, yet was mindlessly accepted by almost all Western politicians and commentators. The idea of a Second Front grew out of the false assumptions that Operation Barbarossa had launched a First Front in June 1941, and that prior to Barbarossa there were no serious fronts to consider.

Like its partner in Soviet vocabulary, 'the Great Patriotic War', it helped to propagate a string of myths – that the USSR had been neutral and passive in the period before Barbarossa; that the Red Army when invading Poland, Finland, Romania, and the Baltic States had not been involved in hostilities; and that the USSR was a 'peace-loving country' and a totally innocent victim of aggression. As Anders pointed out, the First Front had been contested in Poland in September 1939, when the Red Army had been one of the combatants. It follows, therefore, that Finland in 1939–1940, when the Soviet Union attacked its Finnish neighbour with an invasion force of over a million men, was the scene of the war's Second Front; that Scandinavia in May 1940, when the *Wehrmacht* invaded Denmark and Norway, constituted a Third Front; and the subsequent German invasion of the Low Countries and France a Fourth.

The Soviets, of course, were very eager to conceal their activities during the currency of the Nazi–Soviet Pact, and adapted their language accordingly. Roosevelt, Churchill and company swallowed the bait hook, line, and sinker.

NORMAN DAVIES in the children's sector, Polish Cemetery in Pahlevi (2014).

THE CARPATHIAN BRIGADE

CHAPTER 7
1941–1943

'COMRADES-IN-ARMS': AN infantryman of the Carpathian Brigade embraced by a soldier of the Australian 9th Division, North Africa, 1942.

SHOULDER BADGE of the Carpathian Brigade: a cedar of Lebanon over the Polish flag.

CHAPTER 7

1941–1943

THE CARPATHIAN BRIGADE

IN 1941–1942, WHEN THE ANDERS ARMY WAS IN THE PROCESS OF FORMATION, ANOTHER POLISH UNIT, WHICH WAS DESTINED TO SHARE A COMMON FATE, WAS ALREADY ENGAGED IN FRONT-LINE COMBAT.

The **Independent Carpathian** Brigade (SBSK) had been formed in Syria in April 1940 and maintained a separate existence until May 1942. Its commander, from start to finish, was General Stanisław Kopański (1895–1976).

At the end of the September Campaign and the fall of Poland, those Polish soldiers who had not surrendered or been captured were ordered to escape either to France or to French-ruled territories. Most of the escapees made for France via Hungary, Yugoslavia, or Italy. But several thousand headed for the Balkans whence they could make their way to French-ruled territories of Lebanon and Syria. In practice, it was not too difficult to reach the Levant. Once one had entered Romania or Bulgaria, it was a simple matter, with the help of Polish consular officials, to catch a ship from Constança or Varna and to sail through the Bosphorus and the Dardanelles to Beirut. As many veterans would later recount: 'It was a very pleasant voyage'.

In the winter of 1939–1940, France was still the major patron of Poland's exiled forces. French military officials in the Levant took charge of the new arrivals and escorted them to a base camp at Homs in Syria. By March 1940, the Brigade had received its name, had organised its subdivisions, and had attracted about 3,500 officers and men. It was not a force to be belittled.

Designed along the lines of the *Chasseurs Alpins*, which specialised in mountain warfare, it was composed of two infantry regiments (of two battalions each) plus regiments of artillery, reconnaissance, signals and engineers. As new recruits arrived, numbers rose; the aim was to reach the standard size of a division in the *Armée du Levant* of 208 officers and 6,840 men.

SYRIA IN 1940, like Syria today, was a hotch-potch of variegated ethnic groups and religions. The French solution to the considerable problem of governing it was to create half-a-dozen sub-states with far-reaching autonomy, and to control the whole through a Governor and military garrison based in Damascus. Lebanon was one of Syria's sub-states. Homs was a city in the interior known for its cotton industry and for the nearby crusader castle of Krak des Chevaliers.

The French Governorate of Lebanon was run by a local government which became strongly separatist after the fall of France, and which in 1943 was to declare the country independ-

CARPATHIAN BRIGADE in pith helmets disembark at Alexandria.

ent, creating the Lebanese Republic that has survived to the present. Its population was dominated by Maronite Arab Christians, who looked to the 4th century hermit Maron as their founder, and who formed a uniate branch of the Catholic Church. The main city of Lebanon, Beirut, was a prosperous seaport and tourist attraction, the 'Paris of the Middle East', which acted as the international banking centre for nearby oil rich states. Its seaside 'corniche', its elegant boulevards and delightful parks made for pleasant living, and from 1939 it was the place where friends, families and hangers-on of the soldiers of the Carpathian Brigade were naturally concentrated.

In the summer of 1940, however, when France's fall pushed Lebanon towards independence, the French Governor of Syria opted to support the Vichy regime. Thereupon, the exiled Polish government ordered Colonel Kopański to march his men out of Syria, and to take refuge in neighbouring British-ruled Palestine. In this way, the Carpathian Brigade found itself serving under British command in a region where Britain's supremacy was soon to be challenged by the Axis Powers. It was thereon separated from the greater part of its civilian dependants.

The origins of the North African Campaign lay in Mussolini's ill-advised declaration of war on Britain in November 1940. The Italian dictator wished to make a gesture of solidarity with Nazi Germany, whose Luftwaffe had recently failed, thanks in part to significant Polish opposition, to win the Battle of Britain. He also had dreams of expanding his African empire by sending an expedition into British Egypt from Libya. He and his advisers were well aware that nothing would gain him greater credit with Hitler than the conquest of the Suez Canal.

THE OPENING SHOTS of the campaign were fired in minor skirmishes between British and Italian forces on the border of Egypt and Libya. But as the fighting intensified, Britain strengthened its VIII Army in Egypt while the Italians called for assistance from their German allies. To begin with, the neighbouring French colonies of Tunisia and Algeria remained loyal to the Vichy regime, and hence favourable to the Axis. But after the Royal Navy sank the French fleet at Mers-el-Kébir (3 July 1940) and the Free French took control of Tunisia, the conflict widened, and neither side could claim victory until the entire length of the North African coast was secured. In this situation, the German High Command decided to despatch the *Afrikakorps* of Lt Gen. Erwin Rommel to act as the armoured spearhead of the Axis forces.

During this period, the Carpathian Brigade, based at Latrun in Palestine, was gradually expanding until its establishment reached 5,000 men. It could not be used in the Libyan campaign, because Poland had not declared war against Italy. So several units of the Brigade were sent to Egypt, where they guarded POW

RIFLEMAN with MG34 gun.

VEHICLE MARKS of the Carpathian Brigade.

camps and strengthened the fortifications of Alexandria. It was then given the full name of the Independent Polish Carpathian Brigade. After the German invasion of Yugoslavia and Greece in April 1941, the Brigade was despatched to the port of Haifa, expecting to sail for the Balkans. But developments overtook plans. By overrunning Greece so quickly, the Germans eliminated the possibility of the Brigade's despatch to the Balkans. At the same time, by sending the *Afrikakorps* to Libya, they facilitated the Brigade's despatch to North Africa alongside British forces.

The British VIII Army, to which General Anders would later be attached, was one of the most extraordinary and colourful amalgams of modern military history. Although always commanded by senior British officers, its constituent elements were drawn from various parts of the British Empire and of German-occupied Europe. It was called the 'Eighth Army' as an act of bravado, there having been seven French armies in the region, but only one small British Expeditionary Force. At its birth in September, it was commanded by Lt Gen. Sir Alan Cunningham, and consisted of two Army Corps, the XXX and XIII, the 7th British Armoured Division, the 1st South African Infantry Division, and the 22nd Guards Brigade. The XIII Army Corps, with which the Poles would have

GENERAL SIKORSKI'S visit (above).

WATERTANK WITH inscriptions: Acqua potabile, Trinkenwasser, Water point, Woda do picia.

AUSTRALIAN 'DIGGER' with pet dog (right).

SAHARA SCENES.

GENERAL STANISŁAW Kopański.

MEDALLION OF THE 'RATS of Tobruk'.

much to do, consisted of the 4th Indian Infantry Division, the 2nd New Zealand Division, and the 1st Army Tank Brigade.

THE NORTH AFRICAN CAMPAIGN was characterised by a series of rapid movements back and forth along the Mediterranean coast through what the British called 'The Western Desert'. When Axis forces held the advantage, they drove the British eastwards into Egypt; when the British gained the upper hand, they drove the Germans and Italians back westwards through Libya. The SBSK made its entrance in August 1941 to strengthen the defences of the outpost of Tobruk, which had earlier been captured by Australian forces. Tobruk was an isolated port on the Libyan coast which was essential for the purpose of seaborne Allied supplies, and which had been outflanked by the latest

AUSTRALIAN LIGHT gun at the front line (above).

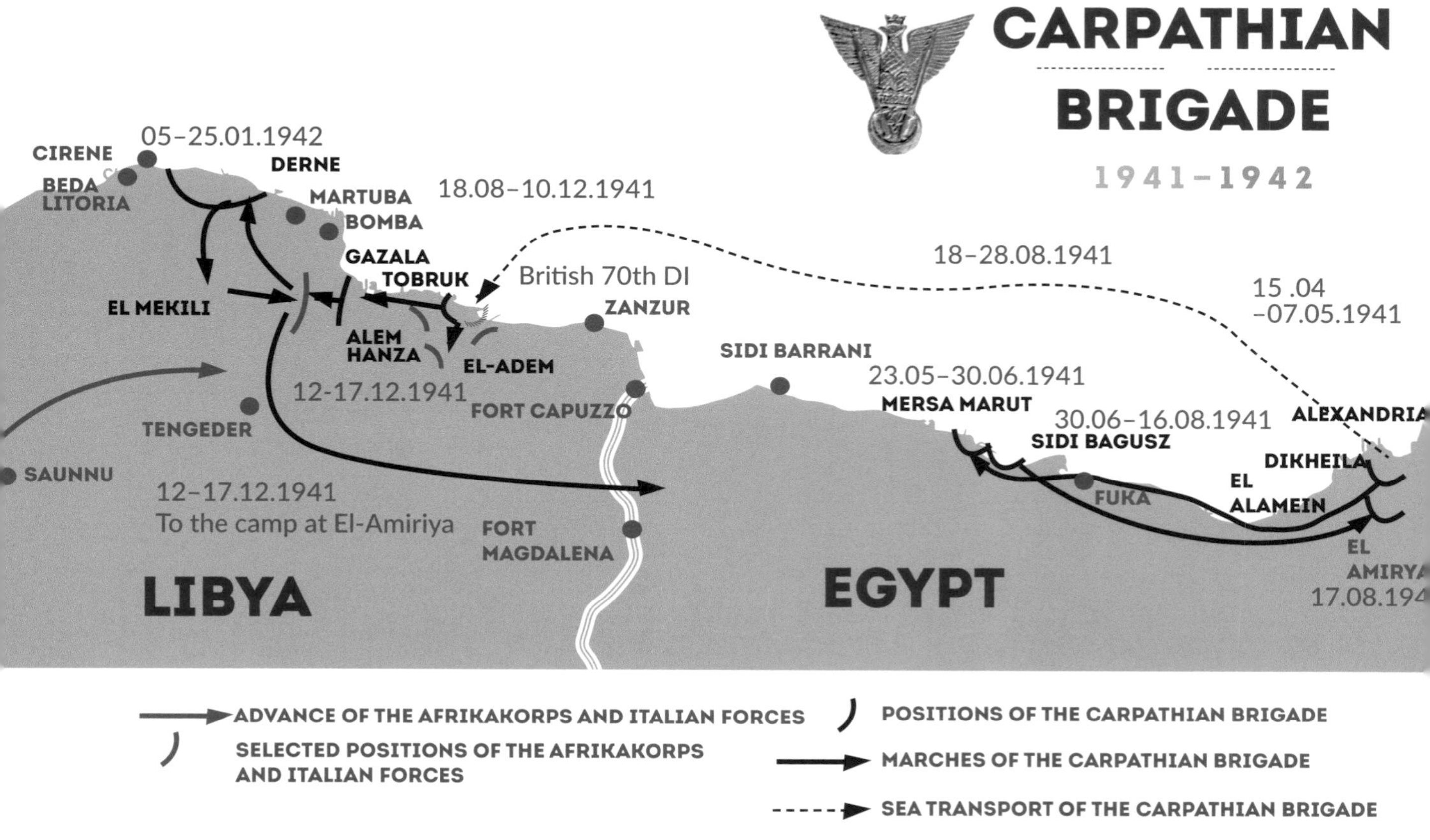

AXIS PRISONERS brought in.

Axis advance. In all, the siege lasted 241 days. The Poles were landed in the company of the 11th Czechoslovak Infantry Battalion at a point when the Australian Government had insisted that its exhausted 9th Division be withdrawn. They held out gallantly, fighting alongside their British, Czech and Australian allies until 7 December, when Rommel was forced to withdraw.

In all, the 'Rats of Tobruk' sustained 3,894 casualties, mainly Australian. They adopted their name after Berlin Radio announced that they were caught 'like rats in a trap'; they called the Royal Navy supply force, 'the Scrap Iron Flotilla' because Berlin had described it as 'a load of scrap iron'. The Australians fashioned Tobruk Medals, bearing the image of a rat, from the bodywork of German planes shot down by captured German guns. Their 'Rats of Tobruk Association' was for decades a motor of Polish–Australian friendship.

After Tobruk, most of the Brigade was attached to the British XIII Corps, with which it participated in fighting, both advances and retreats, round the Axis' Gazala Line. It was withdrawn on March 2.

The Siege of Tobruk coincided with the most intensive phase of the Siege of Malta. In May 1941, Rommel declared that 'without the capture of Malta, the Axis will end by losing North Africa'. As a result, the island was subject to more than 3,000 German air raids launched from southern Italy. But it held out. By the end of 1942, following the victory of El Alamein, the eastern Mediterranean had been secured by the Allies; the centre of gravity of the North African campaign moved to the western Mediterranean; the *Afrikakorps* had been eliminated; and the *Wehrmacht* was placing its hopes on success on the Eastern Front.

During its service in North Africa, the SBSK's *ordre de bataille* consisted of eight elements:

· **HQ Staff:** Gen. Stanisław Kopański (commander)
· **Chief-of-Staff,**
Lt Col. Jerzy Zaremba
Quartermaster + services + Intelligence
· **1st Battalion, Carpathian Rifles**
(Lt Col. Stanisław Kopeć)
· **2nd Battalion, Carpathian Rifles**
(Maj. Antoni Michalik)
· **3rd Battalion, Carpathian Rifles**
(Lt Col. Józef Sokół)
· **Carpathian Artillery Regiment**
(Lt Col. Stanisław Gliwicz)
· **Carpathian Anti-tank Artillery Battalion**
(Lt Col. Antoni Cieszkowski)
· **Carpathian Uhlans Regiment**
(Maj. Władysław Bobiński).[92]

From Libya, the Brigade moved back to Palestine to await further orders.

JERUSALEM

JERUSALEM, VISITED by the Carpathian Brigade in 1941–1942. Church of the Holy Sepulchre (left), Grotto of the Virgin's Dormition (right), the Dome of the Rock (bottom left), sacred to Muslims; *nota bene* the Western Wailing Wall (right), sacred to Jews.

8

CHAPTER

1941–1943

IRAQ

CHAPTER 8

1941–1943

IRAQ

ANDERS' MOVE TO IRAQ WAS PLANNED FOR THE EARLY MONTHS OF 1943, WHILE THE GERMAN THREAT TO THE MIDDLE EAST WAS STILL RATED HIGHLY; AND IT WAS THE NATURAL PRODUCT OF ALLIED DISPOSITIONS IN POWNALL'S PAI REGION.

The move had been confirmed in the latter part of 1942. The British were holding Baghdad with divisions from the Indian Army, and the Iranian oilfields around Abadan with British and Australian troops. The Americans confined themselves to the Persian Corridor. The Soviets were holding the Caucasus and Iranian Azerbaijan with light formations drawn from the region, but would not have willingly invited Poles to Baku. But the oilfields of northern Iraq were unguarded. So Anders was directed to northern Iraq with HQ at Kirkuk. Pownall envisaged his own arrival for an inspection for 3 May 1943, the Polish National Day.

Iraq in 1943 was nominally a sovereign state, which had emerged 20 years earlier from the British Mandate of Mesopotamia and the break-up of the Ottoman Empire. But its monarch, King Faisal II, a relative of the Kings of Jordan, was a British placeman, who had rewarded his patrons by granting them control of the country's security forces. The British, in fact, never left and regarded their Mesopotamian prize as a protectorate of their interests in the Gulf. As the Americans were to discover to their cost at the start of the 21st century, there is not, and was not any such thing as 'an Iraqi nation'. All there was were three disparate, former Ottoman provinces. The province of Mosul in the north, to which Kirkuk belonged, was inhabited largely by Kurds. The province of Basra in the south was inhabited by Shias and Marsh Arabs. The province of Baghdad in the centre was dominated by Sunni Arabs, who, as allies of the Ottoman Sultan, had traditionally ruled over all the others.

THE KURDS, with whom the Polish Army came into contact, formed part of a large ethnic group that was not Turkic, Iranian or Arab. Some 30 million strong, they were the largest such group in the Middle East that had never gained its own state. Instead, their lands were partitioned between Turkey, Iran and Iraq, turning them, like the Poles of the 19th century, into a stateless nation. It would be interesting to know, if any of their Polish guests recognised the similarities.

Iraq's oilfields were grouped in two distinct locations, one in the north-east of the country, the other in the south-east. The former stretched from Mosul and Kirkuk virtually to Baghdad. The latter centred on Basra on the Gulf coast, and geologically belonged to the same basin as Kuwait and Iranian Abadan. The south was well guarded by British and Indian troops, so it was in the North that the Poles were deployed.

The Polish forces in Iraq were distributed over a wide range of localities. Anders established his initial headquarters at Quizil Ribat,

BABYLONIAN LION, 6th Century BC. Part of the original Ishtar Gate from ancient Babylon on display at the Berlin Pergamon Museum.

200 miles to the north-east of Baghdad. A large transit camp stood adjacent to the Iranian border, slightly further north. The base at Mosul lay close to the Turkish frontier. Other centres were at Habbaniyah on the Euphrates near Fallujah in central Iraq, at Qayyarah near Nineveh in Kurdistan, and at Jalawla. Baghdad became the hub for administrative and liaison services.

Polish troops travelling from Iran were usually sent to the transit camp at Khanakin (Hanakin), some 10 or 15 miles beyond the frontier. Dressed in their British uniforms, they passed the dusty frontier post without stopping, and with no questions asked. Rolling through a nondescript town patrolled by British military police, and crossing a rickety bridge over the River Diyala, they saw the plain of the Tigris stretching into the distance. It was as though they were entering the legendary biblical Garden of Eden:

> "What a pleasant surprise we had on arriving at Camp Khanaqin. Everything was ready for us. Two rows of perfectly aligned new tents.

LT GEN. SIR HENRY POWNALL, OC Persia and Iraq; Anders immediate superior, 1943.

FAISAL II, the boy king of Iraq reads an illustrated Polish newspaper *Parada*.

PARADE BEFORE the Duke of Gloucester, Naft-i-Shah.

MOTORCYCLISTS in the desert.

A kitchen with walls of mats made of plaited rushes and roof of corrugated iron. Even piped water. We were not surprised at that luxury. England, we thought, is so rich, it can do anything. What did impress us was the latrine. Screened by a five-foot high burlap fence, the long and narrow septic ditch was covered with rough planks with a row of a dozen square holes cut in them. Each hole had a wooden flap cover with rawhide hinges and a strap for lifting it. A bucket full of quick-lime stood in one corner of the enclosure and sheaves of toilet paper were nailed to the fence posts. Primitive, we would say now, but after the horrid prison and army latrines in Russia it had an air of foppishness. And, perhaps because of the dry desert heat, it didn't stink.

We marvelled at our tents. They were brand new, made in India of hemp canvas and designed for a hot climate. The entrance flaps in front and back could be flung open wide or laced tight. Stitched to the underside of the roof were straps for suspending individual mosquito nets. A second canvas roof hung about a foot above the tent's main roof. It was larger than the roof below and its overhang kept the walls of the tent in shade."[93]

THOUGH THE IRAQI SUMMER was burning hot, the changing seasons brought marked changes in the weather:

"The winter months in Iraq – fraught with rains, winds, cloudy skies – brought abrupt jumps in temperatures. By December we had already changed our shorts and tropical shirts for woollen battledresses and leather jerkins with felt linings. As nights and some days became colder, we were issued lambskin vests. Even they weren't warm enough for guards on night duty. They wore ankle-length sheepskin coats. Sometimes a thin layer of ice would form overnight on the drinking water in our clay jars. Each soldier was issued with eight blankets. We were still sleeping on the ground inside our tents. To conserve body heat dur-

GEN. ANDERS hands over the standard of the 5th Kresowa Infantry Division to Col. Nikodem Sulik.

"HERE, NEAR Baghdad, under the sun's burning rays, on the desert sand on 19 October 1942, the life of the II Polish Army Artillery Group begins."

ing the chilly nights, we had about as many blankets under us as over us and we needed them all. The mornings were cool and misty. However, by ten o'clock we would sweat even in shirt sleeves.

But wintertime brought one bonus for us in this harsh foreign land. We were delighted to see our old friends from Poland, the starlings. The Germans couldn't stop them from seeking freedom. They would land, sit down, and chatter at us for a while before flying off to continue their journey. The birds' tidings were the only news we heard from home. It made us long for the green forests and fields of Poland. The starlings would go back in the spring. But would we?

TWICE WE HAD TORRENTIAL RAIN. Sheets of water came down from low-lying clouds. The deluge produced streams of water everywhere. These joined to create fast-flowing muddy rivers and small lakes. Tents tumbled. It was hard not to think that we were living in the land of the biblical Flood. But a couple of hours after the rain stopped, the ground was bone dry again and our blankets as well."[94]

Though the Polish Army was stationed in Iraq to boost British reserves in the event of a German invasion, there was no defending to be done since no German attack materialised. The Poles dug in, fortified their positions, and practised their defensive routines. But it was essential that they used their time more profitably. Three priorities soon emerged: the three 'M's: merger, motorisation and mechanisation.

The merger that had been long on the cards was with the Carpathian Brigade, which was kicking its heels in Palestine. The Brigade moved to Iraq to be split up and cannibalised; its constituent units were distributed round under-strength elements, before it ceased to exist in March 1943. In its place, there arose a first-class division, the 3rd Carpathian Rifles under their new commander, General Bolesław Duch. The Army as a whole benefited hugely from the injection of trained and experienced officers, whose presence was felt at every level and in all the services. One quarter of the Carpathian Brigade's personnel were university graduates – an unusually high proportion – they possessed the intellectual and cultural potential which all good officer training schemes desire.

The make-up of the 3rd Carpathian Rifles mirrored the British as opposed to the Soviet model of military organisation, which had prevailed in the first year of the Army's existence. Its complement embraced three main frontline services – cavalry, infantry, and artillery, and a wide range of support services. (Heavy armoured formations were organised separately.) Every soldier wore the division's emblem: a shield bearing a deep green cedar of Lebanon emblazoned on the white-and-red Polish flag (below).

Full motorisation had not been a feature of the Polish Army in 1939, but was now considered essential. An Army of 80,000 men required a lorry-park of 15,000–20,000 vehicles.

3RD CARPATHIAN RIFLE DIVISION

Brigade	Sub-units
1st Carpathian Rifle Brigade	1st Rifle Battalion 2nd Rifle Battalion 3rd Rifle Battalion
2nd Carpathian Rifle Brigade	4th Rifle Battalion 5th Rifle Battalion 6th Rifle Battalion
3 Carpathian Rifle Brigade *(from 1945)*	7th Rifle Battalion 8th Rifle Battalion 9th Rifle Battalion
Reconnaissance Units (one of these)	3rd Carpathian Cavalry Regiment 12th Podolian Cavalry Regiment 7th Lublin Cavalry Regiment
Artillery units	1st Carpathian Field Artillery Regiment 2nd Carpathian Field Artillery Regiment 3rd Carpathian Field Artillery Regiment 3rd Carpathian Anti-tank Artillery Regiment 3rd Carpathian Light Anti-aircraft Artillery Regiment
Support Units	3rd Carpathian Medium Machine Gun Battalion 3rd Carpathian Engineers Battalion 3rd Carpathian Signals Battalion
Rear Units	military police, court martial, military hospital, front hospitals, logistics unit, transport battalions and such

ANDERS ARMY IN IRAQ

An important step was taken, therefore, when the Army was motorised following delivery of a fleet of trucks, staff-cars, and motor-bikes. Driving lessons had to be provided for 20,000 drivers, and technical courses for mechanics. More than one British officer commented on the reckless, devil-may-care style of Polish drivers, and General Pownall commented sourly on the cost of replacing damaged clutches and gearboxes. The mechanics learned the mysteries of the magnificent Leyland engines with enthusiasm.

This is the point where the Polish Women's Auxiliary Service (PSK) came into prominence. Before Iraq, these women soldiers, commonly referred to by their acronym as *pestki*, 'apple pips', had been channelled into traditional nursing, administrative or even menial domestic roles as cooks and cleaners. But now the PSK supplied a pool of about 5,000 drivers, the celebrated *drajwerki*, who were to make a strong impression, both in the Arab countries and in Italy.

Mechanisation in the form of tanks and armoured cars featured strongly in the modern army. In this respect, special attention was paid to the cavalry regiments whose role in modern warfare was changing fast. Pownall suggested that Anders, who was an experienced cavalryman, take personal charge and instruct them in up-to-date reconnaissance techniques. Hints were dropped that the 12th Podolian Lancers, in particular, were not up to scratch. (Two years later, it was men from the 12th Lancers who first raised the Polish flag on the ruins of Monte Cassino.)

For the first time, the Army also received a full complement of light and heavy weapons. Infantrymen had to be familiarised with standard British rifles and submachine guns, and artillerymen had to be trained in the deployment, observation, and firing techniques of British guns. General Pownall insisted on the use of British Army manuals, all of which had to be translated and studied.

Pownall's correspondence stressed that the quality of officers was key to success in training. The implication was that too many Polish officers were unable to adapt to their new tasks. Yet Anders needed no lectures on this point. The Army was still suffering from the drastic consequences of the Katyń massacres and by the inevitable advancement to officer rank of poorly qualified substitutes. Up

IRAQ

KURDISTAN (NORTHERN Iraq), land of the ancient Assyrians and of the biblical Garden of Eden. Anders' Army was stationed there in 1942–1943, protecting the Iraqi oilfields from the Germans.

THE RAWANDUZ Canyon in Kurdistan (top).

CLAY TABLET with cuneiform writing (above), invented around 3500 BC and used in Mesopotamia for three millennia.

EARTHLY PARADISE, a print by Lucas Cranach the Elder (16th century) (far right).

ZAKHO, ZAXO in Kurdish (above), northernmost Iraqi town, once known as the 'Assyrian Jerusalem' owing to a sizable Jewish population.

THE CITADEL in Erbil, Hawler in Kurdish (centre bottom), the capital of Kurdistan said by its inhabitants to be "the oldest living city in the world".

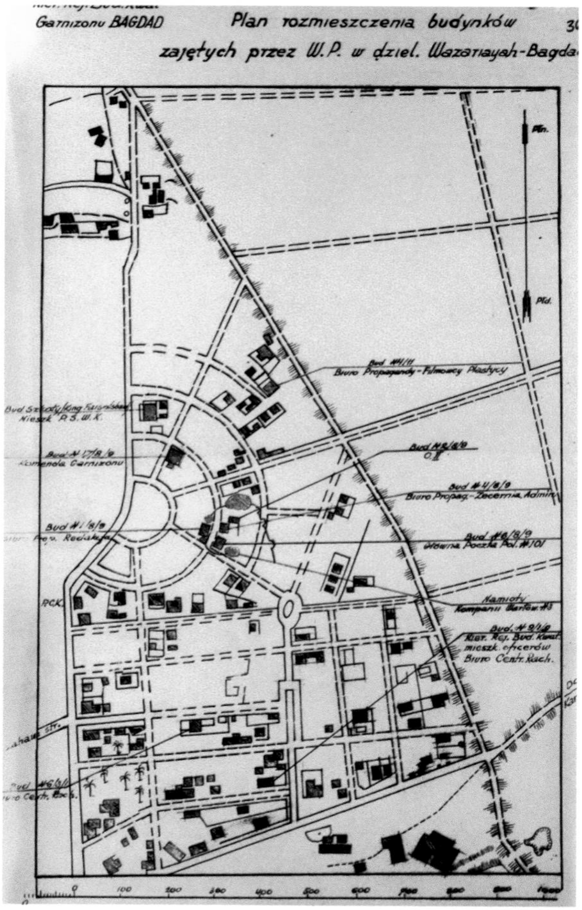

BAGHDAD (2015).

STREET PLAN of Polish HQ in Baghdad.

to 1,000 officers had to be retired, or transferred to clerical duties, and every effort was made to accelerate officer training, and to promote the cadets.

Army life in Iraq was inevitably dominated by extensive and systematic training. Since the German enemy never actually approached Iraq, the troops were kept busy by physical exercises and by numerous courses on military theory and practice. These courses frequently followed the principle of 'Know Your Enemy', and included lessons on the traditions, regulations, and equipment of the *Wehrmacht*:

"OUR CLASSES were held either in the shade of trees or in the army Nissen huts... The lecture area under the trees was laid out with replicas of German trenches, fox-holes, gun emplacements, and other battle devices brought from the Libyan Desert after the German retreat there. And we learned about Germany's astounding new weapons. Artillery pieces with a range greater than anything the Allies had. Six-barrelled *Nebelwerfer* mortars. Their radios, field telephones and even telephone cables, all of them weighing a fraction of those manufactured by the British or the Americans. We admired the German machine gun *Spandau*, known to us at that time as *Solothurn* because its prototype was designed in the Swiss town of Solothurn. Its firing rate was treble that of the outdated British Bren gun that was also of foreign design and was named for the arms factory in Brno, Czechoslovakia.

It is only now that I appreciate how superior the German weaponry was. The new German Tiger tank had not yet appeared on the battlefields but on that course in Baghdad we were given detailed pictures of it, its new gun, the thickness of its armour, and so on. It is clear that by early 1943 the Allies were already fully aware of the Tiger's existence and of its quality, yet had not produced either

BAGHDAD, SHIA
shrine of Musa Al-Khadim (1943).

a tank or an anti-tank gun that could cope with it when it rolled onto the battlefield. My friends from the armoured units told me that, till the end of the war, American and British tanks were no match for the German panzers. They said that you could dent the armour plates of a Sherman tank with a hammer. And a shell fired from a standard German 88mm anti-tank gun would go through a Sherman and out the other side."[95]

Soldiers from the Signal Corps, who were being trained to intercept German communications, needed a high level of familiarity with the *Wehrmacht's* rules and procedures:

"We were given reams of papers and reports to study. We had to learn everything about German documents, orders, pay-books, and instructions. I still remember an instruction to German soldiers in the *Africakorps* warning them about venereal diseases. It went something like this: "*Nur der freigegebene Bordel darfst du besuchen. Benutze dabei ein Kondom als meinst Frauen sind geschlechtkrank* ..." (You may only visit the brothels freely attached to the army units. Use a condom because most of the women have venereal diseases).

The German I had learned in high school from Mrs Geller, an excellent teacher, stood me in good stead, but she had not taught us phrases like that. I enjoyed improving my German and found the whole course fascinating."[96]

Visiting Baghdad on a 24-hour pass, Polish soldiers found that they were besieged by the same temptations that beset the soldiers of *Wehrmacht*:

"The happy cabdriver took us across the long iron bridge over the Tigris river to the

" Why don't you hire my camel to go back to Poland." Polish soldiers in the Near East

POSTCARD PUBLISHED in Iraq. "Why don't you hire my camel to go back to Poland."

ZAKRZEWSKI

"**MIECZYSLAW ZAKRZEWSKI** (1911–1999), professional army officer, one of some 500 officers sent from Britain via Murmansk, to join Anders' Army in Central Asia (5th Infantry Division). A keen amateur photographer, he travelled to Russia with his indefatigable Dollina camera and an extraordinary stock of film. He took more than 3,000 photographs in half a dozen countries."

part of the city forbidden to Allied soldiers. After a short ride through the winding streets, he stopped in front of a jolly villa with a courtyard surrounded by palms. A plump madam ushered us into a salon that was sparsely furnished and had a high ceiling with two large electric fans. There she introduced us to her four equally plump charges. They were clad in heavy jewellery and high-heeled shoes. Sekunda, though only a few years older than me, liked to play the old *roué*. Without hesitation he selected madam herself. She acknowledged his choice with a nod and an approving smile, as if saying 'That guy knows what he wants and what's good for him.' They trotted upstairs, followed by Majewski with another *hanum* (girl) in tow. I chose a very pretty Arab *bibi*. She was much younger than me but she treated me with condescension... She knew that she was good-looking and gave me an eyeful of her physical attributes. Our lovemaking session was brief. But I managed to stay with her longer by asking her for Arabic words for parts of the body and things around the room. We even had a smoke together – my cigarettes, of course. So when I returned with her to the salon, I sighed with relief when I saw Sekunda and Majewski already there. I was afraid that I'd be the first one back.

THE MADAM treated us to a glass of cloudy *arak* and a string of superlatives in rudimentary English with an admixture of some startling Polish words (obviously we were not her first Polish customers) referring to our alleged masculine prowess and gentlemanly behaviour. She implored us to come back to her establishment again. We understood only the gist of her valediction. But then she asked for double the fee we had agreed on... It cost too much. More than a tenth of my monthly pay."[98]

A soldier's life in an isolated desert camp could often be boring, not to say downright depressing. But from time to time a minor sensation could break the boredom:

"Our beloved Commander-in-Chief, General Władysław Anders, had left the Soviet Union with us and, from time to time, made the rounds of our camps. During one of his visits a garage mechanic, wearing his greasy overalls and bedraggled running shoes, came up to him in the desert with a complaint. Anders said, 'Yes, my son.' and heard him out. The mechanic wanted permission to see his wife who was now in Tehran. He hadn't seen her for two years, but every time he asked for spousal leave, it had been denied. Anders asked him 'Aren't you afraid to appear before your Commander-in-Chief in dirty clothes?' The mechanic drew himself up to his full height and pushed his chest up. 'A Polish soldier is afraid of no one, Sir. Not even the devil himself.'

'Well spoken, soldier,' Anders replied, and he told him to tell his officers that their General said they were to grant him leave to see his wife."[98]

On another, later occasion, when General Anders visited the same company, a young cadet was ordered to propose a vote of thanks:

"While Anders was winding up his speech, I was preparing mine in my head. I recalled how my mother told us about a wonderful speech my father had given at the farewell

ARMY GYMNASTS in Hanaqin (opposite top).

SHIA SHRINE of Musa al-Khadim in Baghdad (opposite bottom).

THE RIVER Tigris in Baghdad (left).

DESERT DANCING (below).

dinner for a faculty friend and how well it had been received. He had used a Latin quotation from Horace's most famous poem in his *Carmina* (The Odes) :

Exegi monumentum aere perennius
regalique situ pyramidum altius.

I opened my brief speech to the General on behalf of the assembled students, saying 'Through you we have regained our lives. Our lives are now here for you.' Then I quoted Horace, not in Latin (although I knew it by heart), but in a slightly modified Polish translation.

'To Poland we shall erect a monument higher than the pyramids and harder than granite— a monument of glory.'

General Anders then shook my hand while Maliniak, the hunchback photographer from our public relations unit, snapped a picture."[99]

SHORTLY BEFORE ANDERS and his Army were fully installed in Iraq, they were hit by a political bombshell. The USSR had broken diplomatic relations with the exiled Polish government, to which they owed allegiance. They felt fortunate to have passed beyond the grasp of

Stalin's agents, but they were under no illusion — thousands of friends and compatriots left behind would now suffer repression.

The cause of the diplomatic rupture lay in the Polish government's perfectly reasonable reaction to recent revelations of the Katyń massacres. The Germans, having discovered the corpses of some 3,500 murdered Polish officers in the Katyń Forest near Smoleńsk, declared that the NKVD was the author of the crime. The Soviets responded by declaring that it was all the work of the Nazi SS. The Polish government, under great pressure from its British hosts not to state publicly what it knew to be the truth, referred the matter to the International Red Cross in Geneva. Stalin reacted with fury. Not only did he break off relations, with the help of the worldwide Communist movement, he launched a raucous propaganda campaign against all, especially the Poles, who did not accept the Kremlin's mendacious version of events.

In Britain, Soviet propaganda was believed, and was routinely backed by the War Censorship. The British press did not simply point the finger of blame at the Nazis; with few exceptions it repeated Moscow's slurs against the Poles who

NAH-I-SHAH, MINI-MEMORIAL to Polish soldiers.

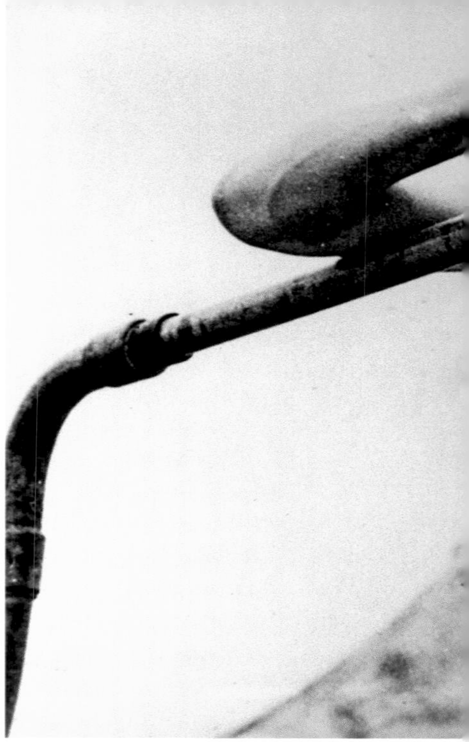

JUNACY

OFFICER CADETS aged 14 to 18 ('Junacy') formed an essential part of the military machine; each expected to be commissioned as soon as he graduated. Owing to the shortage of officers in the 'Anders Army' they were given special priority. After brief stays in Iran or Iraq, they were mainly transferred to schools in Palestine. Some of the older boys, like Alexander Topolski, graduated in time to serve in the Italian campaign; others did not graduate until after the war. Eating (top left), drinking (centre) reading (top right), praying (bottom left), and visiting an air base (bottom right). The War Censor did not permit the name of the air base in this official photo to be published.

BIBLIOTEKA

POLAND
POLAND
POLAND

STAGE DESIGNING for the Army Theatre in Iraq (above).

NEWSPAPER EDITORS (top right).

THE ARMY'S orchestra (opposite).

were painted as 'Fascists', 'Nazi sympathisers', 'poor allies', 'cowards, who feared to fight', and 'anti-Semites'. The British Communist Party, which was never banned, fanned the flames in organs of the military press; soldiers and officials who dared to speak ill of the Soviet ally were threatened with punishment.

The British, like the Americans, viewed the Second World War in somewhat naive, simplistic, and self-righteous terms; and they were strongly influenced by memories of the Great War of 1914–1918, in which the Tsar had been a prominent ally. They convinced themselves they were fighting a 'Good War' and that Adolf Hitler was the embodiment of incomparable evil. In essence, Germany was the enemy, and Russia a traditional friend. True enough, they might say, Stalin had deviated from the right path during the currency of the Nazi–Soviet Pact; but since 1941, he had returned to the fold and was proving his worth as a staunch fighter 'for the Good'. In the climate set by Stalingrad, most Westerners found it impossible to believe that their ally ran concentration camps, committed mass crimes, or operated a totalitarian dictatorship. They discounted stories about 'Stalin's victims'. In their narrow view,

the only victims of the war were people who had been maltreated by the German enemy.

When Anders and Pownall met in Baghdad, therefore, the atmosphere was tense. It was May 1943, and Anders had been personally denounced by Soviet Commissar Andrei Vyshinsky as a 'renegade' and a 'deserter', who had run away from action on the Eastern Front. Pownall, for his part, had sent instructions to his Polish subordinates ordering them "to keep calm" and "to refrain from all criticism" of the USSR. Anders would later challenge the minutes of this meeting from which all references to the facts of the case (as presented by Anders) had been cynically omitted.[100]

Yet worse was to follow. Defamatory smears about Anders' character and the presumed 'ill discipline' of his troops began to circulate not just in the press but in official reports, as if they were established fact. Anders wrote to the British War Office to protest. But the reigning misconceptions about the Soviet Union were too strong. The assessment of Anders by the British Foreign Office characterised him as "a gallant but truculent soldier with a high view of Poland's status... and little respect for some of the realities of modern world politics".[101] By 'the realities of world politics', the Foreign Office was using weasel words to camouflage its fawning deference to Stalin. As later became obvious, Anders' British superiors were wrong, and Anders was right. *Cześć Jego Pamięci!* (Hail to his memory!)

To cap it all, Anders was laid low by malaria. He was wracked by fever at the time when the insults about him and his army were at their height. This was the nadir of his military career. He can only have been relieved when he received orders to move on.

IN THAT SUMMER OF 1943, the strategic prospects for the Middle East clarified. The possibility of a German advance into the region evaporated. The *Afrikakorps* had been driven out of Africa. The Red Army was advancing along wide sectors of the Eastern Front. And in July Anglo-American forces landed in Sicily at the start of a hard-fought campaign against Fascist Italy. The presence of a Polish Army in northern Iraq no longer made sense, and its transfer to the Mediterranean theatre became a matter of urgency.

CHAPTER

9

WHO WERE THE *ANDERSOWCY*?

CHAPTER 9

WHO WERE THE ANDERSOWCY?

ALMOST ALL GENERAL DESCRIPTIONS OF THE ANDERS ARMY DESCRIBE ITS MEMBERS AS 'POLES' – WHICH SOUNDS LOGICAL.

The 'Polish Army in the USSR', as it was originally named, was made up of 'Poles': Poles who had been sentenced to the Gulag; Poles who had been deported to the USSR from eastern Poland; Poles who had benefited from the Amnesty of 1941. In this context, the term 'Pole' means 'citizen of the Polish Republic'. According to Polish law, Polish citizens alone were permitted to serve in a Polish Army.

If one looks a bit closer, however, one finds that Anders' soldiers were very varied in their ethnic, religious, social, and political make-up. They were all Polish citizens, but they were by no means a homogenous group of people; they were a cross-section of the 37–38 million who lived in prewar Poland.

THE QUESTION OF NATIONALITY, for example, was highly complex, and, because the Soviets had their own criteria for determining it, very important. Not without reason, Soviet law distinguished 'nationality' from 'citizenship'. According to the NKVD, no-one could claim to be a Polish national if Polish were not their native language or if Roman Catholicism were not their religious denomination. In this, the NKVD agreed very closely with prewar Polish nationalists, who had promoted the dubious concept of *Polakatolik*, and who loudly proclaimed the slogan of "Poland for the Poles". (It is no accident that at the end of war, when the NKVD created a People's Poland in its own image, it was a new sort of Poland shorn of all national minorities.) The make-up and flavour of the Anders Army owed much to the character of the Kresy, whence most of its men originated, and differed significantly both from the Berling Army and from the army of post-war Poland.

Many of the Polish citizens who joined Anders did not meet the criteria of *Polakatolik* or so-called *Prawdziwy Polak* (Real Pole). Anders himself, who came from a Protestant family of Baltic German origin, was a clear case in point. (In London, after the war, he was driven to such fury by nationalists, who constantly repeated the slur that he was 'not a Pole', that he took them to court and won his suit for libel.) Anders belonged to the same multinational tradition as Marshal Piłsudski, who was born in Lithuania and who regarded loyalty to the traditions of the old Commonwealth as the sole test of nationality. He, like many, followed the lead of the greatest of Polish poets, Adam Mickiewicz, who opens his epic *Pan Tadeusz* with an invocation, not to Poland, but to *"Litwo, ojczyzno moja"* (Lithuania, my fatherland). There was a whole division of such 'Poles' from 'Litwa' in the Anders Army.

PORTRAIT OF GENERAL ANDERS from the Anders Room, Sikorski Museum, Kensington, London.

The Army equally possessed a contingent of Lithuanian-speaking Lithuanians, who came together at Buzuluk and who formed their own battalion. They sang Lithuanian songs, and carried their own yellow-green-red *proporczyk* or standard.

Ukrainians formed the largest national minority in prewar Poland, about 15 per cent of the population, and belonged to a category which the NKVD had sought to exclude. Many of them were conscripts from 1939, who had spent the next two years in Soviet POW camps, and many, especially from East Galicia, were bilingual, had attended a Polish school, or were the product of mixed Polish–Ukrainian marriages. They would not have had too much difficulty in registering themselves as 'Poles', as 'Roman Catholics', or sometimes as *Lemkos, Bojkos* or *Hutsuls*. "No, sir," they might say, "I am not a Ukrainian, but a Ruthenian." They were predominantly Greek Catholic by religion.

It is difficult, however, to calculate their exact numbers. Estimates vary from 5,000 to a grossly exaggerated 20,000. Many Ukrainian recruits declared themselves to be Poles in order to be accepted, and then never bothered to clarify their status. None of them rose to senior positions in the Army, though they were clearly present in strength in the ranks, as evidenced by their gravestones in military cemeteries. But even the gravestones can be misleading. One can meet with complaints that Ukrainian first names were polonised – Mikhailo being changed to Michał, for instance – thereby effacing the soldier's true identity.

Information on the subject can be sought from the Association of Ukrainians in Great

GREEK CATHOLIC Bishop of Lublin, Sava Sovietov, formerly a chaplain of the Anders Army (top).

GREEK CATHOLIC graves, Polish Military Cemetery, Casamassima (Italy) (right).

MUSLIM AND JEWISH graves, Casamassima

Britain, which started up in 1945 as the 'Association of Ukrainians in the Polish Armed Forces'. Literature it recommended includes the memoirs of Mikola Koziy, *For Another's Cause*, published in London in two volumes in 1958–1960.[102] A peasant lad from the village of Bohdanivka in the district of Ternopil, Koziy mentions numerous other comrades-in-arms such as Corporal Teodor Daniliv, a lawyer from Buczacz; Bohdan Durbach; Yurii Yenkal; and Major Volodymyr Yaniv, a Signals officer. He also claims that the first German bunker to be captured at Monte Cassino on the morning of 12 May 1944 was stormed by a Volhynian called Mikhailo Pankivets.

The Belarussians of the Anders Army had a similarly low profile to that of the Ukrainians, although they were less numerous. They came, in the main, from the voivodships of Grodno, Nowogródek, Pińsk, and Brest.

Aliaksandar Bochka (1926–2015), later known as Father Alexander Nadson, was the best-known Belarussian to serve under General Anders. Born in the little town of Haradzieja (Polish: *Horodziej*), he was too young to have been conscripted into the Polish Army in 1939, but was drafted by the Germans in 1944, and sent to France. His subsequent career mirrored that of the future Archbishop Szczepan Wesoły. Fleeing the German service, he made his way to the II Corps in Italy early in 1945, fought at the frontline in the period before VE-Day, and was later transferred to Britain. Educated at the Greek College in Rome, he joined the Belarusian Catholic Mission in Britain, where in 1971 he opened the Francis Skaryna Library and Museum. He served for decades as the Apostolic Visitor for Belarussian Catholics Abroad.

JEWS FACED THE SAME BARRIERS as Ukrainians and Byelorussians. In the USSR, they were classified as a separate nationality, and had special problems with the NKVD. But most were well educated; many were culturally polonised, or had lost their links with Judaism. The majority came from Yiddish-speaking families, although typically were used to conversing in several languages. They possessed a wide variety of political connections, including former Piłsudskites, Zionists, and Bundists. The Zionists (i.e., Jewish nationalists) professed an ideology that was openly hostile to prewar Poland, while the Bundists (Jewish socialists) worked closely with members of the PPS for a better Poland in the future.

Surprisingly perhaps, a small group of radical Zionists enjoyed a close link with the prewar Polish Army. The late Sanacja regime concurred absolutely with the Zionist proposition that Jews should aim to live in Palestine, not Poland, and it supported schemes of Jewish emigration. In 1936–1939, the Polish Army trained thousands of Zionist volunteers, who were preparing to fight the British in Palestine. British Intelligence was alert to the existence of this group, but was not successful in blocking their recruitment.

Although the senior commander of the Army's Medical Corps, General Bronisław Szarecki, was not Jewish, the overwhelming majority of his staff were. This is not surprising, since the greatest part of the medical profession in prewar Poland was Jewish. Yet Jews could be encountered in any of the Army's branches and formations.

The more one studies Polish Jewry, the easier it becomes to realise that there was no such thing as a typical Polish Jew. By the middle of the 20th century, Jews in Poland held a range of attitudes to traditional Judaism: they professed a wide variety of political ideologies, exhibited differing degrees of assimilation, and in terms of socio-economic status, included the richest of the rich, like some of the cotton barons of Łódź, or the poorest of the poor, like the inhabitants of some of the more indigent *shtetls* of the Kresy.

By the same token, it is impossible to depict a typical Jewish soldier of the Anders Army. The archival photos which exist are peculiarly anonymous; they show young men in British battledress, smiling at the camera in a variety of nondescript settings and the captions are bland to a fault:

- Portrait of Jack Roth (Anders Army) in Como, Italy
- Group portrait of Jewish soldiers in the

RABBI PINKAS ROSENGARTEN (Jerusalem 2007) (left).

MIECZYSŁAW BIEGUN (Menachem Begin), Corporal, about 1943 (top).

FATHER ALEXANDER NADSON (formerly Aliaksandar Bochka) – Belarussian Catholic Mission, London (right).

Anders Army
- Jewish soldiers… celebrate Passover, in Como, Italy
- Dr Arthur Haber, a doctor in the Anders Army
- Studio portrait: Lance Corporal Julian Bussgang wearing the Monte Cassino Cross
- Marcus Rosenzweig playing the accordion
- Mark Frueman standing against army trucks in Egypt
- Oskar Littman with two members of his Polish army unit
- Ignac Greenbaum with two other Jewish refugees from the Soviet Union
- Chaim Lingalka… in his British Army uniform (Italy)
- Eva Litman… greeting General Anders with flowers.[103]

One remarkable ex-soldier, whom I met personally, was Edward Kossoy (1913–2012). Born in Radom, he graduated from Warsaw University's Law Faculty in 1934, and five years later, to avoid the Nazi Germans, he fled east to Lwów. There he was arrested by the NKVD, charged with 'counter-revolutionary activity', and sentenced to eight years' penal labour under the notorious catch-all Article 58. By his estimation, from the 20,000 Poles sent to the Gulag at Pechora, only 6,000 were still alive two years later. They were worked to death constructing a railway link between the Pechora river and the southern Urals; fellow Russian inmates told him that two dead bodies lay under every rail.

KOSSOY'S SERVICE in the Anders Army was short. It enabled him to leave the USSR, but came to an end in Tehran, where, suffering from typhus, he was discharged on health grounds.

Kossoy's subsequent sojourn in Palestine–Israel lasted a decade. He fought in the Israeli War of Independence, recruited by his Varsovian classmate, Menachem Begin, and married a woman from Warsaw before leaving to study in Munich.

Kossoy's career as an attorney in Geneva spanned half a century. He specialised in restitution and reparation claims against the German government, reportedly assisting some 60,000 clients – Jews, Poles, and Roma.[104]

In Geneva, Kossoy became inseparable friends with Wacław Micuta, a hero of the Warsaw Rising. When I met them around 2003, both had reached 90, and both were brimming with stories and with good humour.

Menachem Begin, Kossoy's exact contemporary and fellow graduate of Warsaw's Law School, is by far the most commented-on Jewish soldier in the Anders Army.[105] Yet neither of them had much in common with the traditionally ultra-religious Jewish lads, who, on

- Po demobili

POLAND

NAZWISKO
SURNAME
NOM
BORODZICZ
IMIĘ
CHRISTIAN NAME
PRÉNOM
SZCZESNY ZDZISŁAW
DATA URODZENIA
DATE OF BIRTH
DATE DE NAISSANCE
30. 8. 1922 r.
Jest Członkiem Zwyczajnym Stowarzysze
Polskich Kombatantów na podstawie Stat
S.P.K. Art. III. par. 2. lit.
The above is an active Member of the Pol
Combatants Associat
Le sus-nommé est Membre actif de l'Asso
-tion des Combattants Polon
ZARZĄD GŁÓWNY S.P.K.
COUNCIL of MANAGEMENT P.C.A.
COMITÉ GÉNÉRAL DE L'A.C.P.
IN GREAT BRITAIN
PODPIS CZŁONKA
SIGNATURE
SIGNATURE DU PORTEUR

się w Szkocji
25 lipca 1947 roku urodził się mój syn Mirosław,Tadeusz w Diddington.
2 kwietnia 1950 roku urodziła się w Glasgow moja córka Izabella,Barbara.
Baillies of Glasgow
Tu mieszkaliśmy. Glasgow, 18 Balliol Street
(fot. z 1989 r.)

SZCZĘSNY BORODZICZ

SZCZĘSNY BORODZICZ (1922–1993), **SOUVENIRS OF A SOLDIER** — page from the family album (center top). Wife Wirginia shows her husband's uniform (far left); his medals (below). Polish Combatants Association card (below far left); born 1922, served 1941–1946. Polish Red Cross unit in training (below left). Colleague in Tatishchevo camp (below center). Training at the Polish Agricultural School in Glasgow, 22 March 1950 (below).

GENERALS ANDERS, Duch, and Rakowski.

the formation of the Army in 1941, still formed a majority of Polish Jewry.

Tartars and Armenians were far smaller minorities than the Jews. But the Tartars still had their own regiment of Tartar Cavalry in the Army of 1939, and a few individuals found their way to join Anders. Their names are not hard to find. In the Polish cemetery at Loreto, for example, among the crosses and the stars of David one comes across the name of Sulejman Rodkiewicz, an uhlan from the 12th Podolski Uhlan Regiment, died 27 June 1944.

The wife of journalist, Zdzisław Bau, who was attached to the Army's Press Office, was a Muslim woman from Wilno, Zarema Lebiedź (1913–2008), sometime executive secretary of the Józef Piłsudski Institute in New York.

Germans, usually from Silesia, were the only minority whom Anders agreed with the NKVD to exclude. Those who had presented themselves for service at Totskoye were left behind in the USSR. This may appear odd; Anders himself had German roots, and in the September Campaign of 1939 the Polish Army did not attempt to bar citizens of German origin from serving. Yet the NKVD was less flexible. Stalin had recently ordered the USSR's own German community to be deported *en masse*.

ALL ARMIES FUNCTION through the combined activities of specialised 'arms': traditionally cavalry, infantry, and artillery. But numerous other departments are required to support an effective fighting-machine: notably the Observer, Engineers, Signals, Transport, Medical and Intelligence Corps, not forgetting the Quartermaster, Post Office and Pay Corps, and Pioneers.

Each of the services encourages particular skills and builds particular types of character. The cavalry goes for dash and elan; the infantry for stamina and raw courage; the artillery for cool calculation and precision. Each depends on the others.

Anders, like Soviet marshals Zhukov and Rokossowsky, had served his apprenticeship in a Tsarist cavalry regiment and had commanded a cavalry brigade in 1939. Polish lancers had an especially distinguished tradition. But the nature of cavalry warfare was changing fast, and the Anders Army came into being at a moment when the world had been astonished by the success of the German *Blitzkrieg*. Cavalry units everywhere were being mechanised; war-horses were being put out to pasture; and tanks were rapidly becoming the principal offensive weapon.

General Stanisław Rakowski (1895–1950) was typical of the horseback soldiers who had to learn the art of armoured warfare. In the 1930s he had commanded the 18th Uhlan Regiment, and, being a historian, the Army's Historical Bureau. But as from 1943, he was put in charge of the 2nd Warsaw Armoured Brigade, the principal armoured formation of the Polish II Corps. Rakowski's troops fought mainly in Sherman tanks, and were divided into four regiments, each of three or four squadrons. To enable recognition, every tank had a name painted on its side in large capital letters, and every squadron used tank names starting with the same letter. The tanks of HQ Squadron of the 4th 'Scorpion' Armoured Regiment, for example, all had names beginning with 'G': Gustaw, Gdynia, Gdańsk, Grochów, Gardziel, Gryf, Grom and Grodno. The 1st Squadron of the same regiment chose the letter 'T': hence, Tobruk, Tajfun, Turnia,

'GRIZZLY' SHERMAN tank, Stag Hound APC.

MK-I RIFLE (bottom), Thompson sub-machine gun (right)., and Mk hand grenades.

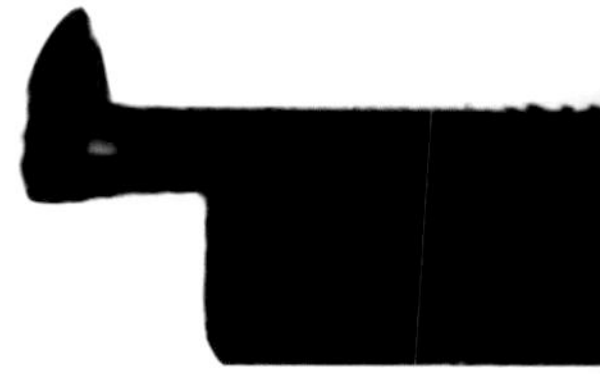

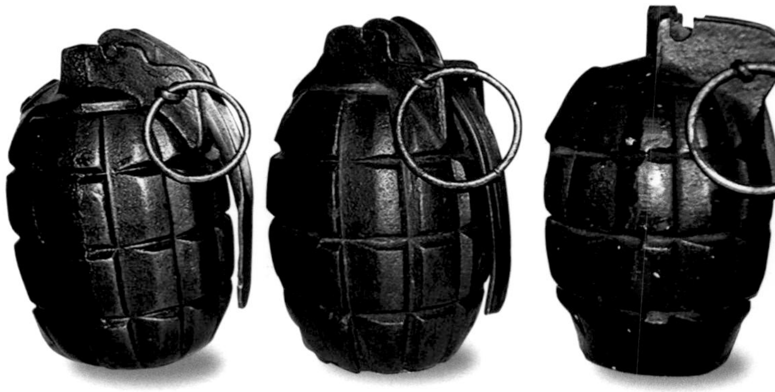

Trzyniec, Tempo, Tygrys, Taran, Tur, Terror, Ter, Topór, Tuchola, Tyran, Tranto, Tapir, Taras, Tarzan, Tomahawk, Toruń, Turoń, Tczew, Toniek, Taranto. Tank crews willingly identified with the dynamic names. General Rakowski died in Buenos Aires.

The Army's best specialist in tank warfare, however, was Col. Stanisław Szostak (1898–1961), sometime *Junker* of the elite Nikolayevka Cadet School in Petrograd. Szostak's experience with tanks began in 1924 when he joined Poland's 1st Tank Regiment, equipped with Renault FT tanks. By 1935, he was director of the Armoured Training School, and in the September Campaign commanded an armoured reconnaissance unit made up of TKS 'tankettes'. Prior to Soviet captivity, he was interned in Lithuania. Anders put him in charge of the Army's preparations for training armoured troops. He wrote all the manuals, designed all the courses, and supervised manoeuvres.

Numerically, the infantry forms the backbone of any army, and the 'Anders Army' was no exception in that infantry divisions constituted the core around which all the other units revolved. In the Second World War, however, infantry tactics had evolved considerably, and the massed assaults, which had led to such massive slaughter in 1914–1918 were abandoned. Infantrymen were taught to take cover, to spread out to avoid presenting an easy target, and to follow armoured vehicles wherever possible. By 1943, they were almost entirely motorised, and they possessed a much greater variety of weapons than their predecessors. The rifle and infantry divisions of the Anders Army were equipped with standard British issue: the Sten gun (SMG), the classic M1928 'Tommy Gun', Lee Enfield rifles, the Bren gun (Light MG), the Vickers Medium MG, Mills handgrenades, 2- and 3-inch mortars, anti-tank guns, Polsten 'ack-ack' guns, and Mark II Lifebuoy flamethrowers.

General Nikodem Sulik-Sarnowski (1893–1954) commanded the elite 5th Kresowa Infantry Division, and earned the *Virtuti Militari* medal. Born in Sokółka in Podlasie, he was always associated with regiments from eastern Poland, and in 1920 had participated in the Żeligowski Mutiny, which secured Wilno's adherence to the Second Republic. In 1939, he had commanded the Border Protection Corps (KOP) on the eastern

front, after which, as deputy of the underground resistance movement in the Wilno district, he evaded capture by the NKVD.

HIGHLY TRAINED COMMANDOS, the Army's 'special forces', were the cream of the infantry. Commanded by Maj. Władysław Smrokowski (1909–1965), their 1 Independent Company and their 2 Motorised Battalion, would be the first to be sent to Italy in January 1944 and suffer the first casualties.

Artillery had been the great failure of the First World War. In the decades before 1914, heavy guns had been designed to deliver many tons of metal and high explosives onto every square yard of the enemy line, and it was widely believed that no defences could withstand such a barrage. Generals persisted in ordering waves of massed infantry into sectors 'softened up' by artillery, only to find repeatedly that defenders had survived and that the enemy could comfortably fill the gaps with reserves.

In the Second World War, therefore, the expectations for artillery were much reduced, while greater emphasis was placed on speed, mobility, flexibility and combined operations. The star of the British gun park was the QF 25-pounder gun-howitzer, which could be easily towed into position. Polish artillery groups were divided into regiments, batteries and troops. In Italy, they were usually competing with superior German opposition, and were forced to rely heavily on air support.

Napoleon started his career as an artillery officer, making his mark with his 'famous whiff of grapeshot' at Paris in 1795. He was the model for many successors.

Brigadier General Roman Odzierzyński (1893–1975) was the leading artillery commander of the Anders Army. Born in Lwów, he joined the Austro-Hungarian Army in 1910, and spent the whole of the First World War as a frontline artillery officer. In the Polish–Soviet War, he commanded a field artillery regiment before rising through the ranks to head Poland's Anti-Aircraft School. Evacuated to France and then Britain, he belonged to a group of Polish officers sent out to Iraq via Archangel in 1942. After the war, General 'Odd', as the British called him, occupied the office of Prime Minister of the Government-in-Exile for three years.

All soldiers started their military careers in a particular branch of the service, but it was not unusual for a versatile man to move from one branch to another. Mieczysław Zakrzewski (1911–1999), born at Kraśnik near Lublin, served before the war as a junior officer in a cavalry regiment, before studying metallurgy at the AGH Academy of Mining and Steelmaking in Kraków. Recalled from the reserves in 1939, he joined Col. Maczek's 10 Motorised Cavalry

Brigade and participated in heavy fighting. Interned in Hungary, active again in France, then transferred to Scotland, he was ordered in January 1942 to sail to Murmansk and to join the Anders Army. To begin with, he commanded a reconnaisance unit of General Okulicki's 7th Infantry Division in Kermine, but then undertook a variety of duties in Iraq, Transjordan, Palestine and Italy. At Monte Cassino he commanded a mortar unit, but in August 1944 returned to the 3rd Silesian Cavalry as a troop commander. In this way, he contrived to serve with cavalry, infantry and artillery. He never rose to the highest rank, but was very important, in that, as a keen photographer, he took thousands of unpublished pictures, some used in this book.

OF ALL THE SUPPORT SERVICES, none was more important than the Intelligence Department. Poland's *Dwójka* or 'Second Department' had a brilliant record, being responsible, among other things, for breaking the Enigma Code. Its work combined politics with military affairs, its main task being to assess the capacity of the enemy and to understand the sector of the world in which the Army was ordered to operate. Intelligence officers were the Army's 'eyes, ears, and brain'.

Yet the *Dwójka* of the Anders Army was obliged to operate in the most hostile of environments. It had no secure home base, and had to conduct its activities on foreign soil and in the shadow of rival secret services. In the USSR, it was in theory the partner of the NKVD; in practice, it was stuck in the territory over which the NKVD sought to exercise total control. In Iran, it entered a sphere in which both the British and the Soviet intelligence services were cooperating closely, and where it was less than welcome. In Iraq and Palestine, it moved into countries where British Intelligence reigned supreme,

CHIEF COMMANDER of the PSK, Władysława Piechowska (top), holding a child.

COLONEL, LATER GENERAL, Klemens Rudnicki (right).

BRIG. GEN. Roman Odzierzyński (right).

THE FUNERAL of General Anders, Monte Cassino, 1970: The General's daughter Anna Maria and widow Irena (kneeling, front); his daughter Anna Anders-Nowakowska (back row); Prince Eugeniusz Lubomirski (standing right).

GENERAL ANDERS in tropical kit following one of his many long distance flights; Gen-Prof. Szarecki (top).

LONDON 1942: The Cabinet of the exiled Polish Government, General Sikorski (centre), Stanisław Mikołajczyk, vice-premier and future premier, on Sikorski's left (bottom).

the other way when youngsters claimed without proof to be eighteen. The *Junacy* or Cadets began their studies at 14, and boys worked in a number of menial jobs such as messengers or orderlies.

Anders, however, encountered some special problems, especially with his officer corps. Due to the 'missing 22,000' who were later shown to have been murdered in 1940 at Katyń and elsewhere, the shortage of trained officers was acute, and urgent measures were taken to fill the gap. Urgent priority was given to the Cadet Schools whose graduates would move up into the Army on completion of their studies; and desperate appeals were made to the General Staff in London to send replacements. Fortunately, the Polish Army in Britain had a surplus of officers. In the meantime, any officer who could report for duty without falling over was kept in post. The shortage did not begin to ease before the Army's reorganisation in Iraq and its successful merger with the Carpathian Brigade.

It is not possible to say who was the oldest soldier in the Anders Army, but General-Professor Szarecki, OC Medical Corps, offered a fine example of someone who overcame the problems of age. He was old enough to have worked as a military surgeon in the Russo–Japanese War, and he was already 67 when he signed on in Buzuluk. By the time of Monte Cassino three years later he had completed his 'three-score-and-ten', and had long passed retirement age. Nonetheless, he is singled out by Melchior Wańkowicz for having put in two successive 24-hour shifts at the height of the battle, toiling at the operating table in Dressing Station No. 1. Courage, skill and stamina are not the preserve of frontline soldiers alone.

It is widely considered that Krzysztof Flizak (born 1932) qualified as the youngest soldier in the Anders Army. He was presented in this way in an illustrated article published in a military newspaper in Iraq in 1943:

> "The youngest soldier of General Anders reports to the head of his company, Sgt Bronisław Dereń, at the Polish Army camp by the lake at Habbaniya."

Flizak's basic story does not raise any serious doubts. Brought up in Dokszyc (Wilno district) the son of a professional soldier, he was deported with his mother and siblings to a workstation in the taiga outside Novosibirsk. The family knew that their father was a POW in the USSR. On hearing of the Amnesty, therefore, he set out without an ID or a ticket to find his father, travelling and sleeping on trains heading south. Helped by Poles whom he met on the way, he found his father at Kermine in Uzbekistan, and was placed under the Army's care.

THE HAND OF PROVIDENCE was manifestly on the boy's shoulder. His father had come to Kermine on a chance errand from some other camp, but was unable to stay long and the little Krzysztof was duly registered as a dependant. Having fibbed about his true age, he was assigned to a *Kompania Młodzieżowa* (Youth Company), a military-sounding euphemism for an orphanage. From then on, as he said, 'the Army was my family'. His only rival for the title of 'youngest recruit' was an Italian orphan whom the Army adopted in 1944.

It is true perhaps, as mean-minded journalists have pointed out, that Krzysztof Flizak was never a serving Polish soldier. He was still a pupil in the Cadet School in Palestine, aged 13, when the war ended, and he did not reach maturity until he was already in postwar Britain. He sailed on the *Queen Mary* to the USA in 1951, when he was old enough to join the US Army. He served in Korea in the 101st Airborne Division,

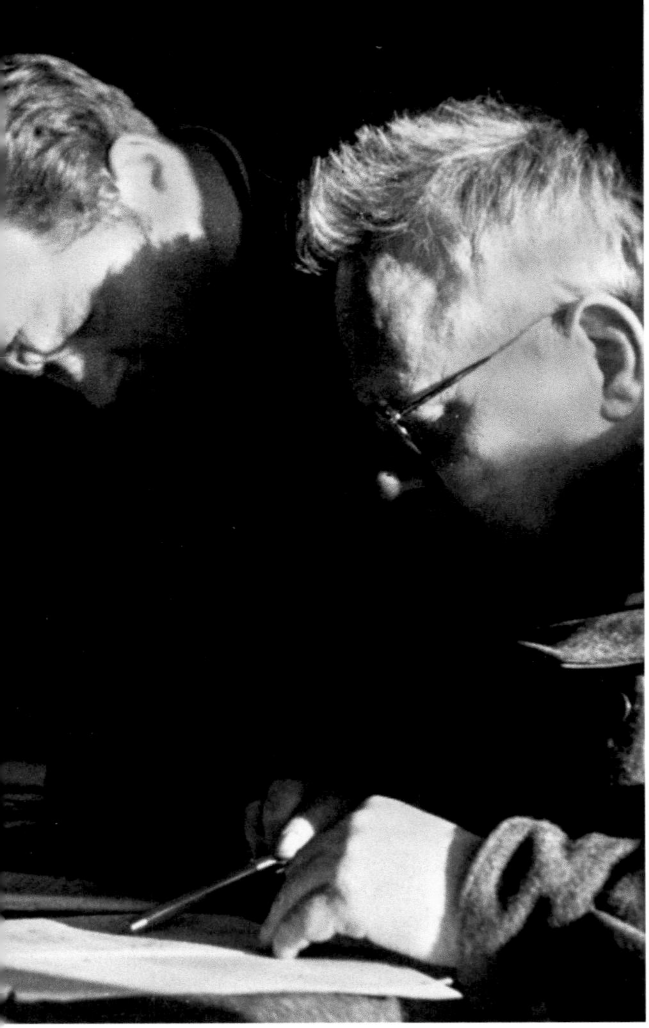

ARMY PRESS Office: Jerzy Giedroyc (left), Gustaw Herling-Grudziński (centre), Melchior Wańkowicz (right), Mottola (Italy), January 1945 (top).

MICHAŁ GIEDROYĆ and his son Niko search for traces of the former family home at Łobzów (now Belarus), around 1997.

the 'Screaming Eagles', spent years recovering from wounds at Fort McClellan, Alabama, and, with the help of a veteran's scholarship, obtained a PhD in Psychology from Wayne State University, Detroit.

Flizak returned to Poland in 2012, his 80th year, attending the ceremony of Soldier's Day at the Grunwald Monument in Kraków. The pedants were not happy that he was wearing both the uniform of the II Corps, and his American insignia.[107]

According to Bolshevik–Communist parlance, Poland was dubbed *Panskaya Pol'sha*, 'Poland of the Landlords' or 'Poland of the Aristocrats'. The Poles were routinely described by Soviet propaganda as *Pany* or 'feudal lords', as if the whole Polish nation were made up entirely of landowners and their lackeys. In reality prewar Poland was still dominated by peasants, who constituted up to 75 per cent of society. The number of industrial workers was small, as were those of members of the intelligentsia and middle-class professions. All these facts were reflected in the make-up of the Army.

It is not often realised, however, that Poland's Second Republic had formally abolished the nobility in 1921, and was imbued with a remarkably egalitarian spirit. (It achieved this effect without conducting a bloody campaign of murder and dispossession like that which stained the name of the Bolsheviks.)

It is also true that the Army enjoyed privileged status, especially after Piłsudski's *coup d'état* in 1926. As a result, military service in prewar Poland offered an exceptional ladder for social advancement.

Lastly one of the great achievements of the Second Republic was to conquer illiteracy, which dropped from about 70 per cent in 1921 to less than 10 per cent in 1939. The first generation of independent Poland was engaged in an educational crusade, well aware that education offered the means to iron out the terrible social inequalities of the period before 1918. The passion for education, including that for girls, was very visible in the Anders Army.

Aristocrats, of course, were present, though they enjoyed no privileges. Anders' own adjutant, Lt Eugeniusz Lubomirski (1895–1982), was a member of one of Poland's wealthiest and most ancient families. Arrested by the NKVD in 1940, he was detained in a special camp for aristocrats, before being sent to Moscow for interrogation. He met Anders in the Lubyanka.

Prince Eustachy Sapieha (1881–1963), sometime Minister of Foreign Affairs, also did time in the Lubyanka. He joined the Anders Army as a means of leaving the USSR, but departed for British East Africa at the first opportunity after reaching the Middle East.

The PSK also had its aristocrats. A splendid photo exists of Princess Monika Radziwiłł-Strumiłło, saluting in Iran, in her full army uniform. Princess Monika, then thirtyish, was a widow, having lost her husband in Soviet captivity.

The most striking fact, however, is not that the Anders Army sheltered a handful of aristocrats, but that none of the 'top brass' belonged to the so-called cream of society. Anders himself was the son of an estate manager; General Sulik was from a rural village in the Grodno district; General Szarecki was the son of a railway worker. These were not feudal '*Pany*' by any stretch of imagination.

The vengeance of the Soviets, however, concentrated less on the 'big fish' than on the class of *osadnicy wojskowi* (military settlers) who had been given land in the Kresy during the interwar period. According to the Military Settlement Act (1920), the aims of the scheme were to strengthen the Polish element of the population, to improve agricultural standards, and to provide employment for ex-servicemen and their families. Roughly 30,000 units were distributed, mainly in the borderlands of Belarus and Volhynia. The greater numbers of beneficiaries were veterans of the Polish–Soviet War, and they accepted their land grants on condition that they conducted armed patrols of the border. In Soviet eyes, they were marked men – political enemies and social parasites. Skirmishes broke out as soon as the Red Army crossed into Poland on 17 September 1939. Communist-led rural committees sequestrated their produce and livestock. And in 1940, 80% of them, some 108,000 people, were deported. Those who remained were targeted three years later by the murderous gangs of Ukrainian nationalists.

BRONISŁAW MŁYNARSKI (above).

JÓZEF CZAPSKI (left).

PREWAR POLISH SOCIETY was widely reported as lacking a middle class; and it was frequently said that the gap was filled by the Jews. These judgements are hardly fair. Poland's middle class, made up of business and com-

POSTCARD SENT from Tatishchev Camp No. 1 by Capt. Feliks Tatarowski on 3 September 1941 to Mrs Józefa Wojciechowski, 1 Jay St, Geneva (NY), received New York, 15 December 1941.

mercial, professional and intellectual circles, was reasonably substantial for a pre-modern, and largely pre-industrial, society. It consisted of Christians and Jews in equal parts and most characteristically it encouraged a *milieu* where people of all religions and none could mingle freely, and where inter-marriage was common. These facts can be observed, as elsewhere, in the make-up of the Anders Army.

Bronisław Młynarski (1899–1971), the brother-in-law of Artur Rubinstein and a friend of Józef Czapski, was one of the more refined figures among Anders' officers. The son of Emil Młynarski, the distinguished composer and director of the Warsaw Opera, he had been studying in Moscow, at the Zyberi Commercial School, when the Bolshevik Revolution broke out, and returned to Poland to fight as a cavalryman in the Polish–Soviet War, during which he was decorated for bravery with the *Krzyż Walecznych* (Cross of Valour). Having trained as an infantry officer in the Cadet School, and then serving in a battalion of sappers, he left the Army to work in business, for the Gdynia–America line. At the outbreak of war he was a reserve officer, and fought briefly at Brześć nad Bugiem (Brest) against the Germans before being ordered to the rear at Dubno, where he was captured by the Soviets.

Młynarski's account of his time in the clutches of the NKVD, *W niewoli sowieckiej* (1974), describes his incarceration at Starobielsk, in the company of men who were to be killed at Katyń, and his psychological fencing-matches with an interrogator convinced that he was a spy.[108] He escaped through the intervention of the German Embassy, and came to the Anders Army at Buzuluk from a second camp at Grazoviets. He stayed with the Army every step of the way to demobilisation in England in 1946. After the war, Młynarski was summoned to the USA to work as Artur Rubinstein's secretary, married a film star, Doris Kenyon, and lived happily ever after in Hollywood.[109]

Poland's working class was small and localised. It formed an important social sector in a few cities such as Łódź, Warsaw, or Katowice, but it was absent in most parts of the country. Białystok, which had a sizeable Jewish working class, and Drohobycz–Stryj, the heartland of the Galician oil industry, were the only places in the Soviet zone of occupation in 1939–1941 where industrial workers were present; they were equally the only places whence working-class men might have found their way into the Anders Army.

POLAND'S PEASANTRY outsized all other social groups in the prewar era, and naturally supplied the largest cohort of army conscripts. It is a logical conclusion, therefore, that the great majority of non-officer POWs, who were held in Soviet detention in 1939–1941 and who subsequently joined the Anders Army, were of peasant origin. They were not farmers in the English sense, but crofters tilling their

TWO SOLDIERS

TWO SOLDIERS OUT OF 80,000 MEN. Their families were often left with a handful of old photos, a few unverifiable stories, and only fragmentary information about their Army careers.

CZESLAW DOBRECKI riding a motorcycle in Palestine, around 1943; enjoying an outing with the '*Pestki*' in Italy, about 1945; and filling up the radiator of a 'One-and-a-Half Tonner'.

CZESŁAW DOBRECKI

BOGDAN ŻUKOWSKI

WŁOCHY, 15 LUTY 1945 R.

SZKOŁA PODOF. ŁĄCZNOŚCI
BRONI PANCERNEJ

Świadectwo ukończenia kursu szkoły podoficerskiej łączności Broni Pancernej w czasie od 15.XI.1944 r. do 15.II.1945 r. w 9 kompanii łączności 2 Brygady Pancernej

przez st.szer. Żukowski Bogdana

z wynikiem pomyślnym, uzyskując z następujących przedmiotów oceny:

1. *Organizacja wojsk łączności w. j.* dostatecznie
2. *Regulamin służby wewnętrznej* dobrze
3. *Regulamin ruchu łączności* dostatecznie
4. *Podstawy elektro i radiotechniki* dostatecznie
5. *Znajomość sprzętu łączności* dostatecznie
6. *Organizacja sieci radio i tele* dostatecznie
7. *Organizacja ośrodka łączności* dostatecznie
8. *Budowa linii telegraficznej* dobrze
9. *Terenoznawstwo* dostatecznie
10. *Miny i pułapki* dostatecznie
11. *Nauka o broni* dobrze
12. *Dowodzenie* dostatecznie

D-two 2 BRYGADY PANCERNEJ 2 POL. ARMOURED BDE.

Dca Szkoły Podofic.
(–) GIERAT kpt.

Dca 9 komp. łączności
(–) KOZAKIEWICZ mjr.

Dca 2 Bryg. Pancernej

BOGDAN ŻUKOWSKI was said to have been captured by the Soviets in 1939 "because his train happened to be in the East". He served with the Anders Army all the way from Russia to Britain, returning to Poland in 1947. He died in 1967 before his son was old enough to understand the details of his past. (Top) preparing for the Holy Mass in the desert; (left) Zukowski's certificate of completion of an NCO's course on 'Communications in Armoured Warfare', Italy, 2 February 1945.

own plots, agriculturalists of the lowest order, sometimes tenants or *fornale* (hired labourers). They were raw, tough, country lads, hardened by back-breaking toil on the land, who were well suited to weather the rigours of exile or of a labour camp. Rarely educated beyond primary level, they were practical men, and, as the memoirs of others often note, they could best withstand the long days of felling trees in an Arctic forest or of picking cotton on a roasting *kolchoz* in Uzbekistan. Coming from the Kresy, they were almost equally divided between Polish-speaking Catholics and Uniate or Orthodox Belarussians and Ukrainians. For them, the differences in language or religion were less significant than the similarities of age-old rural culture. They were famous, when asked by sociologists about their nationality, for saying they were '*tutejsi*' (locals).

For obvious reasons, peasant-soldiers rarely write memoirs, and it is notable that the largest social group in the Anders Army has hardly left a trace of its presence. Nonetheless, there are exceptions, and an excellent piece of oral history, recently recorded in Bradford (Yorkshire), tells the story of Feliks Czenkusz (1920–2013) in his own words. The recording is particularly valuable, because it presents a perspective on the Anders Army as seen through the eyes of a witness who possessed virtually no prior political knowledge or social awareness of the events experienced.

'*PESTKI*' RELAXING on Lake Genazereth, Tiberias, Palestine, 28 January 1944.

As it happened, Feliks Czenkusz hailed not from the Kresy, but from a village called Łąkorz, 12 miles east of Grudziądz and only a mile from the then Polish–German frontier. His father was a saddler making leatherwork for the horse trade. He volunteered for the Polish Army in 1938, and was sent to an Army-run craft training scheme in the Wilno district. He was working in Wilno at the outbreak of war, and on the rumoured approach of the *Wehrmacht* fled through a forest to the Republic of Lithuania. There, in June 1940, he was picked up by the NKVD and deported.

Czenkusz's account of deportation is filled with smart observations. On the station at Molodeczno Soviet officers boarded the trains, forcing all passengers to show their hands, and sorting officers from non-officers, and military men from police. (He, as a peasant boy, was presumably not judged to be a *byeloryki* or decadent 'white hand person', and was left alone.) In the village of Babynino, in the Kaluga *oblast*, to which he was exiled, the windows of the cottages had no glass, only paper. To his surprise, he was not put to work, but, as a youth, was subject to political education. "They came to our huts at 10 am each morning," he recorded without offence or enthusiasm, "and talked to us about Communism." The educators were pleasant enough, unlike the escorts on the train, who "had the brutal faces of men of the steppe".

'*PESTKI*', JENIN, Palestine, 25 November 1943.

The group to which Czenkusz belonged was reloaded onto a train on his 21st birthday, 4 June 1941. "We did not know where we were going. We were never told what the plans were for us. The train was travelling southwards, but as we slept in the night, [it] changed direction towards the north." They arrived at the port of Murmańsk on the White Sea, where they boarded a ship called the *Clara Zetkin*. "We could only guess that our destination would be one of the sub-Arctic islands."

ON THE DAY that the *Wehrmacht* invaded the USSR, 22–23 June 1941, Czenkusz and his colleagues were at sea, 24 hours out of Murmańsk. The ship stopped. "It was 'shaking' with rumours. We knew that the Russian officers were getting instructions from Moscow." After a day becalmed, the *Clara Zetkin* restarted its engines and sailed to the mouth of the Panol river, where earlier Polish exiles were lodged in barracks. "The Russian soldiers opened fire on aeroplanes" over the camp, "and after that they admitted that Russia was at war with Germany."

The uncertainty continued. After one or two months, Russian prisoners arrived to replace the Poles, who were sent by ship to Archangel. "They gave us food for 3 days, some bread and some very nice ham, but I ate up all of my rations during the first day." At a transit camp near Archangel, they saw Russian prisoners held in cages: "These people looked as if they were in a zoo." Re-boarding a train, they travelled south for several days. "I was very hungry. We did not know it... but this was the first step to becoming free men again."

The description by Czenkusz of his reception into the Polish Army at Tatishevo is priceless:

> "We were housed in tents and some of our officers were given buildings within the camp. We now realised that we were in the Polish Army, and more officers arrived. We were loosely organised, but were gradually allocated to units and regiments such as the infantry or the engineers. I found myself in a reconnaissance unit – a poor choice since I was short-sighted and wore glasses.
>
> Then a General Anders arrived in camp to take a look at his future soldiers. He walked with sticks, a reminder of his recent imprisonment... We had not been issued with arms at this point. We were drilled, and full army life began."[110]

It is evident from the wording that Czenkusz had no idea who General Anders was.

To complete the social scene of the Anders Army, one cannot honestly omit the category of criminals. Anders took in his share of anti-social individuals – thugs, gangsters, thieves, fraudsters, and rapists. Caught by the *gendarmerie*, sentenced by military courts, and incarcerated in the Army's prisons, they were a constant drag on the Army's patience and resources. They were never noticed by the rest of the troops, except when they smashed up a train in transit or ran riot on a transport ship. It was little consolation to think that most had learned their evil ways as a survival strategy in Soviet camps. Rumours circulated that incorrigible reprobates and recidivists were occasionally shot.

FROM LEFT:

PROFESSOR STANISŁAW Kot

MARIAN HEMAR

RYSZARD KACZOROWSKI

MIECZYSŁAW BORUTA Spiechowicz

LEON KOZŁOWSKI

GENERAL ANDERS was well known for frowning on politics, which he regarded as divisive and damaging. He had served under three political regimes: the Russian Empire, Poland's constitutional Republic, and the Sanacja regime, all of which had collapsed. Prewar Poland had been wracked by political quarrels, notably between Piłsudski's left-leaning Independence Movement and Dmowski's right-wing Nationalists.

In the wake of the defeat of 1939, Polish opinion was deeply split between those who held the Sanacja regime responsible for the disaster and those who did not. Anders did not want these disputes to weaken the unity of his army.

Nonetheless, it was inevitable that a variety of political views would circulate among 80,000 men and women, and that the prewar parties would exert a degree of influence behind the scenes. Of those parties, four commanded the greatest support: the PSL (Peasant Party), the National Democrats (*Endecja*), the Socialists

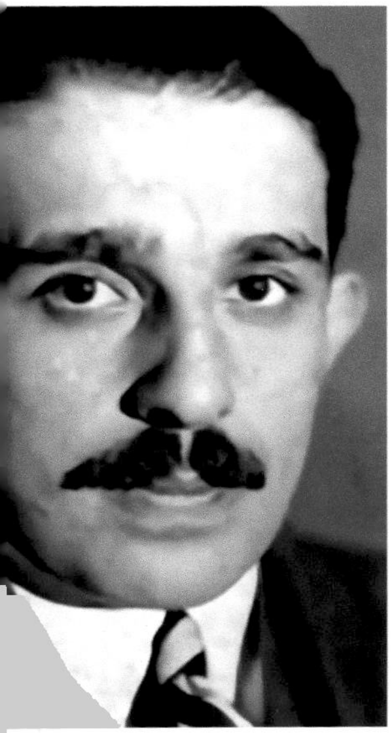

(PPS), and the Christian Democrats (*Chadecja*). All had suffered in the 1930s under the *Sanacja* regime, which had created its own pseudo-political party, the BBWR (Nonpartisan Bloc for Cooperation with the Government), to help oil the wheels of its authoritarian institutions. And all were now competing over conflicting visions of the future both in the exiled Polish government and in the pages of the Polish press abroad.

The Army was supposed to steer clear of politics, of course, and followed the orders of the Commander-in-Chief and the legal government, both embodied in the person of General Sikorski. Party political activities were not permitted. Even so, not least in the Army's press, political issues were raised and passionately debated.

International affairs, and in particular the progress of the war, formed the number one issue. Within that wider context, the growing power of the USSR, and the uncritical views of Stalin expressed by Western opinion-makers, caused grave alarm. Since the National Democrats had always seen Germany as the prime danger, they were traditionally amenable to an accommodation with 'Russia'. The Piłsudskites feared Russia above all, and hoped for assistance from Germany. But with Hitler and Stalin in power, none of these policies could be applied.

On the internal front, the performance of the Government-in-Exile gave rise to increasing unease. Open opposition was muted so long as General Sikorski was alive, but it rapidly spread after his death. From mid-1943 onwards, the sentiment took hold that the ruling circle of clapped-out politicians would have to be replaced, sooner rather than later.

The PSL, which in theory represented Poland's largest social constituency and which had been persecuted by the Sanacja regime, seemed to be the most credible vehicle for change. Its leader, Wincenty Witos, who had been imprisoned by the Sanacja, had been interned in a German jail since 1939. It was no great surprise, therefore, that the PSL's top representative in London, Stanisław Mikołajczyk, succeeded Sikorski as Prime Minister.

The ethos of the PSL, however, was both anti-clerical and anti-military, and the shift was undoubtedly felt in the Army. Anders was decidedly more sympathetic to the Commander-in-

Chief, General Sosnkowski, than to Mikołajczyk. The teachers of the Army Schools, which were controlled by the government's Ministry of Education, equally felt that the traditional priorities of Religion and Patriotism, *Bóg i Honor*, were coming under threat.

The National Democratic Party (*Endecja*) commanded the largest single block of opinion in prewar Poland. Its founder, Roman Dmowski (1864–1939), was dead, but his writings continued to be read, and his divisive opinions undoubtedly enjoyed substantial support among Anders' officers. Dmowski was a trenchant critic of Poland's messianic tradition, and of the long list of failed insurrections; he held sober views on economic development and national education. At the same time, his ideological platform contained a poisonous streak of overt anti-Semitism: not the genocidal anti-Semitism of the Fascists, but a milder recipe which stressed that 'Poland was for the Poles' and that national minorities should somehow find somewhere else to live. (It may be likened to the stance of right-wing Zionists who stress that Israel is a Jewish state and regard Arabs as undesirables.)

Inevitably, therefore, the Jewish issue dogged the Anders Army from start to finish. Accusations and counter-accusations proliferated. It was put about that the Army's relief committees were discriminating against Jews. It was repeatedly stated, even by Menachem Begin, that the Army did not accept Jewish recruits. And it was widely reported that Jewish soldiers were constantly harassed and humiliated. A frequent charge was levelled at the Army's General Staff, which supposedly harboured 'an anti-Semitic clique'. Sometime head of the *Dwójka*, Col. Władysław Michniewicz was the most usual target for such attacks.

The Socialists (PPS) were the long-standing enemy of the National Democrats. Marshal Piłsudski, whose political life started in the PPS, was a lifelong opponent of Dmowski. It was PPS members of the National Council in London, like Józef Beloński or Jan Stańczyk, who drew attention to nationalist excesses and who stressed the principles of toleration and ethnic pluralism. In the so-called Stańczyk Resolution of 1940, the Government-in-Exile formally adhered to the contention that 'Polish Jews, as Polish citizens, shall be equal in duties and rights to the Polish Community in liberated Poland.' Anyone in the Anders Army who was even moderately informed should have been aware of this commitment.

Two Polish political parties were illegal before the war, and stayed banned in all bodies subject to the exiled government. The Polish Communist Party (KPP) was proscribed for opposing the principle of Polish Independence; several thousands of its members fled to the Soviet Union only to perish during Stalin's purges. The National Radical Camp (ONR), an offshoot of the Nationalists, though violently anti-German and anti-Communist, had Fascist leanings inspired by Mussolini. Neither organisation could operate openly among Anders' soldiers, but both undoubtedly had their clandestine sympathisers.

When the Anders Army was formed, therefore, no organised group of Polish Communists existed – neither in Nazi-occupied Poland, nor in the USSR, nor, indeed, in the West. Even so, the most instinctively anti-Communist formation in the world unwittingly sheltered a number of 'reds' and 'revolutionaries' whose devious habits were anathema to most of their comrades. One such invisible company consisted of hundreds of informers and 'sleepers' who had been infiltrated into the Army by the NKVD. As later discovered, many ex-prisoners of the Gulag and inmates of the POW camps had only been released on condition that they undertook to work in secret for their Soviet controllers.

WŁADYSŁAW BRONIEWSKI,
poet; a prewar picture.

Once the Army had left the USSR, it was a common occurrence for these men to confess their fault to their officers, and to beg forgiveness.

In addition, several individuals with Communist convictions or leanings entered the Anders Army, and by keeping a low profile, hoped to avoid the wrath of their comrades. Władysław Broniewski, for example, who joined the 6th Infantry Division in April 1942, initially felt content with his lot. "I feel good in uniform," he told his daughter in a letter, "and [have] rid myself of all worries except for those concerning you." Yet, as Marcia Shore reports, the euphoria soon passed: "[Broniewski] was without close friends, [and] other Polish officers bore hostility towards him for his communist past and continued leftist views." General Anders called him in, and offered him extended leave. He gladly accepted, and travelled to Jerusalem via Baghdad, Damascus, and Haifa.[111]

The second husband of Broniewski's first wife, Romuald Gadomski (1905–1974), did not fare so well. A long-term member of the KPP, he escaped the Stalin's Purges only to be recruited by the Comintern and ordered to infiltrate the Anders Army. When his treachery was uncovered, he was jailed in Palestine. He subsequently became the Consul-General of People's Poland in Jerusalem, and a high-ranking officer of the Communist security apparatus in its worst Stalinist phase.

A heavy cloud of suspicion has equally fallen on Capt. Jerzy Klimkowski (1908–1991), who, having served under Anders in 1939, became one of the General's adjutants. He has been accused both of working as a secret NKVD informer and of fomenting opposition to Commander-in-Chief Sikorski. He was placed before a court martial in 1943 on a variety of charges, and was jailed in Palestine. After the war, he put his name to a scandalous political squib, which appeared to have been prepared by the Polish United Workers' Party's propaganda department, and which appeared under the title of *Byłem adiutantem gen. Andersa* (I was General Anders' adjutant) in Warsaw in 1959.

A WHO'S WHO of the Anders Army looks very different in the 21st century from that in the period of the Army's existence in 1941–1946. Many names prominent in the 1940s disappeared into postwar oblivion. Others, which were relatively obscure in wartime, only met the limelight through later achievements.

Jerzy Giedroyc and Gustaw Herling-Grudziński, for example, worked during the war in the second line of the Army's operations; they emerged after the war as political and literary giants.[112]

Melchior Wańkowicz, who was moderately well known as a war correspondent, rose to much greater heights of fame after he returned to Poland in 1958 and published his classic study of the Battle of Monte Cassino. Daring to air his opposition to the Communist censorship, he was arrested, charged with slandering Poland, and convicted of spreading anti-Polish propaganda abroad. He was rehabilitated posthumously.[113]

LEONID TELIGA aboard *Opty*.

HARDLY ANYTHING IS KNOWN about the war service of Vincent Zhuk-Hryshkevich (1903–1989), except that he joined the Anders Army following release from the Gulag. Before the war, he had worked in the Belarussian Gymnasium in Wilno. After the war, having emigrated to Canada, he became a leading light of the Belarussian–Canadian community, and in 1970, the President of the Belarusian Government-in-Exile.

Leonid Teliga (1917–1970) reached the Anders Army by an unusual route. Wounded in the September Campaign, a soldier of the 44th Infantry Division, he managed to flee to the USSR, to evade the NKVD, and to set up as a fisherman on the Sea of Azov.

Having assisted in the Soviet withdrawal from the Crimean harbours – Sevastopol alone resisted the Nazi onslaught – he made his way across southern Russia to Uzbekistan, joined Anders, and stayed with him till the war's end. One of the few returnees to People's Poland, he cultivated his passion for yachting and in 1967–1969 became the first Pole to circumnavigate the globe.[114]

The entertainer known to the Anders Army as Gwidon Borucki (1912–2009), and to post-war Australians as Guy Lorraine, was born in Austrian Kraków under yet another name. He is best remembered for his handsome looks and for his role as a Polish officer in the film *The Colditz Story* (1955).

Borucki's early fame arose during concerts for the cabaret troupe of Henryk Wars. His stage partner during those performances, and behind the scenes his spouse, competed with him in the art of name-changing. Christened Iryna, the daughter of a Uniate priest, she adopted

JERZY GIEDROYC (top).

IRYNA YAROSEVICH (aka Renata Bogdańska), from 1948, General Anders' second wife.

the stage-name of Renata Bogańska during her prewar career as an actress, and finally, after divorcing and remarrying, she emerged as Irena Andersowa, the General's second wife. The origins of the romance of the glamour girl and her top military commander, 28 years her senior, are concealed in discreet opacity. But at the end of the wartime years of pain and stress, it was recognised as a famous love match. It provides a 'happy ending' to the Army's story, which would otherwise be sadly lacking.

NOT ALL THE *ANDERSOWCY*, not even Anders himself, followed the Army's trail from beginning to end. Thousands died, alas, before they could depart from the USSR. Thousands, for a variety of reasons, left the Army in the Middle East. And thousands were killed, or wounded and released on medical grounds, due to frontline service in Italy.

On the other side of the coin, huge numbers of personnel joined the Army in the course of its progress; the largest influxes to come either from the recruitment of ex-*Wehrmacht* troops or, in early 1945, from ex-Home Army fighters liberated from German captivity. In that final phase of the war, several of the Army's senior officers were posted elsewhere; General Rudnicki, for example, took over command of the 1st Armoured Division in Germany, and Anders served for five months in London as Commander-in-Chief.

Nonetheless, there was a solid body of men and women who kept together all the way 'from Buzuluk to Britain'. They were the Army's backbone. Gustaw Herling-Grudziński was one, Rabbi Pinkas Rosengarten a second, Jadwiga Domańska a third, and there were countless others. They would all have been familiar with Harry Lauder's song, which was very popular with British troops of the era: 'Keep right on to the end of the road'.

10

CHAPTER
1942–1944

CIVILIAN DIASPORA

CHAPTER 10

1942–1944

CIVILIAN DIASPORA

IN 1942–1943, WHEN GENERAL ANDERS WAS CONTENDING WITH HIS MILITARY DUTIES IN IRAN AND IRAQ, THE FATE OF THE 40,000 CIVILIANS WHOM HE HAD BROUGHT OUT OF THE USSR REMAINED AN OPEN QUESTION THAT COULD ONLY BE SETTLED IN STAGES.

The Army, which had organised and managed the exodus, was no longer in a position to cope. But the British authorities in Iran were also hard-pressed, having no facilities or personnel to deal with such a large-scale influx of malnourished and disease-ridden refugees. They turned for assistance, therefore, in the first instance to the Government of Iran, and then to the Colonial Office and to the exiled Polish government in London. The short-term problem was how to keep the refugees alive. The longer-term problem was how and where to provide for them in tolerable circumstances which might last for the rest of the war.

The first task, organised by British reception centres at the main points of arrival, was to count the refugees and to register them. Tens of thousands of questionnaires were distributed, and, sitting in the shade by the beach at Pahlevi or in the park beside the railway station in Mashhad, the newcomers struggled to fill them in. Very few of the refugees understood English, and many of the children had missed years of schooling. In the case of the orphans, of whom there were thousands, many were unaware of basic details, such as age, surname, or place of birth. They were sat down with older children, who could read and write and who endeavoured to extract as much information as possible.

The second task was to break up the mass of refugees into manageable groups and to distribute them among a number of temporary locations where they could be fed and sheltered.

The third task was to set up hospitals, schools, and welfare centres where the refugees' needs could be attended to. Several of these temporary institutions continued to function in Iran till the end of the war.

IN THE MEANTIME, efforts were being made in London to find sponsors who were prepared to take in groups of refugees on a more permanent basis. It must be remembered that in the early 1940s, few international charities like Oxfam (established in 1942) or Save the Children (1919) were functioning, and there was no hope of keeping such large numbers together. Polish government officials in London were obliged to tour the embassies and representatives of other Allied countries to see, if anyone could help. In the following months they succeeded in raising support from five separate sources: the colonial government of British

POLISH ORPHANS welcomed in New Zealand, 1 November 1944, Prime Minister Peter Fraser.

East Africa, the Maharajah of Nawanagar, the Jewish Agency in Palestine, the Government of Mexico, and the Prime Minister of New Zealand. The diaspora was going to be worldwide.

Huge logistical problems remained. Financial subsidies had to be arranged. The War Office had to be approached to provide transport and shipping. And teams of carers had to be raised. It would be well into 1943 before anything positive could start to happen.

RELIEF WORK actually started in advance of the First Evacuation. In December 1942, the Polish Red Cross organised a convoy of lorries which carried food and medical supplies from Bombay to Tehran. These deliveries were destined for the Polish military and civilian refugees who were still in Soviet Central Asia. When the convoy returned in the spring of 1943, completing a round trip of almost 4,000 miles over the wildest terrain, it took with it an advance party which was to set up the camp at Balachadi .

In Tehran, the coordination of relief work was shouldered by the Polish Consulate, and in particular by a team of workers headed by Count Michał Tyszkiewicz and his wife Hanna. The Count, a member of one of Poland's greatest landed families, acted as the link with London and with other participating governments. His wife, Hanna Ordonówna, who had been one of Poland's most popular singers before the war, acted as the link between Tehran and the various groups of civilian adults and children who were preparing to be sent further afield. The process lasted for more than two years, from early 1942 to the end of 1944.

Described chronologically, the despatch of civilians from Iran consisted of a long series of small movements, each with its own collection process, timetable, planned route, and final destination. It was dependent on the capacity of intermediate transit stations, on the availability of shipping, and on information regarding the readiness of distant reception centres. Geographically, the process involved three distinct stages: the first within Iran from initial collection to the point of departure; the second a sea voyage or voyages from a port in the Persian Gulf; and the third involving journeys of distribution within the country of destination. It was spread over four continents: Asia, Africa, North America, and Australasia.

The principal transit camp was built near Ahvaz in south-western Iran, a town within striking distance both of Basra (Iraq) and of the Iranian port of Bandar (now Bandar-e Mahshahr). In addition to rudimentary accom-

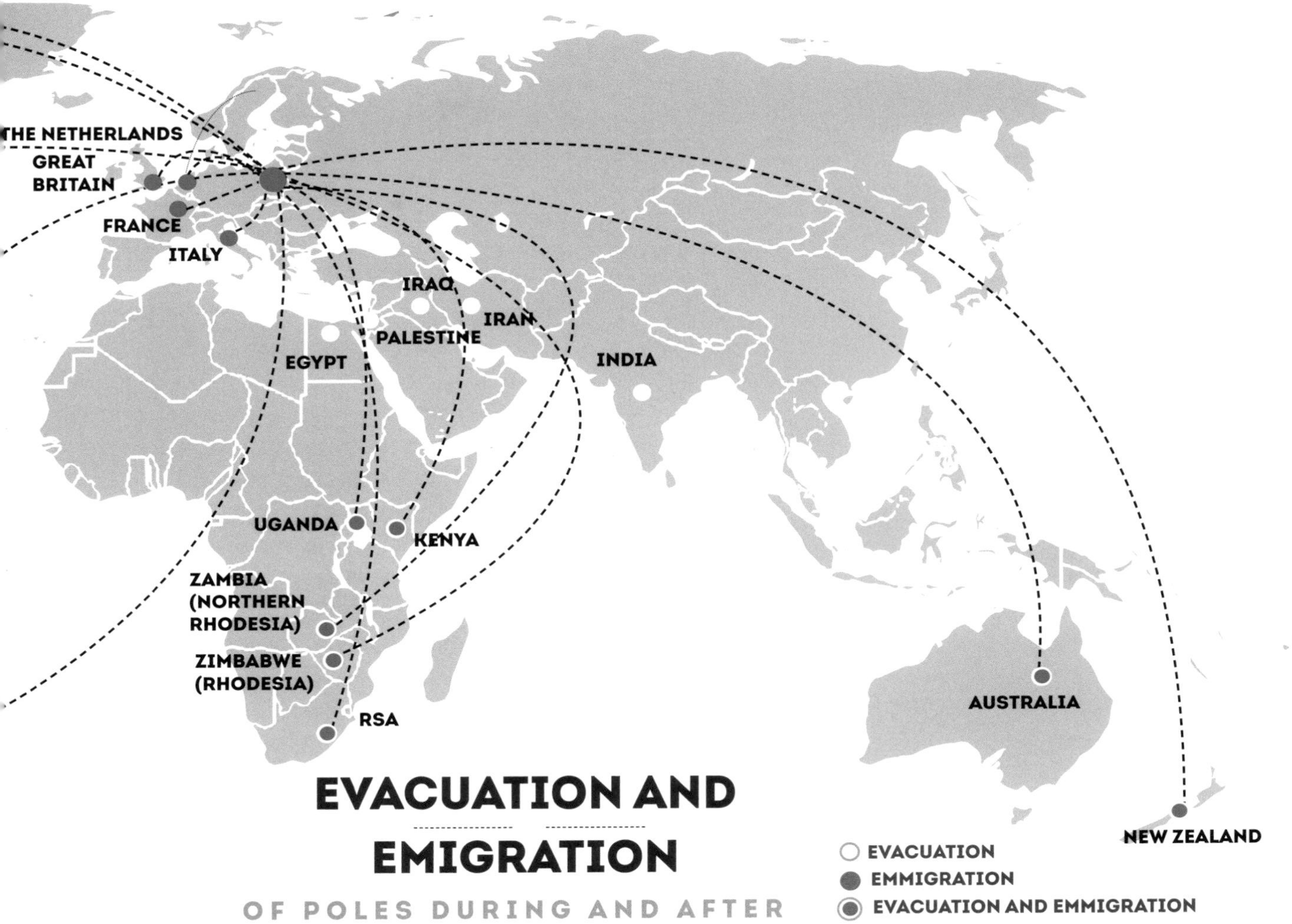

EVACUATION AND EMIGRATION

OF POLES DURING AND AFTER WORLD WAR II

modation blocks, the camp contained an orphanage, a school, a recreation ground, and a hospital. Refugees brought to Ahvaz sometimes waited for weeks or even months before moving on. The more fortunate ones had to wait only hours or days before hearing that the lorries were lined up to take them further towards their port of embarkment.

"I arrived in Ahwaz straight from an orphanage in Tehran. It was August 1943. I stayed there until the end of 1945. Lots of memories, happy and sad, from that camp. Like many others, I came down with malaria, shivering terribly, then having bouts of high temperatures, so they took me to a hospital where I was treated for three weeks. The worst thing was that I felt better after just a few days, but I had to stay at the hospital for the full three weeks of treatment and that was hard. My friends were out there having fun, playing ball, watching movies in the open-air cinema in the evenings and I had to lie in bed. So one evening after the curfew I decided to slip out when the nurse wasn't looking and went to see a movie. Naturally, I was found out even though I had arranged a pillow and sheets under the blanket to make out that I was there asleep. The next day the doctor punished me by taking away all my clothes, pyjamas, shirts, so that I had to lie in bed, completely naked, for 48 hours. I was terribly ashamed as there were also girls and ladies in the hospital room. The other thing I remember is learning to ride a bicycle. We often slipped out of camp without passes to go to the city to rent a bike that we could ride at least for an hour. Food supplies were the barter money: marshmallow, tins of Australian cheese, chocolate etc.

One day in camp it was announced that nobody should go out because it was the Islamic Ramadan and all the stores would be closed, as well as that it could be dangerous. But wanting to ride a bike was stronger than any bans. I and one other boy, we slipped out of the camp and went to town. Everything was closed as announced. We were walking down the main street and suddenly turned into an alley, where we froze with fear.

About a hundred meters before us we saw a crowd of men, some of them shirtless, walking and singing, shouting and lashing one another. We were terribly afraid and started to run as fast as our legs would take us. After a few dozen meters I ran into an American army patrol, stopped them and asked to be taken back to the Polish camp. My friend, who had started running in the opposite direction, did not come back for a long time. Somebody said that he had been kidnapped by the Persians. His mother was in utter despair and people in camp were excited. In the evening a jeep came by with two American soldiers and the Polish boy between them. It turned out that he had also met an American patrol and had gone with them to their camp, where

he was given food and chocolate, sweets and chewing gum. But that was not the end of our adventure. The next day we had to face the camp commandant and were reprimanded by the school director, not to mention what our mothers had to say, but we survived somehow."[115]

At the port, the refugees would board either a small vessel that would take them on a short trip along the Persian Gulf or a larger ship that would take them directly to their new places of exile. Many faced another transit camp in Karachi or Bombay before embarking on the adventure of a major ocean voyage.

IRANIAN LEAFLET on germs and handwashing (top left).

POSTCARD FROM Paris to Lebanon, 5 April 1947, to 'Monsieur St. Kościałkowski', Polish Red Cross (top).

POLISH SCHOOLBOYS, Ajaltoun (Lebanon) (left).

POLISH REFUGEE CAMPS in the Middle East existed long before General Anders left the USSR. The largest of them, in Beirut (Lebanon), was created in 1939 to cater for dependants of the Carpathian Brigade and for other Poles who had reached the Levant via Romania or Turkey. In the course of the war, the number of refugees housed in Beirut swelled to about 6,000, and the Qasqas cemetery contains the graves of close to 150 people who died there. A small memorial marks their presence:

> "Here lie the Poles who escaped gulags and prisons; they passed away on Lebanese land on the way to their Fatherland. Poland remembers them."[116]

The wording of the memorial makes it clear that many of those who died in Beirut had travelled with Anders from Russia.

The first large group to leave Iran, for Lebanon, consisted of about 3,500 boys and girls in the group of 14 to 18 year-olds who were destined for military service as soon as they became adults. Many of them had joined scouting guide troops, which had been formed under

BEIRUT – 'Paris of the Levant'.

Jukowicz Stanisław
STUD. ARCHITEKTURY
Eichler K
STUD. ARCHITE
MAJA ZASZCZYT ZAWIADOMIC
ZE SLUB ICH ODBEDZIE SIE DNIA 18 SIERPNIA
o GODZ 17
W KAPLICY DELEGATURY APOSTOLSKIEJ
W BEIRUCIE

WEDDING INVITATION; Beirut, 18 August 1946. Stanisław Jukowicz and Krystyna Eichler in the Chapel of the Apostolic Delegate.

the Army's auspices in Russia or Central Asia. In Iran they were re-formed into new, pre-military training organisations – the boys as *Junacy* (Cadets) and the girls as *Młode ochotniczki* (literally, Young Girl Volunteers).

The leading party of 500 cadets left Iran by road in May 1942. They enjoyed an extended stay on the shores of Lake Habaniyah in Iraq before crossing the Syrian Desert to base camps at Bashit near Amman, and Rehevot near Tel-Aviv.

The transport operation, which took the young people from Iran to the Levant, lasted from May to August (1942). It was a joyful adventure:

"My long journey to a new life at JSK began at Tehran railway station, where my mother attempted to hand me over to Aunt Rózia Mycielska (*née* Tyszkiewicz) who was travelling with the Polish contingent. She was accompanied by her daughter Zosia, a young woman endowed with a very good figure, daringly poured into a pair of tight trousers. I retired politely to the safety of our hotchpotch platoon of Juniors. The unit was looked after by an elderly sergeant who remembered the Russian Imperial Army. Better him I thought, than female fussing, which at the time I was desperately trying to shake off. In any case there were the fabulous 150 (or thereabouts) railway tunnels to be admired on the way to Basra through Qum and Kazvin, built before the war by the Germans eager to make themselves indispensable to the oil-bearing Middle East.

Basra I remember very well because it was there that I sampled for the first time the 'full English breakfast' cooked by that

GIRL CADETS (*Młode Ochotniczki*), Jenin, Palestine.

superior body of men, the Catering Corps. Fried bacon, and that delicious small pastry that went with it, remain a happy memory. In Basra we were transferred to a narrow-gauge railway and sent on to Baghdad, slowly winding our way through plantations of date palms.

The transit camp on the outskirts of Baghdad was total heaven, because it was presided over by the equivalent of a *Grande École* of the Catering Corps. The pupils of that establishment tried on us their *haute cuisine*, and we embraced their offerings with enthusiasm. Our elderly sergeant wished to return the compliment, and three times a day made us sing in formation as we marched to our feasts.

The third and last part of our journey, the 800 km (500 miles) between Baghdad and Haifa, was a desert ride in a convoy of army lorries. These vehicles were manned by Sikhs, and the column was commanded by a dashing British officer in an open staff car. The Sikhs I found fascinating. Each morning they would perform the ritual of winding their turbans. This they carried out in pairs. One man would walk around his partner in ever-decreasing circles, skilfully depositing new layers of regulation khaki cloth over the other man's head. The roles would then be reversed.

OUR DRIVERS were individualists. Once the dirt track gave way to open desert, they abandoned their formation and started racing. This apparently was a well established Sikh pastime, indulged by the Army provided the CO was able to keep the lid on. Ours was up to the challenge: with panache he herded his lorries by racing round them like a sheep dog, keeping one eye on his compass – the only navigational aid between transit stops. An admiring audience was continuously at his elbow: the most glamorous Polish ATS girls in the convoy were invited to take turns as his passengers. It was a buyer's market.

These goings-on were enjoyable so long as the weather was good. But Iraq's February can be treacherous. We ran into at least one *hamsin*, a desert sand storm whose lashings are as foul as those of a Siberian *buryan*, though for different reasons. We admired the way our CO was able to find his way to our daily destination – the next transit camp – in such conditions. I gather the technique was to look for the outline on the horizon of the regulation water tank on its high stilts.

On the third day the desert, until now a standard yellow-and-grey, turned dark and then almost black. We were approaching Amman, the capital of Transjordan and our last transit stop. This desert 'overnight' was spent in expectant sleeplessness: the next day we were to cross the River Jordan. The approach to that crossing brought with it a dramatic change of scenery. We were suddenly surrounded by orange groves and green farmland; and then greeted by curious glances, and the occasional wave, from the inhabitants of the tidy Jewish settlements, in Haifa, our destination, we caught our first glimpse of the Mediterranean. It was early evening and we were treated to a spectacular sunset.

ST CHARBEL Makhlouf (1828–1898): Maronite monk, beatified 1965, canonized in 1977.

At the Haifa transit camp Polish Army lorries were waiting for the Junior Platoon. The drivers were PSK (Polish ATS) girls who, being gossipy, at once told us that our destination was Camp Barbara near Ashkalon, about 20 km (12 miles) north of Gaza, at the other end of Palestine. We drove into the night, gratefully enjoying the smooth and careful handling of the vehicles by our new lady chauffeurs.

Even in the middle of the night we could see that the camp was as permanent an establishment as a camp can ever be. There were clusters of well made wooden barracks, backed by regular 'quads' of large white tents. We found the camp fast asleep, but at the same time alert. Cadets on night duty could be seen doing their rounds, and armed guards stood at sensitive points. The place radiated confidence.

We were delivered that night to the Distribution Point, where we would await the Army's decision regarding our future. For the newcomers these were tense days. We were interviewed, examined for physical fitness, and our aptitudes, academic and otherwise, were scrutinised. The platoon distracted itself by exploring the camp and admiring its sights, of which the most striking was the enormous red-brick garrison cinema (called for some reason 'Kinema'),

and doubling as chapel, ballroom, concert hall and lecture theatre. The other landmark was the huge water tank at the northern perimeter, elevated high above the tents and barracks, and incidentally providing a perfect vantage point for the press photographers regularly sent down to record the doings of that intriguing Polish enterprise, General Anders' Cadet School".[117]

AFTER ARRIVING AT BASE CAMP and recovering from their journey, the young travellers were directed to one of a dozen schools, most of which had been set up in Palestine and a few in Egypt.

In the months that followed, thousands of exiled Poles made their way to Beirut, either individually or in groups. For those who could afford it, or who had work waiting for them, Beirut was the place to be:

"The Beirut which welcomed my mother and her two daughters no longer exists. After the war it was corrupted by American capitalism and the Sixth Fleet, then torn apart by political and religious strife. But in the mid-1940s, Beirut was a stable cosmopolitan community addicted to commerce, and looking to France for models. Its population of a third of a million was a veritable mixture of races and creeds, with Christians narrowly outnumbering Muslims.

Blue sea, blue skies, green mountains. The city's setting was – and is – unforgettable, on a headland between the bays of St Andrew and St George. The locals claim that St George did exist, and that he was in fact their own exclusive saint before the English came and hijacked him. Hotel Saint George, Beirut's most famous landmark, still proclaims this assertion. The *mise-en-scène* is not as

LEBANESE CEDAR trees.

CRUSADER SEA castle in Sidon.

dramatic as Hong Kong or Rio, but it exudes harmony. Before the arrival of the skyscraper, the architectural tone was dictated by handsome nineteenth-century houses flanked by almond trees, jacaranda and bougainvillea. Many of these houses had roof gardens. Pines and cypresses dominated the high ground, and resplendent palms lined the Corniche and the Avenue des Français, the Levant's centre of gravity. The precious cedar had gone, but a grove of some 400 specimens lingers on at Bcharre, high above Tripoli, familiar to today's tourists as the 'Cedars of Lebanon'.

The Polish Army and its civilian dependants needed doctors and chaplains. The potential remedy was waiting in the ranks: the prewar medical students and seminarians. Someone reminded the Polish Authorities of the reputation of Beirut's faculties of theology and medicine at the University of Saint Joseph. The University's response was positive: the young men would be welcome to come and complete their studies. Such was the beginning of the Polish wartime presence in the Lebanon. Soon the American University of Beirut joined the scheme, and other disciplines were offered to young Poles of promise in anticipation of postwar needs.

For the Polish exiles in pursuit of learning, Beirut was a place of historical significance. The founder of Saint Joseph was after all a Pole (albeit from the Grand Duchy of Lithuania), still remembered in the Levant as *Abuna Mansur*, or Father Conqueror; and by the French as *l'Homme incroyable*. The poet Słowacki stayed in 1837 at the monastery of Beit-Chesh-Ban, where he wrote his great prose poem *Anhelli*. In the sixteenth century a grandee globetrotter, Mikołaj Krzysztof Radziwiłł, had written an early and detailed description of the Levant.

The Lebanese government came to like the itinerant Polish students in uniform. Soon hospitality was extended to several thousand Polish exiles. These people were dispersed among the small towns and villages surrounding Beirut. The dispersion suggested a need for a focus. The Polish Legation and the *Delegatura* responded with a plan to establish in the capital a 'Polish House'. Anna Giedroyć, fresh from her Tehran successes, was designated its organiser and first administrator.

Priority visas were issued, and my mother and sisters arrived in Beirut, courtesy of Nairn Brothers' trans-desert coach service, in late November 1944. My mother's dreams of higher education for Anuśka and Tereska were soon dispelled. They were seduced by our British allies into interesting secretarial work at ENSA. All three moved into what was to become the Polish House, and my mother went into action. In December, Father Kantak (an historian at USJ) blessed the premises and the new venture, and on 1 January 1945 Anna Giedroyć's appointment was formally confirmed.

THE HOUSE WAS IMPOSING. A wide marble staircase adorned by potted palms led to the grand reception rooms upstairs. The location high above the port afforded a view, and the quiet sidestreet peace and seclusion. It was a prime site, where my mother soon created a social and cultural centre, doubling at the same time as a transit hotel for the several thousand new Polish arrivals steadily pouring into the Lebanon. 'Here,' wrote Father Kantak, 'in the principal drawing room, we had meetings, cultural events and lectures; here the new arrivals found hospitality and food.' My mother was particularly proud of her small but ambitious catering staff who three times a day cooked for up to a hundred people. The scale was impressive; so was the quality of the food.

All this I observed from the sidelines during my Easter 1945 break from the Cadet School. At that time my mother was totally – and anxiously – absorbed in Tereska's nuptials, arranged (by special dispensation from the Papal Nuncio) for Easter Sunday. The whole affair proceeded at breakneck speed: it was still wartime, and Tereska was determined. The manner of Stach's and Tereska's engagement, which took place only a few weeks earlier, illustrates the romantic intensity of what my mother described at the time as a *coup de foudre*. Stach, still on crutches, arrived from the front determined to take a discreet first look at his faithful correspondent. He managed this at Halabi's in the Avenue des Français, a restaurant favoured by the Polish community. My sister's friend Helenka Zaleska remembers: 'One day, over lunch with Tereska, I noticed an officer unknown to us holding a photograph and making enquiries. I went up to him and discovered that the photograph was of Tereska! Their first meeting took place at our table. Within days they were engaged.'

The arrival of the bridegroom accompanied by his best man, a regimental colleague called Misiewicz, created a stir. The impeccably turned-out young men who had recently fought their way up Monte Cassino came to us marked with that special confidence, which belongs to those who have seen battle and lived to savour the victory. After the horrors of the previous six years, this seemingly reckless marriage on Easter Sunday became a celebration of life and renewal. The private chapel of the Nuncio, and later the principal drawing room of the Polish House, provided a worthy setting.

On the strength of her success with the Polish House, my mother was asked to set up a new hall of residence for Polish ATS girls studying at the American University of Beirut. This came to be known as the White House. One of my mother's charges remembers, 'We liked our White House and we were proud of it.

ON THE Anders Trail in Lebanon: a group of motorcyclists organised by Father Wiesław Lenartowicz, 2009.

The Warden maintained firm discipline, but at the same time each of us felt able to enjoy a great deal of freedom; we all knew that our shared concerns, and our individual problems, were understood.' This tribute sums up my mother's secret: discipline on loose reins.

The young ladies of the White House were not privy to their Warden's concern about the potentially harmful influence of the Beirut Polish Students' Union (*Bratniak*), dominated by one or two 'eternal students' – carriers of the less laudable habits of Poland's prewar university life. There was one particularly irresistible individual, an ageing 2nd lieutenant in the Polish Army whose reluctance to return to the frontline was matched by his reluctance to immerse himself in his studies. During this man's chairmanship, *Bratniak* was side-tracked into pretentious socialising and dubious politics. My mother's worries about the effect of these distractions on her young charges were shared by Father Kantak and the Legation responsible for the conduct and welfare of the students. In the event, the young ladies of the White House survived *Bratniak's* temptations, and in due course most of them delivered creditable results with cheerful poise.

The White House also benefited from my mother's circle of friends and acquaintances. In Tehran the exiles still lived in the shadow of the Soviet presence. Lebanon, under the control of the Western Allies, seemed a haven of security. Reassured, people rediscovered entertaining and visiting. My mother's position and her comfortable lodgings encouraged social life of almost prewar quality.

Contacts with the British Language School for Arabists, i.e. future diplomats and spies, were interesting. Sometimes my mother and

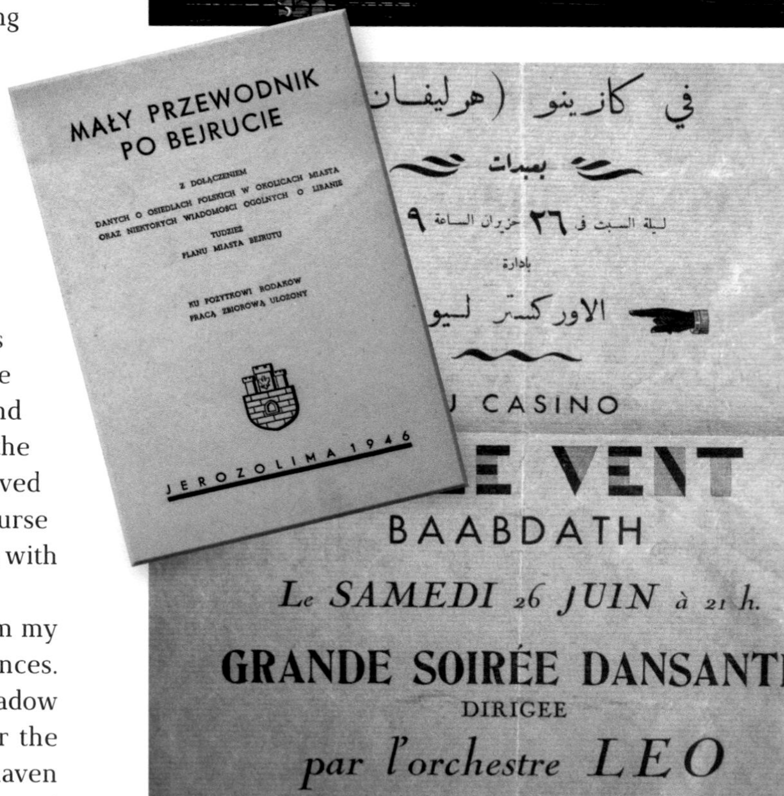

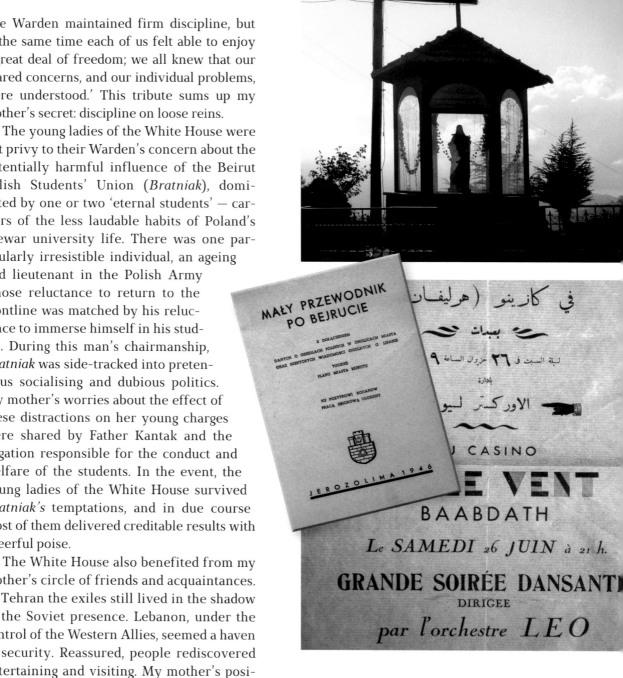

WAYSIDE MARONITE shrine, Lebanon (top).

POLISH 'GUIDEBOOK to Beirut' (Jerusalem 1946) (centre) and invitation to a 'Grande Soirée Dansante' at Baabdath in Lebanon.

my sisters joined them on their excursions to historical sites. The young linguists and their minders were congenial company."[118]

Refugees heading for British East Africa were usually sent by sea from Karachi to Mombasa. The voyage of 2,700 miles took five or six days. On arrival at Mombasa, the weary travellers were taken for rest and recovery to the nearby transit camp at Makindu. Apart from the short trip across the Caspian, most of them had never experienced the rigours of a voyage on the open ocean, and were extremely relieved to reach dry land:

"In 1943, we were shipped across the Indian Ocean... to [East Africa], arriving in Port Mombassa. We were loaded onto barges, and taken down several waterways, and then by road, ending up in Massindi, not far from Lake Albert, some distance from Kampala.

Near Massindi large camps were built to accommodate Polish civilians. The sites for these camps... were chosen by representatives of the Polish government in London, and we were to stay there until the end of the war. We were allocated half a mud hut with a straw-covered roof, [and] with nothing inside but wooden beds on a mud floor. The cooking stove was outside, with just a roof for cover. Toilets were a little further from the hut — just a latrine.

The camp was five minutes from the jungle; there were beautiful flowers, banana trees, papayas and marvellous birds and butterflies. The weather was mostly tropical, hot and sunny, but with violent thunderstorms quite regularly. One day there was a rumour that local Africans were coming to kill us, because they did not want white people on their soil, but nothing happened.

In Massindi, my Mother met Franciszek Silarski, whose wife had died in Siberia... and [whose] three sons were in the Polish Army... They were married in 1944, and I was very happy. He was very kind. My stepbrother Adam was born in September 1945.

One day, my Mother left [Adam] in his crib and went on with her chores. She did not see a little monkey sitting on the roof. A few minutes later she heard my brother screaming and... [his] face was covered in blood. The doctor who stitched the wound said he was very lucky: if [the monkey] had bitten his eyes, he would be blind...

We stayed in Massindi for five years, which I enjoyed very much and made lots of friends... We got on well together in those long sunny evenings after school. I [had] finished five years of schooling when news came that WWII in Europe was now over".[119]

EIGHT POLISH CAMPS were established in East Africa in 1942–1943. One of them, Rongai, was in Kenya, not far from the capital, Nairobi. Two, Masindi and Koja, were in the inland colony of Uganda, and five were in the former German territory of Tanganyika — Tengeru, Kondoa, Kidugala, Ifunda, and Morogoro. Each of the camps had its own character. Koja, for example, enjoyed a beautiful location on the shores of Lake Victoria. Tengeru lay at the foot of the great snow-covered peak of Mount Kilimanjaro.

Karolina Mariampolska (b. 1930 in Stanisławów) was a pupil at Koja Camp. She had been deported to Siberia with her mother, after her father was consigned to the Gulag. She was evacuated with other Army dependants to Iran, whence she sailed for Africa. In 1952, she was to marry Ryszard Kaczorowski, a prominent Polish scoutmaster in London, and in 1989–1990 would become 'Poland's First Lady' when her husband took office as the last President of the Government-in-Exile.

Yet all the camps shared many common features. All of them were little islands of Polishness

MASINDI (UGANDA), Corpus Christi Mass, 1944 (top).

MARKET AT Tengeru in Tanganyika (opposite).

under the African sun, and often in remote bush country. All were designed to receive families, who were housed in simple huts built from local materials. All had schools where the children were taught in Polish, often using prewar textbooks sent from London. All had a church served by a Polish Catholic priest. All had a hospital to care for the sick and elderly and had a director appointed by a Government Delegate sent from London and charged with the welfare of Poles in a particular district or colony. Most of them, however, were entirely self-governing and key decisions were taken by parents or by an elected camp council. Most were remembered by their residents as 'the happiest time of our lives' or 'one long summer holiday'.

Many accounts of life in the Polish camps in East Africa convey the image of an equatorial idyll – peace, calm and an orderly existence after the nightmares of Siberia. Many former residents of these 'little Polands in the jungle' do indeed recall their time there with fondness.

Yet observers, who looked more closely, saw that conditions could be less than perfect:

> "Father Krolikowski's observation was that the majority of the children were fine, but that there were a few boys who were a serious problem and he worried about them. They did not form gangs, nor did they engage in destructive practices, but he was concerned about their attitude nonetheless. He became increasingly alarmed at the growing barbarity of some of them, fuelled by the 'lax conditions in Africa', as he put it. The lack of male teachers to act as role models, and the poor quality of the few male teachers they did have, were important contributing factors. Many of the men who were sent to the camps to act as policemen, and in other offices, and who might have been possible role models were, to

use both Father Krolikowski's and Al Kunicki's word, 'rejects'. Father Krolikowski described them as 'psychopaths, hot-heads, moral degenerates', men dismissed from the army at a time when the army needed soldiers – obviously of questionable character. While not all men would have fit this description, it took only a few to have a disturbing influence.

As well, the camp was already a very unnatural society, unbalanced in a variety of ways. Although the size of a small town, it did not have the same web of economic, social, and political relationships that make up a functioning society. Even the families were incomplete, because most fathers were serving in the military. Husbandless mothers were in the majority and, although they tried to exert influence over their children, by the time the children were teenagers, their mothers had usually lost any influence they might have had. For the orphans, there was not even that leavening agent. The female teachers had little authority over the teenagers, and there was no effective way of imposing sanctions on the children. No matter what the children did, they knew they were guaranteed food, shelter, and clothing. Even if they behaved, the camp had little more to offer them, so there was no tangible reward for good behaviour and no effective punishment for bad. To compound the situation, their experiences in Russia had taught them to distrust all authority and that the only people who would take care of them would be themselves or their siblings."[120]

Refugees heading for Northern or Southern Rhodesia usually sailed to Dar-es-Salaam, 190 miles to the south of Mombasa. From there, they were transported to one of seven camps, four

AFRICAN EXILE

FOLK DANCING (top left); First Communion in national dress (centre); girls at close quarters with a python (top right); Tengeru Camp, Uganda (below centre); Girl Guides meeting with their superior (below right).

of which: Lusaka, Bwana M'kubwa, Livingstone, and Abercorn were in Northern Rhodesia (today's Zambia), and three: Rusape, Digglefold, and Marandellas in Southern Rhodesia (today's Zimbabwe).

Life in the Rhodesian camps was much the same as that in East Africa. The residents lived a simple, peaceful life of everyday chores and education, enlivened by religious festivals, patriotic parades, choral singing and, above all, scouting. It was in this part of Africa that Robert Baden-Powell had first imagined the worldwide scouting movement. And conditions there for practising the skills of trekking, tracking, camping, and cooking in the wild were ideal. Scouts and guides were warned of the dangers of disturbing elephants, lions, leopards, and hyenas:

"One of the schoolgirls, Zofia Wierzbicka from Marandellas, organised scouting at Digglefold. Circumstances being favorable and thanks to the personal interest of the commander of the Local Scout Council of Southern Rhodesia, scoutmaster Stanisława Staszewska-Barska from Salisbury, a team of 15 girl scouts formed one of the best troops in all of Africa. In 1944, the methods of scouting were taught at Digglefold for two weeks by scoutmaster J. Brzeziński and assistant scoutmaster Z. Słowikowski. In 1945, the Digglefold scout troop consisted of three teams counting altogether 117 girl scouts. Assistant scoutmaster Irena Sobocka, who headed them, was honoured as the best girl scout in South Rhodesia. The centre was a base for training courses for the youth club and scout staff. Scout contacts were maintained with the English scouts from Marandellas and Salisbury; the local press wrote of a joint campfire event organised at Digglefold. Other than the scouts at Digglefold, there was also the Marian Sodality and a common room with student store sponsored by the Polish YMCA. There was a rich artistic and publishing life – a newspage was edited. Poetry was written. Embroidery. The schools maintained good prewar Polish education standards. Apart from their classes, the girls were taught everything that they would have learned traditionally in a Polish home."[121]

GRADUATION EXAMS, Tengeru.

Over half of the civilian exiles who left the USSR with the Polish Army found refuge in Africa. Thinking of all the friends and relatives whom they had lost, they could only praise Providence and thank God for their good fortune. Some of them were fortunate enough to see several African countries:

"In the spring of 1944, we travelled by army truck from Iran to Karachi, and then by ship to Africa... and then by train to camp called Bwana M'Kubwa in what was then Northern Rhodesia... We stayed [there] until [Mother, a teacher] was posted to Lusaka, now in Zambia.

MASAI WARRIORS, near Tengeru (above).

SCHOOLBOYS AND schoolgirls at Tengeru (left).

My first, very ordinary childhood memories are from Lusaka: a dark-eyed beauty called Jagódka sitting opposite me in the kids' sandpit; starting school at five in the seven-year-old's class... and the wonder of electric lighting in the commandant's hut.

By 1947, the camps were being liquidated. First a commission from the Polish Communist regime set up by Stalin arrived to persuade us to return to Communist Poland. They received short shrift from people whose homes had been annexed by Russia... and who were still thanking God for delivering them from the Soviet paradise.

The Americans came next, followed by the Canadians, Australians and New Zealanders to take their pick of humanity on offer. In that particular market, my Mother... was inundated with offers. But my grandfather was old, and might be a burden on the host country... To my mother's eternal credit, she turned all the offers down. [So] we were the last to leave Lusaka at the beginning of 1949...

Mother was posted to a camp called Tengeru near Arusha in what is now Tanzania. Tengeru was dominated by a splendid view of

Mount Meru but… it appeared to be in the middle of nowhere. We were allocated a pair of mud huts… These were exciting for us kids, but Mother didn't share our enthusiasm… and we soon moved to one of the large posh square huts with a concrete floor, windows with wire mesh mosquito nets, and a separate outside kitchen. I can't remember if there was any electricity; I have a feeling that even the commandant used paraffin lamps for lighting…

Tengeru was much bigger than [the camp] at Lusaka. It had a primary school, two secondary schools… and a large boarding house for orphans and young people separated from their parents. There was considerable agricultural activity. Apart from the gardens… around people's huts, there were large fields of maize, potatoes and other vegetables like carrots and cabbage…

By early 1950, only those who had been rejected by the [immigration] commissions… were left in the camp. That's when the British commission arrived… I think they knew that leaving people in the middle of Africa was not an option; their main concern were people who had health problems, [particularly] TB, or needed treatment before sailing [to England].

In July, we travelled by train from Arusha to Mombassa, and then sailed on the Dundalk Bay to England, arriving in Hull on 2 September 1950. After a few days, we travelled in a fleet of coaches to Springhill Lodges camp in the beautiful Cotswold countryside."[122]

Refugees heading for South Africa sailed either to Durban or to Port Elizabeth. They were concentrated in one large camp at Oudtshoorn in Cape Province. They found themselves in a bountiful region of rich farmland, orchards, and vineyards. Unlike their compatriots further north, they were not out on the veldt or in the jungle. They were in a well-developed land of rural villages and small towns, and could easily benefit from expeditions to Cape Town or to the beaches of the Cape of Good Hope.

THE DOMINION OF SOUTH AFRICA was one of most pleasant countries to which refugees were directed in the 1940s. The racial conflicts of later times were absent, and the government's policy of *apartheid* was yet to come. The climate of Cape Province was less extreme than in the British colonies further north, and the local population was well disposed:

3 MAY celebrations, Koja (Uganda).

After that first encounter, the boys set off to hunt for peacocks in the wild. At one point, they thought they had succeeded:

> "We surround the cactus on all sides, and start to close the ring. Slowly and silently, we move in, fearing to disturb the bird prematurely. One more step or two, and perhaps we'll catch it.
>
> I am alongside Stefan, who points to the shadows under the bush. Something there is moving. Blinded by the sun, we can't see too well... but one last step and the bird will be ours.
>
> Bending down, we stretch out our hands. Then, we are stopped in our tracks, only a few centimetres in front of us, as if sprung from the ground, we see the huge swollen head of a cobra..."[125]

Defeated in the wild, the lads turned to domesticating a variety of small animals. Some kept lizards in boxes; others caught scorpions, and spiders for frightening the girls:

> "The greatest success fell to our cheeky little friend, Fredzio, who caused a sensation by walking round the Settlement with his pet mongoose on a lead. The mongoose, which was named 'Riki' after Kipling, though trained, was an odd, hairy creature which had lost little of its aggressive nature.
>
> [One day, when a snake was reported in the camp], the Commandant put the garden out of bounds. But we had the idea of putting the mongoose to the test. Approaching the garden, it bristled, and bolted into the bushes, pulling the lead out of Fredzio's hands. For two or three minutes, we heard the commotion of a life-and-death struggle. Then 'Riki' reappeared, dragging his lead and gaining a round of applause. [We found] the remains of a 4-foot snake, to which Fredzio promptly claimed the right, saying he would try to tan its skin."[126]

Valivade, in contrast to Balachadi, was located in the land of the Hindu Marathi people, whose specifics were described in the newsletter *Polak w Indiach* of 13 September 1944. It

DORMITORY UNDER canvas.

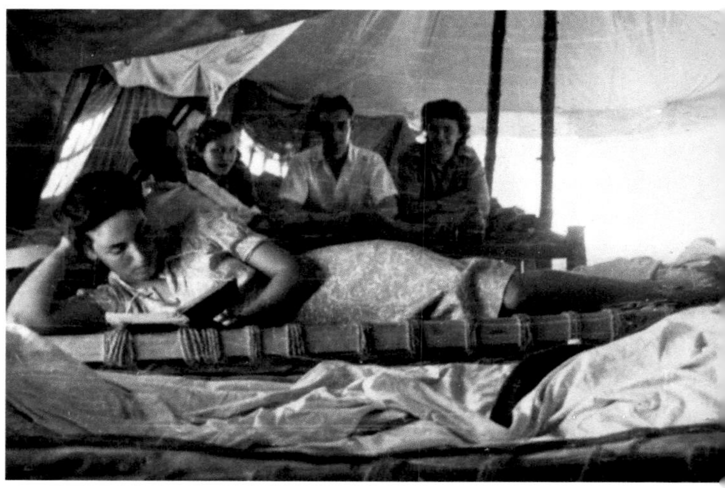

turned out that Valivade was Kolhapur, and that it possessed a dynasty of maharajas of its own:

"Kolhapur probably derives its name from its geographical position because 'Koll' means a depression between the hills, which translates into Kollapur, eventually becoming Kolhapur in the Maratha language.

It was only in the sixteenth century that the Marathas led by Shivaji Bhonsale, later called 'the Great', fought to free themselves from the Mahommedan yoke, creating the Maratha kingdom in the middle of India. In 1674, Shivaji was crowned king of Raigad and assumed the title of Chhatrapati (Lord of the Canopy). He was tolerant in religious matters and supportive of economic development. He had a strong army and a fleet of several hundred ships, plus over two hundred forts.

THE PRINCELY STATE OF KOLHAPUR was over 3,200 square miles. According to the 1941 census, the population was over a million, 93,000 of whom lived in the town itself. Situated half way between Pune and Goa, it lies on the plateau nearly 1,800 ft. above sea level on the Panchganga river, a tributary of Krishna. The state stretched from the Western Ghats covered with evergreen monsoon forests to the fertile Deccan plains in the East. Its main products were rice and sugar cane from which the popular molasses was made. Villagers were weaving rough cloth and making clay pots. The town was famed throughout India for its soft leather shoes and sandals (chappals). In our time, Kolhapur was also an important centre of the film industry and in Panhala one could encounter film crews engaged in making historical and mythological films.

After Shivaji's death in 1680, the fight for succession broke out between his two sons, Sambhaji and Rajaram, and their descendants, culminating in the meeting between the two cousins in 1731 below the fort walls of Panhala. A truce supposedly securing peace and tranquillity was signed. It was a great occasion, the splendour of which purportedly outshone the meeting of Henry VIII and Francis I on 'the field of the cloth of gold' in France, but the martial people of Kolhapur soon found an outlet in piracy and warfare.

When the capital was moved from Panhala to Kolhapur in 1782 the town entered its third

THE MAHARAJAH'S family, Balachadi.

CHRISTMAS IN Quetta – en route to India.

stage with the building of the royal palace behind the temple. The town defences were strengthened and with the establishment of British Superintendence in 1845 the fourth stage of development began and lasted until Indian independence.

In 1821 Maharajah Absaheb was murdered in his own palace in Kolhapur. The assassins were caught and condemned to be trampled to death by elephants in Panhala's courtyard, which we called 'the elephants' yard'. Relative peace followed the nascent of British rule after the 1857 uprising, which the Kolhapur Marathas did not join.

Thus we reach the beginning of the 20th century when the Kolhapur Chhatrapatis received from the British the hereditary title of Maharaj. Shahu was decorated with GCSL, GCVO, GCIE, and Cambridge university gave him an honorary law degree. He was also awarded the 19 gun salute.

He was succeeded by Rajaram II who continued the enlightened policy of his father and started democratic innovations. The town Council responsible for education, health care and communication became electable from 1927. Two years later the High Court and Appeal Law Court was established. He also modernised the drainage, and established free education for women. In 1933 an office of the Resident to Kolhapur was created to have a direct link with the Central Government and the Viceroy.

When he died in 1940 without male issue, the elder of his two wives, Dowager Maharani Tarabai had to adopt an heir, the one year old Pratapsingh, Shivaji V".[127]

Such was the state of play when the infant Maharajah's lands saw the first influx of Polish refugees in 1942. Those Poles insisted that they lived at Valivade not in a 'camp' but in a large orderly 'settlement'. At all events, they enjoyed

INDIA

THE MAHARAJAH'S palace and Rolls-Royce, Jamnagar; Indian children greeting visitors.

UNVEILING OF A MEMORIAL TABLET, Balachadi 1989 (below left); the Maharaja's son with Wiesław Stypuła, one of the schoolchildren from Balachadi. "To the Land of Jamnagar, which gave shelter and hospitality to thousands of homeless Polish children during World War II...". Wiesław Stypuła with his daughter Agnieszka Michałowska in front of the maharaja's palace in Kolhapur (bottom centre) .

NAWANAGAR
7
GJY · 4757

CHILDREN AND teacher waiting for transfer to Balachadi.

conditions that were markedly better than what they had endured in the USSR or in Iran.

The leading work, *The Poles in India,* runs to 644 pages and a good half of it is devoted to Kolhapur-Valivade. It includes every conceivable topic from administrative details and relations with the Government of India's Refugee Organisation to education, sport, culture, scouting, religious life, festivals, expeditions, visits to Hindu temples, and even 'eccentric characters':

> "In Valivade we had a mixture of people from all parts of Poland, from all social classes, different ethnic groups and unconventional individuals. The most mysterious personality was Ćwiek, the tall, dark-skinned King of the Gypsies.
>
> Another colourful character was Radziwoniuk who collected specimens of all Indian snakes, lizards, scorpions, [and] beetles and preserved them in jars or dried them. He had two barracks in which to do his experiments and planned to take his specimens back home to Poland after the end of the war. He tried to become immune to poisonous snake-bites. Many years later in the Polish mountains one of the boys who knew him in Valivade met him again. M. Radziwoniuk caught snakes for the zoo, living in the forest in the wild all through the summer, telling stories of his knowledge acquired from the Indian

snake-charmers about plants which made poisonous snake bites harmless. [...]

Then there was Mr A. Bojko, who was hero-worshipped by boys, because he told them incredible stories of his exploits as a pilot. He might have really been a pilot some time in the past, before he became concussed and confused.

Newcomers to our Camp would often suffer from shock when they came face to face with Adolf Hitler's double. It was Mr Ignacy Kasprowicz who worked as an accountant; however, his hair style, his moustache and his whole bearing were identical with that of the German Fuehrer. He was generally known as 'our Hitler'. Those who were with him at the time of his landing in England after the end of the war, tell the story of the reaction of those standing on the shore with great humour. Nobody knows what happened to him later."[128]

A very precise account exists of Valivade's administration:

"In January 1943, K. Banasińska as a Delegate of the Ministry of Social Welfare, wrote to Minister J. Stańczyk in London that 'Capt. A.W.T. Webb (*the Principal Refugee Officer in the Government of India*) is of the opinion that the Camp Commandant should be a Pole. He thinks that to appoint an Englishman could be unfavourably interpreted as an inability to govern ourselves. He emphasises that the whole administration should be in Polish hands. At the same time he advises against full autonomy, which was tried in camps of other nationalities, and it did not work due to local intrigues and quarrels... He is also against any presence of a Consular representative, as this might encourage a split in the proper functioning of the administration.'

AT THE END OF FEBRUARY 1943 the Foreign Office notified the Polish Embassy in London that the Camp will be ready in March, which was an impossibility, if one takes into account that the permission for its construction was given only a few days previously...

The Administration consisted of the following Departments:

ULICA SIKORSKIEGO (Sikorski Street) in Balachadi.

WIESŁAW STYPUŁA, sometime pupil at Balachadi, shows off his scouting neckscarf.

Administration Office
Building & Technical
Voluntary Fire Brigade
The Post Office
Refugee Records Office
Sports Section
Financial & Management
Cultural & Educational
Camp Security Guards
Army Families Register
Health Service

Their work was based on the Statute of the Polish Refugees in India dated 25 June 1943, which was replaced with minor amendments six months later by the Rules and Regulations.

FROM THE VERY BEGINNING, until his removal caused by his negative attitude during the registration by UNRRA, the Camp Commandant was Capt. W. Jagiełłowicz, at a salary of Rs 500 per month. He had overall control of the Camp administration and represented the Camp to outside Authorities. He was responsible for the management of the approved Camp Budget. He also endeavoured to convey the needs and desires of its inhabitants to the Delegate of the Social Welfare Ministry in Bombay. He was very popular and generally respected as "father figure" of the Camp. To help him in his task he had a deputy, O. Grabianka and a quartermaster Z. Łopiński (@ Rs 300 each, monthly). The rest of the administration consisted of secretaries, interpreters and messengers with remuneration of Rs 40–50 monthly."[129]

One Polish woman from Valivade even had the good fortune to meet Mahatma Ghandhi:

"I worked in the Polish Rest Centre in Panchgani as a teacher and a nurse among the Polish children threatened by tuberculosis, and undergoing convalescent hospital treatment. One day we found out that Gandhi had arrived in Panchgani for relaxation and to restore his health, weakened by one of his consecutive hunger strikes.

In Panchgani at that time we had a number of young people who had previously attended the lectures about India given by Wanda Dynowska, when she lived for a while in Valivade. She was on friendly terms with

THEATRE AT Valivade. Standing next to King Herod and the devil is Hitler as a personification of evil.

Gandhi and talked a lot about him and his great mission. On learning that this Living Legend was near us, we decided to visit him. On the way there we purchased the most beautiful garland of flowers to greet him in accordance with Indian custom.

We trembled with emotion as we stood in front of the house where Gandhi was living. The house was small, with a verandah running around it and surrounded with trees. A beautiful white goat was tied up to one of the trees.

BALACHADI: BOYS with Indian doctor Tavinder Singh (top left).

CHILDREN WITH Maharajah (top right).

CAROUSEL AT Balachadi (centre left).

MAHARAJAH GREETED by boy's band, Balachadi.

A girl, who turned out to be Gandhi's granddaughter, said that Mahatma would come out shortly. In a while a small and frail looking figure appeared in the doorway. The Living Legend was dressed in a white *dhoti* (a cotton garment instead of trousers) sharply

INDIA

STAŚ HARASYMOWICZ with mother Antonina and with Frank Cwetsch, Valivade, 8 July 1943 (below); sewing class at Valivade (top right); the Tyszkiewicz family at Valivade (centre right); on a bicycle outing in Quetta stopped by a flood on the river Tiger (now Pakistan) (bottom right).

COLORFUL PARADE in Kolhapur (opposite centre); the children from Balachadi with a Polish flag from the SS *Kościuszko* (top right); refugee kids in Valivade (opposite centre); street and church in Valivade (opposite bottom).

contrasting with his dark skin, sun burned and dried up by the long lasting fast. Gandhi, leaning on his walking stick, came forward to greet us in the Indian way, hands together, and invited us on to his verandah. We stepped onto the verandah almost on our toes, completely overwhelmed. In front of us stood this small, old Man, emanating such power, that he seemed to be a giant.

GANDHI SAT DOWN on the spread out mats and asked us to do the same. A person from our group presented him with the garland of flowers, and someone else said a few words by way of greeting. I was so thrilled with the excitement of being in the presence of this great man who was shaping the future of India that everything else escaped my attention.

From behind his round spectacles we saw these smiling eyes full of goodwill. His eyes looked young in contrast to his tired face and frail body dressed all in white. Finally he spoke up in a quiet and somehow tired voice, which gained strength as he carried on with the speech. He talked about his friendly feelings towards the Poles and Poland and lamented over the tragedy of the Polish nation. He said that his fellow countrymen and we share the same love for our homeland and desire for freedom, the greatest treasure of all. There is no such sacrifice that is not worth giving for the good of the homeland, not even the sacrifice of life. He also admitted that in the struggle with a foe, *satyagraha* (struggle without the use of violence and hatred) is not always effective, because the conditions are not always suitable, but he warned about hatred, which is a destructive force leading only to disaster. He recalled Christ's teaching about love for fellow men, about forgiving those who harm us and His teaching that our fellow man means not only our friend, but also our foe. It is easy to forgive our friend, but to forgive one's enemy is greater achievement. When we showed our surprise that Gandhi knew the New Testament, he smiled and said

POLISH FOLK dancing, Jamnagar (above).

GŁOS INDIOM

HARCERSTWA

Dnia 4 czerwca 1943 r. odbywa się w Karachi pierwsze w Indiach przyrzeczenie harcerskie, które od 70 chłopców i dziewcząt przyjmuje phm. Bidakowski Władysław. Drugie przyrzeczenie w Indiach odbyło się w Balachadi — Jamnagar dnia 15 sierpnia 43 r., które odbiera phm. J. Ptakowa. Wyjazd drużyn z Karachi do Meksyku i sąsiedniego obozu w Malir powoduje opróżnienie obozu z elementu harcerskiego, jednak nie na długo, gdyż w sierpniu przybywają nowe drużyny z Iranu, składające się z młodzieży dopiero rozpoczynającej swą służbę w harcerstwie. Stąd pietrzą się przed nią trudności z powodu braku zastępowych i drużynowych. W tym czasie na terenie księstwa Kolhapur, w środkowo — zachodnich Indiach, powstaje w Valivade nad rzeką duże osiedle polskie, do którego zostaje przeniesiony cały obóz z Malir.

Bazar w Panhali

Dnia 1 września 1943 r. odbyła się w Valivade pierwsza odprawa kierowników jednostek harcerskich. Na odprawie tej zorganizowano Komendę Hufca Valivadzkiego; w ciągu 10 dni zgłoszono do Komendy Hufca 4 drużyny harcerzy, 8 drużyn harcerek i 4 gromady zuchów.

Dnia 10 listopada 43 r. odbywa się pierwsze przyrzeczenie w Valivade, które jest trzecim z rzędu przyrzeczeniem w Indiach.

Należy na tym miejscu podkreślić kontakty naszego harcerstwa z lokalnymi organizacjami skautów angielskich i hinduskich. I tak, w październiku 1943 r. hufiec Valivade nawiązuje łączność z miejscową organizacją skautów hinduskich „Balewir”: odbywają się wspólne gry i ćwiczenia. Skauci hinduscy wskazują i ułatwiają uzyskanie wspaniałych terenów pofortecznych na płaskowyżu w Panhali pod obozy i kursy. Drużyna skautów hinduskich z Kolhapur odwiedza kurs dru-

209

"SKAUT": PUBLISHED by the Polish Scouting Union in the East for Iran, Africa, Egypt and Palestine.

that among all the other holy books he also owned the Bible and drew from it strength and understanding of the human soul.

Gandhi's face showed signs of weariness. Several times already, his granddaughter had appeared in the doorway looking at him with deep concern. Just before saying farewell to us, Gandhi said that he always remembers in his prayers Poland and Poles scattered around the world and wished us a speedy return to our country, to work and live there. We left in silence, fully aware of the significance of this meeting for us."[130]

The Polish communities in India were destined to stay in the sub-continent for six or seven years, and developed a strong sense of solidarity. They are the subject of numerous memoirs and also scientific studies.

While they were still there, the boy Maharaja of Kolhapur died and was succeeded in 1947 by an older relative, who had served with the 4th Indian Division, the 'Red Eagles', and had fought in North Africa alongside the Carpathian Brigade. Ruling as the Shahaji Chatrapati, he was obliged to surrender his princely state to the Republic of India in 1949. Nonetheless, his son, still entitled the Maharaja of Kolhapur, was present in 1998, when the Association of Poles in India erected a monument at the site of the former Valivade settlement.

MOVING ON TO PALESTINE. Almost 1,000 Jewish children were handed over in Iran by the Polish Army to the 'Jewish Agency', the principal organ of the worldwide Zionist move-

BOMBAY: DIRECTORS of the Polish Group. Hanna Ordonówna in uniform (right).

ment. They were in part the sons and daughters of serving soldiers, but were largely the offspring of parents, who did not themselves qualify for evacuation from the USSR, but who, when stranded in Central Asia, had chosen to place them under the Army's care to ensure their survival.

One such child was Włodzimierz Szus (now Ze'ev Schuss), who had been deported with his mother and two siblings to Uzbekistan. His father, a prewar Polish Communist, was missing, and his unemployed mother had no means of support. She herself could not apply to join the Army, but had heroically decided to entrust her brood to an Army-run orphanage in Tashkent. By so doing, she lost contact with them for seven years, but was happily reunited with them after the war.

One of the girls among them has left a description of her sister Halinka's experiences:

> "Halinka's father succeeded in placing her among what became known as the *Yaldei Tehran*, the 'Children of Tehran'.
>
> 'It was such a difficult decision', recalls Stella Fruchter, Halinka's sister, who lives today in Tel Aviv. 'We were such a close-knit family. But we really had no choice. We loved Halinka, and wanted the best for her... Mother had the feeling she would never see her daughter again...'
>
> The train carrying the Jewish orphans left Samarkand on August 10 1942. It wended its way through the endless desert of Kara Kum... to reach the Caspian port of Krasnovodsk.
>
> Halinka was 13 years old when they disembarked at Pahlevi, a slim speck of a girl with a sack containing all her belonging...
>
> In Tehran... they reached decent, efficient care by the *Yishuu*'s representatives... [After 5 months] they sailed to Karachi because the Iraquis refused to grant them visas, to India and onto Suez... Finally, on 18 February 1943, the 716 'Tehran Children' were welcomed by a rejoicing Yeshuu at Aitlit camp...
>
> Halinka was adopted by Kibbutz Givat Brener. It was a world full of strangers..."[131]

Halinka (Hadassah) Lempel, an Israeli soldier, was killed in the War of Independence in May 1948.

The story of the 'Children of Tehran' is one of great devotion and fortitude. But in time, it was to become the source of controversy. For one thing, the Jewish religious authorities in Palestine regarded the children as victims of 'kidnap' by the Zionists, and, after being allocated to secular *kibbutzim*, to have been deprived of an orthodox Judaic upbringing. For another, in postwar Israel, they were judged not to qualify as Holocaust survivors, and hence were deprived of the compensation which was paid to most other Polish Jewish immigrants. Their unhappy fate became the subject of a long-running court case against the State of Israel that was not settled until the 21st century.

No less sadly, the origins of the 'Children of Tehran' have largely slipped from public memory in the intervening years. Albums produced in Poland, like *Tułacze dzieci* (1995), make no single mention of the Jewish component. Similarly, in many Israeli sources, the fact that the group were survivors not of the Holocaust but of Soviet maltreatment, or that it was the Polish Army, which rescued them, is often overlooked. "The Tehran Children were Polish war refugees," writes the World Zionist Organization, "that were exiled to the USSR and reached Israel after a gruelling three and a half years' journey... The Soviet Union refused to maintain the war refugees living on its share of the Polish territories, and exiled them to Siberia and other remote locations. In the winter of 1941, the refugees were freed and fled

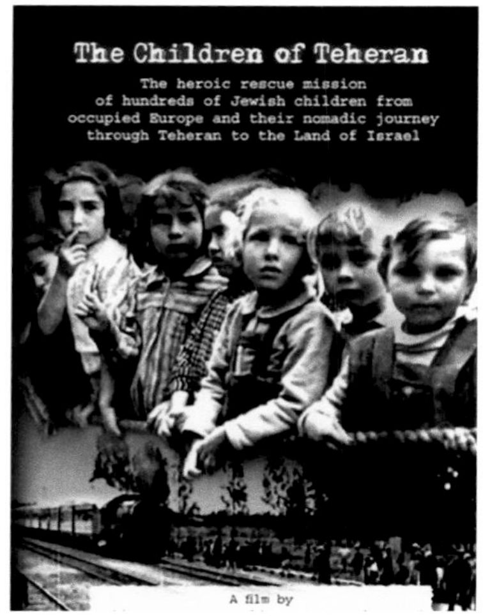

POSTER FOR the film *Children of Tehran* (2010) (above).

NORMAN DAVIES talking with Professor Schuss, Jerusalem, January 2014 (left).

south, to Central Asia. Many died from hunger and disease. Some of the children were given to orphanages, and made their way to Tehran..."[132]

The story of the 'Tehran Children' certainly forms one of the most uplifting episodes of the whole Anders saga – 1,000 boys and girls rescued from the jaws of death – and it would be easy to imagine that they simply settled down and lived happily ever after. In reality, they had a tough time adapting to their new country, and, having survived 'Siberia', 30 or 40 of them were to die in Israel's War of Independence. What is more, the facts of their origins were soon drowned and lost amidst the reigning Zionist myths. The website of the US Holocaust Memorial Museum, for example, defines the group as follows:

> "The 'Tehran Children' is the name used to refer to a group of Polish Jewish children, mainly orphans, who escaped the Nazi-German occupation of Poland. This group... found temporary refuge in orphanages and shelters in the Soviet Union, and was later evacuated with several hundred adults to Tehran, Iran, before finally reaching Palestine in 1943."[133]

WHERE CAN ONE START? Though some of the 'Tehran Children' had escaped from Nazi-occupied Poland in 1939, it was Soviet-occupied Poland from which they had all been deported in 1940–1941, and the chief source of their distress lay in the fact that they were NOT given even temporary refuge in the Soviet Union. On the contrary, they and their parents, like two million other Polish exiles, were left to rot and die either in slave labour camps or in remote exile. And they were not evacuated to safety in Iran by some anonymous stroke of fortune or with 'several hundred adults'; they were saved by the humane policy of General Anders and his Army, who took them and some 40,000 others to safety. Without Anders most of them would have been dead very soon.

Over 60 years later, an Israeli TV team directed by Yehuda Kaveh and with Dalia Gutman as producer set out to make a film about *The Tehran Children.* They regarded it as a forgotten episode, whose central figures had themselves preserved very few recollections. Dalia Gutman relates how she met retired general Avigdor (Janusz) Ben-Gal and how he told her of the moment when, as a five-year old boy, he had to part with his parents. "It was such a heart-rending story, it prompted me to learn more;" and soon she found other stories to tell:

> "On 19 February 1943, Shoshana Gilady saw a photo in the *Palestine Post.* It was a black-and-white picture of two women peering out of the window of a tram. Gilady recognised herself in the photo, which had been taken the previous day. She was one of the two mothers, and the baby was her son, Alex.
>
> Several decades later, Alex Gilady received a copy of the photograph and showed it to a man he had recently befriended. 'I had a copy made', Alex recalled, 'and took it to the office of Arie Mentkavich, whom I had met at a convention of Holocaust survivors. He looked at the picture, and said, 'Alex, we are brothers.'"[134]

"I quickly realised," Ms Gutman continues, "that all these children's stories had become oral history, and that there is no orderly documentation... The film examines what people do when they bury their memories, and how they confront their lack of memories today... [Some] children underwent difficult wandering, have no personal documents and do not even remember their parents. Many of them now travel to Poland in search of landscape that might help them relive the childhood memories that were erased... probably out of necessity to protect themselves."[135]

THE OFFER from the government of mexico to take in a consignment of Polish orphans was made at a time when the largest transfers to Africa or India were already underway. After some delay, one group left Iran in July 1943, another a month later in August 1943.

Iran and Mexico were separated by 8 thousand miles of ocean. The route took their ships from Bombay first round the Cape of Good Hope to Cape Town; then across the South Atlantic to Rio de Janeiro, next through the Panama Canal to the Pacific, and finally up the coast of California to Los Angeles. The final stage, from Los Angeles to León in central Mexico, was to be undertaken by train.

The treatment of the children in California can only be described as bizarre. For reasons that can only be imagined, the US authorities

classified these innocent little Poles as 'enemy aliens'. They disembarked them in Los Angeles under armed guard, and transferred them to an enclosure surrounded by barbed wire, in a camp reserved for Japanese internees. Two days later, they put them on a locked train, still under armed guard, bound for the frontier at San Antonio in Texas, where they passed into the care of their Mexican hosts.

The warmth of the Mexican welcome contrasted strongly with the children's none-too-friendly reception in the USA:

> "Polish children were transported to Mexico in two groups in July and August 1943. On arriving in León they were warmly welcomed by the Mayor and the local community. An orchestra played the Polish and the Mexican anthems. The Mexican government gave the Polish settlers a vast ranch. Santa Rosa was situated in the south-west highlands of Mexico, 6 km (3 miles) from León, in the state of Guanajuato. One thousand four hundred persons, 800 of whom were children, found shelter there. The settlers were looked after by: the Polonia Council, NCWC (National Catholic Welfare Conference), the Polish government in London, and the Felicjanki Nuns. In a short time the settlement had an elementary school, a gymnasium, and a hospital. The staff were Poles, among others: Alfons Jacewicz, Franciszek Sobota, Zofia Orłowska and Father Józef Jarzębowski.
>
> A scout troop was soon formed in Santa Rosa. Trips to learn about the country were organised to almost all parts of Mexico; they were paid for, as were the trade schools and reading rooms, by the (American) NCWC. The first employees of this institution were Irena Dalgiewicz, and an Irish woman, Miss Eileen Egan. The next ones to come to the settlement were Renata Rączkowska and Helena Sadowska."[136]

Owing to the prominence of the Catholic Church in Mexico, it was easy to establish con-

CROSS-COUNTRY JOURNEY to Paricutin (far left).

THE PARICUTIN Volcano (left).

REV. JARZĘBOWSKI, with a teacher and a pupil on horseback (above).

tact with local schools, parishes, and scout troops. Polish children visited their Mexican neighbours, took to wearing extravagant Mexican *sombreros*, and learned Mexican songs. Mexican children frequently visited Santa Rosa, attending concerts, dancing displays, and religious occasions. Joint expeditions on foot or on horseback were arranged, and were seen as a valuable element in the children's education. A schoolboy, Stanisław Jaskołd, has left an account of a trip to see the Paricutin volcano:

> "'Finally,' shouted the students of high school grades 2 and 3 when they moved from the Santa Rosa colony for a one week trip on 4 September. The trip itinerary took them through three states: Guanajuato, Michoacan, and Jalisco.
>
> We got to Michoacan on the same day and spent the night in Moreli, the biggest town in this state. The next day, after seeing the most important monuments, we started off to Uruapan. I was the most interested in a volcano that we passed, just about 38 km (23 miles) from Uruapan. The desire to see it grew when the delegate Sobota started telling us interesting stories about active and extinct volcanoes.
>
> The mountainous road was full of bends, pits and very muddy, so the whole group (40 people) had to take taxis from Uruapan, moving in the direction of the Paricutin volcano.
>
> As we left Uruapan, we could see evidence of the nearness of the volcano everywhere. The forest was sprinkled with ash blown here by the winds. The hot air caused the leaves on the trees to go yellow. Often you could see evidence of copious rains, the

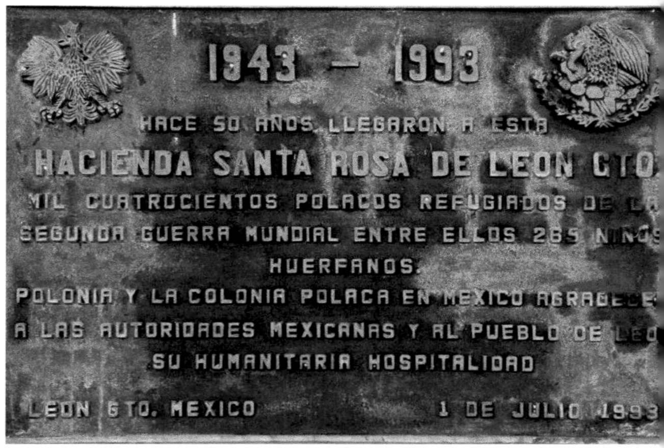

HACIENDA SANTA Rosa (below) and memorial tablet, 1943–1993 (right).

MRS FRANCISZKA PATER DE LUNA returns to her childhood school (top).

THE COURTYARD at Santa Rosa today (above).

The cars followed a wide arc around a huge clearing and came to a stop at the edge of the lava.

In front of us there was a huge volcanic cone. Smoke billowed from it, sending up ashes in booming eruptions from time to time. But there was no time to admire the volcano as we had to go on, on foot or on horseback, to look at this terrible elemental force from close up. With some difficulties we reached the still hot lava bed. Ashes were falling continuously, making it difficult to move forward, but curiosity was stronger.

The farthest that we got were the remains of a Mexican village engulfed by the lava. From where we stood we could see a small town at our feet, covered completely except for a half-destroyed church tower. The volcano was terrible to look at. The ground shook under our feet, adding to the general impression. The still hot lava was sizzling, breaking into small pieces. Huge pillars of steam rose from the cracks."[137]

water causing major devastation and making the road impassable in places. Even so our cars moved forward at a rapid pace, heading for our goal, the volcano. As if to spite us, the mountain hid in a cloud of low-lying mists, so we could not see where it was. Finally, its location was betrayed to us by the boom of frequent eruptions.

MOST IMPRESSIVE perhaps was the strength of the culture, both religious and secular, that the Polish exiles carried with them. At Santa Rosa, they were thousands of miles from their nearest Polish neighbours. Yet they instinctively did all the same things that their compatriots were doing in Africa or India: they

SANTA ROSA

MEXICO. THE FIRST GROUP at the hacienda in Santa Rosa, 1 July 1943 (centre); the first christening, Stanisław Stańkowski 6 October 1943 (bottom left); children helping to renovate the centre (below right).

THE COMMON TABLE – first dinner at Santa Rosa (opposite top); wedding of painter Anna Żarnecka who grew up in Santa Rosa (opposite far right) and the painter today.

NORMAN DAVIES in New Zealand (above).

1944: THE children come ashore (right).

built a chapel with their own hands; they put a sign announcing 'POLAND' outside the gate, and they created a little haven of Polishness.

NEW ZEALAND

Most of the Polish children from Iran were safely lodged in their new homes in Africa, India, Palestine or Mexico before the last big group set sail from Bombay in September 1944. The USS *General Randall* arrived in Wellington, the capital of New Zealand, on 1 November.

It was carrying 733 orphans, some of them as young as two or three, and 105 carers, headed by Rev. Michał Wilniewczyc, who had come from Isfahan, and by Sisters Maria Aleksandrowicz and Anna Tobolska.

A moving film, now in New Zealand's State Archives, was made of the arrival of the Polish Children in Wellington.[138] It shows Prime Minister Peter Fraser in a homburg hat, climbing the gangplank to make a speech of welcome. It shows boys and girls clinging to the burly soldiers who lifted them two at a time from the deck to carry them to the dockside. And it shows the beaming faces and gleeful smiles of the older children who were guided onto *terra firma* by military nurses wearing starched white hats and magnificent red capes. If ever there was a scene of Christian compassion opening its arms to total strangers in need, this was it.

From Wellington, the children were taken by bus into the mountainous interior of North Island, where, near the Maori settlement of Pahiatua, a former POW camp, had been refurbished for their use. It was a second Santa Rosa or Oudtshoorn, "under the Southern Cross".

No one can doubt that the love and concern extended to the Polish exiles by the New Zealanders was unsurpassed. And entries in the children's diaries reveal how well the positive

WELLINGTON HARBOUR today.

MORE CHILDREN come ashore.

feeling was appreciated. At the same time, the children were left in no doubt about the danger of losing their identity:

"*Thursday, 21 December 1944*

We have been trembling from the morning. Second class is Latin and a test. All those awful indicatives, ablatives, becoming more terrible by the minute. The exam was easy. Director Zięciak came to us during the fourth hour and told us that our whole class (nine in all) was going to an English school. She said: 'Girls, remember that you are Polish and you are going there not to fall in love, but to get an education. Remember that you are Polish.' She had tears in her eyes when she said this and we also started to cry.

We had to write our CVs, but we also wrote an application that we wanted to finish our Polish junior high school. We told all our professors and the priest about this during classes and they gave us their full support.

The mathematician said he was satisfied, because we 'were not sleeping'."[139]

Inevitably, news from the outside world brought mixed reactions:

"*Tuesday, 8 May 1945*

From the morning we have been hearing that the war has ended. The Germans have been defeated! The war in Europe is over, finally!

Thursday, 17 May 1945

Another sad anniversary. Mother took it very badly when Józek was killed at Monte Cassino one year ago. He was only 21."[140]

The Children of Pahiatua were sent to New Zealand for the duration of the war. But at war's end, they had nowhere else to go. Not one of them volunteered to go to Communist Poland. So they stayed. And they and their families and descendants are still there today.

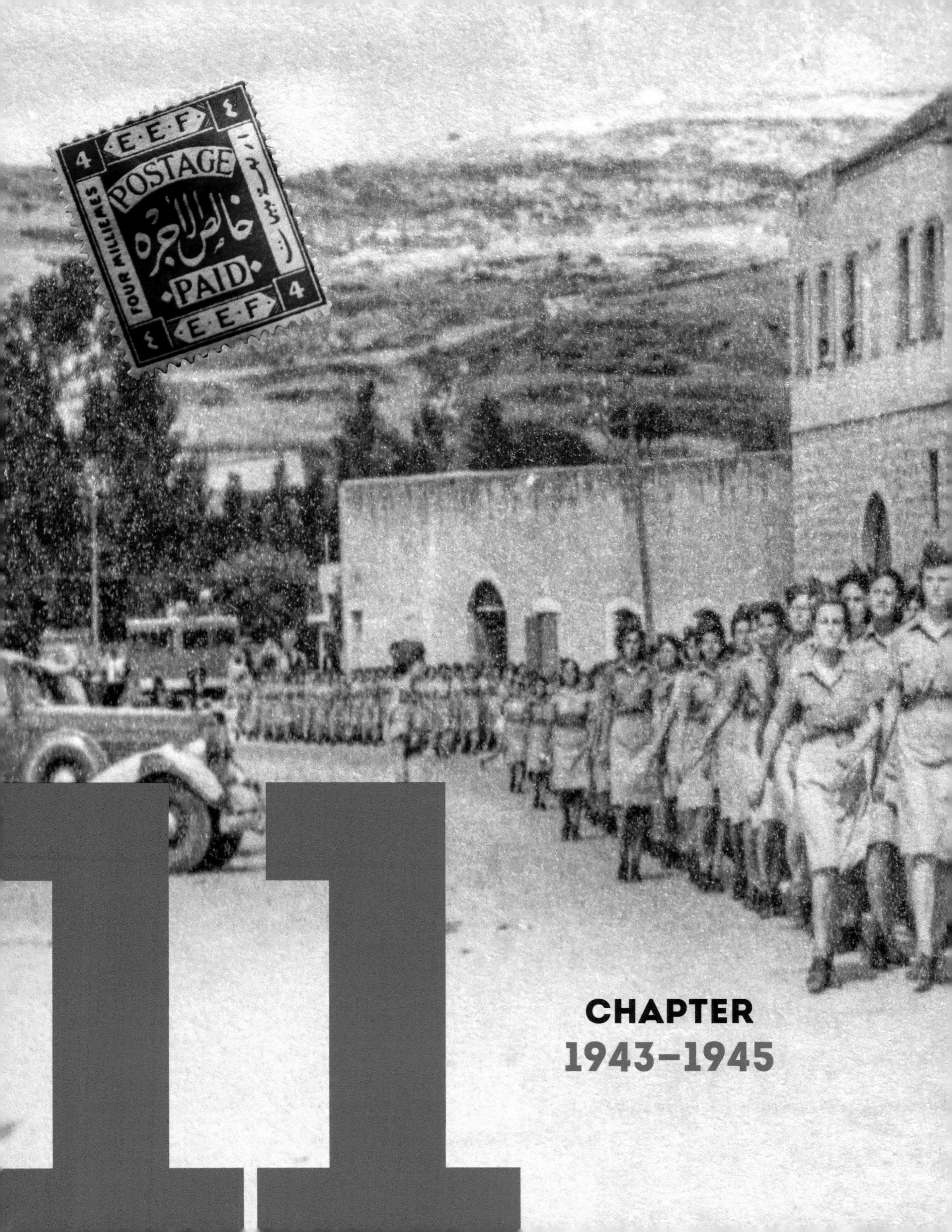

11

CHAPTER
1943–1945

PALESTINE

Flowers from the Holy Land

CHAPTER 11

1943–1945

PALESTINE

DURING THE TIME WHEN GENERAL ANDERS AND HIS ARMY WERE STATIONED IN IRAN AND IRAQ, THE STRATEGIC PREDICAMENT OF THE ALLIED POWERS EASED, AND NEW PRIORITIES EMERGED.

In **October 1942**, at the second battle of El Alamein, Britain's VIII Army under General Montgomery repulsed the Axis advance towards Egypt, and began the long westward drive along the North African coast through Libya, Tunisia, and Algeria. At the same time, on the Eastern Front, the Red Army halted the *Wehrmacht* spearhead on the Volga at Stalingrad, starting a prolonged engagement that would end in February with the annihilation of the German IX Army. The combined effect of these two victorious operations was to dispel Allied fears for the safety of Middle Eastern oil and to render the Poles's current task superfluous. Anders and his men understood very well that a new task would soon be found for them.

By now, the fate of the reorganised Polish force was almost entirely in British hands. The Poles were being fed, clothed, armed, and trained at British expense, and it was generally accepted that they would be despatched at the first opportunity to a destination that best suited British imperial interests. There were two main options. One was to send Anders to India, which was coming at the time of a heightened threat from the Japanese; the other was to send him to the Mediterranean theatre, where the British command in Egypt was crying out for reinforcements. The news that they were heading for the Mediterranean brought a great sense of relief to men, who had no inclination to march still deeper into Asia. As always, the fervent hope of the Anders soldiers was to fight the German enemy who was occupying their homeland. For them, the road that led towards Europe was the only one that beckoned.

IN THE MONTHS AFTER EL ALAMEIN, however, the lines of development in the Mediterranean theatre were far from clear. Britain's lifeline along the sea-lanes between Gibraltar and Alexandria was extremely precarious; the security of Malta, the Royal Navy's halfway house, hung by a thread until the middle of 1943; and the continuing campaign against German U-boats in the Atlantic meant that the USA was still unable to send a full-scale force to northern Europe. The Western Allies had promised Stalin to relieve pressure on the Red Army by opening a new front in the West. But the obstacles to mounting a major amphibious operation were formidable and the advice from naval and military commanders alike held that the necessary resources were lacking.

The decisive moment came, therefore, when London and Washington agreed early in 1943 that Italy was the only place in Europe where a second front could be opened. Longstanding plans for crossing the English Channel to France were postponed to the following year, and all efforts were concentrated on assembling in

North Africa necessary ships and troops for an assault on Sicily.

Stalin felt betrayed. The Red Army had been bearing the brunt of the *Wehrmacht*'s attentions for 18 months, and the Soviet dictator thought himself entitled to greater support from his Western partners. Indeed, he suspected that the dastardly capitalists were deliberately scheming to let the Red Army bleed to the point of exhaustion before launching their own attack on Germany. To assuage Stalin's fears, the Americans made haste to ship vast quantities of food, military equipment, and fuel to the USSR via the Persian Gulf.

The role reserved for the Anders Army was to take up positions on the periphery of the Mediterranean theatre, to train for combat readiness while the outcome of the landings in Sicily was awaited, and then to join the second line of advance of the VIII Army in Italy. Their first destination was Palestine.

CHRISTIANS, MUSLIMS, AND JEWS all called it the Holy Land. For Christians it was the homeland of Jesus Christ. For Muslims, who number both Abraham and Christ among their prophets, it was holy to what Mohammad had called 'the peoples of the Book'. For Jews, it was the land of Zion and *Eretz Israel*, the land promised by God to the Children of Israel.

Jerusalem, the chief city of the Holy Land, had special significance for all three monotheistic religions. It was the site of Solomon's Temple, whose foundations formed the

so-called Weeping Wall. It was the scene of Christ's crucifixion and resurrection. And it was the place from which the Prophet had ascended into Heaven.

But in 1943, it formed the Mandated Territory of Palestine, ruled by the British in accordance with a League of Nations mandate. And it was a country riven by conflict. The Arab majority fought the Jewish minority, both sides believing fervently that the land was 'theirs'

CHURCH OF the Dormition, Jerusalem (top right).

NORMAN DAVIES in the Holy City (right).

STREET IN Jerusalem, 1943 (below).

and that they had an absolute right to control it in the future. The British garrison, depleted by wartime transfers of troops to other destinations, struggled desperately to hold the ring, convinced that the end of the war might bring an uncontrollable explosion.

Palestine had been conquered from the Ottoman Empire by the British in 1916. Before that, it had formed the southern part of the Ottoman province of Syria, ruled from Damascus. It had also been a key element in the secret Anglo–French Sykes–Picot Agreement,

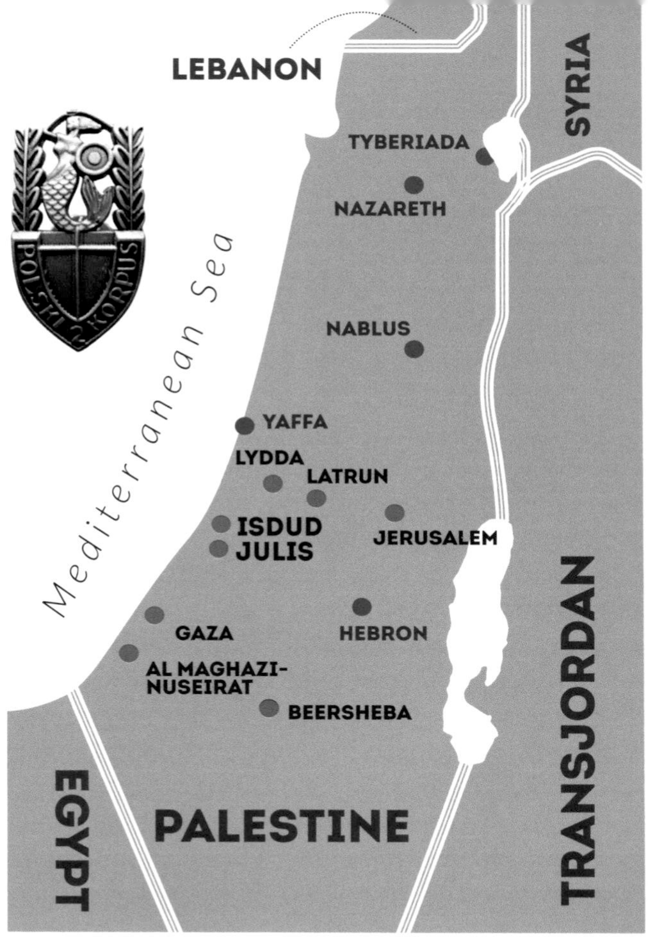

ANDERS ARMY IN PALESTINE

which had carved up the Ottomans' Arab provinces between France and Britain. In 1918, the French were formally installed in northern Syria, which included Damascus, Aleppo, and Lebanon, while the British set themselves up in Palestine and Mesopotamia. The League of Nations mandates confirmed the arrangements three years later.

The British, however, faced a serious political problem. During the First World War, they had made extensive promises both to Arabs and to Jews, thereby arousing incompatible expectations. Seeking Zionist support, they had promised in the Balfour Declaration of 1917 that Her Majesty's Government would approve of the creation of a 'Jewish Homeland' in Palestine. (They carefully avoided using the term 'Jewish State'.) Seeking Arab support, they promised the Hashemite Sheriff of Mecca, that, if he joined them in the war against the Ottomans, they would make him an independent ruler in Palestine. This second promise underlay the Arab Revolt of 1916–1918, and the romantic adventures of Lawrence of Arabia.[141]

The problem was solved in one morning in March 1921 by the British Colonial Secretary, Winston Churchill. Emboldened by the League of Nations mandate, he called a conference in Jerusalem, and announced to the assembled leaders that Palestine was to be divided into two halves. The eastern part – east of the River Jordan – was to become the British-protected Emirate of Transjordan (now the Kingdom of Jordan). The western part – west of the River Jordan – was to remain under direct British rule as Mandated Palestine, within which the Zionists would be free to build their 'homeland'. Both the Arabs and Zionists felt cheated. Both had wanted the whole of Palestine, and both had received only half.

Not surprisingly, therefore, the following decades were wrecked with turmoil. Riots, murders, and intercommunal disturbances were commonplace. Zionist migrants poured in, especially from Poland, although not in the numbers that their leaders had hoped for; Tel Aviv grew into a major city; *kibbutzim* spread round the countryside causing "the desert to bloom"; and Jewish settlers established their own defence force, the *Haganah*.

By 1936, the Arab Palestinians could take no more. The second part of the Balfour Declaration, which the Zionists never quoted, had guaranteed "the rights of the indigenous population". But it had been blatantly ignored. In 1936–1939, a second Arab Revolt, this time against the British, caused much blood to be spilt and strained intercommunal tolerance to the limit. At this stage, the Zionists backed the British authorities against the Arabs.

In 1939, the British produced a compromise scheme, the so-called Peel Plan, which foresaw separate designated areas of Arab and Jewish settlement. Once again, both sides were bitterly disappointed. The Zionists, in particular, saw that London was not prepared to concede their demands for a Jewish state, and radical Zionist groups laid plans for their own armed rising. To this end, they reached an unpublicised agreement with the Polish government.

Such was the state of play in Palestine when the Second World War broke out. Britain and its ally Poland were pitted against Nazi Germany, and Hitler's undeclared partner, the Soviet Union. The leadership of the Zionist movement, seeing the Nazis as the main enemy, called a truce with the British. But the radicals pressed on with a terrorist campaign. The Arab leaders were in disarray, but some placed their hopes in liberation by the Germans. Released from prison by the British, the Grand Mufti of Jerusalem, Haj Amin al-Husseini fled to Berlin, courted the favour of the Nazis, and longed for a German victory. It is not that these Arabs harboured special sympathies for Fascism; they were simply looking for a Power that would save them both from the British and from the Zionists.

DURING THE EARLIEST YEARS of the Second World War, little was known abroad about the fate of the Eastern Europe's Jews under German occupation. Rumours spread about deportations, executions, ghettoes, and concentration camps. But in 1942, the news deteriorated. Following the Wannsee Conference and the instigation of Operation Reinhard, the Nazi SS launched what they called The Final Solution – a concerted campaign to kill every Jew in Europe. Dedicated death-camps like Treblinka, Bełżec, and Sobibór were built, and gas chambers began to consume millions of victims. Thanks to daring emissaries such as Jan Karski, who had personally visited the Warsaw Ghetto and allowed himself to be incarcerated in the camp at Bełżec, hard information was brought to Britain. Despairing at the inactivity of the Allied governments, the Bundist deputy to the Polish National Council in London, Szmul Zygielbojm, committed suicide. But in December 1942, Poland's Minister of Foreign Affairs, Count Edward Raczyński, published an official report entitled *The Mass Extermination of Jews in German-occupied Poland*, and sent a copy to every member state of the United Nations. The truth about what would later be called 'The Holocaust' or 'The Shoah' was out.

In Palestine, knowledge of the Holocaust had two obvious consequences. One was that the flow of Jewish refugees would greatly increase. The other was that the temper of the Zionists would harden, as the postulates of militants and radicals seemed increasingly realistic.

Both these developments would take place under pressure from Zionist organisations in the USA, and by extension from resolutions in Congress and the Roosevelt administration's policies. Behind the scenes, the Chairman of the Foreign Affairs Committee of the House of Representatives, Sol Bloom, was badgering the State Department, and American officials were starting to use Zionist vocabulary about "the opening of Palestine to immigration and its constitution as a democratic Commonwealth." The British Ambassador to Washington, Sir Ronald Campbell, was called in by the State Department, and subjected to some heavy hints. For the time being, however, the pressure did not have the desired effect. The US Ambassador in London warned that "the British Government have no intention of caving in," and on 7 February 1944 the Secretary of War, Henry Stimson, writing to the Chairman of the Senate Committee on Foreign Relations, Senator Connally, who was preparing to introduce a pro-Zionist resolution, cut the matter short:

> "Dear Senator Connally,
>
> I have your letter of 5 February 1944 enclosing a copy of Senate Resolution 247...
>
> I feel that the passage of this resolution... or even public discussion thereon, would be apt to provoke dangerous repercussions in areas where we have vital military interests. Any conflict between Jews and Arabs would require the retention of troops in the affected areas... The consequent unrest in other portions of the Arab world keep resources away from the combat zone against Germany. I believe, therefore, that our war effort would be seriously prejudiced by such action.
>
> Sincerely yours,
>
> Henry L. Stimson"[142]

Registered at the G.P.O. as a Newspaper — THE JEWISH STANDARD — Friday, November 27

THE JEWISH STANDARD

NATIONAL JEWISH WEEKLY

THE MEANIN[G] OF ZIONIS[M] By Sidney Lati[...] (See p. 4)

Third Year/No. 33 — Friday, November 27, 1942 — Kislev 18, 5703

GERMANS TRY TO EXTERMINATE EUROPEAN JEWRY

Mass Murder in Eastern Europe

REPORTS GIVING HARROWING DETAILS OF THE SYSTEMATIC POLICY OF EXTERMINATIONCARRIED OUT AGAINST THE JEWS BY GERMANY HAVE BEEN PUBLISHED IN THE WHOLE OF THE PALESTINE PRESS ON NOVEMBER 23rd AS A BEGINNING OF WORLD-WIDE ACTION TO AROUSE THE FREE WORLD FROM COMPLACENCY AND SILENCE, AND TO BRING ABOUT A CONCERTED MOVE FOR ARRESTING THE CAMPAIGN OF EXTERMINATION AND ALLEVIATING DISTRESS.

The reports were published on the front page of all the Hebrew newspapers which appeared with black borders. According to the reports the systematic annihilation of the Jewish inhabitants of Polish towns and townships began after Himmler's visit to Warsaw last spring. A special Annihilation Committee (Vernichtungskommission) was established, which toured the entire territory of the Gouvernement General directing the destruction of "Jewish Communists." Children up to the age of 12 years were executed in the thousands without mercy, and all elderly people were also murdered. Able-bodied males were registered and sent in groups to an unknown destination. Every trace of them has been lost. In many places the Jewish women were also arrested and deported.

MASSACRES IN GHETTOS

According to an eye-witness account, 27,000 of the 30,000 inhabitants of the Kielce Ghetto were rounded up for deportation six months ago, and whilst the deportation was being carried out 1,500 Jews were murdered on the spot. There are rumours that the remainder was slaughtered during the journey.

In Brest Litovsk thousands of Jews were flung by the Nazis into the River Bug and drowned. In Piotrkow only 2,600 Jews survived out of a total of 20,000, and the survivors included only 160 women and children. At Czenstochowa only 2,000 Jews remained of the former 40,000 Jewish inhabitants. The population of the Radom Ghetto was reduced from 32,000 to 3,500, and a similar mass slaughter was carried out in most of the other ghettoes.

The Great Synagogue at Bialystock was set on fire after 1,500 Jews had been herded together there. In the township of Tiktin most of the Jews were buried alive.

Reports received from the Warsaw and Lodz ghettoes reveal an alarming decrease of the Jewish population during the last few months.

According to messages from the same sources the deportation of Jews from

LAVAL'S BLOOD GUILT

The first list of names of Jewish refugees who by order of the Laval regime were surrendered to the Nazis for deportation to unknown destinations in Germany and countries occupied by the Nazis, was received by the Hebrew Sheltering and Immigrant Aid Society in New York. The list covers the victims who were formerly interned in the French concentration camp, Camp de Gurs.

THE ZIONIST AIM—BISHOP AND MUFTI—BRODETSKY v. BRODETSKY

(From Our Political Correspondent)

THE political resolution adopted by the Old Zionist Organisation's Actions Committee in Jerusalem has already produced such a state of uncertainty and confusion that even many supporters of the resolution are now beginning to doubt the wisdom and to suspect the purpose of the whole affair. Thus both in England and America Jewish Agency propagandists are explaining that the term "Jewish Commonwealth" was used in order not to outrage non-Zionist liberal opinion in this country and an elaborate process of reasoning is employed in order to explain that Jewish Commonwealth means the same as Jewish State and why—despite this identity of meaning—it was necessary to use the one in preference to the other.

On the other hand both the Misrachi and Jewish State Party representatives in Jerusalem voted *for* the resolution although they are pledged to the Jewish State formula. This is now explained by them on the ground that the Hebrew version of "Jewish Commonwealth" employed in the resolution was *Medina Iwrith*, which means Jewish State. Thus it would appear that after reaching an agreement with non-Zionists in America, the Jewish Agency in Jerusalem used "Jewish State" as the Hebrew translation of "Jewish Commonwealth," hoping perhaps that the people in America will not get to know about it. There you get a characteristic example of that form of political duplicity and expediency which has destroyed the reputation of Jewish Agency leadership either as reliable or resolute.

The question now arises, what is to become of all the explanations now being offered by Old Zionist propagandists for explaining away the use of the word "Jewish Commonwealth" when at the same time the people who voted for the resolution will be justified in claiming that they voted for a "Jewish State." On the other hand the people in America who

THE death of Dr. Graham Brown, Bishop in Jerusalem, removes a man who for a long time played an important role behind the Palestine political scene. He was notoriously anti-Zionist and maintained close contact with anti-Zionist circles, not least among them being the infamous Mufti of Jerusalem. All Jewish defeatist sections, as well as Christian and Moslem groups that were opposed to Jewish political growth in Palestine found in him a supporter of influence. It should be a warning to us that the Jerusalem Bishopric is a political rather than an ecclesiastical position and that Zionist leadership should regard and treat it as such.

THE growing chaos in this country in the matter of communal representation, aggravated by the office of the so-called World Jewish Congress, entered an interesting stage last week when the Board of Deputies set up a special committee to go into the whole matter. It is understood that the setting-up of this Committee followed a heated debate at a recent meeting of the Joint Foreign Committee when Dr. Brodetsky was challenged to justify his position of a Vice-Chairman of the World Jewish Congress, at the same time while he holds the position of President of the Board of Deputies. He was attacked on the ground that the World Jewish Congress office in this country is regarded as attempting to undermine the influence of the Board of Deputies by going to authorities, governmental and others who are now completely bewildered by having to face sometimes conflicting memoranda, the headings of which bear the name of Dr. Brodetsky in both cases. It is understood that Dr. Brodetsky offered to resign his position in the World Jewish Congress, but the Joint Foreign Committee preferred to have the whole matter first investigated, so that his resignation—if it comes about—should result from the Committee's investigations and report, rather than as a

MURDER CAMPS IN POLA[ND]

THREE SPECIAL CAMPS [...] BEEN ESTABLISHED BY TH[E GER]MANS IN POLAND FOR TH[E PUR]POSE OF EXECUTING JEW[S DE]PORTED FROM THE WARSA[W AND] OTHER GHETTOES UNDE[R THE] PRETEXT OF "RESETTLEME[NT IN] THE EAST, ACCORDING [TO RE]PORTS RECEIVED BY THE [...] GOVERNMENT. ABOUT [...] JEWS HAVE BEEN DEPOR[TED] THIS WAY FROM THE W[ARSAW] GHETTO ALONE, THE [...] STATES.

The persecution of the [...] Poland, it was declared in [...] Government circles, which h[...] in progress from the very [...] of the German occupation, ass[...] tremely acute forms since Mar[...] when Himmler ordered the e[...] tion of 50 per cent. of the Jewish [...] tion in the Gouvernement Gene[...] carried out by the end of 1942.

Not satisfied with the results [...] termination campaign during [...] part of this year, Himmler, on [...] sion of his visit to the Gouv[...] General last July personally iss[...] decrees aiming at the total destr[...] Polish Jewry.

Warsaw Massacre

The persecutions in Warsaw [...] on July 21st, when German p[...] suddenly drove into the Ghet[...] soldiers immediately started [...] into houses, shooting the inhab[...] sight. The first victims belonge[...] to the educated classes. On [...] almost all the members of th[...] Council were arrested and [...] hostages.

On July 22nd the Jewish [...] was ordered to proclaim a d[...] the German authorities deali[...] the "resettlement" of all [...] Jews, regardless of sex or ag[...] Eastern part of Poland, with [...] exception of persons working [...] man factories or members [...] Jewish militia. The daily q[...] people to be resettled was [...] 6,000, and members of the [...] Council were ordered to ca[...] the decree under pain of dea[...]

On the next day, however, [...] 23rd, the German police ap[...] peared at the offices of the [...] Council, demanding to see th[...] man, Mr. Czerniakow. A[...]

FIRST NEWS of the Holocaust: *The Jewish Standard*, 27 November 1942 (opposite).

NORMAN DAVIES and Col. Radosław Janczura talking with Gen. Zvi Kan-Tor at the Israeli Army Tank Museum in Latrun (2014) (opposite below).

POLISH SOLDIERS in Jerusalem (right).

FORMER RAILWAY station at Semakh Junction (below).

THE ARRIVAL IN PALESTINE of 70,000 armed Polish soldiers could not fail to cause a stir and to alter the balance of forces. Serving under British command, they greatly increased the total number of troops at the Governor's disposal, even though they were not intended for garrison-style duties. British Intelligence was well aware of the large number of Jews in the Polish ranks, and measures were taken to keep them apart from the civilian population.

General Anders, like British Intelligence, was well informed of the Zionist sympathies of some of his men; but he also knew that many Polish Jews were not pro-Zionist, and he could not have been certain of their reactions. In any case, the last thing he wanted was to embroil his Army in the politics of the Middle East. For him, as for the great majority of his men, Palestine was no more than a stage on the long road that led from Russia to Europe. His main concerns were to complete the reorganisation that had been started in Iraq; to restore his men to full health and strength; and through intensive training, to bring them closer to battle readiness. The chance of visiting the Holy Land was merely a fortunate bonus.

The journey from Iraq to Palestine involved a long trek of 540 miles across Syria. In 1943, the route was completely controlled by the British Army, which had taken over when the French authorities in Syria failed to sever their links with the Vichy regime. It formed the central section of Britain's overland communication network that ran from Egypt at one end to Tehran and Baghdad at the other.

Convoys of British military trucks began to arrive at the Polish camps in northern Iraq in August 1943. Men, weapons, and supplies were loaded up, and day after day lines of 20 or 30 trucks carrying 500–600 men set off towards the West. The tracks across the Syrian Desert were rough and sandblown. The men took cover under the trucks during midday breaks, and bivouacked in the open at night. They spent anything from 4 to 7 or 8 days in transit, and the whole operation lasted weeks. Heavy equipment, including the artillery, followed later. The first of the units to leave Iraq was the newly formed 3rd Carpathian Rifle Division, which started its journey to Palestine on August 3.

Arrival in the Holy Land was the cause of much rejoicing. Though few of the Polish soldiers had been there previously – the *Karpatczycy* excepted – they were approaching a part of the world that had been familiar to them from childhood. Bethlehem, Jerusalem, and Nazareth were names that had been impressed upon them throughout their upbringing. Those who were lucky enough to enter Palestine down the coastal road from Lebanon were especially excited to see the Mediterranean. Like Xenophon's men who shouted "*Thalasos*! *Thalasos*!" on sighting the sea at the end of their march from Persia, they knew that the ships that sailed on that sea would take them much nearer home.

Once in Palestine, the troops of the Anders Army were distributed round a score of camps, none of them in close proximity to the main ports or cities. Anders established his HQ at Julis, later at camp 'Kilo 89', both near Gaza. The 3rd Division was also stationed at Julis. The 5th Division was located at Mughazi-Nuseirat, the Armoured Brigade at Latrun, the Artillery at Isdud, the Sappers at Beit Yirya, and all other services in Gaza.

Polish soldiers were not stationed in Palestine for recreation. They were subject to a rigorous regime of physical exercises, weapons training, and educational courses. They lived in tented encampments, far from the main urban centres and enjoyed little free time. They were left in no doubt that they were being brought towards a peak of fitness and skill that was steadily transforming a rag-tag collection of refugees into a modern fighting force.

Yet few of them complained. Many were still scarred by the desperate struggle for survival in the Gulag or in remote exile, and were more than content to be living a secure and purposeful life where all their basic needs were cared for. They were well fed, well clothed in new British uniforms, well tanned by the fresh air and sunshine of the desert, and well satisfied (in the main) to be surrounded by their compatriots in a 'little Poland' far from Poland.

It was on the training grounds of Palestine that the reorganisation started in Iraq was completed, and that men who had come together from very different directions began to merge into one formation and to adopt a common identity. At the outset, the *Prawosławni* who had come out of Russia, kept themselves apart from the *Lordowie,* who had been sent out from England, and from *Ramzesowie* (mainly from the Carpathian Brigade, who had served in Egypt and North Africa). But now, redistributed among a mass of new or expanded units, they lost their former allegiances, and rapidly gelled into 'The II Corps'.

As part of the reorganisation, numerous men with special skills were despatched from Palestine to other branches of the Polish Armed Forces in Europe where their services were urgently required. Radiotelegraphers, for example, like the young Zbigniew Siemaszko, were sent to London to serve in the HQ Communications Centre at Stanmore. Volunteers were sent to the Polish Parachute Brigade that was forming in England; others like

ROADSIDE SCENES (left).

THE DESERT road from Iraq to Palestine (below).

Michał Zawadzki (father of my friend, Hubert Zawadzki) were posted to General Maczek's 1st Armoured Division, or, like Stefan Knapp, the future artist, who worked in enamel-on-metal, to the RAF. And experienced officers like Colonel Leopold Okulicki were redirected to the Polish General Staff and thence to the *cichociemni*, who were dropped by air into occupied Poland to strengthen the Home Army. On leaving Palestine, all these men faced an arduous sea voyage, which took them via the Suez Canal to Cape Town, Rio de Janeiro, and eventually to Britain.

The reorganisation also foresaw that numerous military units would remain in the Middle East after the Army's deployment elsewhere. To this end, an umbrella command called the *Jednostki Wojskowe na Środkowym Wschodzie* (JWŚW) was formed as from March 1943 under General Karaszewicz-Tokarzewski, who was replaced as commander of the 6th (Lwów) Infantry Division. In due course, when the Army was redesignated as the 'Polish II Corps', the JWŚW was to become the 'Polish III Corps' with its HQ in Cairo.

Contact between the Polish soldiers and the local population was limited. A language barrier kept them apart from the Palestinian Arabs, and the main camps were located far from the main centres of Jewish population like Tel Aviv. Nonetheless, regular outings were organised to the Holy Places, notably to Nazareth, Bethlehem, and Jerusalem, and on these outings the troops learned much about the people and problems of the country. If they did not know earlier, they realised that Arabs and Jews were at 'daggers drawn', and that both were locked in deep conflict with the ruling British authorities on whom the Polish Army was dependent.

Since most Jews in Palestine at that time spoke fluent Polish, however, men and women from the Anders Army rapidly established close relations with them. These relations were, at first, mainly commercial: the soldiers had money to spend, and Jewish merchants had goods to sell. But soon it became clear that Zionist agents were active, seeking out soldiers and civilians with a Jewish background and urging them to desert.

Before that, news arrived that the Army was to be inspected by the Commander-in-Chief in person. General Sikorski's imminent arrival would finalise the Army's reorganisation, and strengthen its progress towards battle readiness. At the same time, given the revelations of the Katyń murders in April 1943, and the subsequent break in diplomatic rela-

PALESTINE – definitely not Siberia.

tions with the USSR, it was bound to provoke political discussions and to heighten emotions. The greater number of Anders' soldiers had good reason to fear Soviet intentions, and to lament the complacency which characterised Allied perceptions of Stalin. They would leave the Commander-in-Chief in no doubt that they expected him to defend Polish interests with courage and determination.

In 1942, the Polish Government-in-Exile took steps to publicise the Polish cause in the Middle East by creating two important institutions in Palestine – the Polish Information Centre in the East (PCIW) and the Delegate's Office for Education and Schooling. The former, which complemented similar information centres in London and New York, supported the Jerusalem branch of the Polish Telegraphic Agency (PAT), and published an English language newsletter, *The Polish Digest.* It also assisted the work of press organs outside Palestine such as the *Kurier Polski* (*The Polish Courier*) in Baghdad and *Parada* (*Parade*) in Cairo.

The Delegate for Education and Schooling, Łukasz Kurdybach, was admirably active in supporting numerous Polish schools, in providing them with textbooks, and, through the Publication Section, in producing an astonishing range of books and newspapers. Between 1942 and 1946, over 200 titles, both school textbooks and literary works, were put into circulation. The Polish press in Palestine included dailies such as *Gazeta Polska* (*Polish Gazette*), *Głos Polski* (*The Polish Voice*), *Dziennik Żołnierza APW* (*Daily of the Soldier of the Polish Army in the East*), *Ochotniczka* (*The Female Volunteer*), and *Przez Lądy i Morza* (*Through Lands and Seas*); the weekly *Orzeł Biały* (*White Eagle*), and the fortnightly *W Drodze* (*On the Way*).

The cultural and informational activities of both Government and Army in Palestine brought together a close-knit circle of remarkable men and women, many of whom were to gain greater prominence in the postwar era. One need only mention the names of Jerzy Giedroyc, director of the Polish Army's Press Office; Melchior Wańkowicz, the future historian of Monte Cassino; Gustaw Herling-Grudziński, author; Wiktor Weintraub, literary scholar and Harvard professor; Zygmunt and Zofia Hertz, Julian Mieroszewski, Maria Danilewicz, Ignacy Pokrywa, and many more. Their ethos was both patriotic and liberal. "The greatest dangers for Poland," wrote Jerzy Giedroyc, "are nationalism and clericalism."

SOLDIERS ARRIVING in Palestine after months in the wastelands of Iraq received only the most favourable impressions. They saw little of the tensions that were simmering under the surface:

> "[Palestine] had everything a soldier in the desert could wish for – modern cities, asphalt highways, orange groves, and masses of fresh water. Every army camp had washrooms and showers galore. The Jewish population was friendly. It seemed as if nearly all of them spoke Polish. You felt at home there, they told us, especially in a Jewish restaurant. Just imagine! Scrambled eggs with real Polish pork sausage, even though it's taboo for Jews and Arabs alike. But pigs are easy to raise and cheap to feed on scraps. And if others wanted to eat it and pay well to do so, why should restaurant owners not attract and please their *goyim* clientele? What's more, there you could wash down the pork sausage with a glass of Wolfschmidt Polish vodka, albeit manufactured in Palestine. Young Jewish women were wearing short shorts, they said. Now all of us wanted to go to the land of Abraham...
>
> What I remember of our drive through Palestine are green trees and orange groves. There were winding asphalt roads and many road signs and people. But we went through town after town without stopping, head-

POLISH PATROL on the Via Dolorosa (right).

DOCUMENT FOR Stanislaw Fujarczyk certifying guard duty at the Holy Sepulchre in Jerusalem during Easter 1944 (top right).

STONE DOORWAY and III Station of the Cross, carved by Polish soldiers in the Armenian Church, formerly the Polish church (opposite bottom).

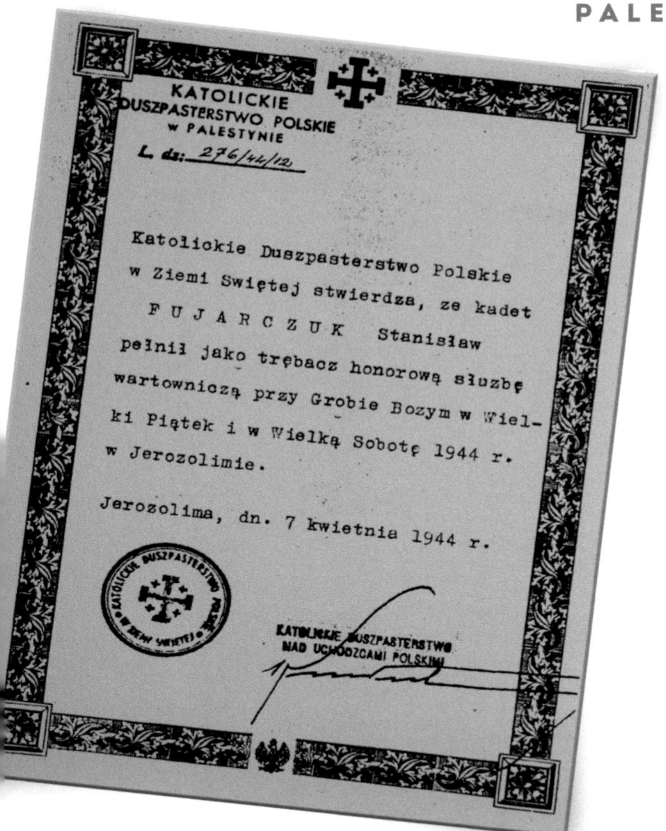

KATOLICKIE
DUSZPASTERSTWO POLSKIE
W PALESTYNIE
L. dz: 276/44/12

Katolickie Duszpasterstwo Polskie w Ziemi Swiętej stwierdza, ze kadet F U J A R C Z U K Stanisław pełnił jako trębacz honorową słuzbę wartowniczą przy Grobie Bozym w Wielki Piątek i w Wielką Sobotę 1944 r. w Jerozolimie.

Jerozolima, dn. 7 kwietnia 1944 r.

KATOLICKIE DUSZPASTERSTWO
NAD UCHODZCAMI POLSKIMI

ing straight for our camp which was near where the Gaza strip border now is. It was called Camp Kilo 89 for the distance southeast from the port of Tel Aviv. Now we had huts of planks complete with showers and dining rooms – luxury after the tents of Iraq and four days of crossing the desert. I regarded that crossing of the desert as an accomplishment and felt sure I now knew how Columbus and his sailors felt after crossing the ocean.

We showered and showered and kept flushing the toilets just to marvel at them. The windmill that fed the showers complained like a rusty hinge day and night...

Exploring north from Camp Kilo 89 we saw the villages of Julis, Qastina, and Barbara, soon nicknamed Jula, Kasia, and Basia, good Polish diminutives of women's names. There was a striking difference between the Arab and Jewish villages and towns. The Jewish ones were laid out in order with ugly concrete modern buildings lacking character. Their farm fields and orange groves were the picture of modern agriculture. They were surrounded by high fences with barbed wire, watchtowers and concrete bunkers in the corners. Everything was well irrigated. The spraying jets of mist that pointed in a different direction each time we passed made it look as if children were playing with water hoses. The Arab villages were old, pleasingly unaligned and organic in the way they had grown as needed. The houses were of adobe and rock.

They fitted comfortably into the landscape. And there were scattered date palms, wild lemons and the original water hole that had been in use since the village began. Black-clad women gathered at the well or spring with their earthenware jugs. Donkeys and goats filled in the Biblical scenery. We saw no enmity between the two cultures but nei-

ENSA GARRISON Cinema and cafeteria under NAAFI management, Camp Barbara (top).

SELF-IMPROVEMENT IN spare time (centre bottom).

GENERAL ANDERS in Nazareth (opposite).

ther did we see any neighbourliness. The Jews were wealthy and suspicious of the Arabs. The Arabs were poor and felt the growing strength of the newcomers moving into their lands."

Before long, the author of this memoir, Aleksander Topolski, was taken by the Army on an outing to Jerusalem:

"Like many others who had barely survived imprisonment and starvation under

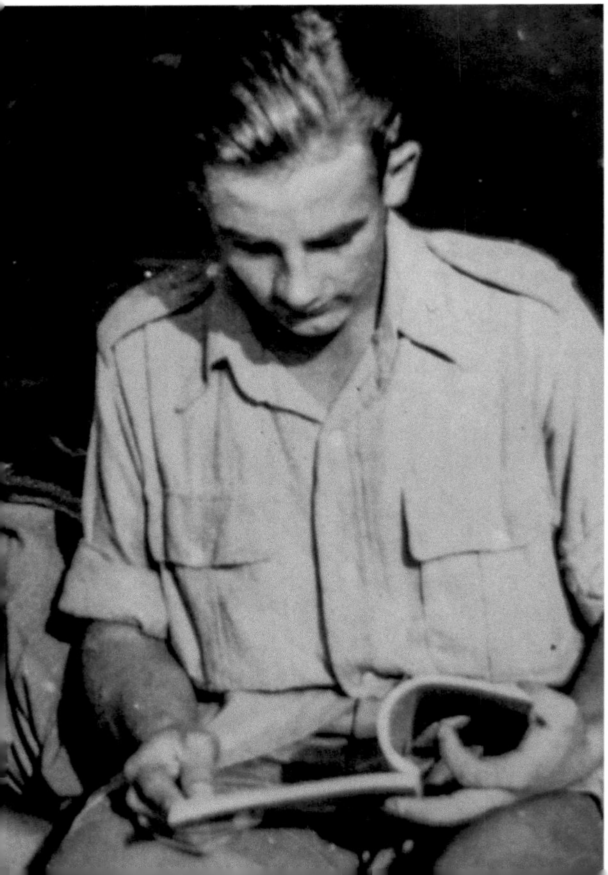

the Communists, I had vowed to make a pilgrimage to Jerusalem, if only God would spare me. I had often wondered how I could fulfill that promise – perhaps by walking there from Poland. I never thought it would be so easy to make good on my pact with God. But I must admit I was not impressed by Jerusalem. What I remember best is the sight of an Armenian monk wielding a candlestick to whack a Greek Orthodox priest who happened to cross the dividing line inside the Church of the Holy Sepulchre. The church had been partitioned amongst different Christian faiths by lines painted on the floor. I attended the mass there and gave my silent prayers in thanks for getting out of the Soviet Union and for letting me off so easily in making good my promise."[143]

WHILE THE SOLDIERS settled in, many young Polish exiles were beginning their education. Palestine was the place where many of them received their very first lessons.

"[In May 1942] we arrived in Rehevoth where the Third Carpathian Division's Artillery was stationed. The official language here was English, as Palestine was under the control of the British. Every few months my father was able to come and visit us. We lived in a sea of tents... [but] after two months, we were moved to Abo Kebir where there were many Polish families. I remember we were near St. Tabitha's supposed grave, where a light burned all the time...

I was eight years old at the time and could neither read nor write... In Abo Kebir, all the teachers were Polish and under the control of the Delegature of the Government-in-Exile. We had books as there was a Polish publishing house in Jerusalem. My sister was in a different school, for girls. We also

JEROZOLIMA

STREETS IN OLD JERUSALEM (above).

WALLS OF OLD JERUSALEM (above).

OUR LADY OF KOZIELSK (top right).

POLISH GRAVES at the cemetery (bottom centre).

ZEEV BARAN (on the right), Honorary Consul of the Republic of Poland in Jerusalem, Rev. Tadeusz Nosal, Rector of the Polish Catholic Mission in the Holy Land, sister Róża, Norman Davies. The New Polish House in Jerusalem.

THIRD STATION of the Passion (below): "I could see that the III [and IV] Stations... were too ruined for people even to go inside to pray... it proved possible to rent them and to make them good again". (Chaplain Rev. Stefan Pietruszko-Jabłonowski). Lt Tadeusz Zieliński, an ex-prisoner of the the Kozielsk II camp, sculpted the figures. Christ Falling under the Cross carved from Carrian marble is set against the backdrop of a painting showing the "Passion of the Poles".

MEMORIAL PLAQUE at the New Polish House (bottom).

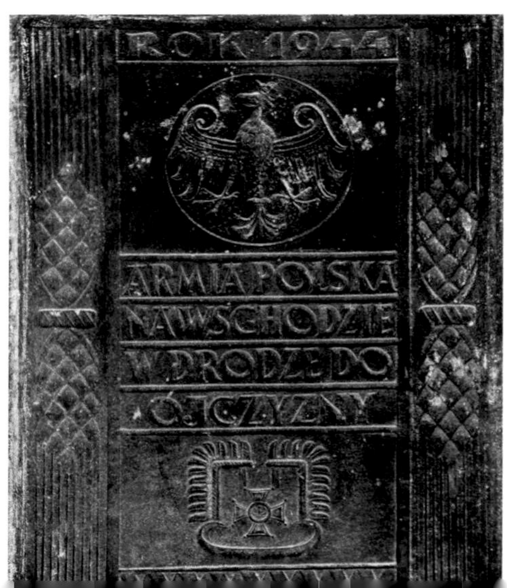

NAZARETH, 1944. Parade of the 4th Company of the PSK (right)..

NAZARETH: POLISH bookshop (below).

***OCHOTNICZKA* JAGÓDKA** with her dog (opposite).

had pastoral care there. We had our First Communion and spent the Christmas of 1942 in Bethlehem.

I saw this as the land of milk and honey. We had everything we wanted... [And] we had news, a Polish newspaper was published in Jerusalem. I remember that we learned of the death of General Sikorski in 1943...

I visited Tel Aviv, where everything was in Polish; you could get Polish food everywhere, and everyone was good to us. The locals liked us better than the British. [I went to] a Polish secondary school in Tel Aviv. Half of my class from Abo Kebir was Jewish. We had lessons together, and they recited all the Polish nationalist poems with us. We just had separate religious lessons. I thought nothing of this; I thought this was how things were supposed to be...

In 1944, my sister and I were finally together in a school in Tel Aviv. That's where I was when the war ended. We lived in a Polish house in Jaffa...

All of a sudden, the family moved to Nazareth and I was sent to the *Junacy* school.... This was the end of my childhood, as these were real barracks with real discipline.... My mother worked for a Catholic organisation in Nazareth called *War Relief*. [The] British soldiers were always asking for tea. The standard reply was: 'with milk or lemon.' Milk was not a good option, as it was condensed or evaporated... so English soldiers had to learn to drink tea with lemon.

The *Junacy* or 'Young Soldiers', as we were known, moved to [Camp] Barbara in early 1946... The Communist Polish Repatriation Commission was active at the time, but was not generally well received... Three nationalist Jewish organ-

isations, Irgun, Haganah and Stern were [also] active... Irgun blew up the King David Hotel in Jerusalem, where the British HQ was located, [and] the explosion was heard in Barbara...

Jewish legions came to Barbara to play football with the British, and Italian POWs were allowed to watch... In 1947, we saw German POWs at Port Said when we were leaving for England. Someone went over to talk to them. Immediately, the Principal of our School said, "absolutely no fraternizing with the enemy!".[144]

WHILE THE YOUNG ZYGMUNT KOPEL went to secondary school in Tel Aviv, an older boy, Michał Giedroyć, was already buckling down to life as an Army cadet:

"My hand-delivered posting to the Sixth Company, First Platoon, arrived about 20 February 1944, by which time I was well briefed. The bearer of good news was the duty cadet of the Sixth in full fig – epaulettes, white belt and white spats. He looked me up and down (he was much taller than me), and offered to help me with my kit. We Juniors were trained to carry all our gear unaided, but this was obviously a gesture of welcome. I accepted the offer, and the two of us set off happily on foot towards the other, 'senior', end of the camp. There, in the shadow of the garrison Kinema and the water tank on stilts, I was to be initiated into military life.

The cadet school was a five-company battalion. This was an attempt to match the six-year cycle of Polish secondary education (a company for each year) – but with a downward adjustment for natural wastage in the last two (toughest) years. Each company had three platoons, and each platoon was made up of four sections of eight cadets. Total numbers fluctuated: at the beginning of 1944 the headcount rose well over the battalion establishment, reflecting an unforeseen bulge at the end of Year Four. The Army responded by adding a supplementary company, the 6th.

The school curriculum as designed to provide both general education and military training. The former was based on the Polish prewar model, in which a four-year *Gimnazjum* (roughly, GCSE level) was followed by a two-year *Liceum* (equivalent of A-Levels). The *Gimnazjum* course was broadly based across some 11–13 subjects, aiming at a generalist type of education at the expense of study in depth. A concession was made to the arts/sciences divide, by allowing two kinds of *Liceum*: humanist (arts) and mathematical/scientific. The distinction remained one of emphasis. Interestingly, our Cadet School initially opted for the humanist variant. Presumably the choice matched the traditional self-im-

age of the Polish officer corps. A technological *Liceum* with emphasis on civil and structural engineering was eventually added at JSK in the academic year 1945/1946.

Military training was thorough. It amounted to basic infantry training, followed by more advanced work up to the level of platoon command. The more promising cadets could expect promotion to this level while still at school by taking charge of their peers. These were challenging assignments. Four times as many appointments were also available at the less exacting level of section command. All these 'martial arts' (I find the term particularly suitable for my subject bearing in mind the humanist character of our *Liceum*) were matched by demanding PE, with an input from the British Army. Needless to say, the equipment made available for these pursuits – martial and physical – was extensive and of high quality. The academic disciplines were less well equipped. The School lacked

ON THE roof of the Austrian Institute (top).

RAMLA CEMETERY: Polish and British graves (above).

WORLD WAR II Monument in Jerusalem: Norman Davies with Polish Consul Wiesław Kuceł (opposite).

even the most elementary science laboratories.

After graduation from the *Liceum*, the cadets could look forward to promotion to one of the Cadet Officer Schools of the Polish Second Corps in Italy. There, after some six months of intensive specialist training, the freshly promoted Cadet-Officers would be assigned to their units, usually regiments of their choice.

In normal circumstances the age spectrum for our School would have been from 12 or 13 at entry to 17 or 18 at graduation – almost identical to that of the Royal Naval College, Dartmouth prior to 1955....

Of course, the circumstances of boys emerging from Soviet captivity were far from normal. On the academic front, virtually all entrants were behind by at least two years. In my platoon, the normal age of entry would have been 15–16. In fact, the actual average age of my peers was around 18. In February 1944, I was just 15. This created some problems.

My first impression of the Sixth Company was the impeccable orderliness of its sleeping quarters. Significant numbers of cadets still suffering from malaria were billeted in barracks, but the majority were allowed to move into tents. These were, I believe, Indian Army issue, spacious and comfortable. The perfect geometric layout – each platoon in four tents in a row – encouraged good housekeeping. In no time small gardens appeared around each tent, voluntarily tended by the green-fingered members of each section. This kind of gardening was a labour of love, because our camp was on the edge of the Negev Desert, where plants had to be carefully matched to climatic conditions and frequently irrigated. The favourites were, I think, the eucalyptus and the castor-oil plant.

The company mess occupied the central barrack. Its furniture was basic: enough for dining, but only just adequate to double-up as a venue for the wireless and private study. It was staffed by locally recruited Arabs and supervised by two Polish PSK ladies of a certain age.

The cadets discovered that their Arab waiters had a knack for Polish obscenities, and naturally this linguistic sideline was encouraged. Personal animosities among the waiters were stoked in the knowledge that at the height of each quarrel the antagonists would slip into Polish abuse of the most elaborate kind. These were moments to be savoured – with an eye on the reaction of the PSK supervisors.

My new colleagues struck me as extremely well turned-out; they were in fact very concerned with their appearance. This was encouraged by the dress privileges that matched their officer standards, made possible by our caring sergeant-quartermaster. My Tehran kit and uniform was somewhat short of these exalted standards, and there emerged an instant consensus that something had to be done about me for the sake of the reputation of the Sixth. The quartermaster saw to it within days. But even in my smart new clothes I was still a *Junak*, a mere Young Soldier on probation...

THE HARD CORE of our teaching staff consisted of experienced prewar teachers; all of them touchingly dedicated to the task before them: the mental rehabilitation of young men saved from captivity. Alongside these professionals the Army placed at our School's disposal a motley collection of gifted

ISRAELI INSTITUTE OF FOREIGN AFFAIRS, Jerusalem. (From back, left to right) Director Lawrence Weinbaum, Polish Consul Wiesław Kuceł, Norman Davies, and Ambassador Mordechai Palzur.

YEARBOOK OF the first graduation (*matura*) class of the State Pedagogical Liceum in Nazareth (left).

and often eccentric men of stature: university dons, men of letters, one or two senior civil servants, not to mention an outstanding pre-war actor-director. These provided the fizz, and encouraged undergraduate attitudes. The appearance of our teachers was not exactly warrior-like, but this was treated by the cadets with friendly indulgence. By contrast, our English instructors, all seconded by the Education Corps, brought with them standards of military *chic* compatible with our own. And so on the whole did our own military commanders, although they tended to be older men (an unkind wit observed that most of them, as they walked, left behind them a trail of dry rot). The fact was that younger officers were needed on the Italian front. In the meantime, we had the benefit of more mature guidance.

Dr Wit Tarnawski, a well known physician, had the most daunting task of all, bearing in mind the physical condition of his charges so soon after release from Siberia. Not only was he responsible for its repair; he also had to monitor the escalation of the targets set by the PE instructors, so that the strength and endurance of the young men would not be overtaxed.

The success of the Tarnawski rehabilitation scheme was resounding. Within two years the School began winning matches against senior teams of major Allied units.

The doctor always attended home games: watching his cadets win was his reward. He also enjoyed other successes. A true Renaissance man, he was an acclaimed expert on the writings of Joseph Conrad and a man of letters in his own right. Such was the calibre of those gathered together by General Anders to educate his cadets.

Year Four of *Gimnazjum*, which I entered in mid-February, was compressed into five-and-a-half months instead of the usual nine. This was done in order to accelerate the progress of all those delayed by exile. At the same time everything possible was done not to compromise standards: working hours were stretched to the limit, leave was cut to the minimum, and quality was still demanded without excuses. In comparison with Tehran's gentle canter, this was nothing short of the Spanish Riding School. For me it was a challenge on a par with the Siberian *desyatiletka*.

The school was consciously elitist: Anders's breeding ground for junior officers. Other boys were directed to Young Soldiers' Schools offering technical education and army trades. There was also a Preparatory School (*Szkoła Powszechna*) based alongside us at Camp Barbara, from which Year One of *Gimnazjum* was drawn.

The Cadet population was fiercely democratic. Our periodical, *Kadet*, declared: 'For three years our School was home for the sons of cabinet ministers, generals and staff officers; for princes and counts; and for the sons of NCOs and smallholders. There were no differences among us.' It could not be otherwise among young men – one third of them either orphans or unaware of their parents' whereabouts. We all shared the scars of Siberia... We had learnt that solidarity is a powerful weapon, and this knowledge bound us into a community.

The officers and the NCOs in charge of the School saw themselves as a part of this brotherhood. They, too, were victims of the Soviet experience; and for that reason were well qualified to guide the School. The bonds of solidarity were further cemented by the shared motherland: three quarters of the cadets came from Kresy, the eastern Borders of the Polish Second Republic.

The social nuances behind the formal façade were subtle. I soon discovered that to the outside world our Fifth Company appeared the most fashionable... In the hands of the legendary Sergeant Major Wilczewski, the Fifth was impeccably turned-out, and drilled to perfection. In 1943, it was they who represented the Polish Army before General 'Jumbo' Wilson at the military parade in Cairo.

An informal club, calling itself the Aristocrats, appeared in the midst of our platoon. This group was led by Romek Brąglewicz and Żenek Klar, my old chums from Tehran. This pack of young blades were not enam-

NAZARETH: PSK memorial tablet, 20 May 1944. *Zwróć Ojczyźnie Naszej Wolność* (Bring Freedom to Our Country) (above).

ST PETER'S Church in Jaffa (far left).

TEL AVIV street view (centre).

oured of learning, driven by hormones, they pursued girls and there were plenty of them at the Polish Junior PSK School in Nazareth. [They doused] themselves with eau-de-cologne, dressed sharply, and polished... their social skills, above all others the dancing steps of the tango. One Aristocrat called Szuszkiewicz was particularly conspicuous, because he smoked scented cigarettes – the height of sophistication. He kept them under lock-and-key in a small suitcase under his bed, unaware of the skills of my dear friend nicknamed 'Umfa', who was not an Aristocrat but an expert lock-picker..."[145]

THE TRANSFER of the Anders Army to Palestine coincided with further momentous events both on the Eastern Front in Russia and in the Mediterranean Theatre. In July 1943, Marshal Zhukov emerged victorious from the greatest armoured battle in world history at Kursk. His victory meant firstly that the *Wehrmacht* had lost its momentum in the East and would not be capable of mounting another major offensive. Ominously for the Poles (and particularly for Anders' men), it also meant, barring surprises, that the Red Army was going to surge forward in the coming months, and that the Germans were going to be driven from Poland not by the Western Allies but by Stalin's forces.

In those same weeks, British and American forces wrapped up the campaign in North Africa, and on 9 July 1943 landed in Sicily. This meant that in all probability Anders would not be despatched to North Africa, but to Italy. During his inspection of the Polish Armed Forces in the East, the Commander-in-Chief already recognised this prospect. "You will walk the trail well known in Polish history: from Italy to Poland." Polish soldiers in Palestine began to practise their Italian grammar: '*Buona sera, Signorina: che bella giornata!*'.

SIKORSKI'S LAST MISSION

CHAPTER 12

1943

GENERAL SIKORSKI — the last picture.

CHAPTER XII

1943

SIKORSKI'S LAST MISSION

IN THE SUMMER OF 1943, THE POLISH ARMY IN THE MIDDLE EAST WAS NO LONGER JUST A COLLECTION OF UNITS IN THE PROCESS OF FORMATION. IT WAS RAPIDLY APPROACHING THE POINT WHERE IT COULD BE FULLY INTEGRATED INTO THE ALLIED FORCES IN THE MEDITERRANEAN AND WOULD SOON BE DESIGNATED AS THE 'II CORPS' WITHIN THE BRITISH VIII ARMY.

It was by far the largest of the military organisations subject to the Polish General Staff in London, and was ripe for a high-level inspection.

General Sikorski's inspection tour, therefore – he spent five weeks in the Middle East between 27 May and 3 July – was in essence a routine measure.

Yet there were special reasons why Sikorski wished to make the journey, and to talk to General Anders. Sikorski knew of Anders' record and of his achievements in bringing his men and their dependants out of Russia. But he also knew of Anders' strong opinions about Stalin and Communism, and needed to discover exactly where he stood on the political issues arising from Stalin's rupture of diplomatic relations. Already in the previous December, he had received a strongly worded letter from Anders, warning of the dangers for Poland that Stalin was creating:

> "The whole world feels that Germans will be defeated, but we have a terrible sense of unease in our hearts, because we feel the victory of Bolshevism [will be] a deadly menace to Poland... It is absolutely clear to us that the Soviets have cheated us; and that fact needs to be declared everywhere."[146]

AFTER THE REVELATION of the mass grave at Katyń, however, Sikorski had not spoken out publicly. He had not told the world that Poland had been deceived by Stalin, or that, as all Poles suspected, the massacres had been perpetrated by the NKVD. Instead, fearing that speaking the truth might cost Poland dearly in the eyes of the Western Powers, he had taken a cautious line and had referred the matter to the International Red Cross. But his caution had not worked. Stalin was not assuaged; he wanted all the Allies to state that the massacres were the work of the Germans. And he cut Sikorski's government off. What is more, many Westerners followed suit. Feebly informed about Soviet realities, they lapped up Soviet propaganda uncritically, and blamed the Poles. It was in this context that the brilliant political cartoonist, David Low, published his notorious picture of Polish soldiers firing from their dugout both at the Germans and at the Russians. The caption read: "Troublemakers".

GENERALS SIKORSKI and Anders (the two in the centre): "Differences resolved".

In the weeks that followed, Sikorski's attitude to the USSR provoked a huge wave of discontent among Poles abroad. The Commander-in-Chief was called a coward and a hedger. There was talk about an unspecified group of disaffected officers, who were plotting to unseat him. If those rumours were true, Anders was the most likely candidate whom the alleged plotters would choose to replace him.

Much was made at the time by political commentators, and later by historians, about an alleged rift between Sikorski and Anders. Sikorski was painted as the 'moderate', and Anders as the hardline, 'anti-Soviet extremist'. In reality, the two men understood that their contrasting reputations derived from their different roles, not from any irreconcilably different views. Sikorski, as Prime Minister, was constrained by the prevailing climate among Allied leaders, who were greatly impressed by the Red Army's performance on the Eastern Front. Anders, who knew the Soviet Union from hard practical experience, felt few such constraints.

Sikorski landed in Cairo on 27 May 1943. He was so satisfied with the flight that he asked for the same plane, a Liberator, and the same Czech pilot, Flight Lieutenant Eduard Prchal, to be reserved for the return journey.

Sikorski's first task was to discuss the future of the Polish Army in the Middle East, first with General Anders and then with General Henry Maitland Wilson, Britain's top military representative in Egypt. The talks produced no surprises and no problems. Anders was eager to move as quickly as possible from the reserve to combat duties in Italy.

From Egypt, Sikorski flew to Iraq, where most of the troops were still based. Rumours had been spread that the Polish Army's morale was low, and that officers with connections to the prewar Sanacja regime were discontented.

None of those fears were substantiated. "You are fighting for Poland," he assured the troops, "you will return as victors."

From Iraq, the Commander-in-Chief flew to Lebanon, visiting a number of schools, hospitals, and military installations. Once again, he was well pleased by what he saw.

FROM LEBANON, the General travelled to Palestine, where some of the Army's main units were starting to concentrate. Many of the participants would later recall with pride the huge parade which took place in the camp at Qastina on 28 June 1943. A makeshift triumphal arch had been erected bearing the inscription 'Witaj Wodzu' (Hail to the Commander). The General arrived in the company of Ambassador Romer, Bishop Gawlina, and the General's own daughter, Lieutenant Zofia Leśniowska. Before the parade, he inspected the living quarters of the Cadet School, the Young Women Volunteers, and the Mechanical School. He was presented with a massive piece of metalwork made by apprentice mechanics; it took the form of a map of historic 'Greater Poland', and was engraved with the words: *"Wodzu Naczelny, wykuwaj szczęśliwie granice Polski"* (Commander-in-Chief, forge Poland's frontiers with good fortune). He then took the salute at a march-past in which contingents from all the services took part. The band struck up with a medley of patriotic melodies and Border Songs (*piosenki kresowe*), and the strains of Dąbrowski's *Mazurek* rang out repeatedly. In the evening, a performance of Moniuszko's *Halka* was staged in the camp cinema. At the end, the General mounted the stage, apologised that his dancing skills were a little rusty,

LIBERATOR OVER the Rock of Gibraltar.

and invited the whole company to join him in a mazurka in Warsaw.

Before leaving, General Sikorski issued a formal condemnation of Zygmunt Berling, who had served under Anders in 1941–1943 but who had stayed behind in the USSR. (He had been in command of the evacuation port of Krasnovodsk, but had failed to leave with the departing units.) The condemnation was a response to the formation in Russia of the 1st (*Kościuszko*) Infantry Division, which was headed by Berling, and which had been integrated into the structures of the Soviet Red Army without the Polish Government's approval. Anders had earlier posted Berling's name on the list of deserters, but Sikorski now declared him to be a 'traitor'. He characterised the *Kościuszko* Division as 'a subversive Communist formation' possessing 'a diversionary character'.

All in all, therefore, General Sikorski was well pleased by the inspection. He concluded that the Anders Army was fit, loyal, and in good spirits.

Nonetheless, the bitterness of Polish–Soviet relations weighed heavily on him. He had been reminded of the burning patriotism of Poles from the Kresy, and realised that a fierce conflict was brewing over the definition of Poland's future eastern frontier. Despite the Katyń affair and the break in relations, he still hoped that the Western Allies would help him to reach some sort of accommodation with Stalin. To this end, on his return to Cairo, he conceded, without mentioning details, that the frontiers of the Second Republic would have to be modified.

ON 3 JULY 1943, General Sikorski and his entourage reboarded the B-24 Liberator II piloted by Flight Lieutenant Prchal. A technical fault forced them to postpone take-off. But the Liberator took to the air at the second

SEARCHLIGHTS IN Gibraltar, 1942.

attempt, flying westwards over the moonlit Mediterranean to Gibraltar. It was not bothered by German or Italian fighters.

Landing in Gibraltar, General Sikorski was welcomed by Governor MacFarlane and informed of an inconvenient situation. A plane carrying the Soviet Ambassador to Britain, Ivan Maisky, was expected shortly, and, since the Polish and Soviet governments no longer shared diplomatic relations, it was imperative that the General and the Ambassador did not meet. Sikorski and his party would be entertained in the Governor's private residence, while Maisky and his staff would be directed to a VIP reception area at the airbase. Sikorski's plane would be parked in a remote spot, and specially guarded by a platoon of British soldiers carrying fixed bayonets.

Such was the setting for General Sikorski's last day on this Earth. He and his daughter, Zofia Leśniowska, and his British companion, Victor Cazalet MP, were wined and dined in style. The Liberator's pilot, Flight Lieutenant Prchal, retired to sleep. The Spanish sun blazed down, and the only mishap of the day occurred when one of the soldiers guarding the General's plane fainted in the heat. According to a later report, the unconscious soldier was dragged into the shade under the wing, and relieved of his gun and bayonet; the army knapsack that he was wearing was placed inside a small open hatch at the rear of the Liberator's fuselage, and forgotten.

In the evening, General Sikorski was informed that Ambassador Maisky had departed, and that he was free to resume his journey to London. His party, 16 people in all, walked down the runway in good spirits, and mounted the steps to take their seats. According to that same official report, Flight Lieutenant Prchal was the only person aboard to obey regulations and to don a lifejacket.

At 23:06, the Liberator's engines roared; the plane sped along the runway, and climbed into the sky at a steep angle.

GOVERNOR MASON MacFarlane (left).

UNDERWATER WRECK of the Liberator (centre).

LIEUTENANT ZOFIA Leśniowska, the General's daughter (right).

All observers of that take-off agreed that it was executed perfectly.

After less than a minute, however, when the plane was still in sight, one or two of the observers noticed something unusual. Instead of levelling out as expected, the plane continued to climb, putting increasing strain on the engines. The pilot later reported that the joystick had jammed and that he was unable to alter the plane's angle of flight; he barely had time to shout into the intercom: "Attention! Crash!" The moment soon came when the engines stalled; the aircraft lost all power and plummeted into the sea like a stone.

Rescue boats set out from the shore almost immediately. But in those few minutes the Liberator had travelled nearly five miles, and nearly half an hour passed before the crash scene was reached. Flight Liutenant Prchal, floating in his lifejacket, was the only person to be pulled out of the sea alive. General Sikorski's body was recovered by divers. His daughter's body was never found. When the wreck was dragged from the seabed, it was found to have been carrying large quantities of contraband: whisky, cigarettes, and fur coats.

LIKE ALL DISASTERS which result in acute political consequences, the fateful crash at Gibraltar aroused many suspicions and conspiracy theories. To this day, many Poles refuse to believe that it was an accident. They usually point their accusing fingers at Stalin's NKVD, the authors of the Katyń massacres, though blame has also been directed at Winston Churchill, British Intelligence, and Sikorski's many enemies among Polish politicians and military figures in London.

Two circumstantial facts encourage these theories. One is that an attempt had been made to sabotage Sikorski's plane during a previous trip to Canada; it looks probable, therefore, that someone somewhere was trying to do Sikorski

harm. The other is that Kim Philby, the British intelligence officer and notorious Soviet agent, was serving in July 1943 in Gibraltar, whence he conducted intelligence operations in the Iberian Peninsula. His traitorous activities would not attract attention for several more years, but he would have been privy to confidential information about Sikorski's and Maisky's flights.

On balance, however, there is no hard or credible evidence to link the crash with assassins, saboteurs, or conspirators. On the contrary, there is every reason to accept the findings of the official RAF report which concluded that the crash was caused by a technical malfunction of the Liberator's guidance system. The malfunction occurred when a piece of baggage (probably the soldier's knapsack) slipped backwards as the plane climbed steeply, jamming the open cables that worked the ailerons at the rear. With the ailerons blocked, the pilot would not have been able to operate the controls. All this makes sense. Unfortunately the report was not made public for decades, and its concealment encouraged conspiracy theories to flourish.[147]

What is certain, General Sikorski's death permanently weakened the Polish cause during the Second World War. He had no successor of comparable authority or experience. His official posts were separated. His role as Prime Minister was handed to Stanisław Mikołajczyk, the leader of the Peasant Party, who had little familiarity with foreign affairs. His role as Commander-in-Chief passed to General Kazimierz Sosnkowski, a fine officer and man of principle, who nonetheless did not possess Sikorski's diplomatic talents. Winston Churchill lost a partner who had loyally held the Anglo–Polish alliance together and who had gained his admiration. General Anders lost a commander whom he respected and valued. Of Sikorski's death, Anders later wrote:

> "It was a profound shock to the whole army. To me it brought great grief, for we respected each other, and his death had come at a time when the difference in our points of view – which had mostly arisen over our attitude to Russia – had been resolved. I felt sure that he would have shown the greatest prudence in the future with regard to Russia, and I knew that there was no other Pole who would carry the same weight with the Allies... There is every reason to believe that, if it had not been for his death, the Polish cause would have been much better defended."[148]

THE GENERAL'S remains en route to Britain (opposite).

KIM PHILBY, Esq. on a Russian postage stamp (opposite).

THE SIKORSKI MONUMENT in Gibraltar (below).

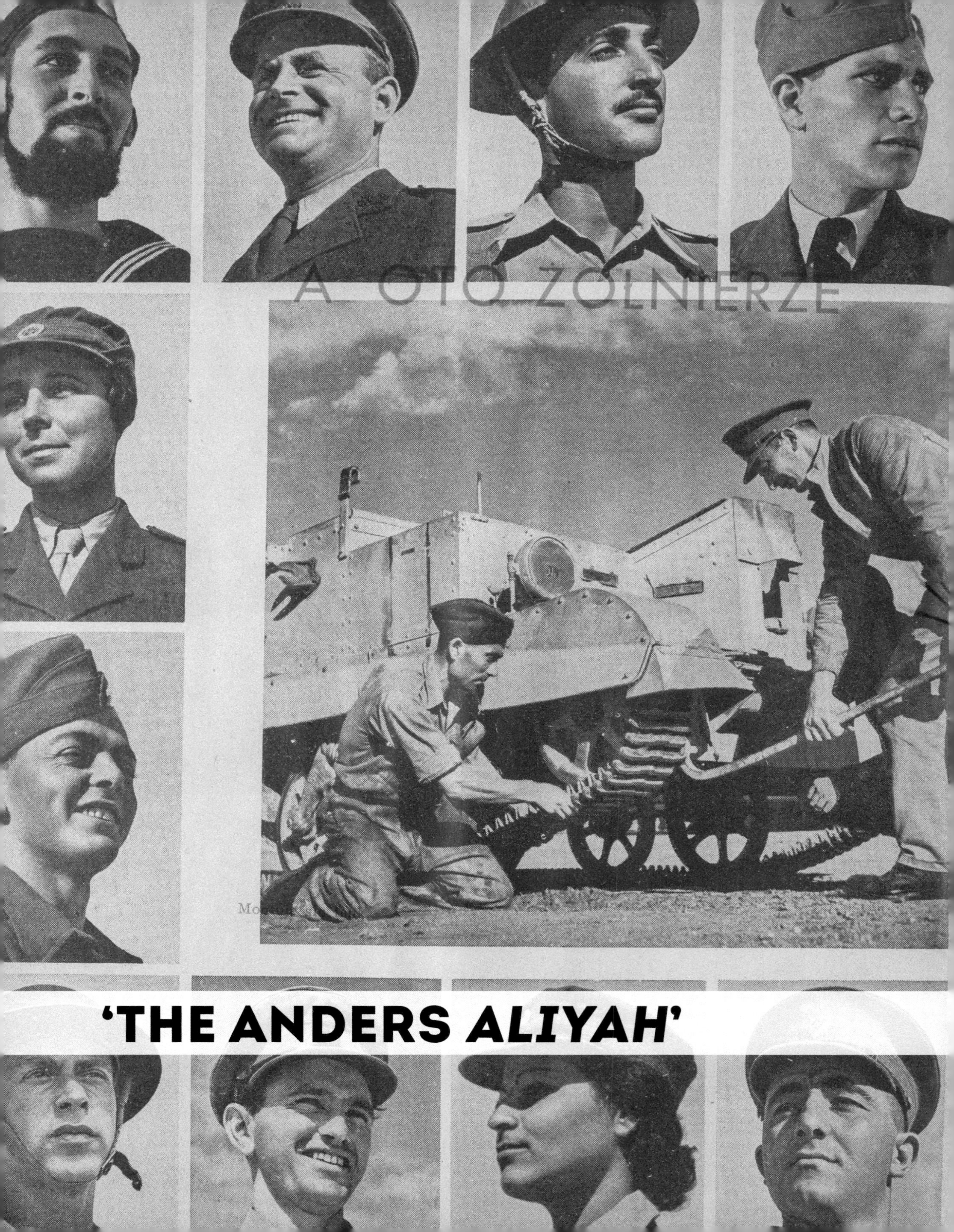

'THE ANDERS *ALIYAH*'

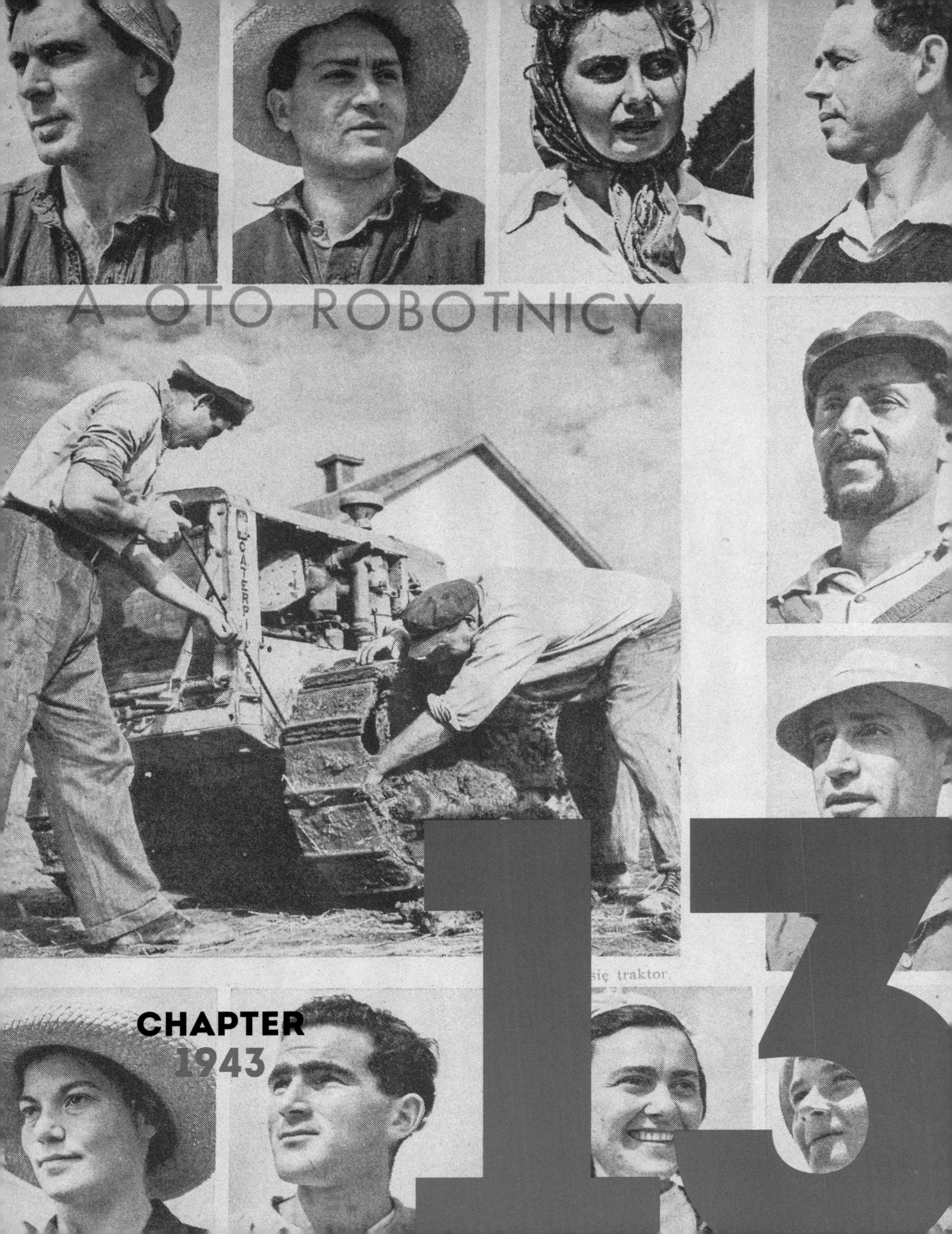

CHAPTER 13

1943

ZIONIST PROPAGANDA: “To Arms, to Work”.

CHAPTER 13

1943

'THE ANDERS *ALIYAH*'

IF POLISH–SOVIET RELATIONS DOMINATED THE AFFAIRS OF THE ANDERS ARMY DURING ITS FORMATION IN THE USSR AND ITS SUBSEQUENT EVACUATION TO IRAN AND IRAQ, POLISH–JEWISH RELATIONS CAME TO THE FORE DURING THE ARMY'S SOJOURN IN PALESTINE.

Contrary to ill-informed reports, General Anders had welcomed the enlistment of Jews, and opposed the attempts of the NKVD to exclude them. Some 4,500 Polish soldiers under Anders' command claimed a Jewish heritage, representing about 5-6 per cent of the total force. This percentage was lower than that of the Polish Army of 1939, when universal conscription had applied; but it was nonetheless a substantial number, whose arrival in wartime Palestine was bound to cause complications.

ZIONISM – meaning Jewish territorial nationalism – it should be said, was never so popular among Polish Jews as among the more secular and more emancipated Jewish communities of Germany, Austria or the USA. Like its left-wing counterpart, Soviet Communism, it offered a radical right-wing escape route from the closed, stultifying world of the ultra-Orthodox Jewish communities of Eastern Europe. Unlike Communism, however, which demanded that recruits abandon their Jewish identity and become in Isaac Deutscher's phrase internationalist 'ex-Jews' and 'non-Jews' – as were the majority of Bolshevik leaders – Zionist ideology encouraged its recruits to strengthen their Jewish identity, to reject the assimilationist tendencies of the preceding era, and to press for the creation of an exclusively Jewish state. Their aims, as formulated in Theodor Herzl's founding tract, *Der Judenstaat* (1896), was to flood the historic 'Land of Zion' with Jewish settlers, to make the desert bloom through hard work and modern science, and in the final stage to launch a sovereign, self-governing State of Israel. In this, they were following a parallel path to that of other nationalists who in the same era were calling for an 'Ireland for the Irish', a 'Lithuania for Lithuanians', or a 'Poland for the Poles'. In the inter-war period, many Jewish families were torn apart by these contending ideologies. It was not uncommon for one brother to be attracted to Communism, and another to Zionism. The obvious example is that of the Berman brothers from Warsaw. The elder brother, Jakub Berman (1901–1984), joined the KPP, and climbed up the Soviet-run Communist hierarchy until, in 1944–1945, he served as the NKVD's chief representative in Poland. His younger brother, Adolf Berman, a Zionist, was active during the Second World War in the Żegota organisation, found life in the PRL unbearable, and ended his career as a member of the Israeli Parliament.

Thanks to these divisions and complications, the dreams of Polish Zionists were hard to realise. They were not well viewed by Piłsudski's Sanacja regime or by the Jews in his legionary movement, although they had some success in the local elections which the Sanacja initiated. They were seen as an obstacle by Jewish politicians who sought to strengthen the Jewish presence in Poland's parliament, and were the sworn opponents of Bundists and Communists. As a result, despite the formation of numerous social organisations and youth leagues, they never mobilised strong support for their migration schemes. Only tens of thousands of migrants left Poland for Palestine in the 1920s and 1930s, instead of hundreds of thousands or millions, and many only went to Palestine because the USA was operating a restrictive quota system. This paltry flow of migrants represented a signal failure from the Zionist perspective.

WHAT IS MORE, one has to report deep political divides within Zionism itself. Most of the movement's founders, including Herzl and David Gruen, born at Płońsk near Warsaw in 1886, who changed his name in Palestine to Ben-Gurion, were visionaries of moderate disposition. They assumed that Zionist settlers would live in harmony alongside the Arabs of Palestine. Herzl even wrote an idealistic novel entitled *Altneuland* (1902) which predicted an Arab–Israeli *utopia* of peace and prosperity. And they encouraged political pluralism in their ranks, welcoming a variety of socialist Zionists, religious Zionists, and cultural Zionists to the movement.

Yet their mild, optimistic vision of the future soon came under fire from hardline Zionist militants who held that the Jews would have no option but to conquer Palestine by force of arms, and, in order to create a cohesive Jewish

THEODOR HERZL (top); the founder of Zionism.

MARCHING SOLDIERS: photo used for the propaganda poster on the previous page.

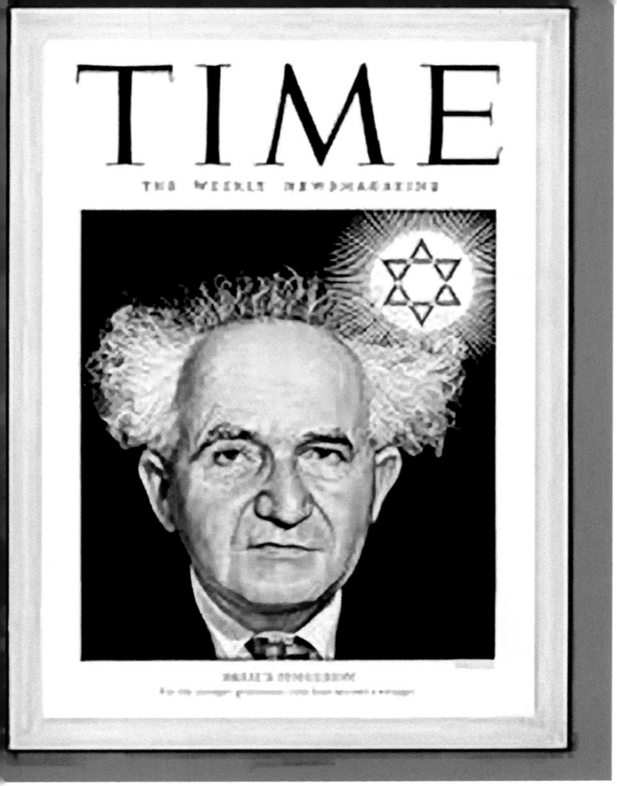

DAVID BEN-GURION, the first President of Israel, born David Gruen.

VLADIMIR JABOTINSKY, the leader of the radical Revisionist Zionism.

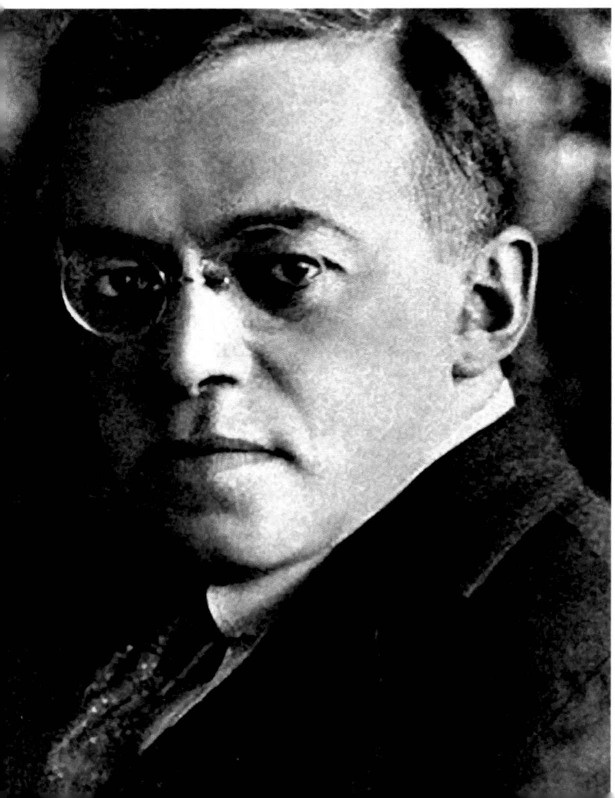

state, would have to drive the Arab Palestinians out. This alternate, militant strategy, which became known as Revisionist Zionism, was best expounded in a work by Vladimir Jabotinsky, *The Iron Wall* (1923). Its ruthless, uncompromising stance grew in credibility during the 1920s and 1930s with the rise of Pan-Arab Nationalism. Its central propositions are easily stated:

First, "every indigenous people will resist alien settlers as long as they see any hope of ridding themselves of the danger... That is what the Arabs of Palestine will persist in doing as long as there remains a solitary spark of hope that they will be able to prevent the transformation of 'Palestine' into the 'land of Israel'."

Secondly, "Zionist colonisation must either be terminated or carried out in defiance of the will of the native population. This colonisation can only continue and develop under the protection of a force independent of the locals, an 'Iron Wall' which the native population cannot break through."[150]

Nearly a century after *The Iron Wall* was published, Israel's government is headed by Benjamin Netanyahu, a man steeped in the Revisionist tradition, and one can only conclude that Jabotinsky's followers have won the argument. Indeed, their policies were already beginning to get the upper hand within Zionism by the late 1930s without due attribution. One set of Palestine's inhabitants were shouting 'The Land of Zion for the Jews', and another 'Arab Lands for the Arabs'. Conflict was unavoidable.

In 1933, the Revisionists served notice of their ruthlessness. A Zionist emissary, Haim Arlosoroff, had been sent to Berlin to explore the possibility of cooperation with Hitler's incoming regime. He returned to Palestine empty-handed, but was promptly murdered. A Polish Jew, Avraham Stavsky, a former classmate of

Menachem Begin in Brześć, was charged with the murder, but acquitted.

In 1936, the Palestine Arabs rose in revolt against what they regarded as pro-Jewish bias of the British authorities. For three years, they pursued a guerrilla war against British police and British soldiers, demanding a fair settlement based on an even-handed interpretation of the Balfour Declaration. During this 'Arab Revolt', the Zionists assisted the British.

In that same year, the Revisionists sought to strengthen their position with the assistance of Poland's so-called 'Government of Colonels' that was formed after Marshal Piłsudski's death. They had recently created their own clandestine military organisation, variously known as 'Irgun' or 'Etzel',[151] but they lacked both training and weapons. One of their most dedicated leaders, Avraham Stern (1907–1942), an immigrant from Suwałki in Poland, obtained an introduction to Colonel Beck from the Polish Consul-General in Jerusalem, Witold Hulanicki, and a deal was done. In the next three years, up to 10,000 Irgun fighters were trained in secret camps at Zakopane, Andrychów, Poddębie, and Zofiówka (Volhynia), and substantial consignments of Polish guns and ammunition were smuggled into Palestine.[152]

Official Polish attitudes to Zionism are often misrepresented. At first sight, one might assume that representatives of Poland's nationalist and military-run prewar regime would have been instinctively hostile to their nationalistic Jewish counterparts. But in practice they were surprisingly friendly, and for very sound reasons. Polish nationalists and Jewish Zionists were in close agreement on the proposition that Palestine, not Poland, was the right place for Jews to live. Attitudes of this sort were undoubtedly present among the officers of the Anders Army.

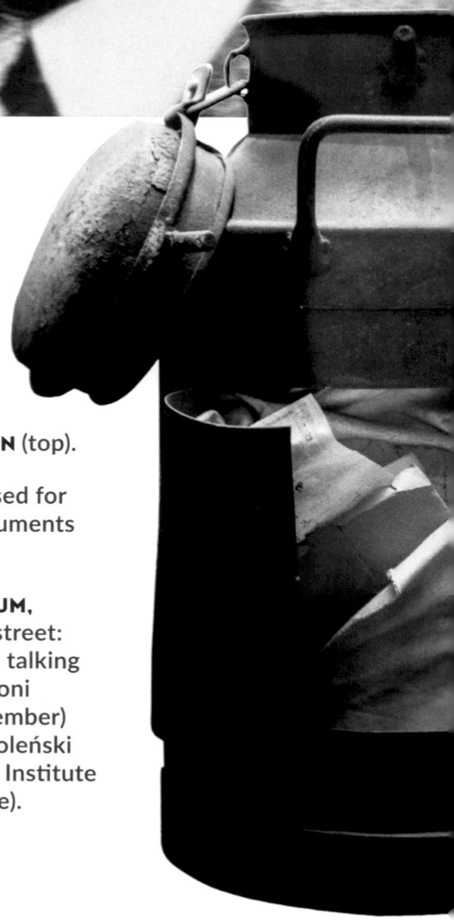

AVRAHAM STERN (top).

MILK CHURN used for concealing documents (right).

THE LEHI MUSEUM, Tel Aviv, Stern street: Norman Davies talking with Hana Armoni (former Lehi member) and Tadeusz Woleński from the Polish Institute (2014) (opposite).

THE OUTBREAK OF WAR caused a deep rift in the Zionist underground. One faction led by Stern maintained that the struggle against the British should continue regardless. He and his comrades, calling themselves *Lehi* (Fighters for the Freedom of Israel) resorted to a terrorist campaign of bombings and murders against the British that earned them the label of the 'Stern Gang'.

Irgun's main faction, however, adopted a position which held that the campaign against the British should be suspended for the duration of Britain's conflict with Nazi Germany, and they encouraged recruitment for Jewish units into the British Army. David Ben-Gurion once called Vladimir Jabotinsky, 'Vladimir Hitler'. As a result, fierce rivalry broke out between Lehi and Irgun at the very time that an army of Britain's ally, Poland, was arriving on the scene.

Thanks to the restraint of the mainstream Zionists, the British police scored several successes against the Revisionists. Jabotinsky was formally exiled, and died abroad. David Raziel, a militant leader, was arrested, and perished in mysterious circumstances in Iraq. And on 12 December 1942, detectives tracked down Avraham Stern, and shot him dead in his hiding place in Tel Aviv. Witold Hulanicki, who had lost his job as Consul but was still living in Jerusalem, was one of the few to attend Stern's funeral.

IN BROAD TERMS, attitudes to Zionism among Polish Jews could be placed in three groupings. First, there was a vocal minority of convinced Zionists, who had been active in Zionist circles in pre-war Poland, and who believed in the mission to recruit fellow Jews to their cause. Menachem Begin, the future Prime Minister of Israel, was the archetype. Active in *Betar*, the Zionist-Revisionist Youth movement, in his native Brześć, he had been arrested by the NKVD as a political activist,

BEIT GUVRIN

ANCIENT ROMAN
Eleutheropolis, today the Beit Guvrin–Maresha National Park in central Israel. One of scores of underground caves at the site is called the 'Polish Cave' from the graffiti left on the walls by Polish soldiers, 1942–1945.

AN EXAMPLE: 'POLSKA–RYSIEK' (bottom right).

POLSKA
RYSIEK

SUNSET AT Jaffa.

and saw the march towards Palestine as the road to the Promised Land.

Secondly, a larger minority opposed Zionism from principle. They did so either for religious reasons regarding Herzl's secular doctrine as offensive to strict Judaic practice, or more frequently as convinced Bundists or socialists, who disagreed fundamentally with Zionism's nationalistic rhetoric. And it was not just a political quarrel.

The Bundists were dedicated to preserving the Yiddish language, and Yiddish-based education. They had no time for the Zionist campaign for Modern Hebrew, or for the Zionists' relentless carping against 'Polish oppression'.

The third group, probably the largest, was made up of a variety of people who wanted nothing to do with the pro-Zionist and anti-Zionist factions. Some, like those who flocked to Piłsudski's Legions, regarded themselves primarily as Poles, but of 'Mosaic descent'. Others came from religious families, either rabbinical or Hasidic, who looked down on all forms of secular politics. Others again were atheists, who had little in common with Judaism or Catholicism. And a few were communists, whose movement had been illegal in prewar Poland, whose Party has been proscribed by Stalin, and whose policies were despised by Zionists and Bundists alike. Many were just people who had dedicated themselves to non-political pursuits, whether music, or science, or cycling, or whatever – bird-watching, for instance.

TEL AVIV: site of a reception centre for deserters (2015).

THE PROSPECT of large-scale desertion by Jewish soldiers when the Anders Army reached Palestine had been foreseen long in advance. British officials had expressed fears on the subject before the Army left Persia, and Polish commanders did not need to be reminded of Zionist sentiments that were circulating in the ranks. But neither the extent of the Zionist sympathies nor the willingness of soldiers to break their oath could be put to the test until the Holy Land hove into sight.

Desertion is a serious offence in any army. During the Second World War, all armies subjected deserters to the harshest discipline. Offenders could be summarily shot, with or without a court-martial, and military police were under orders to pursue and arrest all unauthorised escapees.

The Polish Army was no exception. All its soldiers had sworn an oath to stay loyal to the Polish Republic and to accept military discipline. In the Anders Army, recruits were given the choice between swearing one version of the oath with Christian content and another designed for non-Christians. But the effect was the same. In theory and principle, any soldier who broke the terms of the oath could expect the severest consequences.

THE POLISH COMMAND, however, faced an acute dilemma. On the one hand, it would have been aware both of pre-war policy and of widespread sympathy among the officer corps for Zionist goals. At the same time, it could not ignore the sensitivities of its British patrons, who were vehemently opposed to a move that could only strengthen Zionism in Palestine.

The Zionist leaders in Palestine faced a similar conundrum. They had been in close correspondence with people within the Anders Army from the moment that the first evacuees reached Iran in April 1942. They were no doubt assured that substantial numbers of Jews were willing to skip the Polish service if the opportunity occurred. At the same time, they knew that they could not count on an easy success, and that encouraging Poles to desert might be seen by the British as a breach of the terms of the truce. No-one, in fact, was in a position to foresee what would actually happen.

David Azrieli, born in 1922 in Maków Mazowiecki (Poland) was one of Anders' soldiers who deserted while still in Iraq. In a memoir written nearly 60 years later,[153] he makes it clear that he and his friend, Adam Fogiel, had only joined the Army as a means of escaping from the Soviet Union. Equally, he casually claims to have been the victim of discrimination and of 'brutal antisemitism'. "General Anders", he wrote, "publicly stated that Jews were treated decently as equals of others, but that in practice, he [the General] encouraged antisemitic behaviour among officers and soldiers." At all events, having been granted leave to celebrate the Jewish New Year in the small Iraqi town of Hanaqin and having visited the local synagogue, he saw the chance to make his break. A sympathetic Jewish family gave him a hearty meal; a friendly Jewish merchant gave him a railway ticket to Baghdad; and dressed in the tattered garments of an Arab peasant, he waved farewell to military service:

KING DAVID Hotel, Jerusalem.
"On 22 July 1946, the Jewish Underground Irgun Zvai Leumi... blew up the southern wing."

JERUSALEM · THE BUILT HERITAGE
מלון המלך דוד
מלון היוקרה של ירושלים, אשר נבנה ב-1931 על ידי בני משפחת מוסרי
היהודית-מצרית. בתקופת המנדט שימש בחלקו למשרדי ממשל בריטיים.
ב-22.7.1946 פוצצה מחתרת אצ"ל את האגף הדרומי. אדריכלים - אמיל
פוכט ובנימין צ'ייקין. שתי הקומות העליונות נוספו ב-1967.
فندق الملك داود
أفخم فنادق أورشليم القدس ، أقيم عام ١٩٣١ من قبل عائلة موسيري ، اليهودية
المصرية . في عهد الانتداب استخدم قسم من المبنى مقراً لمكاتب الحكم البريطاني . في
٢٢/٧/١٩٤٦ قامت منظمة " إيتسيل " السرية بتفجير الجناح الجنوبي للمبنى
المهندسان : اميل فوخت وبنيامين تشايكين.في عام ١٩٦٧ أضيف اليه طابقان.
KING DAVID HOTEL
JERUSALEM'S MOST PRESTIGIOUS HOTEL WAS BUILT IN 1931 BY THE
JEWISH-EGYPTIAN MOSSERI FAMILY. DURING THE BRITISH MANDATE
PERIOD PART OF THE BUILDING SERVED AS THE OFFICES OF THE BRITISH
ADMINISTRATION. ON 22 JULY 1946 THE JEWISH UNDERGROUND IRGUN
ZVAI LEUMI (NATIONAL MILITARY ORGANIZATION) BLEW UP THE
SOUTHERN WING. ARCHITECTS: EMIL VOGT AND BENJAMIN CHAIKIN.
THE TWO UPPER STORIES WERE ADDED IN 1967.
משרד התיירות | החברה הממשלתית לתיירות | החברה לפיתוח מזרח ירושלים | הרשות לפיתוח ירושלים | עיריית ירושלים

"On the appointed day, I left the tent in the camp knowing that I would not return. I reached the house of a friendly family without problems, and changed into the clothes of an Arab peasant – an old blouse, tattered trousers, and sandals. We decided that I should pretend to be deaf and dumb, seeing that I lacked all knowledge of Arabic and of local customs. When I left, the whole family gathered round to bid me farewell, and I was reminded of my departure from Maków three years earlier."[154]

Azrieli was destined to make a huge financial fortune in Tel Aviv. He no doubt got there before General Anders did.

Zionist organisations had clearly been on the lookout for such recruits from the time of initial contacts in Tehran, and they were assisted in their aims by Jewish soldiers and employees of the British forces (such as Maj. Moshe Dayan). Few of Anders' Jewish troopers could have been unaware of the fact that, once in Palestine, they would be offered all forms of inducements to start a new life there.

THE PROGRESS OF DESERTIONS in Palestine has not been described in detail anywhere, but it appears to have taken place in several distinct phases. To begin with, when the troops were busy setting up their camps in remote places, desertion was all but impossible. But in August 1943, when the Army began to issue its soldiers with passes for temporary leave, the first rush of desertions occurred. In the course of 2–5 weeks, some 800 soldiers failed to return to their units. Many made their way straight to the Immigration Centre on Allenby Street in Tel Aviv. They were greatly assisted by Zionist organisations, which operated a network of agents, often young women, assigned to make contact with the fugitives in each of the main cities, and which laid on a rota of lorry convoys to spirit them away to safe houses and friendly *kibbutzim*. Once out of sight, they were given civilian clothes, urged to change their names, and issued with false documents in order to satisfy searches by the British police.

General Anders wasted no time in requesting advice from his superiors in London. The reply from General Kukiel, the Minister of National Defence, was unequivocal. Deserters should not be pursued by the *gendarmes* (military police); should not be readmitted to the ranks, if they returned; and should not be deprived of their citizenship. Action should be limited to drawing up a list of deserters' names, and handing it to the British authorities.[155]

This instruction suited Anders' personal inclinations. "The Jews are fighting for their

MENACHEM BEGIN, still in uniform, reunited with his wife (1943).

freedom", he told a group of officers, "and I do not intend to stand in their way."[156]

Many of his officers reacted likewise. A discussion in an officers' mess showed uniform views. "If the loyalty of these deserters is to Israel, let them go."[157]

Asked about the issue 20 years later, Anders admitted that he issued secret orders not to pursue the deserters. "I gave precise instructions not to pursue the deserters. I considered that Jews who saw their first duty in the struggle for Palestine's freedom, had every right to that view."[158] For obvious reasons, these orders were confidential and not made public.

In September 1943, therefore, the stream of desertions became a flood. Over 2,000 more departed. The Army command let it be known that it was turning a blind eye. Jewish soldiers were told that they were free to leave with no questions asked, but that they should go promptly, while the going was good. Witnesses have reported near-comical scenes:

"Captain, I am reporting that tomorrow I shall desert!"

"In that case, soldier, I wish you success."

INDEED, IT HAS EVEN BEEN SUGGESTED that some of the departees were offered special training in sabotage and were allowed to leave with their weapons. Zionist agents visited the camps openly.

In the final phase, in October, Army policy changed, and would-be deserters were encour-

THE MENACHEM Begin Heritage Center and Museum, Jerusalem (left).

NORMAN DAVIES in conversation with Director Herzl Makov (below).

aged to apply for official release, which was readily granted. The total number of Jewish soldiers who left was calculated at 2,982, roughly two-thirds of the whole.

According to an official document drawn up in January 1944, the ex-Polish soldiers headed for four different destinations[159] first the Jewish Legion within the British Army; secondly, rural *kibbutzim* with a variety of political orientations; thirdly, political organisations; and fourthly, family and friends, who were often connected in 'landsmen associations'. It is far from certain, therefore, that a majority of the deserters passed directly into paramilitary bodies like Haganah or Irgun.

The document also analyses the deserters' motives. Uppermost was the appeal to Jewish identity, and to the need to defend Jewish settlements in the coming struggle with the Arabs. Uncertainty about conditions in postwar Europe was also important, as was the fear of anti-Semitism. One should never dismiss this last factor, but one can be fairly sure that it has frequently been exaggerated. Another, Israeli, source states that news about the Holocaust played the key role. "We have nowhere to return to" was the most convincing argument.[160]

Moshe Szymon Sawicki (1916–1979) was just one deserter among thousands. Born in Radziłów near Białystok to a family of Jewish butchers, he walked out of the Anders Army with a temporary pass, and met former neighbours from Radziłów, who took him in. He fell in love with his protectors' daughter, and stayed on in Palestine to marry her. This looked as good a reason as any. To avoid detection he changed his name to Bursztyn/Bourstein.[161]

When the British saw that the Polish gendarmerie was not making serious efforts to pursue the deserters, they were – to put it mildly – less than overjoyed. And their discontent was not unreasonable. In 1943, the radical wing of the Zionist underground was

DR WEIZMANN'S appeal of November 1941, in Polish: *Zgłaszajcie się w coraz większej mierze* (Join up in ever greater numbers).

assassinating British soldiers and bombing British police stations; and the moderate wing was collecting arms and recruits in readiness for an offensive against the British presence at the end of the war. British decision-makers expected their Polish allies to show solidarity. But the Poles prevaricated. When British detectives demanded lists of names and photographs of the missing soldiers, the information could somehow not be found; and when the British military police requested cooperation in mounting joint patrols, excuses were found to avoid them.

Nonetheless, it is interesting that few protests were lodged by their Polish comrades against the departure of so many Jewish soldiers. If the average Polish 'Kowalski' had proved true to stereotype, one might have expected him to complain bitterly over 'preferential treatment'. Yet nothing of the sort seems to have occurred. Most people in the Army accepted the decision of their Jewish colleagues with equanimity:

"Towards the end of our stay in Palestine, when the troops were getting ready to leave for Italy, Jewish soldiers began disappearing from our units. It was a trying time for them. In Palestine there were Jewish paramilitary organisations like Hagana and the radical Stern Gang. They were the forerunners of the future Irgun Zvai Leumi (National Armed Forces) that evolved into the Israeli army. Our Jewish comrades kept vanishing one by one or in small groups. Some would take their weapons with them. Some would not. Some even took care to mail back the uniforms they wore when they left. They hid in kibbutzes and small Jewish towns. We bumped into them now and again. During the 'Virile' war games, we met some in the fields working on the land and exchanged greetings. There was no ill feeling on either side.

The British Military Police, who had an excellent network of informers, offered to bring the deserters back. But Anders refused the offer. He understood the problem facing Jewish soldiers – the problem of divided loyalty. And he saw that for most of them the fight for their own country, the Jewish state, was of prime importance. As Poles we had suffered through centuries of occupation and we could understand how they felt...

Some Jewish soldiers stayed with our troops throughout the war. The number of Stars of David among the crosses in our Polish war cemeteries bears witness to their loyalty and sacrifice.

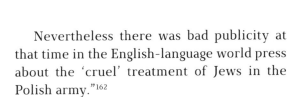

NORMAN DAVIES browsing the press archives in the Begin Center (above).

READING THE Pentateuch (right).

Nevertheless there was bad publicity at that time in the English-language world press about the 'cruel' treatment of Jews in the Polish army."[162]

ONE MUST ALSO PRESUME that Polish soldiers who were invited to visit a kibbutz, as sometimes happened, were given much food for thought. Many of the early Zionist pioneers were devotees of a unique brand of utopian agrarian socialism, where communal living and a collective, moneyless economy were practised, yet where the principles of democracy, frugality, equality, and self-sufficiency were also upheld. After 1936, most of the kibbutzim were armed, and protected by self-defence units. How very different from the realities of the Soviet kolkhoz collectives, which they had experienced in the USSR.

Despite the inaction of the Polish Command, the British police persisted in their own attempts to detain deserters, but with little success. A raid on the kibbutz of Ramat Ha-Kovesh on 16 November 1943 led to the spilling of blood. The inhabitants refused to cooperate; the policemen opened fire and 35 people were either wounded or killed. After that, the British found a simple solution. They reduced the quota of Jewish immigrant licences to Palestine by the same number as that of the deserters from the Anders Army.

ZIONIST PROPAGANDA of the wartime period.

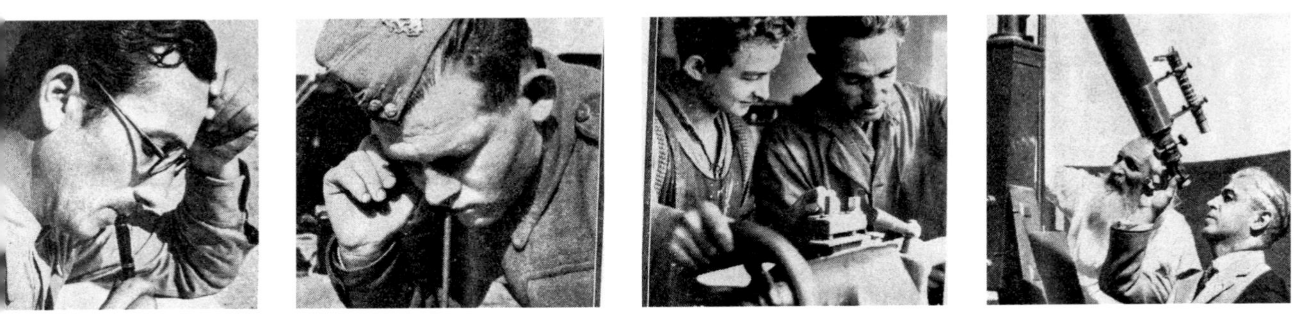

STILL MORE Zionist propaganda: "Work, fight, plan, and make the desert bloom."

THE CAREER OF MENACHEM BEGIN, original name Mieczysław Biegun, has long attracted attention. The future Israeli Premier was on record as saying that "a deserter from any army is still a deserter, and any man who deserted an army that was fighting Hitler could under no circumstances stand at the head of a national militia." Begin certainly did not flee at the first opportunity, and seems to have stayed on in the Polish service until the end of 1943. Forty years later, when he was writing his memoirs, he instructed his lawyer to write a letter to the Sikorski Museum in London to obtain a copy of the document authorising his honourable discharge. I myself happened to be present when the staff of the Museum were searching in vain for such a document; Begin's name figured neither on the list of deserters nor on the list of discharged soldiers. The answer to the puzzle is that Begin was granted 12 months' temporary leave of absence from the Army by an order signed by General Tokarzewski on 31 December 1943. Reunited with his wife, he disappeared immediately into the Revisionist underground, rose to the command of Irgun/Etzel, and lived in disguise for more than a year as the Reverend Rabbi Sassover, with a £500 price on his head. On 22 July 1946, he was co-responsible for the bombing of the King David Hotel in Jerusalem, the most grievous terrorist act in the history of Palestine. Notwithstanding, together with Egyptian President Sadat, he was awarded the Nobel Prize for Peace in 1978.

There can be no doubt, therefore, that former soldiers of the Anders Army greatly strengthened the Zionist underground. Indeed, by supplying several key commanders of Irgun, they must have contributed to the fraternal warfare between Irgun and Haganah at the end of the war. Already in 1944, a Zionist delegation headed by Lewis Namier demanded an explanation from the Polish Defence Minister in London of the suspected continuing cooperation between Polish Intelligence and the Revisionists.

Yet the full story does not stop there. Numerous deserters and departees had nothing whatsoever to do with Zionism. Romuald Gadomski, for example, a pre-war Communist, was one of the Comintern agents that had infiltrated the Anders Army. The poet, Władysław Broniewski (1897–1962), once a soldier in Piłsudski's Legions, had been personally invited by Anders to join his army. He stayed on in Jerusalem with Anders' permission to write poetry. One of his poems from that period was *Bagnet na broń* (*Bayonets ready,*):

When they come
to set your house on fire,
The one in which you live — Poland,
When they hurl at you thunder,
and kindle the pyre
Of iron-clad monsters of war,
And they stand before your gate at night,
And their rifle butts pound on your door,
Rouse yourself from sleep — fight.
Stem the flood.
Bayonets ready!
There is need for blood.

There are accounts
of wrongs in our land
Not to be erased by a foreign hand.
But none share spare his blood;

ramię broń
ją armatę
Zaopatrzenie armii w pustyni
Dostawa piasku dla budowy
Na lewe ramię siekiera
Przecinają drut kolczasty
Odprawa patroli →
Odcinają zamarłe gałęzie
← Objaśnienie planu nowego osiedla

We shall draw it from our hearts and song.
No matter that our prison bread
Not once did have a bitter taste.
For this hand now over Poland raised
A bullet in the head!

O Firemaster of words and hearts,
O poet, the song is not your only stand.
Today the poem is a soldier's trench,
A shout and a command:

"Bayonets ready!
Bayonets ready!"
And should we die with our swords,
We shall recall what Cambronne said.
And on the Vistula repeat his words.[163]

Returning to Poland in 1945, Broniewski compromised his reputation by subservience to the Communist regime. Teodor Parnicki, in contrast, who had served in the Polish Embassy in Kuibyshev before joining the Anders Army, stayed on in Jerusalem, and later in Mexico, to write his historical novels. He did not return to Poland until 1967, and played no part in politics.

The death of Consul Hulanicki, who had remained in Jerusalem and stayed loyal to his Revisionist friends, provides an aptly tragic and mysterious epilogue to these events. Together with a Polish journalist, Stefan Arnold, Hulanicki was assassinated on 26 February 1948

AZRIELI CENTER, Tel Aviv (left).

CONSUL WITOLD Hulanicki (1890–1948) (right).

in an execution-style killing. His murderers belonged to the Lehi, the left-leaning offshoot of Irgun. Squeezed between the British Army and the mainstream Zionists, Irgun turned to the Soviets for help in 1947–1948. The assumption is that misinformation from Soviet agents had misled the gunmen of Lehi to kill one of their best friends. Hulanicki did not live to see the Independence of Israel.[164]

In Zionist terminology, the Hebrew word *Aliyah*, which means 'ascent', refers to the act whereby Jews of the worldwide diaspora have 'ascended' or 'returned' to Eretz Israel. The First Aliyah of 1882–1903 was made by Jewish colonists who settled in Palestine before the formal launch of the Zionist movement. The Second Aliyah of 1904–1914, mainly from Russia, was undertaken by pioneers dedicated to laying the foundations of the Jewish state. The Third, Fourth, and Fifth Aliyahs came in the inter-war period mainly from Eastern Europe. The wave of Jewish immigrants who reached Palestine with the Polish Army is widely referred to as the 'Anders Aliyah'.

WHEN GENERAL ANDERS left Palestine at the end of 1943 to recover in the hills of Lebanon from a bout of malaria, roughly one-third of the Jewish soldiers who had left the USSR under his command, remained in service. And they stayed with the Army to the end. To be exact, by one estimation, there were 850 soldiers and 126 officers.[165] Quite a few of them were to be decorated for bravery in battle, or became casualties.

One of those who stayed was Rabbi Pinchas Rozengarten. He was the chaplain who had personally inducted the first big group of Jewish recruits at Totskoye and who thousands of times over had heard them swear the oath containing the biblical prayer 'Listen, o Israel'. He would eventually settle in Israel, but not till after the war. He was still alive in 2015.

Another was the military nurse, Stefania Witkowska. She belonged to Bundist circles, which objected to Zionist nationalism in principle, but which equally could find no place in Communist Poland. She ended the war in Scotland, before emigrating to the USA.

There is a strong tendency among outsiders to treat the 'Jews' as a homogenous collectivity. The Jewish story within that of the Anders Army emphasises the Jews' diversity.

EGYPT

CHAPTER 14
1941–1945

POLISH SOLDIERS with the Great Sphinx in Giza. October 1943.

EGYPTIAN POSTAGE stamp with a portrait of King Farouk.

CHAPTER 14

1941–1945

EGYPT

EGYPT IS A COUNTRY TOO INTENSE TO COMPREHEND. IT HAS MORE LAYERS OF CIVILISATION, AND GREATER DEPTHS OF HUMAN EXPERIENCE, THAN ANYWHERE IN EUROPE, OR NEAR TO EUROPE. WHEN THE POLISH ARMY REACHED IT, IN THE EARLY YEARS OF THE SECOND WORLD WAR, IT WAS IN A STATE OF TURMOIL, SIMMERING WITHIN, AND THREATENED FROM WITHOUT, YET SOMEHOW ETERNALLY THE SAME.

Egypt was the fascination of a young expatriate English writer, who struggled to condense the unique phenomenon into poetic prose. Some of the Poles would have known him; he worked during the day as the press officer of the British Embassy. And many, being exiles themselves, would have shared the emotional instability and psychological complexes that framed his work:

> "Ancient lands, in all their prehistoric intactness: lake-solitudes hardly brushed by the hurrying feet of the centuries where the uninterrupted pedigrees of pelican and ibis and heron evolve their slow destinies in complete seclusion. Clover-patches of green baize swarming with snakes and clouds of mosquitoes. A landscape devoid of songbirds yet full of owls, hoopoes and kingfishers hunting by day, pluming themselves on the banks of the tawny waterways. The packs of half-wild dogs foraging, the blindfolded water-buffaloes circling the waterwheels in an eternity of darkness. The little wayside chancels built of dry mud and floored with fresh straw where the pious traveller might say a prayer as he journeyed. Egypt! The goose-winged sails scurrying among the freshets with perhaps a human voice singing a trailing snatch of song. The click-click of the wind in the Indian corn, plucking at the coarse leaves, shumbling them. Liquid mud exploded by rainstorms in the dust-laden air throwing up mirages everywhere, despoiling perspectives. A lump of mud swells to the size of a man, a man to the size of a church. Whole segments of the sky and land displace, open like a lid, or heel over on their side to turn upside down. Flocks of sheep walk in and out of these twisted mirrors, appearing and disappearing, goaded by the quivering nasal cries of invisible shepherds. A great confluence of pastoral images from the forgotten history of the old world which still lives on side by side with the one we have inherited. The clouds of silver winged ants floating up to meet and incandesce in the sunlight. The clap of a horse's hoofs on the mud floors of this lost world echo like a pulse and the brain swims among these veils and melting rainbows."[166]

CAIRO, THE CAPITAL OF EGYPT, was home to the HQ of British Forces Command, Mediterranean Theatre. It was the hub for a network of military and civilian formations which guarded the Suez Canal, administered Egypt and

Palestine, organised the North African campaign, and managed shipping on sealanes linking Gibraltar and Malta in the West with Aden and India in the East. After the fall of Singapore in January 1942, it was probably the most important transport centre in the British Empire.

The British forces stationed in Egypt, some 20,000 strong, included the British Army, whose main bases were located at Alexandria, Ismailia, Abbassia, and at Kasr-el-Nil in Central Cairo; the Royal Air Force with bases at Aboukir and Fayid; the Royal Marines; and the Royal Navy which ran the ports of Alexandria, Port Said, and Suez (on the Red Sea). The general officer at the head of Middle East Command in 1943 was General Sir Henry Wilson. His headquarters lay in the Garden City compound in Cairo, which also housed the British Embassy.

Cairo was equally a major centre for the activities both of British Military Intelligence and of the Special Operations Executive (SOE). The presence, not to mention the notorious rivalry of these agencies, added greatly to the inimitable air of mystery and intrigue which permeated wartime Egypt:

> "GHQ was famous for its seemingly futile obsession with secrecy. The archaeologist, Max Mallowan, Agatha Christie's husband, who was stationed in Cairo with RAF Military Intelligence, recalls hearing of the disastrous fall of Tobruk to Rommel from a waiter at the Continental Hotel, before the news had officially reached GHQ. On another occasion he heard from a tram-driver that Churchill was in town, despite the Prime Minister's top-secret visit."[167]

OLD CAIRO, medieval fortifications, 1943 (top left).

SAILING ON the Nile (above).

CAIRO, AL-AHZAR Grand Mosque (opposite).

The task of Military Intelligence was to coordinate information coming not just from North Africa and the Mediterranean, but also from southern Europe and East Africa. It was complicated by the fact that in 1941–1943 Italian forces were active in neighbouring Libya and Abyssinia, and German forces had turned Crete into a major fortress. The focus of the SOE, in contrast, was directed solely to the Balkans. Its agents, who belonged to a parallel section to that of the *Cichociemni*, who focused on occupied Poland, tended to plan their operations in Cairo before being implanted into Greece, or increasingly into Yugoslavia.

British Egypt was well known to the Carpathian Brigade, of course; the *Karpatczycy* had passed through Egypt on the way both to and from Tobruk

KING FAROUK, Queen Farida and Princess Firyal (1940).

(which lies on the North African coast only a short distance beyond the Egyptian frontier). But the 'Land of the Pharaohs' did not appear on the horizon of the Anders Army until it had moved from Iraq to Palestine. In Iraq, Anders had been subordinated to British command in Baghdad; in Palestine and beyond, he answered to British command in Cairo.

EGYPT HAD FALLEN into British hands in 1883 as the result of a power play encouraged by the steady disintegration of the Ottoman Empire. Though owing nominal allegiance to the Ottoman Sultan in Constantinople, Egypt's rulers had run their own affairs for decades – ever since the departure of Napoleon – and their desire to preserve a measure of independence coincided with Britain's desire to impose greater control over the Suez Canal. (As from 1874, Britain already possessed a majority holding in the French-founded Suez Canal Company.)

According to the Anglo–Egyptian Treaty of 1936, Britain was given full possession of the Canal Zone, and full control over Egypt's foreign policy, while guaranteeing to uphold the Egyptian government's sovereign rights over internal affairs. British military and naval bases were established for purposes of external defence but not for maintaining internal order. Henceforth the country was ruled by an uneasy alliance between its British masters and a subservient Egyptian regime based on the shaky dynasty of the House of Muhammad Ali. The arrangements differed little from those current before 1922, when Egypt had been a formal British protectorate.

PYRAMIDS OF Giza (centre).

POLISH CAVALRY in front of the Great Pyramid of Chufu, 1943.

The reigning monarch of wartime Egypt was King Farouk I (1936–1952), son of Fouad I, who had adopted the royal title, in place of that of Sultan, at the end of the British protectorate. The English-educated Farouk was a caricature of decadence. He was said to eat 600 oysters per day, grew to be repulsively obese, kept a huge collection of pornography (that was discovered after his abdication), maintained a string of mistresses, rode round Cairo in a red-painted Bentley coupé, and cruised round the Mediterranean in his oversized motor yacht, the *Mahroussa*. Most curiously, he stubbornly upheld Egypt's neutrality, refusing to declare war on Nazi Germany until 1945, notwithstanding the earlier presence of the *Wehrmacht* on Egyptian soil. One rumour had it that he had written a note to Adolf Hitler, intimating that a German invasion would be most welcome. Another held that he had personally pilfered Winston Churchill's pocket watch. His second queen, Farida, tolerated his conduct for a dozen years, before accepting divorce. His sister, Fawzia, was married until 1943 to the Shah of Persia.

King Zog, the exiled monarch of Albania, was a close friend of Farouk, and was to take up permanent residence in Egypt at the end of the war. Both belonged to Albanian families, both enjoyed playing cards, and both understood how fragile were Europe's surviving royal thrones. "Soon there will only be five kings left", Farouk once said to Zog; "the King of England, the King of Spades, the King of Clubs, the King of Diamonds and the King of Hearts."

For Polish observers, the Egyptian monarchy and its peculiar relationship with the British was nothing exceptional. They had entered Iran soon after Reza Shah had been overthrown by the Anglo–Soviet invasion. They reached Iraq soon after the anti-royalist rising had been violently suppressed in Baghdad. And they came into Egypt at a juncture when tensions between the British and the royal government were becoming explosive.

EGYPTIAN POLITICS revolved round the royal court and a number of competing movements which included the Pan-Arab nationalists, prominent among army officers; the Islamist Moslem Brotherhood, founded in 1922; and the

KING ZOG of Albania, King Farouk's friend (left).

TANK TRAINING in the desert.

liberal *Wafd* party, which had formulated the prewar constitution. The British, unlike the King, found the Wafdists most congenial, and in January 1942, having surrounded the Abdin Palace with tanks, they forced Farouk, under threat of dismissal, to accept a Wafdist premier. Five months later, they themselves were in desperate trouble. The *Afrikakorps* had finally captured Tobruk at the second attempt, and drove to a point less than 80 miles from Alexandria. On 19 July 1942, the British panicked. The officials of Garden City were ordered to burn their archives, creating an event known as 'Ash Wednesday'.

None of these events endeared British officialdom to the natives, who already felt offended by the hordes of foreigners who had descended on them. Cairo was ringed by a score of tented military camps, whose inmates would regularly come into town for riotous evenings of drinking, brawling, shouting, and whoring. The Birka, a road in the heart of a particularly seedy district, was marked by girls advertising their services from the balconies, and by cheap, all-night peep-shows touting for customers at street level. One observer wrote:

> "Not surprisingly, given the excesses of the Birka and of the troops themselves (of whom the rowdiest were said to be the Australians), many Cairenes resented the presence of the soldiers. The foreigners were exposing the city still further to European influence and control. This gave rise to support for the Axis among poorer [people]... The British community of wartime Cairo expected gratitude from the Egyptians, and were pained to find themselves barely tolerated."[168]

Meanwhile, the rich and powerful lived as if there were no tomorrow. The suave British entertainer, Noël Coward, who was brought in to perform for higher circles, remarked that Cairo was "the last refuge of the *soi-disant* international set":

> "All the fripperies of prewar luxury are still present here: rich people, idle people, cocktail-parties, dinner-parties, jewels and evening dress. Rolls-Royces come purring up to the terrace steps; the same age-old Arabs sell the same age-old carpets and junk; scruffy little boys dart between the tables shouting 'Bourse',

Bourse (meaning *The Times*)... The hotels' stocks of good champagne and hock did not run out until 1943."[169]

Many of the Poles, who witnessed these extravagancies, had barely recovered from life in Stalin's Gulag archipelago. What they made of it can only be imagined.

British officialdom was specially worried by the conduct of the SOE and its agents, who were responsible neither to the diplomatic service nor to the standard military hierarchy. The SOE, which answered solely to the Prime Minister's office, was a law unto itself, and did nothing to restrain the high spirits of personnel, who made the most of their free time in Egypt. Not surprisingly, it soon gained the reputation of being a wasteful, undisciplined, ineffective, and even disloyal outfit. A stranded English aristocrat, the Countess of Ranfurly, who was working as a secretary in the SOE's Cairo office, passed on incriminating documents to the Embassy, and denounced her colleagues as 'good-time Charlies'. Her spiteful comments, it has been suggested, were not entirely accurate:

"In fact, SOE did not have a monopoly on 'good-time Charlies', and life in wartime Cairo seems to have been one long party for anyone if they moved in the right circles and had adequate funds. The BBC's Richard Dimbleby got into hot water for wanting to broadcast a radio article critical of the hedonistic lifestyle of staff officers at Command HQ. They spent their days playing polo and their nights at parties; their cult of foppish dressing, with uniforms tailored in the finest cloth, had given Dimbleby his theme of 'the Gaberdine Swine'...

A favourite haunt both of SOE and of regular officers was the bar of Shepheard's Hotel. It was here that an [Army Captain] in search of excitement heard of SOE's existence from an inebriated SOE operative... and, getting instructions from the barman on how to find its offices, found his way there and wangled his way into the organisation. If the barman had not known the location of the 'secret offices', then most Cairo taximen would have driven him there."[170]

CAIRO HOUSED the headquarters of the International Red Cross (Mediterranean), which attracted a growing number of distressed Poles in the early years of the war. In November 1941, therefore, when he passed through Cairo on his way to the USSR, General Sikorski ordered

SOE AGENTS:

JERZY IVANOV-SZAJNOWICZ and Krystyna Skarbek (Christine Granville) (right).

that a separate branch of the Polish Red Cross be established there. The person whom he put in charge was the 25-year-old Countess Zofia Tarnowska; it was an inspired appointment.

Zofia Róża Maria Jadwiga Elżbieta Katarzyna Aniela Tarnowska (1917–2009), who was known after the war as Sophie Moss, was a woman of exceptional vitality and of extraordinary social connections. She was the grand-daughter of Professor Stanisław Tarnowski, sometime Rector of the Jagiellonian University and a leading light in the intellectual life of Austrian Galicia, and through the female line, a direct descendant of Empress Catherine the Great. In 1937, she had married a relative from the senior branch of her family, Count Andrzej Tarnowski, but in the following years suffered a series of personal tragedies. Both of the sons to whom she gave birth before the outbreak of war died in infancy. She is said to have burned her passport in September 1939 to squash the temptation of leaving Poland, but she was forced to flee after German planes bombed her home, and crossed into Romania in the company of her husband, her brother, her brother's fiancée, and her one surviving baby son. The Tarnowskis found temporary shelter in Belgrade. But her baby died, and in 1941, after reaching Palestine, she was abandoned by her husband. When her brother, Stanisław Tarnowski, joined the Carpathian Brigade, she was alone, and accepted the invitation of a family friend, Prince Kamal ed-Dine, to visit Cairo.

LAWRENCE DURRELL, author of *The Alexandria Quartet.*

Remarkably, once in Egypt, Countess Tarnowska regained her composure and blossomed. She became close friends with Lady Lampson, the wife of the British Ambassador, with whom she had worked at the International Red Cross, and before long was a regular participant in social events at the Court of King Farouk and Queen Farida. Indeed, she rapidly became an intimate acquaintance of the royal couple. Most significantly perhaps, since she was still a glamorous young woman in her mid-20s, she befriended a circle of effervescent British SOE officers who stayed in Cairo during the intervals of their hair-raising adventures in the Balkans or the Levant. In 1942, she raised many an eyebrow by moving into the notorious *Villa Tara*, the chief hideout of SOE officers on leave, and by acting as hostess to their many riotous parties.

The so-called *Villa Tara* was a rambling old house on Gezira Island in the middle of the River Nile in Cairo's Zamalek district. Its inhabitants were a cross-section of devil-may-care characters from Britain's secret services. They included Capt. Stanley 'Billy' Moss, a dashing Japanese-born and Russian-speaking expatriate, who was famous for having kidnapped a German general in Crete and who, as author of *Ill Met by Moonlight* (1952) was to inspire a popular post-war film; Major Xan Fielding, who was charged during his service in Cairo with reconciling the hostile factions of the Greek underground; Col. David Smiley, the prototype for James Bond's fictional boss, and Maj. Patrick Leigh Fermor (1915–2011), a friend of Lawrence Durrell, an erudite Balkanist and travel-writer, who lived for much of the war in the mountains of Crete organising the anti-German resistance. Zofia

CAIRO

MOSQUE WINDOW, Cairo (right).

CAIRO AT night (opposite).

MOSQUES OF Sultan Hassan and Al-Rifai in Cairo (centre bottom).

THE HANGING Church (Al Moaalaqa) in Coptic Cairo (bottom right).

CAIRO BAZAAR (below).

LG SAMSUNG
SODIC

PATRICK LEIGH Fermor (left) and William Stanley 'Billy' Moss (right), in disguise in Crete, prior to the abduction of General Heinrich Kreipe, commander of the German occupation forces operating on the island.

Tarnowska was emotionally tuned to the ethos of these characters.

In 1942, when the *Afrikakorps* was approaching Egypt, she was ordered by the Polish Delegation to retire to Palestine. Instead, she moved to an empty hotel on the coast behind the frontline at El Alamein, living alone and tending to the needs of the troops. Back in Cairo, she moved into the Villa Tara, arriving, it was said, with no possessions except a swimming costume, an evening gown, a uniform, and two pet mongooses.

The villa was named 'Tara' by its occupants after the home of the ancient Irish kings, and differed in every respect from the official residence of the SOE, which they called 'Hangover Hall'. It had spacious rooms, servants, an ever-open door, and a splendid ballroom, which soon became the favourite resort of diplomats, officers, local aristocrats, writers, and war correspondents. A piano was borrowed from the Egyptian Officers' Club; Countess Tarnowska, now known as 'Kitten', drew on her knowledge of moonshine-distilling (as practised by the peasants on her father's estate); and no excuse was missed to organise a carefree evening. Guests arriving at the villa were greeted by their hosts disguised by suitable pseudonyms; Capt. Moss was introduced as 'Mr Jack Jargon', Col. Smiley as the 'Marquis of Whipstock', Patrick Fermor as 'Lord Rakewell', and Zofia Tarnowska as 'Princess Dnieper-Pietrovsk':

COUNTESS ZOFIA Tarnowska.

"The evenings grew steadily more rowdy. Usually glasses were smashed. One night chairs were broken when a mock bullfight was staged. On another, Sophie's Polish friends shot out all the light-bulbs, and on yet another a sofa caught fire and was hurled through a plate-glass window... [The moonshine] was prepared in the bath in which prunes were mixed with raw alcohol from the local garage... One night King Farouk appeared with a crate of champagne."[171]

Another account describes the Countess as "wilful, lively, bloody-minded, [and] with an almost total recall... of prewar Poland". It also mentions (though not entirely accurately) the villa's most unusual visitor:

"Another resident was a beer-drinking, house-trained bear acquired in Russia by Poles who had been let out of Stalin's gulags to form the Second Polish Army. Worried that the British authorities would not allow the bear to keep fighting with them in Europe, [the Poles] asked Capt. Moss to take him in while they retrained. [Tarnowska] appealed to King Farouk, who declared: "You are my guest, and so is the bear!"; he delegated Egyptian policemen to take it for walks. The bear went on to experience many battles, including Monte Cassino, and died in Scotland of old age."[172]

Zofia Tarnowska described her stay in Cairo as her 'university'. In 1945, having divorced her husband, she married Stanley Moss and moved to England. After her death, a collection of poems which she had written in Cairo was found. In one of them, she wrote: "If I fear death / it is of dying of boredom."[173]

THREE OTHER POLES, who were present in wartime Cairo, demand mention. The first, Krystyna Skarbek *aka* Christine Granville (1908–1952), was probably the most effective female secret agent in the history of British Intelligence. Recruited in 1940, when she was running clandestine trips into occupied Poland from Hungary, she escaped Hungarian internment, and fled via the Balkans to Palestine and Egypt. In Cairo in 1941, she came under suspicion from the British for her alleged connections with Stefan Witkowski's 'Musketeers', but she remained in the service and moved to a parachute-training course in Haifa. Her most celebrated exploits were carried out in 1944–1945 in German-occupied France.

The second colourful Pole was Skarbek's childhood friend, lover, and partner, Lieutenant Andrzej Kowerski *aka* Andrew Kennedy (1912–1988). The couple met up in Hungary and travelled together to Palestine and Egypt. Despite losing a leg in a prewar hunting accident, Kowerski had served with Colonel Maczek's cavalry during the September Campaign. He, too, was recruited by British Intelligence, but came under suspicion from General Kopański for failing to rejoin his regiment in the Carpathian Brigade. The situation had to be explained by a personal letter to General Kopański from Colonel Gubbins, the head of SOE. After the war, he joined Tarnowska's husband, Stanley Moss, on a two-year search for the Reichsbank's gold. His remains were buried at the foot of Krystyna Skarbek's grave in London's Kensal Green Cemetery.

The third figure of note was Jerzy Ivanov-Szajnowicz (1911–1943), 'hero of Poland and Greece'. Born in Warsaw, the son of a Russian father and Polish mother, he was brought up in Thessaloniki, Greece, but retained his Polish citizenship. He represented Poland at water polo. A polyglot celebrity, he was recruited first by Polish and then British Intelligence, and was one of the SOE agents who frequented Cairo between expeditions to Greece. Specialising in marine sabotage, he achieved many successful strikes in conjunction with the Greek underground, but was eventually caught by the Gestapo and shot.

IT IS EASY TO DEPRECATE the idea that soldiers in a foreign land might be seriously interested in the culture and history, which they encounter. But at least some of the Poles who came to the Middle East in 1942 were exceptions to the rule, and the story of the *Muzeum w Plecaku* (Museum in a Rucksack) is truly remarkable.

From 1932 to 1939, Dr Jarosław Sagan (1903–1979) had been curator of the small museum at Truskawiec, near Drohobycz. Mobilised for the September Campaign, he fought in the Polish

DESERT SIGNALS station.

Army, escaped from a German POW camp, and made his way via Hungary and Romania to Syria, where he joined the Carpathian Brigade. Stationed for a time in Egypt with the *Karpatczycy,* he was fascinated by the antiquities on sale in the local bazaars, and started the habit of going into town with a rucksack on his back, and of filling it with ancient objects that he bought or obtained through exchange and barter. Sagan was badly wounded at Tobruk, and spent several months recovering in hospital in Alexandria. By that time, the Brigade had moved to Iraq, and it looked as if his days of collecting antiquities were numbered. But he conceived a scheme whereby all his comrades in the Brigade would be encouraged to follow his example and to look for ancient objects wherever they could be found. He argued that Poland's museums were undoubtedly being plundered by Nazis and Soviets, and at the end of the war would need replenishing.

In 1943, he persuaded his superiors to approve the creation of the Carpathian Brigade's Field Museum, to which all and sundry were invited to contribute. Hundreds, if not thousands of Polish soldiers volunteered to become amateur archaeologists, and were given crash courses in the history of Pharaonic, Hellenic, and Roman Egypt and in the rudimentary techniques for distinguishing genuine relics from fakes.

Soon after its creation, the Field Museum acquired a geological division that was placed in the hands of a professional geologist, Dr Jan Rogala. Sagan, meanwhile, having made contact with the Egyptian State Archaeological Museum in Cairo, was able to work there on a temporary basis and, in lieu of a salary, to obtain duplicate objects from their cellars.

By 1945, 200 large crates of archaeological and geological samples were waiting for shipment. The archaeological collection included pottery, jewellery, terracottas, amphora handle stamps, Greek inscriptions, lamps, coins, sarcophagi and mummies. The geological collection contained some 6,000 items.

Sagan stayed on in Egypt to supervise the final inventorying and shipping of the collections. With some delay he accompanied them on their final transport, first to England and thence to Poland in 1948.

The contents of the 'Museum in a Rucksack' forms an important part of the displays at the Archaeological Museum in Kraków, where there is a permanent exhibition entitled 'The Gods of Ancient Egypt', and at the *Muzeum Przyrodnicze PAU.* They are proof of the fact that the Polish soldiers did not lack cultural interests.

AS FROM 1943, THE POLISH III CORPS, increasing its presence in Egypt, ran its own internal postal service and issued postage stamps inscribed: "Polska Poczta Polowa JWŚW". Each block of stamps carried the message: "50% of the income will be transferred to the widows and orphans of Polish soldiers who have died or have been killed".

TANK TRAINING at Al-Abassi (1943).

3

ARCHAEOLOGICAL MUSEUM

'THE GODS of Ancient Egypt', part of a permanent exhibition in the Archaeological Museum in Kraków, containing many artifacts of Ancient Egyptian origin collected by Jerzy Sagan in his 'Museum in a Rucksack' (left).

ANCIENT EGYPTIAN animal mummies and minor crafts (bottom left and centre).

OSTRACA: SHORT notes on ceramic sherds (below).

A PAGE from Dr Jaroslaw Sagan's notebook inventorying his collection (bottom right).

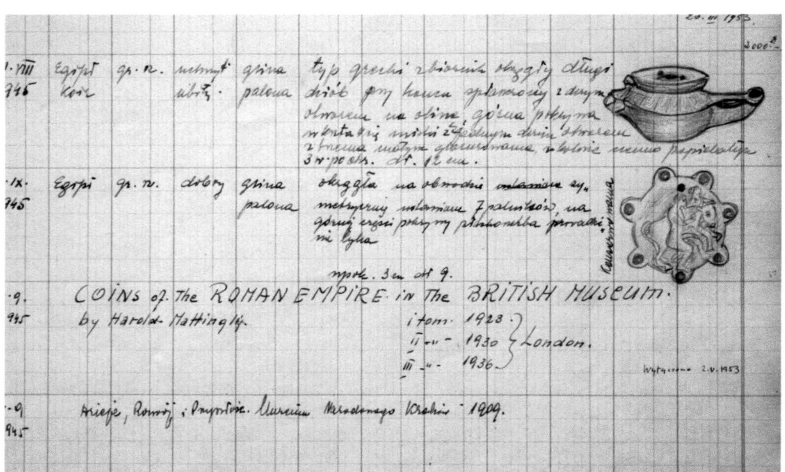

The list of units of the III Corps illustrates the variety of services provided:

- **HQ Polish Army in the East (APW)**
- **APW Staff**
- **APW Quartermaster's Department**
- **13th Military Court**
- **Army Reserve and Training Centre**
- **11 Battalion of Railway Sappers**
- **Military Hospital No. 4**
- **Military Hospital No. 5**
- **Supply and Transport Department**
- **Reinforcement Command No. 3**
- **Reinforcement Command No. 4**
- **Military Prison**
- **Baggage Stores**
- **Accounting Office**
- **Territorial Units – Palestine, Syria, Iran**
    - **15th Military Court**
    - **Administrative Department**
    - **Collection Station**
    - **Junior Cadet School (*Junacy*)**
    - **Cadet School**
    - **Civil Administration Course**
    - **Documentation Office**
    - **Publications Section**
    - **Soldiers' Savings Office**

General Karaszewicz-Tokarzewski stayed with the III Corps until December 1944. He was replaced by his deputy, General Józef Wiatr, who served until the final liquidation of the III Corps in 1947.

VERY FEW OF THE THOUSANDS of Poles who passed through Egypt during the war spent much time there. The men and women of the Anders Army, for example, were transported in military trucks from Palestine, accommodated in transit camps far from the great cities and driven thence straight to the dockside. Most of them could hope for little more than a hurried

Needless to say, many of those Polish soldiers – tanned, fit, and well fed – must have pinched themselves in disbelief. Less than two years earlier they had been starving prisoners struggling to stay alive in a Siberian winter, and now they were basking in the Egyptian sun, joking with their pals, and hobnobbing with the Pharaohs!

Apart from the pyramids, the guidebooks of the era emphasised three other compulsory 'sights'. One was Cairo's Archaeological Museum; the second Cairo's Grand Mosque; and the third, the 'Dead City', the ancient necropolis. Twenty years earlier, the British archaeologist, Sir Howard Carter, had discovered Tutankhamun's tomb, and Tutankhamun's golden treasure was on display for all to see. Many of the Polish visitors would have read at school the brilliant allegorical novel *Faraon* by Bolesław Prus, and would have been well prepared intellectually for the visit.

Having passed through Central Asia, Iran, Iraq, and Palestine, almost all would have been equally familiar with mosques and, at least in outline, with the religion of Islam. Yet Cairo was a bit special. Islam does not boast one Holy City, to match the status of Rome in the Christian world. But Cairo is the largest of Muslim cities, the trendsetter both of Muslim theology and of Islamic art; and it makes a strong impression. Most of the Polish visitors knew that they were *en route* for Italy. They were largely Roman Catholics. Few would not have been fired by the thought, "Now we have seen Cairo; next we must fight our way to Rome."

SOLDIERS VISITING the Great Sphinx in Giza, 1943 (above).

POLISH OFFICER visiting an ancient Egyptian temple with a local guard, 1943 (left).

coach ride to Cairo or a day's leave exploring the brief delights of Alexandria.

For those who made it to Cairo, the favourite destination was undoubtedly the Great Pyramids of Giza. In those days ancient monuments were less protected than at present. Visitors were free to scramble to the top of the pyramids or to clamber atop the Sphinx. Many would hand a couple of pennies to the ubiquitous Bedouin boys to be taken for a camel ride or to be photographed with their mates in typical Arab dress. Alexander Topolski recalls in his memoir that he refused to pay the exorbitant sum demanded by the photographer. So he never got his photograph, and regretted it ever afterwards.

ALEXANDRIA WAS NAMED after Alexander the Great, king of the Greeks who overturned the Pharaohs and brought centu-

KARNAK TEMPLE in Luxor — in 1943 (left) and today.

ries of Hellenistic culture to Egypt. But it was also the city of Anthony and Cleopatra, the ill-starred lovers: one a Roman general, and the other, the last queen and ruler of the Greek Ptolemaic dynasty. This was a tale to stir the most somnolent of soldiers.

In 1942 Lawrence Durrell made Alexandria his home. The part-time press attaché from the British Embassy took a similar position in the Consulate at Alexandria, and began to write. In his *Alexandria Quartet* he summoned up unforgettably exotic images of the city which ever since has been linked to his name:

> "Capitally, what is this city of ours? What is resumed in the word Alexandria? In a flash my mind's eye shows me a thousand dust-tormented streets. Flies and beggars own it today — and those who enjoy an intermediate existence between either.
>
> Five races, five languages, a dozen creeds: five fleets turning through their greasy reflections behind the harbour bar. But there are more than five sexes and only demotic Greek seems to distinguish among them. The sexual provender which lies to hand is staggering in its variety and profusion. You would never mistake it for a happy place. The symbolic lovers of the free Hellenic world are replaced here by something different, something subtly androgynous, inverted upon itself.
>
> The Orient cannot rejoice in the sweet anarchy of the body — for it has outstripped the body. I remember Nessim once saying — I think he was quoting — that Alexandria was the great winepress of love; those who emerged from it were the sick men, the solitaries, the prophets — I mean all who have been deeply wounded in their sex."[174]

Durrell was reported to have missed the Nobel Prize for Literature, for which he was nominated in 1961 and 1962, through his "monomaniacal preoccupation with erotic complications". Eroticism certainly occupies a central position in his mindset:

> "The women of the foreign communities here are more beautiful than elsewhere. Fear, insecurity dominates them. They have the illusion of foundering in the ocean of blackness all around. This city has been built like a dyke to hold back the flood of African darkness; but the soft-footed blacks have already started leaking into the European quarters: a sort of racial osmosis is going on. To be happy one would have to be a Moslem, an Egyptian woman – absorbent, soft, lax, overblown; given to veneers; their waxen skins turn citron-yellow or melon-green in the naphtha-flares. Hard bodies like boxes. Breasts apple-green and hard – a reptilian coldness of the outer flesh with its bony outposts of toes and fingers.
>
> Their feelings are buried in the pre-conscious. In love they give out nothing of themselves, having no self to give, but enclose themselves around you in an agonized reflection – an agony of unexpressed yearning that is at the opposite pole from tenderness, pleasure. For centuries now they have been shut in a stall with the oxen, masked, circumcised. Fed in darkness on jams and scented fats they have become tuns of pleasure, rolling on paper-white blue-veined legs.
>
> Walking through the Egyptian quarter the smell of flesh changes – ammoniac, sandal-wood, saltpetre, spice, fish..."[175]

All one can say is that Durrell's erotic fancies must surely have been shared by a substantial proportion of the lonely young soldiers who passed through Alexandria on their way to fight in another distant land.

GENERALLY SPEAKING, contact between Polish and British troops in the Middle East was limited. Senior officers met for consultations; junior officers worked together in matters such as supplies, accommodation, and transport; and British specialists were often brought in to supervise training or to provide technical instruction about weapons and equipment. But there were few joint manoeuvres, and no shared experience in battle. The *Karpatczycy* had established a very close bond with their

A MYSTERIOUS ancient world: temple walls covered with hieroglyphs.

ALEXANDRIA: EASTERN harbour.

Australian comrades during the first siege of Tobruk, and numerous lifelong friendships were established. But no other Polish unit was given the same opportunity to fraternise.

As a result, the likeliest places for ordinary Poles and 'Tommies' to meet were in the bars and back streets of Cairo or Alexandria. They would have watched Noël Coward's musical film, *In Which We Serve* (1942), that was showing in cinemas all over Egypt; and those with a smattering of English would have struck up a matey conversation with their British counterparts or would have listened to them singing their bawdy army songs like *Eskimo Nell, The Good Ship Venus,* or *Abdul the Bulbul Emir*. How much they understood, or how much the 'Tommies' understood of their attempts to explain the Anders Army's travels, is anyone's guess. But the Poles would have learned two things about British attitudes. One was that few British people in those days had a good word to say about the local Egyptians, whom they routinely described with the derogatory, not to say racist term of 'wogs'. (The acronym stands for 'worthy Oriental gentleman'.) Another was that the British held the Egyptian monarch in the deepest contempt (as did many Egyptians). Whenever the National Anthem was played, to a magnificent melody composed by Verdi, they solemnly intoned their own version of the words:

King Farouk, King Farouk,
Hung his bollocks on a hook.
Queen Farida will not play
Because she's in the family way.

As Poles who learned English found out, the versification skills of the British Army were very advanced:

The sexual life of the camel
is stranger than anyone thinks,
At the height of the mating season
he tries to bugger the Sphinx.

But the camel's posterior orifice
is clogged by the sands of the Nile
Which accounts for the hump of the camel
and the Sphinx's inscrutable smile.

Alexander Topolski was one of the few to attempt to translate this superb poetry into Polish.

IN NOVEMBER 1943, when thousands of Polish troops were pouring into Egypt in preparation for the voyage to Italy, Prime Minister Churchill and President Roosevelt flew into Cairo to hold the first of three secret conferences. Arriving on the 22nd, they stayed at the New Mana Hotel for three days during which they discussed developments in the Far East with their chief guest, General Chiang Kai Shek, before coordinating plans for the D-Day landings. They even found time one afternoon to stroll out of the hotel and to look around the Pyramids. "The conference was so security-conscious and Roosevelt brought such a huge contingent with him that residents were thrown out of nearby villas." As usual, none of the 'lesser powers', like Poland, were invited to send a representative. They then left for their meeting with Stalin in Tehran.

A week later, following the Tehran Conference, the 'Big Two' returned. This time their chief guest was President Inonu of Turkey, whom Churchill, in his eagerness to attack the Reich through 'the soft underbelly of Europe', was hoping to persuade to abandon its neutrality. Roosevelt jibed at the idea. He would not agree to anything that might divert attention from preparations for Operation Overlord. So Churchill's plan was dropped; Turkey remained neutral; and the Western Powers lost their last chance of intervening in Eastern Europe in advance of the Red Army's forthcoming invasion. The leaders went their separate ways on 7 December. It happened to be the day when General Anders, having consulted General Wilson, gave the order for the II Corps to sail for Italy.

IN 1943, ALEXANDRIA was the eastern terminal of the Mediterranean sealanes which carried the lifeline between beleaguered Britain and her imperial possessions in India and the Middle East. At the beginning of the year, those sealanes were still under regular attack by German and Italian bombers and raiders. But in December 1942, the critical siege of Malta had been broken. In May 1943, the *Afrikakorps* was driven out of North Africa, and in September 1943 British and American forces crossed from Sicily to the Italian mainland. For more than two years, Allied commanders had feared to send troopships from Egypt to Europe: the route was too unsafe. But by the last months of the year, the dangers had been greatly reduced, and the troopships sailed. The Poles of the II Corps joined Indians and New Zealanders, who would now be despatched from Alexandria to reinforce the Italian Front.

In preparation for the coming campaign, a new march was composed for the II Corps, and lyrics with suitably defiant words:

We are the soldiers of the Second Corps.
The Crusader's shield adorns our arm.
We are the soldiers of the Second Corps.
We've given the lie to all our slanderers!

The 3rd (Carpathian) Division was already waiting, in expectation of the order, at the giant Qassassin Camp near Cairo. The very next day they began the complicated operation of packing up and of moving to the port at Alexandria. A small advance party of commandos was the first to board ship. The main elements of the 3rd Division set sail on 16 December, escorted by the Polish destroyer *Ślązak*. Arriving in Taranto on the 21st, they stood on Italian soil for the first time, just in time for Christmas, and learned that they were to be sent to positions on the River Sangro.

In the next three months, 55,000 men and women of the II Corps were conveyed from Egypt to southern Italy. The 3rd Division was followed by the HQ Staff, by the 5th (*Kresowa*) Division, and finally by the 2nd Armoured Brigade. General Anders himself landed by plane in Naples on 6 February 1944.

ALEXANDER TOPOLSKI'S Signals Unit found themselves at sea in the last wave of transports in the spring. They were aboard the 20,000-ton Cunard liner, *Franconia,* which before the war had been used for round-the-world winter cruises, but was now a large but humble troopship. None of them were accustomed to sea travel:

> "The first night on shipboard our entertainment was trying to get into our hammocks and laughing at other landlubbers trying to do the same. Getting one leg in is easy, but when you lean a bit to bring in the other leg the ruddy thing has a way of dumping you out the other side. The hammocks were crowded in everywhere, stretched between every beam and pillar. We had to shuffle sideways to squeeze between them. At night it looked like a mezzanine floor of sleeping bodies swaying in unison. Our dorm was also our living space. With few other places to go, we spent most of our time during the voyage resting, talking or playing cards there...
>
> During daylight hours they let us smoke anywhere. But at night there was just one place on the ship where we could go for a cigarette without violating the blackout. It was behind the big funnel where we stood on a grating and could feel the warm air rising from the engine room below. Around us everything was black and silent. Thousands of soldiers on board and yet we heard next to nothing...
>
> Thirty or more ships, including several destroyers, surrounded us from horizon to horizon. Fast frigates steamed around the edge of our convoy like collie dogs keeping a flock together. I learned later that two of

the destroyers and a couple of the troop ships were Polish. Our course lay close to the North African shore. By hugging the coast we stayed as far as possible from the German bombers based on Crete.

Our first evening out was smooth sailing, but next morning the Mediterranean began to show us what it could do in March. By then most of us were feeling woozy. As long as we lay in our hammocks, we didn't vomit. But, sick or not, we had to get up, dress, and report on deck for roll-call and lifeboat drill at our assigned muster stations wearing our drab kapok life-jackets.

Far from inspiring confidence, these elderly unbleached cotton life-jackets looked as if they would sink if you tossed them overboard. The Mediterranean was the colour of gun metal – a bluish grey – broken by whitecaps. The swell was rising and the ship rolled from side to side, making it hard to keep in straight lines for roll call. Our faces became greyer, as if to match the sea. We walked with our legs wide apart, planting our feet firmly on the deck.

A sudden list of the ship would throw us off balance and force us to run in a curve with ever smaller and faster steps to the nearest wall or railing."[176]

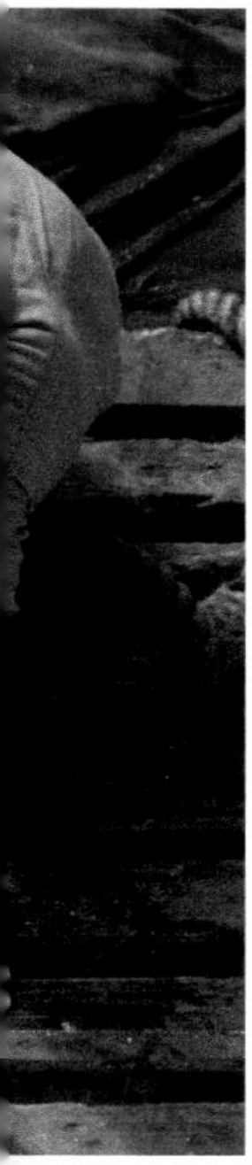

STUDYING THE map of Italy while *en route* (opposite).

ALEXANDER TOPOLSKI in 1944 (left).

SHIPPING AT Port Said, 1943 (below).

15

CHAPTER

1944

ITALY: THE ROAD TO MONTE CASSINO

CHAPTER 15

1944

ITALY: THE ROAD TO MONTE CASSINO

POLISH VIEWS OF THE ITALIAN CAMPAIGN ARE OVERWHELMED BY AN UNDERSTANDABLE PREOCCUPATION WITH THE BATTLE OF MONTE CASSINO.

For most Poles, the Second World War appears as an unending story of humiliations, injustices, and defeats. So an episode which is marked not only by bravery and sacrifice but also by victory and success has irresistible attractions. For every book or article which reflects on the Italian Campaign as a whole, a hundred celebrate the glory that was Monte Cassino.

Yet the overall balance-sheet of the war in Italy cannot be judged on the outcome of one single, though important, episode. It can only be established by examining the aims and expectations of the combatants, and by measuring the extent to which those aims were achieved and the expectations were fulfilled. In the case of the Allied Powers, the principal aims were first to knock out Mussolini's Fascist regime, and second to mount an attack on the Third Reich across its southern, alpine frontier. The first aim was met; the second was not. In the case of Nazi Germany the predominant aim was to tie down Allied forces in Italy, to slow their progress, and thereby to prevent them from crossing the Alps into Austria. Whether one likes the conclusion or not, it is a simple fact that Germany's main objective in Italy was achieved.

The Italian Campaign, which lasted from July 1943 to May 1945, can be divided into three distinct phases:

In Phase 1 (July–August 1943), Allied forces landed on Sicily, and conquered the island in little more than a month. They quickly overcame weak Italian defences in the south, before spreading out along the coastal areas. The Americans turned west heading for Marsala and Palermo; the British VIII Army turned east, heading for Syracuse and Catania. German reinforcements, sent from the mainland, arrived too late to rescue their Italian partners. Pinned down in Messina by the Anglo–American pincer movement, they resisted briefly before cautiously retreating, and recrossing the Straits of Messina to safety.

THE ABBEY as it was on a prewar postcard (right).

GENERAL ANDERS discussing strategy, Apennines, 1944.

ITALIAN CAMPAIGN

(PART I) TO MONTE CASSINO

TARANTO DOCKS – a Polish unit waits for transport.

The Polish II Corps, which was still in the Middle East at the time, did not take part in the Sicilian operation.

In Phase 2 (August 1943–June 1944) the Allies crossed from Sicily to the 'toe of Italy' before embarking on the hard task of fighting their way northwards up the mountainous peninsula. Once again, the Americans turned west, heading for Cosenza and Naples, while the British turned east, securing the ports of Bari, Brindisi, and Taranto before heading up the eastern coast towards Termoli and Foggia.

German tactics became evident from the outset. They were directed less at defeating the Allies outright or pushing them back and more at slowing them down and inflicting the maximum amount of casualties.

To this end, a series of fortified defensive lines were built from coast to coast, inviting the Allies to attack and to suffer unbearable losses by doing so. The German command had little faith in the capacity of the remaining Italian Fascist forces. Nor had they any special interest in occupying Italian territory. Their task was to tie the Allies down as far from the Reich as possible, and to ensure that Italy could not be used as the springboard for attacking the Reich's 'Alpine Wall'.

THE II CORPS BEGAN TO ARRIVE in Italy towards the end of the initial part of Phase 2. Allied forces had already secured the largest part of southern Italy, but their plans for moving further up the peninsula towards Rome were meeting stiff resistance. An amphibious American operation on the western coast, at Salerno (9 September) had nearly ended in disaster; and the British were still to mount a major offensive against the so-called Gustav Line.

Polish troops coming ashore in southern Italy often received a rude shock; reality did not always match expectations:

> "One grey cloudy afternoon in early spring 1944, we docked in Taranto on the instep of Italy. Trucks took us Poles from the port to San

Basilio, a small town with a railway station. Its few houses straddle Highway #100 which runs northeast from Taranto to Bari, a major port on the Adriatic Sea. Along the highway we saw a few white crosses on the graves of soldiers from the British First Parachute Division. It reminded us that we had come to where there was a war. San Basilio was also the base for our Seventh Reserve Division and training centre for the II Polish Corps. We were dropped off in the mud between the trees in an olive grove along with a pile of soggy tents badly rolled up.

'That's your place here', the driver said and drove off.

Heavy wet snow began to fall, and it was getting dark. This was our introduction to sunny Italy."[177]

The Battle for Monte Cassino (January–May 1944) occupied a key place in the second part of Phase 2. It broke the Germans' hold on south-central Italy, and opened the road to Rome.

In Phase 3, which followed the fall of Rome, the Allies pressed on with their drive to the north, while the Germans sought to block their progress at every possible opportunity. Key battles were fought at Ancona (16 June–18 July) [see below], at the Gothic Line (September, October 1944), and at Bologna (April 1945). Yet, when peace came, the front still lay far from the Alps. Churchill, who believed in attacking Germany from the south via its 'soft underbelly', had dreamed of Allied armies pouring

TARANTO

ANCIENT 'TARAS, once a major Greek colony in Magna Graecia; in 1943 destination of the II Corps sailing from Egypt.

MARINA MILITARE
★STAZIONE NAVALE★

THREE ITALIANS from San Castell Terme display a memorial tablet to the liberation of their town by the Poles (2010) (above).

KING VICTOR EMMANUEL III of Italy (far left) dismissed Mussolini in July 1943, appointing as head of government Marshal Pietro Badoglio (left).

through the so-called Ljubljana Gap into Austria. But Ljubljana, like all the other possible alpine routes, remained tantalisingly out of reach.

It must also be said that during Phase 3 the Italian Campaign was significantly downgraded in the overall priorities of the Western Powers. During Phases 1 and 2, it had been the Western Allies' sole theatre of conflict on the European continent, and, as such, had received the undivided attention of governments and military planners. In June 1944, however, the fall of Rome coincided closely with the D-Day landings in Normandy. Henceforth, the Allied campaign in northern Europe was given top priority, and operations in Italy were relegated to secondary status.

The German Command had calculated well. German forces in Italy had enjoyed the advantages of mountainous terrain and of direct supply lines from the start. But now, as their own supply lines shrank, they saw that their Allied opponents found increasing difficulty in sustaining former levels of pressure. Hence, though Stalin's armies were able to cross the eastern frontier of the Reich in the autumn of 1944, and the Americans and British succeeded in breaking into the Reich from the west in the spring of 1945, Allied forces never reached the point where they might have stormed into the Reich from Italy.

THE POLITICAL STATE of Italy, at the time of the II Corps' arrival, had passed through great turbulence. The fall of Sicily threw Mussolini's none too popular regime into question, and in July 1943 the King of Italy, Victor Emmanuel III, dismissed Mussolini and appointed Marshal Badoglio as head of government; Il Duce was imprisoned in a mountain refuge on the Gran Sasso d'Italia in the Abruzzi province; and the Italian armed services withdrew to their barracks, having been ordered to remain neutral in the conflict that continued to rage between Allied and German forces. In spite of this order, a number of Italian units joined the Allies.

Not surprisingly, the uneasy compromise of summer 1943 soon collapsed. On 9 September,

German paratroopers mounted a daring raid on the Gran Sasso, and rescued Mussolini from imprisonment. Emboldened by this sensational strike, the Germans then created an Italian puppet state, the Italian Social Republic, in the territory which it still controlled, and put Mussolini at the head of it. By so doing, they outraged Italian opinion, and in 1944–1945 substantial German forces were diverted to pursue savage operations against left-wing Italian partisans.

Il Duce was reduced to little more than a puppet. Living in style on the shores of Lake Garda, he was nominally in charge of the Government of Salo, which claimed to rule over the whole of Italy, but in practice ruled nothing that the Germans did not control. Italy, in fact, was split into two. The north was taken up by the slowly shrinking German Zone. The south, into which the II Corps was injected, was governed quite amicably by agreement between the Allied Command and the Badoglio government.

Throughout these twists of fortune, a defenceless Vatican City had no choice but to accept whatever conditions were imposed upon it. Under the Fascists, these conditions were not too onerous. After all, it was Mussolini who had restored the sovereignty of the Papal State by the Concordat of 1929, thereby bringing to an end the 'Roman Question', which had been unresolved for the past 60 years.

Under direct German occupation, however, which followed Mussolini's fall, Rome and the Vatican City suffered a dose of the vile oppression that had been inflicted on many other European cities. The Gestapo and the SS arrived in force, and pursued the programme of persecution, arrests, and murders that marked their presence elsewhere. Pope Pius XII bore the ordeal with stoicism. He has been fiercely criticised for failing to protest against the Holocaust. He could be equally criticised for failing to protest publicly against anything. He signally failed to protest against the mass arrests of Polish Catholic priests, his own flock, who were cast into Nazi concentration camps in 1939–1940. Protesting was not his style. His advocates would argue that personal intervention by him with ruthless and godless totalitarians like the Nazis would have destroyed any margin of influence that he still enjoyed. At all events, under the Allied occupation that followed in the wake of Monte Cassino, the Vatican experienced a true liberation that has characterised its existence ever since.

As for relations between Italians and Poles, it is important to remember that Italy and Poland were not at war and that Italians did not view the Polish II Corps as an occupying enemy force. For most Italians, Germany and Austria were the historic enemy, most recently in the bloody battles of the First World War; and anyone engaged in fighting the *Tedeschi* was generally welcome. In any case, the soldiers of the II Corps were overwhelmingly male, and their success with Italian women was famous. Both Poles and Italians were Catholics, and numerous

STRUGGLING UP Italy: an APC crosses an improvised bridge made from two Churchill tanks.

lasting marriages ensued. It is no accident that *i Polacchi* are fondly remembered throughout the length and breadth of Italy.

HAVING LANDED IN ITALY, the Polish troops found themselves in a trilingual environment. They spoke Polish to each other, of course. But they also had to learn the English terminology of the VIII Army, and, as far as possible, the Italian dialects of the locals:

"Superintendent Wilk, who was just finishing his afternoon shift, stayed with me for half an hour or so explaining the intricacies of the superintendent's job. He sounded a bit officious and used a lot of Polonised versions of English technical terms. Occasionally, he would throw in an Arab word. This made it clear that he was a veteran of the Carpathian Brigade's North African campaign, where British troops peppered their army lingo with Arabic words. I thought he was showing off, but it was not so. In time we all started using English words. Even the lowly foot messengers, former village boys with little formal education, found it easier and faster to blurt out 'dee-ay-kew' (an abbreviation of Deputy Assistant Quartermaster-General) in English than to recite *Pierwszy Zastępca Kwatermistrza Kwatery* Głównej in Polish. Or to ask for a 'docket' instead of a '*kwitariusz*'. In the Polish language we lacked the knack of acronyms and shortened forms. Like French and German, Polish tends to be more formal and correct, when spoken, than English."[178]

HAKA, MAORI war dance. The Maori Battalion and the 2nd New Zealand Division were to accompany the Polish II Corps at Monte Cassino.

Polish soldiers who visited Italian homes faced many tricky situations; they were bombarded both with wine and with demands for scarce goods, like cigarettes and ladies' stockings; and they fell easily into the pitfalls of speaking a foreign language without proper preparation:

"'And how do you say Napoli in Polish?'

'Neapol.'

'Good! That's even better than Italian. It's closer to the original Greek – Nea Polis, 'new town'. Do you know how the English say it? Naypullz. Naypullz!?! One cannot even pronounce it.'

The conversation about the similarities between Polish and Italian continued throughout the meal. At dessert time it took an unexpected twist. The old lawyer took a fresh fig from the tray and, holding it up, asked me 'And what do you call that in Polish?'

'Figa', I replied in all innocence. At that Leandro and his cousin burst out with loud guffaws, spewing half chewed food out onto the tablecloth. Then they jumped up holding one hand to their mouths and the other to their stomachs and bolted for the door. The women folk turned their red faces away and busied themselves talking about other things. The old lawyer kept his composure.

'Figa'" he repeated slowly. 'I see. It's from the Latin. *Ficus*.'

I still didn't know what had caused the outburst. How was I to know that *'figa'* was the Italian four-letter word for an intimate part of a woman's anatomy?"[179]

SIKH SOLDIERS of the 10th Indian Division.

WHEN THE II CORPS landed at Taranto, it was raring for action. Formed in Russia nearly three years earlier, it knew that patriotic military service was its *raison d'être*, yet it had been constantly denied the chance of seeing 'the whites of the enemy's eyes'. That chance was now approaching.

The distance between landing and front line combat, however, was considerable. Base camps were established in the region of Bari and Brindisi where a major operation was located. The transfer of all the Corps' constituent units from Egypt took weeks to accomplish; and integration into the structures of the British VIII Army was no simple matter.

The British VIII Army was one of the most extraordinary military outfits ever assembled. First brought together in Egypt's Western Desert in 1941, it had originally consisted mainly of British, Indian, and Commonwealth regiments. But in the course of its odyssey through North Africa and Sicily, its ranks were swelled by the addition of new and ever more exotic formations. Prominent among them were the 'Free French', who, since France itself was still under German occupation, were made up almost entirely of colonials, including Algerians, Moroccans, Madagascarians, and even Tahitians. If Anders' Poles could claim to have travelled a long way from Siberia, the Polynesian *Régiment d'infanterie de marine du Pacifique* could claim to have travelled still further.

AMERICAN SOLDIERS of the 92nd Division, US V Army (above).

Unlike many contemporary Poles, the soldiers of General Anders were familiar enough with multi-ethnic and multi-lingual societies. They themselves included Poles, Ukrainians, Belarusians, Jews, and Lithuanians, and in the Soviet Union had learned to distinguish between Russians and scores of other nationalities. But in Italy they came into contact with comrades-in-arms from every continent and every ethnicity in the world. They were surrounded not just by Canadians, Australians, and South Africans, but also by Maoris from New Zealand, by Brazilians, by Sikhs and Ghurkhas from India, by Senegalese from West Africa, and by Muslim Moroccan *spahis* and *goumiers*. It must have seemed that every nation on Earth had been mobilised to fight the Nazi beast.

MARSHAL ALPHONSE Juin of the French Expeditionary Corps on a French post-war 100-franc coin (left).

The VIII Army's *ordre de bataille* makes impressive reading. Though constantly in flux, its front line consisted in early 1944 of six formations. Some of the units, but not the Polish II Corps, were to be moved around between the British VIII and American V Armies:

- **British V Corps**
  (Lt Gen. Charles Keightley)
  I Armoured Division
  4th Infantry Division
  4th Indian Division
  46th Infantry Division
  56th (London) Infantry Division
  78th (Battleaxe) Infantry Division
  25th Army Tank Brigade

- **I Canadian Corps**
  (Lt Gen. Eedson Burns)
  1st Canadian Infantry Division
  2nd New Zealand Division
  5th Canadian Armoured Division
  21st Army Tank Brigade (UK)
  3rd Greek Mountain Brigade

- **Polish II Corps**
  (Lt Gen. Władysław Anders)
  3rd Carpathian Infantry Division
  5th Kresowa Infantry Division
  2nd Armoured Brigade

- **British X Corps**
  (Lt Gen. Sir Richard McCreery)
  54th (East Anglian) Infantry Division
  59th (Staffordshire) Infantry Division
  10th (Indian) Division
  9th Armoured Brigade (UK)
  Royal Artillery Units

- **British XIII Corps**

(Lt Gen. Sidney Kirkman)
4th Infantry Division
8th (Indian) Infantry Division
1st Canadian Armoured Brigade

- **French Expeditionary Corps**
  (Gen. Alphonse Juin)
  1st Free French Division
  2nd Moroccan Infantry Division
  3rd Algerian Infantry Division
  4th Moroccan Mountain Division

From this one sees that General Anders controlled 15–20 per cent of the VIII Army's strength. When it came to Operation Diadem (see below) and the final assault on Monte Cassino, the Poles represented three of the twenty Allied divisions, which participated in the assault.

Among these numerous formations, three were dependent on exiled governments based in London. General Juin's French Expeditionary Corps, which counted some 112,000 men and which saw service under both the Americans and the British, answered to General de Gaulle's Free French Committee (which was not yet recognised as France's *de iure* government). It included the Foreign Legion's 13th Demi-Brigade, in which a number of Poles were serving. The Polish II Corps, which initially numbered about 55,000 servicemen, was next in size. At the time of Monte Cassino, the largest part of the Corp's strength was held in reserve. The 3rd Greek Mountain Brigade, which numbered about 18,000, answered to the Royal Hellenic government and to its exiled king, George II.

The history of this Greek Brigade was similar to that of the Polish *Karpatczycy*. It was formed in 1941 from Greek soldiers who had escaped to Turkey after the fall of Crete and who found their way to British-controlled Egypt. Exactly like the Carpathian Brigade, it was organised, trained, and armed by the British Army in Palestine, and subsequently sent to North Africa, where it fought in 1942 at El Alamein. In Italy, it was attached to General Freyberg's New Zealand Division, and saw action during the advance on Rimini. Unlike the Poles, however, the Greeks returned to their homeland, being used by the British to help quell the Communist-run ELAS insurgency in Athens in the winter of 1944–1945.

THE US V ARMY under Lt Gen. Mark Clark was the VIII Army's partner in the Allies' XV Army Group, the overarching military organisation for the Italian Campaign. It was made up of three army corps: the US II Corps (Maj. Gen. Geoffrey Keyes); the US IV Corps (Maj. Gen. Willis D. Crittenberger), which included both a South African division and the Brazilian Expeditionary Force; and the British XIII Corps of Lt Gen. Sidney Kirkman. Generally speaking, the V Army was deployed on Italy's south-west coast, and the VIII Army on the Adriatic, with units of both armies deployed in the centre. But it was standard practice within the XV Army Group to switch units from one army to the other. The French Expeditionary Corps, for example, which was allocated to the VIII Army on landing in Italy, was transferred to the US V Army in the summer of 1944. (The Polish II Corps was one of the major formations that was NOT so switched.)

The Allied XV Army was opposed in early 1944 by *Wehrmacht*'s Heeresgruppe C commanded by a former *Luftwaffe* officer, Field-Marshal Albert Kesselring, who was fondly known to his troops as 'Onkel' (Uncle). The German XIV Panzer Corps (General Fridolin von Senger) was deployed on the west side of the German frontline, and was charged with holding up the US V Army. It consisted of the 1st Parachute Army (General Alfred Schlemm),

TRANI

TRANI, ROMAN TIRENUM, 'Pearl of the South', a small Adriatic port north of Bari; it was prominent in the Middle Ages as a departure point for crusaders sailing to the Holy Land. It was occupied early in 1944 by Polish soldiers of the Second Corps who were pushing northwards towards the frontline on the River Sangro. The army stayed there until 1946.

NAVE OF the Cathedral of St Nicholas the Pilgrim (above).

THE PORT with the cathedral in the foreground and the Old Fort of Emperor Frederick II beyond (top right) .

BRONZE DOORS of the cathedral (AD 1180) with accordionist; the west facade of the cathedral (left and opposite bottom).

THE MONASTERY of the Rogationist Fathers, which in 1944–1946 housed a Polish school and orphanage (opposite centre left and bottom right).

TOWN BARRACKS once occupied by units of the Polish II Corps (opposite centre right).

REGGIMENTO FANTERIA 'BARI'

and the LXXVI Panzer Corps (General Traugott Herr). The larger German 10th Army (General Joachim Lemelsen), in contrast, was deployed in the centre and east, and was the British VIII Army's principal adversary. It, too, consisted of two corps: the 51st Mountain Corps (Lt General Max Schrank) and the *Gruppe Hauch* on the left wing. Kesselring's defence lines were strong, and the quality of his troops and their equipment high; his only weakness lay in a severe shortage of aircraft. He possessed only 300 planes as opposed to the 4,000 on the Allied side. It is not unreasonable to conclude that the Germans enjoyed superiority on the ground; the British and American wielded massive superiority in the air.

The VIII Army's line of command centred on General Oliver Leese, the Army's British commander, and former OC of the XXX Corps and hence a comrade-in-arms of the Carpathian Brigade. Leese, a supercilious old Etonian, who had replaced Bernard Montgomery when the latter returned to England to plan the Normandy operation, was the equal and counterpart of US General Mark Clark of the V Army. Above them stood General Sir Harold Alexander, OC of the XV Army Group and supreme Allied commander of the Mediterranean theatre. Below them in the military hierarchy were the corps commanders, of which Anders was one of eight. Given that the Polish II Corps owed allegiance to the exiled government in London, internal affairs within the corps were subject to Polish military regulations. But all operational matters were subject to rules and procedures laid down by the higher British command. To find his way through this labyrinth, Anders was assisted by a score of British liaison officers, most of whom had joined him in the Middle East.

One of the problems which General Anders shared with his Canadian neighbours at the front has been summarised by a historian as "participation without representation".[180] As from 1941, the Allies' Grand Coalition, as Churchill called it, had been set up in an old-fashioned style, which assumed that all strategic decisions could be taken by a handful of self-appointed 'Powers' and that all other coalition members were expected to obey those decisions without discussion. This arrogant manner of doing business would be unacceptable today, in international organisations like NATO, but in the Second World War it was still the unspoken norm. Britain, the USA, and the Soviet Union were regarded as 'the Big Three', to whom all the other allies were supposed to cede automatic priority. As representatives of an independent Dominion, the Canadians were particularly galled. In 1943–1944, they hosted two important interallied strategic conferences – one held in Quebec codenamed 'Quadrant', and the other, also in Quebec, codenamed 'Octagon' – and at neither conference were they given a seat at the table. "There is an inherent British tendency", one Canadian general lamented, "to treat Dominion troops as colonial auxiliaries."

GENERAL OLIVER Leese, OC VIII Army, Anders' immediate superior.

MAPLE LEAF emblem of the I Canadian Corps, who shared the Poles' experience of "participation without representation".

MUSEUM OF Monte Cassino (2015): George Leśniak (centre, son of a Monte Cassino veteran, wearing his father's battledress, with Norman Davies

The Polish II Corps, however, suffered far more painful anxieties. As from April 1943, the government to which it owed allegiance had been formally rejected by one of the Big Three, thereby, by no fault of its own, losing much of its political credibility. By the time that the II Corps landed in Italy, Stalin's influence in Allied counsels was unrivalled. General Anders was under no illusions about his inevitably subservient position.

THE ABBEY OF MONTE CASSINO, founded in AD 537 by St Benedict, was the oldest Roman Catholic monastery in the world, and one of the most venerated shrines of Christendom. Its library and archives sheltered a priceless collection of mediaeval books and manuscripts, and its cellars were filled with art treasures deposited for their safety by galleries and museums in southern Italy. Aware of the monastery's unique place in Europe's cultural heritage, the German officer commanding the sector had assured the abbot that the site would not be directly occupied or used for observation purposes.

Unfortunately, the abbey occupied a key strategic location. It stood atop a huge promontory, guarded by a steep escarpment that dominated all the surrounding peaks and valleys. So long as it remained in German hands, it could frustrate every attempt by the Allies to seize the central Apennines and open the road to Rome. The capture of Monte Cassino, therefore, became a prime Allied objective as soon as the XV Army Group began to push north from their strongpoints in the Mezzogiorno.

Monte Cassino, however, was in no way an objective that could be isolated from several others. The abbey itself was dominated by half a dozen peaks and ridges that lay behind it, and no attack on Monastery Hill could be successful without a series of coordinated flanking manoeuvres in all the adjacent sectors. And the

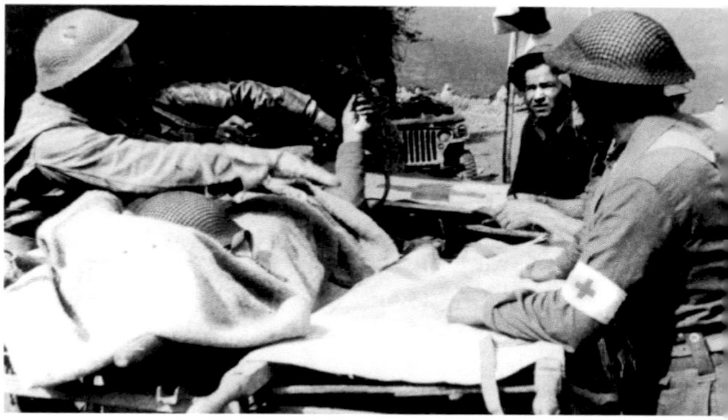

US B17 bomber over the Abbey.

German defence line in the centre was strong enough to support its right and left wings under pressure.

The Allied offensive against Monte Cassino, therefore, was conceived as the focal point of a complex chain of movements stretching from

POLISH INFANTRY storm German dugouts on Monastery Hill (top centre).

AN AMBULANCE unit withdraws a casualty (above).

APENNINE ROADS (top right).

coast to coast. The central assault on Monastery Hill was but one element in a range of operations involving all the front line units of the V and VIII Armies. In particular, it was designed to coincide with a complementary amphibious landing north of the main frontline at Anzio, which aimed to turn the German flank, to put Rome in Allied sights, and to force the bulk of German forces to retreat. Monte Cassino and Anzio were twin pillars of the same plan. The attack on Monte Cassino was entrusted to the British VIII Army; the landing at Anzio to the US V Army.

YET THE WINTER of 1943–1944 was harsh. Heavy snows blanketed the Apennine Peaks, blocked the valleys and swelled the rivers. Climatic conditions favoured the defenders, and it was mid-January before the Allied armies had consolidated their starting positions. General Leese was optimistic; he talked of "breaking the Germans' hold on central Italy". In the event, more than five months would pass before significant gains were made. Not one, but four battles for Monte Cassino would be fought, at terrible cost, before the ruins of the Abbey were finally be conquered.

In the first battle (17 January–11 February), lead roles were given to the British X Corps and the US II Corps, who soon found that Germans dug into well-fortified positions could not be attacked with impunity and that every assault

I FIRST heard about Monte Cassino from a colleague at Oxford, when I was still a student there. My informant's father had been a British general in the Italian Campaign, and had personally witnessed the battle. "Never in all my life," the general had told his son, "have I seen such bravery under fire as shown by the Poles at Monte Cassino."

would provoke a devastating counterattack. In the first three days, the X Corps suffered 4,000 casualties; in the three following days, the US 35th Division was badly mauled, and its 141st Regiment annihilated. In the second week, the US 34th Division and two Moroccan divisions attempted a 'right hook' in the mountains to the north of Cassino. They came tantalisingly

SCENES FROM the main offensive against the German lines at Monte Cassino, 12–18 May 1944. Victory came four months after the start of the battle.

close to their goal. At one stage, they occupied Point 445 only 400 yards from the Abbey. But they could not hold on, and were driven back at great cost. The Moroccans suffered 80 per cent casualties in their infantry battalions. Total Allied casualties approached 11,000.

As the battle proceeded, the US V Army launched its surprise landing at Anzio and almost came to grief. Total surprise was achieved initially, and a lone American jeep was reported to have driven unopposed into the suburbs of Rome. But the American commander, Maj. Gen. John Lucas, was slow to exploit his advantage, and the bridgehead was soon surrounded by a variety of units from the German XIV Army. Over 60,000 Allied troops were pinned down on the beaches and in the coastal villages. They were to be trapped there for 16 weeks of incessant combat.

ST. BENEDICT'S Abbey: in May 1944 (above) and today (opposite).

Meanwhile, the Allied Command convinced itself that the Abbey of Monte Cassino had been secretly occupied by Germans and had thereby become a valid target. As one American officer remarked, "they have been looking so hard, they can see what they are looking for." In reality, apart from a company of monks and a gang of local labourers, the Abbey was empty. Nonetheless, on the morning of 15 February 1944, a fleet of USAAF Flying Fortresses dropped a vast quantity of high explosives onto the sacred building, reducing it to smoking ruins. Pope Pius XII kept silent, but his Secretary-of-State, Cardinal Maglione, told the US Ambassador that the bombing was "a colossal blunder" and "a piece of gross stupidity".

IN THE SECOND BATTLE (15–18 February 1944), which the bombing heralded, inadequate Allied forces failed to make any advance on the marginal gains of the first. This time, the lead was handed to the V Corps of the VIII Army. An initial night-time assault by a battalion of the Royal Sussex Regiment was repulsed with the loss of 11 out of 15 officers, and of 162 of 313 men. The principal attack on Monastery Hill by the 4th Indian Division produced similar results. A bold movement by the 28th Maori Battalion started with the capture of Cassino Station, but ended with hurried retreat. The stalemate was complete. At this stage, the Polish II Corps still lay far from the front.

In those same days, the German XIV Army mounted a concerted attack on the Anzio

bridgehead. Panzers made significant inroads before being halted by American air power. The lesson, as at Monte Cassino, was simple: defensive actions were far more likely to succeed than offensive ones.

IN THE THIRD BATTLE (15–22 March), the lead was given to the 2nd New Zealand Division, greatly expanded by additional units to the strength of an Army Corps. But to no avail. All the advances made by New Zealand and Indian forces were nullified by a fierce and effective counterstroke by the 1st German Parachute Corps. The Allied Command was forced to realise that no progress was likely to be made unless a far larger strike force could be assembled.

The fourth and final battle for Monte Cassino, therefore, could only take place after two months of elaborate preparations. Most elements of the British XIII Corps and the Polish II Corps were moved to the centre in great secrecy. General Anders entered his front-line HQ on 24 April. Kesselring's staff estimated that they were facing six divisions: in fact, they were facing 17. By the time that Operation Diadem was in place, 20 Allied divisions were poised to strike along the 22-mile front of what the Germans called their Winter Line.

General Leese, commander of the VIII Army, had talked to Anders on 24 March 1944, raising the possibility that the II Corps could participate in the coming battle and confirming that the Cassino Massif would be the target of their involvement. His initial approach was tentative, since protocol required that non-British military leaders be given time to consult their governments. Anders, however, agreed to the proposal without hesitation, signally failing to consult his superiors in London. He knew very well that his men were eager to prove themselves in battle, and that to have declined or quibbled could have seriously damaged the reputation of the Corps. He also knew that the number of combat-ready troops – 11 infantry brigades and one tank brigade – was less than half the number at the disposal of the adjacent XIII Corps and French Corps. Nonetheless he accepted, and the proposal became an order. Soon after, he received a memorandum from the Polish Commander-in-Chief in London, General Sosnkowski, protesting that the II Corps was too weak for the assigned task. It was too late. "The smallest corps in the 8th Army was given the most difficult task."[181]

As the deadline for the Polish attack approached, few soldiers possessed detailed information about the plans. But they all noticed subtle changes around them, and they all reflected on the 'hazards of battle':

"When I arrived at the 5th Division Signals Office, about a 20 km (12 mile) trip from us, I saw that this was for real. There were sandbags everywhere. Millions of sandbags, it seemed. Around the tents. Around the dugouts. Alongside trenches. Even around the few vehicles kept there.

Any vehicle, including our jeep, that came that close to the front line had the windshield removed to avoid any tell-tale glint of sun off the glass that might alert the Germans. The

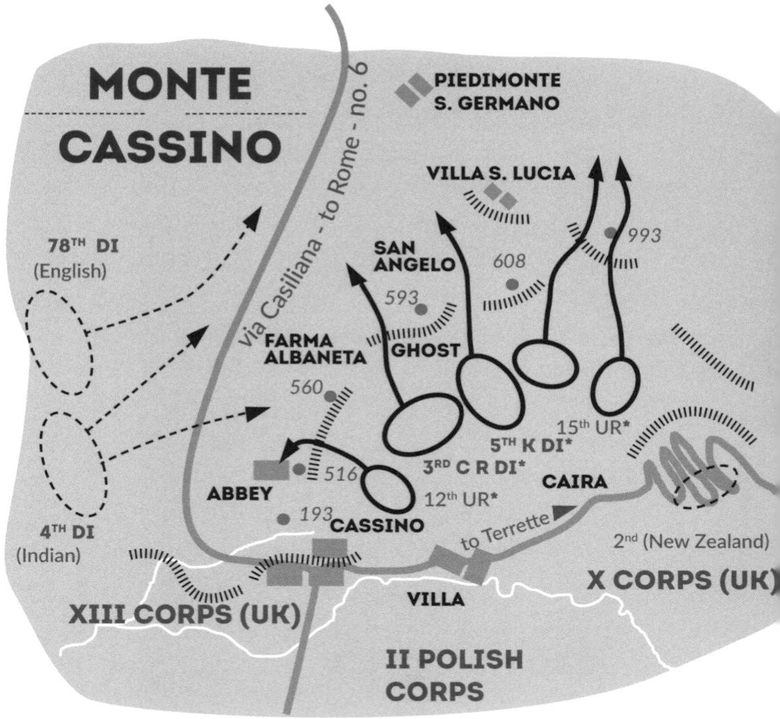

THE BATTLE of Monte Cassino – troop movements (right).

GENERAL ANDERS surveys the ruins (below).

*15th Uhlans Regiment *12th Uhlans Regiment ***5TH KRESOWA DI** ***3RD CARPATHIAN RIFLE DI**

GEORGE LEŚNIAK from York, son of a Monte Cassino combatant, and Norman Davies (left).

SOLDIERS FROM the 5th Infantry Division inspecting a burned tank (below).

odd jeep had a hinged windshield that could be laid flat on the hood of the engine with a canvas slip-cover...

The day of the big push by all the Allied forces across Italy was getting closer and closer but we didn't know when it would start. We thought about the other troops who had tried and failed since December 1943 to take the hilltop Abbey. First came the unseasoned Americans who suffered tremendous losses during their ill-conceived and badly executed attacks across the rivers. Then the hard-driving French colonial divisions with their incredibly courageous soldiers from Tunisia, Morocco, and Algeria led by professional French officers, but denied support from American and British troops at the point when they were about to break through the German defense lines. Third were seasoned British Divisions: the Guards Brigade, and Indian and Gurkha troops along with the New Zealand Corps, who bombed the town of Cassino into oblivion and tried a frontal attack up the hill to the Monastery only to be stymied by their inability to drive through the rubble of the town or the flooded plain and by fierce German resistance on the slope. Now it was our turn."[182]

On 11 May 1944, General Anders issued his momentous Order of the Day:

"Soldiers!
The moment for battle has arrived. We have long awaited the day of revenge and retribution over our hereditary enemy.
Shoulder to shoulder, will fight British, American, Canadian and New Zealand divisions, together with French, Italian and Indian troops.
The task assigned to us will cover with glory the name of the Polish soldier all over the world.
At this moment, the thoughts and hearts of our whole nation are with us.
Trusting in the Justice of Divine Providence, we go forward with the sacred call in our hearts: God, Honour, Country."

Władysław Anders, Lt. General
Commander, II Polish Corps"[183]

GERMAN–ITALIAN ALLIANCE: placid Italian cow tethered to a ruined Sturmgeschutz III mobile gun.

As the Army moved forward, so, too, did the chaplains. By this time, the *Duszpasterstwo Katolickie* (the Chaplaincy) was greatly expanded, and practically every unit was served by its own priest. Rev. Lt Col. Franciszek Studziński (Father Francis Studziński) was the spiritual pastor of the 4th Armoured Regiment:

"After landing in Italy in April 1944 the Fourth Armored Regiment, where I was the chaplain, took quarters in Capriati near Venafro, just 20 km (12 miles) from Monte Cassino. It was clear where Polish soldiers were going to be fighting...

The last intensive joint exercises of the infantry and tanks took place at Capriati, taking one of the hills that people said was very similar to Monte Cassino. At the same time that these purely military exercises were taking place, confessions started in the different units, preceded by short religious sermons delivered by the chaplains during free time in the evenings. The soldiers had to be prepared spiritually for a very difficult task. They came to confession and partook of Holy Communion willingly, knowing that they needed moral strength at a time like this.

The chaplains helped one another in this pastoral service. I worked together with Father Huczyński, former Carmelite prior in Buczacz...

Just before the offensive I went to Aquafondata, where the Fifth Frontier Division had its region of concentration. I wanted to see the field and contact the nearest chaplain in the region and at the same time visit the tank company from my regiment, which was moved there. I found the chaplain in the neighbouring town of Viticuso. He was not in a happy mood, because he had to say farewell to his unit for the duration of the offensive and move to the a.d.s. [advanced dressing station], which did not have a chaplain and had to have one. Aquafondata and its vicinity presented a sorry sight. The town was deserted and everywhere one could see the effects of war."[184]

INTERIOR OF the Abbey Church in 1944 (opposite) and today.

The three divisions of the Polish II Corps had indeed been handed the toughest task of all. While two British corps were to surge forward on either side of them, and the I Canadian Corps was to drive into the nearby Liri Valley, the Poles were asked for the near-impossible: to take Monastery Hill by frontal attack. The German defenders enjoyed every advantage: firing down from long-prepared and carefully hidden positions.

THE POLISH INFANTRYMEN had somehow to charge uphill, scrambling from crag to crag, dragging their weapons and ammunition with them. Their every move exposed them to withering fire. Not surprisingly, therefore, the first Polish assault on 12 May on a peak suitably called Monte Calvario did not bring the desired result. No less than 281 officers and 3,503 men were lost in the attempt. But the survivors were clinging on to terrain on the high sides of the mountain, and the defenders were growing fearful of encircling movements that threatened their line of retreat. In the early hours of 18 May, elements of the 78th British Division joined Polish units on the flanks of the Liri Valley, and the Germans began cautiously to pull back from the heights. Eventually, the leading Poles could see that the monastery had been evacuated, and soldiers from the 12th Podolian Cavalry Regiment girded their failing strength to creep forward and to raise their red-and-white flag above the ruins. At midday, Master Corporal Emil Czech raised his bugle to sound the *hejnał mariacki* (St. Mary's Trumpet Call) to signal victory. On that same day, at Castelforte, the Americans announced

POLISH CEMETERY (above) near the small rural town of Casamassima in Apulia near Bari, where a wartime Polish Military Hospita treated casualties from Monte Cassino. Several hundred wounded who did not survive were buried here. Most Polish military graves in Italy can be traced on the website <www.polskiecmentarzewewloszech.eu.it.

MONTE CASSINO

THE POLISH MILITARY CEMETERY, constructed by the Government-in-Exile in 1944–1945 on the site of the so-called *Dolina Śmierci* (Valley of Death) between Monastery Hill and Hill 593 (opposite).

AMBASSADOR TOMASZ Orłowski in the company of Italian dignitaries (below).

GRAVE OF General Anders (opposite bottom).

ONE OF the eagles gracing the entrance (bottom left)

THE COURTYARD of the Abbey today (bottom right).

THE ABBEY cloister then (above) and now (below right).

that the *Wehrmacht* had been reduced to deploying boy soldiers.

It is sometimes said misleadingly that the Poles conquered Monte Cassino. It would be more accurate to say that they reached the summit of Monastery Hill in the crowning moment of a joint Allied operation. Yet it would be equally misleading to suggest that the Polish contribution was no greater or no less than that of all the others. The soldiers of General Anders had triumphed in face of unequalled adversity, and they had paid the heaviest price. Their triumph provided an iconic moment that lifted the hearts of everyone in the Free World, and that put a stop forever to the nasty, Soviet-inspired propaganda which had been claiming for years that the Poles could not fight.

The end of fighting marked the start of the chaplain's most poignant duties:

> "I went to Aquafondata again directly after the fighting ended at Monte Cassino. I went there to consecrate the cross on the grave of the late Lt Bortnowski, commander of the 1st tank company, who was killed at Monte Cassino. His own company made the cross for him out of tank caterpillars. The Virtuti Militari order that Bortnowski received for the battle at Gazala in Libya was placed as a symbol on the cross. His tank crew, who survived, stood by the grave as the delegation. It was a sad and moving ritual. When the heavy iron cross was set up and when I sprinkled it with holy water, the crew, who had been quiet until then, started to weep on the grave of their commander, whom they had loved like a brother, because he was truly a good man. I wept with them."[185]

MELCHIOR WAŃKOWICZ, the future historian of Monte Cassino, shows the site to some of the earliest visitors.

This scene was multiplied thousands of times. The telegram which General Anders sent to his Commander-in-Chief, General Sosnkowski, was extremely laconic:

> "Victory due to heroism of soldier... commanders set an example... exceptional comradeship with the British formations."[186]

FIVE DAYS AFTER Master Corporal Czech's bugle had rung out at Monte Cassino, the US V Army finally broke out from its encirclement on the Anzio beachhead. Thousands of American GIs poured through gaps in the German defences, and their enemies, after five months of dogged fighting, began to pull back. Anzio and Monte Cassino had proved after all that they were opposite ends of the same great struggle.

The pursuit began in the wake of victory. On 25 May Polish units burst through the Gustav Line at Piedimonte (to the rear of the Winter Line) and forced the German X Army into headlong retreat. At this point, the seven rearmost divisions of the X Army were heading for disaster. All that was needed was for the US VI Corps, now well clear of Anzio, to wheel about and to seal off their escape route.

Alas! For reasons best known to himself, General Mark Clark made one of the direst decisions of the whole campaign. Instead of ordering his VI Corps to intercept the retreating Germans, he ordered them to march directly on Rome. Worse still, having issued the order, he disappeared beyond contact for the rest of the day, leaving his astonished subordinates in confusion. But that's what happened. The Americans rolled into Rome, scattering cigarettes and candy and basking in the adulation of the crowds. But the German X Army escaped. The battles of Monte Cassino and Anzio had caused over 100,000 Allied casualties, far more than German losses. And the two German armies in Italy had been routed. Yet, at the very last moment, the fruits of victory were squandered and Adolf Hitler's legions were left to fight another day.

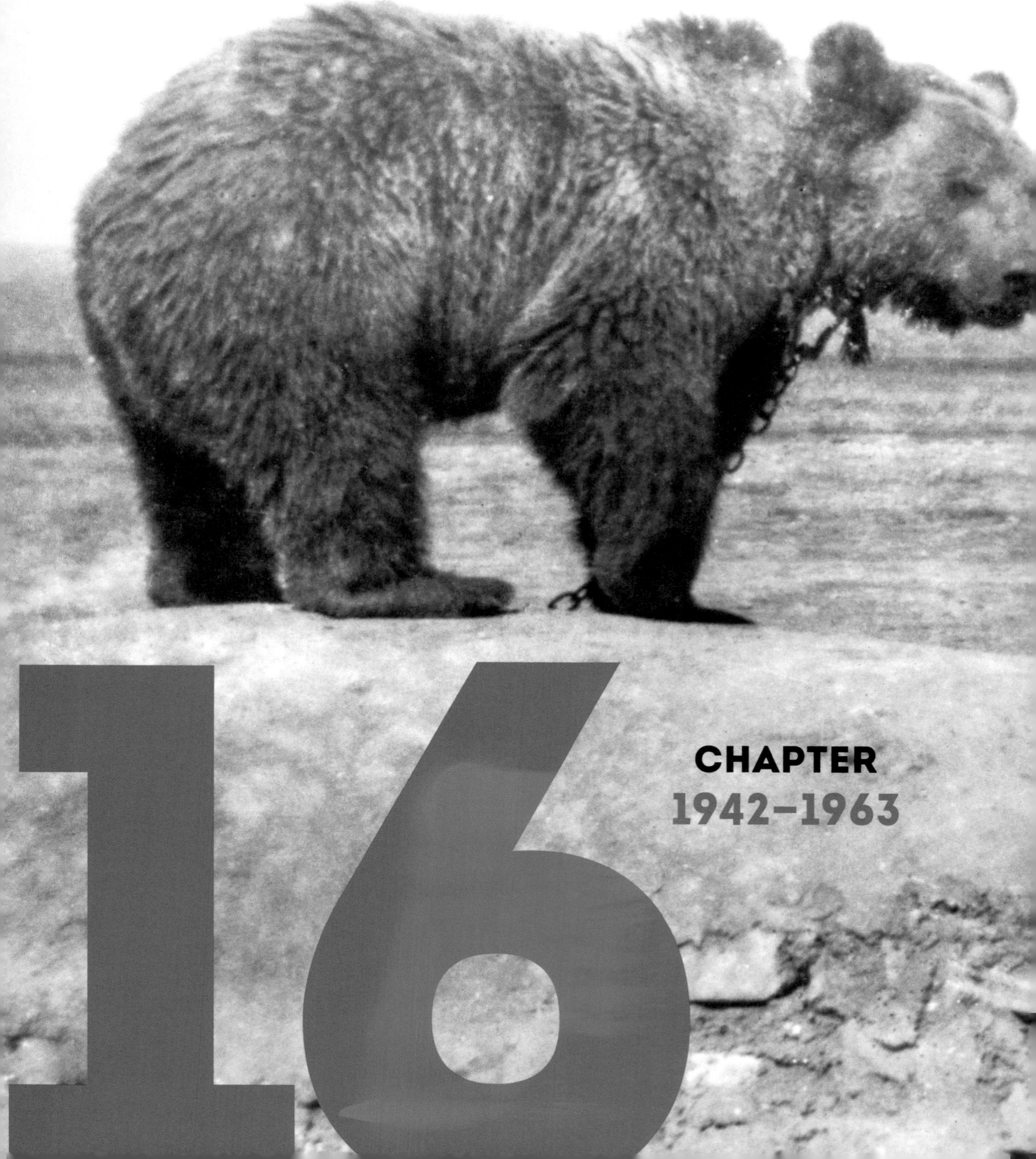

16 CHAPTER 1942–1963

WOJTEK, THE SOLDIER BEAR

CHAPTER 16

1942–1963

WOJTEK, THE SOLDIER BEAR

LEGEND HELD THAT WOJTEK – PRONOUNCED VOI-TEK – CAME FROM SIBERIA. SINCE MANY OF ANDERS' MEN HAD BEEN IN SIBERIA THEMSELVES, IT WAS LOGICAL TO THINK THAT THEY HAD BROUGHT THE BEAR WITH THEM. BUT IT WAS NOT TRUE.

Nor was it true that the bear carried a gun and fought at the front line. Such tales are pure invention. But it is correct to say that Wojtek was registered as a soldier – with name, number, regiment, and rank – that he travelled with the Anders Army for most of its long odyssey.

The story started in Iran: to be exact in a street market in Hamadan. Mrs Bokiewicz (whose husband would later be the owner of a philatelic shop on The Strand in London) saw a cuddly little mountain bear cub for sale, and bought it as a pet. She weaned it, fed it, and looked to its every need. It was in spring 1942, soon after the First Evacuation.

Several months after, the tiny cub had grown into a much larger and heavier animal, and was still growing. It could no longer be cared for in private quarters, and was transferred to the barracks of a military unit. There it was trained to obey basic Polish commands like 'sit' and 'stand', and adopted the loyal and friendly attitude that characterised the rest of its life.

In 1943, when the Army moved to Iraq, Wojtek went with them. The men, who were caring for him, were attached to a unit, the 16th Artillery Transport Company, commanded by Capt. A. Kipiniak, and the bear became their mascot. By now, nearly two years old, he was nearly six feet tall, immensely strong and weighed 500 pounds. He was taught to lift and carry the heaviest artillery shells, which normally could only be handled by two men and a trolley. He would happily load these shells onto lorries, or unload them, and particularly enjoyed riding on the back of a lorry with the wind blowing in his face. His favourite pastime was wrestling. He would wrestle with any soldier who was brave enough to try. But his best

3522 – number of the 22nd Transport Supply Company (above).

WOJTEK THE Cub, still in his native Iran (opposite).

wrestling partner was a large Dalmatian dog that belonged to a Brtish officer.

A major problem arose in Palestine when the company was preparing to leave for Italy. The British officers, who were drawing up passenger and cargo lists, refused to accept a live animal; and it looked as if Wojtek would have to be left behind. But then the ideal solution was found. The bear was formally admitted to the Polish Army, was registered, and issued with a number, identity card, and regulation dog tags. As far as is known, he did not swear the oath of loyalty, but sailed to Italy, not as a cargo or as a mascot, but as a private soldier.

Before leaving Palestine, Wojtek got into a scrap with another bear called Michał (Michael) which had been named after General Michał Tokarzewski and which had been presented by the Shah to a battalion of the 16th Regiment of Lwów Rifles. Michał and Wojtek did not hit it off. Michał attacked Wojtek viciously, without warning, and in the ensuing struggle was nearly killed. He was then given away to some Iraqi soldiers at Kirkuk, but escaped and rejoined his battalion. But he was not to enjoy the same career as Wojtek, being gifted to the Tel Aviv zoo. "I thank you sincerely for the bear", the Mayor of Tel Aviv said. "He will be a souvenir of the Polish Army."

Wojtek, in contrast, returned to his old life. He slept in a bathtub, and consumed a diet of

WOJTEK WORKING in commercial beer sales (centre).

WOJTEK THE wrestler (below).

WOJTEK AT the wheel (below right).

BOOKS ABOUT Wojtek: The legend lives on (above).

NORMAN DAVIES with Wojtek's statue at Park Jordana in Kraków (right).

condensed milk, fruit, marmalade, honey, and syrup. He would be given a bottle of beer as a reward, and was particularly partial to cigarettes, which he ate. Fastidious by nature, he would only eat lighted cigarettes. If offered an unlit cigarette, he would chew it once, and then spit it out. By now the 16th Artillery Transport Company had been renumbered as the 22nd Transport Company

Private Wojtek served for two years throughout the Italian campaign, from Bari to Bologna. Contrary to legend, he did not climb the heights of Monte Cassino, but he was certainly active with his unit. He adapted quickly to artillery fire, and would perch in a tree to see where the sound of the explosions was coming from. His fame was spreading, and he was widely photographed. Each day, he consumed the rations of two or three soldiers. He was not forced to wear a uniform, and was not chained, except at night.

In the summer of 1946, Wojtek sailed from Italy to Britain with his company. Eventually, when the unit was disbanded, he was transferred to Edinburgh Zoo where he became a firm favourite with visitors, especially with children. He continued to be visited regularly by his former comrades-in-arms, until he died from natural causes in 1963.

THE STORY OF WOJTEK the Bear has inspired books, films, poems, pictures, and sculptures.

The books include: Wiesław Lasocki, *Wojtek spod Monte Cassino* (1968); Aileen Orr's *Wojtek the Bear: Polish War Hero* (2010); *Private Wojtek: Soldier Bear* (2011) by Krystyna Mikula-

Deegan, and Jenny Robertson's *Wojtek: War Hero Bear* (2014).

One statue to Wojtek-Bear stands in the grounds of Edinburgh Zoo. It was made and paid for by the veterans who had shared their army life with him. It shows Wojtek out on a stroll, and a young soldier holding onto his leash with difficulty.

A second statue in bronze can be seen in the Sikorski Museum, London, where the main archive of the Anders Army is kept. In the 1970s and 1980s, when I regularly took groups of students to the museum, Wojtek was the one exhibit that everyone remembered.

In 2014, a statue to Wojtek-Bear was finally unveiled in Poland, in Kraków. It was produced through the great enthusiasm of an English resident of Kraków, Richard Lucas, who recruited me to speak to members of the City Council, before the project was approved. It now stands in the Park Jordana which is adorned by the statues of numerous other famous Poles, including Kochanowski, Mickiewicz, Kościuszko, and Pope John Paul II.

'WOJTEK' IS BEST REMEMBERED by Professor Wojciech Narębski (b. 1925), now professor *emeritus* of geochemistry at the Jagiellonian University, celebrated his 90th birthday in April 2015. But 73 years ago, in November 1942, he was a 17-year-old recruit who reported for duty in Palestine with the Anders Army.

Having passed his exams for the *mała matura* (O levels), he was posted to the 22nd Transport Company, and told to report to its commander, Maj. Antoni Chełkowski. Outside the Major's tent, he was astonished to meet a tethered bear cub, "the size of a big dog":

PATIENT WOJTEK with friends at the Edinburgh Zoo (above).

NORMAN DAVIES with Wojtek, statue at the Sikorski Museum, London (right).

"Are you Wojtek?" the Major enquired. "In that case we're going to have two Wojteks in the Company, because that's the bear's name, too. You will be 'Little Wojtek', and he will be 'Big Wojtek'."[188]

Wojciech Narębski was the son of Wilno's city architect, and attended the same *gimnazjum* as Czesław Miłosz and Tadeusz Konwicki. Arrested by the NKVD as a schoolboy, he was incarcerated for many months in the prison at Gorki, weighing only 42 kg when he finally reached the Army. Sent to Iran during the First Evacuation, he completed his basic secondary education in Palestine, before reaching military age.

As a corporal in the 22nd Transport CompanyNarębski followed the Italian Campaign from start to finish. "I never say that I fought at Monte Cassino", he says modestly. "I participated." And he frequently recalls his comrade-in-arms, 'Big Wojtek'.

BIG WOJTEK with friends on the wartime trail (above).

WOJCIECH NARĘBSKI as 'Little Wojtek' (top left) and the veteran Professor Narębski today.

The bear loved nothing better than swimming in the sea. He terrified the Italian girls who were sunbathing on the beach, but all he wanted to do was to charge down to the water's edge, and to plunge into the surf.

At war's end, Narębski passed his '*matura*' in 1946 at the Polish *Gimnazjum* at Alessano in Puglia; and, after a brief spell in England, opted for repatriation. He rejoined his family at Toruń, studied mineralogy at the Mikołaj Kopernik University, and obtained a Ph.D. at the AGH Academy of Mining and Steelmaking in Kraków. A straightforward scientific career awaited him.

Until recently, Professor Narębski was one of a trio of veteran *Andersowcy* who were living in retirement in Kraków. One of the others was Lt. Col. Mieczysław Heród (1918–2013), who had served in the Carpathian Brigade and who later became a professional artillery officer in the Polish People's Army. The third was Col. Tomasz Skrzyński (1923–2015), the 'last of the Carpathian lancers', who had been the first soldier to enter liberated Ancona.

Col. Skrzyński's funeral took place with full military honours at the Rakowicki Cemetery in June 2015. A telegram was read out from the Mayor of Ancona. The eulogy was given by the commander of the present-day II Corps. And the band played '*Brygada Karpacka*'. The honour guard was provided by scouts and guides from the NZH troop, 'Czerwony Mak' (Red Poppy) from Skawina, dressed in uniforms of the Carpathian lancers and of the 4th Armoured 'Skorpion' Regiment. Schoolchildren from the

A HUNGRY Wojtek.

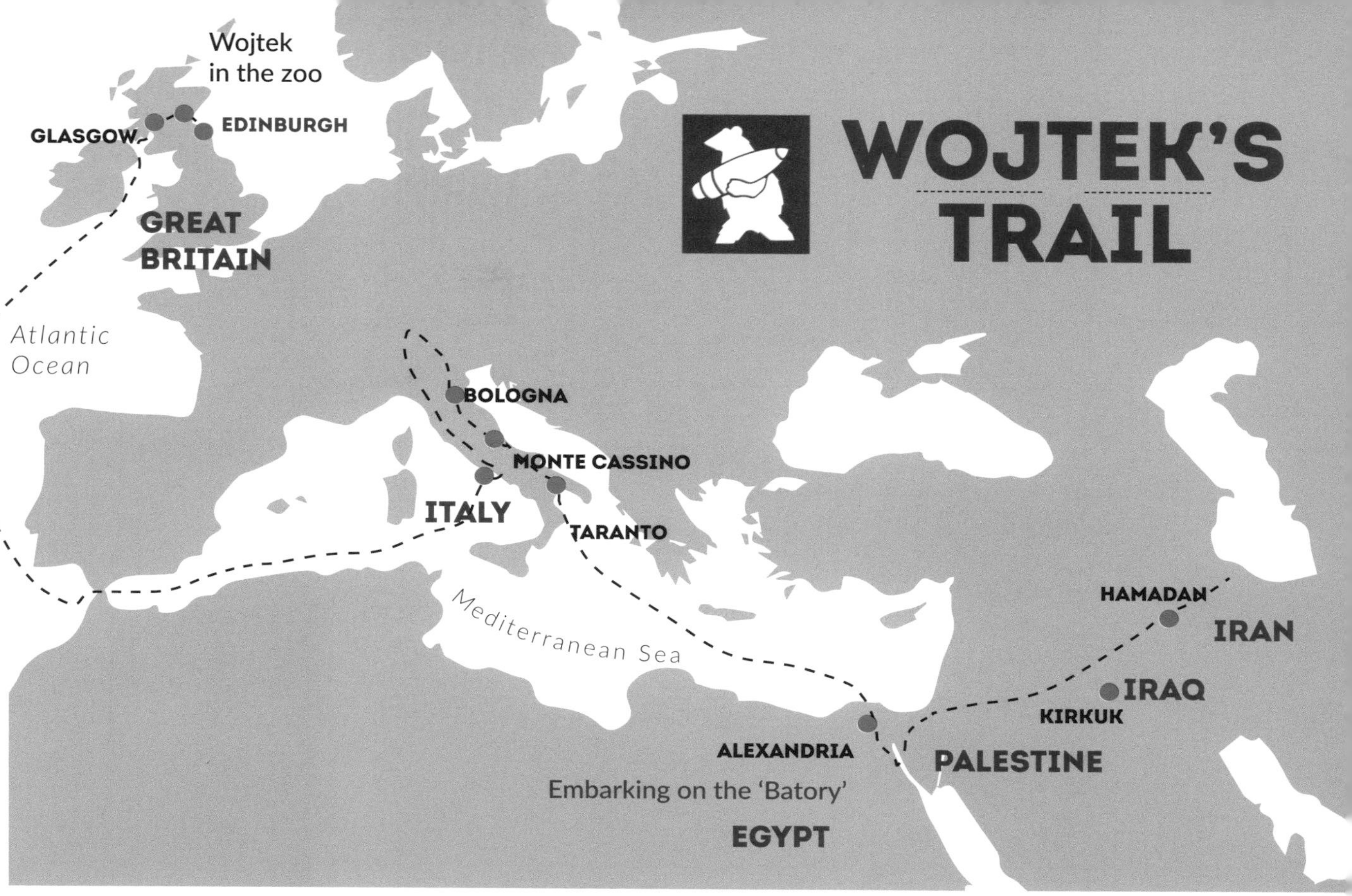

General Władysław Anders Gymnasium No. 42 also attended.

Cześć ich pamięci! (Hail to their memory!)

THE QUESTION REMAINS: Why did Wojtek-Bear evoke such great admiration? There are several possible answers. Animals are frequently taken to personify human qualities: we say 'as cunning as a fox', 'as strong as an ox', and 'as brave as a lion'. And Wojtek in many ways was the ideal soldier – indefatigable, loyal, fearless, and silent. But there's something, too, about Poland's tragic history, which contains more than enough episodes that are sad, depressing and full of despair. But Wojtek's heart-warming story has none of that; it makes you gasp and it makes you smile; and it helped Anders' men to bear their travails and to reach their goal. Wojtek never doubted, never wavered, never deserted, and never turned back.

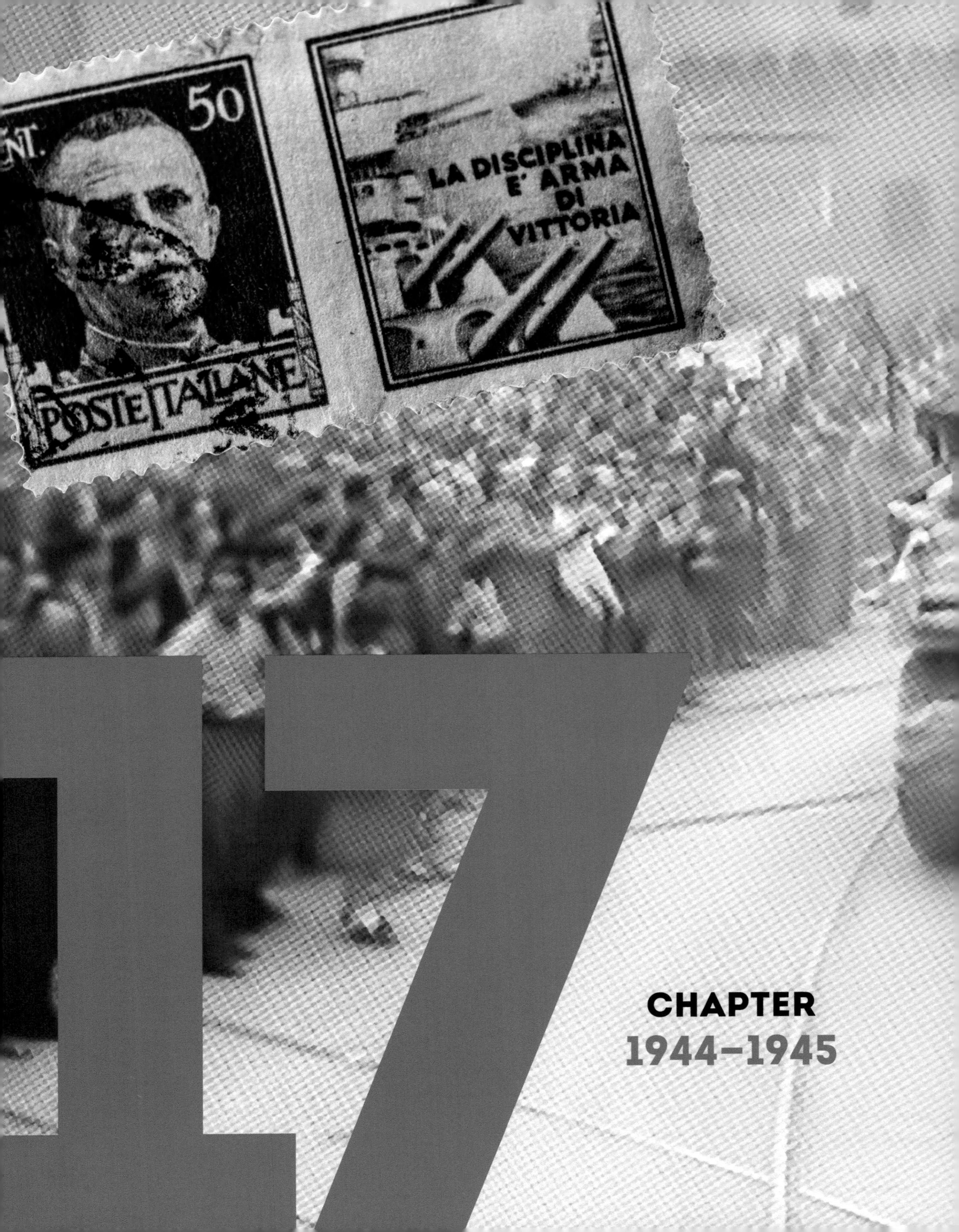

17

CHAPTER

1944–1945

ITALY: THE ROAD FROM MONTE CASSINO

ST PETER'S Basilica (left).

GENERAL ANDERS presents Pope Pius XII with the Abbot's walking stick, found in the ruins of Monte Cassino (opposite).

CHAPTER 17

1944–1945

ITALY : THE ROAD FROM MONTE CASSINO

AFTER THE BATTLE, THE DEAD WERE BURIED; PLANS WERE LAID FOR A PERMANENT CEMETERY; THE WOUNDED WERE TENDED IN A STRING OF BRITISH AND POLISH FIELD HOSPITALS; AND THE REST OF THE II CORPS WAS WITHDRAWN FROM THE FRONT LINE FOR A PERIOD OF REST AND RECUPERATION.

Busloads of Allied troops, including Poles, were taken to Rome to see the sights of the 'Eternal City'. General Anders was received in audience by the Pope, who was well aware of Poland's Catholic roots. Many of Anders' men came from Lwów, whose motto of '*Semper Fidelis*' (Always Faithful) dated from 1657 when King Jan Casimir declared the Virgin Mary to be 'Queen of Poland'. And paeans of praise rang out on all sides. British leaders, who often forgot to express thanks to their allies and associates, did not withhold expressions of admiration on this occasion. General Leese wrote a letter of extravagant praise. And he recommended that General Anders be awarded the prestigious honour of the Order of the Bath.

Later critics of Monte Cassino, of whom there were many, were to suggest that the II Corps' attack on Monastery Hill was an unnecessary act of folly, in which excessive numbers of valuable lives were wasted. This ill-willed view is not credible. It is a matter of fact the losses of the II Corps were no greater than those of the adjacent British X Corps and were actually less in proportion. General Anders' eagerness to put his men to the test under fire should not be mistaken as a vainglorious demonstration of bravado.

Two days after the fall of Rome, news arrived that Allied forces had landed in Normandy, and a couple of weeks later that General Maczek's Polish 1st Armoured Division formed part of the invasion force. The men of the II Corps,

who were no longer the only major Polish formation in active service, could not fail to take notice. For four weeks, the Allies were hemmed into the districts surrounding the beaches, and, as in Italy, made painfully slow progress. But then the breakout came. British, American, and Canadian armies streamed into the plains of northern France, driving the Germans back towards their own western frontier.

Rest and recuperation, however, did not last for long. In the aftermath of Monte Cassino, the Germans had pulled back beyond Rome in the centre, but were still hanging on to the important port of Ancona on the Adriatic Coast. Early in June, General Leese informed Anders of his advancement to be commander of the whole of the Adriatic sector, designating the capture of Ancona as the II Corps' next task and indicating that all aspects of the operation would be in Polish hands. If Monte Cassino had been a test of raw courage, the battle for Ancona would provide the occasion for demonstrating a wider set of military skills, including staff planning, inter-service coordination, and front-line tactics.

The battle for Ancona was to last 34 days, from 16 June to 18 July, and would pass through three distinct phases. Ancona, capital of the Marche Region, is perched on the rocky promontory of Monte Conero, overlooking the sea, and is surrounded by hilly countryside criss-crossed with deep valleys and rivers flowing down from Italy's Apennine spine. The Germans were well dug in behind concentric defensive lines. Approaching from the south, the Allies were forced to fight a series of intricate battles against an enemy that was constantly preparing a dogged line of retreat.

A POLISH soldier's funeral in Piedimonte.

II POLISH Corps' trail: from Monte Cassino to Bologna.

Anders brought three main formations to the front: the 3rd Carpathian Rifle Division on the left, the 5th Kresowa Infantry Division in the centre, and the 2nd Warsaw Armoured Brigade on the right, moving up the Via Flaminia along the coast. They were strengthened by the transfer of a British mechanised cavalry regiment, the 7th Queen's Own Hussars, by an Italian battalion, and by air support from the USAAF.

The Poles were facing elements of the German X Army commanded by Generaloberst Heinrich von Vietinghoff, who had been in charge of the 5th Panzer Division during the invasion of Poland in 1939. Units from both the LXXVI Panzer Corps and LI Mountain Corps were present in the Ancona sector. Once again, the Germans enjoyed superiority in terms of training and equipment, but could not match the Allied forces' resources in air support.

In the first phase, on 16–18 June, Anders mounted a ferocious assault on German positions along the Chienti River, which flows from west to east some 30 miles to the south of Ancona. In this action, the German 278th Infantry Division was severely mauled, suffering heavy losses.

In the second phase, from mid-June to mid-July, the fighting surged back and forth among the valleys and hill towns north of the Chienti. The Poles took control of Macerata, Recanati, Castelfidardo, Ossimo, and Loreto, site of the Santuario della Santa Casa.

Kazimierz Nycz (1914–1944), a prewar cavalryman serving in the 15th Regiment of Lancers, died in the battle for Ossimo, and was buried at Loreto. He was the uncle of the future Cardinal and Archbishop of Warsaw, who took his name. He had been a Soviet POW, had left the USSR in the Second Evacuation, and had followed the trail through Iran, Iraq, and Palestine. As the Cardinal remembers, his few possessions were returned to his family after the war by Britain's War Office; they included letters, two clothing coupons to the value of money found in his pocket, and a rosary from Jerusalem, that was laid in his mother's grave.[189]

LORETO

BASILICA DELLA Santa Casa (centre).

STAINED GLASS window (right) showing Polish soldiers extinguishing a fire in the sanctuary caused by German shelling.

MILITARY CEMETERY (far right).

APOTHEOSIS OF *Victory*, painting (below).

GRAVES, OLIVES, orchards and sea (bottom right).

342-III St. strz. KRYWULEC
13 Baon strz.

Another casualty, who fell on the approaches to Ancona, was Adolf Bocheński (1909–1944), a soldier and political writer, who has been described as the leading conservative thinker of the interwar generation. Returning from studies at the 'Sciences-Po' in Paris, Bocheński had joined the staff of the *Bunt Młodych* (Youth Rebellion) journal, and produced a string of influential works including *Tendencje samobójcze narodu polskiego* (1927) (The Suicidal Tendencies of the Polish Nation), *Ustrój a racja stanu* (1928) (Political Order and Reasons of State), and *Imperializm nacjonalistyczny a imperializm państwowy* (1927) (Nationalist and State Imperialism). His study, *Między Niemacami i Rosją* (Between Germany and Russia), published in 1937, is now considered a classic of the age.

In 1939, Bocheński left journalism for soldiering. He fought in the September Campaign, escaped to France, fought again at Narvik, where he was decorated for bravery, and escaping once more to Syria, joined the Carpathian Brigade. Wounded at Tobruk, he was withdrawn to Palestine, whence he was transferred with his regiment to the II Corps. He was known among his comrades-in-arms for his contempt for danger, and was killed clearing mines at the front line.

Though Bocheński's prewar work was highly praised both by Jerzy Giedroyc and Józef Czapski, they never managed to persuade him to join them in the Press and Information Office of the Corps. But after his death, they republished a couple of his most recent articles that had appeared in the pages of *Orzeł Biały*. One on the *Duch Imperatorowej* (The Spirit of the Empress) was historical, and explored similarities between the strategy of Catherine the Great and that of the Soviet Union. The other, entitled *Polska w polityce Stalina* (Poland in Stalin's Policy) was prophetic. Though published in June 1944, ahead of the formation of the Lublin Committee, it correctly predicted that the Soviet

APENNINE GUN position (above).

ADOLF BOCHEŃSKI, portrait sketch by Józef Czapski (below).

takeover of Poland would be incremental, evolutionary, and heavily disguised. It also contained a long passage about Anglo–Saxon attitudes and the future of the Kresy region:

> "The present situation appears to be that the English and Americans, even if they are united in thinking that Poland's eastern Borders should fall to Russia, are not prepared to accept the idea of the whole of Poland being annexed by the USSR. I do not intend to examine the reasons why public opinion has turned against Poland with regard to the Kresy. We are dealing here with a tragic misunderstanding. In England and America, it is generally considered that the majority of the citizens of our eastern lands want to belong to Russia. In reality, the opposite is the case. The persistence of such a false conception can only be blamed on our public propaganda and on our passive policy towards the minorities."[190]

This contribution to the issue which worried the men of the II Corps more than anything else was composed exactly one month to the day before Bocheński was killed.

IN THE MIDDLE OF THIS ACTION, Allied press and radio began to carry reports of a massive operation launched by the Soviet Army on the Eastern Front. In an onslaught of unparalleled ferocity, Marshal Rokossovsky – who had been brought up in Warsaw, the son of a Polish father and a Russian mother – performed a feat unparalleled by other wartime generals; he routed the entire German Army Group Centre, and before Operation Bagration drew to a close in August, had destroyed more German divisions than were present under Kesselring's command in Italy. This awesome development, which took the Soviets to the banks of the Vistula and put the whole of eastern Poland

THE BATTLE OF ANCONA

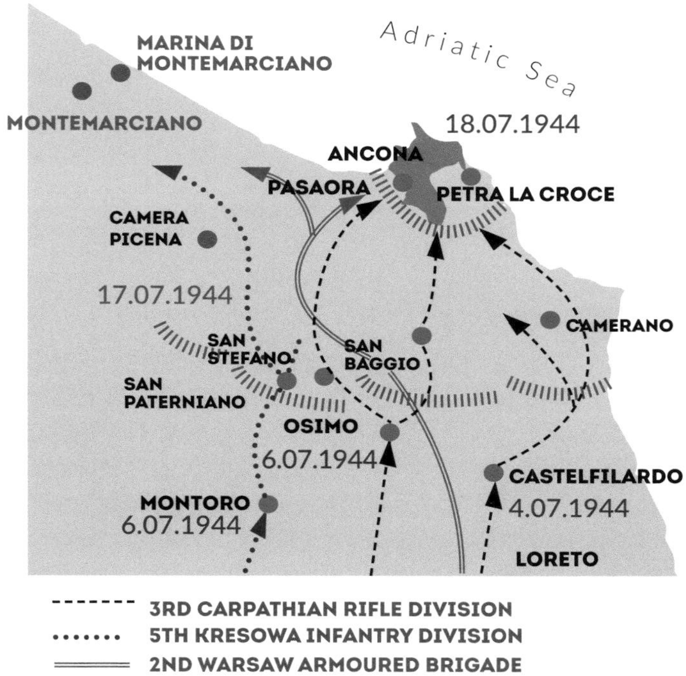

under Moscow's control, inevitably sent a chill down the spines of Anders' men. It was the point when they were forced to realise that the Soviets (not the British or the Americans) were the strongest Allied country in Europe, and hence that their homes in the Kresy were probably lost for ever.

In the third phase, 17–18 July, a succession of infantry attacks secured local positions on the outskirts of Ancona, before a powerful surge of armoured units cut through the German defences and opened the way for the final assault. The 2nd Carpathian Rifles Battalion completed the capture of the city. The 7th Queen's Own Hussars, for their part, were awarded the honorary title and badge of 'The Maid of Warsaw'.

LARGO
2° CORPO D' ARMATA POLACCO
2° KORPUSU POLSKIEGO
IN RICORDO DELLA LIBERAZIONE
DELLA CITTA' DI ANCONA DAL NAZI-FASCISMO
18 LUGLIO 1944 - 18 LUGLIO 2004

ANCONA

THE CITY with its harbor (top left) lies near Cape Conero (bottom left) in a bucolic landscape (centre).
MEMORIAL PLAQUES commemmorate its liberation by the II Corps (left and centre left).
BASILICA DI San Ciriaco (far left centre).
STREET IN Ancona where the II Corps HQ was stationed (below).

Praise for the Poles was lavish. Even President Roosevelt, who was not known for his involvement in Polish affairs, joined the chorus, issuing a public commendation to "Władysław Anders, Lt-General, Polish Army, for exceptionally meritorious conduct in the performance of outstanding services to the United States and the Allied Nations in Italy from October 1943 to July 1944."

The news from the Eastern Front was less heartening. On 22 July 1944, three days after the capture of Ancona, the Moscow-run PKWN, the so-called Lublin Committee, was set up as Poland's temporary executive body, thereby starting the process which would ensure long-term Soviet dominance. While the Polish forces attached to the Western Powers were still inching their way forward in Italy and France, Berling's 1st Polish Communist Army was already stationed on Polish soil.

As 1944 proceeded, the news went from bad to worse. First the Warsaw Rising, then the catastrophe at Arnhem, and finally, the Government-in-Exile's failure to re-establish dialogue with the Soviet Union, showed that Britain and America were not committed to protecting the Polish cause. In the months that followed Ancona, the II Corps fought loyally on, knowing that most of Poland was still occupied by Germans and

TRIUMPHANT ENTRY of the II Corps to Ancona (above).

GENERAL TERENZIO Morena and Norman Davies at Recanati (2015) (opposite).

CHURCHILL AND ANDERS with the interpreter, August 1944 (below).

believing that a just settlement could somehow be secured. But hearts were starting to sink.

On 1 August, Poland's underground Home Army launched the ill-fated Warsaw Rising. The order to launch was issued by the exiled govern-

ment in London. The principal aims were first to assist the Soviet Army in driving the *Wehrmacht* from Warsaw, secondly to prevent an uncontested Communist takeover, and thirdly to ensure that representatives of the legal government were present when new political arrangements were established. (The idea that the Home Army leaders somehow sought to defeat Germany, "to compel Stalin to recognise the Polish Government in London" or "to carry out an anti-Soviet coup" is pure poppycock.) The

Home Army's policy was to continue the struggle against Germany in line with Allied policy, and, if possible, to seek an understanding with Stalin. To this end, Stanisław Mikołajczyk, the Polish Prime Minister, had flown to Moscow, and was waiting to hear what Stalin's intentions were. In the meantime, General Anders left his superiors in no doubt that he viewed the Rising as a catastrophe, even "a serious crime" and "madness". He maintained from the outset that the insurrection did not have "a remote chance of success" and that the capital would be "annihilated".[191] His views were close to those of General Sosnkowski, the Commander-in-Chief, but did not command a majority among Polish leaders in London.

Nonetheless, thanks to their fame as the victors of Monte Cassino and Ancona, the men of the II Corps received visits from a stream of VIPs. One of the visitors was King George VI, who appeared for security reasons as the 'Duke of Richmond' and who, after reviewing the troops, stayed on for a campfire sing-song. The King was a quiet and modest man, who had won great admiration by refusing to leave Buckingham Palace during the Blitz. But he was the Commander-in-Chief of all British and imperial forces, and it was an unusual honour when he insisted on listening to the soldiers' concert and joined in the singing. He was particularly attracted to a sentimental song, whose lyrics he asked to be written down:

Niech inni sy jadą, dzie mogą, dzie chcą,
Do Widnia, Paryża, Londynu,
A ja si zy Lwowa ni ruszym za próg!
Ta mamciu, ta skarz mnie Bóg!

Bo gdzie jeszcze ludziom tak dobrze, jak tu?
Tylko we Lwowie!
Gdzie pieśnią cię budzą i tulą do snu?

GERMAN PROPAGANDA

GERMAN PROPAGANDA targeting Polish soldiers in Italy, 1944 (from top left clockwise):
"YOU ARE marching round Italy, while the Bolsheviks invade Poland".
"SO LIFE in your homeland proceeds without you".
"DEAR POLISH colleague".
"YOUR LONG, long road".
"THE HOPELESS road".
"IN SPITE of the offensive in Italy the English will not be able to prevent it [the tragedy]".
"ARE THESE the colours of your country?".
"POLES, YOU must choose the road, right or left".

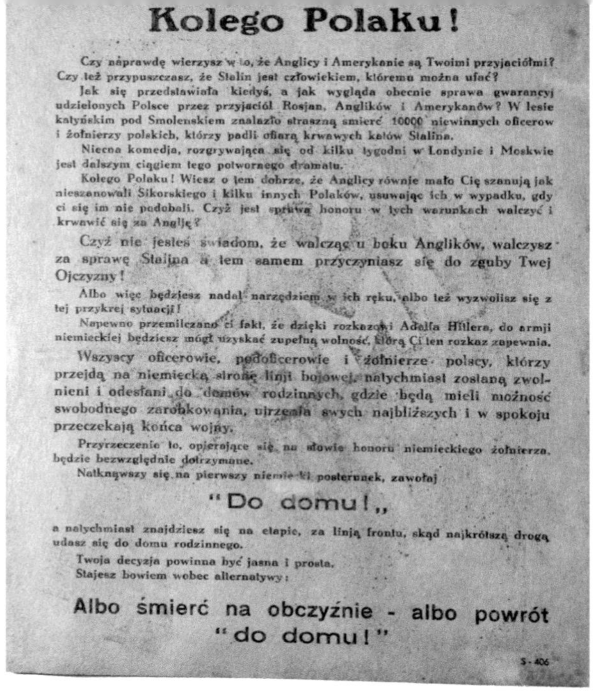

Kolego Polaku!

Czy naprawdę wierzysz w to, że Anglicy i Amerykanie są Twoimi przyjaciółmi? Czy też przypuszczasz, że Stalin jest człowiekiem, któremu można ufać?

Jak się przedstawiała kiedyś, a jak wygląda obecnie sprawa gwarancyj udzielonych Polsce przez przyjaciół Rosjan, Anglików i Amerykanów? W lesie katyńskim pod Smolenskiem znalazło straszną smierć 10000 niewinnych oficerow i żołnierzy polskich, którzy padli ofiarą krwawych katów Stalina.

Niecna komedja, rozgrywająca się od kilku tygodni w Londynie i Moskwie jest dalszym ciągiem tego potwornego dramatu.

Kolego Polaku! Wiesz o tem dobrze, że Anglicy równie mało Cię szanują jak nieszanowali Sikorskiego i kilku innych Polaków, usuwając ich w wypadku, gdy ci się im nie podobali. Czyż jest sprawą honoru w tych warunkach walczyć i krwawić się za Anglję?

Czyż nie jesleś świadom, że walcząc u boku Anglików, walczysz za sprawę Stalina a tem samem przyczyniasz się do zguby Twej Ojczyzny!

Albo więc będziesz nadal narzędziem w ich ręku, albo też wyzwolisz się z tej przykrej sytuacji!

Napewno przemilczano ci fakt, że dzięki rozkazowi Adolfa Hitlera, do armji niemieckiej będziesz mógł uzyskać zupełną wolność, którą Ci ten rozkaz zapewnia.

Wszyscy oficerowie, podoficerowie i żołnierze polscy, którzy przejdą na niemiecką stronę linji bojowej, natychmiast zostaną zwolnieni i odesłani do domów rodzinnych, gdzie będą mieli możność swobodnego zarobkowania, ujrzenia swych najbliższych i w spokoju przeczekają końca wojny.

Przyrzeczenie to, opierające się na słowie honoru niemieckiego żołnierza, będzie bezwzględnie dotrzymane.

Natknąwszy się na pierwszy niemiecki posterunek, zawołaj

"Do domu!,,

a natychmiast znajdziesz się na etapie, za linją frontu, skąd najkrótszą drogą udasz się do domu rodzinnego.

Twoja decyzja powinna być jasna i prosta.
Stajesz bowiem wobec alternatywy:

Albo śmierć na obczyźnie - albo powrót "do domu!"

S-406

Tylko we Lwowie!
Let others go wherever they can,
wherever they want,
To Vienna, Paris or London,
I'm not leaving Lwów!
Yes, mother, may God punish me for it!

'Cause where else people
have such a good life as here?
Only in Lwów!
Where you're woken and lulled to sleep
by a song?
Only in Lwów!

It is doubtful if anyone was able to explain to him that Lwów had recently been liberated from the Germans, and then permanently occupied by the Soviet Army.

WINSTON CHURCHILL called on General Anders in late August. According to the General's account, the Prime Minister became very emotional when discussing Poland's predicament. At the time, the Warsaw Rising was still raging. Tears filled Churchill's eyes when he said that Poland would never be abandoned. He was hoping against hope that Britain's 'First Ally' could somehow be saved. But matters were already moving beyond his control. A few days earlier, Churchill's plea to Roosevelt, begging him to send a joint note of protest to Stalin over Soviet conduct towards the Warsaw Rising, had been ignored. After their talks, Churchill and Anders drove to the front to observe the Gothic Line from close quarters.

Polish forces were performing well on the Western Front. At the Battle of the Falaise Gap (7–21 August 1944), Maczek's division distinguished itself, catching the retreating German 7th Army in a deadly trap and achieving what the Americans had notably failed to achieve after Anzio.

Operation *Market Garden* was the brainchild of Field Marshal Montgomery, and aimed to leapfrog the Western Front and seize a key crossing of the Rhine 60 miles behind enemy lines. But it was poorly planned, and ended in disaster. What is more, it consumed General Sosabowski's Polish 1st Parachute Brigade, an elite formation which had been trained for service in Warsaw and which had subsequently been transferred to Montgomery's command. Still more painful than defeat was Montgomery's unjust, not to say vicious treatment of Sosabowski, who had correctly warned the Field Marshal of his flawed plans and who was thereupon forced to retire (without pension) from army service. A statue to General Sosabowski now stands in the town square of Oesterbeck in Holland, erected by the subscriptions of grateful British veterans and Dutch citizens. But 60 years passed before his memory was properly recognised.

The case of General Sosabowski followed hard on the heels of the still more humiliating case of General Sosnkowski. In the summer of 1944, the Polish Commander-in-Chief had publicly vented his wrath at Britain's half-hearted support of Poland's exiled government. As a result, in the wake of official protests from the War Office, he was forced to relinquish his post. General Anders, who shared many of Sosnkowski's opinions, could only watch in despair. Despite his success on the battlefield, he was becoming increasingly isolated politically.

On 4 October 1944, news reached Italy that the Home Army had capitulated in Warsaw after 63 days of heroic and unequal fighting. Anders could take no pleasure from the fact that his predictions had proven correct. But he could not fail to notice that Poland's cause was sinking. Poland was the ally of the Western Powers, and had served them loyally. Yet it was becoming increasingly obvious that the West had no effective means of influencing Poland's fate.

Meanwhile, the Italian Campaign had slowed dramatically. One reason was that numerous Allied divisions had been transferred to France. But another cause lay in the fact that Field Marshal Kesselring had spent months

JEEP TOUR of Ancona (far left).

HAPPY GERMAN POWS captured near Ancona by the 4th 'Scorpion' Armoured Regiment (top left).

NORMAN DAVIES at the Polish Military Cemetery in Loreto (2015) (below).

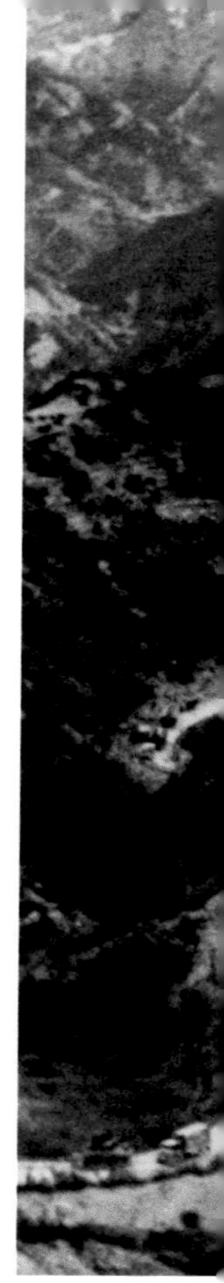

BELFRY FILM point (top left).

FIELD MARSHAL Albert Kesselring and staff (top right).

building the strongest defence line that the Allies had ever confronted. The Gothic Line or *Gotenstellung* ran for nearly 200 miles across extremely mountainous country from the Ligurian Sea at La Spezia to the Adriatic coast between Ravenna and Pesaro. Constructed by 15,000 slave-labourers, it was ten miles deep and filled with thousands of gun-pits, machine-gun nests, anti-tank ditches, and barbed-wire obstacles. It advertised Germany's determination to keep fighting. It was defended by 14 German divisions, which almost matched the reduced Allied strength of 18 divisions. The advantage lay with the defenders, especially when winter rains set in.

The Allies' original plan of attack envisaged an offensive through the mountainous centre. But General Leese argued strongly that the withdrawal of specialist French mountain troops made the concept impractical, and that a combined operation of infantry, artillery, and armour, that had proved its worth at Ancona, would be more effective. Operation Olive, therefore, foresaw a further northwards assault up the Adriatic coast by the VIII Army, to be followed by an American drive into the centre. Once again, the Poles, in the company of the Canadian Corps, were to lead the spearhead on the eastern sector. But progress was painfully slow, and casualties were heavy. Operation Olive was launched on 23 August, but gradually ground to a halt. Apart from the capture of Rimini in September, in which the Greek Brigade distinguished itself, there were few signal victories. The greater part of the Gothic Line was still intact in the New Year.

In that winter of 1944–1945, it became clear that the Western Powers possessed neither the manpower nor the momentum that was propel-

MILITARY TRAFFIC cop at a signposts for the numbered units (above).

MOUNTAIN TERRAIN favouring defenders (left).

ling the Soviet Army forward. The Netherlands, which was not liberated as expected, suffered a winter of hunger. After Arnhem, the *Wehrmacht* launched a major offensive in the Ardennes, and at the Battle of the Bulge (December 1944–January 1945) the Americans lost a couple of months before their line was stabilised. In that same period, observers learned the soundness of Stalin's strategic decision in August 1944 to halt the direct westward advance on Berlin via Warsaw and to pour his reserves into the Balkans. As Western armies stalled, the Soviet Army overran much of Eastern Europe – including Romania, Bulgaria, and large parts of Yugoslavia, Hungary, and Slovakia.

COMPARED TO THE HORRORS of Warsaw, a soldier's life in Italy was relatively benign. The winter weather was harsh, fighting at the front was arduous, and casualties continued to be heavy. But the troops were well fed, well armed, and well housed; they lived in small compact camps, where they were among their own, could speak their own language, and were subject to their own army's rules and discipline. The II Corps formed a self-contained Polish 'family', in which conditions were Spartan, but familiar. The soldiers' determination to fight the German enemy did not waver, and expectations rose about the growing prospects of the Third Reich's demise. At the same time, nagging doubts were creeping in concerning the war's ultimate outcome. Germany was heading for its *Götterdammerung*; but Poland did not seem to be headed for a resounding triumph.

All the time the II Corps was liberating Italian towns and villages, particularly in the Marche region. The Italians never forgot them.

ENGINEERS CROSSING a fast-flowing stream (above).

SUPPLY CONVOY negotiates flooded road (opposite top).

SEARCHING FOR mines (right).

"After the Germans retreated from Recanati", General Terenzio Morena told me in 2015, "we were expecting the English; but it was the Poles who liberated us. They were fine lads, '*bravissimi*', and very religious."

"*Si, si*", the General's wife added; "under the Germans food was very scarce, and we had to eat black bread. But the Poles brought us white bread, and chocolates, and cigarettes."

"Yes, the white bread tasted wonderful", the General, who was 14 at the time, continued, "and the cigarettes were 'Craven A'. And alongside the Poles came the dark-skinned Gurkhas, from Nepal. We were very scared of them. They wore pigtails, and carried a scimitar as well as a gun. They would catch a chicken, and with one stroke – whoosh – cut off its head. And another thing", the General recalled, "the pretty young Polish girls driving enormous military trucks; we had never seen anything like that before."

"*Vero, vero*", his wife agreed; "Italian women weren't allowed to drive in those days."[192]

Unlike the *Wehrmacht*, neither the British, nor the American, nor the Polish Army provided official brothels. But they did take care of the personal hygiene of their soldiers:

The real explanation of the phenomenon was entirely prosaic. In the 1930s, in an attempt to boost Italy's population, Mussolini's Fascist regime had banned the production and sale of all contraceptive devices. As a result, the black market in contraceptives was huge. The ever-resourceful Poles were simply filling a demand in the market.

"Some of those Englishmen in their PACs [Prophylactic Antiseptic Centres] were naive about the ways of the world. Any soldier could walk in and get a few condoms on request. But more than one Pole would ask for a dozen and then show up the next day or so and ask for a dozen more. If the soldier on duty in the PAC remembered him from before, it made quite an impression. Perhaps this fostered the Poles' reputation not so much as great lovers but as sex maniacs."[193]

IT WAS A GREAT COMFORT that Polish soldiers in Italy could correspond with their friends and families who had been left behind in the Middle East or sent to Africa or India. The British Forces Post Office worked well, and letters could be exchanged without excessive delays between Italy and Africa or India. The same could not be said about correspondence with Poland, which was cut off both on the German and on the Soviet side. The International Red Cross in Geneva conducted a service to locate missing persons, but the results were often meagre. Commercial firms took orders for food parcels to be delivered to Poland via Portugal but parcels sent in that way were hostages to fortune.

Polish servicemen in Italy could benefit from a lively press and from broadcast radio programmes. Since its origins in Palestine, the Army's Department of Culture and Press (OKP) had expanded, and consisted of six main sections: press, documentaries, radio, films, theatre, and entertainment. It was headed by Józef Czapski followed by Jerzy Giedroyć.

The Newspaper Section (*Wydział Czasopism*) increased the number of its published titles to 51. In addition to older papers like *Orzeł Biały* (The White Eagle), new ones appeared such as *Ku Wolnej Polsce* (Towards Free Poland), *Na Szlaku Kresowej* (On Kresowa's Trail), or *Wiadomości Wojskowe* (Military News). Numerous political poisitions were represented, and reports were issued about military developments on other fronts, on news from occupied Poland, and on opinions gleaned from Britain and USA. The Polish military press was in theory subject to British War Censorship, but in

VICKERS MACHINE gun nest (above).

POLISH OBSERVATION point on Apennine summit (below).

POLISH SOLDIER over conquered Matera (opposite).

practice was largely left alone until the post-Yalta crisis.

The Studies Section (*Biuro Studiów*) concentrated on longer publications of in-depth analysis, and in particular on ground-breaking studies of the Soviet system. In this respect, working in conjunction with its counterparts in London, it may be considered one of the founders of the discipline of Sovietology, then in its infancy. Its publications included *Sprawiedliwość sowiecka* (Soviet Justice, Rome 1945) by Kazimierz Zamorski (Sylwester Mora) and Stanisław Starzewski. A companion volume entitled *Ustrój sowiecki* (The Soviet System, 1946) was authored by Jerzy Niezbrzycki (*aka* Ryszard Wraga), an intelligence officer based in London. The book opens with a quotation from Thomas Masaryk: "The Bolshevik state is terrorist in nature and purely political." The members of the Section were to play a significant role in the postwar Institute 'Reduta'.[194]

Given the fact that many soldiers had either missed their schooling completely or had been unable to complete it, the work of the Army's Educational Department held prime importance. Schools were organised at every level, and short courses provided on every conceivable subject, from history and literature to science, technology, music and art. The Army's main schools and colleges, opened in Iran and Palestine in 1942–1943, continued to function, but the passion for education accompanied the II Corps into Italy. Beata Obertyńska (1898–1980), poet and writer, was one of the Army's activists in this field. Born in Lwów, and arrested by the NKVD in 1940, she served time in the Brygidki Prison, in Starobielsk and in Vorkuta, before following the Anders trail through Iran, Palestine, Egypt, and Italy. As a corporal of the Educational Corps, she worked in the II Corps' educational centre in Rome. Her memoir, *W domu niewoli* (In the House of Captivity), published in 1945, was written in South Africa.[195]

THE RADIO STATION of the II Corps, *Radio Kościuszko*, was charged with broadcasting programmes that entertained, informed, and raised the spirit of the troops. Its favourite voice was that of Włada Majewska (1911–2011), who was well-known later in Radio Free Europe. But it had a special problem. From 1944, it found itself competing directly with *Radio Wanda*, the *Wehrmacht*'s Polish-language station, which constantly broke into programmes with a stream of political propaganda. It described the II Corps as the 'dupes of Churchill and Roosevelt' and it emitted appeals for patriotic Poles to join Germany in the struggle against Bolshevism. A Polish radio-operator whose task was to monitor enemy broadcasts reported that even before Monte Cassino the Germans realised that Polish troops were facing them across the front:

"The sugary voice of *Wanda* began to be heard on German radio each evening speaking to us in Polish. The Nazis knew that we weren't conscripts but volunteers.

'What are you poor boys doing fighting in Italy?' *Wanda* asked. 'The Bolsheviks are entering your homeland and burning your houses and raping your women. It's easy for you to get home to your loved ones. You are close to the front lines now. All you have to do is cross over and say "Do domu" to the first German soldier. He will know that means you want to go home and they will help you to get there.'

Messages like that cut us to the quick. We hated being reminded of Soviet cruelties – most of us had suffered them ourselves – and of what might be happening to our loved ones in Poland while we were stuck in Italy and unable to defend them. The Germans knew all too well how to needle us with such broadcasts. The taunts made us upset and angry but we had no way to silence them.

One evening one of our radio operators, on his own and against all rules, tuned our transmitter to the frequency used by *Wanda* and broke our strict radio silence with a message we all heard interrupting *Wanda*'s syrupy tones.

'Just you wait, you old whore. We'll hang you yet.'"[196]

***THE END** of the Fight for Piedimonte*, **print by Stanisław Gliwa (1944) (above)**

DANCE TROUPE performs '*A Silesian Wedding*' on the Gothic Line.

The film unit in the II Corps, continuing earlier work in the Middle East, was run by two experienced directors, both Jewish. Józef Lejtes (1901–1983) had directed his first film, *Huragan* in 1928, and was attracted in the 1930s to historical films. Michał Waks (Waszyński) (1904–1965), a Catholic convert, had fled to the USSR in 1939 and had succeeded in pursuing his film career for a brief period in Moscow. But after joining General Anders in Russia, he became the Army's most prolific filmmaker. His principal achievement in 1944–1945 was the filming and production of the documentary record of Monte Cassino.

The Theatre Section of the II Corps was managed from start to finish by Jadwiga Domańska (1907–1966). Born in Dąbrowa Tarnowska, Domańska was a professional actress, who had made her name on the stage in prewar Warsaw. In 1940, as an underground courier of the nascent Home Army, she attempted to cross illegally from the German to the Soviet occupation zone; she was captured by the NKVD and cast into a labour camp. After the Amnesty, she enlisted in the Anders Army, and, as a former clandestine soldier, was given the rank of captain. In Baghdad, she created the Polish Dramatic Theatre in Exile, and in Italy the Army's Drama Theatre. The Section's ambitions were set high, both in quantity and quality. Plays, concerts, and revues were put on at every opportunity, at desert oases, at base camps, and, in Italy, at the immediate rear of the front line. Polish classics, such as Fredro or Wyspiański, were favourites; but the repertoire even extended to productions of *Les Fourberies de Scapin* (*Szelmostwa Skapena*) by Molière and of Puccini's opera *Turandot*. The attraction of *Turandot* may well have lain in its Persian setting and its central theme of riddles and dicing with death.

Much encouragement was also given to individual creative artists, especially to painters, photographers, and poster designers. An early exhibition was held in Tehran showing pictures and photos relating to the Army's experiences in the USSR. A professional Union of Polish Artists (ZZPAP) was formed in Baghdad, where it held its opening exhibition in the British Institute. Another signal vernissage was held in the Museum Bezald in Jerusalem in August 1943. In Italy, several soldier-artists including Stanisław Westwalewicz,

Karol Badura, Aleksander Werner, Zygmunt Turkiewicz, and Stanisław Gliwa entered into combat at Monte Cassino, and later participated in the collection of pictures for the pictorial publication, *Monte Cassino* (1944). Józef Czapski was the Nestor of the Army's painters; Zygmunt Turkiewicz the most productive; Stanisław Gliwa specialised in lithographs, and after the war in hand-printing. He belonged to the Polish Neopagan society, the *Szczep Rogate Serce*, and in England was to attain a high reputation among traditionalist typographers. He selected the illustrations for Melchior Wańkowicz's book on Monte Cassino.

In the realm of popular song, it is notable that several tunes attained international appeal during the Second World War, crossing all frontiers and front lines. The beautiful German song, *Lili Marlene*, for example, composed in Poland during the First World War, was broadcast from the *Wehrmacht* radio in Belgrade in 1941, and became a hit with men of the British VIII Army in North Africa, and via the Carpathian Brigade with the II Corps. Another universal number originated in prewar Czechoslovakia as *Škoda Lásky* (Wasted Love). It was adopted and adapted by Germans as *Rosamunde*, by Poles as *Banda*, and by the British as the *Beer Barrel Polka*. The II Corps sang it to the carefree words:

We're young. We're young.
We'll not be harmed by moonshine.

From its earliest days, the Anders Army attracted a large group of talented cabaret artists – singers, musicians, songwriters, comics, and assorted entertainers. Their leader was Henryk Wars (Warszawski) (1902–1977), who had been prominent in prewar Warsaw, and who had escaped in 1939 from German detention. Forming an ensemble called *Tea Jazz* in Soviet-occupied Lwów, he was able to perform, surprisingly, in Odessa, Kiev and Leningrad. Renata Bogdańska joined him on that tour, and decided with the rest of the troupe to throw in her lot with the Anders Army. Gwidon Borucki was another close associate. Kazimierz Krukowski (1901–1984), a cousin of the poet Julian Tuwim, enjoyed similar prominence as a singer and comic raconteur. A graduate of Warsaw University's Department of Philosophy, he had appeared in cabaret under the stagename of 'Lopek' as early as 1927, and starred in many films in the 1930s. His signature-tune, in tango time, was *Najpiękniejsza signorina* (Most beautiful Signorina). No one, however, outshone Feliks Konarski (1907–1991), pseudonym 'Ref-Ren', poet, actor, novelist, songwriter. Born in Kiev, he had toured the USSR with a theatre troupe, like Henryk Wars, and was in Moscow at the time of Barbarossa and of the Amnesty. Together with the composer, Alfred Schütz, he was the author of the Polish exiles' most heart-searing ballad.

The lyrics and the melody were put together in the night on 17–18 May 1944 and were ready to be performed by the time that the victory was officially proclaimed. Some doubt exists as to who sang at the first performance; it was either Guido Borucki or Renata Bogdańska backed by Alfred Schütz's field orchestra. A picture has survived showing men of the 3rd Carpathian Division sitting on the grass under the Italian sky, watching the orchestra play on an improvised stage, and listening intently to a uniformed singer who is definitely male.

Attempts to render the song into English so lack the original's rhyme and rhythm that a literal translation is the best that can be offered:

Can you see those ruins on the summit?
There your foe is cowering like a rat.
You must! You must! You must!
Buckle to, and tear him from the clouds.
So they went, like crazy and fierce;

FELIKS KONARSKI, author of *The Red Poppies on Monte Cassino* (far left).

RED POPPIES growing today on Monte Cassino (left).

They went to kill and to avenge,
They went, stubborn to the end,
To fight, as always, for their honour.
(Chorus)
The scarlet poppies on Monte Cassino
Drank in blood instead of dew,
Through them, the soldier walked to die;
Though, from death, the anger will be stronger.
The years will pass, and the centuries will pass
Only traces of bygone days will remain.
But all the poppies on Monte Cassino
Will be redder, having grown from Polish blood.

The condemned rushed on through the fire
Not a few of them caught it, and fell.
Like the madmen who took Somosierra
Or those, long ago, at Racławice.
They charged with furious elan,
And they made it; the charge
was crowned with success.
And they planted
their red-and-white banner,
On the ruins, high above, in the clouds.

The melody, an archetypal Polish march in a minor key, mixes melancholy with proud cadences. The words and the sentiment are unmistakably reminiscent of Joseph Piłsudski's haunting *First Brigade*.

Music of all sorts flourished. The II Corps had its own orchestra and every major unit its brass band. One might ask where all the expensive instruments came from, and part of the answer would be 'America'. Already in Iran, the Anders Army had received the gift from Cardinal Spellman of New York of a complete set of instruments, music sheets and manuals for a full-size military band. Not that orchestras or bands were necessary. The Army's trail through the Middle East and Italy promised many starlit evenings where accordions purred seductively, guitars were strummed, and lonesome exiles sang along beside the campfire.

DRAMATIC NEWS from the Eastern Front reached Italy in the second half of January. In one fell swoop, two large formations of the Soviet Army had overrun the whole of Poland, from the Vistula to the Oder, in the space of two weeks. The Western Allies had no such achievements to report.

Soviet victories on the field of battle were matched by similar victories in the political and diplomatic sphere. At Yalta, between 4 and 11 February 1945, the Big Three decided that Poland was going to be assigned to the Soviet sphere of influence, that the Polish–Soviet frontier would be fixed on the Bug (as Stalin had consistently demanded), and that the Communist-run Lublin Committee would form the basis of Poland's postwar government.

Roosevelt was determined that nothing in Eastern Europe would deter Stalin from joining the war against Japan. Churchill by this time was playing a minor role, in which he could not defend the interests of his Polish allies. The exiled Polish government in London, to which the II Corps owed its allegiance, was brutally sidelined, and would never regain its influence. Poland's eastern Kresy, which the men of the II Corps regarded as their homeland, had been allotted, by interallied decree, to the Soviet Union. Henceforth the big question, both for the VIII Army's commanders and for General Anders himself, was: Would the II Corps continue to fight?

In his memoirs, Anders writes that Yalta "confirmed his worst fears". For more than two years he had hoped that, put to the test at the conference table, Western leaders would defend Poland's cause. Those hopes were now dashed, and on 13 February he tendered his resignation in a telegram to the Polish President:

> "The II Polish Corps cannot accept the unilateral decision by which Poland and the Polish nation have been surrendered to the spoils of the Bolsheviks. I have applied to the Allied authorities to withdraw Corps units from battle sectors; I cannot in conscience demand any further sacrifice of soldiers' blood."[197]

The Allied generals in Italy urged Anders to reconsider. General Mark Clark, the American, showed special understanding:

> "My sympathies were entirely with Anders, but I could see no advantage to impulsive action on his part... He was very depressed and tears were in his eyes...
>
> "'We are done for', he exclaimed referring to the territory that was to remain in Russian hands. 'My people come from there'.
>
> 'What are you going to do about it?' I asked him. 'Your men will follow your lead...

YALTA: ROOSEVELT'S last appearance in the 'Big Three' (right).

GENERALS ANDERS and Alexander (centre).

TANK PATROL (far right).

If you quit now, you will lose the respect of the Allies, and they are your only friends'."[198]

Ordinary Polish soldiers were, in Anders' words, "numbed and bewildered". There was a violent reaction in the army as the men realised the great injustice that had been done to them. Aleksander Topolski describes how he found out:

"I escaped from the hospital [in Palagiano] for a day and went to Bari. Somehow I linked up with [the journalist], Tadzio Siuta, who was there on a job for the Polish Daily. It was maybe a week after the end of the Yalta Conference... Tadzio was the one who told me that the 'Big Three'... had met in Yalta for secret negotiations that lopped off the Eastern Part of Poland as a present to Stalin. As a result, Anders had resigned... The giveaway to the USSR included both the Pripet Marshes and the former province of Galicia, where I grew up... But there was even worse news. The Russians... were given control of our homeland and of the elections there after the war."[199]

The Yalta Agreement provoked one of 'Ref-Ren's most furiously ironic lyrics. His 'Yalta' was not his usual bittersweet; it was bitter:

They went off somewhere beside the sea
To confer in a secret place
And to fix the fate of the world.
That day saw the death of my brother,
Killed by a German P-lot shell.

They talked of democracy, peace and rule of law,
Of matters connected with war at the front...
Meanwhile it was Corporal Jóźwiak who fell
On some sort of distant Monte...

With genius they laid their genial plan,
The basis for a new slavery...

THE CAMPAIGN continues: defusing a booby-trap.

And the press was writing: "In our sector
no change to report, routine patrol."
They played with the map, not seeing the blood
That was drawn by the lancet at Lublin
In two months and just a few days
Falls a full year since Monte Cassino.

Poetic inspiration... friendship... vicious circle
Of slogans long since worn down bare.
Instead of the pieces of silver,
Judas settled for the Atlantic Charter. [200]

Such were the intense feelings of betrayal that 30 officers and men in the II Corps were said to have committed suicide. On 20 February, Anders flew to London for consultations with President Raczkiewicz and for an interview with Prime Minister Churchill. Raczkiewicz somehow persuaded him not to resign, but instead to accept the vacant post of Commander-in-Chief. (The nominal post-holder, General Bór-Komorowski, was being held in a German POW camp.)

Churchill was not apologetic. He told Anders coldly that the Poles should have reached an agreement with Stalin earlier — as if such an agreement were possible.

If Churchill did not already know, he was forcibly reminded during post-Yalta negotiations that reaching an agreement with the exponents of Stalinism was a pipedream, if only because there was no common terminology. He had clashed with Molotov at Yalta over

abuse of the terms 'Fascism' and 'democracy', and was soon asking Roosevelt whether at Yalta they had not promoted 'a false prospectus'; misunderstandings persisted until the onset of the Cold War finally closed all attempts at discussion.

In Italy, Field Marshal Alexander confessed that he had been present at Yalta, but that he had not participated in the political exchanges. He conceded that the II Corps should be relieved of all offensive operations, and that now, under the command of Anders' deputy, General Bohusz-Szyszko, it should merely defend its existing positions.

ALLIED LEADERS IN ITALY were close to despair. As Marshal Allanbrooke, the Chief of the Imperial General Staff, was to recall, "Without the Second Corps, the series of offensives carried out from Cassino onwards would hardly have been

RE-STOCKING THE shells for a big gun.

possible." At the same time as Harold Macmillan, the British government's representative at Allied HQ, noted in his diary: "At the worst, [the Poles] will disintegrate into a rabble of refugees."[201]

The sceptics were proved wrong. In his farewell message, Anders asked his comrades to maintain their "dignity and discipline", and he was not disappointed. When the Allied Spring Offensive started, the II Corps took part, and played the key role in the Bologna sector. Bologna, which had been under attack since October, finally surrendered on 25 April, and Polish soldiers, many of whom had been captives in Stalin's Gulags, found themselves welcomed as liberators:

"They were surrounded by crowds of smiling, cheering people, many of them shouting '*Viva la Polonia*'.

Women threw flowers, men handed them glasses of wine, girls hugged and kissed them. For the Poles it was bittersweet time. 'On the one hand, I was happy that I could bring freedom to these people,' recalled a soldier; 'on the other hand I was sad that this was not a Polish street...'"[202]

And Harold Macmillan was content to eat his words. "I had underestimated the marvellous dignity and distinction in the last battle of the war, in the front of the attack. They had lost their country, but had kept their honour."[203]

AS GERMANY'S STAR FELL, two unexpected problems gained increasing prominence. One concerned desertions from the *Wehrmacht*; the other, the fate of people who Stalin was demanding should be 'repatriated'.

At an early stage in the Italian Campaign, men of the II Corps became aware that numerous Poles were serving in enemy ranks. They could hear their *Radio Wanda* which was broadcast in Polish from *Wehrmacht* transmitters. (The audience of *Radio Wand*a was drawn largely from conscripts from Pomerania or Silesia who had been drafted into German ser-

GENERAL RUDNICKI leads the liberation cavalcade in Bologna.

POLISH JEEP meets American jeep.

vice after the annexation of their native provinces in 1939.)

But in 1944–1945, an increasing number of these conscripts crossed the lines and demanded to join the II Corps. The VIII Army's top brass were deeply suspicious of this trend, wondering what sort of loyalties these 'German Poles' might possess. Yet, as the trickle became a flood, the trend could not be stopped, and the depleted ranks of the II Corps started to be replenished by a welcome wave of recruits. Despite its heavy casualty rate, the II Corps ended the campaign with far more men than it started with.

Kazimierz 'Togo' Fałat was one of tens of thousands of ex-*Wehrmacht* conscripts who in 1944–1945 found their way to the II Corps. Grandson of the famous painter, Julian Fałat, 'Togo' was himself an artist, and, thanks to an Italian mother, spoke fluent Italian. As a result he was drafted into the German X Army's cartographic section, and helped to design successive German defensive lines. During the battles surrounding the Salerno landings in September 1943, he was wounded and taken to a field hospital, from which, when it was overrun by the Americans, he made no effort to escape. Held as a POW, he was presumably among the very first who volunteered to join the II Corps later that year.

Another conscript who crossed the lines somewhat later was Stefan Wesoły (b. 1926), later Archbishop of the Polish Diaspora. Born and educated in Katowice, he had been living during the early war years in a district that had been annexed by the Reich. As a result, he was subject not only to military conscription, but to all the other forcible methods that were applied to German youth. Prevented from completing his secondary education, he was assigned in 1943 to a work gang building bunkers at Cuxhaven near Hamburg, and in the following year, when still seventeen, was drafted into the *Wehrmacht* and posted to occupation forces at Cannes in southern France. This was his opportunity. Leaving his unit and crossing the front line, Wesoły surrendered to an American patrol, and after brief detention as a POW, was re-directed to the II Corps in Italy. He served as a radio-telegraphist, travelled to England with the Corps, and set out on the long road to the priesthood and the Catholic hierarchy.

POLISH SOLDIERS who had followed Anders out of the USSR were intensely curious about their compatriots who had served in the *Wehrmacht*, and about their conduct under fire:

> "Anders took the risk of forming two infantry brigades mostly from soldiers who'd come over from the German army. Could we count on the loyalty of these soldiers who'd spent years fighting in the German army in Russia and then in Italy? Any such fears proved to be unfounded. Anders was right. Those patriotic Poles who crossed over turned out to be *'plus catholique que le pape'* – fiercely loyal. They were well trained and cautious, yet courageous when need be. Survival after years on the Russian front had taught them caution. They also knew what would happen if

POLISH TANK on the streets of Bologna (left).

LANCE CORPORAL Jan Szatsznajder of the 1st Regiment of Krechowiecki Lancers with a liberated lady (above).

they were taken prisoner and recognised as a turncoat. As the Germans retreated, we found a few such soldiers left out in full view with their throats slashed."[204]

The fears of the doubters were put to rest.

The issue of 'repatriation' was more complicated, but of still greater interest for Anders' men. The armed forces of the Reich did not consist solely of 'Germans'.

They included people of many nationalities drawn from every occupied country. The Waffen SS, in particular, contained numerous divisions of Belgians, Dutchmen,

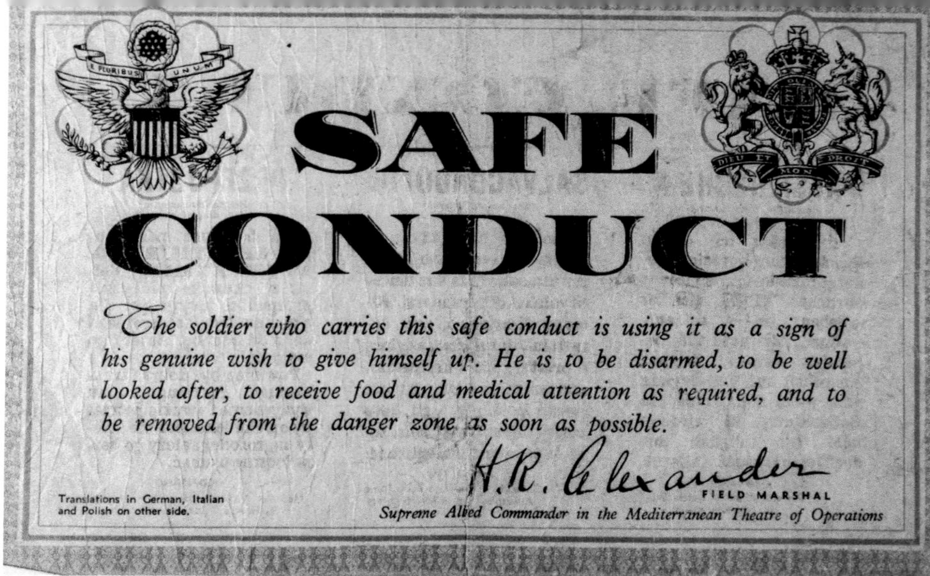

SAFE CONDUCT

The soldier who carries this safe conduct is using it as a sign of his genuine wish to give himself up. He is to be disarmed, to be well looked after, to receive food and medical attention as required, and to be removed from the danger zone as soon as possible.

H.R. Alexander
FIELD MARSHAL
Supreme Allied Commander in the Mediterranean Theatre of Operations

Translations in German, Italian and Polish on other side.

BENITO MUSSOLINI, Prime Minister of the Italian Social Republic, talks to an adolescent militiaman (below).

D-326/99/7/10,- Rps 416 26

SAFE CONDUCT

PASSIERSCHEIN

(wörtliche Uebersetzung des umstehenden Textes)

Der Soldat, der diesen Passierschein vorzeigt, benutzt ihn als Zeichen seines ehrlichen Willens, sich zu ergeben. Er ist zu entwaffnen. Er muss gut behandelt werden. Er hat Anspruch auf Verpflegung und, wenn nötig, ärztliche Behandlung. Er wird so bald wie möglich aus der Gefahrenzone entfernt.

SALVACONDOTTO

(Traduzione letterale del testo a tergo)

Il soldato che porta con se questo salvacondotto lo usa per dimostrare la sua sincera volontà di arrendersi. Bisogna disarmarlo, aver cura di lui, dargli da mangiare e prestargli, se necessario, assistenza medica. Al più presto possibile, egli deve essere allontanato dalla zona delle operazioni militari.

PRZEPUSTKA

(Dokładne tłomaczenie tekstu na drugiej stronie)

Dla bojowych posterunków SPRZYMIERZONYCH ARMII: Żołnierz, okaziciel niniejszej przepustki, używa jej dla okazania swej szczerej woli do poddania się. Należy go rozbroić.
Powinien być dobrze traktowany. Przysługuje mu wyżywienie i w razie potrzeby opieka lekarska. Że strefy zagrożonej należy go bezzwłocznie usunąć.

Scandinavians, Hungarians, Bosnians, and assorted Slavs, who had succumbed to German recruiting drives. The million-strong Vlasov Army consisted almost entirely of Russians and Ukrainians, who had served in the Soviet Army before being made prisoners-of-war.

AS FROM 1944, however, Stalin had made it clear to the Western Allies that he expected all those 'traitors' to be handed over to Soviet justice; and from fear or naivety, the British and American authorities began to comply.

The first shiploads of 'repatriates' were sent from Normandy to Murmansk in the aftermath of D-Day. British officers were astonished to find that many of these people preferred to commit suicide than to 'return home'.

In Italy, the problem of 'repatriation' reared its head in the early months of 1945. A British officer, Major Dennis Hills, who had worked as a liaison officer with the II Corps, accompanied a ship taking 'repatriates' from Naples to Odessa. On his return, he reported that the ship's passengers had been summarily executed by machinegun on arrival. For his temerity in slandering the Soviet Union was hauled in front of a courtmartial, and demoted.[205]

Unlike the British, the Poles needed no reminders of Stalin's evil intentions. Indeed, since most men in the II Corps had been forcibly given Soviet citizenship in 1939–1941, they

TRILINGUAL SAFE conduct for would-be POWs. (opposite).

GERMAN POWS at the war's end (left).

LVIV, 11 May 2013, concert to mark the 70th anniversary of the founding of the 'Haliczyna' Division (SS 14th Waffen Grenadier Division). "They fought for Ukraine" (below).

rightly feared that they, too, might be in line for repatriation.

Yet the most immediate problem arose when the II Corps took charge of the SS 14th Waffen Grenadier Division (1st Galician) who had surrendered to the Allies and were located in POW camps at Rimini.

These men were Ukrainians, who had been recruited in southern Poland in 1939–1941, and who, by Polish law, were still Polish citizens. Anders ruled that they would not be handed over for repatriation, and that the only courts they would face would be Polish military courts. In effect, he saved their lives.

At the end of the war, they would all be sent to Britain alongside the Poles, whose citizenship though not their values they shared. At least, 176 ex-members of the SS *Galizien*, duly screened, were judged fit to join the II Corps.

Peace was declared on 9 May 1945. Italy rejoiced. With the help of the Allies, the Italians had thrown off both the remnants of the Fascist regime and the hated Germans. The men and women of the II Corps watched with mixed feelings. They could take satisfaction from a job well done, but could not return to their homeland. They would never participate in Poland in the sort of heartwarming, patriotic scenes that they witnessed in Bologna.

ITALIAN ALPS

THE ITALIAN Alps or 'Triglav' (above): The Allied Campaign in Italy never achieved its objective of crossing the Alps into Austria, thereby invading the Third Reich from the South. Churchill's dream was to force the Ljubljana Gap into Slovenia.

FORLÌ, BETWEEN Bologna and Rimini, a city familiar to the II Corps (opposite).

MEMORIAL TABLET IN FORLÌ: "On the road of their pilgrimage, the soldiers of the 5th Kresowa Infantry Division, faithful to Christ and to the Polish Republic, covered themselves in glory in the fierce battle for the freedom of their homeland and of all the world's peoples. The hospitable thresholds of the city of Forli raise to God fervent prayer for the freedom of oppressed Poland and for a better tomorrow in Italy" (below centre).

MATERA NEAR BARI, another haunt of the II Corps (below).

A STREET sign in San Paterniano (far right).

LUNGO LA STRADA DEL NOSTRO PELLE-
GRINAGGIO NOI SOLDATI POLACCHI DEL-
LA QUINTA DIVISIONE KRESOVA FANTERIA.
FEDELI A GESÙ CRISTO E ALLA REPUB-
BLICA POLACCA COPERTICI DI GLORIA
NELLA LOTTA TENACE PER LA LIBERTÁ
DELLA NOSTRA PATRIA E PER LA LIBERTÁ
DEGLI UOMINI NEL MONDO MENTRE AB
BANDONIAMO L'OSPITALE CITTÁ DI FORLÍ
PORGIAMO A DIO LA PREGHIERA PIÚ CALDA
PER LA LIBERTÁ DELLA OPPRESSA POLO-
NIA E LA PROSPERITÁ DELL'ITALIA
FORLI 24 OTTOBRE 1945
22 SETTEMBRE 1946
NA SZLAKU SWEGO PIELGRZYMSTWA
ŻOŁNIERZE 5 KRES. DYW. PIECHWIER-
NI CHRYSTUSOWI I RZECZYPOSPOLI-
TEJ POLSKIEJ, OKRYCI CHWAŁĄ W
NIEUGIĘTEJ WALCE O WOLNOŚĆ
SWEJ OJCZYZNY I WSZYSTKICH
LUDZ I NA ŚWIECIE OPUSZCZAJĄC
GOŚCINNE PROGI M. FORLI - ZANOS-
ZĄ GORĄCĄ MODLITWĘ DO BOGA
O WOLNOŚĆ UMĘCZONEJ POLSKI I
LEPSZE JUTRO ITALI I.
FORLI, 24 PAŹDZIERNIK 1945
22 WRZESIEŃ 1946

PARCO
GEN. W. ANDERS

18

CHAPTER

1945–1946

WAR'S END: FROM ITALY TO NOWHERE

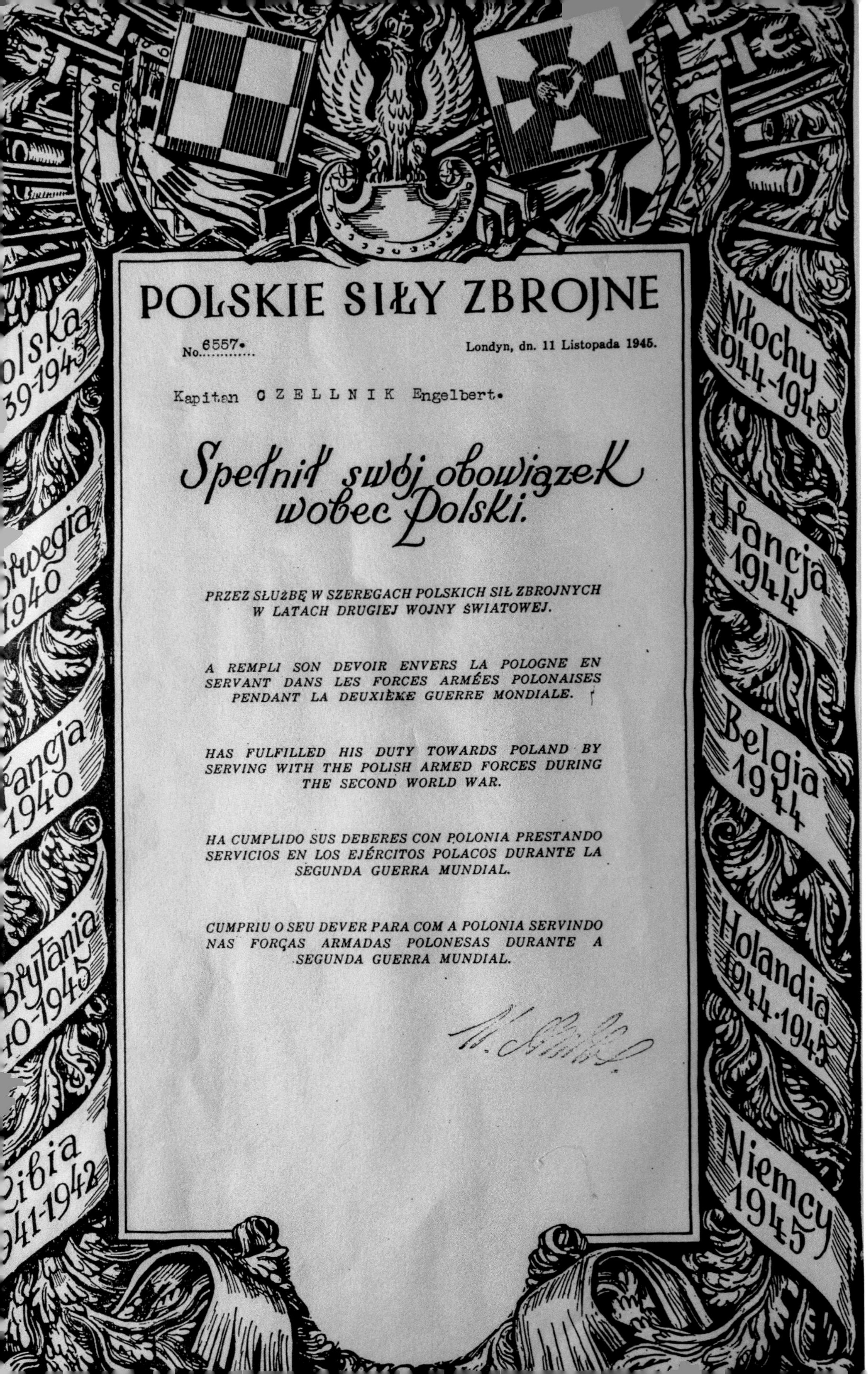

POLSKIE SIŁY ZBROJNE

No. 6557. Londyn, dn. 11 Listopada 1945.

Kapitan CZELLNIK Engelbert.

Spełnił swój obowiązek wobec Polski.

PRZEZ SŁUŻBĘ W SZEREGACH POLSKICH SIŁ ZBROJNYCH W LATACH DRUGIEJ WOJNY ŚWIATOWEJ.

A REMPLI SON DEVOIR ENVERS LA POLOGNE EN SERVANT DANS LES FORCES ARMÉES POLONAISES PENDANT LA DEUXIÈME GUERRE MONDIALE.

HAS FULFILLED HIS DUTY TOWARDS POLAND BY SERVING WITH THE POLISH ARMED FORCES DURING THE SECOND WORLD WAR.

HA CUMPLIDO SUS DEBERES CON POLONIA PRESTANDO SERVICIOS EN LOS EJÉRCITOS POLACOS DURANTE LA SEGUNDA GUERRA MUNDIAL.

CUMPRIU O SEU DEVER PARA COM A POLONIA SERVINDO NAS FORÇAS ARMADAS POLONESAS DURANTE A SEGUNDA GUERRA MUNDIAL.

POLISH ARMED Forces Service Diploma issued to Captain Engelbert Czellnik, 11 November 1945. (Signed: W. Anders).

CHAPTER 18

1945–1946

WAR'S END: FROM ITALY TO NOWHERE

AT THE END OF THE SECOND WORLD WAR, ROUGHLY ONE-QUARTER OF EUROPE HAD BEEN LIBERATED BY THE WESTERN POWERS; THE LIBERATED NATIONS IN FRANCE, ITALY, THE LOW COUNTRIES, DENMARK, NORWAY, GREECE, AND WEST GERMANY WERE FREE TO REJOICE AND TO FORM GOVERNMENTS OF THEIR OWN CHOOSING.

A **second quarter** of the continent – in countries such as Sweden, Spain, Switzerland, and Ireland, which had remained neutral – was unaffected by the new postwar arrangements. But the eastern half of Europe, from which the forces of the Third Reich had been driven by the Soviet Army, quickly crystallised into a solid Soviet-run Block, where Soviet security services ruled supreme and where dictatorial Communist parties loyal to Moscow were successively imposed in every country. In Churchill's famous phrase, an 'Iron Curtain' was descending on Europe, dividing East from West.

The Polish II Corps found itself on the wrong side of this Iron Curtain. In normal circumstances, General Anders and his soldiers would have returned to a heroes' welcome in Poland. But circumstances were not normal. The Polish Provisional Government of National Unity, which in line with the Yalta decisions was installed under Soviet auspices, made no secret of its hostility to the General, whom it denounced as an agent of imperialism. What is more, in a massive campaign of so-called repatriation, it was busy transporting millions of Poles from the lands east of the Bug, which was home to most of Anders' soldiers and which had now been arbitrarily annexed to the USSR.

Shortly After VE-Day a Polish Military Mission under Colonel Kazimierz Sidor arrived in Italy, charged with organising the transfer of the II Corps to Communist-run Poland. Backed by the British authorities, they were given access to the Polish camps and made their appeals to soldiers' meetings. But smooth words weighed less than hard experience, and painful memories of the realities of life in the Soviet Union made most men resistant to the Mission's blandishments. In any case, few members of the II Corps would have considered going to Poland, while their friends and families were still in Africa or India. In the end, only 14,000 volunteered to leave, mainly Pomeranian and Silesian ex-POWs who had originally been conscripted into the *Wehrmacht*. They were sent to transit camps at Cervinara and Polisi near Naples, whence they were despatched either by sea to Gdańsk or by rail to Zebrzydowice. They would find that their reception in Poland was far less friendly than promised.

MONTE CASSINO Commemorative Cross, with diploma, issued 1 March 1945, to Corporal Szczęsny Borodzicz, of the 15th Battalion of Riflemen; "Polish eagle" badge from a soldier's cap (upper right).

Departures notwithstanding, the numbers who remained with the II Corps far exceeded those who had arrived in 1943–1944. Thousands joined in the spring of 1945, after Allied armies liberated POW camps in western Germany; one of the biggest contingents consisted of men and women from the Home Army who had been imprisoned after the fall of the Warsaw Rising and who took the first opportunity to cross the Alps and to answer General Anders' call. As peace came, the total of serving members of the II Corps passed the 100,000 mark, including 10,000 women.

IT IS MORE THAN IRONIC that the Polish II Corps had grown to its maximum size at the very time that its raison d'être was ending. The proportions and complexity are well demonstrated by the list of units which had been awarded the Monte Cassino Commemorative Cross (*Krzyż Pamiątkowy Monte Cassino*) by the Polish Government-in-Exile in recognition of their services[205] (see right and overleaf):

In 1944–1945, 48,847 crosses were awarded from a total of 50,000 produced. The recipients who are listed by name include 13 senior commanders starting with General Władysław Anders and including Bishop Józef Gawlina; war correspondent Melchior Wańkowicz; US Army Liaison Colonel Henry Szymanski (USA); and Brigadier Sir Eric Frith from the 26th British Liaison Unit.

II Corps Headquarters
3rd Carpathian Rifle Division
5th Kresowa Division HQ
5th Wilno Infantry Brigade HQ
13th–14th–15th Wilno Infantry Battalions
6th Lwów Infantry Brigade HQ
16th–17th–18th Lwów Infantry Battalions
4th–5th–6th Light Artillery Regiments
5th Anti-tank Regiment
15th Poznań Lancers Regiment
5th HMG Battalion
5th Engineers Battalion
5th Signals Battalion
5th–6th Sanitary Companies
5th–6th–15th–16th Supply Companies
5th–6th Workshop Companies
5th Provost (Military Police) Squadron
Military Court
2nd Warsaw Armoured Brigade HQ
1st Krechowiecki Lancer Regiment
6th Children of Lwów Armoured Regiment
4th 'Scorpion' Armoured Regiment
9th Signals Company
9th Medical Company
9th Supply Company
9th Electro-Mechanical Engineers Work shop Company
9th Forward Tank Replacement Squadron
6th Field Court
2nd Artillery Group HQ
7th Horse Artillery Regiment
9th–10th–11th Medium Artillery Regiment
7th Anti-tank Regiment
7th Light Anti-aircraft Regiment
8th Heavy Anti-aircraft Regiment
1st Artillery Survey Regiment
Carpathian Lancer Regiment
2nd Corps Engineers
10th Battalion Corps Engineers
10th Bridging Company
301st Engineering Company
304th Mechanical Equipment Platoon
10th Bomb Disposal Park
11th Signals Battalion

II Corps Signals Traffic Control Team
II Corps Artillery Fire Control Platoon
12th Special Radiotelegraph Platoon
12th Special Information Platoon
386th Signals Platoon
389th Medium Radio Platoon
II Corps Signals Park
Air Support Signals Section
Aerial Photographic Section
II Corps Medical Services
3th–5th Casualty Clearing Stations
2nd Military Hospital
6th Field Hospital (Venafro)
1th–3rd Military Hospitals
31st Sanitary Company
32nd Field Hygiene Platoon
34th Anti-Malaria Station
45th–46th–47th–48th–49th Surgical Teams
49th–50th Transfusion Teams
341st Field Medical Dump
Bacterio-Chemical Unit
II Corps Transport and Supply
21st–24th Transport Companies
29th Ambulance Company
30th Independent Workshop Platoon
326th–328th Supply Dumps
61th–62nd Anti-Aircraft Artillery Supply Units
331th–332nd Field Bakeries
334th Propellant Fuel Dump
336th Office Materials Dump
318th Field Canteen and Library Company
26th–28th Forward Supply Companies
II Corps Materiel Service
Materiel Park Delivery Platoon
Field Officers Shop
Field Ammunitions Laboratory
350th Materiel Supply Company
375th Field Laundry
377th–378th Field Baths
Corps Electro-Mechanical Engineers Service
13th–15th–35th Electro-Mechanical Engineers Workshop Company
Corps Ordinance Workshop
36th Rescue Company

12th Geographical Company
312nd Field Map Store
II Corps Provost (Military Police)
11th–12th Military Police Platoons
Army Service Corps
Guard Battalion
12th Field Court
War Graves Registration Office
II Corps Field Postal Service
Military Censors' Office
Metereological Section
II Corps Paycorps
II Corps Press and Culture Office
Command Station No. 1
Smoke Screen Unit
Soldiers Welfare Section
Concert and Entertainment Unit
Reserve Liaison and Translators
111st Bridge Security Company

Health Service Inspectorate
Independent Commando Company
Cipher Office and Radio Station
7th Light Anti-aircraft Regiment
7th Anti-tank Regiment
301st Engineering Company
389th Medium Radio Platoon
II Provost (Military Police) Platoon
318th Field Canteen and Library
35th Electro-Mechanical Engineers Workshop
5th–162nd Military Hospitals
Aerial Photo Interpretation Unit
8th Heavy Anti-aircraft Regiment
3rd Casualty Clearing Station
31st Sanitary Company
7th Anti-tank Regiment
1st Artillery Survey Regiment
Convalescent Home

The surplus crosses, 1153 in all, were eventually sold off to dealers. It appears that no awards were made to the Polish Auxiliary Women's Service. Eight awards, nos 48400–48407 were made to the Health Service Inspectorate (WAS), but it is unclear whether or not the inspectors were female.

The ranks of the II Corps continued to be swelled and pushed over the 100,000 mark by the arrival of further *Wehrmacht* soldiers of Polish origin, who had surrendered to the Allies *en masse* on 28 April 1945. Some of those men had surrendered in France, not just in Italy. An eyewitness, who sailed in early May on a British ship between Marseilles and Taranto, described the extraordinary kaleidoscope of people on the move at that time. The biggest group on the ship were the *Titovcy*, that is, Yugoslav partisans recently released from a German POW camp, and the others were Poles still wearing their *Wehrmacht* uniforms.

None of this helped the British authorities, who faced a deep quandary. Their intention of sending Poles to Poland was looking increasingly impractical. The idea of sending them to Britain when British demobilisation was at its height seemed unrealistic. So, after much debate, they decided to leave them in Italy until alternative and more definite arrangements could be made.

IN ALL COUNTRIES IN EUROPE where Western armies had been deployed, joint British and American organisations were set up to supervise civilian administration behind the front. During the war, Allied Control Councils acted as the link between military commands and local officials. When peace came, the Allied Military Government (AMG) took over, providing a temporary stabilising authority pending the restoration of democratic institutions. In Italy, the AMG based in Rome was

STANDARD BEARERS of the II Corps awaiting Field Marshal Alexander, Iesi near Cignol (Marche), 1945 (above).

GALLIPOLI (APULIA) (right).

ITALIAN STAMP overprinted with the initials of the Allied Military Government, 1945 (centre).

charged with maintaining law and order, with making preparations for a national referendum, and in the north, with curbing the ambitions of Communist partisans, who were threatening to stage a revolution.

The II Corps, with headquarters at Casarano near Lecce, provided the largest military contingent at the AMG's disposal. It performed guard duties and sent out patrols from Vibo Valentia to Verona and Venice, but was largely held in reserve in case of serious disorders. Given the bitter civil war that had erupted in similar circumstances in neighbouring Greece, British political leaders had good reason to take precautions.

From the soldier's point of view, life in Italy had its attractions. In some ways, it mirrored the conditions that had prevailed in Iran or Palestine. There was food, shelter, safety, and friendly locals. But there was little to mitigate the anxieties of an uncertain future.

To keep the troops happy, or least occupied, the leaders of the II Corps put great emphasis on education. Thousands of soldiers, who had missed out on schooling during the war, attended classes to pass their grades and to qualify for university studies of for technical training. The Polish secondary school at Casarano was filled to overflowing. A second *gimnazjum* functioned at nearby Matino, and the *Szkoła Podchorążych* at seaside Gallipoli.

Politics, both Polish and Italian, however, disturbed the idyll in seaside Gallipoli. Colonel Sidor and his mission were notorious for links with Italian Communists, whose press organs like *Unità* regularly smeared the II Corps as 'Fascists' and 'imperialist lackeys'. Violent incidents occurred when the Poles reacted against Communist agitators; full-scale street battles took place. Windows were smashed in Casarano, when local comrades festooned the town with posters reading "Vivat Stalino". Similar scenes recurred across Italy. In Recanati, as General Morena recalls, the Communists flew the red flag over the town hall, and the Poles came along and pulled it down.

Since the Fascists had been defeated, the Communists assumed that political power should now be theirs. They dragged the local mayor, the *sindaco,* to the Polish commander and demanded that he be shot. "He may have served the Fascist regime", the General said, wringing his hands in disgust, "but he was not a Fascist." General Anders wanted nothing of that sort of behaviour.

In Poland, meanwhile, the Moscow-run Provisional Government vented its anger on the II Corps which was refusing to recognise its authority. It denounced General Anders as a warmonger, who was supposedly planning to mount a white horse, to lead his troops on a march against People's Poland, and thereby to provoke the Third World War. In due course, the General would be stripped of both his Polish citizenship and his officer's rank. (These were meaningless acts of petty bureaucratic revenge that had no practical consequences.)

VICTIMS OF YALTA MONUMENT, Kensington, London.

Rumours of an impending Third World War, however, were not entirely fanciful. The world press was speculating about it, and, as later revelations confirmed, British and American leaders were weighing the pros and cons of drastic action. Their relations with Stalin deteriorated fast, once the Third Reich had collapsed; and some strategists argued that the West should launch an attack earlier rather than later. (At the time, neither side possessed nuclear weapons.) Winston Churchill went so far as to draw up a secret plan, codenamed Operation *Unthinkable,* which proposed an offensive by 50 British and US Divisions against Soviet positions on the Polish–German border in the region of Dresden. The aim was 'to impose the will of the United States and the British Empire' on Central Europe. The reaction of Churchill's professional military advisers was to reject it out of hand. Given that the war against Japan was still in progress, the US government would never have approved such a risky adventure.

Early in June 1945, the Moscow Trial of 16 Polish resistance leaders took place. Obscenely, a group of political leaders, who had led the underground struggle against the German Occupation, were charged with 'collaboration'. The chief defendant, General Leopold Okulicki, who had served under Anders in Russia and Iran, remained defiant. His tragic fate convinced his former colleagues – if they needed convincing – that there was no place for them in Poland. Okulicki was to die a year later under Soviet detention.

LATE IN JUNE 1945, in line with the Yalta Agreement, the USA and the UK withdrew their recognition of the exiled Polish government in London, shortly after extending recognition instead to the Provisional Government of National Unity in Warsaw. Their decision turned their Polish allies,

LANCE CORPORAL Janina Piołunowicz/ Iwandziuk, II Corps, 5th Division (left).

LANCE CORPORAL Feliks Milaszkiewicz, Rome, 1946 (centre).

LIEUTENANT COLONEL Eryk Janowski who stayed in Italy (right).

SOLDIERS' DOG TAGS (centre bottom)

who had served them loyally for the preceding six years, into virtual outlaws, stateless persons, and mercenaries. General Anders and his men, who had sworn their oath of allegiance to the Government-in-Exile, found that their political leaders had lost all international standing. The II Corps was still serving under British command, but all the formal treaties on which its service depended had ceased to be valid. Only then did the British authorities begin to realise what a terrible legal, bureaucratic and humanitarian mess they had created.

General Anders, who had returned to Italy only recently from his post in London as Acting Commander-in-Chief, reacted angrily to the shabby treatment of his Government by Britain and the USA; his Order of the Day of 6 July bristled with defiance:

> "Men! I am turning to you at a time of extreme difficulty... The Governments of the Western Powers have decided to recognise the so-called Government of National Unity imposed on Poland by her occupation and thus to withdraw recognition from the legal Polish Government in London...
>
> The World Powers bypass our constitution and lawful authorities... and have agreed to the *fait accompli* created with regard to Poland and the Poles by a foreign force.
>
> Men, at this moment we are the only part of the Polish Nation which is able, and has the duty, loudly to voice its will... we must prove today by word and deed that we are faithful to our oath of allegiance... and to the last wishes of our fallen comrades who fought and died... for an independent Poland... We will fulfil our duty towards our country and its lawful authorities. Long live the glorious Republic of Poland!"[207]

JUNIOR OFFICERS' School (above).

MATERA, 1945. Snack lunch (left).

CLEMENT ATTLEE (GB), Harry Truman (USA), Joseph Stalin (USSR) at the close of the Potsdam Conference, August 1945 (opposite).

Never had Poland's case been put more cogently. A Foreign Official described it as "lamentable". The British government reacted by demanding that Anders be replaced, either by General Tadeusz Kutrzeba, who had spent the war in a German POW camp, or by General Boruta-Spiechowicz, who had served under Anders in the USSR and Iran, but who in 1945 had returned in Poland. But Anders had his admirers in high places. Many high British officers supported him. What is more, the War Office was well aware that the II Corps was heavily armed and could not be coerced. So Anders survived without difficulty and a month later published another defiant document, his 'Oath':

> "Our tradition, which is a thousand years old, binds us with Western Civilisation and we do not intend to be forced into a [foreign and hostile] Eastern system. We shall therefore remain loyal to our allies... even if they do not at the moment see eye to eye with us... We believe that the true liberty of nations will be achieved through the triumph of truth over falsehood and of Christian culture over barbarism."[208]

In August 1945, the 'Big Three' met at Potsdam for the third and last time. President Truman replaced Roosevelt, who had passed away, and Churchill was facing an imminent General Election. They succeeded in agreeing on interallied arrangements for the governance of occupied Germany, and, despite Churchill's initial opposition, they redrew the Polish–German frontier on the Oder and western Neisse. (Churchill had said at the start of the conference that Breslau would be given to Poland "over [his] dead body"; but he had to leave Potsdam to attend Britain's General Election [which he lost], and in his absence the Russians and Americans swiftly reached agreement). Before that, President Truman let it be known that the USA had dropped an atomic bomb on Japan. Stalin betrayed no surprise – probably because he had already been informed – and the world passed into the nuclear age. The new Poland, whose boundaries the conference confirmed, bore little resemblance to the prewar Poland where Anders and his followers had grown up. It was, for them, a foreign country.

After Potsdam, the chances that the Western Powers would do something to modify their stance on 'Poland' diminished to almost nil. The Poles left stranded in Italy had to digest the fact that they were now facing a life of permanent exile.

General Anders summarised the political outcome of the Second World War in two sentences:

> "Tehran, Yalta and Potsdam laid the foundations for a new enslavement of Poland. At Tehran, we were pushed into the Russian zone of influence; at Yalta, a new partition of Poland was carried out... and at Potsdam, these crimes were confirmed and sealed."[209]

His judgement on Tehran can be questioned. But the general tenor of his remarks is repeated by the great majority of Poles today.

IN THE WINTER OF 1945–1946, the decision whether to stay abroad in exile or not hung over every soldier in the Anders Army and their dependants. On one side of the argument, both the British and the Warsaw governments were urging them 'to return', talking about their 'patriotic duty' and the need to support Poland's postwar reconstruction. They also stressed the example of Stanisław Mikołajczyk, the former Prime Minister of the Government-in-Exile, who had agreed to join the Provisional Government of National Unity and who professed the view that an attempt to work with the Communists must be made.

On the other side, three lines of argument proved particularly persuasive. One, based on hard experiences, was that Communist assurances could not be trusted; the Polish press

abroad publicised the case of the 'Sixteen', the leaders of the non-Communist underground state, who had all been promised safe passage by the NKVD, and who all found themselves on trial in Moscow. Secondly, political commentators were widely predicting that political repression would intensify as soon as Stalin had established his control of Eastern Europe more completely. Thirdly, as Ernest Bevin was eventually forced to concede, the annexation of eastern Poland to the USSR meant that the homes of most *Andersowcy* were now in the country from which they had spent the last five or six years trying to escape.

The English writer, Bernard Newman, took the trouble to interview a Polish ex-soldier, who was refusing to return. He soon heard a convincing explanation of the attitude that often puzzled British public opinion. After years of wartime Soviet propaganda, few Britishers could imagine the realities of life in the USSR:

> "I was in a lumber camp in North Russia", the soldier told Newman, "almost in rags... We were worked shockingly hard on a minimum of food. One day, I said to a Russian officer who appeared friendly. 'But why do treat us like this? In your own interest you should feed us, so that we could work properly.' 'Why should we?' was the reply. 'We have tried out the system; at the present rate you will last about five years. Then you will be used up, but there are plenty more where you came from."[210]

Soviet propaganda was greatly helped by an unexpected campaign which claimed that Jewish soldiers in the II Corps were being held against their will. In a telegram sent to the British government, the Secretary of a US Trade Union Committee wrote: "The Fascist, anti-Semitic character of the Anders Army is too well known to warrant elaboration... This [forcible detention of Jews] is comparable to the hideous practices of Nazi beasts, who forced Jews to dig their own graves before despatching them."[211] No comment is required.

The Polish government in Warsaw chimed in with accusations that Poles were being used for

UMBERTO II, 'King of May', dethroned by the Italian Referendum of June 1946. *Corriere della Sera* announced: "The Republic of Italy is born".

'LOCKED OUT': Soldiers of the II Corps find the gates of postwar Poland barred. "We fought for Independent Poland," they say. "We don't know you," replies the watchman of Soviet Poland. Caricature, 1944–1945.

unpaid labour, as if they were German POWs. Then, on 20 February 1946, Warsaw announced that the Polish Armed Forces in the West no longer existed; it was an astonishing legal fiction. If soldiers wished to travel to Poland, they would have to apply to Polish Consulates abroad as individuals.

On the other side of the coin, a series of sensational events was publicised which served to counter Communist claims. A former soldier of the II Corps, Franciszek Ferenc, who had been repatriated, managed to return to Italy, and in newspapers of the Corps to denounce the repressions that awaited returnees. Colonel Sidor tried to discredit him by saying he was a *Volksdeutsch*. Then, in January 1946, the world press carried reports of shocking scenes in the former Nazi concentration camp at Dachau. When US soldiers attempted to collect former inmates for repatriation to the USSR, many preferred to commit suicide rather than return to their 'Soviet homeland'. Fears inevitably rose in the II Corps that Poles, too, might be forcibly repatriated. An artist from the II Corps produced a poster which showed a Polish soldier as a mouse and Poland as a mousetrap.

British war censors were still busy reading the correspondence of Polish soldiers in Italy to gauge their morale. "We were fighting for your freedom and ours", one soldier wrote, "but now only for yours." Another officer actually addressed the censor. "You are probably wondering whether to cut off certain sentences of this letter. Don't do it. It's not propaganda – it's the truth. If you order us to close our mouths, what are we fighting for?"[212]

Civilians as well as soldiers waited to learn their fate. A UN Relief and Rehabilitation Administration (UNRRA) camp was opened at Bari, and other camps for displaced persons (DPs) at Barletta and Trani. Americans could be found who thought DP stood for 'Dumb Polack' or 'Damned Poles'. Repatriation camps, largely empty, were established at San Basilio and Cervinara.

The position that most people took was that they were not going anywhere near the Soviet Bloc unless circumstances improved – and, as it proved, the circumstances only deteriorated. The sole substantial group which agreed to go to Poland consisted of ex-*Wehrmacht* conscripts from Silesia, who knew nothing of Soviet/Communist methods, and whose homes were within the postwar frontiers. Apart from

ERNEST BEVIN, Britain's Foreign Secretary, 1945–1950, author of the 'Keynote Message' (1946) and of the Polish Resettlement Corps, 1946–1948.

them, the only returnees were a small number of individuals who gave absolute priority to rejoining their families, and a still tinier element, who were working for Western intelligence. Men and women who had fought under British or American command were loyal to the legal Polish government, and believed in the 'Free World', regarded the Soviets and Communists as usurpers, and had no moral qualms about continuing to serve their wartime allies. Rotmistrz Witold Pilecki (1901–1948) was one such person. He had been a prisoner in Auschwitz, had fought heroically in the Warsaw Rising, and had joined the Anders Army after release from a German POW camp. He left Italy for Poland, in unclarified circumstances, in 1945.

Throughout those months, the British Foreign Secretary, Ernest Bevin, was wrestling with a multitude of problems connected with Britain's erstwhile Polish allies. Apart from the II Corps in Italy, he had somehow to find a solution for a large group of Polish soldiers that had remained in Britain: for the 1 Armoured Division of General Maczek that was performing occupation duties in northern Germany, and for tens of thousands of Polish civilian refugees still living in Africa, India, and elsewhere.

He decided to set out British policy in a 'Keynote Message' to be sent individually to every Polish soldier serving under British command; 215,000 copies of the message were sent out from London to be read on 20 March 1946. Members of the II Corps were put on parade before being handed their copy.

Bevin told them two things: first that the British government still wanted them to return to Poland, and that the assurances of the Warsaw government regarding their safety and welfare were 'satisfactory'. "On behalf of His Majesty's Government", he wrote, "I declare that it is in the best interests of Poland that you return to her now." Secondly, he declared that provision would be made for anyone who declined to go to Poland, to stay in Great Britain. Most soldiers decided there and then that they would go to Britain.

THE KEYNOTE MESSAGE was intended to make a forceful appeal. But its impact was ruined by an appalling translation and by inept presentation:

> "I can tell you what happened in my company", wrote Zbigniew Wysecki. "There was a British officer, I believe it was a major, and he was the person who handed this letter to every soldier personally. It wasn't just distributed... every soldier walked individually up to that major, he sat behind a table, and the major handed him that letter, and, if I'm not mis-

taken, fourteen or fifteen accepted the letter. All the rest just saluted and turned around... So he was left holding a pile of letters."[213]

The leaflet had been translated into what Anders described as "a very queer sort of Polish", which increased suspicions. There was also hostility to Bevin personally because back in 1920, during the Polish–Soviet War, arms shipments for Poland had been blocked by a strike organised by Bevin and Bevin's trade union.

That week a letter was published in *The Times*:

"Sir,

As a member of the Polish forces who has received a copy of the Foreign Secretary's appeal, may I suggest that more care might have been exercised in translating it into Polish? It contains at least 25 errors of grammar and syntax, which do anything but sweeten a bitter pill... The poor quality of the language in which a document is couched does not contribute to its intended effect.

L.R. Lewitter, Christ College, Cambridge"[214]

The important thing was that the II Corps' future was clarified. If the men preferred Britain to Poland, they were free to go. If they chose Poland, the way was open. Professor Lucjan Lewitter became a major figure in Slavonic Studies in Britain for the next forty years.

What actually happened to the returnees is a complicated matter. Despite what the Western media stated, the war had not really ended in Poland. The Provisional regime was conducting a low-level civil war against remnants of the Home Army and new organisations like Freedom and Independence (WiN), and a vicious campaign of ethnic cleansing codenamed Operation *Vistula* was in progress in the Podkarpacie Region. The all-powerful security force, the UB, regarded anyone who had been abroad as suspicious and *ipso facto* hostile. Hundreds of thousands of Poles were being

TRIAL OF members of the secret WiN organisation, Warsaw, 1946.

OPERATION *VISTULA* village burned by UPA bandits in 1946.

GUSTAW HERLING-GRUDZIŃSKI

THE WRITER'S DAUGHTER Marta with books written by her father in their home in Naples (top left).

HERLING-GRUDZIŃSKI TYPEWRITER (top centre).

THE FIRST COMMUNION pendant that Lidia Croce, daughter of famous Italian philosopher Benedetto Croce, gave Gustaw before the battle of Monte Cassino. They were married years later.

LIBRARY OF Italian philosopher Benedetto Croce with memorabilia of Herling-Grudziński (right), his books (top right) and his medals: the Virtuti Militari Cross for the Battle of Monte Cassino and the Order of the White Eagle awarded in 1998 (far right).

A WORLD APART: *The Journal of a Gulag Survivor*, Herling-Grudziński's memoir published in 1951 (bottom right).

GUSTAW
HERLING-
GRUDZIŃSKI
DZIEŁA
ZEBRANE tom 2.

Gustaw
Herling-
Grudziński
Dziennik
pisany nocą
TOM 3
1993–2000
Gustaw
Herling-
Grudziński
Dziennik
pisany nocą
TOM 2
1982–1992
Gustaw
Herling-
Grudziński
Dziennik
pisany nocą
TOM 1
1971–1981

A WORLD APART
GUSTAV HERLING
The shocking personal experiences of a man who spent two years in Soviet prisons and labor camps.
A Mentor Book

恍如隔世
中一出版社出版

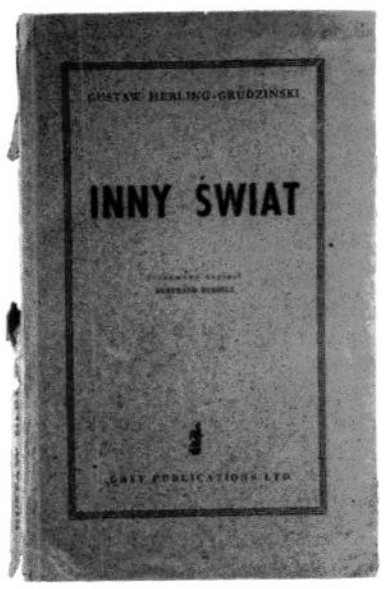
GUSTAW HERLING-GRUDZIŃSKI
INNY ŚWIAT

'repatriated' from the Kresy, and the so-called Recovered Territories were in a state of disorder as the German population was expelled and Polish settlers moved in. The 'returnees', therefore, could not expect an easy life. At the very least, they were 'filtered' by the UB, and 'verified', that is, obliged to sign a statement of loyalty. If they showed anything less than total deference, they would be arrested, accused of offences, great or small, and imprisoned. If they were considered dangerous, they could be added to groups of interned ex-Home Army people, and shipped off to camps in the USSR.

Witold Pilecki, one of Poland's greatest wartime heroes, was arrested on 8 May 1947 after only two years of freedom. He was brought before a 'People's Court', charged with treason and shot.

My own experience of these events was necessarily very limited, but 20 years after the war in England I met a group of ex-II Corps soldiers, who were working as farm labourers at a village called Dursley in Gloucestershire. They originated from the district of Tarnopol in the Kresy; pleased to meet someone who spoke Polish, they told me their story. They were simple peasant lads, talked with a strong eastern accent, and were probably Ukrainians. At the end of the war, they said, they had wanted to go home. They had served in the Polish Army as conscripts in 1938–1939, and found their way to General Anders via Soviet POW camps. Their families had not been deported, and were waiting to receive them back. But they feared for their safety. Their home villages near Tarnopol, now Ternopil, were in the USSR, not Poland,

and they had heard rumours that the NKVD killed servicemen returning from service abroad.

Their decision was to draw lots, to send three of their number back to Tarnopol, and to await news that it was safe to travel. The man who drew the shortest straw departed first, promising to send a letter or postcard bearing a suitably coded message. Nothing was heard of him. After three months, the second man left. Nothing was heard of him either. Finally, after six months, the third man went, and never managed to send a message. So the group then resigned itself to staying abroad, and they determined to stick together come what may.

This is just one anecdote. But it underlines the terrible uncertainty that reigned in 1945–1946. There was much uncertainty about Poland's future, and almost total uncertainty about the future of all those thousands who had followed General Anders out of the Soviet Union.

In the summer of 1946, attention turned to two referenda: one in Italy, the other in Poland. The Italian Referendum, fixed for 2 June, was to decide whether the country should remain a monarchy or become a republic. In the south, where most Poles were stationed, majority feelings were strongly monarchist. But in the north, where the Communists were most active, republicanism dominated, and in the vote, the republicans triumphed, 54% to 46%. The crest-fallen king was forced into exile. The Polish Referendum, fixed for 30 June, was a very poor substitute for the 'free and fair elections' promised by the Yalta Agreement.

ROTMISTRZ WITOLD Pilecki (left).

GENERAL ANDERS decorates men of the 7th Queen's Own Hussars, whose standard bears 'the Maid of Warsaw'. Sait'Elpidio (marche), May 1946 (centre).

POLISH REFERENDUM, 30 June 1946. Voters were invited to vote, 'Three Times Yes': for kicking out senators, landowners and Germans, but not for kicking out Communists (right).

It took the form of a vote on three innocuous questions, which had little or no relevance to the existing power structures. The Soviet and Communist organisers claimed a triumphant victory, and no one could effectively protest. The men and women of the II Corps could only watch. They were unable to participate in either of the referenda.

THE REPATRIATION ISSUE raised its ugly head again through an incident at Ancona on 18 June 1946, when a group of some 50 soldiers jumped from a moving southbound train. They claimed to have been ex-*Wehrmacht* POWs at Klagenfurt who volunteered to join the Polish forces but had been 'kidnapped' en route by Soviet officials. Anders lodged a protest to the British authorities. What emerged was that the NKVD was treating anyone born to the east of the Bug as a Soviet citizen, even if they had never lived a single day in the USSR; and that they were taking high-handed measures to enforce their claim. In response to Anders's protest, however, Supreme Allied Command Mediterranean (SACMED) was bombarded by counter-protests from two Soviet generals, asserting that 30,000 Soviet citizens were being held against their will by the Anders Army 'at gunpoint'. General Alexander replied coolly that if General Anders wished to invite Soviet inspectors to examine his troops, he was free to do so. This unpleasant affair was known as 'the case of Jan Rasimowicz'.

MAJOR ERIC Frith, Chief Liaison Officer to the Polish Army in the Middle East and to the II Polish Corps, 1943–1946 (above).

THE BOOK by Major Dennis Hills, one of Frith's staff, who actively opposed forcible repatriation to the USSR (left).

It was in a climate of considerable tension, therefore, that preparations began for the transfer of the II Corps from Italy to Britain. The formal order, issued on 5 June by the War Office, envisaged that 103,000 Poles would make the voyage. Shipments were to begin in September, and would continue to the end of the year.

Almost exactly at the time that the II Corps' departure for Britain was decided, a grand Victory Parade was staged in London on 8 June 1946. Soldiers, sailors, and airmen from all over the world took part, but virtually no Poles. The absence of comrades-in-arms from the Battle of Britain, the Battle of the Atlantic, from Monte Cassino, and Arnhem was quickly noticed by the press and provoked questions. The story then arose that the Poles had not been invited or alternatively that the Soviet government had banned their appearance. The truth is probably more prosaic. Some idiotic British bureaucrat, it seems, sent the official invitation not to the Government-in-Exile, which was on hand in London, but to the Government in Warsaw. The Provisional Government of National Unity, which had recently declared that the Polish Forces Abroad no longer existed, did nothing, neither accepting nor refusing the invitation. Only at the very last minute did the British organisers realise that no Polish contingent was preparing to attend. A hurried telephone call from Ernest Bevin to an appropriate official or go-between brought a curt 'Thank you, but no.' Such at least is the best, but unverified version. The important thing to remember, however, is that the Poles in London had no desire to participate. They had no sense of victory. They took pride in having done their duty, but they knew that the Polish cause had been defeated. "If I had received an invitation", one veteran told me, "I would have turned it down."

GENERAL ANDERS stayed on in Italy until the autumn. His description of his departure carried a characteristic sting in the tail:

> "I left Italy on 31 October 1946, travelling by way of Verona, through lovely mountain scenery marred by never-absent signs of war-bombed towns and villages, wrecked railway coaches and vast dumps of unusued ammunition... I was not going home, but into exile. Somewhere in the east there was a red glow in the sky as from a distant fire."[215]

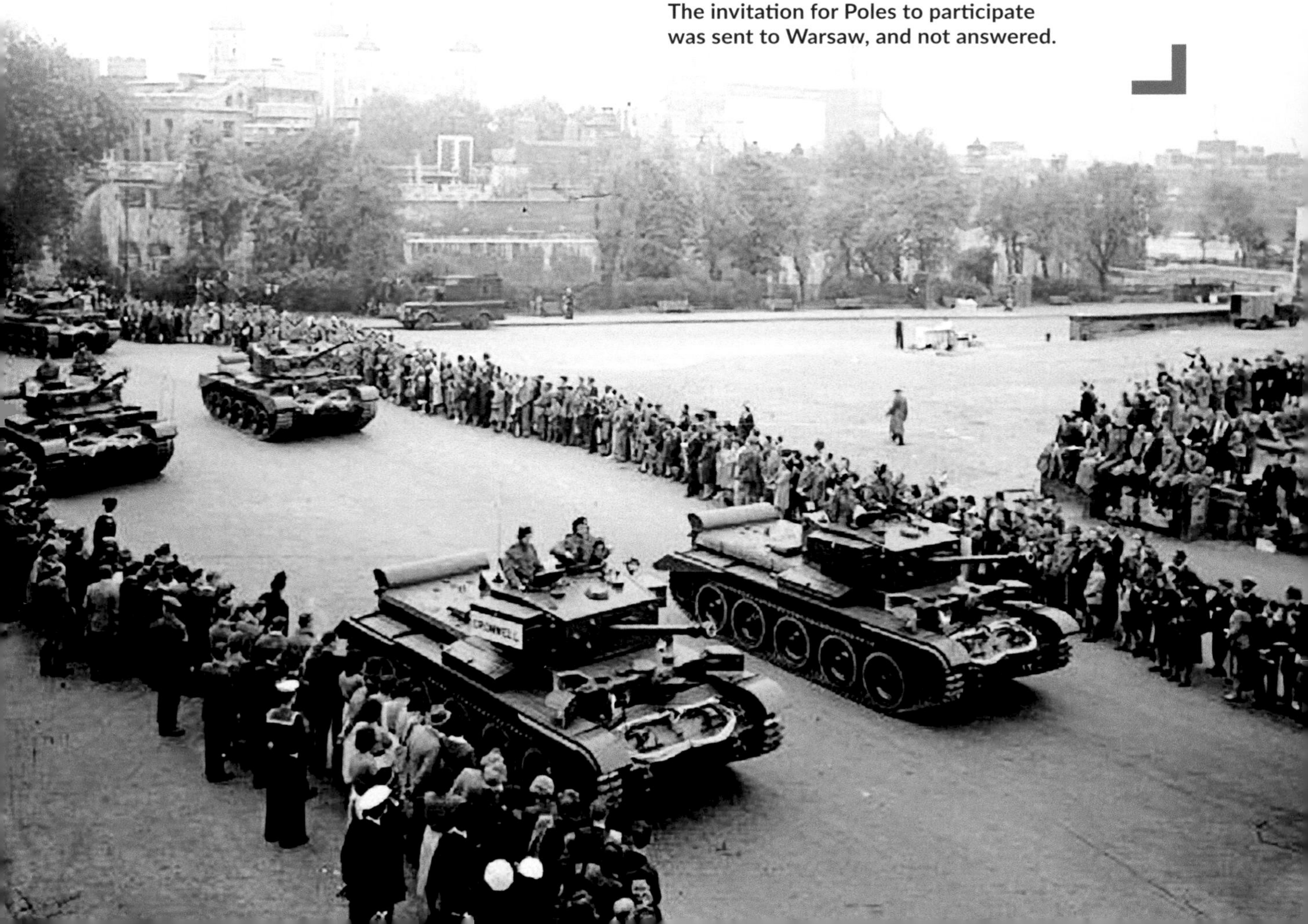

VICTORY PARADE, London, 8 June 1946. The invitation for Poles to participate was sent to Warsaw, and not answered.

CABINET OF Democratic Socialist Tomasz Arciszewski, October 1944–July 1947 (above).

THE SEAT of Poland's Government-in-Exile, Eaton Place, London (bottom right) and plaque (left).

DISCARDED POWER. Poland's legal Government, successor to the prewar Republic, to which the 'Anders Army' owed allegiance, operated in exile, 1939–1945; it lost its international standing in June 1945 as a result of the Yalta Agreement, but continued to function in London until 1990.

BOLESŁAW BIERUT arriving in Warsaw, June 1945, after consultations in Moscow (above).

STAMPS FROM the Bierut era: Joseph Stalin and Bolesław Bierut (below).

IMPORTED POWER. Comrade Bolesław Bierut headed a small group of Communist activists, appointed by Stalin to run postwar Poland. Unelected, almost totally unknown, and enjoying little popular support, they relied on the NKVD/KGB and its Polish subsidiaries, and the military. They exercised dictatorial power on Leninist lines through the secret decisions of a so-called 'Party', first the PPR and then the PZPR, which controlled all state institutions. After building a Soviet-style 'One Party System', they founded of the People's Republic that lasted from 1948 to 1989–1990.

BRITAIN:
END OF THE TRAIL

CHAPTER
1946–1948

19

CHAPTER 19

1946–1948

BRITAIN: END OF THE TRAIL

1946 WAS THE YEAR OF LEAST CLARITY. THE MAIN WAR HAD ENDED, BUT FIGHTING CONTINUED IN SEVERAL PARTS OF EASTERN EUROPE, AND THE SOVIET TAKEOVER WAS NOT COMPLETE.

Czechoslovakia, for example, which had been broken up during the war, had largely reunited, and a democratic government was in place in Prague. Although the Czech Communist movement was historically much stronger than its Polish counterpart, a typical Communist one-party state had not been constructed. In Germany, four Allied zones of occupation were in operation, but there were no signs yet of West Germany breaking away from East Germany. In Poland, where support for Communism was particularly weak, the opposition Peasant Party (PSL) of Stanisław Mikołajczyk had not been supressed, and the Democratic Socialists (PPS) had not yet been merged with the Communists. In short, though Churchill had already spoken publicly of the 'Iron Curtain', the rigid division of Europe had still to be implemented. Stalin held all the levers of control in Eastern Europe, but the growing rift with the Western Allies had not yet become an unbridgeable chasm.

TWO MONTHS AFTER his Keynote Message, Ernest Bevin unveiled his solution to the problem of providing for the 160,000+ Poles, who were still in British service but who could not be demobilised in the normal manner. His solution centred on the formation of two quasi-military organisations: the Polish Resettlement Corps (PRC) for army and navy personnel, and the Polish Air Force Resettlement Corps (PARC) for airmen. Both organisations were run by British military officers, and were subject to military law and discipline. Their members were technically volunteers, who were paid regular rates according to rank while they were prepared for release into civilian life. Their service was to last two years, during which they would be given tuition in English, trained in crafts, and sent on work experience. Men and women from the II Corps, and their dependants, formed over two-thirds of the membership. The details were not fully in place before the passage in Parliament of the Polish Resettlement Act (1947), Britain's first piece of legislation on organised mass immigration.

Before the scheme could be launched, however, the War Office was obliged to mount a massive naval operation to bring the candidates for resettlement to Britain. Priority was given to the transfer of military personnel, in the first place to the II Corps from Italy, and then to the III Corps from the Middle East.

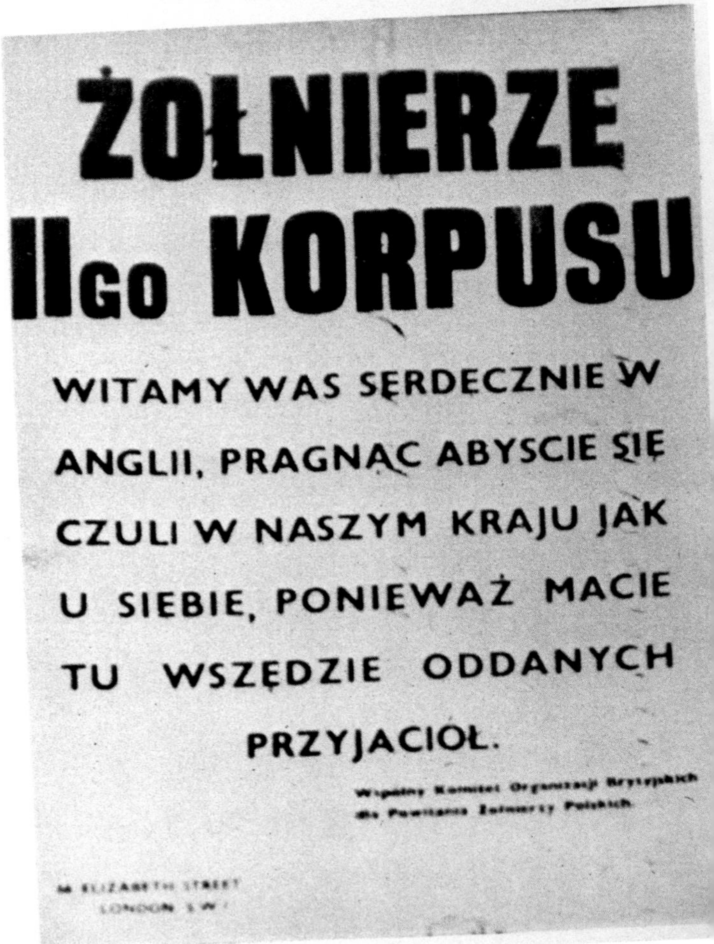

ŻOŁNIERZE
IIgo KORPUSU
WITAMY WAS SERDECZNIE W ANGLII, PRAGNĄC ABYSCIE SIĘ CZULI W NASZYM KRAJU JAK U SIEBIE, PONIEWAŻ MACIE TU WSZĘDZIE ODDANYCH PRZYJACIOŁ.

ADDRESS TO welcome Poles from the 'Committee of British Organisations': "We sincerely welcome you to England, wishing you to feel at home in our country, seeing that you have so many devoted friends everywhere" (1946).

Last in line were the civilians and Army dependants who had to be shipped to Britain from numerous distant countries, especially from Africa, India, and the Levant. The operation as a whole was not completed for three years. Throughout this period, the British government was planning to encourage the reemigration of a substantial proportion of the Polish exiles to Canada, Australia, South Africa, or New Zealand.

The complicated story of the multiple transfers of soldiers and civilians to Britain in 1946–1948 can be followed on a number of websites, in particular the section "Ships and Passenger Lists of Polish WWII DPs" which forms part of the site <http://www.polishresettlementcampsintheuk.co.uk>. It is the story of ships sailing back and forth between Italy, Africa, and India on one side and Southampton, Liverpool, Hull, and Glasgow, on the other, bringing their consignments of refugees to safety in Britain. The names of the vessels are highly evocative: MV *Winchester Castle,* SS *Asturias,* HMT *Empire Trooper,* SS *Atlantis,* RMS *Empress of Scotland,* SS *Cilicia* etc.; and the passenger lists are extremely valuable in that they often include not just names and ages but ranks, occupations, destinations, and War Office registration numbers.

Soldier Józef (Ziutek) Raginia, a member of the II Corps, boarded one of the earliest ships. His diary of the voyage has survived on the back of an old 1946 calendar:

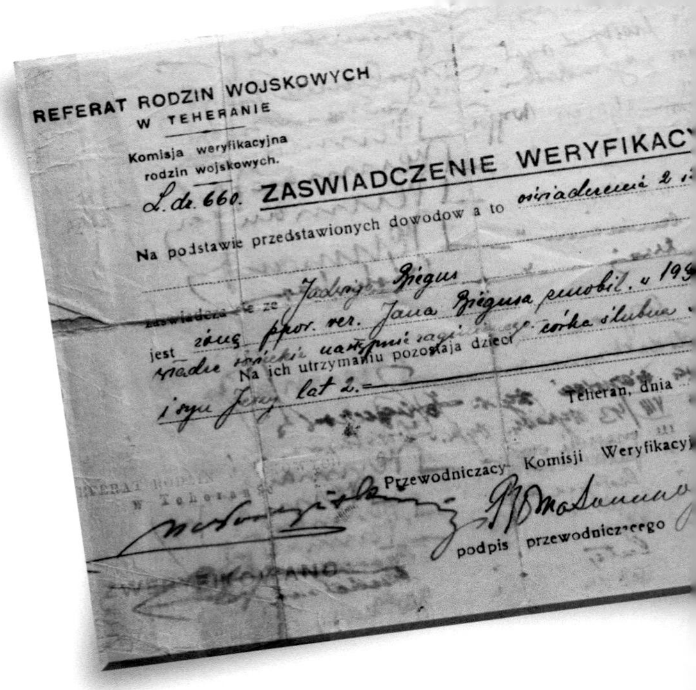
REFERAT RODZIN WOJSKOWYCH
W TEHERANIE
Komisja weryfikacyjna
rodzin wojskowych.
ZASWIADCZENIE WERYFIKAC
Na podstawie przedstawionych dowodów a to
jest
Na ich utrzymaniu pozostają dzieci
Teheran, dnia
Przewodniczący Komisji Weryfikacyj
podpis przewodniczącego

IDENTIFICATION CERTIFICATE issued by the Association of Polish Families in Tehran. Jadwiga Biegus, widow of the late Reserve Corporal, Jan Biegus; children Krystyna 5, Jerzy 2. 5 October 1942, Tehran.

"21 July – We left Senigallia for Falconara, [and thence] at 10:40 at night for Naples... [We] stayed in a camp in Naples until the 25th, watching Vesuvius and swimming in the swimming pool.

25 July – At 12:20 we left the soil of Italy and boarded the English ship, Cilicia, [and sailed] at 16:30 that same day... In beautiful weather, we sailed past the island of Capri, known for its songs... We all felt a sense of sadness... because we were parting from surroundings... where we experienced the most beautiful days of our wanderings.

26 July – Beautiful weather, calm sea, pleasant journey.

27 July – We watched many dolphins as they chased the ship; as evening approached we could see the shores of Spain.

28 July – Holy Mass aboard ship.

29 July – Uneventful day...

30 July – The sea is very rough: sea sickness.

31 July – From early morning, we can see the shores of Ireland... From 17:00, we are sailing close to the Scottish shore, we can see very nice seaside villas making a pleasant impression.

1 August – At 10:35 my foot touched the soil of Scotland for the first time, while going to customs clearance. At 20:00 we left Glasgow by train...

2 August – We arrive at Keele Hall, our new place of residence."[216]

The II Corps was transported in relays usually to Liverpool or Glasgow. On landing they were required to hand over their arms, and were invited to enrol in the PRC. After that, they were allotted to one of the PRC's five regional commands, each of which had dozens of military camps at their disposal. The effect was that the constituent units of the II Corps were broken up into much smaller groupings that were scattered round many different parts of Great Britain.[217]

UNION CASTLE Line, RMMV *Carnavaron Castle*, 20,122 tons.

CAMPS	REGION	COUNTIES	NUMBER OF PEOPLE	
51	SCOTCO	Berwickshire, Roxburghshire, Wigtownshire	**4,640**	HQ Artillery
31	NORCO	Derbyshire, Lincolnshire, Northumberland, Yorkshire	**16,170**	HQ 2nd Armoured Division
26	SOUTCO	Wiltshire, Gloucester, Berkshire, Oxfordshire	**15,990**	HQ 5th Division
	EASTCO	Buckshire, Hertfordshire, Norfolk, Suffolk, Huntingdonshire, Sussex	**23,290**	HQ 14th Armoured Brigade HQ 3rd Infantry Division
	WESCO	Cumberland, Lancshire Cheshire, Anglesey, Merionethshire, Shropshire, Staffordshire, Montgomeryshire, Brecon, Herefordshire, Pembrokeshire, Glamorgan	**60,720**	HQ II Polish Corps
			TOTAL: **120,810**	

The Carpathian Division was accommodated at Hodgemoor Camp, Chalfont St Giles, Buckinghamshire.

In all, the PRC possessed over 150 sites, many in remote rural locations. Most had been used during the war either as army training camps or as POW camps, and hence were often in poor repair. Conditions were Spartan, especially in the winter; heating was rarely adequate, and sanitation facilities extremely basic. Communication between one camp and another was difficult, increasing the sense of isolation.

Nonetheless, a secluded camp with a strange-sounding English name was destined to be home for the foreseeable future, and the exiles buckled down to the task of turning it into a more comfortable setting. In just one region, in the English Midlands for example, no less than 26 camps were distributed round the countryside: Each of those camps had their own character and

COUNTY	CAMP	UNIT
Cheshire	Delamere	II Corps HQ
	Calveley	II Corps Transport Company
	Petty Pool Sandiway	663rd Polish Air Observation Post Squadron
	Oulton Park	11th Signals Battalion, Machine Park
	Doddington Park	Camp II/40
Shropshire	Alderley Hall	1st Polish Survey Regiment
	Gwernheylod	2nd Squadron Traffic Control
	'R' Camp, Donnington	26th Supply Company
	Ellesmere	Polish General Hospital No. 11
	Mile House, Oswestry	23rd Transport Company
	Tilstock, Whitchurch	Camp for Military Families
	Hardwick Hall	9th Workshop Company, 19th KIO, 7th Anti-tank Regiment
Derbyshire	Blackshaw Moor 1	Sapper Unit, 30th Independent Workshop Platoon
Staffordshire	Blackshaw Moor 2	5th Brigade Group
	Blackshaw Moor 4	Armoured Forces Training Centre
	Baron's Cross	Camp for Military Families, Military Hospital No. 340
Herefordshire	Foxley Canadian Camp	II Corps HQ
	Shobdon Camp, Kingsland	1st Railway Engineer Batallion
Gloucester	Daglingworth	333th Field Butchery, Divisional Artillery Command, 5th Kresowa Infantry Division
		25th Wielkopolski Uhlan Regiment, 1st and 2nd Polish Motorised
		Artillery Regiments
	Stowell Park	6th Lwów Light Artillery Regiment
	Ullenwood, Cheltenham	5th Lwów Light Artillery Regiment, 5th Kresowa Light Anti-aircraft Artillery Regiment, 6th Kresowa Sapper Company, Divisional Artillery Platoon, 1st Anti-tank Artillery Regiment
		1st Anti-aircraft Artillery Regiment
	Fairford	18th Lwów Rifles Battalion
Oxfordshire	Stanton Harcourt	S13th Rifles Battalion
	Nettlebed South	15th Rifles Battalion
Warwick	Marlborough Farm	66th Pomorski Infantry Battalion
	Yscoyd Park	Military Hospital No. 1

SHOBDON CAMP, Kingsland (Herefordshire), 1946.

history. Delamere, for example, placed in the part of a grand country house, had been constructed to accommodate 15,000 US troops. Blackshaw Moor was another ex-US camp. Fairford was based on an airfield, which has since become the main testing ground of British Aerospace.

Most of the memoirs of life in these military camps have been written by the children and grandchildren of the postwar exiles. One such account refers to Penley in North Wales, near Wrexham, which housed Polish Military Hospital No. 3. Penley Camp had been constructed during the war for the 129th US Army General Hospital, which was closed after D-Day in 1944 and which by 1947 was derelict:

> "Andy Bereza was born in Penley in 1949. He and his younger brother Stanley, and sister, grew up in the camp, attended the schools there, and were part of the established Polish community. 'We spoke Polish until the age of six, then learned English at school with a Liverpool accent, because that was where the teacher came from.'
>
> Andy's father, Dr Michael Bereza was born in Poland in 1903... and at the beginning of the [Second World] War was a Colonel in the Polish Medical Corps. After the invasion he escaped to Romania... and the Middle East, where he was the Chief Medical Officer of the famous Carpathian Brigade, which fought with the British VIII Army in North Africa and Italy... He met his wife, Zofia Gallot, the daughter of the former Polish Transport Minister, while on leave in Palestine.
>
> After Dr Bereza arrived in Britain, he was appointed Deputy Head of the Polish Medical Corps, supporting Polish Forces for the whole

of the UK... After demobilisation in 1947, he administered Penley for the Ministry of Health and later under the NHS. He continued a struggle to keep Penley open... pleading with Enoch Powell, the then Minister of Health... Dr Bereza had developed an unusual management style. 'When in Africa, [Dad] was used to taking a break between 1 pm and 3 pm because of the heat. At Penley, he insisted that the rest of the staff take [a break], too.'

In the beginning conditions were hard... Most families lived in shared accommodation. Andy's family was the only one with an indoor toilet... [but eventually the facilities improved]. 'We didn't have to leave the camp for anything... It was a memorable lump of prewar Poland stuffed into North Wales.'"[218]

RMS *QUEEN* ***Elisabeth*****, photo in the building of the Southhampton harbor.**

Once the installation of military units was complete, it was the turn of the Cadets and of schoolchildren from various army-run schools in the Middle East. By 1947, Michał Giedroyć was 18 years old and had finished both his *matura* and his officer training:

"We travelled to Port-Said for embarkation. The troopship *Empire Ken* (to this day the 'Ken' remains a puzzle) was a handsome vessel of a certain age. I distinctly remember her three funnels and the steel-grey camouflage. Later we discovered notices, badly painted-over, saying "*Herren*" and "*Damen*". We concluded that the good ship was a liner, and a war prize.

The tedium of boarding was enlivened by the presence of Captain Dzieduszycki, in whose otherwise distinguished family eccentricity ran deep. He was apprehended struggling with an immensely heavy piece of hand luggage. Challenged, he explained that he was carrying an anvil, from which he would not be parted. 'When you strike it', he said, 'it responds with a most beautiful sound.' Apparently, he had carried it across Siberia and Central Asia. The English, appreciative of eccentricity, allowed him on board with it.

The Polish contingent was sizeable and the captain asked for a full-time interpreter. I was chosen for the job, which came with a comfortable corner in the ship's office next to the bridge. I was instructed to remain on stand-by to duplicate all the English announcements on the tannoy. This was sufficient excuse to avoid emergency drills, tug-of-war competitions and the like. There were plenty of opportunities for reading, chatting up the girls, and watching flying fish from a deck chair. In the bar at night a contingent of Welsh Guardsmen broke into song at the slightest opportunity. Their spontaneous harmony was perfect. The Mediterranean was as flat as a mill pond and I, in the knowledge that my mother and Anuśka were to follow me in a matter of months, felt at ease with the world whatever the future.

At Gibraltar we put on battledress, and were told to brace ourselves for the Bay of Biscay. But even the Bay was kind to us. On 1 August 1947, Empire Ken entered the port of Southampton. Later in the day I was told that it was a 'Bank Holiday'. Out of the morning mist there emerged a tall figure in uniform wearing a matching tall hat. I nudged an English neighbour at the rail and enquired who this mysterious personage was.

THE SOUTHAMPTON-HYTHE ferry (left) and dockside buildings (right): first sights of England.

'It is one of our policemen,' was the proud answer.

That misty Bank Holiday morning in Southampton docks marked the beginning of the rest of my life."[219]

As from the winter of 1946–1947, wives, families, and dependants began to arrive from Africa, India and Lebanon last of all, their ships landing in Plymouth, Southampton, or Liverpool. Wherever possible, they were sent to the same camps as their waiting husbands and fathers. It was a time for tears and rejoicing. Most of the families had been split up for four or five years, frequently wondering if they would ever meet again.

Between 200 and 300 Polish soldiers and civilians who came to Britain refused to accept the British government's terms; they steadfastly refused either to depart for Poland or to join the PRC. They were classified as 'recalcitrants', and were imprisoned.

SOUTHAMPTON BY NIGHT, (top left). Built in Italy for the P&O Line and launched in 2013, the MV Britannia (141,000 tons) is Britain's largest passenger ship (top right). A misty morning in Southampton (bottom centre). The best way to see Southampton docks is to sail across the harbour on the Hythe Ferry (bottom left). The first views of England were not always inspiring (bottom right).

SOUTHAMPTON IS the principal commercial port on England's South Coast, whereas neighbouring Portsmouth is the Royal Navy's principal naval base. Southampton grew up in the Middle Ages through the cross-Channel trade with France, and later developed routes to the West Indies and North America. It was the port from which sailed both the Pilgrim Fathers, who founded New England, and in 1912 the doom-struck Titanic. Home to the prestigious Cunard Line, it frequently welcomed the greatest liners of the mid-20th Century such as the 'Queen Mary' and the 'Queen Elizabeth'.

SOUTHAMPTON

POLES FROM THE 'ANDERS ARMY' began arriving in Britain in 1946. Though many of the soldiers were landed at Liverpool or Glasgow, Southampton was the destination for most of their civilian dependents. Arriving on the 'Empire Ken' from Port Said on 1 August 1947, one of those immigrants wrote: "On that misty morning in Southampton, the rest of my life began."

Scanning the passenger lists for familiar names can be a time-consuming but rewarding exercise. I myself struck lucky perusing the list of the voyage of the RMS *Scythia*, which sailed from Singapore, "picked up a handful of Polish Army Officers and relatives at Port Said for the North-West Command HQ, Shrewsbury" and landed at Liverpool on 27 January 1948. There, among the passengers, was my late friend, Zofia Litewska and her four children:

"325 LITEWSKA, Zofia, F, 42, Housewife
326 LITEWSKA, Maria, F, 18, Student
327 LITEWSKA, Halina, F, 14, Student
328 LITEWSKA, Zofia, F, 12
329 LITEWSKI, Jerzy, M, 17, Student"[220]

The ship's name was highly appropriate. That fatherless family had every reason to feel like survivors of 'The Scythian Steppes'.

It is hard to describe the moral triumph which those bare details conceal. Mrs Litewska, deported to Arctic Russia in 1940, had lost her husband, who died in Tehran, but she had successfully protected, reared and nourished her four children all along an eight-year trail and brought them to safety. She was to live in England for the next half century, and support them as they all gained a university education and entered an independent adult existence. To my way of thinking, it was a towering achievement. If her youngest daughter, Zofia was 12 in 1948, she must have been carried off to the icy wastes of the North aged three or four.

The *Empress of Scotland* landed in Liverpool on 15 February 1948 carrying among other passengers, 220 Poles from Bombay:

"650 BARANOWSKA, Rozalia, 45, Housewife
651 BARANOWSKA, Kazimiera, 15, Student
652 BARANOWSKI, Remigiusz, 9, Student
653 BARANOWSKA, Alfreda, 25, Widow...
753 KOZŁOWSKI, Kazimierz, 46, Priest
904 ZAK, Władysław, 50, -

RMS *SCYTHIA*, 19,000 tonnes, a former transatlantic liner converted into a troopship, 1939–1945; later used by the International Refugee Organisation.

905 ZAK, Maria, 48, Housewife
906 ZAK, Anatol, 13, Student
907 ZAK, Irena, 15, Student"[221]

Men were few and far between the women and children.

SCHOOL OF Foreign Commerce, London, 1946; (Michał Zawadzki, second from right, front row).

The SS *Atlantis* sailed from Naples to Southampton under the care of the Polish military authorities, landing on 8 November 1948. During the voyage of just over a week, eight babies were born, principally to the Italian wives of Polish servicemen.

Sailing from Durban, the *Empire Trooper* picked up 475 Polish personnel from Beira and Dar-es-Salaam before docking at Southampton on 21 April 1948. The ship's manifest lists each passenger's Personal Record Number, and War Office Number:

"From Beira:
Group leader, DOMANSKA, Urszula
SR 473 BADICZ, Maria, F, 24, RUS.A.1
SR 413 BALDIN, Jadwiga, F, 47, DIG.A.1
SR 415 BALDIN, Wanda, F, 21, DIG.A.3
SR 416 BALDIN, Maria, F, 20, DIG.A.2
SR 15 BAROWOCZ, Tekla, F, 38, MAR.A.11
SR 16 BAROWOCZ, Jan, M, 16, MAR.A.12
SR 1476 BORTKILWICZ, Lidia, F, 47, RUS.A.11...

From Dar-es-Salaam:
Group leader, SZCZYGIEL, Elonora
T 4692 FROSZTEGA, Maria, F, 26, IF.A/62
T 707 GŁOWACKA, Wanda, F, 34, IF.A/79
T 708 GŁOWACKI, Ryszard, M, 14, IF.A/80
T 709 GŁOWACKI, Andrzej, M, 11, IF/A/81
T 7608 KUBINSKI, Jan, M, 42, KID/B/10"[222]

The War Office Numbers help greatly in tracing their subsequent fate in British Army records.

The Lists of Ships and Passengers are too absorbing to put down easily. The twin-funnelled, diesel-engined MV *Georgic*, 27,000 tons, built in 1931 in Belfast, was a first-class modern liner of the White Star Line. Almost sunk by German bombs at Port Taufiq in July 1941, during the North African campaign, she had to be totally reconstructed and refurbished before resuming duties as a troopship. In June-July 1948 she sailed from Kilindini Harbour, Mombasa to Southampton. The passengers aboard, mostly from East African camps, were required to state their proposed address in the UK:

"552 KOŁODZIEJ, Magdalena, F, 50, Woodlands Hostel, Baldock Herts.
553 KOŁODZIEJ, Roman, M, 17, Woodlands Hostel, Baldock Herts.
554 KUCHARSKA, Janina, F, 42, 257, Stafford Rd., Cannock Staffs.
555 KUCHARSKA, ?, F, 18, 257, Stafford Rd., Cannock Staffs.
556 KUCHARSKA, Helena, F, 11, 257, Stafford Rd., Cannock Staffs.
557 KUCHARSKI, Marian, M, 19, 257, Stafford Rd., Cannock Staffs.

558 KUCHARSKI, Józef, M, 13, 257, Stafford Rd., Cannock Staffs.
559 KUCHARSKI, Helena, M, 43, King George V Sanatorium, Middleford Surrey
560 KUCHARSKI, Tadeusz, M, 17, King George V Sanatorium, Middleford Surrey
561 KUREK, Regalia, F, 58, Anglesey, North Wales
562 KUREK, Stefania, F, 21, Anglesey, North Wales
563 KUREK, Kazimierz, M, 18, Anglesey, North Wales"[223]

Descriptions are extant of the first hours, which the refugees and exiles spent in Britain:

"The SS *Oxfordshire* left Beirut on 10th July arriving in Hull on 22 July 1950 with 654 Polish DPs aboard including c. 100 children. She docked in the King George Dock, Hull at 11 am, and disembarkation started at 12 (midday). The W.V.S. and British Red Cross were in attendance with cups of tea and medical assistance.

Customs inspection was carried out quickly, and the people were transferred by bus to a transit camp at Priory Road Hull. On arrival, the refugees were checked off by the National Service Hostels Corporation staff, and were given an I.D. card, a meal ticket, knife, spoon, fork, mug and towel.

One man about 60 brought two hives of bees with him, and subsequently took them with him to Haydon Park Camp.

On Sunday morning, mass was celebrated by a priest from Cottingham, and on Monday, 24 July, the new arrivals were transported by bus to their allocated destinations: 39 went to private accommodation provided by relatives and friends, and the other 612 were transported to their allotted camps — to Damfield Lane 33, East Moor 83, Haydon Park 91, Husbands Bosworth 43, Lowther Park 142, Marsworth 55, Mepal 79, Northwick Park Gloucestershire 47, Springhill Lodges Gloucestershire 28, Stover Park Devon 11."[224]

IN THE DECADES since the PRC ceased to operate, the vast majority of its camps have been dismantled, often leaving no trace of their former existence. But one at least has survived, and though used for other purposes, can be visited and can evoke something of the prevailing atmosphere there some 60 years ago.

Northwick Park is a fine country house that belongs to a branch of the Spencer-Churchill family; it lies half way between Oxford and the Severn Valley in luscious hilly countryside. Northwick Park Camp was built in the grounds of the house for an American military hospital, which arrived in 1943 and left in 1945. The first Poles arrived in 1946. Every single feature smacked of wartime austerity and hasty construction. The central area was taken up by a communal dining hall, a shop, a storage depot, a communal ablutions block, and a laundry. A small school building and a chapel stood alongside. Living accommodation was provided in prefabricated Nissen huts, the so-called *beczki śmiechu* (barrels of laughs), which were rightly regarded as the lowest form of human habitation. The tube-shaped huts were served by electricity, but not by running water or sanitation, and were divided into two halves — one half per family. Heating was supplied by a primitive wood-burning or coal-burning stove: ventilation by a crude pipe stuck through the corrugated roof. Residents might easily long for their mud huts in Africa or the tented cities of the Middle East, especially when the weather turned inclement. The winter of 1946–1947 saw heavy snowfalls, and was the coldest in British history.

When I visited Northwick Park recently, my guide was a man who had attended school there as a child but who had lived with his

POLISH YMCA Officer's Identity Card – Wiktoria-Maria Łotecka (Polish Forces).

family in the nearby sister camp of Springhill Lodges. "We never knew luxury", he said, "so we never missed it." It was a happy, busy life, he recalled; his parents were content to raise their children in peace and quiet after so many turbulent years. "Our world was entirely Polish", he added, showing us the memorial-shrine to *Matka Boska Częstochowska* (Our Lady of Częstochowa), which is still in place despite the surrounding buildings being used now for car repairs and for a craftsman's workshop. "The *Angoli* were a foreign tribe; we had little to do with them." And when the spring came, and the summer, the children could roam in the woods, and climb trees, and pick flowers, or enjoy the treat of ride on the country bus to the market at Moreton-in-Marsh. They knew nothing of their parents' earlier troubles. Indeed, some of them, like Zosia Hartman and her future husband, Jerzy Biegus, stayed on long after the PRC handed the camp over to the National Assistance Board. The Bieguses, husband and wife, are authors of the standard introduction to the subject, *Polish Resettlement Camps in the UK* (2013).[225]

Zofia (Zosia) Biegus' own memories of Northwick Park go back to 1948 when she arrived on the back of an army truck with a crowd of others. "I can see barbed wire and watch towers," one of them said. "It's a prison," decided another. "For God's sake, there are children here after all," chimed in those at the back. "It can't be true," someone else said, calming us down, "this is Great Britain."[226]

As Zofia explains, it was not a pleasant experience for the parents. "But for the children the idyllic surroundings had much to offer... We felt ourselves free at last."

The barbed wire soon disappeared; it was only there because the camp had briefly been used for German prisoners. Cooking stoves were installed in the huts, and many families abandoned the communal kitchen, preferring to cook their '*raszyn*' (rations) for themselves. After a few weeks, the initial fears evaporated.

Children of school age were encouraged to visit local families, and by way of preparation were handed brochures telling them the rules of English etiquette. "Don't drink too much, and control your appetite", they were told; "and boys, whatever you do, don't kiss ladies' hands."

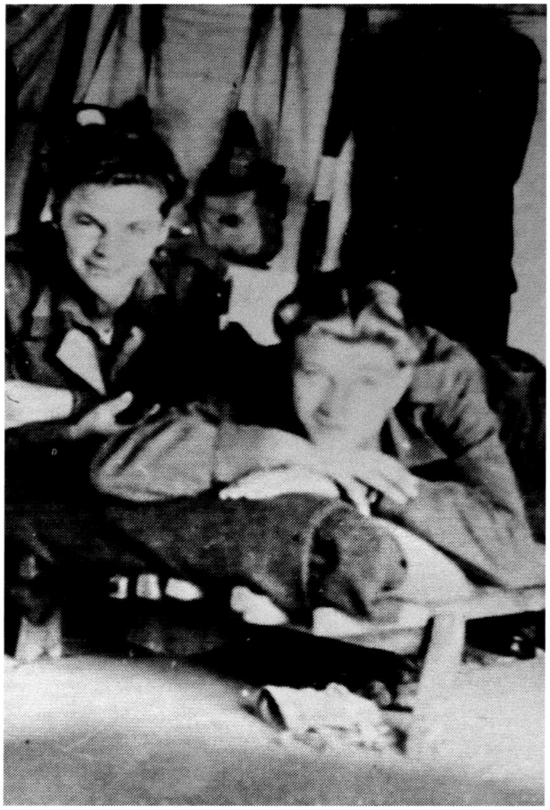

DAGLINGWORTH CAMP (Gloucestershire) (left).

LUXURY ACCOMMODATIONS (right).

For many years, Zofia believes, the inhabitants of Northwick Park thought that they would sometime return to Poland. That's why integration with the British was not a roaring success.

"We had new schoolfriends, of course, and we visited each other, and we watched the coronation, and took part in the life of the nearby village; but in the evenings we came home to our 'Little Poland'."

The PARC came into being shortly after the PRC. All the Polish Airforce Squadrons were disbanded at Coltishall (Suffolk) in November 1946 and their personnel distributed between a dozen camps including Castle Combie (Wiltshire) and Tweedsmuir (Scotland). The 318 Polish Fighter-Reconnaissance Squadron, which had accompanied the II Corps in Italy, was among them.

LIFE IN THE PRC resembled nothing more than that of a Polish village. As often as not, the buildings were prefabricated Nissen huts rather than the typical Polish *chata*. But every camp had its chapel and its chaplain, its school and its teachers, and daily routine centred on religious services, educational classes, and communal dinners. The men wore uniform and were addressed according to military rank. The women would dress up in folk costume for church festivals, and no occasion was missed to mark a national day with a procession and a feast. Owing to the lack of teachers familiar with Polish, and also to the elementary linguistic skills of many pupils, compulsory English lessons presented an ordeal for all concerned, and rarely produced satisfactory results. Agricultural courses, in contrast, or training in electrics, plumbing or carpentry, attracted enthusiastic participants. Many of the younger men, conscripts from 1939 or volunteers from Siberia in 1941–1942, had never learned a trade, and were eager to equip themselves for the world of work.

The Polish Education Association (PEA) opened for business on 1 January 1947 and closed down in 1954. With the assistance of British government agencies, it was charged with raising standards at all levels and, in particular, with opening channels whereby immigrant Poles could better integrate with British society. For example, since the PRC camps were typically located in remote rural districts, it founded and ran six boarding schools where talented secondary pupils could be taught for O-level and A-level exams, and thereby qualify for university entrance. Two of these schools, Fawley Court at Henley for boys and Pitsford in Staffordshire for girls, were to enjoy careers that stretched to the end of the century. Other PEA schools active in the 1940s and 1950s included Scone Palace, Dunalister and Grendon Hall in Scotland, Stowell Park (Gloucestershire), Bottisham (Cambridgeshire), Diddington (Huntingdonshire), Lilford (Northamptonshire) and Shephalbury (Hertfordshire).

At the tertiary level, several universities in Britain opened their doors to Polish students who were able to qualify. The Polish University Abroad (PUNO) had been brought from France to London in 1940, and offered studies in Polish based on prewar practices. But several Polish University Colleges, teaching in English, prepared students for professional careers in Britain. Among them were the Polish School of Medicine and Veterinary Science in Edinburgh, the Polish Faculty of Law at Oxford, the Polish School of Architecture at Liverpool, and the Polish University College of Engineering and Technology in London. Many ex-servicemen from the II Corps passed through these institutions and flourished professionally thereafter. Dr Ryszard Gabrielczyk, an ex-Junak and later president of the *Macierz Szkolna* (Polish School Motherland), worked for 40 years in London as a distinguished civil engineer. Mr Zbigniew Siemaszko, who had served under Anders in the USSR and Iran, before being sent to Britain as a radio operator, entered the world of electronics. He kept up his passion for history, writing numerous fine books, including a biography of General Anders.[227]

Two unpleasant developments, however, clouded the exiles' life. One centred on the nefarious activities of the Polish Consulate in London, the other on the open hostility of the British Trades Union Congress (TUC).

Ever since the establishment of postwar diplomatic relations, the Polish Consulate in London was firmly under the control of the Communist security and ultimately of the Soviet NKVD. Not surprisingly, therefore, it was a nest of spies, who busily monitored the activities of the emigré community and of political officers who were tasked not just to speak Communist propaganda, but also to harass and badger the inhabitants of the PRC camps, which they frequently visited. In those days, under Jakub Berman – though not later – the security officers often presented a profile similar to Berman's, and dubious figures like Marcel Reich-Ranicki (best known for his subsequent role as a literary guru in Germany) played an active role. (Isaac Deutscher, the prototype of 'the non-Jewish Jew' and a former comrade of the KPP was at the height of his fame in British left-wing circles.) These people missed no opportunity to blacken the reputation of General Anders, to stress the 'patriotism' of Poland's new regime and to promote the soldiers' return. Typical of their work was a book

NORTHWICK PARK CAMP

NORTHWICK PARK CAMP (1946), now 'Northwick Business Park' (right).

NISSEN HUT — 'barrel of laughs', term of endearment for huts designed during WWI by Major Peter Nissen (bottom left).

NORMAN DAVIES asks a tenant of the business park about past history (centre).

'YES, TWO FAMILIES used to live in each of these huts," says a former tenant, Hubert Zawadzki (bottom right).

Tel : 01
PO5

DANGER
Fragile
Roof

by Kazimierz Sidor entitled *W niewoli u Andersa* (Anders' Captives).[228]

The ill-will of the TUC, which was at the height of its power under Clement Attlee's socialist government, was motivated by two considerations. First, it saw its first duty in championing the cause of demobilised British soldiers, whose chances of employment were supposedly threatened by the influx of Poles. Secondly, in all things East European, it was strongly influenced by the views of British Communists and pro-Soviet fellow travellers. In 1948, a popular but obnoxious history of Poland (*Six centuries of Russo–Polish Relations*) was published in London by two Communist authors, William P. Coates and Zelda Coates.[229] As a result, whenever Poles from the PRC sought employment, pressure was applied on contractors and on the labour exchanges either to refuse them work or, most typically, to restrict them to the unskilled, lowest-paid jobs.

Nonetheless, the news from Poland in 1947–1948 was unexceptionally bad. The Polish General Election, long delayed, was subject to manifest fraud when it happened in January 1947. The US Ambassador in Warsaw, Arthur Bliss Lane, resigned in protest, and the Western Powers declared, to no effect, that the conditions of the Yalta Agreement had been flouted. Stanisław Mikołajczyk, former Prime Minister and leader of the Peasant Party, the only leading politician from London to join the Provisional Government of National Unity, was forced to flee in fear of his life. And the political scene moved inexorably towards the formation of a dictatorial one-party state. Poland's two best supported parties, the PSL and the PPS, were destroyed, and the Soviet-guided United Polish Workers' Party, the PZPR, assumed monopoly power in December 1948. If the inmates of the Polish Consulate in London thought that they could win over the members of the PRC in such conditions, they were sadly mistaken.

Already in 1946, Ernest Bevin had been obliged to protest to the Provisional Government of National Unity about the unsolved murders of opposition politicians in Poland, and the arrest of many ex-servicemen who served in Britain during the war. But as the Polish Communists gained confidence, they openly subjected their opponents to Soviet-style show trials and resorted to judicial murder. Two such state crimes attracted attention. One was the trial and execution of General Fieldorf 'Nil', a hero of the Home Army; another was the death in similar atrocious circumstances of Capt. Witold Pilecki (1901–1948). Given such news, the rate of return dropped from a slender stream to a trickle.

Yet the shelter provided by the PRC was temporary. The majority who joined in the autumn of 1946 were due to be released in the autumn of 1948. Some left earlier, if they decided to emigrate or if they gained permission to take a permanent job. Those who joined in 1947 could not expect to stay beyond 1949. All feared the brown envelope from the British War Office which carried the notice announcing that their service in the PRC was coming to an end.

The possibility of a Third World War, and hence of a renewed fight for Poland's independence, hung in the air for several years after 1945. Propagandists both in Warsaw and in London raised the spectre that General Anders would mount his white horse and lead his men across Europe to free his country from the Soviets. No one really knew what plans may or may not be in the making, so precautions were taken. The Polish Army in Britain was never fully demobilised. The *Biuro Historyczne* (Historical Bureau), headed by General Kukiel, the wartime Minister of Defence, acted as the core of a camouflaged General Staff, and so-called *Koła Oddziałowe* or Departmental Circles were retained as organisational cadres that could be rapidly expanded. At

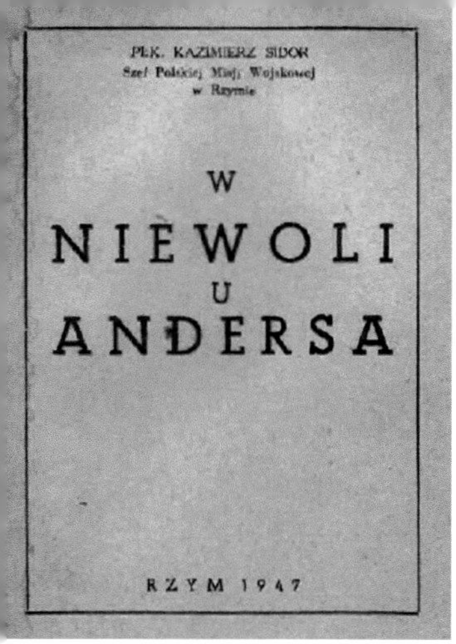

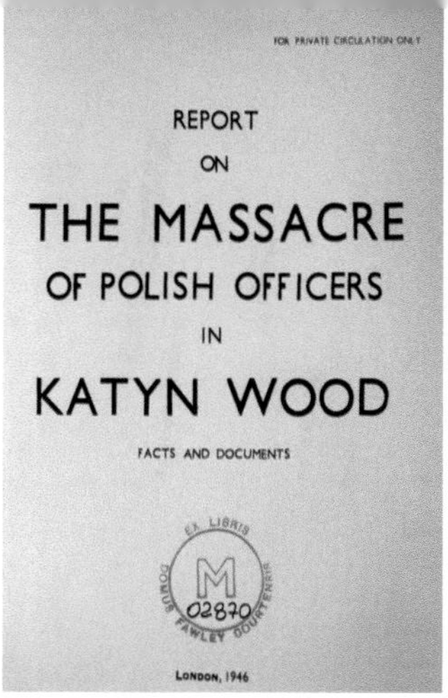

CLASHING WORLD views: Kazimierz Sidor, *In Anders' Captivity* (Rome, 1946–1947) (above left).
REPORT ON *the Massacre of Polish Officers in Katyn Wood* (London, 1946) (centre).

CYCLE RIDE: 1 mile from Bodney Camp in Norfolk (top right).

***JUNACY* IN ENGLAND** without the sun of Palestine (below).

the same time, under Lt Col. Zygmunt Czarnecki (1900–1989), a body called the *Brygadowe Koło Młodych Pogoń* aimed to train a pool of reserves. Dr Jan Ciechanowski, among others, recalls playing wargames in Richmond Park under the suspicious eyes of London policemen. The assumption – or at least the wishful idea – appears to have been that the British Army would have provided the equipment for two motorised divisions which would have swept into Poland from Germany, and, after eliminating the *politruks*, would have merged with the Polish People's Army.

After 1949, when the USSR developed an atomic bomb, the equation changed and no-one in their right mind could envisage a conventional attack to overrun the Soviet Block. During the Cold War, which set in thereafter, it was clear that Poland could be devastated by nuclear exchanges between East and West. The one element which remained active was the so-called Polish Link whereby officers of the former *Dwójka* continued to work closely with the British intelligence services.[230]

BY THE LATE SUMMER OF 1948, nine years had passed since the outbreak of the Second World War; eight years had passed since the deportations to Siberia and Kazakhstan; seven since the formation of the Anders Army; six since the start of the evacuations to Iran; five since the Army's sojourn in Palestine; four since

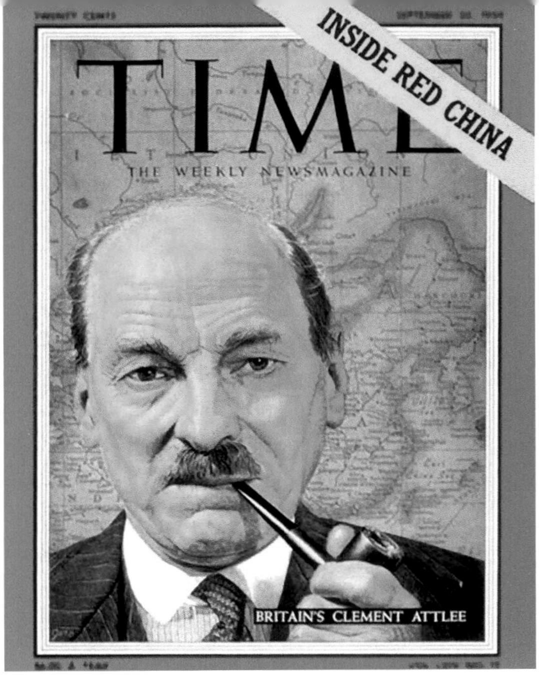

CLEMENT ATTLEE, Prime Minister in 1945–1950, victor over Churchill in 1945 and Britain's finest exponent of democratic socialism.

GEORGE ORWELL, novelist and democratic socialist and Britain's finest critic of Soviet communism, author of *Animal Farm* (1946).

Monte Cassino; three since the end of the war; and two since the launch of the Resettlement Corps. The men and women who had come together during that extraordinary odyssey were now taking responsibility for their future. There would be no Third World War. There was no chance that the Kresy, or even part of the Kresy, would somehow be re-joined to Poland. There was no point in thinking about a journey to their former homes in the Soviet Union or to a hostile 'People's Republic'. The Soviet empire in Eastern Europe was solidifying. The Iron Curtain had clanked shut. Hitler had gone, but Stalin still held sway – victorious, all-powerful, impervious to the pleas of the Western Powers, and soon to be nuclear-armed.

Ernest Bevin's Keynote Message contained an honest but chilling clause, which outlined the limitations of Britain's offer to members of the PRC. At the end of their two-year service, they would not receive British citizenship automatically; they would not be given reserved housing; and they would not be guaranteed employment. In short, they would have to fend for themselves. Bevin also reminded them, in addition to the option of going to Poland, that there would be a third possibility: that of applying to emigrate to one of the countries of the British Commonwealth. For many in the difficult days of 1948, emigration looked promising. In the end, roughly half of the PRC members stayed in Britain, and roughly half emigrated.

Postwar Europe was swarming with millions of displaced persons, refugees, and demobilised soldiers from all ends of the continent, all seeking safety, work, funds, and relief from their distress. The Poles from the II Corps, therefore, were far from unique, and were obliged to compete with masses of others in seeking a solution to their problems. The number of foreign countries, which were offering assisted emigration schemes, was limited. Jewish people were leaving for the new state of Israel, and anyone with American friends or relatives willing to sponsor them were able to travel with no difficulty to the USA. Certain South American countries, such as Argentina or Brazil, were also potential destinations. But for many reasons Australia and Canada presented the best prospects. Both were huge countries with small populations which published their need of immigrants. Both were strong democracies, which welcomed people fleeing totalitarian oppression. And both had expanding economies which promised a decent standard of living, even to immigrants who had to start on the bottom rungs of the social ladder.

As the PRC slowly wound down, many of its members sent off for application forms to both Australia and Canada, not knowing which of the two to choose. They had many weeks to wait before being called for an interview at the offices of the High Commission in London, and often decided that they would accept the first offer that was made. What they wanted was to start their new life as soon as humanly possible.

THE POLES WHO WENT TO AUSTRALIA left Europe with little expectation of ever returning. They were making a leap of faith, knowing that they were making a decision for a lifetime. Twenty years before the age of jet travel, the voyage by ship lasted for weeks and was very expensive. Immigrants who sailed on a £10 ticket were setting out on a one-way journey. On arrival in Australia, they were bound to work for two years in government-designated occupations, after which, as free residents, they could not hope to save the equivalent of a return fare for a very long time.

Nonetheless, thousands took the plunge, and it was men of the Carpathian Division who showed the way. Prior to joining the II Corps, they had served in North Africa alongside Australian soldiers. Friendships had been made, trust established, and a favourable image formed of life in the sun-drenched antipodes.

Polish migration to Australia resulted from an agreement reached in 1947 between the

THE ZAWADZKIS: family life at last.

OUTING TO Bystock Court (Devon), i.e. 'Bajstok', near Exmouth (above).

"HERE'S THE place I am living in now, a Lord's Manor." Feliks Ziębicki. Bystock, 17 June 1946 (right).

Australian Government and the International Refugee Organisation in London. Over the next eight years, 160,000 European migrants would benefit; 60,000 of them were Poles.

In October 1947, an advance party of 280 Polish ex-servicemen from the 'Rats of Tobruk' landed at Hobart, before moving to the Hydro-Electric Commission's construction camps in central Tasmania. They were soon followed by almost a thousand of their comrades:

> "The majority of them spent two years working in isolated construction camps in Tarraleah, Bronte Park, Butler's Gorge, Waddamana, and Liawenee. They worked 44 hours per week, in very rough weather conditions, living initially in provisional barracks with primitive facilities. In some of the camps, Polish rather than English was the main language of communication. After completing their work contracts, [several] ex-servicemen stayed with the H.E.C.... but most moved to Hobart or Launceston."[231]

MIGRANTS WHO WERE DIRECTED to mainland Australia usually passed through the vast camp at Bonegilla, out in the bush of Victoria State. Landing at Port Melbourne, they were ferried to 'as close an equivalent to Ellis Island as Australia has ever had'.

Poles made up the biggest groups among crowds of Hungarians, Latvians, Lithuanians, Estonians, Ukrainians, Slovenians, Germans, Romanians, and Czechs. First impressions were to prove lasting:

"When the first transport ship, *General Stuart Heintzelman* arrived in Melbourne in December 1947, with its 839 [passengers], the newcomers were to experience a very iconic journey into the mysterious interior of an unknown land. Once out of the port, [they] would have seen the outskirts of Melbourne, the ever smaller towns with ever smaller weatherboard houses. They would have glimpsed the increasingly open horizons, where the pale-green-grey eucalyptus trees and the telegraph poles were the only thing to see against a stark blue sky. They would have seen the sun shimmer on faded green foliage and brown earth, with the innumerable shades of intermingled yellow, brown, and grey... In time, the outlines of the bush would have become dark and spidery, in the quiet shadows of the night. And so, one might say, as these newcomers passed from one life to the next, an ancient dreaming touched a new one."[232]

FOREMOST AMONG THE 60,000 POLES who settled in Australia in those years was Professor Jerzy Zubrzycki (1920–2009). Though not a member of the II Corps, Zubrzycki was well known to them; in the summer of 1944, at the airfield at Bari, he was the intelligence officer from SOE charged with briefing aircrews before their perilous flights to assist the Warsaw Rising. Gaining a PhD in sociology from the London School of Economics in 1950, he accepted a chair at the Australian National University in Canberra, where he lived and thrived for over half a century. His wife Aleksandra (Ola) née Królikowska was an ex-servicewoman from the WSK of the Anders Army. She had been snatched from her schoolroom in Wilno by the NKVD, and deported with her mother to Semipalatinsk in Kazakhstan.

Jerzy, who had known her briefly before 1939, heard of her misfortune, and was waiting for her 'at the end of the trail' in London, where they married. Together, they not only made a happy family life for themselves, with their four children; they helped to transform Australia. They belonged to the wave of immigrants who believed that the traditional 'White Australia' was morally wrong, and that the narrow Anglo-Saxon culture of this huge empty continent had to be prized open to new influences:

"A small, politically involved minority ushered in multiculturalism in Australia... Zubrzycki was a key player in this small minority. The issue he grappled with... was how to create a society, in which people of different cultural backgrounds could live in harmony and make their contribution to Australian life. It was a vital issue. A million migrants had been welcomed in the ten years after the Second

World War... [These] migrants were expected to adopt the values, traits, loyalties and enthusiasms of the country's Anglo-Celtic majority.

However, by the late 1950s, questions were being asked about these policies. Australia's Asian neighbours... saw the White Australia policy as an affront to everything they stood for... And there was discontent among European migrants..."[233]

POLISH-AUSTRALIANS – a community grouped around the website <www.kresy-siberia.org>, Melbourne (2014).

THE POLES WHO WENT TO CANADA benefited from an Order in Council from 1946 which gave special preference to European immigrants. In later times, this policy was to be denounced as racist; at the time, the Canadian government was merely looking for immigrants who would blend easily into the existing population. It was minded to attract Dutch people who had been ruined by the famine of 1945, DPs who were crowding refugee camps in Germany, and Polish ex-servicemen stranded in Italy or Britain. The first quota of 4,000 subsided places was awarded to the Poles.

Alojzy Bach had served in the *Wehrmacht*, in the Polish II Corps, and in the PRC:

"At the Hensley camp in Liverpool, where I spent some time, several commissions were accepting applications for emigration to various Commonwealth countries. I chose Canada. Before long, I was called before a commission, which enquired about my knowledge of farming and examined my physical condition to make sure I could work in the fields. Today we laugh at their questions – they asked us, for instance, if we could tell wheat from oats – but it did not seem funny then. I must have met all their criteria, for I got my two-year contract as a farm labourer and some time later arrived in Halifax with a group of 550 Polish ex-servicemen. Then we boarded a train for what we had been warned was going to be a very long ride. We knew we were going to Manitoba, but no one knew exactly where it was. Finally, we got off the train at the station in Winnipeg and transferred to the awaiting trams, which took us to the barracks. We were all still wearing our uniforms, and on June 1, we took part in the Decoration Day parade. They divided us into two companies, led by 2nd Lieutenant Baranowski and 2nd Lieutenant Panek. The Polish Gymnastic Association Sokół loaned us their colours, and we marched with them before the stand.

I remember our welcome in Winnipeg. Not all the locals were delighted that we had arrived; some openly asked, 'What the hell did they come here for?' But the majority opened their hearts and their families to us. They invited us to dinners and introduced us to their friends in the parish of the Holy Spirit. I was most graciously received by the Rakowskis in Transcona. We have been close friends ever since.

After two weeks in the barracks, we were split into three groups: one destined for Emerson, one for Lettelier, and one for Roland. I found myself in the Lettelier group and went to work in the sugar beet fields. We were paid not by the hour, but by a mile-long row. The more rows we thinned, the more we earned, but even the hardest working among us did not make much. When the sugar-beet season was over, we were assigned to individ-

TORONTO AND Lake Ontario with the CN Tower (1976). It was not there when the biggest influx of Poles occurred.

CHILDREN OF PAHIATUA in 2009 on their 65th anniversary reunion, Wellington, New Zealand.

ual farmers; here I was lucky, for my farmer in La Salle, of French descent, turned out to be a very decent person and good to me. After the harvest, we returned to the sugar beet camps and worked on that contract until the first frost. In November, we were brought back to Winnipeg and told to look for farm work..."[234]

Between 1945 and 1955, the Polish-born community in Canada rose from 6,000 to over 50,000. A substantial element of these immigrants originated in the II Corps; and 50% of them settled in the province of Ontario.

It is a well-observed feature of migration that uprooted individuals possess an in-built tendency to stick together with others of their own kind and to home in like racing pigeons on locations already settled by immigrants of the same nationality. In Canada, therefore, incoming Poles made for the district of Roncesvalles in Toronto, for places like Wilno or Rawdon (Quebec), which already had Polish connections, or for industrial towns like London (Ontario) or Hamilton, where work could be found. (London (Ontario) is immediately adjacent to the US city of Detroit, which possessed a large and old-established Polonia.)

Some immigrants, however, ventured further afield. Professor Bogdan Czajkowski, for example, poet and literary critic, made a long career at the University of British Columbia in Vancouver.

THE POLES WHO EMIGRATED to South America did so largely because they already had friends or family living there. The numbers mov-

POLISH CHILDREN OF PAHIATUA Memorial, Wellington Harbour. "They say thank you to the New Zealand Government, New Zealand Army, Catholic Church, caregivers, teachers and all who extended a helping hand."

ing to Argentina or Brazil in the postwar years were thousands rather than hundreds. They homed in on the large group of Poles long since resident in Buenos Aires, or on the Polish settlements dating from the 'Brazilian Fever' of the 1890s in the province of Rio Grande do Sul.

Among the Polish civilians returning to Europe from Africa or India, a larger percentage agreed to go to Poland than was the case among military veterans. As Anna Kajak relates, they, too, had their 'difficult beginnings':

> "Our decision to return to Poland was taken without too much hesitation. We had no one in the Polish army in the West, our relatives were in Poland and we considered that our place was there too. It was winter 1947/48. Sailing from Bombay, we sang carols aboard our ship *Georgic*. Our first contact with Poland took place in Italy, in Rome, where waiting for us was a Polish Red Cross train. Clean, neat and comfortable, it made a good impression on us. Our life in Poland began in a transit camp in Koźle, where we underwent quarantine.
>
> Our closest relative lived in the Silesian town of Bielsko, where my grandparents resided before the war and where I spent my early childhood. Our first unpleasant impression occurred when we had to change trains at the Katowice railway station. While handling the heavy trunks containing all our possessions, we were rudely abused by a young man who did not even think of helping women struggling with the heavy loads.
>
> Arrival at Bielsko, a cordial welcome from relatives and then the start of a prosaic life. The housing situation turned out to be disastrous. People waited for years for the housing bureau to allot them living quarters. My married uncle lived in an allotted room, part of a beautiful house, but to reach the kitchen or bathroom, he has to cross two rooms occupied by the main tenants... The uncle's wife occupied a room in a house divided between three families. The main tenant, unhappy with the situation, tries to make life unpleasant for the others. When she goes out, she takes the bath plug with her so that others cannot use the bath...
>
> During the first years after the war, there were no difficulties with provision of food. In Poland, we had adequate supplies during a period when most European countries were experiencing malnutrition and rationing...
>
> It is worth mentioning a network of milk bars that was established during those years. They served vegetarian food, mainly dairy-based, reminding one of homecooking and

SERDEC

ILFORD PARK

POLISH HOME (2015): Norman Davies meets residents for 'Memory Time' (left).

VETERANS OF the II Corps and veteran Helena Edwards (bottom left and centre).

KRAKÓW STREET / West Wing (bottom right).

ANNA ZIĘBICKA, sometime owner of the famous 'Lost Bag', passed away at Ilford Park in 1992 aged 90, and is buried at the nearby Newton Abbot Cemetery.

they were cheap. We often ate there while living away from home...

The most important matter for us youngsters was the 'how and where' to find further education. My secondary school level reached in India was one year before matriculating. I realized that the standard of science and mathematics taught in India was much lower than in Warsaw secondary schools, leaving gaps difficult to fill...

There were a number of distinct groups amongst the students. There was the 'Golden

FAREWELL TO AFRICA, Tengeru Camp, 1949.

Youth': children of privileged parents, talented, certain of matriculating from this school. They were mostly interested in other matters and did not put much effort into study. There were a number of students who were forced to work because of their living conditions. They fought fiercely in an attempt to prevent the school's standards rising too high and wanted it to be exclusively for working students. Others strived to obtain both high marks and to leave school with a favourable opinion as an assurance of access to higher education. Membership of the ZMP, the first step to Communist Party membership, served towards that end. Some of us were just ordinary people who kept their beliefs, such as religious sympathies, to themselves. To me, having spent time in the Soviet Union, joining the ZMP was out of the question. I had seen too much at close range and I knew. Nonetheless I thought that events taking place in Poland were something entirely different...

I thought that many beneficial changes took place in Poland after the war.

Nationalisation of factories and an agrarian reform seemed to us as a great achievement. Similarly, the access of village youth to schools and the widespread migration from the country to town and city also seemed to be an achievement. It took time to notice the negative side of the changes and gradually, our subjugation to Russia became obvious."[235]

THE POLES WHO STAYED IN BRITAIN did so either because the pull of distant unknown continents was too weak or because the advantages of the old continent were too strong. Many feared, if they were to find Australia or Canada uncongenial, that they would lack the means to escape. Others felt, if they did not leave Europe, that conditions in Poland might improve and that they might be able to return. Parents with children valued the provision of free state schooling, the newly introduced National Health Service, and the support of the Polish Catholic Mission. Those who could not easily decide for themselves followed the example of friends and neighbours with whom they had shared their life over the preceding years.

The process of quitting the PRC and of moving into civilian life often took weeks and months. It involved job-seeking, house-hunting, and finally the fateful day of removal from camp to a new home.

BINGLEY MILLS, Bradford.

Poles who applied to labour exchanges were most frequently directed to Britain's big industrial cities, where they found work in textile mills, food factories, and engineering works. Compact Polish communities began to form in Glasgow, Manchester, Bradford, Birmingham, Coventry, and in particular districts of London. Towns like Slough, because of the railway yards, or Bedford because of the brickworks, also took in Poles. At the same time, numerous job seekers simply sidled along from the camp to the nearest village or market town and accepted whatever positions were available as dish-washers, chambermaids, street-sweepers, and drivers, or if their English was good enough, sales assistants. Due to language problems and to the non-recognition of Polish qualifications, colonels worked as waiters, lawyers as shoeshine boys, and qualified teachers as seamstresses, packers, or gardeners.

The experiences of Poles who sought employment on leaving the PRC can only be described as mixed. Some thrived, some did not:

“The Polish Resettlement Corps was a joke,” recalled one dissapointed customer; “they pushed us to the worst jobs. I was just a corporal. They sent us to a camp near Cambridge. Many of my friends were being demobilised and I was still a secretary in the Polish Army.

I went to report to an officer, and he said that I could stay in the Army as long as he saw fit. I said that I would only stay until I got a job. I found a job with the British American Optical Company. It was terrible work.”[236]

SATURDAY, JUNE 18,

Prima donna's paintings raise funds for Huddersfield Poles

From Our Huddersfield Staff

A former prima donna at the Warsaw Opera House, Mrs. Irene Valdi-Golebiowska, now a music teacher in Huddersfield, staged a one-woman exhibition of paintings at the Huddersfield Polish White Cross Club yesterday.

Most of the paintings have been seen previously in Beirut, the Lebanon and in London, but new water colours on view were completed as recently as Saturday. They included pictures of Castle Hill, Huddersfield, and the Green-head Park War Memorial.

The exhibition, which is being held to raise money for the newly formed club, will continue to the end of the month. Within 20 minutes of its opening a portrait in oils, “Leila, daughter of the sheik in Lebanon,” had brought in 15 guineas, and a water colour of

Mrs. Irene Valdi-Golebiowska

June 22,

THE DAILY MIRR

ties.

PRIMA DONNA Valdi-Golebiowska, once a star in Warsaw, now a music teacher in Huddersfield, Yorks, is showing paintings to help build a Polish White Cross club in Huddersfield.

MADAME VALDI-GOŁĘBIOWSKA, opera singer turned painter.

The way that many Poles found work is described in the oral memoir of Feliks Czenkusz. It was the autumn of 1947:

“A friend of mine who had experience of working in textiles in Poland had been informed that a mill in Bingley, West Yorkshire, that was owned and run by a Polish Jew, Mr David Pike, was seeking workers with previous textile experience... I think the mill was called Ebor Mill, and was situated alongside the Leeds-Liverpool Canal in Bingley.

My friend applied for a job there, and though I had no textile experience, I decided to go with him... David Pike had many orders for cloth, but not enough workers... I obtained

WŁADYSŁAW ANDERS

ANNUAL COMMERCIUM of the Arkonia Student Corporation in Warsaw (May 1937). Polish Marshal Edward Śmigły-Rydz addressing the company, Anders seated opposite him (above).

ANDERS TRAINING his favourite mare. Warsaw, after 1935 (top centre).

AS LIEUTENANT Colonel, commander of the 1st Wielkopolski Regiment, after April 1939 (top right).

WITH CHILDREN at Northwick Park, 1953 (right).

CHRISTMAS 1955. Anna Maria Anders with mother Irena and bemedalled Father.

FATHER JÓZEF JARZĘBOWSKI, M.I.C. (1897–1964); born in Wilno, he crossed the USSR and the Pacific to the USA in 1941; worked at Santa Rosa, Mexico, and in 1953 founded the Marian College at Fawley Court, Henley-on-Thames, together with the school and library.

release papers from the Army commandant, a train ticket, and directions to both the Bingley Mill and to a lodging house in a street situated behind Busby's Store...

When I first came to civilian life, I thought I might be discriminated against by English people, but I found that I faced discrimination from fellow Polish people... I went to work at Bingley Mill on the night shift. Most night shift workers were ex-army Polish men, whereas the day shift workers were mainly English... I was the first person to work there that was 'outside the group', the only one not to have worked in textiles previously... The experienced men were supposed to teach me the skills, but were not keen to do so. They were not very friendly and often unhelpful... [It] was not a good experience, and after 18 months I decided to leave."[237]

Fortunately, a generation of Poles who had survived Arctic labour camps and remote Soviet collective farms knew how to work as well as how to fight. They found that their British neighbours came to respect them, and to accept them as valued members of the community. They also found, although Britain was a predominantly

Protestant country, that a strong Catholic Church, usually of Irish origin, was ready to welcome them. Once the initial period of struggle and anxiety was over, many marriages took place, and new waves of children and grandchildren were born, creating an air of normality.

And Polish ex-servicemen took their place in a country where the sacrifices of the past are systematically honoured. By a happy coincidence, the 11th of November, which is Britain's official Day of Remembrance, is equally Poland's National Day. Never a year passes without a delegation of men and women from the Polish Veterans' Association (SPK) lining up before the war memorials of British towns and cities, dressed in their black berets and red-and-white sashes.

On Remembrance Day 2014, when the BBC broadcasted its annual programme from the ceremony at the Cenotaph in London, attended as always by the Queen, the commentator caught sight of the Poles as they marched past, banners flying and heads held high. "These are the men of Monte Cassino", he said, "seventy years on." "Yes," added a British ex-combatant, speaking to the camera, "They reached the top!" General Anders himself lived in England with his second wife and daughter for 24 years. Having served under British command, he received an officer's pension – unlike General Bór-Komorowski – but never ceased to care for his former soldiers' welfare. He played a prominent role in exile politics, being one of the 'Group of Three', who opposed the presidency of August Zaleski.

In 1960, he successfully fought a libel case in court against a band of nationalist compatriots (*narodowcy*), who had claimed in their newspaper, the *Narodowiec* (The Nationalist), that he was not a Pole. He died aged 77 in 1970, and was buried, in accordance with his wish, alongside his fallen comrades at Monte Cassino.

Having been taken from Poland by his Soviet captors in 1939, he never saw his homeland again. His widow, Irena Andersowa, died in London aged 90 in 2010, and was buried in the same grave.

THE TRAIL, which started with the deportations in the period of the Nazi-Soviet Pact, led tens of thousands of people to the four ends of the earth. There are survivors of the exodus still living in Tehran, in Santa Rosa, in Israel, in Italy, in Tasmania, Canada, Africa and in Britain. The 'Pahiatua Club' still functions in Wellington, New Zealand. And the 'Children of Tehran' have recently won their case in the Supreme Court against the State of Israel. And the memory of the *Andersowcy* lives on, particularly among the veterans, their friends and their descendants.

In the former Kresy, nothing much changed for the better until the Soviet Union collapsed. In 1991, the Supreme Court of the Belarusian SSR ruled that the deportations of 1940–1941 had been illegal, and suspended all proceedings against ex-soldiers who had served in the West. Compensation was paid for loss of property. In 2003, 23 veterans of the II Corps were still alive in Belarus, but without normal ex-combatant rights.

So the trail had many ends, not one; it led to all the continents of the world (except perhaps Antarctica). But Poland itself must not be forgotten. The great majority of men and women who left the Soviet Union in the ranks of Anders Army, or under its care, had dreamed of reaching 'Poland'. The Poland of their dreams, however, was dissolving, even as they journeyed to find it. It is said that the number of persons, who had started in the USSR and yet agreed to go to postwar Poland, did not exceed 300, that is, one quarter of one percent; there were 46 in total who opted freely to go to the USSR. What they found was not the Poland they had left, but something very different.

20 CHAPTER

RETROSPECT: HISTORIOGRAPHY, FILMS, MUSEUM, MEMOIRS, INTERNET

CHAPTER 20

RETROSPECT

HISTORIOGRAPHY, FILMS, MUSEUM, MEMOIRS, INTERNET

IN MAY 2015, SOME OF THE COMBATANT POWERS OF THE SECOND WORLD WAR CELEBRATED THE 70TH ANNIVERSARY OF THE ALLIED VICTORY IN THEIR DIFFERENT WAYS. IN LONDON, QUEEN ELIZABETH II ATTENDED A SOLEMN CEREMONY REMINISCENT OF REMEMBRANCE DAY.

In **Gdańsk**, the Polish President convened a meeting where a score of statesmen and stateswomen from all parts of Europe, in the company of the Secretary-General of the United Nations, made pronouncements on their understanding of war and peace in our time; he then led his guests to the monument at Westerplatte, to pay their respects at a place where the first shots of the war had been fired on 1 September 1939. In Moscow, President Putin hosted a Soviet-style military parade in Red Square. Little or no mention was made at any of these events of General Anders and his Army, or of their extraordinary story.

At Monte Cassino, however, on 19 May, a modest gathering of a couple of hundred veterans and their well-wishers assembled at the Polish Cemetery to mark the 71st anniversary of the battle. Holy Mass was celebrated in the bright Italian sunshine by Archbishop Stefan Wesoły, himself a veteran of the II Corps. Diplomats, military officers, Italian dignitaries, local officials, and Catholic nuns mingled with the friends and families of soldiers who had served in Italy over seven decades ago. The choir sheltered under the improvised awning as they sang the anthems. The sermon talked of patriotism and the high price of patriotism, of memory and identity, and of the European heritage based on a Christian tradition. The scene must have been similar to that of the many field services (*msze polowe*) that were regularly held throughout the Army's progress. Later, wreaths were laid at the grave of General Anders and of his wife, Irena, who rejoined him after a separation of 40 years. Photographers scurried among the guests. TV presenters staged interviews on the margins. Dressed in his father's battledress, with 'POLAND' emblazoned on the shoulder, a British man from York greeted a Maori from Auckland, the grandson of a soldier from the Maori battalion that had fought alongside the Poles. A historian in a fine straw hat was taking notes. And a young man from London, fascinated by the inscriptions on the gravestones, was walking along the rows of crosses, taking pictures, and marvelling at the Borderland names:

+ 12.5.44 Edward Kuźnicki, 2 Baon Strz. (2nd Rifles Battalion), Wilno–Troki
+ 12.5.44 Bronisław Iwaszko, 3 Baon Strz. (3rd Rifles Battalion), Nowogródek
+ 17.5.1944 Bazyli Jewtuch, 5 Baon Sap. (5th Sapper Battalion), Stolin
+ 12.4.44 Kan. Jan Daniliszyn, 1 P.A.L. (1st Light Artillery Regiment), Lwów

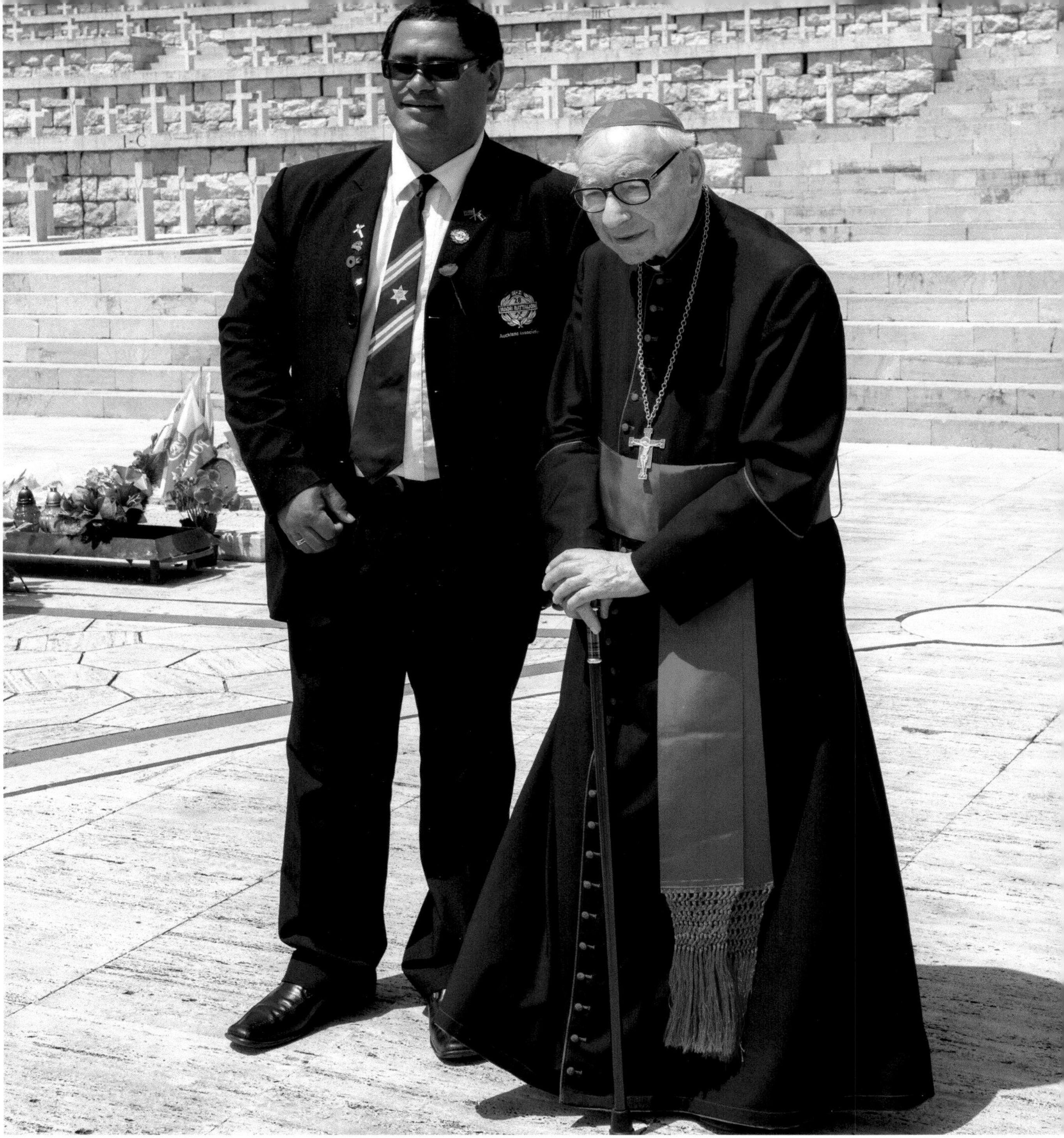

ARCHBISHOP SZCZEPAN WESOŁY (right), formerly Director of Pastoral Care for the Polish Diaspora, with Mr Joe Shelford-Tuki, Vice-President of the Auckland Association of the New Zealand 28th Maori Battalion and grandson of a Monte Cassino veteran, following the anniversary Mass, 18 May 2015. Unit badge at left.

WITH MICHAŁ GIEDROYĆ, Oxford (2015) (right).

***JUNAK* MICHAŁ GIEDROYĆ** reports to General Anders, 1946 (far right).

+ 20.5.44 Kpr. Andrzej Silberberg, P.6 Panc. (6th Armoured Regiment), Petersburg

Overlooking everything, the rebuilt monastery of Monte Cassino, founded by St Benedict, Patron of Europe, gleamed in the bright light at the top of hill, exuding a sense of calm, peace and reconciliation.

AFTER 70 YEARS, the accumulated literature on the history of the Anders Army is considerable, though no definite study has yet appeared. The most thorough, factographical biography of General Anders, by Zbigniew Siemaszko, does not go beyond 1942; and the planned second volume is, as the author confesses, never going to appear.[238] A lively investigation into Anders' later years, by Ewa Berberiusz, looks at the great man in decline, but not at the height of his powers.[239] No authoritative biography which catches the spirit of the man has been written. On Anders as a military leader, the best example remains the work by the late Harvey Samer.[240]

The saga of the Anders Army, and its odyssey through a dozen countries, makes for a complicated subject, and no author to date has been able to treat the whole adequately. The segment of the story that deals with the deportations and forced exile of 1939–1941 has been well addressed since 1989, notably in the works of the late Keith Sword.[241] But other segments are less well documented. Polish–Jewish relations, and the passage of the Army through Palestine, tend to be addressed by historians with an axe to grind.[242] The shortcomings of the Italian Campaign are regularly overlooked in favour of the glory that was Monte Cassino. Polish readers have much to digest, starting with the accounts of Melchior Wańkowicz and Jan Piekałkiewicz,[243] but they would be advised to consult some of the more critical assessments, including those of Ellis or Hapgood and Richardson.[244] A French historian has gone so far as to call his study of the Italian Campaign *Une Victoire Inutile* (A Useless Victory).[245] The fate of civilians, and their dispersal to several continents, is well summarised in publications such as *Dzieci tułacze*;[246] Polish accounts often omit the Tehran Children, while Zionist accounts of the Tehran Children repay the compliment by saying nothing or little about the experiences of non-Jewish exiles. The collection edited by Jan and Irene Gross, *War through Children's Eyes*, remains a key work on the children's terrible experiences.[247] The postwar life of Polish exiled communities awaits an inspired author, but much basic information can be gleaned from

books by Sword, Ciechanowski, and Davies.[248]

Individual memoirs undoubtedly supply the largest source of information. In the nature of things, they are confined to the experiences of one person or of one family, and are not usually intended to paint the broader picture. Yet the best of them do explain the causes and considerations underlying successive stages of the saga; also, since they were often written for the benefit of children or grandchildren, they are usually available in both English and Polish versions. The top position is obviously occupied by General Anders' own memoir, *Bez ostatniego rozdziału* (1949), published in English as *An Army in Exile.*[249] My own favourite happens to be *The Last of the War Horses* (1974)[250] which I read long ago, having met General Rudnicki in person in London. Rudnicki was very adept in providing the political and geographical background to his personal experiences; unfortunately, he did not give the same attention to the later stages of the odyssey as to those in the Soviet Union and the Middle East.

In the intervening decades, the list of memoirs has steadily grown, so that it now contains scores, if not hundreds of titles; one can be sure that for every memoir that was published, ten were not. It is only possible to put forward a personal selection:

- Wesley Adamczyk, *When God Looked the Other Way*
- Władysław Anders, *An Army in Exile*
- David Azraeli (Azrylewicz), *One Step Ahead*
- Menachem Begin, *White Nights*
- Józef Czapski, *Inhuman Land*
- Alick Dowling, *Janek: a story of survival*
- Helena Edwards, *Days of Aloes*
- Michał Giedroyć, *Crater's Edge*
- Maria Hadow, *Paying Guest in Siberi*a
- Gustaw Herling-Grudziński, *A World Apart*
- Eugenia Huntingdon, *Unsettled Account*
- Zofia Litewska, *A Memoir*
- Sandra Oancia, *Remember: Helen's Story*
- Sławomir Rawicz, *The Long Walk*
- Klemens Rudnicki, *Last of the War Horses*
- Aleksander Topolski, *Without Vodka and Without a Roof*
- Stefan Wajdenfeld, *The Ice Road*
- Zoë Zaidlerowa, *Dark Side of the Moon*[251]

For understandable reasons, most of these memoirs concentrate on the early phase of Anders' story, in the Soviet Union, where the greatest pain and suffering were endured. Aleksander Topolski's work, however, is exceptional, partly because it follows the whole length of the trail, and partly because it is written with great verve, humour and irony. In terms of literary quality, it is only equalled by *Crater's Edge* by Michał Giedroyć.

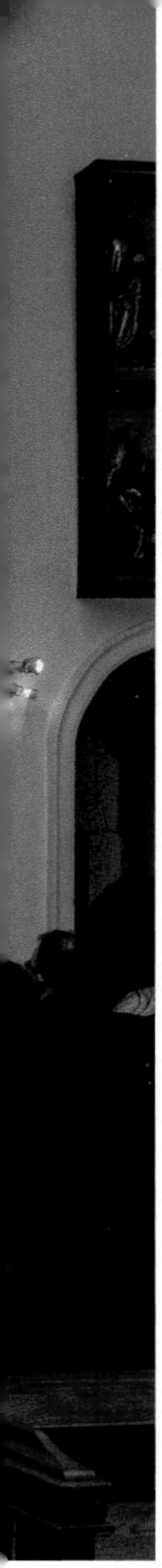

SOLDIER'S FAREWELL

MEMORIAL SERVICE for the late Kazimierz Michalski, born in Jaroslaw, Galicia, veteran of the Anders Army, longtime resident of Oxford. The Polish Army's Field Cathedral, Warsaw (2014) (top left).

A WORD OF APPRECIATION (top right).

THE LAST BLESSING (bottom left).

A WREATH OF REMEMBRANCE (bottom right).

THE ABBEY benignly overlooking flags from Polish schools in Rome and Ostia (right).

POLISH TV interviews a passing historian: Monte Cassino (2015) (below).

In the realm of fiction, the Anders story is not well represented, even though it provides a rich setting for tales of romance, intrigue, endurance or adventure. One novel that explores the theme is William Makowski's *The Uprooted* (Mississauga, 2002).[252] Andrzej Kunert has published an anthology of poetry inspired by Monte Cassino.[253]

More, too, might be expected from the realm of film, even though the censorship of People's Poland suppressed anything that could be suspected of paying tribute to Anders and his followers. A 90-minute documentary, *General Anders and his Army* was produced by the Wytwórnia Filmów Dokumentalnych i Fabularnych (WFDiF) in Warsaw in 1987. A similar production, *As Crosses are the Measure of Freedom*[254] emerged in the USA a little later. Both have been shown on Polish television. One of the earliest films on the subject, directed by Michał Waszyński, was *The Long Road* (1946), starring Renata Bogdańska.[255]

The late Jagna Wright heroically produced a valuable documentary, *A Forgotten Odyssey* (2000), but not without overcoming extraordinary indifference and obstruction.[256] Peter Weir's *The Way Back* (2010), inspired by the memoir of Sławomir Rawicz, is the only film of the genre to date to reach major cinema outlets.[257]

Several lesser known productions have been devoted either to the subject of exiled children or to particular personalities. In the former category are Andrzej Czulda's *Perskie ocalenie / Persian Salvation* (2012)[258] and Yehuda Caveh's *Children of Tehran* by Israeli films;[259] in the latter are *Songster of Warsaw* (2006) about Henryk Wars,[260] and Ryszard Bugajski's *The Death of Captain Pilecki*.[261] An extraordinarily beautiful and uplifting documentary, *Mit Iranske Paradis* (*My Iranian Paradise*) (2008) was made by Katia Forbert Petersen, a Danish–Polish woman, who was born in Tehran and who is deeply interested in the origins of her mother and the exodus of the Anders Army. It compares and contrasts the wartime and postwar Iran, which her mother knew, with the Iran of today, which she re-visited after 50 years' absence.[262]

None of these modern items, however, can detract from the unique value of the films made by the Anders Army's own film unit. Assembled in Central Asia by the director, Michał Waszyński, the unit's first film, *From Reveille to Fire's End* (1943) chronicled the daily life of soldiers only recently released from camps, prisons and remote exile. It was followed by *The Children, General Sikorski in the Near East, Polish Parade, Garden of Eden,* and *The Invincibles* shot on location at Monte Cassino.[263] The arrival of Polish orphans in New Zealand in 1944 was caught by cameramen of the New Zealand National Film Institute in *Children of Pahiatua.*

ANYONE INTENDING to do primary historical research will have two meccas in mind: the Polish Institute and Sikorski Museum (PISM) in Kensington and the Hoover Institution at Stanford, California. The former holds the archives of the Polish Government-in-Exile and part of its military forces, including the Anders Army. The latter's holdings include the Władysław Anders Papers, the Zygmunt Berling Papers, the Stanisław Mikołajczyk Papers, and 'Miscellaneous Records of the Polish Armed Forces Abroad'. The Hoover recently acquired the *Memoirs of Stanisław Kroczak*, an officer of the 22nd Artillery Transport Company whose most famous member was Wojtek, the Soldier Bear. Other interesting files are located in collections such as 'The Polish Research Center (Jerusalem), 1943–1944', 'Poles Deported to the Soviet Union' and 'Polish Ministry of Information, 1939–1945'.

Many archival resources remain untapped. There are few important deposits in Poland, though the *Archiwum Akt Nowych* (The Archive of Modern Records), the Central Army Records Office in Rembertów, and the *Ośrodek Karta* (The 'Karta' Centre) have been collecting materials since 1989. Nonetheless, discoveries can undoubtedly be made in all the countries through which the Anders Army passed, from Russia to Britain. The archives of wartime British Intelligence stay firmly shut, but the files of War Office are available at the Public Record Office and have yet to yield up many details of relations between Anders and British officialdom from 1941–1946.

MUSEUMS PLAY A VITAL ROLE in the preservation of memory, but for 50 years

ZBIGNIEW SIEMASZKO, born in Wilno, soldier of the Polish Army in the USSR and Middle East, radiotelegrapher of the General Staff, member of the PRC, engineer, publicist, historian, biographer.

after the formation of the Anders Army, the Sikorski Museum in London was the only place in the world where a relevant exhibition could be viewed. Since 1989, however, the Polish Army Museum in Warsaw has recognised the *Andersowcy* as part of Poland's military heritage, and a private Museum of the II Corps has been opened at Józefów.[264] In 2007, declared 'the Year of General Anders', a comprehensive exhibition was mounted under the auspices of Studio Historia and curated by Dr Andrzej Kunert. The catalogue of the exhibition, entitled *Dom jest daleko, Polska jest wciąż blisko* (Home is far away, but Poland is still near), adds a valuable item to the subject's literature.[265]

IN THE 21ST CENTURY, however, the Internet is rapidly establishing itself as the primary repository of historical information in general and of knowledge about the Anders Army in particular. Two websites are especially relevant: one called Kresy-Siberia is well established, run out of Australia, and contains an excellent Virtual Museum.[266] The other, http://andersarmy.com, which is linked to the preparation of the present album, is much younger; it is an experiment in crowdsourcing aimed at gathering and presenting historical narratives, photographs. and souvenirs from the worldwide public.[267]

Yet those are just two sites from thousands or even tens of thousands. The online encyclopaedia, Wikipedia, which, despite its obvious drawbacks, is not to be lightly dismissed, has ready-made articles on all the main personalities, on all phases of the Army's progress, and on many aspects of its organisation and composition. All the books, films, archives, and museums listed above can be checked out on the Internet. And it is increasingly the practice for people to place their memoirs and photographs on a virtual website, and to forget the old idea that serious matter has to be put into print. A good example, which vividly illustrates the mentality of the deportees would be the website of the Rymaszewski family from Australia.[268]

TOMB OF the Unknown Soldier, Warsaw (2015).

I FIRST HEARD OF GENERAL ANDERS and his Army more than 50 years ago. I admired him then, and I admire him still; and I feel a special bond with the men, women, and children whom he rescued from hunger, disease, and official abuse. Theirs is a story of endurance and fortitude that gives one faith in the human spirit.

Of the Poles from the Anders Army that I personally had the privilege of meeting in England, three in particular stand out in my memory. Mr Michał Giedroyć, scion of a princely family, was deported as a child to Central Asia in 1940, was saved by the evacuation to Iran, and now lives in Oxford with his Scottish wife of 60 years,

Rosemary. He has recently published an excellent memoir, *On the Crater's Edge*[2.6]. Michał and Rosemary are the patriarch and matriarch of a very loving large family of children, grandchildren, and great-grandchildren, who are the living proof that, given the will, great good can be snatched from adversity. Some years ago, when Michał returned to his birthplace at Łobzów near Nowogródek in Belarus, he found that his parents' house, a substantial *dwór*, once so common in the Kresy, had been destroyed without trace.

Mrs Zofia Litewska, a schoolteacher in prewar Poland, was deported to a labour camp in the Arctic Circle near Archangel with her four children. She taught in the Polish School in Isfahan in Persia, where her husband died. But she and her offspring pulled through to reach safety in England in 1948. She was the sweetest and most dignified old lady that I've ever met. She taught Polish to my elder son. Despite the traumas of her life, she achieved a wonderful state of equanimity, and, thanks to her deep religious faith, a radiant inner peace. She, too, wrote and published a memoir.

Yet Judge Kazimierz Michalski was the toughest of the lot. Reunited with his family in Delamere Camp, he worked in the immediate postwar years in a dirty and menial job in the Cherry Blossom boot polish factory in Birmingham. I met him in 1958 or 1959, when I was a student in Oxford and he was the manager of foreign books in Blackwell's University Bookshop. It took ten more years before he obtained a position more suited to his professional qualifications as librarian at the Oxford Faculty of Law. He was very active in the Ex-Combatants' Association and in our local Catholic parish. He died aged 104 in 2012 whilst visiting his native Jarosław. He belonged to the

NATIONAL MEMORIAL ARBORETUM

BLOCKLEY

MONUMENT OF Polish Soldiers and Wall of Remembrance (top left and centre).

NATIONAL MEMORIAL Arboretum, Alrewas (Staffordshire), Great Britain: inscriptions on the obelisk: "They Died Serving their Country" and "We will remember them" (bottom left).

BLOCKLEY CEMETERY, Gloucestershire (top right). Hubert Zawadzki and Norman Davies beside Hubert's father's, Michał's grave (bottom right).

category of human being for which there is only one adjective – indestructible. I was always asking him questions. During my last conversation with him, I asked if he could remember the Austro-Hungarian Army and the siege of Przemyśl during the First World War. He not only remembered; he could remember the names and numbers of the regiments that he had seen as a boy.

Hardly a day goes past, therefore, when I am not reminded of the Anders Army. On the day that I completed the first draft of the present text, I was having lunch with a friend, a banker from Wrocław, in the Winosfera Restaurant on Warsaw's Chłodna Street, sitting on high chairs by the window. As usual, he asked me what I was writing. I replied that in the evening I would be writing the last couple of pages of a publication on the odyssey of the *Andersowcy*. "Oh yes", he said, "my father's brother was one of them. He followed the trail from beginning to end: a very typical case – deportation, Siberia, Iran, Palestine, Monte Cassino. He died a couple of years ago in Doncaster [in Yorkshire]. We brought him home. He's buried in Wrocław."

Another friend of mine, John Martin, is both a professor of cardiology and a poet. I chose to finish my panorama of the Second World War, *Europe at War*, with one of his poems. I selected it because of its line about 'the infinite value of every human life'. But then I noticed that it was inspired by a dying veteran of the II Corps:

"My patient lay in the hospital bed
Unshaven, smelling of urine,
And bitten by lice,
Of no fixed abode,
Living on the street,
And unemployed,
Without family or friends.
In his Slavic accent
He declared
'I fought at Monte Cassino.'
And my junior doctors in their ignorance

THE ANDERS ROOM, SIKORSKI MUSEUM, London (2015): trophies and exhibits from the 17th to the 20th centuries.

GENERAL ANDERS fêted at the Daglinworth PRC Camp, around 1950 (above).

THE DAQUISE Restaurant, Kensington (2015) (below), established 1947 by a certain Mr Dakowski and his French wife; the walls are decorated with pictures of the restaurant's most famous clients, including General Anders, Count Edward Raczyński and Roman Polański.

Remained unmoved by man or by history.
And I turned to them
With my hand on the shoulder
Of my patient,
To address them on the greatness
Of the Second Polish Corps
And the infinite value
Of all human beings."[270]

Most recently, when this book was very nearly complete, I was adding a few paragraphs here and there, on topics that needed strengthening. And I inserted a new paragraph into Chapter 13, on the 'Anders' Aliyah'. The paragraph outlined the case of a young Polish Jew, born in Lwów, who had volunteered to join the Army at a juncture when many Jewish soldiers were leaving it. His name was Julian Bussgang. The very next day, as if by telepathy, an e-mail arrived from Dedham (Mass.) in the USA. It read:

> "Dear Professor Davies, Are you writing a new book about the Anders Army? As a former soldier of that army, can I help? I also could connect you with a few other veterans."

It was signed "Julian J. Bussgang". As I discovered, Dr Bussgang is a distinguished mathematician and inventor after whom a theorem of stochastic analysis, the Bussgang Theorem, has been named. I enjoyed a long telephone conversation with him.

Even then I was not done. On the day after the final version of *Trail of Hope* was closed, my wife came home from Poland, and put a book on my desk. It was Zbigniew Wawer's splendid monograph, *Armia generała Władysława Andersa w ZSRR, 1941–42* (*The Army of General Władysław Anders in the USSR, 1941–42*). I had bought the book a couple of years ago in Poland and left it on the bookshelves of our apartment in Kraków. I had looked for it in vain in Oxford, when writing the first chapters of my own book. Even at a glance, I could see that I would have benefited greatly from Professor Wawer's detailed chapters and organisational diagrams, not least about the earliest phase of the Army's development. I also noticed a large number of first-rate photographs; I was particularly envious of the shot of *Instruktorka* (Instructor) Piechowska with General Sikorski at Buzuluk: the rare picture of the 5th Mounted Division at Tatishchev, and the wonderful portrait of Generals Anders and Sulik at Dzalal-Abad. What could I do but wring my hands and bemoan a missed opportunity? Well, since historians always start reading from the back, when picking up a colleague's book, I could perhaps quibble with Professor Wawer's last sentence. He writes of the *setki grobów* (hundreds of graves) which give witness all over Europe to the patriotic devotion of General Anders's soldiers. The graves are counted not in hundreds, but in thousands.[271]

AFTER MY RESEARCH was done, and I had visited a series of foreign countries, from Russia and Iran to Israel and Italy, I decided that I ought to seek out a couple of locations which symbolised 'the end of the trail'. My search took me first to Stover Country Park in Devon and then to a quiet churchyard at Blockley in the Cotswold hills of Gloucestershire.

Stover Park is a nature reserve; it has woods and lakes, an arboretum and a heritage trail, and special areas reserved for walking, camping, bird-watching, and lepidoptera. But it is also neighbour to the last remaining Home for Polish Veterans in Great Britain, known since its restoration as 'Ilford Park'.

There has been a Polish camp, hospital, and hostel at Stover since 1948. It was set up originally by the Polish Resettlement Act, and housed ex-Army veterans, their families and DPs. After the closure in 1969 of Northwick Park, it was reputedly the last of its kind in the country. In 1992, a completely new establishment was built for 100 residents to the most modern standards. It is financed by Britain's Ministry of Defence, administered by the National Health Service, and staffed almost

APPOINTMENT WITH Cardinal Kazimierz Nycz, Metropolitan Archbishop of Warsaw, who was named after an uncle killed at Ossimo, 1944.

JUREK AND Zosia Biegus, née Hartman, children of the Anders Army, and guardians of the memory of the II Corps and the PRC.National Memorial Arboretum, Wall of Remembrance (2015).

entirely by Polish-speaking carers, nurses, and social workers. It has been known for decades to local Devonians as 'Little Poland'.[272] (The only place in Great Britain where similar arrangements have been made is at Penrhos on the Lleyn Peninsula in North Wales, where a private organisation, the Polish Housing Association, supports a contented community of elderly Polish people.)

Our visit to Ilford Park in March 2015 involved a long day's drive of some 160 miles from Oxford. We arrived by prior arrangement at lunchtime, and were invited to share a midday meal with a dozen men and women, all of an advanced age and all connected in one way or another to the Anders Army. Among them were a former military postman, a former military nurse, and a former parachutist, who had left the USSR with Anders before volunteering to join General Sosabowski's Brigade. The youngest, I estimated, was 88 years old.

The first thing one notices on entering 'Little Poland' is a quotation from Winston Churchill which hangs on a glass panel in the vestibules and which 'honours Britain's debt' to her wartime Polish allies. The second thing is that the entire environment of the home is Polish: the corridors are called Lwów Street or Poznań Street; the menu at dinner consists of *barszcz* (borsch) or *żurek* (sour rye soup), followed by *bigos* (cabbage stew) or *de volaille* (Chicken Kiev), and *naleśniki z jabłkami* (apple pancakes); the chapel, served by a Polish priest, is dedicated to the *Matka Boska Częstochowska* (Our Lady of Częstochowa); and a small shop is filled with souvenirs, trinkets, publications, pictures, and food products from Poland. The third thing is the very high quality of the accommodation. A gentleman called Zbigniew, a widower in his nineties, showed me his suite of rooms. He enjoyed a large living room with glass doors looking out to a spacious balcony, with separate bathroom, kitchen and bedroom. The balcony provided a view over sunlit flowerbeds, lawns and trees. The resident's hat and Tatra-style walking stick hung in the hallway, indicating his habit of strolling round the footpaths of the 91-acre site. "You couldn't dream of something better", he told me. This was the first time since he was brutally deported from his home in the Kresy in 1940 that he could make such a statement. He would certainly not have been treated so generously on first arriving in Britain. One British citizen at least felt proud.

EXAMINING THE original protocols from 1941–1942 of meetings between Generals Sikorski and Anders and Joseph Stalin; Norman Davies under instruction from his former pupil, Dr Andrzej Suchcitz, Chief Archivist, Sikorski Museum.

Blockley is a tiny Cotswold village halfway between Chipping Campden and Moreton-in-Marsh. It is an epitome of rural England in miniature. Its recorded history goes back to AD 855 when King Burgred of Mercia granted a monastery there to the Bishop of Worcester for the price of 300 solidi. The parish church of SS Peter and Paul, Catholic in origin but Anglican since the 16th century Reformation, was founded in 1180, and is built in late Norman (Romanesque) style. The quaint old High Street is lined by a few higgledy-piggledy honey-stone cottages and a handful of pokey stores. The railway station, which was closed in 1966, stands on the Oxford–Worcester line. The post office closed in 2007. But two public houses remain – the Crown Inn and the Great Western Arms. The surroundings are characterised by steep rolling hills, by extensive woods of oak, beech and elm, and by rich farmland. Cattle graze, horses run in the pasture, and corn ripens in a peaceful, apparently changeless setting.

I WAS TAKEN TO BLOCKLEY by my friend, colleague, and fellow historian, Dr Hubert Zawadzki. We went to visit the graves of his parents. Blockley Cemetery lies outside the village on the side-slope of a wooded hill. It is entered from Station Road through an arched gateway that leads onto the ascent of the central path. The older and lower sector is reserved for Protestant graves; the upper sector for Catholic burials, which started in the early 1950s thanks to the nearby Polish Resettlement Camps at Springhill Lodges and Northwick Park.

Michał Zawadzki and Irena Protassewicz met in Polish Military Hospital No. 1 in Taymouth Castle in Scotland in 1946. He was a patient still

MICHAŁ AND IRENA ZAWADZKI, born respectively in Kiev and in the district of Slonim, deported to the USSR, served in both the 'Anders Army' and the Polish I Corps, met at Polish Military Hospital No. 1, Taymouth Castle, Aberfeldy, Scotland (above).

ANNA-MARIA ANDERS, the General's daughter with Norman Davies (2014); in the background a photo of the 'Children of Pahiatua' (left).

recovering from severe war wounds received at the Battle of the Falaise Gap. She was an army nurse, who had served General Anders at all points of the trail from Russia to Palestine, before being transferred to the Polish I Corps in Britain. He, too, served in the Anders Army from Russia to Palestine, whence he was directed to Maczek's 1st Armoured Division. He was born in Kiev to a family from Polesie and she came from the district of Słonim near Nowogródek.

They were married in Scotland, before moving south with their growing family first to a resettlement camp and then to Stratford-upon-Avon, where Hubert attended secondary school. Their graves lie in a beautiful, peaceful corner of the land where they found refuge. Alternately shaded by the trees and warmed by the sun or cooled by the breeze of the hills, their last resting place is surrounded by flowers and shrubs, and by the graves of fellow exiles. When they were torn from their Polish homes by war and deportation, they would have known nothing of their future destiny, and could have had no thoughts of living and dying in England. Yet they were among the survivors, who outlasted the whirlwind; and in their hearts, among a jumble of other emotions, burned the still, small flame of hope – the hope to live, the hope of doing their patriotic duty, the hope to return home, and, if homegoing was not possible, the hope to pursue a normal, happy, and purposeful life. In their memory, and in that of tens of thousands like them, this book has been entitled 'Trail of Hope'.

ENDNOTES

Chapter 1

1. Ruth Turkow-Kamińska, *Mink Coats and Barbed Wire*, London: Collins 1979. | **2. Józef Czapski,** *The Inhuman Land, London:* Chatto and Windus, 1951; **Gustaw Herling-Grudziński,** *A World Apart*, London: Heinemann, 1953; **Joseph Scholmer,** *Vorkuta*, London: Weidenfeld and Nicolson, 1954; **Menachem Begin,** *White Nights*, London: Macdonald, 1957. | **3. Anne Applebaum,** *Gulag: a History of the Soviet Camps*, London: Allen Lane, 2003. | **4. Jurek Biegus,** *Siberian Baby*. Available at: <http://www.polishresettlementcampsintheuk.co.uk/stories/biegus.htm>. | **5. Michał Giedroyć,** *Crater's Edge*, London: Bene Fatum Publishing, 2010. | **6. After Ryszard Kapuściński,** *Imperium*, London: Granta, Chapter 1. | **7. Klemens Rudnicki,** *The Last of the War Horses*, London: Bachman and Turner, 1974, pp. 132–133. | **8. Private diary of Czesława Wierzbińska** (now Panek), with permission. | **9. Eugenia Huntingdon,** *The Unsettled Account*, London: Severn House, 1986, p. 143. | **10.** *Ibid.*, p. 98. | **11.** *Ibid.*, p. 99. | **12.** *Ibid.*, p. 114. | **13.** *Ibid.*, p. 99. | **14. S.V. Utechin,** *Everyman's Concise Encyclopaedia of Russia*, London: J.M. Dent and Sons, 1961, pp. 260–261.

Chapter 2

15. Władysław Anders, *An Army in Exile*, London: MacMillan & Co., 1949, p. 47. | **16. Giedroyć,** 2010, *op. cit.*, pp. 52–56. | **17. Rudnicki,** 1974, *op. cit.*, pp. 168–169. | **18.** *Ibid.* | **19.** *Ibid.*, p. 168. | **20. Biegus,** *op. cit.* | **21. Danuta Skiba** from 'Stories' at http://www.polishresettlementcampsintheuk.co.uk. | **22. Giedroyć,** 2010, *op. cit.*, pp. 66–69. | **23. Ryszard Kaczorowski,** private conversation, 2009. | **24. Sławomir Rawicz,** *The Long Walk*, New York: Harper, 1956; The Way Back, dir. Peter Weir, USA, 2010. | **25. Interview with Professor Palusor (Plutzer)**, Jerusalem, January 2014. | **26. Zofia Litewska,** *A Memoir*, Oxford 1995. | **27. Norman Davies,** *Od i do. Najnowsze dzieje Polski według historii pocztowej*, vol. II, Warszawa: Rosikon Press, 2008. | **28. Krystyna Orzechowska-Juzwenko,** *Dlaczego? Wspomnienia syberyjskie i inne*, Wrocław: Instytut Pamięci Narodowej, 2011. | **29. Wierzbińska**, *op. cit.* | **30. From Stanisław Kot,** *Conversations with the Kremlin and Dispatches from Russia*, Oxford: Oxford University Press, 1963. | **31. Israel Gutman,** *Jews in General Anders' Army in the Soviet Union*, Jerusalem: Yad Vashem, 1977. | **32. Menachem Begin,** *White Nights: The Story of a Prisoner in Russia*, New York: Harper & Row, 1979, *passim*. | **33. Interview,** 9 January 2014, Jerusalem. | **34. Sylwester Strzyżewski,** *Dezercje Żydów z Armii Andersa w świetle dokumentów Instytutu Polskiego... w Londynie*, „Zeszyty Naukowe WSOWL" 2012, no. 3(165), p. 232. | **35. Henryk Markiewicz,** *Mój życiorys polonistyczny z historią w tle*, Kraków: Wydawnictwo Literackie, 2002. | **36. Ks. Marek Wesołowski,** *Duszpasterstwo w II Korpusie gen. Władysława Andersa*, Kielce: Color Press, 2004. | **37. Ks. Andrzej Chibowski,** *Kapłańska odyseja ks. Michała Wilniewczyca*, Ząbki: Apostolicum, 2012, pp. 1–69.

Chapter 3

38. Zbigniew S. Siemaszko, *Generał Anders w latach 1892–1942*, London: Wydawnictwo LTW, 2012, p. 24. | **39. Giedroyć,** 2010, *op. cit.*, pp. 97–105. | **40. Stanisława Jasionowicz,** *Pamiętam... I nie pamiętam...*, Paris 2006, pp. 25–35. | **41. Rudnicki,** 1974, *op. cit.*, pp. 233–234. | **42. Utechin,** *op. cit.*, pp. 582–583. | 43. *Ibid.*, pp. 276–277. | **44. Rudnicki,** 1974, *op. cit.*, pp. 218–219. | **45.** *Ibid.* | **46. Anders,** 1949, *op. cit.*, p. 110. | **47. Helena Edwards,** *Days of Aloes*, Halwell: Sandpiper Press, 1992. | **48. Skiba,** *op. cit.* | **49. Rudnicki,** 1974, *op. cit.*, p. 242. | **50.** *Ibid.*, p. 241. | **51.** *Ibid.*, p. 247. | **52. Anders,** 1949, *op. cit.*, p. 115.

Chapter 4

53. Rudnicki, 1974, *op. cit.*, p. 192. | **54. Siemaszko,** 2012, *op. cit.*, pp. 333–334. | **55.** *Ibid.*, p. 342. | **56.** *Ibid.*, p. 352. | **57. Rudnicki,** 1974, *op. cit.*, pp. 223–224. | **58. Markiewicz,** 2002, *op. cit.*, pp. 64–65. | **59. Rudnicki,** 1974, *op. cit.*, p. 213. | **60.** *Ibid.*, pp. 234–235. | **61.** *Ibid.*, pp. 200–201. | **62.** *Ibid.*, p. 226–227.

Chapter 5

63. Edwards, 1992, *op. cit.* | **64.** *Ibid.* | **65. Skiba,** *op. cit.* | **66. Giedroyć**, 2010, *op. cit.*, p. 98. | **67. Edwards,** 1992, *op. cit.* | **68. Rudnicki,** 1974, *op. cit.*, p. 248. | **69. Giedroyć,** 2010, *op. cit.*, p. 99. | **70. Skiba,** *op. cit.* | **71. Agnieszka Jaskuła,** *Biskup polowy Wojska Polskiego Józef Feliks Gawlina* (1892–1964), „Biuletyn Wojskowej Służby Archiwalnej" 2007, no. 29, p. 297. Available at: <http://archiwumcaw.wp.mil.pl/biuletyn/b29/b29_6.pdf>. | **72. Zbigniew S. Siemaszko,** *General Anders – Addenda to Biography*, London, 2014, pp. 74–78. | **73. Harvey Sarner,** *Zdobywcy Monte Cassino*, Poznań: Zysk i S-ka, 1999, p. 114. | **74. Feliks Bilos** in: ***Providence Watching****: Journeys from Wartorn Poland to the Canadian Prairies*, ed. K. Patalas, Manitoba: University of Manitoba Press, 2003, pp. 38–48. | **75. Rudnicki,** 1974, *op. cit.*, pp. 249–250. | **76.** From **Paweł Chlipalski's account;** *Chlipalski family archives*. London. | **77. Edwards**, 1992, *op. cit.* | **78. Tomas Venclova,** *Aleksander Wat: Life of an Artist and Iconoclast*, New Haven: Yale University Press, 1996, p. 155. | **79.** *Ibid.*, p. 147. | **80. Elżbieta Kurkiewicz z Kordońskich,** *Wykaz zmarłych zesłańców, więźniów i łagierników: suplement* [List of deceased deportees, prisoners and lagerniks: supplement]. Available at: <http://www.stankiewicze.com/index.php/index.php?kat=31| sub=631>.

Chapter 6

81. Wiesław Stypuła, *W gościnie u „polskiego" maharadży*, Warsaw, 2000, pp. 36–37. | **82. Ervand Abrahamian,** *A History of Modern Iran*, Cambridge: Cambridge University Press, 2008, pp. 112–158. | **83. Polska Szkoła w Isfahan...** | **84. Stypuła,** 2000, *op. cit.* pp. 23–32. | **85. Giedroyć,** 2010, *op. cit.* | **86. Edwards**, 1992, *op. cit.* | **87.** *Ibid.* | **88. Giedroyć**, 2010, *op. cit.*, pp. 128–131. | **90.** *Isfahan, City of Polish Children*, ed. by **Irena Beaupré-Stankiewicz** et al., Isfahan | Lebanon: Association of Former Pupils of the Polish Schools, 1987. | **91. Jasionowicz**, 2006, *op. cit.*, pp. 47–48.

Chapter 7

92. See *Short History of Polish Carpathian Brigade*, 1940–42, London: Zarząd Główny Związku Tobrukczyków, 1985; **Stanisław Kopański,** *Wspomnienia wojenne*, London: Veritas, 1972.

Chapter 8

93. Aleksander Topolski, *Bez dachu. Moje wojenne przeżycia*, Poznań: Rebis 2012, pp. 34–35. | **94.** *Ibid.*, pp. 67–68. | **95.**

Ibid., pp. 85–86. | **96.** *Ibid.*, pp. 86–87. | **97.** *Ibid.*, pp. 89–90. | **98.** *Ibid.*, passim. | **99.** *Ibid.*, pp. 136–137. | **100. WO 201/1395, Anders to Pownall**, 22 May 1943, cited by Maresch, p. 37. | **101. FO 371/56469 N 8734.** Notes by Mr. Bourdillin, 3 July 1946, quoted by Maresch, p. 38.

Chapter 9

102. Mikola Koziy, *For Another's Cause*, 2 vols, London 1958–1960. | **103. United States Holocaust Memorial Museum:** Photo Archives, Online Catalog searched under <Anders Army>. Available at: <http://www.ushmm.org/search/results/?q=anders+army>. | **104. Edward Kossoy**, *Na marginesie*, Gdańsk: Słowo/obraz terytoria, 2006. | **105. Eric Silver,** *Begin: A Biography*, London: Weidenfeld and Nicolson, 1984. | **106. Rudnicki,** 1974, *op. cit.* | **107.** *Krzysztof Flizak, najmłodszy żołnierz 2. Korpusu Polskiego Generała Andersa* [film], Youtube, 15.08.2012. Dostępny w WWW: <https://www.youtube.com/watch?v=7MQNsvT_m9Y>; *Najmłodszy żołnierz Andersa*, 24.05.2012. Available at: <http://wiadomosci.onet.pl/prasa/najmlodszy-zolnierz-andersa/thjby>. | **108. Bronisław Młynarski,** *The 79th Survivor*, London: Bachman and Turner, 1976. | **109. Piotr Lisiewicz,** *Gdy enkawudzista gra na bałałajce*, "Nowe Państwo" 2013, nr 5(87). | **110. Maggie Smith**, *An extraordinary journey to find work in Salts Mill, Saltaire. The story of* ***Feliks Czenkusz***, Bradford, 2013. Available at: <http://www.saltairevillage.info/people_0002_Feliks_Czenkusz_1920_2013.html>. | **111. Władysław Broniewski,** *Pamiętnik: wydanie krytyczne*, Warszawa: Wydawnictwo Krytyki Politycznej, 2013; **Marci Shore,** *Caviar and Ashes: A Warsaw Generation's Life and Death in Marxism*, 1918–1968, New Haven: Yale University Press, 2006. | **112. Jerzy Giedroyc,** *Autobiografia na cztery ręce*, Warszawa: Czytelnik, 1994; **Zdzisław Kudelski,** *Studia o Herlingu-Grudzińskim: twórczość, recepcja, biografia*, Lublin: Towarzystwo Naukowe Katolickiego Uniwersytetu Lubelskiego, 1998. | **113. Aleksandra Ziolkowska-Boehm,** *Melchior Wańkowicz: Poland's Master of the Written Word*, Lanham: Lexington Books, 2013. | **114. Leonid Teliga,** *Samotny rejs Opty*, Gdańsk: Wydawnictwo Morskie, 1976.

Chapter 10

115. Eugeniusz Knurek, *'Pamiętne przygody'* in *Tułacze dzieci / Exiled Children*, Warsaw: Muza, 1995, p. 48. | **116. Lysandra Ohstrom,** *'Polish cemetery: last remains of refugee community'*, The Daily Star, Lebanon, 28 Jan 2013. | **117. Giedroyć,** 2010, *op. cit.*, pp. 143–145. | **118.** *Ibid.*, p. 171–73. | **119. Skiba,** *op. cit.* | **120. Lynne Taylor,** *Polish Orphans of Tengeru. The dramatic story of their long journey to Canada 1941–49*, Toronto: Dundrum Press, 2009, pp. 83–84. | **121. *Tułacze dzieci***, *op. cit.*, pp. 231–236. | **122.** *Ibid.* | **123. Ks. Dr Jan Jaworski,** *'Wspomnienia, 1939–2007'*, in *Rycerze, Infułat i Pastor czyli wojenne wspomnienia spod Krzyża Południa*, ed. by **A. Krzychylkiewicz, A. Romanowicz,** Warsaw: Urząd do Spraw Kombatantów i Osób Represjonowanych, 2013. | **124. Leszek Bełdowski, Jan K. Siedlecki,** *'Kolhapur and Panhala'*, in ***Poles in India****, 1942–1948*, ed. by **Teresa Glazer** et al., London: Association of Poles in India 1942–1948, 2000, pp. 78–79. | **125. Stypuła,** *op. cit.*, Chapter 26. | **126.** *Ibid.*, p. 203–207. | **127. Bełdowski, Siedlecki,** 2000, op cit., pp. 165–170. | **128.** From *Poles in India, 1942–1948*, *op. cit.*, 2000, pp. 422–433. | **129.** *Ibid.*, pp. 183–190. | **130.** *Ibid.*, pp. 454–455. | **131. Alexander Zvielli,** *With so much to live for...* Available at: <http://www.zchor.org/tehran/children.htm>. | **132. The Central Zionist Archives:** *Tehran Children.* Available at: <http://www.zionistarchives.org.il/en/datelist/Pages/tehran-children.aspx>. | **133. United States Holocaust Memorial Museum:** *Holocaust Encyclopedia*. Available at: <http://www.ushmm.org/learn/holocaust-encyclopedia>. | **134. Nirit Anderman,** *'The lost memories of the Tehran Children'*, Haaretz, 3 Jan 2007. | **135.** *Ibid.* | **136. J. Wójtkowski,** in *Tułacze dzieci*, *op. cit.*, p. 272. | **137. Stanisław Jaskołd,** in *Ibid.*, p. 278. | **138. National Film Archive,** New Zealand (1944). See *Tułacze dzieci*, *op. cit.*, pp. 256–261. | **139. Anna Bednarska**, in *Tułacze dzieci*, *op. cit.*, s. 63. | **140.** *Ibid.*, p. 64.

Chapter 11

141. T.E. Lawrence, *Seven Pillars of Wisdom: A Triumph*, Oxford, 1922. | **142.** *'Behind the headlines: the nefarious role of Henry Stimson'*, Jewish Telegraphic Agency, 27 Dec 1984. | **143. Topolski**, 2012, *op. cit.*, pp. 123–124. | **144. Zygmunt Kopel,** in *Waiting to be Heard; the Polish Christian Experience under Nazi and Stalinist Oppression*, ed. by **Bogusia Wojciechowska,** Bloomington, Indiana: AuthorHouse, 2009, pp. 204–206. | **145. Giedroyć**, 2010, *op. cit.*, pp. 146–151.

Chapter 12

146. Quoted by **J. Kirszak,** *Generał Władysław Anders*, Warsaw: Instytut Pamięci Narodowej, 2014, p. 14. | **147.** See **Keith Sword,** *Sikorski. Soldier and Statesman: A Collection of Essays*, London: Orbis Books, 1990. | **148. Anders,** 1949, *op. cit.*, p. 204–205.

Chapter 13

149. Ze'ev Jabotinsky, *The Iron Wall*, quoted by **Daniel Gordis**, *Begin: The Battle for Israel's Soul*, New York: Schoken, 2014, Chapter 3. | **150.** *Ibid.* | **151.** See **Michael Cohen,** *The Rise of Israel: Jewish Resistance to British Rule in Palestine, 1944–1947*, New York: Garland, 1987. | **152. Jan Bodakowski**, *Polska pomoc nowo powstającemu Izraelowi.* Available at: <http://www.wicipolskie.org/index.php?option=com_content| task=view| id=977>. | **153. Danna J. Azrieli,** *One Step Ahead: David J. Azrieli (Azrylewicz). Memoirs, 1939–1950*, Jerusalem: Yad Vashem, 2001. | **154. D. Azrieli,** *Ze wspomnień Davida Azrieli o służbie w Armii Andersa* (fragment), trans. K.D. Majus, Tel Aviv 2014, p. 4. | **155. Strzyżewski,** 2012, *op. cit.*, p. 232. | **156.** *Ibid.*, p. 233. | **157. Jan Zaściński,** *Pieśń o Warze*, Warsaw: Bellona, 1999, p. 137. | **158. Zbigniew S. Siemaszko,** *'Generał Anders, życie i chwała'*, *Kultura* 1970, no. 5–8, p. 36. | **159. Strzyżewski,** 2012, *op. cit.*, p. 230. | **160. Dov Levin,** *'Hayalav shel Anders [Anders' soldiers]'*, Et-Mol 1993, no. 5(109), pp. 9–11. | **161. Yoel Bourstein,** *The story of my father, Moshe Shimon Bursztyn.* Available at: <http://www.radzilow.com/bursztyn.htm>. | **162. Topolski,** 2012, *op. cit.*, pp. 159–160. | **163. Translated by A. Gillon, L. Krzyżanowski** in *Introduction to Modern Polish Literature: An Anthology of Fiction and Poetry*, New York: Twayne, 1964, pp. 422–423. | **164. Isabella Ginor,** *Gideon Remes, A Cold War casualty in Jerusalem, 1948: the assassination of* ***Witold Hulanicki***, „Israel Journal of Foreign Affairs" 2010, vol. IV, no. 3, pp 137–158. | **165. Levin,** 1993, *op. cit.*, p. 6.

Chapter 14

166. Lawrence Durrell, *The Alexandria Quartet*, London: Faber and Faber, 2012, p. 686. | **167. Andrew Beattie,** *Cairo: A*

Cultural History, Oxford: Oxford University Press, 2005. | **168.** *Ibid*., p. 167. | **169.** *Ibid*., p. 166. | **170. Heather Williams,** *Parachutes, Patriots and Partisans: The Special Operations Executive and Yugoslavia*, 1941–1945, London: C. Hurst | Co., 2003, pp. 51–52. | **171.** *'Obituaries: Sophie Moss'*, The Telegraph, 3 December 2009. | **172. Elisa Segrave,** *'Lives Remembered: Sophie Moss'*, The Independent, 22 February 2010. | **173. Zofia Tarnowska-Moss,** *Wiersze*, Tarnobrzeg, 2008. See also, **Andrew Tarnowski,** *The Last Mazurka: A Family's Tale of War*, Passion and Loss, London: Aurum, 2006. | **174. Durrell,** 2012, *op. cit*., p. 17. | **175.** *Ibid*., p. 59. | **176. Topolski,** 2012, *op. cit*., p. 111.

Chapter 15

177. Topolski, 2012, *op. cit*., p. 188. | **178.** *Ibid*., p. 203. | **179.** *Ibid*., p. 298. | **180. Christine Leppard,** *Fighting as a Colony? 1st Canadian Corps in Italy, 1943–45*, PhD thesis, Calgary: University of Calgary, 2013. | **181. Michael Polak,** *'An alternative view – the controversy surrounding military decisions taken by General Władysław Anders'* in *General Władysław Anders: soldier and leader of the free Poles in exile*, pod red. Joanny Pyłat, Jana Ciechanowskiego *et al*., London: Polish University Abroad, 2008, p. 102. | **182. Topolski,** 2012, *op. cit*., pp. 236–237. | **183. Anders,** 1949, *op. cit*., p. 174. | **184. Adam (Franciszek) Studziński,** *'Wspomnienia z Monte Cassino'*, in *Wspomnienia wojenne kapelanów wojskowych*, 1939–45, ed. by J. Humeński, Warsaw: Caritas, 1974, pp. 399–401. | **185.** *Ibid.* | **186. Anders**, 1949, *op. cit*., p. 181.

Chapter 16

187. Wiesław Lasocki, *Wojtek spod Monte Cassino*, London: Gryf Publications, 1968; **Aileen Orr,** *Wojtek the Bear: Polish War Hero*, Edinburgh: Birlinn, 2010; **Krystyna Mikula-Deegan,** *Private Wojtek: Soldier Bear*, Leicester: Matador, 2011; **Jenny Robertson,** *Wojtek: War Hero Bear*, Edinburgh: Birlinn, 2014. | **188. Bogdan Gancarz,** *'Prof. Wojciech Narębski ma 90 lat'*, Gość Krakowski, 17/4/2015.

Chapter 17

189. Interview with Cardinal Kazimierz Nycz, April 2015. | **190. Orzeł Biały,** no. 107, 18 June 1944. | **191. J. Ciechanowski**, *'General Anders, the Home Army and the Warsaw Rising of 1944'*, in *General Władysław Anders: soldier and leader...*, *op. cit*., p. 158. | **192. Interview with General (retd.) and Signora Morena**, Recanati, 19.5.2015. NB. The Gurkha's traditional knife was not a scimitar, but a kukri. | **193. Topolski,** 2012, *op. cit.* | **194. Kazimierz Zamorski**, *Sprawiedliwość sowiecka*, Rome 1945. | **195. Beata Obertyńska**, *W domu niewoli*, Rome: Oddział Kultury i Prasy 2. Korpusu Armii Polskiej, 1946. | **196. Topolski**, 2012, *op. cit*., pp. 238–239. | **197. Anders**, 1949, *op. cit*., p. 251. | **198. Mark W. Clark**, *Calculated risk*, New York: Harper, 1950, p. 421. | **199. Topolski**, 2012, *op. cit.* | **200. Feliks Konarski**, *'Jałta'*, in „Zapomniana piosenka, gdzieś pod sercem ukryta", opr. Aleksander Markowski. Available at: <http://www.readbag.com/wszechnica-cieszyn-pl-doc-zapomniana-piosenka>. | **201. Lynne Olson and Stanley Cloud**, *For Your Freedom and Ours: The Kosciuszko Squadron – Forgotten Heroes of World War II*, London: Arrow Books, 2003, p. 375. | **202.** *Ibid.* | **203.** *Ibid.* | **204.** Topolski, 2012, *op. cit*., p. 281. | **205. Denis Hills**, *Days of Aloes*, Sandpiper Press, San Anselmo, 1992.

Chapter 18

206. ***Monte Cassino Commemorative Cross***. Available at: <http://en.wikipedia.org/wiki/Monte_Cassino_Commemorative_Cross>. | **207. Anders**, 1949, *op. cit.* | **208. Anders' Oath**, quoted by **Mark Ostrowski**, *To Return to Poland or not to Return*, London University, Ph.D. thesis, 1996, p. 87. Available at: <http://www.angelfire.com/ok2/polisharmy>. | **209. Anders**, 1949, *op. cit*., p. 304. | **210. Bernard Newman**, *The story of Poland*, London: Hutchinson, 1945, *passim*. | **211. Ostrowski**, *op. cit*., p. 69. | **212.** *Ibid*., pp. 72–74. | **213. Zbigniew Wysecki**, quoted by **Halik Kochanski**, *The Eagle Unbowed. Poland and the Poles in the Second World War*, London: Allen Lane, 2012. | **215. Anders**, 1949, *op. cit*., p. 448.

Chapter 19

216. Józef (Ziutek) Raginia, *Italy to Glasgow*. Available at: <http://www.polishresettlementcampsintheuk.co.uk>. | **217.** *Army units in Polish Resettlement Corps camps in the UK, 1946–1948*. Available at: <http://www.polishresettlementcampsintheuk.co.uk/PRC/PRC.htm>. | **218.** *Growing up at Penley*. Available at: <http://bbc.co.uk/legacies/immig_emig/wales/w_ne/article_2.shtml>. | **219. Giedroyć**, 2010, *op. cit*., pp. 181–182. | **220.** *Ships and passenger lists* of Polish WW2 DPs arriving from Africa and Europe. Available at: <http://www.polishresettlementcampsintheuk.co.uk/passengerlist/shipsindex.htm>. | **221.** *Ibid.* | **222.** *Ibid.* | **223.** *Ibid.* | **224.** *Ibid.* | **225. Zosia Biegus, Jurek Biegus,** *Polish resettlement camps in England and Wales, 1946–1969*, Ashingdon: PB Software, 2013. | **226. Iwona Kadłuczka,** *'Mój dom to obóz'*, 4.06.2011. Available at: <http://m.wiadomosci.gazeta.pl/wiadomosci/1,117915,9725905,Moj_dom_to_oboz__Kawalek_zapomnianej_historii.html>. | **227. Siemaszko,** 2012, *op. cit.* | **228. Kazimierz Sidor,** *W niewoli u Andersa*, Rome, 1947. | **229. William P. Coates, Zelda Coates,** *Six Centuries of Russo-Polish Relations*, London: Lawrence | Wishart, 1948. | **230. Piotr Zychowicz,** *'Jak Polacy mieli iść na III wojnę światową'*, Rzeczpospolita, 2.10.2010. Available at: <http://niniwa22.cba.pl/jak_polacy_mieli_isc_na_3_wojne.htm>. | **231.** *The Polish Community in Tasmania*. Available at: <http://polishassociationhobart.org.au/home-2/the-polish-community-in-tasmania>. | **232. Wanda Skowrońska,** *To Bonegilla from Somewhere*, Ballarat: Conor Court Publishing, 2013, p. 8. | **233. John H. Williams, John Bond,** *The Promise of Diversity: the story of* ***Jerzy Zubrzycki****, architect of multicultural Australia*, Toorac, Vic.: Grosvenor Books, 2013, pp. 90–91. | **234. Alojzy Bach**, in *Providence Watching*, *op. cit*., p. 30. | **235. Anna Kajak (Ostrihanska),** *'Difficult Beginnings'*, in ***Poles in India***, *op. cit*., pp. 523–526. | **236. Józef Szkudłapski,** in *Waiting to be Heard*, *op. cit*., p. 287. | **237. Smith,** 2013, *op. cit*., pp. 25–27.

Chapter 20

238. Siemaszko, 2012, *op. cit.* | **239. Ewa Berberyusz,** Anders spieszony, Londyn: Aneks, 2002. | **240. Harvey Sarner,** *General Anders and the Soldiers of the Second Polish Corps*, Cathedral City: Brunswick Press, 1997. | **241. Keith Sword,** *The Soviet takeover of the Polish Eastern provinces, 1939–41*, London: School of Slavonic and East European studies, University of London, 1991; Id., *Deportation and exile: Poles in the Soviet Union*, 1939–48, London: School of Slavonic and East European studies, University of London, 1994. | **242. Gutman,** *op. cit.*

| **243. Melchior Wańkowicz,** *Bitwa o Monte Cassino*, Rzym: Wydawnictwo Oddziału Kultury i Prasy Drugiego Polskiego Korpusu, 1945–1947; **Janusz Piekałkiewicz,** *Monte Cassino: dwadzieścia narodów w zmaganiach o jedną górę*, Warszawa: Agencja Wydawnicza Jerzy Mostowski, 2003. | **244. John Ellis,** *Cassino: the hollow victory*, London: Aurum, 2003; **David Hapgood, David Richardson,** *Monte Cassino*, New York: Congdon | Weed, 2003. | **245. Pierre Le Goyet,** *La campagne d'Italie: une victoire quasi inutile*, Paris: Nouvelles Éditions Latines, 1985. | **246. Tułacze dzieci, op. cit.** | **247. Irena Grudzińska-Gross, Jan Gross,** *War through children's eyes. The Soviet occupation of Poland and the deportations, 1939–1941*, Stanford: Hoover Institution Press, 1981. | **248. Keith Sword, Jan Ciechanowski, Norman Davies,** *The formation of the Polish community in Great Britain, 1939–1950*, London: School of Slavonic and East European studies, University of London, 1989. | **249. Anders,** 1949, *op. cit.* | **250. Rudnicki,** 1974, *op. cit.* | **251. Wesley Adamczyk,** *When God Looked the Other Way*, Chicago: University of Chicago Press, 2004; **Anders,** 1949, *op. cit.*; **Azrieli,** 2001, *op. cit.*; **Begin,** 1979, *op. cit.*; **Czapski,** 1951, *op. cit.*; **Alick Dowling**, *Janek: a story of survival*, **Letchworth**: Ringpress, 1988; Edwards, 1992, *op. cit.*; **Giedroyć,** 2010, *op. cit.*; **Maria Hadow**, *Paying Guest in Siberia*, London: Harvill Press, 1959; **Herling-Grudziński,** 1951, *op. cit.*; Huntingdon, 1986, *op. cit.*; Litewska, 1995, *op. cit.*; **Sandra Oancia,** *Remember: Helen's Story*, Calgary: Detselig Enterprises, 1977; **Rawicz,** 1956, *op. cit.*; **Rudnicki,** 1974, *op. cit.*; **Aleksander Topolski,** *Without Vodka*, Ottawa: UP Press, 1999; **Topolski,** 2012, *op. cit.*; **Stefan Waydenfeld,** *The Ice Road*, Edinburgh: Mainstream, 1999; **Zoë Zajdlerowa,** *The Dark Side of the Moon*, London: Harvester Wheatsheaf, 1946. | **252. William Makowski,** *The Uprooted, Mississauga*: Smart Design, 2002. | **253. Andrzej Krzysztof Kunert,** *Bitwa o Monte Cassino w poezji*, 1944–1969, Warszawa: LTW, 2007. | **254. Bo wolność krzyżami się mierzy..., dir. Krzysztof Szmagier,** Poland, 1989. | **255. Wielka droga, dir. Michał Waszyński**, Poland–Italy, 1946. | **256.** *A Forgotten Odyssey*, dir. **Jagna Wright**, Great Britain, 2000. | **257.** *The Way Back*, dir. Peter Weir, USA, 2010. | **258.** *Perskie ocalenie*, dir. Andrzej B. Czulda, Poland, 2013. | **259. Children of Tehran**, reż. Yehuda Kaveh et al., Israel, 2009. | **260. Henryk Wars.** Pieśniarz Warszawy, dir. Wiesław Dąbrowski, Poland, 2007. | **261. Śmierć rotmistrza Pileckiego,** dir. Ryszard Bugajski, Poland, 2006. | **262. Mit Iranske paradis**, dir. Katia Forbert Petersen, Denmark, 2008. | **263. Charles Ford, Robert M. Hammond**, *Polish film: a Twentieth Century history*, Jefferson, NC: McFarland | Co., 2005, Chapter 6. | **264. Muzeum 2 Korpusu Polskiego w Józefowie**. Available at: <http://www.2korpus.pl/>. | **265. Andrzej Krzysztof Kunert,** *Dom jest daleko, Polska wciąż jest blisko. Generał Anders i jego żołnierze*, exhibition catalogue, Warszawa: Studio Historia z Ograniczoną Odpowiedzialnością, 2007. | **266. Kresy Siberia Virtual Museum.** Available at: <http://kresy-siberia.org/museum/en>. | **267.** http://andersarmy.com | **268.** *http://www.rymaszewski.iinet.net.au* | **269. Giedroyć,** *op. cit.* | **270. John Martin,** quoted by: **Norman Davies,** *Europe at War: No Simple Victory*, London: Macmillan, 2006, p. 490. | **271. Zbigniew Wawer,** *Armia generała Władysława Andersa w ZSRR*, 1941–1942, Warsaw: Bellona, 2012. | **272. Ilford Park Polish Home**, Stover, Newton Abbot, UK. Available at: <http://www.veterans-uk.info>.

CREDITS

A .M. Anders: 571 | A. Ledóchowska i A. M. Zakrzewski: 50, 72, 83, 84, 85, 89, 107, 112, 113, 138, 139, 154, 155, 198, 202, 216, 236, 245, 246, 247, 248, 249, 250, 342, 347, 400, 402, 414, 415, 418, 419, 420, 421, 424, 451, 474, 492 | Z. Biegus: 172, 173, 465, 519, 538, 539, 541, 549, 550, 552, 558, 559, 566, 567, 570, 589 570, 589 | W. Bizon: 152, 153, 282, 283, 339, 358, 362 | W. Borodzicz: 102, 103, 264, 265, 514 | Czelnik: 513, 528 | Ch. Davies: 114 | N. Davies: 336, 337, 562, 563 | J. Eddis-Topolski: 425 | M. Giedroyć: 276, 352, 353, 354, 579, 537, 550, 555 | G. Górny 262 | M. Herling: 276 | E. Jankowski: 517, 519 | St. Kościałkowski, Rome: 94, 126, 189, 191, 195, 196, 197, 198, 202, 204, 206, 207, 217, 294, 296, 302, 340 | Rev. W. Lenartowicz: 35, 66, 94, 113, 116, 118, 119, 122, 123, 129, 148, 149, 176, 298, 301, 302 | W. Narębski: 460, 462, 464, 465 | W. Seliwanowska: 59, 84, 136, 141, 156 | Z. Siemaszko: 175, 182, 571 | A. Stebelski: 142, 143, 314, 315, 321, 324, 325, 326, 334, 335| W. Stypuła: 314, 316, 317, 318, 319, 320, 323, 324, 325, 326, 327 | K. M. Ujazdowski: 478 | H. Zawadzki: 547, 556, 569, 593 | A. Żarnecka 335 | New Zealand Embassy in Warsaw: 291, 336, 337 | Australian War Memorial: 222, 226, 228 | Central Military Library: 8, 65, 106, 124, 195, 236, 237, 238, 354, 355, 266, 272, 358, 359, 378, 380, 392, 393, 395, 406, 444, 445, 446, 447, 448, 450, 452, 478, 488, 489, 490, 491, 492, 495, 499, 501, 506, 507, 523 | Polish Army Central Archives in Warsaw-Remebertów: 62, 91, 105, 109, 117, 127, 150, 151, 180 | Centre for the Documentation of Deportation, Displacement and Relocation in Kraków: 36, 64, 83, 211, 297, 304, 305, 306, 307, 308, 309,310, 311, 324, 325, 355, 356 | The Menachem Begin Heritage Center and Museum in Jerusalem: 262, 347, 390 | The Wanderers' Photographic Archive Foundation: 294, 311, 313, 322, 330, 331 | Instytut Pamięci Narodowej in Białystok: 348, 349, 350, 405, 456 | The Rev. Józef Jarzębowski Museum in Licheń: 29, 41, 42, 43, 69, 71, 73, 74, 76,77, 78, 80, 82, 86, 101, 102, 104, 108, 110, 111, 121, 125, 128, 135, 147, 211, 244, 252, 253, 484, 485, 572 | The Lehi Museum in Tel Aviv: 382 | Narodowe Archiwum Cyfrowe: 8, 56, 140, 163, 190, 191, 203, 204, 210, 274, 278, 370, 374, 397, 434, 446, 447, 452, 457, 482, 486, 501, 502, 503, 504, 505, 525, 570 | wikipedia: 18, 19, 20, 22, 23, 24, 27, 30, 32, 34, 37, 38, 49, 5Ô, 51, 54, 70, 146, 158, 159, 164, 169, 171, 179, 181, 185, 190, 192, 212, 220, 224, 225, 226, 229, 236, 242, 243, 260, 263, 267, 268, 269, 270, 273, 274, 278, 284, 285, 287, 289, 368, 371, 372, 373, 375, 380, 381, 404, 406, 408, 409, 434, 435, 436, 437, 438, 442, 444, 473, 482, 488, 497, 498, 506, 507, (This file is licensed under the Creative Commons "Attribution-ShareAlike 2.5 Italy" Licence, Vincenzo Gianferrari Pini): 508, 521, 522, 524, 528, 530, 531, 532, 534, 546, 556, 568 | Fotolia: © Rod: 188, © Lucian H Milasan: 235, © bestimagesever: 403, © wizdata: 404, © Leonid Andronov: 410, 420, © markobe: 410, 412, © juan_g_aunion: 411, © Claudio Colombo: 497 | Depositphotos © Leonid Andronov: 411 | Dreamstime.com: © Kmiragaya: 242, © Sadikgulec: 243, © Rasoulali: 244, 248, 249, © AnnaOmelchenko: 296, 299, © Bigevil600: 298, © Asakalaskas: 422, © Mediaimagephotography: 544, © Electropower: 545 | PAP: 288 | platforma armiaandersa.pl: J. Niebrzydowski: 37, 177, J. Nosal: 7, K. Dobrecki: 280, J. Żukowski: 281, www.warrelics.eu

G:BR:OMN:REX ET INDIAE IMP:
GEORGIVS VI D:G:BR:OMN:REX F:D:IND:IMP.

THE 1939–1945 STAR
THE AFRICA STAR
GRI

MILI
VIR
TUTI
TARI

MONTE CASSINO
ANKONA
NA
POLU
CHWAŁY
1920

ACKNOWLEDGEMENTS

We wish to thank:

The President of the Republic of Poland

The Ministry of Foreign Affairs of the Republic of Poland

The Embassies of the Republic of Poland in Mexico, Moscow, Rome, Tehran and Tel Aviv, New Zealand Embassy in Warsaw and Embassy of the Russian Federation in Tehran

Bank Zachodni WBK, Archaeological Museum in Kraków, Central Military Library name after Marshal Józef Piłsudski, Centre for the Documentation of Deportation, Displacement and Relocation in Kraków, Kresy - Siberia Foundation, History of Poland Museum, Knights of Columbus in Poland, The Lehi Museum in Tel Aviv, The Marian Fathers' Congregation, The Menachem Begin Heritage Center and Museum in Jerusalem, MillionYou, National Culture Centre, Polish Army Central Archives in Warsaw, The Polish Institute in New Delhi, The Polish Institute and Sikorski Museum, The Polish Soldiers' Family Association in Italy, The Rev. Józef Jarzębowski Museum in Licheń, The Wanderers' Photographic Archive Foundation,The World War II Museum in Gdańsk, ZAiKS

Anna Maria Anders, Marek Adamski, Krzysztof Babraj, Renata Balewska, Dorota Barcińska, Andrzej Bednarek, Zosia i Jurek Biegus, Kazimierz Bilanow, Władysław Bizon, Danuta Boczek, Wirginia Borodzicz, Estela Czekierska, Lidia i Engelbert Czelnik, Maria i Grzegorz Czerniak, Christian Davies, Krzysztof Dobrecki, John Dunn, Maciej Dworzański, Joan Eddis-Topolski, Suzanna Eibuszyc, Wojciech Ejchorszt, Kenneth Fedzin, Nina Finbow, Janusz Fogler, Mateusz Frankowski, Maciej Gablankowski, Andrzej Gaca, Michał Giedroyć, Karen Gladysz-Gryff, Ryszard Golis, Karolina Gorzała, Grzegorz Górny, Rev. Wiktor Gumienny MIC, Bartłomiej Grzesik, Tymoteusz Gurbin, Ewa Gwóźdź, Bożena Hersztowska, Krzysztof Jabłonka, Teresa Jabłońska-Matysiak, Lucyna Jadowska, Halina Janda, Eryk Jankowski, Witold Jarczyk, Magdalena Jarkowska, Paweł Jaroszewski, Paula Jędrzejczyk, Rev. Krzysztof Jędrzejewski MIC, Tomasz Kapitaniak, Bronisława Karst, Mateusz Kawczyński, Adam Kiełbiński, Andrzej Kindler, Janina Kmieć, Janusz Kolbuszewski, Aldona Kostanecka-Matraszek, Robert Kowalski, Kinga Koźmińska, Andrzej Krajewski, Maria Krywult, Ewa Krzymień, Zbigniew Krzywosz, Małgorzata Kucharska, Andrzej K. Kunert, Miłowit Kuniński, Tomasz Kurzątkowski, Bartosz Kwaśniewski, Przemysław Kwiatkowski, Beata Lamkiewicz, Anna i Jan Ledóchowki, Piotr Lemieszek, Rev. Wiesław Lenartowicz, Joanna Lockwood, Zdzisława Matusiak-Kowieska, Maria Mazurek, Katarzyna Meissner, Agnieszka Michałowska, Dominik Mika, Elżbieta Miros, Alicja Morawiec, Mateusz Morawiecki, Marianna Murawska, Giovanni Murro, Paweł Myszkowski, M. Nadwyczawski, Wojciech Narębski, Jan Niebrzydowski, Elżbieta Nikoniuk, Szymon Nosal, Jolanta Nowakowska, Magdalena Nowek, Janina Nowicka, Janusz Nowicki, Nunzio Olivieri, Wiesław Ośrodek, Michał Paluch, Przemysław Papis, Tomasz Pater, Bożenka Pearson, Magdalena Piechowiak, Katarzyna Pisarska, Iwona Radwanska, Jakub Rak, Cezary W. Rembowski, Włodzimierz Rędzioch, Rev. Jan Rokosz MIC, Karolina Saar, Marek Schwetz, Marta Sielska, Tomasz Sierakowski, Janusz Skarzyński, Paweł Skiba, Anna Skład, Jan Skrzypczak, Alfred Stebelski, Iwona Stefańska, Waldemar Stopczyński, Wiesław Stypuła, Andrzej Suchcic, Maria Sulma, Michał Szota, Walter Szwender, Tomasz Szydłowski, Michał Szymański, Rev. Jarosław Szymczak, Zdzisława Świniarska, Marek Świto, Jerzy Piotr Talaga, Janina Tenderenda, Krystyna Tokarska, Jan Tumiel, Mark Turkiewicz, Kazimierz M. Ujazdowski, Regina Villmo, Sławomir Wawer, Irena Wawrzyniak, Abp. Szczepan Wesoły, Witold Wiliński, Stefan Wiśniewski, Adrian Wojtczak, Bożenna Wójcik, Zdzisława Wójcik, Elżbieta Zachara, Dagmara Zandman, Andrzej Zakrzewski, Marcin Zakrzewski, John Zarecki, Hubert Zawadzki, Bogumiła B. Zimna, Jan Zwierzchowski, Jerzy Żukowski

This edition published in Great Britain in 2015 by Osprey Publishing,

Photographs: © Janusz Rosikoń
Layout: Maciej Marchewicz
Collaboration: Jan Kasprzycki-Rosikoń
Copyediting: Mary Murphy, Iwona Zych

A CIP catalogue record for this book is available from the British Library

ISBN: 978 1 4728 1603 0
ePub ISBN: 978 1 4728 1605 4
PDF ISBN: 978 1 4728 1604 7

Osprey Publishing, part of Bloomsbury Publishing Plc

PO Box 883, Oxford, OX1 9PL, UK
PO Box 3985, New York, NY 10185-3985, USA
E-mail: info@ospreypublishing.com

www.ospreypublishing.com

Printed in Poland